I0819315

WATER-WISE PLANTS *for* MEDITERRANEAN GARDENS

WATER-WISE PLANTS *for* MEDITERRANEAN GARDENS

Graham Payne

THE CROWOOD PRESS

CONTENTS

INTRODUCTION

The title of this book demonstrates the basis of the selection in the plant directory, which comprises a wide range of plants for different subtropical and drier climates, with particular emphasis on those that can survive with little water. The book aims to assist gardeners in selecting plants that can thrive in their specific climate, using plants from regions with comparable climates, not only Mediterranean plants in summer-dry areas but also others for winter-dry areas.

How extremely fortunate are those living in such a climate where you can grow an immensely wide range of plants from cool temperate to tropical regions of the world. Low shrubs and succulents are perfect for covering extensive areas of infertile soil, offering diverse colours, fragrances and textures. The most important aspect is planting naturally, allowing dominant species to thrive while other varieties spread organically.

You will see from a glance through this book looking at their origin that the plants that grow in drier regions come from such diverse countries as Mexico, South Africa, Australia, Madagascar, China and Malaysia. If you are lucky enough to live in a frost-free area with a modest water supply, you should be able to grow all the plants in this book that are suitable for your soil. Many plants are also suitable for regions with light to moderate frosts.

Whether you live in a home with a large or a small garden, there is a wide range of attractive and colourful plants to create a beautiful garden with interest throughout the year. Even in a residential flat or apartment, it is still possible to grow some attractive plants. A flat with a small balcony can happily accommodate a few pots or a trough.

I hope this book will provide some help to the many people who enjoy growing dry-climate plants in their garden. Whether you live in the Mediterranean region itself or an area of the world that has a similar climate, you can enjoy these plants.

CHAPTER 1

DRY CLIMATES

What is a Dry Climate?

In this book, I have listed plants that will grow in a subtropical or dry climate: but what are they? The Mediterranean climate is recognised as one with about four months of dry, hot sunny weather in summer and cool wet winters. Temperatures may differ, but the plants in this book are chosen for areas with little or no frost in winter. There are also regions with wet summers and dry winters, in the eastern cape of South Africa, eastern Australia, southeastern North America and northern Argentina.

Regions of the World with a Subtropical and Dry Climate

- **The area surrounding the Mediterranean Sea.** In this region, plants such as Olive, Figs, Oleander, Cistus, Lavender and Rosemary are frequently found. The Cape Floral Region of South Africa, stretching from the Peninsula to the Eastern Cape, is unmatched regarding flower power. Accounting for less than 0.5 per cent of the continent of Africa, the Cape Floral Region holds an astonishing 20 per cent of its flora, most of it indigenous to this specific region, containing a staggering 465 species. Commonly found plants from this region are Pelargonium, Osteospermum, Gazania, Nemesia and bulbs, including Nerine and Amaryllis.
- **California's central and southern coastal region.** The main period of rainfall is winter and spring. A Mediterranean climate is found mainly along the coast, though some areas are affected by summer fog. Many popular garden plants originate in coastal California. Eschscholzia, Ceanothus, Carpenteria, Romneya and *Epilobium canum* (*syn.* Zauschneria) are only a few.
- **Southern and southwestern Australia region.** A biodiversity hot spot with an estimated 8,000 species evolving. Most of the east coast has a summer rainfall climate, varying from dry scrubland and open forests around Sydney to wetter forests in the Blue Mountains. Common plants include Eucalyptus, Banksia and Anigozanthus.
- **Central Chile, parts of Argentina and other regions of central South America. Also eastern China and southern Japan.**
- **Northern parts of New Zealand** have produced spectacular plants such as Clianthus, Phormium and Cordyline.
- **Coastal southern England, Ireland and even western Scotland** have a mild climate affected by the warm Gulf Stream. Large European cities such as London with radiated heat and shelter from buildings create their own warm microclimate, where many tender plants can be grown. As the global climate warms, many areas of western Europe and the British Isles now have a warmer climate, especially in southern and eastern England, where the normal lowest winter temperature is no lower than -5°C, a moderate frost at which many of the plants in this book will survive. Those plants that will not take any frost – the tender tropical plants – have been individually described as being tender. Many factors will affect the climate locally, such as proximity to the sea or altitude.

Climate Change

Gardeners in dry subtropical and Mediterranean climates are facing a race against time as they experience the growing impact of climate change in their own gardens. Gardeners find they need to question traditional gardening practices. Climatic shifts, such as prolonged droughts and erratic rain patterns, are driving gardeners to adopt more resilient and sustainable practices to ensure their gardens' health and thrive under increasingly harsh conditions. Home gardeners are discovering the need for climate-resilient gardening to support vibrant and productive gardens.

Climate change is increasingly causing global disruption. Humans have an inherent desire for certainty, and the predictability of weather has been a given in modern societies. However, as each year is hotter than the last, wildfires rip through extensive areas and are followed by floods and hurricanes of unparalleled force and extent. It appears no part of the world is now spared extreme weather events.

The ebb and flow of warm and cold periods continues as it has always done. However, 2023 was the hottest year on record, and 2024 has broken many records. Canada experienced its worst fire season and there were catastrophic blazes in Hawaii, the Mediterranean, central Amazonia and Chile. The ferocity and speed of the growth are escalating, resulting in indirect repercussions. As wildfires rage, American cities are experiencing blackouts. China continues to grapple with an ongoing drought. Greece is in a battle to protect its monuments from being consumed by flames. India and tropical Africa are experiencing scorching temperatures approaching 50 degrees Celsius. Even the east of England is now designated as semi-arid.

By prioritising soil health, biodiversity and water conservation, regenerative gardening forms the basis for climate-resilient gardening. This method helps reduce the negative effects of climate change and promotes overall environmental sustainability. For home gardeners, developing a personal climate change action plan involves specific steps such as improving soil quality, selecting appropriate plants, reducing water usage and designing the garden layout to group together plants with similar water requirements. By implementing these strategies, gardeners can transform their spaces into resilient gardens that not only survive but also thrive under changing conditions, while playing a part in mitigating climate change effects.

Dry Gardens and Xeriscaping

For those with a limited water supply or those who only spend a short time in the home, a dry garden may be the answer. A term that is often used is 'Xeriscaping', a concept for garden design with efficient use of water, which originated in the state of Colorado, USA.

The term xeriscape comes from '*xeros*' the Greek word for dry, combined with 'scape', which literally means a picture or a view of a type of scene – thus, we have the term for a dry landscape. Many people have a negative association with this

A beautiful garden can be created with little water.

word, thinking that all xeriscapes are hot, hostile and thorny. Some associate the term with minimal plant material and lots of rock. Actually, xeriscaping can be and often is attractive, quite lush and extremely colourful. One feature that is often used is that of a 'dry riverbed'. A natural-looking river is created using rocks and careful planting with the water represented by well-worn riverbed stones carefully laid to create the illusion of a dry river. When well constructed, this can look stunning.

Using water-efficient plants does not mean drab plants full of thorns or just cactus, as many natives of dry regions will look attractive with little or no water. Plants such as Kalanchoe species come in many forms, *K. beharensis* with its huge silver leaves, *K. blossfeldiana* with its attractive red flowers, while Aloe species have stunning foliage and attractive flowers. Drifts of *Lampranthus spectabilis* covered with flowers, an iridescent bright reddish-purple, red, white, or pink, look spectacular in spring. There are so many colourful plants that you can use successfully.

Reduce the Size of Your Lawn, or Create a Lawn-Free Garden

Lawns require up to 25mm of water per week in dry periods in order to keep them lush, whilst a water-wise bed will require far less water. So, reducing the size of your lawn and changing it to an indigenous garden bed is a great way to reduce your water requirements. If you really want a lawn, keep it small. Place modest quantities of grass in areas where it will be used for cooling the environment, or for play and recreation. There is no sense in placing extensive areas of grass where no one will use it. Consider using alternatives to grass. Some areas can be paved, while some can be planted with drought-tolerant ground cover plants such as *Gazania rigens*, *Vinca major*, *Santolina chamaecyparissus* or Junipers. Different types of gravel can be laid in large sweeps to give a pleasing effect.

Narrow strips of lawn enhance low borders beside a path.

CHAPTER 2

PLANTS FOR THE GARDEN

Plant Selection

Plant selection is an important part of dry, subtropical and Mediterranean-climate gardening, given the challenges of droughts, erratic rainfall and temperature extremes. The key to a healthy and sustainable garden is choosing plants that can adapt to changing climate conditions. Native plants thrive in your garden's soil and climate, needing little water or maintenance and promoting local biodiversity. Many plants have developed to thrive in dry climates, making them more resistant to local pests and diseases and providing food and shelter for native animals and insects. Gardeners should only plant non-native plants if they are not considered invasive. Local councils usually provide lists of invasive species to avoid as well as native plants that are recommended.

Gardeners should give more attention to perennial plants, since they are better suited to withstand climate extremes compared to annuals. Perennials have roots that go deep into the water table. By planting perennials with little digging, the integrity of the soil is preserved. Planting ground covers or mulching to avoid exposed soil will prevent water evaporation during droughts and the erosion of fertile soil during extreme rains. Enhance biodiversity and save water by replacing extensive lawn areas with native alternatives in your garden.

Companion planting is another useful approach for a climate-resilient food-producing garden. It promotes biodiversity and can reduce the spread of pests. It also strengthens soil health through varying root structures and diverse nutrient supply, improving soil fertility and structural integrity. By carefully selecting the right plants for your garden and local conditions, you can reduce garden maintenance, protect the soil and establish a sustainable and resilient garden ecosystem. The plants in this book have been selected mainly for their resistance to drought. As you can see from the pictures, a drought-tolerant garden can still have plenty of attractive and colourful plants.

Getting Started

Whether you are building a new home on an empty plot, buying an existing one or already own a house with a garden, consider the overall design that you want. You need to give some serious thought to the garden before putting in new plants. What sort of garden is it going to be? Personal choice will be a great deciding factor. We all have our own ideas of what we want in a garden, but there are many other factors that have to be considered. The shape, size and orientation of the plot are all relevant. The contours of the land will make a difference, as will the position of the house and its entrance. Any mature trees must be looked after carefully and worked into the design.

Is it on a hilltop where most of the topsoil has been washed away, or is it in a valley with deep, rich soil? If it is on a hilltop, then wind may be a problem, while a valley may be a frost pocket. Is it close to the sea? This is ideal for the beach, but what about those salt-laden winds that can decimate so many

plants? What is the soil like? Is it mostly chalky or acid? Is it a deep, rich loam or more likely is it poor and rocky?

Maintenance is a key consideration. How much time can you spend in the garden? If you work or have many commitments, then you will have less time to spend in the garden than if you are retired.

Cost is also an important factor. Many people take great pride in creating a wonderful garden from seeds or cuttings given to them by friends, which is an extremely economical way to make a garden. Other people feel time is more important, wanting an instant garden, and are prepared to pay for large trees and shrubs to fill it.

Your Design Choices

When planning a garden from scratch, we all have certain features that we want to include: perhaps a covered archway giving summer shade; a path leading to a shady corner with a seat; or a pool with a bubbling fountain. Choosing a style is important. Some people envisage a more formal style with straight paths, tall trees and neatly-clipped shrubs as architectural features along with restrained plantings, while others prefer a more natural look.

Some will go for colour – mixed borders themed by colour or plantings where one colour will merge into another. This will mean that all plants are carefully chosen and planted according to their colour. Other people, such as myself, just love plants, and enjoy the thrill of finding unusual ones that will grow well in the area. We enjoy a genuine thrill from seeing a rare plant flower for the first time. This means that the overall design is based on the plants, their needs and how they grow.

To design a garden effectively, it is important to have a knowledge of the plants that are available locally and the way that they will grow. I hope that those listed in this book will help you choose successfully.

Most people never have the opportunity to design an entirely new garden. They move into a house with one existing which is usually possible to redesign and improve. Keen gardeners can always think of changes or add new plants for variety or to create a different effect. The main deciding factor is that you are happy with your garden, since after all, you are going to live with it, be there every day. You must be comfortable with the feel of the garden.

The gentle sound of running water adds a soothing touch.

Planning a Garden

Draw a scaled plan of your property on squared paper. Consider natural characteristics such as existing vegetation, drainage, type of soil, wind exposure, direction of sun and local climate.

Plan what the various areas will be used for and consider views and areas requiring screening. Think how you intend to water your garden (for example, irrigation system or hand watering). Plants need varying amounts of water and maybe at different times of year, so group plants according to their water, soil and sun requirements.

For example, grass areas require watering more frequently than garden beds or trees and should be planted in separate areas. Start with hard features such as paved or tiled terraces, walls, pergolas and so on. Then mark the important trees, allowing them enough room to grow, then fill in with the beds and borders. Transfer your ideas to the ground, marking paths, walls and other hard features out with string or sand to show the structure and shape the garden will take.

If you choose to have any hard landscaping, it is far easier to construct it before the planting begins. Raised beds can add interest on a flat site, as well as being easier to look after, especially if they are for growing vegetables. If any earth has to be moved to create a raised bed or to move rocks to make a feature, it can be done with an earth-moving machine, which can do a great deal of work in a short time at reasonable cost. Think about this carefully before any planting is carried out, as a machine may not have access later. Determine how much maintenance you are prepared to take on.

Consider Your Budget

When you are ready to plant, begin with any trees. These are important to provide shade, both for you when you sit in the garden and to shelter other plants. Trees are usually slow growing and will be important features of the garden. Some will eventually become large, so think of what they will look like when they are mature. Will they block the light to the house or obscure the view? With any planting, think of where the drains are, because roots seek moisture and can block them. If wind is a problem, then planting a windbreak is important. Acacia, Eucalyptus and Juniperus are examples of windbreak plants.

A big question is 'Do you want a lawn?' If you are used to living in a cooler region, then you will probably be used to having one, but is it right for a dry garden? To plant a lawn, the ground needs a lot of preparation, constant maintenance, cutting about once a week, feeding regularly, and plenty of water. If you decide not to have a lawn, areas of gravel are practical, or ground-cover plants in areas where you do not walk.

One of the many attractions of living or holidaying in a dry climate is being able to eat 'alfresco' on warm evenings. So, it is wonderful to create an intimate outdoor living room. A paved or tiled area with some night-scented plants around it such as *Choisya ternata* with sweet-scented flowers in spring and autumn, and aromatic leaves, *Nerium oleander* with perfumed flowers or a *Jasminum officinale* growing over a pergola will create the conditions for a memorable meal.

Consider what style of outdoor furniture you like, which is both comfortable to use and durable. To improve the atmosphere of your outdoor space, add shade trees and perhaps some plants with lush foliage such as Strelitzia, phormiums and a palm if there is room. In a large garden, choose the position carefully so that it is sheltered from the prevailing wind and, in cooler climates, faces the evening sun. If you have a small garden, you may decide to devote the whole to an outdoor room, where it can be intensively planted with climbers on the walls and shade-loving, colourful plants growing low down and in pots in the corners.

Pots and Containers Add Interest

Wherever you go in the Mediterranean regions, you will see plants growing in pots or containers. These are on steps, windowsills, balconies, terraces or anywhere that colour is wanted. Plants are grown in containers for many reasons. Because of the large number of people living in flats or home units, gardening on windowsills or balconies has become a necessity. Potted plants in attractive containers are highly decorative, even for gardeners with plenty of outdoor space. Patios, courtyards and garden areas can be enhanced by adding features that soften and beautify the space or create focal points. This way you can give plants a suitable microclimate or show them off when they are looking their best.

There are, of course, many other reasons that the popularity of this form of gardening is growing. Garden centres now offer a much bigger range of attractive tubs, pots, troughs, hanging baskets, vertical garden kits and window boxes and an even greater variety of plants to grow in them.

It may be difficult to grow plants well in containers in a hot, dry climate. When planting up a container, it is important to remember that there will be wet periods, and a badly drained container can soon become waterlogged, resulting in the plant dying. Good drainage is essential. If the container has a flat base and is going to stand on a flat surface, check to see if the hole in the bottom will let the water drain out. It may be necessary to raise the container up on a support such as some tiles, to allow it to drain freely.

Soil in containers in the scorching sun will heat during the day. The larger the pot and the thicker the sides (preferably terracotta or concrete) the less this will happen. As plants in pots have only a relatively small amount of soil, which gives them a small reserve of water to draw on, watering the pots is crucial. Do this frequently, especially in the hottest part of the year. As containers will dry out fast, be sure to have a large saucer under each pot to allow it to sit in water for a while. This will help extra moisture absorb into the pot and help soak the soil area (water often runs through too fast to do this the first time).

It is a pleasure to walk under a leafy pergola on a hot day.

Plants in pots can add colour to a garden. A *Clivia minata* is a spectacular plant when in full flower; it can be brought onto a shady terrace near the house to be seen at its best, but for the rest of the year, it is rather dull. Many plants can be treated this way, flowering annuals, bulbs, ferns, creepers, herbs, shrubs and trees. Another advantage of having plants in pots is that they can be moved around like furniture in the house, which can be rearranged to suit your moods.

Climbing Plants and Pergolas

All gardens are greatly enhanced by climbing plants, whether they are used to clothe walls, hide unsightly objects or give some shade. On hot summer days, there is nothing better than sitting, or strolling in the shade, while catching a cool breeze. In hot gardens, it is essential to create shade to enhance this feeling. Many people opt for rustic constructions such as pergolas and patios. Training a fast-growing climbing plant to create a canopy atop the structure will earn praise from friends.

Courtyards possess a cosy atmosphere that distinguishes them from gardens. A well-designed courtyard can transform a small space and give it a sense of purpose. City dwellers can find a much-needed break from indoor living in a courtyard. If you live in a larger home with multiple garden spaces, consider incorporating courtyard designs for an additional meditative area, or use enclosed courtyards as distinctive features within the home.

Walls of houses cry out for climbers that are carefully sited. A *Trachelospermum jasminoides* on the wall near a living room that will fill the air with its scent at night is wonderful. Any plant that is against a wall must be placed with care, as a wall in full sun all day can become extremely hot, and many plants will suffer. Some wall plants are rampant and become a problem while others, such as Hedera species, can damage walls. A well-sited and managed wall plant can add great beauty to a house. Probably the most popular one for Mediterranean regions must be Bougainvillea. There are many spectacular varieties that come in vibrant shades of many colours. As it can make 2 metres of growth a year, it will quickly cover a large area and it thrives in the hottest location. Often large old plants of *Bougainvillea glabra* with its purple bracts can be seen covering abandoned ruins, where it receives no water or attention but yet flowers so profusely.

Plant Names

Why do gardeners use the difficult-to-understand Latin or botanical names for plants? The reason is that each country, region, nursery or even individuals can have their own names for plants, and this can be confusing or misleading. There is only one botanical name for each species, hybrid or cultivar, and this is recognised worldwide. The botanical name comprises two or three words. First is the genus name followed by the species, then maybe a variety or cultivar.

You will see that following the plant name comes the family name. This name is like a human family's name. All the plants that belong to the same family are related. Although, like humans, they may not look as though they are related.

A botanical name tells you something about the plant. The genus name is usually a Greek or Roman classical name or named after a person. The species name is usually a descriptive name. It may tell you about the place that the plant comes from, the colour of the flower or leaves, or the form of the leaf. It may tell you the shape of the plant, or about any peculiarities that the plant has, such as heart-shaped leaves, edible fruit, or if it grows tall, when fully grown. The same descriptive words are used often, so whenever you see '*africanus*' you know it comes from Africa, or '*grandiflora*' that it is large-flowered. Once you know the meanings of these words, they become easy to understand and help you identify a plant.

Carl Linnaeus (1707–78) is famous for creating a system of naming plants and animals – a system we still use today. This system is known as the binomial system as set forth in his *Systema Naturae* (1735) and subsequent works. Each species of plant and animal is given a genus name followed by a specific name (species), with both names being in Latin. He based the system on the sexual reproductive parts of the flower. Until then, all gardeners had their own pet names of plants, which led to total confusion when trading plants. There was much resistance to this idea initially, but over time, it became the standard way to name plants and still is.

With the introduction of DNA testing of plants in the 2000s, it has been found that many plants have been wrongly named. Some plants now have a new species name and others have moved genus or family. In principle, each genus should form a 'clade', containing plants that are more closely related to each other than to any other plants. You will note that many plants have the word '*syn.*' for synonym, followed by the old name. As in Linnaeus' time, many gardeners are reluctant to use the new or unfamiliar name of their plants. In writing this book, I have tried to use the most up-to-date name available. All names have been checked with World Flora Online, an internet-based compendium of the world's plant species, launched in October 2012 to publish an online flora of all known plants by 2020, created by the Royal Botanic Gardens, Kew and Missouri Botanical Garden.

CHAPTER 3

SOIL AND WATER

Organic Matter is Important

Many dry-climate and Mediterranean soils are short of organic matter because dryness inhibits the formation of humus, and also because the geological structure makes them almost devoid of plant foods. Incorporating organic matter into the soil improves the structure enormously. This can be done before planting, but it should also be a continuous process.

Once the garden becomes established, one of the best pieces of equipment to buy is a shredder. This reduces prunings into chips or mulch that can be spread over the garden. Any material that will compost such as leaves, grass clippings and kitchen waste should go directly onto a compost heap.

Plants need many nutrients in the soil so that they can grow, flower and fruit. Some of these are elements usually found in the soil naturally in sufficient quantities, but in some soils some elements may be unavailable. Plants may suffer and show signs of deficiency. In such cases, you may add the missing nutrients by manure or a chemical fertiliser. If using a general chemical fertiliser, choose one with added trace elements, as these are beneficial.

Soil is Important

Soil erosion is a major problem throughout many regions. So often, owners of hilltop houses find that the topsoil has been washed away and only the poor subsoil is left. Thought must be given as to how to manage the soil well. Avoid steep slopes, which allow water to remove the valuable soil. Terrace a slope whenever possible; even a row of rocks will break the force of the water and prevent gullies from forming. Just as bad is a poorly-drained soil. If the garden is low-lying or in a basin, the water may collect during the winter and plant roots may rot. A well-aerated soil is important for a healthy root structure.

Mulch

Mulching is an essential element of a water-efficient garden. Using mulch liberally and regularly helps retain soil moisture. It does this by reducing evaporation, restricting weed growth and improving soil structure as it breaks down. Some people worry that leaves look 'messy' and rake them up and dig the soil. But this leads to poor-quality soil, resulting in a lower water infiltration rate, drainage problems, soil erosion and dust around the home. Mulch also protects soil against erosion, improves plant growth by providing insulation for plant roots and moderates extremes in soil temperature.

There are many types of mulch to choose from. You can use almond shells, mushroom compost, straw or pine needles, or better still, any manure that may be available from a local farm. Organic mulch, such as sugar cane mulch or pine bark, will decompose over time and help improve your soil. Organic mulch should be reapplied frequently, preferably in autumn and

Rock walls hold back soil on a steep slope.

spring, to replace the broken-down mulch. The ideal thickness of the mulch layer depends on the particle size of the mulch material. If using large chunks, such as pine bark, a deep layer of 5cm or more is needed. Be sure to keep the mulch at least 6cm clear of plant stems, or they may rot.

Inorganic mulch such as pebbles will help reduce evaporation but will not help to improve the soil. Flat stones and coarse gravel, of varied size and 15cm or more deep, and as locally sourced as possible, are much more natural and attractive. Any rain that does fall is protected from evaporation, and in the driest areas the stones can be laid around a depression, so they direct rain to the roots of the plants.

Water in the Garden

Gardeners dread the word 'drought'. It is so much easier to garden when we get rain. However, drought is a fact of life, so as gardeners, we need to come to terms with it and learn how to garden with it.

Right now, drought is being exacerbated by climate change, making gardening through the drought a bit more challenging. One of the greatest challenges of climate change is that we cannot know what those changes will be – except that they are likely to be extreme. Most of our plant watering is more shallow than we think and can actually do harm. Plants will direct their roots to seek water in the soil. If water is only ever to be found in the top 10 or 20 centimetres, the roots will not bother growing deeper into the soil. Even when the surface soil dries up, there is often moisture further down, so we aim for the roots to be deep in the cooler soil, where there is still moisture for longer. When watering, a deep soak is needed, rather than a light sprinkle. While most of us are familiar with the concept, we often lack a true comprehension and appearance of a deep soak.

In summer-rainfall climates, water is rarely a problem, and enough rainwater can be stored to survive any dry spells. But summer-dry climates have much greater difficulties. Even in England, known for its rainfall, summer droughts are common, and public water supplies are insufficient for the growing population in southern England, leading to restrictions on garden watering before the start of the growing season. In regions with arid summers, water scarcity and rising costs are compounded by population growth. However, the acceleration of climate change has prompted gardeners worldwide to reconsider their plant choices. In the past few decades there has been a tremendous movement to make gardens with drought-tolerant plants that use little, or no, summer water once established. This does not mean that the garden will be dull. By the careful selection of plants, a really colourful garden can still be achieved.

When and how often to water

Watering in the early morning is the best time, before the heat of the day when plants need it most. While automated systems can be programmed to operate in the early morning, this time may not be favoured by later risers. For hand-watering, late evening is the most popular and recommended time. This is fine, as little moisture is lost during the night. Try not to water during the heat of the day unless you find a plant that is suffering.

How much water to give? This is a much harder question to answer. The amount to give a plant depends upon so many factors. Individual species will need different amounts. Plants require most water when in active growth. The soil type affects water retention, with heavy clay holding more water than light sandy soil. Size of the plant will make a difference, with a small one needing less water than a large tree, but then as plants become established and send their roots down, they may need less water. Another important consideration is the season; increase watering as it gets hotter and decrease as it cools down after summer. Once plants are established, after the first few weeks in the ground, they may be allowed to dry out for short periods between waterings. Many plants in this book need watering only occasionally. Some plants have a dormant period, when they need no water at all. The key is experience – observe your plants and water them only when needed.

A watering can allows you to water sparingly.

A TO Z OF PLANTS

A

ABELIA *see* LINNAEA

Abutilon vitifolium see *Corynabutilon vitifolium*

ACACIA
Fabaceae
Wattle, Mimosa
Native to dry tropical or warm temperate regions of Australia

The 2005 Botanical Conference decided – and confirmed at the 2011 Conference – that the name Acacia should be kept for the Australian species and that the (mainly) African species should be reclassified into the genus Vachellia.

A vast genus of about 1,000 species of deciduous and evergreen shrubs with many species having thorns or spines. Leaves are typically compound in arrangement, the shape of the leaflets varying among species. Small, often fragrant flowers, usually yellow or cream-coloured, are in dense, spherical clusters or spikes. Species are found in a wide range of habitats, from arid deserts to tropical rainforests. Some species have a symbiotic relationship with nitrogen-fixing bacteria in their root nodules, allowing them to thrive in nutrient-poor soils. They are among the most popular and colourful trees in Mediterranean gardens. Of the many species known, only a few are commonly planted in gardens. Many have escaped and become naturalised. In some regions, species have become invasive and can displace native vegetation.

Acacia baileyana
Golden Mimosa, Cootamundra
Native to southeastern Australia

A fast-growing evergreen tree to 6m or more with a spreading and open canopy. Bark of young branches is smooth and greenish, but as the tree matures, it becomes rougher and may develop fissures. Leaves are 4 to 6cm long and doubly pinnate with many small leaflets 5mm long and silvery-blue grey. Clusters of small, often globular, yellow fragrant flowers in racemes up to 8cm long appear profusely from winter to early spring, giving the tree an attractive and ornamental appearance when in bloom. Easily grown in well-drained soil in full sun. Drought and frost tolerant, it is well-suited to Mediterranean climates. This is one of the most commonly planted acacias, making a wonderful multi-stemmed tree. The cultivar 'Purpurea' has purple-tinged foliage, which should be cut back to encourage fresh growth that has the best colour. Unfortunately, more tender than the species.

Acacia dealbata
Silver Wattle, Mimosa
Native to Australia, New South Wales to Tasmania

A relatively fast-growing tree that can reach to 10m or more with an equal spread. It has a graceful, spreading canopy. Bark on younger branches is smooth and greenish, but as the tree matures, it may develop a rougher texture and become fissured. Leaves are bipinnate and feathery, with a silvery-blue or greyish-green colour up to 12cm long. Fine, fern-like foliage gives the tree an elegant appearance. Terminal branches produce masses of tiny, fragrant, spherical clusters of bright yellow flowers. Inflorescences are typically abundant and can create a striking display when in bloom. Easily grown in a variety of soil types and climates. It tolerates drought and light frosts and is well suited to coastal climates. Much appreciated for its flowers, which provide the florists' Mimosa.

Acacia longifolia
Sydney Golden Wattle

A medium to large shrub or small tree growing to 10m high with a willowy spreading habit. Leaves are typically bright green or greyish-green, leathery, 8 to 15cm long and linear, giving the plant its specific epithet. Bright yellow, fragrant, golden-yellow flower heads are in loose cylindrical spikes to 6cm long. These appear along the branches in late winter until early spring. Grows best in sandy well-drained soil in full sun. Drought, salt, frost and wind tolerant. Often planted near the beach, where it makes a good soil binder, where wind will make it prostrate and branches may root in the sand. It has a useful life of about ten years. A light prune after flowering will help keep it bushy with prolific flowering.

Acacia paradoxa syn. *Acacia armata*
Kangaroo Thorn, Hedge Wattle, Prickly Wattle

Native to New South Wales, Australia

This spreading and often densely-branched shrub can form thickets to about 3m high and as wide. Stems and branches are armed with sharp, often curved, 1 to 2cm long thorns. Leaves are typically phyllodes, which are modified leaf-like structures 2 to 3cm long rather than true leaves, a widened petiole that takes on the appearance of a leaf. They are often linear, grey-green to bluish green. Round, bright yellow flower heads, on stalks 6 to 20mm long, are borne singly (rarely in pairs) at the bases of the phyllodes in early spring in abundance. It is adaptable to various habitats, including open woodlands, grasslands and disturbed areas. Grows in most well-drained soils. Drought tolerant. As with many species, it has nitrogen-fixing nodules on its roots, contributing to soil fertility. Because of its thorniness, it can make an impenetrable hedge, or it can be used as a sand barrier.

Acacia saligna
Blue Leaf Wattle

Native to Western Australia

A fast-growing shrub or small tree growing 8m or more high spreading to 3 to 5m in perhaps three or four years, with a somewhat weeping habit. Leaves are narrow, blue green, 15 to 30cm long, resembling willow leaves, hence the common name. Rich yellow flowers appear in late winter and early spring, in groups of up to ten bright-yellow spherical flower heads. Grows in most well-drained soils. Drought tolerant. Stems are brittle and large limbs can be damaged by wind, so prune to keep an open centre. It is sometimes cultivated, particularly in arid and coastal areas, where it is valued for its attractive foliage and showy flowers.

ACANTHUS
Acanthaceae

Native to the Mediterranean region

A genus of about 30 species of large-leaved perennials or subshrubs known for their distinctive, deeply-lobed leaves and striking architectural appearance. The genus includes both evergreen and deciduous species. Plants produce tall spikes of tubular flowers that usually have a hood-like structure, with colourful bracts surrounding them, commonly white or pale pink, rising above the foliage. The Acanthus leaf motif has a long history in art and architecture, having been a popular design element in classical Greek and Roman art, often used in the Corinthian order of columns. The motif has continued to be used throughout history in various forms of decorative arts.

Acanthus spinosus
Bear's Breeches, Greek Acanthus

Native to the Mediterranean region

A clump-forming perennial with obovate, deeply-lobed, dark-green leaves, shiny above to 1m long with spiny margins. In summer, white flowers with purple shaded bracts are borne in 1m long racemes, often with purple-tinged stems above the foliage. Grow in a rich, well-drained soil in full sun, but it will tolerate shade. It thrives in the shade of trees where few other plants can survive. Drought tolerant. Relatively low maintenance once established. Cut back stems after flowering. Flowers are sometimes used for floral arrangements. The bold foliage and striking flower spikes make it a favourite among gardeners, looking to add a touch of classical elegance to their outdoor spaces.

Acca sellowiana see *Feijoa sellowiana*

ACHILLEA
Asteraceae
Yarrow

Native to Europe and western Asia

The genus includes a diverse group of perennials well known for their fern-like foliage and flat-topped clusters of small, daisy-like flowers that come in white, yellow, pink and red. Species are often cultivated in gardens for their attractive flowers, aromatic foliage and ability to attract pollinators such as bees and butterflies. They are also valued for their drought tolerance and ability to thrive in a variety of soil types, making them popular choices for xeriscaping and wildflower gardens.

Achillea filipendulina
Fern-Leaf Yarrow, Golden Yarrow

Native to parts of Europe and western Asia

A clump-forming, evergreen perennial to 120cm high with rosettes of linear, pinnate, lobed and serrated, hairy and rough fern-like foliage, which emits a spicy scent when crushed. Strong, leafy stems bear golden yellow flower heads 13cm across from mid- to late summer. It thrives in well-drained soil in full sun but can tolerate some light shade. Drought, heat and humidity tolerant, once established. It is also relatively low maintenance. A beautiful and versatile plant that adds colour and texture to garden borders, meadows and cottage-style landscapes. Valued for the quality of its cut flowers.

ACHNATHERUM
Poaceae
Needle Grass

A genus of nineteen species. Several species have been switched between Achnatherum and genus Stipa. Taxonomy between the two closely related genera is still uncertain.

Achnatherum calamagrostis syn. *Stipa calamagrostis*

Native to southern Europe

A deciduous, fountain-like, ornamental, perennial free-flowering grass, which forms rounded mounds to 1m high and 1.2m wide. Leaves are rush-like, cylindrical, blue-green to 30cm long. During summer, these are embellished with a haze of silvery white flower plumes up to 80cm long. As they mature, both flowers and foliage undergo a gorgeous transformation, taking on a beautiful, light brownish yellow that remains throughout the winter, elegantly swaying with the wind. Easy to grow in full sun in any moderately fertile, well-drained soil. Drought tolerant once established. Grown for its early blooming feathery flowers, it is an attractive grass for borders in a dry garden, requiring little care.

ACIS
Amaryllidaceae
Snowflakes

Native to Europe and north Africa

A genus of nine species of perennial, herbaceous spring-blooming bulbs. Species are relatively short, up to 45cm. Though the flowers and foliage are like snowdrops, Acis grows at least twice as tall and blooms at a different time. Pure white, bell-shaped flowers are decorated with lime green accents and dangle in clusters from arching stems. Bulbs are reliably perennial, and summer dormant, so you can expect them to bloom every year for years to come.

Until 2004, the genus Leucojum included species now placed in Acis.

Acis autumnalis syn. *Leucojum autumnale*
Autumn Snowflake

Native to the Mediterranean, north Africa

A bulbous perennial with upright, narrow, grass-like leaves to 16cm long, which are produced at flowering time. Each bulb produces up to four slender stems to 25cm high from late summer into autumn. Individual flowers are good for two to three weeks, but on a well-established clump there will be a continuous succession. These carry two to four glistening white bell-shaped flowers, 1cm long. The bulbs are ideal for planting in a rock garden or a well-drained border. A delicate-looking plant that prefers full sun. Summer dormant so give little water, allowing the bulbs to dry out. They should remain undisturbed for many years.

Acis longifolia syn. *Leucojum trichophyllum*
Three-Leaved Snowflake

Native to southern Portugal, southwest Spain and Morocco

A bulbous perennial growing to a height of 10 to 20cm. Each plant produces long, thin, thread-like leaves, usually three, referring to its old species name. These appear before flowering. In winter, flowers are borne on a single, thin round erect stem, 8 to 30cm high, with one to four beautiful, small, nodding, individual white flowers, which are often flushed with pink at the base. They are six-petalled with three inner petals and three outer petals, all with a sharply pointed tip, bell-like at first, with the petals continuing to spread outwards as they mature. A pretty plant to grow in sandy, well-drained soil in full sun. Give little water during summer to allow the bulbs to become dormant.

ACOELORRHAPHE
Arecaceae

Native to south Florida, West Indies and Central America

A genus containing a single species of clumping palm. Panicles of bowl-shaped hermaphrodite flowers are borne among fan-shaped leaves that are produced it terminal tufts. Often used in Florida as a street tree and for park decoration.

Acoelorrhaphe wrightii
Silver Saw Palmetto, Everglades Palm, Saw Cabbage Palm

Native from Mexico to Central America

A clustering palm, which can spread from 2 to 6m wide with stems up to 6m high. Its slender stems are less than 15 centimetres in diameter and are covered with brown fibres and old leaf bases. Leaves are palmate (fan-shaped), with segments joined to each other for about half of their length, and are 1 to 2m wide, light green above and silver underneath. Leaf petiole is 1 to 1.2m long, and has orange, curved, sharp teeth along the edges. Flowers are minute, inconspicuous and greenish, with six stamens. The fruit is pea-sized, starting orange and turning to black at maturity. Grow in full sun or partial shade in fertile soil, but it can also take poor soil. Fairly drought tolerant, but grows better with generous watering and will even tolerate occasional boggy conditions. Surprisingly hardy, it will re-sprout even if the stems are killed by severe frost. A mature clump of this palm makes an attractive specimen. In its native habitat, it grows in swamps and periodically flooded forests.

Acacia baileyana purpurea.

Acacia saligna.

Acanthus spinosus.

Achillea filipendulina.

Achnatherum calamagrostis.

Acis autumnalis.

Acoelorrhaphe wrightii.

Adenium obesum.

Adenocarpus hispanicus.

ADENIUM
Apocynaceae
Desert Rose

Native to Africa and the Arabian Peninsula

A genus of about twelve species of thick-stemmed shrubs up to 3m tall, with branches that are often twisted or gnarled. Leaves are a thick, leathery, glossy green with a lighter midvein, obovate, 4 to 15cm long. They are adapted to growing in dry places. The flowers are large and trumpet-shaped, with a range of colours including white, pink, red, purple and bicolour.

Adenium obesum
Desert Rose

Native to tropical and subtropical eastern and southern Africa, Arabian Peninsula

A variable succulent shrub with a thick, usually bottle-shaped, twisted, greyish brown stem of up to 3m high and tapering to many branched tips. Upright succulent branches produce opposite, thick, obovate 4 to 12cm long leathery leaves that have somewhat squared or rounded tips. Red, pink or white flowers, narrowly bell-shaped, 6 to 8cm long, are borne from one to several in terminal corymbs throughout spring and summer. It lends itself well to pot culture and makes a lovely specimen with its swollen basal trunk (caudex). The best showy flowers come from specimens that are pot bound and have been pruned each year. Outdoors grow in well-drained, slightly alkaline soil in full sun. Drought tolerant. As subspecies readily hybridise, there are many cultivars in many colours. It is widely used as an ornamental plant around the world. The plant's sap is highly toxic.

ADENOCARPUS
Fabaceae

Native to the Mediterranean region and sub-Saharan Africa

A genus of about fifteen species of deciduous and evergreen shrubs with alternate three-pinnate leaves. They are valued for their broom-like, yellow flowers borne in terminal racemes on the previous year's growth in spring or summer.

Adenocarpus hispanicus

Native to the Iberian Peninsula in Spain and Portugal

A variable, upright or spreading, deciduous shrub to 4m high. Leaves are three-pinnate, tiny, 7 to 25mm long and light green. In summer, yellow flowers 2cm long cover the shrub in dense terminal racemes. Grow in well-drained mildly acidic to mildly alkaline soil in full sun. Drought, high wind, salt and light frost tolerant. It can be dry for extended periods to constantly moist. Suits Mediterranean and dry-style garden designs and informal screens. Remove half of the flowering wood to prevent seeding and remove the oldest branches to the base after flowering.

AEONIUM
Crassulaceae

Native to the Mediterranean region and Canary Islands

A genus of about 36 species of beautiful, evergreen, perennial succulents or sub-shrubs. Stems can be simple or branched, usually thick, succulent, in various colours. Neat rosettes of fleshy, often glossy leaves are produced at the ends of clustered basal shoots. Leaf colour ranges from green to shades of red, purple or black, and some are variegated. Terminal cymes, panicles or racemes of many star-shaped, many-petalled flowers 8 to 15mm across emerge from the centre of the rosettes on long, slender stems in spring to summer. They are adapted to arid rocky environments and semi-arid regions, often found growing in coastal areas, on cliffs and rocky slopes in regions with mild, frost-free conditions. Grow in full sun in well-draining soil, which is essential to prevent waterlogging. Drought tolerant, so are commonly used in xeriscaping, succulent gardens, and as container plants. Some species go dormant in summer, during which they may drop their leaves when not requiring any water. This adaptation helps them conserve water during periods of intense heat and drought.

Aeonium arboreum 'Velour'
Purple Pinwheels

Native to the Canary Islands

An upright-growing succulent 60 to 90cm high and 30 to 60cm wide. Many branched stems end with 15 to 20cm, magnificent rosettes of leaves, giving an appearance of a miniature tree. Leaves are fleshy, 7 to 8cm long, dark chocolate to dark purple and lightly fringed. If grown in full sun, the foliage turns almost black. Bright golden racemes containing many small yellow star-like flowers are produced in pyramidal heads to 30cm high during summer. Commonly grown on tops of banks and walls, or in rock gardens. Especially good in hot, dry, sunny situations, as it is drought tolerant once established.

Aeonium canariense
Velvet Rose

Native to the Canary Islands

A short-stemmed succulent up to 20cm high that usually branches at the base, producing large, beautiful, symmetrical, deep cup-shaped rosettes of leaves up to 40cm across. Leaves are dark green and spoon-shaped, up to 25cm long with sticky hairs. Small bright yellow flowers are produced in a pyramidal spike in spring up to 1m high. Suckers are produced readily, giving rise to many new plants. It can be grown in full sun but grows better if given partial shade. Best grown in fertile, well-drained soil. Drought tolerant but give it deep, infrequent summer watering. Withstands light frosts.

Aeonium cuneatum

Native to the Canary Islands

A low-growing succulent reaching around 50cm high, spreading with no stem. This is a massive growing species, forming large rosettes to over 50cm in diameter. Leaves are smooth and often coated in a white farina, giving the plants a frosted look to the upper surface. The flower is yellow and more open than some other species. Best suited to growing in the ground where the plants can have plenty of room to grow and spread rather than in pots. It offshoots easily, making a large group across the ground. Naturally found growing in filtered light, so avoid excessive sun exposure. Ideal for a rockery or dry garden. Protect from frost.

AESCULUS
Sapindaceae
Buckeye, Horse Chestnut

Native to North America, southeast Europe and east Asia

A small genus of about fifteen species of deciduous trees and shrubs. They are characterised by their distinctive, palmate leaves, usually with serrated edges. Tubular, usually white, cream, yellow or pink flowers are in panicles or spikes and are usually quite showy. Flowers are often fragrant and attract pollinators such as bees. The fruit is a capsule that contains one or more seeds. These capsules are often spiny or husk-covered, giving the appearance of a chestnut or buckeye. The seeds, commonly known as 'conkers' or 'buckeyes', are large and shiny, with a smooth surface.

Aesculus californica
California Buckeye

Native to California

A large deciduous shrub or small tree, often with several stems up to 8m high, spreading to 10m wide with silvery trunk and branches. It is summer deciduous in dry areas, with leaves appearing with autumn rains. Dark green leaves are palmately compound with five to seven leaflets 8 to 10cm long with a finely-toothed margin and (particularly in spring) downy surfaces. Leaves are tender and prone to damage from both spring frost or snow and summer heat and desiccation. In early summer, it produces a mass of fragrant, white or pink-tinged flowers, with long protruding stamens in dense erect panicles up to 20cm long. These are followed by rough-skinned fruit 5 to 7cm long. The seeds are poisonous and are among the largest of any temperate (non-tropical) plant species. It has adapted to its native Mediterranean climate by growing during the wet late winter and spring and entering dormancy in dry summer months, though those growing in coastal regions hold on to their leaves until mid-autumn. Full sun is necessary for the tree to have the best appearance. It can grow effortlessly in any soil, thriving abundantly. Summer drought tolerant.

Aesculus pavia
Red Buckeye

Native to southeastern USA

A deciduous shrub or small tree typically reaching about 3 to 6m high. It has an open, spreading form with multiple stems. The medium to dark green leaves are palmately compound, usually composed of five to seven lance-shaped leaflets and serrated along the edges. Striking, tubular, red to orange-red nectar-rich flowers, in upright panicles, are borne in spring, attracting birds and other pollinators. Fruit is a capsule that contains one or two large, shiny seeds, often referred to as buckeyes. Grow in well-drained soil in full sun. Because of its attractive flowers and manageable size, it is often used in landscaping. Suitable for gardens, naturalised areas, and as an understorey plant. It is valued for its vibrant flowers and makes a lovely addition to gardens in its native range and beyond.

AGAPANTHUS
Amaryllidaceae
African Blue Lily, Lily of the Nile

Native to southern Africa

A genus of about ten variable species of perennials with thick rhizomes. Long, strap-like, arching, evergreen or deciduous leaves arise from a central basal rosette. Large, rounded clusters to 20cm of trumpet-shaped, 3cm-long flowers are held on tall, erect stalks, in a range of colours, including shades of blue, purple, white and occasionally pink. Flowering occurs in summer, and the display can be quite striking. The inflorescences are good for cutting and are followed by decorative seed heads. Some species are found in the winter rainfall area of the Cape of South Africa, others in summer rainfall areas.

Agapanthus africanus
African Lily

Native to Northern, Western and Eastern Cape, South Africa

A clump-forming, evergreen perennial growing 25 to 70cm high, with attractive, leathery, metallic green leaves to 30cm long. In early summer, stout flower stalks grow 60 to 90cm high from within the leaves. Each stalk is topped with umbels of 12 to 30 deep violet blue, trumpet-shaped flowers up to 4cm long. Flowers are thick-textured with a dark blue stripe running down the centre of each petal. These may last for up to a month. It thrives with ample water during the spring growing season, but when established can survive without summer water. It is best grown in fertile, well-drained soil in full sun or partial shade. This species is often confused with *A. praecox* but is much less common in cultivation.

Agapanthus praecox subsp. *orientalis*
Lily of the Nile

Native to Eastern Cape, South Africa

A clump-forming perennial with evergreen leaves 2.5 to 5cm broad and arching up to 60cm. Rounded large umbels 15 to 30cm across comprise trumpet-shaped, light-blue to deep violet and white, 5cm or more long flowers on stems 60 to 90cm high. The immense umbels can be up to 200 blooms on a single head. Grow in well-drained soil in

onium arboreum 'Velour'.

Aeonium cuneatum.

Aesculus californica.

sculus pavia.

Agapanthus praecox orientalis.

Agapetes serpens.

gave americana flower.

Agave americana 'Variegata'.

full sun or part shade. Thrives with plenty of water during spring but can withstand drought when established. If grown in containers or tubs, it can make attractive displays on terraces or balconies. Free drainage, especially in winter, is important, as it must not become waterlogged. There are many cultivars including 'Albiflorus' with white flowers, 'Nanus', which is dwarf and compact, and 'Variegatus' with striped leaves.

AGAPETES
Ericaceae
Agapetes, Chinese Lanterns

Native to warm temperate regions of east Asia, western Pacific, Australia

The genus includes around 170 species of semi-climbing shrubs. Species are typically epiphytic or lithophytic, meaning they grow on other plants or rocks rather than directly in soil. Stems are pendulous or trailing with small, elliptical, alternate leaves. Attractive pendulous clusters of flowers are usually bell-shaped or tubular, ranging from white to pink to red with prominent sepals giving them a lantern-like appearance, hence the common name. Species are often grown in hanging baskets or containers with well-draining, acidic soil. With proper care, they can make beautiful additions to gardens.

Agapetes serpens
Himalayan Lantern

Native to the Himalayas

An evergreen, epiphytic shrub producing long, slender shoots that can clamber into branches of trees. Often grows in nooks of trees, creating arching shoots to 1m high and wide, covered in dainty leaves around 2cm long on either side of the hairy stem. It often has a swollen trunk to hold onto its host branch. During winter, the foliage turns the most wonderful bronze. The 2.5cm long flowers run along the length of its branches. Each flower is in a cluster up to 5cm long and 1cm wide. Drought and frost tolerant. Grow in slightly acid soil in shade or partial sun. Good in a coastal area.

AGAVE
Asparagaceae
Century Plants

Native to Mexico and southern United States, specifically Texas

A large genus of over 300 species of small to giant succulent herbs. All species have thick, stout, fleshy, strap-like leaves in rosettes, usually with spines on the margins. Almost all species are trunkless, but a few produce stems to 10m high. Most species flower only after attaining some age and then die, but usually sucker and produce offshoots. Inflorescences are usually of considerable size and arise from the centre of the rosette of leaves, often to a great height. Flower clusters occupy only the top half of the inflorescence. All species need well-drained soil in full sun. Leaf fibres of many of them are used for making rope and twine. The rosette hearts of other species are used in Latin America to make an alcoholic drink known as 'mescal'.

Agave americana
Century Plant

Native to Mexico, but now naturalised over a wide area of the Mediterranean

A stemless succulent that forms a large rosette next to the ground. Blue-green, stiff, thick and fleshy lance-shaped leaves are up to 30cm wide and 2m long with hooked spines along the edge, and a stout spine at the tip. A flower spike, which is produced in early summer on mature plants, can grow to a gigantic 10m high before producing its masses of small 9cm-long greenish flowers on many short branches. Once the plant has flowered it dies, but usually leaves a rosette of suckers at the base of the old stem. Grow in full sun in any soil. Summer drought tolerant. It is often referred to as the Century Plant, which is misleading as it was originally thought only to flower once a century. In fact, it can flower from ten years old to perhaps 60 years depending on the soil and situation. There are many variegated forms, such as 'Marginata', which has attractive yellow margined leaves, 'Mediopicta', which has a broad central splash of yellow, and 'Striata', which has yellow or white stripes. It can be a beautiful addition to a container garden when it is still young.

Agave angustifolia 'Marginata'
Caribbean Agave, Century Plant, Maguey, Narrow Leaved Century Plant

Native to Mexico and Central America

A small to medium-sized, clump-forming, long-lived succulent, forming large rosettes of leaves 0.5 to 1m tall and 1 to 1.5m across. Older individuals develop a short woody trunk at the base. Smooth, stiff linear leaves up to 30 to 80cm long and 3 to 10cm wide are light green with cream-coloured margins and a sharply pointed apex ending in a spine. White to greenish-yellow flowers are in a terminal panicle on an inflorescence stalk up to 2.5m tall. Plants flower only once, starting from ten years of age or more. Grow in full sun in well-drained soil. While fairly drought tolerant, it is not as drought tolerant as other species and cultivars.

Agave attenuata
Swans Neck Agave, Fox Tail Agave

Native to tropical regions of Mexico

A small perennial succulent that grows between 2 and 3m high. Grey-green, wavy-edged leaves are up to 1m long, with no spines and a hint of ivory powder. Some older plants make a clump of 2m across. It gets its common name from its unique flower stem that curves elegantly, resembling the neck of a swan, and can grow up to 4m tall. Flowering stems emerge from the heart of the plant in summer and produce yellow or orange clusters of fragrant flowers along its spike. Grow in dry, well-draining soil in full sun to light shade.

Agave geminiflora
Twin Flowered Agave, Two Flowered Agave

Native to Mexico

A stemless, slow-growing succulent that forms a large dome of foliage next to the ground with a symmetrical rosette of sharply tipped, narrow dark-green foliage. Each leaf looks like it has a tangled silver thread wrapped around it. Grows 60cm to 1m high and wide. After around ten years, a huge 4m spike of masses of little yellow flowers appears. It usually flowers only once, then dies afterwards. Grow in full sun in well-drained soil. Drought tolerant. An architectural feature plant for containers, desert gardens, rockeries, water-wise planting, adding a modern look to the garden. Requires little maintenance and looks great in a group.

AGONIS
Myrtaceae

Native to southwestern Australia

Agonis formerly contained several other species, but the genus was recently split, with the majority moved to Taxandria.

Now a small genus of evergreen trees and shrubs that make attractive specimen trees.

Agonis flexuosa
Peppermint Tree, Australian Willow Myrtle

Native to southwestern Australia

A small and robust tree, usually less than 10m high and 5 to 10m wide, with a fibrous brown bark. Leaves are bright green, lance-shaped to 15cm long, densely covering the branches. It grows in a weeping habit and looks remarkably like a weeping willow from a distance. It is most readily identified by the powerful odour of peppermint emitted when leaves are crushed or torn. Many axillary clusters of two to three small white, fragrant flowers to 1cm across are produced in summer. Grow in full sun in fertile, well-drained neutral to acid soil. Drought tolerant once established. Makes an elegant specimen tree.

Agonis flexuosa 'Burgundy'
Burgundy Willow Myrtle

The deep burgundy foliage is truly eye-catching. This medium-sized tree has a weeping habit and grows 5 to 8m tall. Its burgundy colour provides a beautiful contrast to landscapes. It is complemented by clusters of small white flowers in spring. Because of its aesthetic appeal and resilience, it is highly desired for gardens, avenues, and as a feature tree in landscapes.

ALBIZIA
Fabaceae subfamily Mimosoideae

Native to tropical and subtropical regions of Africa, Asia to Australia

A genus of about 150 species of mostly deciduous trees or shrubs and climbers They are grown as ornamentals in tropical and subtropical gardens for their light, feathery, attractive foliage.

Albizia distachya see *Paraserianthes lophantha*

Albizia julibrissin
Mimosa Tree, Silk Tree, Persian Silk Tree

Native to southwestern and eastern Asia

A deciduous tree to 10m high with a spread to 6m and a domed crown. Branches have a spreading and often weeping form. The tree is known for its fern-like leaves, which are bipinnately compound, giving it a feathery appearance. Light-green pinnate leaves are 30 to 45cm long and are light sensitive, so they fold at night. It produces attractive, fluffy, pink to lavender-coloured flowers that resemble pom-poms. Beautiful fragrant flowers are pink in terminal fluffy clusters 7 to 15cm wide, appearing in summer. These are followed by thin seed pods that are 15cm long. Its flowers look their best when viewed from above. This tree can be difficult to establish. It can make an excellent shade tree with its flat top, ideal for a patio or terrace. Grows best with high summer heat and is known for its ability to tolerate drought conditions, making it suitable for areas with limited water availability. The variety 'Rosea' has richer pink flowers. The tree has been cultivated for its ornamental value in gardens and parks, appreciated for its showy flowers. Pruning is often necessary to maintain a desirable shape and prevent the tree from becoming overly leggy. In some regions, it has become invasive, particularly in the southeastern United States and parts of Australia.

Albizia lophantha see *Paraserianthes lophantha*

ALCEA
Malvaceae

Hollyhocks

Native to temperate regions of Europe and Asia

A genus of about 60 species of biennials or short-lived perennials. The foliage can be coarse, and some species have a slightly hairy texture. They are grown for their tall flower spikes. Only one species is usually grown in gardens.

Alcea rosea

Native to Turkey, but naturalised around the Mediterranean region

A tall, vigorous, upright, leafy-stemmed, hairy biennial up to 3m high. Large, alternate, roundish, heart-shaped leaves up to 4cm long are usually three to seven-lobed and roughly hairy. They are known for their prolonged summer flowering. Large, showy single, semi-double or double, open, funnel-shaped flowers 8 to 15cm wide appear on distinctive long terminal spikes. Colours range from white, pink, rose, red and purple to yellow, apricot and deep chocolate-maroon. Easily grown in well-drained soil with added organic matter. Drought tolerant once established. They are popular in cottage gardens and are often used as

Agave angustifolia **'Marginata'.**

Agave attenuata.

Agonis flexuosa **'Burgundy'.**

Albizia julibrissin **'Rosea'.**

Alcea rosea.

Allium caeruleum.

Allium giganteum.

Allium moly.

Allium sphaerocephalon.

background plants or against walls and fences, providing interest and can be a focal point in the garden. Easily raised from seed sown in autumn or winter. 'Charters Double' is a fine double strain, while 'Majorette' is a dwarf strain growing only 60cm high.

ALLIUM

Alliaceae

Onion

Native mainly in the Northern Hemisphere

A vast genus of perhaps 700 species of spring-, summer- and autumn-flowering bulbous or rhizomatous perennials that have a strong smell when bruised. The following are just a selection from the many that are worth growing in the garden. All alliums are easy to grow in most well-drained soils in full sun or partial shade. They are drought tolerant but need water while in growth. Effective plants in borders and rock gardens. Many make good cut flowers.

Allium caeruleum

Blue Allium

Native to north and central Asia

A bulbous perennial with bulbs that are nearly round. Linear, stem-clasping leaves, 7cm long, die before the flower spike appears in early summer. The flower spike, up to 60cm high, is topped with a dense, round cluster 5cm across of 30 to 50 bright-blue, star-shaped flowers each 2cm across. Known for attracting bees, butterflies and other pollinators to the garden. Stunning in beds and borders. Spectacular in large sweeping drifts. Looks great when planted in groups of 10 to 15 bulbs. Excellent as cut flowers for both fresh and dried arrangements.

Allium flavum

Yellow Flowered Garlic

Native to the Mediterranean

A bulbous perennial with narrow, blue-green, semi-clasping leaves to 20cm long. 1 to 2cm wide, yellow, bell-shaped, pleasantly scented flowers with prominent stamens in pendant clusters of up to 60 appear on stalks of 10 to 30cm in summer. Attracts bees, butterflies and other insects.

Allium giganteum

Giant Allium

Native to central and southwestern Asia

A bulbous perennial with strap-shaped leaves up to 45cm long and 5cm wide, which die before the flower spike appears on stout stems in summer. At up to 1.5m high, it is perhaps the tallest of the ornamental onions. Spectacular, dense, ball-like clusters, 12 to 15cm wide, may contain 50 or more lilac, star-shaped flowers with prominent stamens. Long-lasting blooms remain ornamental well into summer. This perennial makes a perfect background plant. An eye-catching species that makes good cut flowers. Attracts bees, butterflies and other insects.

Allium moly

Golden Garlic, Lily Leak

Native to the Mediterranean

A bulbous clump-forming perennial with lance-shaped, grey-green leaves up to 30cm long and 5cm wide. In summer, bright yellow, star-shaped flowers are borne in open clusters to 5cm across, containing up to 40 flowers on stalks 25 to 45cm high. Spreads rapidly, ideal for naturalising around shrubs. Excellent as cut flowers, both fresh and dried arrangements.

Allium sphaerocephalon

Drumstick Allium, Round Headed Allium, Round Headed Leek

Native to Europe, Caucasus, Iran, north Africa

A bulbous perennial with linear, mid-green, basal leaves to 35cm long. Each long-lasting, small, spherical flower head grows on a green stem resembling a drumstick 50 to 90cm high. Flowers emerge green in late spring to early summer and gradually gain colour, from the top to the bottom, lasting a gloriously long time in their rich, purple hue, then finally turn a shade of straw. Suited to beds and borders, plant in drifts of fifteen bulbs and allow to naturalise. An excellent cut flower, both fresh and dried. Attracts bees and butterflies, making it a splendid choice for pollinator gardens. They are fantastic for cutting, looking good for a couple of weeks in a vase. Bulbs are best left to naturalise, only lift and divide them when overcrowded.

ALOE

Asphodelaceae

Native to arid parts of Africa, Madagascar and the Arabian Peninsula

A large genus of around 300 species of succulents, shrubs and trees, usually stemless but sometimes with simple branched stems. These plants are known for their thick, fleshy leaves that store water, making them well-suited to arid environments. Leaves vary from green to greyish green or bluish green, typically long, narrow and pointed, with a serrated edge. Some species also have distinctive white spots or bands on their leaves. Tall, slender flower spikes reach to about 1m high, bearing tubular flowers ranging from yellow to orange or red. Some species bloom in winter, while others bloom in summer. They are showy and easily grown.

Aloe arborescens

Tree Aloe, Torch Plant, Candelabra Plant

Native to southern Africa

This much-branching succulent forms clumps up to 4m high with an equal spread. Grey-green, sword-like, fleshy, tapering leaves are curved with spikes along the edges to 60cm long, forming rosettes. In winter, it produces terminal racemes to 80cm high bearing cylindrical, bright-red, 4cm-long flowers. Ideal for coastal planting, as it withstands salt-laden sea spray. It thrives in heat and drought, happily growing in the poorest of soils, does best in gritty, well-drained soil in full sun. When older, it makes a most impressive and beautiful mound of leaves. 'Variegata' has yellow striped leaves.

Aloe cameronii
Red Aloe
Native to Malawi and Zimbabwe

An attractive shrubby succulent with erect stems branching from the base, growing up to 1.5m. The many branches are ascending, or the basal ones are shortly decumbent. Stems are topped by a lax rosette of green leaves that turn a beautiful coppery red in summer, which are persistent. Leaves are erect to spreading, lance-shaped with margins lined with brown-tipped teeth and up to 50cm long and 7cm wide. They are a rainbow of colours depending on sun and water. Flowers are usually bright red with paler tips or orange and occasionally creamy yellow, slightly curved, up to 4.5cm long. They appear in racemes up to 30cm long on a branched stalk, usually in late autumn and winter. Grow in sandy or gravelly well-drained soil in full sun. Drought tolerant. If over watered, the foliage will remain green. Ideal for rock gardens, succulent gardens, Mediterranean gardens. Great as an accent plant for sunny borders or in containers.

Aloe ferox
Ferocious Aloe, Bitter Aloe
Native to southern Africa

A single stemmed, tree-like succulent to 2m high and 1 to 1.5m wide with a bold rosette of leaves. Fleshy, broadly lance-shaped leaves are hollow above, curved underneath and often spiny. They are grey green to bronze green, edged with brown-red teeth and up to 1m long. Old leaves remain after they have dried, forming a 'petticoat' on the stem. Upright, terminal, candelabra-like inflorescences have five to eight branches 30 to 80cm long held above the foliage. These bear showy, large tubular scarlet or orange-red flowers 2 to 3cm long, with dark-orange stamens protruding from the mouth in summer. It thrives in heat, full sun or partial shade, and drought, although it grows better if given occasional summer water. Gives a beautiful display in sunny borders or decorative containers. This large, slow-growing, bold plant is ideal for a dry garden. Great for attracting nectar-feeding birds.

Aloe marlothii
Native to South Africa

A large evergreen succulent on a central stem 2.4 to 3m high, it forms a dense rosette of fleshy grey-green leaves to 1.5m long dotted with reddish spines tapering to a sharp point. The large leaves remain after they have dried, leaving a skirt around the base. Multi-branched, spreading flower panicles, with up to 30 almost horizontal racemes, bear tubular flowers varying from orange-red to yellow or bright red in autumn and winter. The overall effect is quite dramatic. Extremely drought tolerant, it needs little to no irrigation. Grow in full sun in well-drained soil. One of the largest species of aloe. Ideal for rock gardens, succulent gardens, Mediterranean gardens. Great as an accent plant for sunny borders or in containers.

Aloe plicatilis see *Kumara plicatilis*

ALOYSIA
Verbenaceae
Native to the warmer parts of North and South America

A genus of around 30 species of aromatic tender shrubs with opposite or whorled, simple aromatic leaves. Small salverform flowers are borne in spikes or racemes. One species is common in cultivation.

Aloysia triphylla
Lemon Verbena
Native to Argentina and Chile

A deciduous or partially evergreen shrub that makes straggly open growth to 2m high and wide. It is mainly valued for the lemon scent of its leaves. These are narrow lance-shaped, 8 to 10cm long, normally in whorls of three or four along the stems. Tiny pale lilac insignificant flowers are borne in spiked terminal panicles 12cm long during summer. Grows best in full sun, in well-drained soil, with little summer water. Fragrant leaves of lemon verbena are commonly used in teas, potpourris and as a culinary herb to add a lemony flavour to various dishes. It can be grown in pots or containers near the house so that its lemon scent can be appreciated. For this purpose, it should be kept small by frequent pinching of the shoots.

ALSTROEMERIA
Alstroemeriaceae
Peruvian Lily, Lily of the Incas
Native to South America

A genus of about 60 species of clumping or spreading perennials 30 to 60cm across with thick elongated fibrous roots that can be rhizomatous. Erect stems are 30 to 90cm tall with alternate linear to lance-shaped, mid-green leaves 7 to 12cm long. Some species may have variegated or striped foliage. Showy funnel-shaped flowers 3 to 10cm long are borne in summer. Many species and hybrids are popular choices for cut-flower arrangements, because of the long-lasting blooms and vibrant colours. Some species can be invasive in certain regions.

Alstroemeria aurea
Peruvian Lily
Native to Chile

A tuberous perennial with leafy stems to 1m high. Pale green, lance-shaped leaves are about 10cm long and may have a twist that exposes the underside of the leaf. Terminal clusters, held above

oe arborescens.

Aloe ferox.

Aloysia triphylla.

stroemeria aurea.

Alyogyne huegelii.

Amaranthus caudatus.

Amaranthus cruentus.

Amaranthus tricolor.

the foliage, of small, brilliant-orange or golden-yellow orchid-like flowers about 5cm across are often adorned with spots or streaks with chocolate brown. These bloom profusely for several weeks during summer. Performs best in full sun or light shade in fertile, moist, well-drained deep sandy soils. An excellent border plant and spectacular in mass plantings. Ideal for Mediterranean gardens, as the flowers are produced in significant quantities during summer, making masses of colour in a border. The tops will die down once the flowering has finished. Easy to grow, low maintenance and loved by butterflies and other pollinators. Many selections and hybrids are available in a variety of colours. One of the hardiest Alstroemerias.

Alstroemeria ligtu hybrids

Peruvian Lily

Garden origin

These hybrids, which are the most attractive, are also the ones most commonly available. The growth resembles the species above, yet the trumpet-shaped flowers exhibit a diverse array of colours such as pink, whitish, orange or yellow, frequently adorned with streaks or speckles of darker hues. Cultivation is the same as the above species. They are easily raised from seed sown in autumn or early spring.

ALYOGYNE

Malvaceae

Native to southern and western Australia

A genus of about six species of small flowering shrubs with a spreading or upright growth habit. They range from smaller varieties suitable for containers to larger shrubs suitable for garden borders. Leaves are usually green, with a lobed or serrated margin. Some species may have silver-grey foliage. The species produce large, showy flowers with a resemblance to hibiscus blooms. Flowers have five petals in varying shades of purple, blue, pink and white, produced in upper leaf axils from spring to autumn. Grow in well-draining soil in full sun. Drought tolerant once established. They are well suited to warm and arid climates, making them popular choices for gardens in regions with a dry Mediterranean or sub-tropical climate.

Alyogyne huegelii syn. *Hibiscus huegelii*

Lilac Hibiscus or Native Hibiscus

Native to western Australia

A fast-growing, evergreen shrub that has an upright to spreading growth habit up to 1.2 to 2.4m high and wide. Stems are usually covered in a fine bloom. Small coarsely hairy leaves are deeply three- to five-lobed, dark green and up to 6cm long with a serrated margin. Some varieties may have silver-grey foliage. The many large, hibiscus-like, trumpet-shaped, lilac-blue to deep-purple single flowers 10 to 12cm wide last two to three days each and are produced in flushes throughout the year. Grow in shrub borders or as an accent plant in Mediterranean gardens, water-wise and xeriscape gardens. There are different cultivars available, offering variations in flower colour and growth habit. Pruning helps shape the plant and encourages more prolific flowering.

Alyssum maritimum see *Lobularia maritima*

AMARANTHUS

Amaranthaceae

Native to tropical regions of the world

A genus of about 60 species of annual or short-lived perennials that grow from 1 to 2m tall, although some species are smaller. They have simple, alternate leaves that are often colourful and can be smooth or hairy. Flowers are usually small and inconspicuous, in dense upright clusters that can be terminal or axillary. The seeds are small, shiny and black.

Amaranthus caudatus

Love-Lies-Bleeding

Native to tropical regions of Central and South America

A stout, branching, upright, annual or short-lived perennial to 2m high. Ovate, light-green leaves are up to 15cm long and 10cm wide. Some cultivars have red or purple-green leaves. Tiny, extremely showy, vividly coloured red flowers appear in long trailing tassels 45 to 60cm long. Grow in well-drained soil in full sun or partial shade. Some water may be needed during the summer. Plants are easily raised each year from seed, indeed it may self-seed. Cultivated in India for food, the seeds are used as grain and young leaves are edible.

Amaranthus cruentus

Red Amaranth, Princes Feather

Native to tropical regions of Central and South America

A widely grown, summer-flowering, coarsely hairy annual to 2m high with stems often splashed with red or entirely red. Large ovate to lance-shaped leaves, up to 15cm long, are highly variable from pale green to splashed or marked with red, or reddish-green with a brilliant red or bronze underside. Minute flowers are in a large, branched red or purple inflorescence to 60cm long from summer to autumn. Grow in full sun with some summer water. Easily raised from seed.

Amaranthus tricolor

Joseph's Coat

Native to South and Southeast Asia

A vigorous, erect, much-branching annual to 1m or more high. Grown for their ovate or lance-shaped multicoloured leaves to 20cm long, blotched and marked with colours of crimson, marbled red, green and yellow. The slender flower spikes are insignificant and should be removed for better leaf colour. Grow in full sun or partial shade with some summer water. Easily raised from seed. Green-leaved strains are grown in tropical Asia as a vegetable.

AMARCRINUM
Amaryllidaceae
Garden origin

Amarcrinum is the only species within the genus, an inter-generic hybrid comprising crosses between Amaryllis and Crinum.

Amarcrinum memoria-corsii

A cross between *Amaryllis belladonna* and *Crinum moorei*, both of which are native to South Africa. This tender perennial hybrid typically grows to 0.6 to 1m tall and as wide, featuring a clump of strap-shaped leaves to 60cm long and 5cm wide. It inherits characteristics from both parent plants, producing large, showy flowers similar to those of Amaryllis, but with a more robust growth habit akin to the Crinum. Large, fragrant, trumpet-shaped flowers are typically shell-pink or white and bloom on tall stems each 8 to 10cm wide. Showy flowers bloom late summer into autumn in umbels of 10 to 15 flowers atop 60cm tall leafless stalks. This makes them popular ornamental plants in gardens and landscapes. They are relatively low maintenance. Grow in organically rich, moist, well-drained soil in full sun to light shade.

AMARYLLIS
Amaryllidaceae
Belladonna Lily, Jersey Lily, Naked Lady, Amarillo, Easter Lily

Native to the Western Cape region of South Africa

A small genus of flowering bulbs now considered just a single species. For many years, there was confusion among botanists over the names Amaryllis and Hippeastrum. As a result, the common name 'amaryllis' is mainly used for cultivars of the genus Hippeastrum, which are widely sold in winter for their ability to bloom indoors. This is one of many genera with the common name 'lily' because of the flower shape and growth habit, but they are only distantly related to the true lily, Lilium.

Amaryllis belladonna
Naked Lady, Belladonna Lily

Native to South Africa, particularly the Cape region

A seasonally-dormant bulbous perennial, with each bulb 5 to 10cm in diameter. Several long, strap-like, fleshy, green leaves to 60cm long grow in a basal rosette during spring and early summer. However, the most eye-catching feature is its tall, leafless flower stalk that emerges in late summer to early autumn. Reaching 60 to 90cm high, bearing clusters of trumpet-shaped, delicately fragrant flowers 5cm wide, a soft to deep pink, though variations in shade can occur. Each flower has six distinct tepals, which are petal-like structures, and a prominent central pistil and stamens. The striking contrast of the leafless stem and the pink flowers makes it a dramatic garden feature. Relatively easy to grow in well-draining soil in full sun or light shade. Water when in growth and keep dry when dormant. They are commonly grown as potted plants in regions with colder winters, where they are often cultivated indoors, and can be forced to bloom during the winter.

AMPHILOPHIUM syn. DISTICTIS
Bignoniaceae
Native to South America

A genus of about 43 tender species of woody, evergreen, flowering vines that climb by tendrils to 9m or more. Opposite leaves comprise two lush, glossy, ovate to lance-shaped leaflets and three tendrils. They are valued for their highly colourful tubular flowers up to 10cm long. These vines are adapted to summer heat, but not extreme winter cold. For the fastest growth, they should be grown in loamy soils and exposed to sun or partial shade. Pruning can keep them smaller.

Amphilophium buccinatorium syn. *Distictis buccinatoria*
Blood Red Trumpet Vine

Native to Mexico

A spectacular, strong-growing evergreen climber 6 to 9m or more high with square stems. Rough leathery, oval leaves 5 to 10cm long have two leaflets with a terminal forked tendril. Trumpet-shaped, waxy flowers 15cm long, with yellowish throats start orange-red and fade to blush-red with age. These are produced abundantly in racemes 15 to 25cm long throughout the warm months. If grown in full sun, it will cover itself with spectacular flowers. Grow the climber against a sunny wall or through a tree. Easily grown in any well-drained soil in full sun to part shade. Tolerant of summer drought once established, but water occasionally in summer as needed, to keep it growing and flowering well. Can be cut back hard each year to keep under control.

ANEMONE
Ranunculaceae
Windflowers

Native to temperate and subtropical regions of Africa, Asia, Europe and the Americas

The genus Anemone has recently been split into several genera, including Anemonoides and Eriocapitella.

A genus of low-growing perennials with rhizomatous or tuberous roots. The basal leaves with long leaf-stems are simple or compound with lobed, parted, or undivided leaf blades that can be upright or prostrate.

Anemone blanda see *Anemonoides blanda*

Anemone coronaria
Poppy Anemone, Spanish Marigold, Windflower

Native to the Mediterranean region

A tuberous perennial growing 20 to 40cm high, spreading to 15 to 25cm

Amarcrinum memoria-corsii.

Amaryllis belladonna.

Amphilophium buccinatorium.

Anemone coronaria.

Anemonoides blanda.

Anigozanthos bicolor.

Anigozanthos 'Yellow Gem'.

Anisodontea capensis.

Antigonon leptopus.

wide, with a basal rosette of a few dark green fern-like leaves, each with three deeply lobed leaflets. Flowers are 3 to 8cm across, borne singly on tall stems above the foliage. These are usually red, but may be white or blue with five to eight showy petal-like tepals and a black centre with a whorl of small leaves just below the flower, which blooms in late spring. Grow in well-drained average soil in full sun. Easy to grow, it has been cultivated in the Mediterranean region for centuries. Known as the florist's anemone, the vibrant blooms are ideal for floral arrangements.

Anemone hupehensis see *Eriocapitella hupehensis*

Anemone nemorosa see *Anemonoides nemorosa*

ANEMONOIDES
Ranunculaceae

Native to temperate regions of Asia, Europe and North America

As of August 2020, Kew's Plants of the World Online accepts 35 species and named hybrids in this genus that has been split off from Anemone, to which they are similar. The bulbs flower in spring, with the flowers wilting and the plant entering a dormant phase during the summer and autumn, only to return to life in the following spring.

Anemonoides blanda syn. *Anemone blanda*
Balkan Anemone, Grecian Windflower

Native to eastern Mediterranean region

A hardy rhizomatous perennial growing 10 to 15cm tall with a similar spread. Basal leaves are alternate, toothed, finely divided and fern-like in a whorled pattern. It is valued for its vibrant daisy-like flowers, which are usually an intense purple-blue but may be shades of pink and white. Each blossom is about 5cm across, with six to ten petals surrounding a bright yellow centre. These appear in early spring, a time when little else is in flower. Grow in full sun or partial shade in well-drained average soil. Give water when in growth and leave dry when dormant. Great when planted in a large group. Perfect for pathways and front of borders.

Anemonoides nemorosa syn. *Anemone nemorosa*
Wood Anemone

Native to Europe and Near East

A rhizomatous, shade-loving, herbaceous perennial 15 to 25cm high. Compound, basal, palmate leaves grow from underground rhizomes and die back down by midsummer (summer dormant). Plants bloom in spring, soon after the foliage emerges from the ground. Flowers are solitary, poppy-like, held above its foliage on short stems, with a whorl of three palmate or palmately lobed leaflike bracts beneath. Flowers are 2cm in diameter, with six or seven (and on rare occasions eight to ten) tepals (petal-like segments) with many stamens. In the wild, flowers are usually white but may be pinkish, lilac or blue, and often have a darker tint on the backs of the tepals. Easily grown in humus-rich, slightly acidic well-drained soil in part shade. Drought tolerant while dormant. Great for planting under trees. For best effect, grow in a large group.

ANIGOZANTHOS
Haemodoraceae

Kangaroo Paws

Native to Australia

A genus of eleven species of evergreen, clump-forming perennials up to 2m high with short rhizomes. Leaves are lance or strap shaped, light to dark green to 90cm long. Renowned for their tubular, velvety and brightly coloured flowers with distinctive paw-like structures clustered at the ends of leafless stalks. Many hybrid cultivars offer a wide range of colours, including shades of red, orange, yellow, green and pink.

Anigozanthos bicolor

A clump-forming perennial to 70cm high, spreading to 40cm wide, with mid-green leaves 30 to 40cm long, usually with bristly margins. Attractive red and green-yellow flowers, 3 to 6cm long, appear in clusters of four to ten on short stalks that emerge from the base of the leaves in spring and summer. Easy to grow in full sun in well-drained soil. Can adapt to a range of soil types, including laterite, and can withstand wet areas. Drought- and frost-tolerant once established but needs water in spring. Ideal size for small gardens or containers. Looks great when mass planted, in borders, as feature plants and for cut flowers. Prune back after flowering to promote fresh growth.

Anigozanthos flavidus
Kangaroo Paw

Native to southwest Australia

An evergreen, clump-forming perennial 60 to 80cm wide. Narrow, dark green, lance-shaped leaves are 35cm or more long. From late spring to autumn, it produces stiff branching flower spikes to 1m or more high, bearing panicles 4 to 7cm long of yellow and green, but may also be in shades of red, pink, orange, or brown curious woolly flowers to 5cm long, with a long-bent tube. Grow in well-drained humus rich sandy soil in full sun. Drought tolerant once established. They are well adapted to the Mediterranean climate. Often used in cut-flower arrangements because of the long stems and distinctive flowers. They are well-known for their bird-attracting flowers and strappy foliage. These hybridise freely both in the wild and in cultivation. Popular in gardens and landscapes for their unusual and striking appearance. Remove old flower heads from the base.

Anigozanthos manglesii
Mangles' Kangaroo Paw

Native to southwest Australia

An evergreen perennial with rosettes of upright grey-green leaves to 60cm long. From mid-spring to autumn, it produces stiff flower spikes to 1m or more high, covered in red hair. These carry racemes 5 to 14cm long of up to seven yellowish-green, woolly 8cm tubular flowers. These are red at the calyx with dark green lines, while the lip is reflexed and darker. Cultivation is the same as *A. flavidus*.

Anigozanthos 'Yellow Gem'

Garden origin

A beautiful perennial, which grows in a neat clump to approximately 1.5m high and 1m wide. Evergreen, strap-like leaves are up to 25cm long arising from underground rhizomes. Clusters of beautiful, furry, claw-shaped, bright yellow flowers up to 4cm long are supported on highly branching, reddish stems up to 1.5 m high. Flowering occurs over a long period from late spring to midsummer. Each stem flowers once, so after the blooms are finished, cut it back to the base. Tolerant of light frost. Cultivation is the same as *A. flavidus*.

ANISODONTEA

Malvaceae

Cape Mallow

Native to South Africa and Namibia

A genus of nineteen species of evergreen shrubs and woody perennials, found in a range of habitats, from open grasslands to rocky slopes. Leaves are toothed and have a somewhat fuzzy or hairy texture. They vary in size and shape depending on the species. Flowers are typically five-petalled and come in shades of pink, purple and white. Blooms are often solitary or in clusters. Species are cultivated for their ornamental value and are suitable for gardens in regions with a Mediterranean climate. Drought tolerant, preferring well-drained soil and full sun.

Anisodontea capensis

African Mallow, Dwarf Hibiscus, Cape Mallow, False Mallow

Native to the Cape Provinces of South Africa

A fast growing, woody subshrub up to 2m high and spreading to 1m wide with hairy stems. Growth is open and freely branching. Slender branches are sparsely covered with evergreen, hairy leaves 2 to 3cm long, with three or five deep lobes, each of which may be lobed or toothed. The 2 to 3cm wide showy flowers are pink with raspberry red veining and a dark basal spot. These are single or in two to three flowered racemes from leaf axils appearing in profusion, mainly from summer until autumn but may continue throughout the year. Ideal as a backdrop in smaller gardens, it provides excellent definition to borders and is a wonderful specimen for container planting. Ideal for hedging. Easily grown from seed.

ANTIGONON

Polygonaceae

Queen's Wreath Vine, Coral Vine

Native to tropical Mexico, Central America

A small genus of only three species of tendril-climbing vines, with branching stems and a tuberous root system. Their 10cm long leaves are alternate, with flowers borne in raceme-like clusters, often toward the ends of stems. Bell-shaped flowers have five tepals, usually pink, red or purple, sometimes yellowish or white. The stamens are joined at the bases, forming a tube. Only one species is commonly grown.

Antigonon leptopus

Mexican Creeper

This rapidly growing, tropical climbing vine with tuberous roots may grow 2 to 3m in a season. The vine is evergreen in the tropics but deciduous in cooler climates. Leaves are pale green and somewhat arrow shaped. Flowers are coral-pink clusters that bloom most of the summer. Flowers may also be red or white depending on the cultivar. The tendrils and its vining habit help the plant attach itself to arbours, trellises, fences or walls. It can survive in arid conditions but will grow in any well-drained soil in full sun. Water during the flowering season for it to look its best. The vine is classified as invasive in some places because of its aggressive growth.

ARBUTUS

Ericaceae

Strawberry Tree, Madrones

Native to temperate regions of the Mediterranean, western Europe, the Canary Islands and North America

A genus of about fourteen species of evergreen and deciduous trees and shrubs. Bark is often smooth and reddish-brown, but as it matures, the bark may peel away in thin sheets, revealing a smooth, coppery surface underneath. Species typically have leathery, glossy leaves that are alternate and simple. Leaves are often lance-shaped or elliptical. Flowers are urn-shaped and typically hang in clusters. They are usually white or pink and can be quite showy. Blooming period varies depending on the species. Fruit of the species is a berry-like drupe, often red or orange and may resemble strawberries, giving rise to its common name. Species are often found in a variety of habitats, including woodlands, coastal areas and mountainous regions. They can be adapted to different soil types and are sometimes tolerant of slightly acidic soils.

Arbutus unedo

Strawberry Tree

Native to southern Europe

An evergreen shrubby tree up to 8m high spreading as wide, often with basal suckers and a reddish bark that peels. As it ages, the trunk twists and takes on a gnarled look. Leathery, glossy green leaves are oval to elliptic to 10cm long. Small white or pinkish bell-like flowers open in pendant panicles to 5cm long in autumn. The 2cm round red fruit ripens the following autumn, so that the flowers and fruits are produced simultaneously. The tree grows well in a wide range of soils and climates, being unusual among ericaceous plants for its lime tolerance. It grows well in coastal gardens as it withstands salt-laden sea breezes.

Grows best in full sun or partial shade. Drought tolerant once established. The fruit is sometimes distilled into a fiery spirit called 'Medronho'.

ARCTOTIS
Asteraceae
African Daisy
Native to South Africa and Namibia

A genus of about 50 species of spreading annuals or perennials, occasionally subshrubs. Leaves form basal rosettes, often deeply lobed or divided, silvery green or greyish green. Solitary, daisy-like, brightly-coloured flowerheads are borne on long stems from summer to autumn. Species are well adapted to dry, sunny environments and are often found growing in sandy or rocky soils, in coastal areas, grasslands and scrublands. Many are cultivated for their attractive flowers and drought tolerance.

Arctotis × hybrida
African Daisy

This hybrid species has been bred for its large, colourful flowers and is widely cultivated as an ornamental plant. An evergreen stemless perennial growing to 30cm high, spreading 30cm or more wide. The 15cm-long entire, indented or lobed, silvery-green, lance-shaped leaves are felted and grow from the base in rosettes. Solitary, daisy-like flowers come in many colours: cream, yellow, orange, pink, red or purple, often with central zones of contrasting colours. They are 8 to 12cm across, borne on stems up to 45cm high, blooming from spring to early summer. The best flowers are produced in the first year. Flowers close in the afternoon or during dull weather. Summer drought tolerant once established, needing water only during the winter growing season. Excellent, quick-growing ground cover for sunny dry areas, especially on slopes. Ideal for regions with Mediterranean or arid climates. Highly valued for their colourful flowers, long blooming period, and are suitable for rock gardens, borders, containers and mass plantings. If conditions are right, they will self-sow, but will probably revert to orange.

ARGYRANTHEMUM
Asteraceae
Marguerite Daisy
Native to the Canary Islands and Madeira

A genus of 23 species of evergreen subshrubs with a mounding shape, about 60 to 90cm high and wide. Opposite or alternate leaves are lobed or deeply divided, 5 to 10cm long, fern-like, often green or grey-green, and may have a fuzzy or hairy texture. Loose corymbs of daisy-like, single flowers come in a variety of colours, including white, yellow, pink and purple, usually with a central disc surrounded by ray florets. They bloom profusely, especially in warmer months. Species are native to coastal regions and are often found growing in sandy or rocky soils. Valued for their long blooming period, vibrant flowers, and tolerance of heat and drought.

Argyranthemum foeniculaceum
Canary Islands Marguerite
Native to the Canary Islands, particularly the island of Gran Canaria

A compact evergreen subshrub growing 30 to 60cm high. Feathery, glaucous blue-green leaves are finely divided, fern-like, 5 to 10cm long and aromatic when crushed. Single daisy-like flowers 3 to 5cm wide comprise a central yellow disc floret with radiating white ray florets. These are produced mainly during winter, but can appear almost continuously. Flowers are attractive to pollinators such as bees and butterflies. Grow in well-drained soil in full sun. Fairly drought tolerant needing little summer water, but will flower better with an occasional soaking. It is quick growing, but should be replaced every three to four years to look its best. Excellent for the front of a sunny border. Great in regions with a Mediterranean climate. Makes an ideal pot or container plant for a sunny terrace. Do not prune back into hard wood as it seldom shoots out. With care, it can be trained into a standard, which looks wonderful in a pot.

Argyranthemum frutescens
Paris Daisy

A variable, evergreen, strongly-branched, perennial shrub to about 70cm high with an equal spread. Alternate, more or less fleshy, bright-green leaves are pinnatisect, 1 to 8cm long and 4 to 6cm wide. Inflorescences are loose with 4 to 30 single, daisy-like flower heads, white with a yellow centre, up to 2cm in diameter and appear for most of the year, but mainly in spring. It is fairly drought tolerant, needing little summer water, but will flower better with an occasional soaking. Grow in any well-drained soil in full sun. For continual flowering, prune lightly and frequently. Replace the plant every three to four years as it becomes old and woody with few flowers.

Argyranthemum hybrids

Much hybridising has taken place, resulting in a wide range of attractive flower colours and forms. The foliage and cultural requirements are like the above. 'Jamaica Primrose' bears primrose yellow, single flowers. 'Mary Wootton' bears anemone-centred light pink flowers. 'Powder Puff' is compact with pale-pink double flowers. 'Snowflake' has semi-double white flowers.

ARISTEA
Iridaceae
Native to tropical and southern Africa, Madagascar

A genus of about 50 evergreen, clump-forming, rhizomatous perennials that produce slender, grass-like leaves and bear striking blue or violet flowers. Flowers are usually in clusters atop tall, wiry stems. Species are adapted to various habitats, including grasslands, rocky slopes and marshy areas. They play important ecological roles in their native ecosystems and are used in gardens for their attractive flowers. Once established, they resent being moved.

Aristea ecklonii

Native to central and southern Africa

A strong-growing, evergreen, rhizomatous perennial that forms a clump to 40cm or more with sword-like basal leaves to 60cm long. A branched flower stalk rises from among the leaves, bearing smaller stem-clasping leaves. Bright-blue six-petalled saucer-shaped flowers, 2cm across, are borne throughout summer. Each flower is short-lived with new ones continually being produced. Grow in full sun or partial shade in well-drained soil. Moderately drought tolerant once established, but flowers better with occasional water. Easily raised from seed. Seed pods should be removed to prevent it from becoming invasive.

ARMERIA

Plumbaginaceae

Sea Pink, Thrift

Native to coastal regions of Europe, Asia and North America

A genus of perhaps 80 species of evergreen, low-growing, tufted perennials or subshrubs. Leaves are typically narrow and grass-like, forming dense, tufted mounds. Flowers are small, usually less than 2cm in diameter, in compact, rounded clusters atop slender stems. They come in various colours, including shades of pink, white and purple. Many species within the genus are native to coastal habitats, where they thrive in sandy or rocky soils. However, some species are also found in inland areas, particularly in mountainous regions. Their attractive foliage and long-lasting flowers make them popular ornamentals in gardens and landscapes. Plants are relatively low-maintenance and can tolerate a range of soil conditions, as long as it is well-draining. Thriving in coastal environments. A popular choice for gardeners and landscapers around the world.

Armeria maritima

Sea Thrift

A cushion-forming, small evergreen perennial 15 to 30cm high, spreading to 30cm wide. Dense, narrow-linear, rich green basal leaves are up to 12cm long. Small flowers are in round clusters to 2cm diameter on stiff stems to 20cm long. These are normally pink to lavender to rose-pink or white, but selections have been made with brighter- or deeper-coloured flowers. Blooms profusely from spring throughout summer. Easily grown in full sun in dry, well-drained soil. Drought tolerant once established. Ideal for edging paths and borders, ground cover and coastal gardens. Also, they make good container plants.

ARTEMISIA

Asteraceae

Native mostly to dry areas of the Northern Hemisphere, with a few from South Africa and western South America

The genus is a diverse group of 500 or more species of mostly aromatic annuals, biennials, perennials, evergreen and deciduous shrubs. Many species are valued as ornamentals for their attractive silvery-grey foliage, which is frequently used to create contrast or to smooth the transition between intense colours. A number are cultivated for their essential oils, which are used as flavourings or in herbal medicine.

Artemisia abrotanum

Southernwood, Lad's Love

Native to southern Europe

A popular, small perennial subshrub to about 1m high and as wide, forming an upright bushy mound. Silky hairy, grey-green leaves are highly aromatic to 5cm long with threadlike lobes that have grey hairs underneath. Its foliage emits a fruity camphor-like fragrance when touched and has historically been used as an air freshener. It has tiny insignificant clusters of small yellowish-white flowers that appear in late summer. Grow in full sun or light shade in rich well-drained soil. Drought tolerant once established, perfect for hot and dry sites, it dislikes hot humid conditions. It is largely grown as an unusual and textured foliage plant. Useful near paths where its scented leaves can be appreciated. Ideal for the herb garden. Easy to maintain, apart from a light clipping after flowering to keep shape.

Artemisia arborescens

Tree Wormwood, African Wormwood

Native to the Mediterranean region

A woody-based, shrubby perennial or shrub to 1m or more high and wide with silver-grey stems. Finely divided, silver hairy leaves are up to 10cm long, aromatic when crushed. Small yellow flower heads are borne in leafy clusters to 30cm long in summer to autumn. A most attractive silver shrub, which can become untidy with age. Cut back hard in spring to maintain a compact habit. It is heat, frost, drought and coastal tolerant and thrives in well-drained soil, making it suitable for xeriscaping and landscaping in arid regions. Grow in full sun in borders with little summer water. This delightful aromatic perennial is an excellent background plant or border filler.

Artemisia 'Powis Castle'

Garden origin

A beautiful evergreen subshrub that forms a silvery, dense bushy mound, 60 to 90cm high and as wide. Deeply cut fragrant silver-grey leaves are up to 6cm long. It is highly valued for its fern-like, silvery-white foliage, that blends with other perennial plants. Insignificant panicles of yellow flower heads appear in late summer. Thrives in poor to moderately fertile, well-drained soil in full sun. Excellent drainage is essential. Drought tolerant. It makes a good background for bright flowers and an excellent ground cover.

butus unedo.

Arctotis hybrids.

Argyranthemum frutescens.

stea ecklonii.

Armeria maritima.

Artemisia schmidtiana.

rum italicum.

Arundo donax 'Versicolor'.

Artemisia schmidtiana
Angels' Hair, Silver Mound, Wormwood
Native to Japan

A small, mat-forming, evergreen tufted perennial that forms a dome 30cm high and 45cm wide. Fragrant, downy, silver semi-evergreen leaves are much divided and about 4cm long. Tiny yellow flowers appear in pyramidal panicles to 10cm long in summer, attracting butterflies. Grow in a well-drained normal, sandy, poor or clay soil. Drought tolerant once established. Looks good in beds of perennial flowers or herb gardens and in containers. Like many artemisias, it is cultivated for its foliage rather than its flowers.

Artemisia stelleriana
Dusty Miller, Beach Wormwood
Native to Asia and North America

A compact, almost prostrate, rhizomatous, evergreen well-branched perennial to 15cm high, spreading to 45cm wide. Stalkless, deeply-toothed or pinnatifid white hairy, silver-grey leaves are 5 to 10cm long. When brushed against, it has a delightful, earthy aroma. Small golden flowers open from summer to autumn, but it is really for the foliage that this plant is grown. Drought tolerant, grows best in a sunny, well-drained spot. It provides a lovely contrast amid the green of the garden and adds beautiful texture. A splendid choice for garden beds, embankments, pots and more.

Several forms have been selected as garden cultivars. 'Boughton Silver' (aka 'Silver Brocade') is probably the best known cultivar. It is a prostrate form with prettily cut broad white leaves and was originally known as 'Mori's form'.

'Nana' is more erect to 30cm, but a lax-stemmed form with less deeply-cut silverish leaves. It has been grown for many years in the UK, where it is used as a filler between other plants in the herbaceous border.

'Elsworth' is a taller to 45cm, more strongly erect stemmed form with more deeply cut silver leaves.

'Shemya' is a short form of 30cm with silver green leaves.

ARUM
Araceae
Lords and Ladies
Native to southern Europe, northern Africa and western Asia

A genus of 26 species of tuberous perennials. They are grown for their glossy, often shield-shaped leaves and sometimes brightly coloured spathes. All parts of the plant are poisonous, and the sap is a skin irritant.

Arum dioscoridis
Spotted Arum
Native to the eastern Mediterranean

A handsome tuberous perennial 20 to 30cm high that is summer dormant. The thin arrow-shaped, dark glossy green leaves appear during autumn, borne on long leaf stalks. In spring, a short-stalked inflorescence appears up to 30cm high, comprising a black, rod-shaped spadix surrounded by a yellow-green, purple-mottled brown or even purple bract (spathe). This encloses thin spadices of tiny flowers that are unpleasantly scented. Grow in a humus-rich, well-drained soil in a sheltered site in sun or partial shade. Summer-dormant, so it only needs winter rains. Water during any dry spell in winter. Can be grown as an ornamental plant in rock gardens in Mediterranean regions. Also grown indoors as a pot plant.

Arum italicum
Italian Arum
Native to Europe, Turkey and northern Africa

A robust, tuberous perennial 30cm high with mostly cylindrical tubers that are summer dormant. Arrow-shaped, dark glossy-green leaves, 20cm long with whitish veining, appear in autumn. They gradually wither during early summer. In spring and early summer, greenish-white spathes 15 to 40cm appear. These are upright at first, then fold over and conceal the short yellow spadices of tiny flowers. Often followed by spikes of attractive, berry-like, fleshy fruit which turn scarlet-red as the foliage withers and may last until new leaves appear. Grown mainly for its decorative seeds. It prefers a humus-rich, well-drained soil in a sheltered site in partial shade. Summer-dormant, so it only needs winter rains. Water during any dry spell in winter. 'Marmoratum' has pronounced cream-veined leaves.

Arum pictum
Black Calla
Native to Corsica, Sardinia and the Balearic Islands

A tuberous perennial 15 to 25cm high with arrow-shaped, dark glossy-green leaves 25cm long, which are carried on long leaf stalks. These have fine, creamy white veins. The spathe, which is a dark purple, almost black, up to 20cm long, appears in autumn, with the dark purple spadix extending beyond it. Like other Arums, it is best grown in a humus-rich, well-drained soil in a sheltered site in partial shade. Summer-dormant, so it only needs winter rains. Water during any dry spell in winter.

Arundinaria murieliae see *Fargesia murielae*

ARUNDO
Poaceae
Native to the Mediterranean region, Asia, and parts of Africa

A genus of about six species of giant rhizomatous grasses or reeds. Growing 3 to 6m tall, occasionally to 10m, with leaves 30 to 60cm long and 3 to 6cm broad. There are a few other species within the genus, though they are less well-known and not as widely distributed.

Arundo donax
Giant Reed
Native to the Mediterranean region

A rhizomatous perennial with somewhat woody stems 2 to 5m high that resemble bamboo. It has hollow stems, which are sturdy and can form dense thickets that can spread almost indefinitely. Arching, broadly linear, flat green leaves are up to 60cm long and 8cm wide, with rough margins. The inflorescence is a slender erect white to green or purplish plume to 60cm high. Grows best in full sun in any soil, even coastal sand dunes that are always moist. For best foliage cut the stems to ground level annually, or for flowers, leave canes for a second year. However, it is also considered an invasive species in many parts of the world. The variety 'Versicolor' has beautiful grey-green leaves striped creamy-white with stems to about 2m high and is less invasive. This looks most impressive with its bold, bamboo-like canes and variegated leaves, making it a much more attractive garden plant.

ASCLEPIAS

Apocynaceae

Tropical Milkweed, Silkweed

Native to North and South America, Africa

A large genus containing about 200 species of perennials that mostly have a milky latex sap in their stems and leaves. Usually opposite, leaves are typically simple. They are often broad and can vary in size and shape among different species. Plants produce distinctive, intricate flowers that typically have five united petals. Flowers are in clusters and come in shades of pink, orange, red and white. Monarch butterfly larvae feed only on leaves of milkweed plants.

Asclepias curassavica

Blood Flower

Native to South America

A showy evergreen subshrub up to 1m high with upright single or branched stems. Dark-green pairs of lance-shaped leaves are up to 15cm long. Eye-catching clusters of small orange flowers, 5 to 10cm across, appear terminally and in leaf axils. The five-parted corolla is brilliant red and reflexed, exposing the crown of five orange or yellow hoods. These are produced from summer to autumn, then give way to long, narrow seed pods. Flowers are a significant source of nectar for butterflies, bees and other insects. Grows well in dry, moist and wet soils, preferring full sun. It requires some summer water to flower well. It is easily grown and will self-seed readily. Perfect for sunny borders, butterfly gardens and tucking into odd spots. The stem produces a toxic milky sap, hence its common name; do not let this prevent you from growing this rewarding and easily cared-for plant.

Asclepias fruticosus see *Gomphocarpus fruticosus*

ASPARAGUS

Asparagaceae

Native to Europe, Africa, Asia

A genus of around 200 species of evergreen and deciduous perennials, climbers and subshrubs. The most commonly cultivated species is *Asparagus officinalis*, which is widely grown for its edible shoots. Other species are grown for their ornamental foliage and are popular in gardens or as houseplants.

Asparagus densiflorus

Foxtail Fern

Native to west Africa

This evergreen, arching, tuberous perennial forms dense clumps with arching, upright stems covered with small, needle-like leaves, giving it a fluffy, foxtail-like appearance. Grows to a height of 60 to 90cm, with a similar spread. In summer, it bears axillary racemes of small white flowers followed by red berries. Grow in well-drained, slightly acidic to neutral soil. Tolerant of short periods of drought once established. It thrives in well-lit locations and can tolerate some shade. Avoid exposing it to direct sunlight for extended periods, especially in hot climates. A versatile and low-maintenance plant, making it a popular choice for both indoor and outdoor gardens.

Asparagus densiflorus 'Myersii'

Myers Fern

Has dense, arching, foxtail-like fronds 30 to 40cm long of needle-like leaf-like stems each 2 to 3cm long. Prune away any yellow or damaged fronds to maintain the plant's appearance. You can also trim back stems to shape or control its size.

Asparagus densiflorus 'Sprengeri'

Asparagus Fern

Native to Mozambique and South Africa

A rounded evergreen perennial with arching then pendant stems, to 1m long, which emerge directly from the ground and become woody and spiny, giving an open, loose appearance. True leaves are scale-like and inconspicuous. The structures that most refer to as leaves are actually leaf-like branchlets called cladophylls, which are linear, flattened structures that are bright green occurring singly or in groups of three or more at a node. Axillary racemes produce tiny white flowers followed by attractive, red, ovoid berries appearing throughout the year. Prefers medium warmth, regular watering in the spring to autumn growing season and sparingly in winter. It is intolerant of direct sunlight and wet soils. It is often grown for the graceful, feathery-like, fern-like foliage that is used in floral arrangements. Used in a hanging basket and as ground cover for a partially shady spot. It suits a container well and is beautiful if trained to cascade over a wall.

Asparagus setaceus syn. *Asparagus plumosus*

Lace Fern, Common Asparagus Fern, Climbing Asparagus

Native to southern Africa

A scrambling evergreen perennial with tough green stems and leaves, which may reach several metres. Leaves are actually leaf-like cladodes up to 7mm long by 0.1mm in diameter, which arise in clumps of up to fifteen from the stem, making a fine, soft green fern-like foliage. Sharp barbed thorns occur on the stem. From spring to autumn, small greenish-white bell-shaped flowers are 0.4cm long, and followed by small green berries, which blacken with maturity. The plants perform best in organically rich, well-drained soil, with regular summer water and little in winter. It is cultivated as an ornamental in gardens and containers, and as a house plant. The attractive foliage is also used in floral arrangements.

ASPHODELINE
Asphodelaceae
Native to the eastern Mediterranean region

A genus of seventeen species of biannuals and perennials with fleshy roots. Leaves are blue-green and grassy, both basal and along stems. Tall, narrow flower spikes to 1.2m high have fragrant, starry, yellow flowers, which always make an interesting addition to the late-spring garden. Individual flowers on the spikes open in a random order and do not last long, being replaced quickly by other flowers.

Asphodeline lutea
King's Spear, Yellow Asphodel
Native to Turkey

A rhizomatous perennial forming a clump 30 to 60cm wide of narrow, linear, grassy, grey-green leaves to 30cm tall. In spring, a conical, leafy flower stalk 8 to 10cm is topped by a dense cylindrical raceme 30 to 45cm long of flowers all along it. Flowers are fragrant, large-bracted, bright yellow, to 3cm across with large, ovate bracts. Flowers give way to globose green seed pods that mature to an attractive brown. Easily grown in average, medium moisture, well-drained soils in full sun. Prefers deep loam with good drainage. Grow in a border or on a dry sunny bank.

ASPHODELUS
Asphodelaceae
Native to Europe, Africa and the Middle East

A genus of sixteen species of perennial herbs. Many species have a small rhizomatous crown and thick, fleshy roots. These plants are characterised by their tall, slender stems and clusters of white or yellow flowers.

Asphodelus albus
White-Flowered Asphodel
Native to the Mediterranean region

A clump-forming perennial growing to 50 to 120cm high with fleshy, thickened rhizomes. Leaves originate from the base of the stem and are keeled and glaucous (covered by a waxy coating), about 50 to 70cm long. Leafless flowering stems bear white flowers, funnel-shaped, 4cm diameter, with six elongated petals from spring to early summer. Attractive to wildlife. After pollination, the yellow-green seed capsules are egg-shaped. Best grown in light, humousy, moderately fertile, well-drained soil in full sun. Tolerates part shade. Drought tolerant once established. Not well adapted to hot and humid summers. Plants drop their leaves in summer after bloom.

Asphodelus ramosus
Branched Asphodel
Native to the Mediterranean region

A winter-green and summer-dormant perennial species. Leaves grow to 60 to 80cm long from a central basal, large leaf rosette. Impressively tall leafless stems up to 1.2 m of branching spikes carry many flowers, coffee-coloured in bud, opening to white stars narrowly striped in coffee colour. In flower for several weeks during late spring and early summer. Grow in rich, acidic, well-drained soil in a sunny spot. Summer drought tolerant.

ASPIDISTRA
Asparagaceae
Native to Asia, China, Japan

A genus of about eight species of evergreen perennials that form thick roots. Although often thought of as a houseplant, it can be grown outside in mild areas, where they are often used as ground cover.

Aspidistra elatior
Cast-Iron Plant
Native to China

A rhizomatous perennial with basal leaves rising singly from the roots, which slowly spreads to 60cm wide. Arching leaf blades are ovate to lance-shaped, dark blackish green, glossy and 30 to 75cm long. Inconspicuous purple bell-shaped flowers 2 to 3cm across appear on a short stem at soil level in spring or summer. The plant is tolerant of neglect and unfavourable conditions, including low light. Happiest when grown in shade in a humus-rich sandy loam, with moderate summer water. It is rare for them to flower, but these are small, somewhat insignificant, and just above the surface of the soil. They are usually pollinated by slugs, which is why the flowers are at ground level. Perfect for creating ground cover in shady border areas. Root systems are fairly large in proportion to the above-ground foliage and it is this that enables them to compete particularly well in areas where roots from other trees and palms would otherwise be a problem. 'Variegata' is an attractive variegated form, having creamy, white-striped leaves. These plants burn when exposed to bright light.

Asteriscus maritimus see *Pallenis maritima*

AUBRIETA
Brassicaceae
Aubretia
Native to dry rocky places of eastern Europe, Asia

A genus of about twelve species of hardy evergreen mat-forming perennials. Species typically have small, violet-purple flowers, although cultivars are available in pink, blue and white. These bloom in early spring and attract pollinators such as bees and butterflies. Low maintenance, thriving in well-drained soil and full sun to partial shade. These are often used as ground covers or in rock gardens because of their spreading habit and ability to tolerate poor soil conditions. They are grown for their colourful spring

lepias curassavica.

Asparagus densiflorus **'Myersii'.**

Asparagus densiflorus **'Sprengeri'.**

aragus setaceus.

Asphodeline lutea.

Asphodelus albus.

idistra elatior.

Aubrieta deltoidea.

Aucuba japonica.

flowers and the ability to cascade over walls or rockeries, also in containers and hanging baskets.

Aubrieta deltoidea

Native to the eastern Mediterranean region

A hardy, evergreen, mat-forming perennial with straggly stems 5 to 15cm high, spreading to 60cm or more wide. Small grey-green leaves up to 1cm long are oval with toothed edges. Tiny four-petalled flowers 3cm wide are borne in elongated clusters covering it during spring. These vary from violet to red-purple, rose to deep red, and sometimes white. Grow in any well-drained soil with plenty of organic matter in full sun. Somewhat drought tolerant, but needs moisture for flowering. Ideal for rock gardens and for dry sunny walls. Also looks good when grown among gravel or between paving. After flowering, shear off spent flowers to keep plants looking neat. Easily raised from seed. Many named varieties have been raised, including some with variegated leaves.

AUCUBA

Garryaceae

Native to eastern Asia, from the eastern Himalayas east to China, Korea and Japan

A small genus of about ten species of dioecious evergreen shrubs. They are valued in landscaping for their tolerance of shade and ability to grow in a variety of soil types, although preferring moist, well-drained soil. Often used as specimens, hedges or screens. Also can be grown in containers for their ornamental foliage and colourful berries. Aucubas are low-maintenance and relatively pest- and disease-resistant. Only one species is in common cultivation.

Aucuba japonica

Spotted Laurel, Japanese Laurel

Native to China, Korea, Japan

An evergreen, rounded to spreading shrub, which grows slowly up to 3m high and wide. Dark-green leaves are opposite, broad lance-shaped, 5 to 8cm long, 2 to 5cm wide, irregularly and finely toothed. Small, purplish red flowers appear in spring, 4 to 8mm in diameter, each with four purplish-brown petals in clusters of 10 to 30 in a loose cyme. The fruit is a red drupe approximately 1cm in diameter, which ripens in autumn and is avoided by birds. Male and female flowers appear on separate shrubs, so both sexes should be grown together to ensure a fruit crop. Thrives in shade or even deep shade. A tough shrub that will tolerate pollution, coastal conditions and a wide range of soils. Drought tolerant, but looks better with adequate moisture. It grows well in containers in shady terraces or courtyards. There are many cultivars that have brightly-marked leaves that are more often grown than the type. 'Crotonifolia' has leaves that are heavily marked with golden yellow and is female. 'Goldieana' has dark green leaves with white or yellow marks. 'Variegata' is the best known Aucuba, has dark-green leaves spotted with yellow and is male or female.

B

BABIANA

Iridaceae

Baboon Flowers

Native to west and southwest of South Africa and southwestern Namibia

A genus of about 65 species of cormus perennials with ribbed or pleated, often hairy bright-green leaves. Spikes of funnel-shaped, often strongly-scented flowers 2 to 4cm across are borne mainly in spring.

Babiana dregei

Native to the Northern Cape of South Africa

A perennial corm growing up to 15cm long with an erect, branched stem. Sword-shaped leaves are slightly pleated with thick veins and margins, and a sharp, ridged tip. Flowers range from deep purple-blue to magenta with white splashes, with three lower tepals appearing in late summer. Grow in well-drained soil in full sun. Summer drought-tolerant, but needs water in the winter growing season. Ideal for pots and containers but also excellent for naturalising in borders and rockeries. They grow best in clumps and go well between shrubs and amongst perennials at the edge of a path.

Babiana rubrocyanea

Native to the Western Cape of South Africa

A perennial corm growing 5 to 15cm high that appears above the ground during winter and spring with leaves and flowers. Leaf blades are pleated, lance-shaped and hairy, emerging from the soil in late autumn and early winter. Beautiful purplish-blue funnel-shaped flowers with a sharply defined glowing carmine red centre bloom from late summer to autumn. This species is adapted to survive dry and hot summers by shedding its leaves and stems, with the corms remaining dormant underground. Grow in well-drained soil in full sun. Summer drought-tolerant, but needs water in the winter growing season. Frost tender. Great in containers on a terrace in cooler regions. They look superb coming up through gravel mulch between other plants. This species will increase every year, gently but steadily.

BALLOTA
Lamiaceae
Native to Europe, the Mediterranean region and west Asia

A genus containing about 35 species of clump- or mat-forming perennials or small evergreen subshrubs. Ballota species are often aromatic and have a strong, somewhat unpleasant odour when crushed, which can deter herbivores. They typically prefer dry, rocky habitats and grasslands. Ballota species are cultivated as ornamental plants for their attractive foliage and flowers, but are not as common as other members of the mint family.

Ballota acetabulosa syn. *Pseudodictamnus acetabulosus*
Native to Greece and Turkey

An extremely woolly, bushy subshrub growing to 60cm high, spreading to 75cm wide with cottony erect stems. Heart-shaped, grey-green leaves up to 5cm long, with rounded toothed margins, are wrinkled with woolly upper surfaces and dense white cotton underneath. Flowers 1 to 2cm long are white or pink, flushed with purple, and are produced in leaf axils during late summer. It can be grown in poor, dry, free-draining soil. To grow well, it needs to be in full sun. For the best results, it should be cut back hard in autumn or early spring to promote strong fresh growth.

Ballota pseudodictamnus
Native to Greece and Turkey

A low spreading subshrub that forms a dense mound to 60cm high and wide that is entirely covered in greyish-white wool. Small heart-shaped leaves, up to 3cm long, are also covered in silver hairs. Tiny two-lipped lilac-pink flowers 1 to 2cm long are produced in whorls in summer. For the best results, it should be cut back hard in autumn or early spring to promote vigorous growth. Looks most effective when planted in groups of three or five or as an edging to a path. Makes an attractive foliage plant. Grows well in a sunny, well-drained position, drought tolerant during summer.

BANKSIA
Proteaceae
Native to Australia

This genus of around 170 species ranges in size from prostrate woody shrubs to trees up to 30m tall. Some species grow as erect shrubs, but several species are prostrate, with branches that grow on or below the soil. Leaves vary in size, from narrow needle-like 1 to 1.5cm, to large up to 45cm long, mostly with serrated edges. Many species have differing juvenile and adult leaves. The flower spike, often several centimetres long, is an elongated inflorescence comprising a woody axis covered in tightly-packed pairs of flowers attached at right angles, often containing hundreds or even thousands of flowers. These come in shades of yellow, orange, red and even pinkish hues. Grow in well-drained soils in a sunny position.

Banksia coccinea

A shrub to about 4m high, but can grow taller. Leaves are broad with toothed margins. The conspicuous flowers are fairly squat in comparison with other banksias and bright orange or red. Spikes are about 10cm wide by a similar length, held terminally on the stems. These are seen in late winter through to early summer. Seeds are enclosed in follicles attached to a woody cone and are kept within the cone until burnt. The plant is fire-sensitive because it does not have lignotuber for vegetative regeneration after bushfires. This species relies on seed for regeneration. It is a desirable garden plant because of its dramatic habit and spectacular flowers. However, it readily succumbs to root rot fungus, which flourishes in areas of summer rainfall and humidity. It prefers sandy, well-drained soils. Summer drought tolerant. The terminal flowers are ideal for cut flower arrangements.

Banksia integrifolia
Coast Banksia
Native to eastern Australia

A highly variable species most often encountered as a tree up to 25m high, but in sheltered locations it can reach 35m. The tree usually has a single stout trunk, which is often twisted and gnarled, with the characteristic rough grey bark. Leaves 4 to 20cm long are dark green with a white underside and occur in whorls of three to five with entire margins. The flower spike is roughly cylindrical, 10 to 12cm high and 5cm wide. Flowers appear from late summer to autumn, usually pale yellow but may be greenish or pinkish in bud. Each individual flower comprises a tubular perianth made up of four united tepals and one long, wiry style. Popular in gardens for its attractive foliage, flowers and unusual seed pods. It is cultivated as an ornamental tree or shrub in gardens and parks, particularly in coastal areas where it thrives. Drought tolerant. Its deep root system also helps stabilise coastal soils and prevent erosion.

BAUHINIA
Fabaceae
Royal Poinciana
Native to tropical regions around the world

A large genus of 300 species of evergreen or briefly deciduous trees, shrubs and large vines. Most species have distinctive two-lobed leaves that are shaped like a cloven-hoof print. Their flowers are easy to recognise, with five spreading petals that resemble orchids. The uppermost petal, called 'the standard', is usually larger than and differently coloured from the other four. These plants do not thrive in alkaline soil.

Babiana dregei.

Babiana rubrocyanea.

Ballota pseudodictamnus.

Banksia coccinea.

Banksia integrifolia.

Bauhinia variegata.

Beaucarnea recurvata.

Beschorneria yuccoides.

Bauhinia variegata
White Orchid Tree, Buddhist Bauhinia

Native to northern India, southeast China

A fast-growing tree to 6m high with a 6m spread, the slender trunks topped with arching branches. These are clothed in large, 10 to 20cm long, heart-shaped, two-lobed, deciduous leaves, which are not actually variegated. Before shedding its leaves in autumn, the tree is adorned with many delightfully fragrant, lemon-green marked, orchid-shaped blossoms that measure 13cm wide. These are followed by 30cm long, slender, brown, flat seedpods. When the flowers appear, they are a beautiful sight to see. Easy to cultivate, it prefers a sunny spot in average well-drained soil. Drought tolerant.

BEAUCARNEA
Asparagaceae

Ponytail Palm, Elephant's Foot

Native to arid regions of Mexico

A small genus of about six large succulent species, sometimes of tree-like proportions, often forming a basally swollen trunk. Leaves are in large terminal rosettes, with each long blade narrow and grass-like. Only one species is commonly grown.

Beaucarnea recurvata

Native to drier parts of eastern Mexico

This tree can reach a height of up to 9m and 1.5m wide and is usually sparsely branched with thick, fissured bark. Young plants typically have a single trunk, but as they age, smaller trunks and sparse branching near the top can also develop. A swollen basal portion of the trunk can be up to 1m in diameter. Long, narrow, dark green leaves about 2cm wide grow up to 1.5m long in a rosette formation at the top of the trunk. As they mature, plants produce tall stalks with small white or yellow flowers that emerge from the centre of the rosette. These flowers are followed by small, dry fruit. Plants are slow-growing, taking several years to reach full size. Grow in well-draining soil in full sun. Drought tolerant. In the wild, they are often found growing in rocky, sandy soils in areas with low rainfall. They are attractive and easy to care for, making them a popular choice for dry landscaping. Frequently used as pot plants on terraces or in courtyards.

BESCHORNERIA
Asparagaceae

Native to semi-arid areas of Mexico and Central America

A small genus of about ten species of evergreen, clump-forming, perennial succulents with rhizomatous stems. This genus includes several species of evergreen perennials known for their striking foliage and unique inflorescences. Species are typically adapted to arid or semi-arid climates and thrive in well-drained soil and full sun to partial shade. They are drought tolerant once established and require little maintenance, making them suitable for xeriscaping and low-water gardens. Overall, the genus is valued for its striking appearance, low-maintenance requirements, and ability to add architectural interest in gardens and landscapes, an alternative to more common succulents and agaves.

Beschorneria yuccoides

Native to Mexico

Mexican Lily, False Red Agave

A succulent that forms a clump 1.5m high, spreading to about 1m wide, with a rosette of about 20 lance-shaped grey-green leaves 60cm long and 5cm wide. Although it is related to Yucca and Agave, the soft leaves contain no spikes and therefore make it a more usable architectural, handsome plant. Once plants have been established for a few years, in summer, a thick, often arching pinkish-red flower stalk reaching 90cm to 2m high appears. It bears nodding, bell-shaped, bright-green flowers adorned with showy red bracts. Dislikes being waterlogged in winter, or shallow chalky soils. Looks good as a specimen plant, or near the front of a border, where it makes a bold architectural form throughout the year. It is worth growing for the striking glaucous swordlike foliage and exotic arching flowers. Great for coastal and Mediterranean gardens.

BILLARDIERA syn. SOLLYA
Pittosporaceae

Native to Australia

A genus of about 25 species, mainly light climbers or small shrubs. All occur only in Australia, with the majority being found in Western Australia. The genus includes species formerly included in the genus Sollya. Few species are cultivated for their bell-shaped, usually blue flowers.

Billardiera heterophylla syn. *Sollya heterophylla*
Bluebell Creeper, Climbing Blueberry

A slender, moderately vigorous climber whose branches twine around stems of other plants up to 2m or more if given support. The light and delicate leaves are variable, usually oblong to lance-shaped 2 to 5cm long and glossy deep green. Clusters of 1cm long, brilliant blue, bell-shaped flowers appear throughout most of the summer. Small cylindrical fruits have many seeds. It is available in several forms, including white- and pink-flowering forms. Easily grown in most well-drained soils in full sun but prefers some shade. Drought and frost tolerant once established. Cut back frequently to keep it in shape. Can be used as a ground cover or grown against a low wall that it can scramble over. It also makes a good container plant. It has become an environmental weed in many areas.

BILLBERGIA
Bromeliaceae

Native to Mexico to Argentina

A genus of about 62 species of rosette-forming, evergreen perennials, usually epiphytic, occasionally terrestrial, mostly medium-sized species with small funnel diameters. Most species are epiphytes, growing on plants or rocks, others directly on the ground. Water collects in the leaf funnels. The rough leaves are always reinforced on the edge, with a spiked tip. Some species and varieties have beautifully coloured leaves. They are cultivated for their erect or arching panicles or racemes of colourful, tubular but short-lived flowers. In their native surroundings they thrive on trees, but if they fall, they will find a new home on the ground.

Billbergia nutans
Friendship Plant, Queen's Tears
Native to South America

A variable epiphytic bromeliad with short rhizomes growing about 50cm high. Narrowly funnel-shaped rosettes have twelve to fifteen linear or strap-shaped, pointed, sometimes red-flushed, narrow grey-green leaves to 70cm long. In late winter and spring, it bears striking pink-bracted flower stems 15cm long with slim, pendant blooms coloured pink, green and blue, with curled-back petals that are relatively short-lived. It rapidly forms a large clump and can make a good ground cover. Being epiphytic, it can be grown in the fork of a tree, where the cascading flowers can be well displayed, but can also be grown in the ground or in a pot. Like most bromeliads, it will survive in dry, shaded garden beds. Divide clumps every few years. Give them a spray of water every so often in summer if it is dry. This bromeliad is reasonably frost hardy. One of the easiest bromeliads to grow.

BISMARCKIA
Arecaceae
Native to Madagascar

A genus containing a single dioecious species of solitary, moderately tall, attractive tropical palm characterised by a round crown of large, fan-shaped, silvery-blue or grey-green leaves.

Bismarckia nobilis

A spectacular palm that grows up to 8m high or more. The trunk of mature palms is typically thick and robust, often covered with persistent leaf bases. Huge fan leaves up to 3m across are deeply divided into segments, heavy, thick and a beautiful waxy blue-grey. Leaf stalks are streaked with a scurfy white. The palm is slow-growing, especially when young. With age, female trees produce 3cm plum-like brown fruit in huge clusters 1m or more long. They prefer full sun and well-draining soil but can tolerate a range of soil types, including sandy or rocky soils. Fairly drought tolerant once established, but grows better with some summer water. Well-suited for coastal areas, tolerating salt spray and windy conditions. Often used as focal points in tropical and subtropical landscapes, providing a dramatic accent with their large, architectural leaves. In colder climates, they can be grown in containers and brought indoors during winter. Difficult to transplant when young, they should not be moved bare-rooted.

BOLUSANTHUS
Fabaceae
Native to southern Africa

A genus containing a single species of deciduous tree that is grown for its clusters of highly-coloured, pea-like flowers.

Bolusanthus speciosus
Tree Wisteria, Vanwykshout

A slow-growing, deciduous small tree 4 to 6m high spreading to 4m wide with a grey trunk. It has a rounded crown and a single trunk with smooth grey bark. Branches are often drooping, giving it a graceful appearance. Leaves up to 15cm long are compound, comprising up to fifteen lance-shaped leaflets along a central stalk. Each leaflet is lance shaped or oblong, with a glossy green upper surface and a paler underside. The briefly deciduous pinnate leaves appear after the flowers open. It is best known for its spectacular display of blue-violet, 2cm-long flowers, which appear in pendulous racemes to 25cm long in profusion in late winter to early spring. Flowers are pea-shaped and highly fragrant, attracting bees, butterflies and other pollinators. These are followed by 6cm-long seed pods. For best flowering, the tree should be grown in full sun in a rich well-drained soil. It can tolerate both drought and frost once established, but grows better with summer water. This handsome tree is easily propagated by seed. Pruning may be necessary to maintain a desired shape or remove dead or damaged branches. It is often planted as a shade tree in parks, gardens and along streets. The tree's stunning flowers make it a popular choice for landscaping projects.

BORAGO
Boraginaceae
Native to the Mediterranean region

A genus of just two or three species of hairy annuals and perennials. Typically growing to around 60cm to 1m high. They have rough, bristly stems and leaves covered in fine hairs. Leaves are alternate and often oval or lance-shaped. Clusters of small, star-shaped flowers are typically blue or purple, although white and pink varieties also exist. Flowers have five petals and are borne on terminal racemes. They are attractive to bees and other pollinators. One species has long been cultivated as a herb. Species are often grown as ornamental plants in gardens and landscapes for their attractive flowers and foliage. Borage, in particular, is valued as a companion plant in vegetable gardens for its ability to attract pollinators and repel certain pests. It is also used as a green manure or cover crop to improve soil fertility.

Borago officinalis
Borage
Native to Europe

A freely-branching annual 20 to 60cm high and 45cm wide. Hairy grey-green basal leaves are 10 to 20cm long, ovate and toothed. Lance-shaped stem leaves are up to 15cm long. Leaves and flowers are edible with a cucumber-like flavour. Pure blue flowers 2cm wide are produced

'ardiera heterophylla.

Billbergia nutans.

Bismarckia nobilis.

›lusanthus speciosus.

Borago officinalis.

Bougainvillea × buttiana.

›ougainvillea hybrid.

Bougainvillea spectabilis.

Bougainvillea 'Raspberry Ice'.

during spring, opening to a star with dark-purple projecting anthers. Grow in full sun or shady areas. Does exceptionally well in parched, low-nutrient soil. Drought tolerant. Although it seeds itself freely, it does not transplant well. Cultivated throughout the Mediterranean region as a culinary herb. Use tender leaves in salads and drinks, and the attractive flowers as a garnish. 'Alba' has white flowers.

BOUGAINVILLEA
Nyctaginaceae
Paper Flower

Native to tropical and subtropical South America

A genus of eighteen species of semi-deciduous shrubs or woody vines to 6m or more with thorny stems and persistent, spine-like inflorescence stalks. Three species are grown throughout warm regions of the world. Plants need full sun, as plants prefer the hottest, sunniest spot in the garden. Needs water when young but is drought tolerant when mature. Use it as a warm season, colour accent vine. Plant vines to cascade over walls, banks, fences, trellises, arbours and container rims. It can also be used as a cut flower or a security barrier. It will even withstand sea spray.

Bougainvillea x buttiana
Garden origin

This cross between *B. peruviana* and *B. glabra* has produced a vigorous, woody climber easily growing 10 to 12m high. The ovate leaves are up to 8cm long. Clusters of wavy floral bracts, 3 to 5cm long, ranging from yellow to red and purple, are produced from summer through autumn and into winter. This garden hybrid has been used to produce many named varieties.

Bougainvillea hybrids
Garden origin

Bougainvillea has been hybridised a great deal, predominantly from *B. spectabilis*, *B. glabra* and *B. peruviana*. There are many spectacular varieties that come in many shades, including some double varieties and some with variegated leaves. Some varieties have more compact growth, which are suitable for growing in containers, while others are rampant growers.

Bougainvillea spectabilis
Native to Brazil

A vigorous and dense climber growing 7 to 10m high. Stems have many large, curved thorns. The ovate leaves are up to 10cm long and downy underneath. Purple, pink or reddish bracts 5 to 6cm long are produced during spring and summer. This is the primary parent of the many differently coloured and free-flowering hybrids that are now grown.

Bougainvillea spectabilis 'Raspberry Ice' syn. 'Tropical Rainbow'
Garden origin

A bushy scrambling evergreen climber to 12m or more, high. The ovate, deep green leaves 8cm long are beautifully edged with cream. Flowering bracts up to 3cm long are deep pink to red. These are produced from summer through to autumn and into winter, making a spectacular sight.

BRACHYCHITON
Malvaceae
Bottle Tree

Native to Australia and New Guinea

Around 30 species of trees and shrubs known for their striking appearance, growth forms and vibrant flowers. They vary in size and habit, with some species growing into large trees reaching over 30m, while others are shrubs. Some are known for their swollen trunks. Leaves are alternate and entire to palmately lobed or compound, from 4 to 20cm long and wide. Foliage may be deciduous, shedding leaves during dry seasons or in response to drought. All species are monoecious with separate male and female flowers on the same plant. Petalless flowers with five or six colourful tepals are profusely borne in axillary or terminal panicles, creating a spectacular display. These showy blooms are rich in nectar, attracting birds, bees and other pollinators. They are particularly well-suited to drier environments and are often found in arid or semi-arid regions of Australia.

Brachychiton acerifolius
Flame Tree

Native to subtropical Queensland and New South Wales in Australia

An evergreen or briefly deciduous tree growing to 30m or more in the wild, but usually 6 to 12m in cultivation. The tree usually forms a pyramidal shape but may spread wide. Usually the green trunk is smooth, solid looking and may be swollen at the base. Attractive, glossy, bright green, palmate leaves have five to seven deep lobes and are 8 to 20cm across on long stalks. In summer, the tree covers itself with terminal clusters of bowl-shaped bright coral red tubular flowers 2cm across, over the entire tree when it is leafless, giving it the common name. A large tree in full flower is a spectacular sight, especially as it usually drops its leaves at the time of flowering. It needs to be grown in full sun in well-drained soil. Drought tolerant once established.

Brachychiton bidwillii
Little Kurrajong, Bidwill's Bottle Tree

Native to eastern Australia

A variable species, mostly an open shrub of about 2m tall, but sometimes a small tree on a single stem reaching to 4m. Leaves are five-lobed, felty and purple-brown when young. Most forms drop their leaves immediately before flowering, which enhances the spectacular floral display. Spectacular bell-shaped flowers up to 30mm long and 15mm wide vary from orange-red to salmon-pink and are held in clusters in spring. As the plants age, flower production increases. After eight years, they may produce spectacular massed displays of hundreds of flowers almost covering the trunk, besides the typical flowers growing in clusters on twigs and branches. Grow in well-drained soils in full sun to part shade. Resistant to drought, partial shade to deep shade, light frost. It flowers best in full sun and responds well to pruning in order to increase flowering. Suitable for large pots, containers and tubs.

BRACHYGLOTTIS
Asteraceae
Native to New Zealand

A genus of about 30 species of small trees, shrubs, herbaceous perennials and climbers. Many species formerly listed as Senecio are now listed as Brachyglottis. They are grown for their attractive foliage and flowers.

Brachyglottis greyi syn. *Senecio greyi*
Daisy Bush

Native to New Zealand

An evergreen shrub up to 2m high and 3m wide with stout, spreading branches covered in white felt. Oblong 10cm-long leathery leaves are dark green, margined silver-grey with white felt underneath, while young leaves are densely covered in white felt. Clusters of 14cm wide daisy-like, deep yellow, 3cm-wide flowers appear profusely during summer, attracting pollinators like bees and butterflies to the garden. Grow in full sun in well-drained soil. Drought tolerant once established, it can tolerate salt spray and windy conditions. It is easy to grow and can be pruned to maintain its shape and size, making it a versatile choice for various garden settings. Looks great in shrub borders, particularly in coastal areas.

BRACTEANTHA *see* XEROCHRYSUM

BRAHEA
Arecaceae
Hesper Palm

Native to Mexico and Central America

A genus of about sixteen species of mostly low or medium, single-stemmed palms, characterised by large, fan-shaped leaves and stout trunks. They typically prefer well-draining soil and are relatively drought tolerant once established, making them suitable for arid or semi-arid climates. These palms are often used in landscaping to create a tropical or Mediterranean ambiance, and they can also be grown in containers indoors or on patios in cooler climates. They are all slow growing, making attractive specimen trees. Some species produce edible fruits or seeds, which are consumed locally in their native habitats.

Brahea armata
Mexican Blue Palm, Blue Hesper Palm

Native to Mexico

An upright-growing palm that makes slow growth 6 to 12m high with leaves spreading to 7m wide. The solitary stout trunk of mature trees is usually straight, thick and grey. It may either be covered with persistent dead leaves or be smooth and free from leaf bases. Its distinctly silver-blue leaves are deeply divided into about 50 fan-like segments, stiff, 1 to 2m wide, with 1m-long petioles, armed with stout, curved teeth. Spectacular, arching or pendulous inflorescence, extend out beyond the crown, reaching to 5m. Showy clusters of yellow or creamy flowers are 1.5cm across, borne on mature plants over twenty years old during summer. A wonderful palm for a dry garden, making an excellent specimen. In the moonlight, its beautiful blue leaves can look almost white. It can be temperamental, and difficult to transplant.

Brahea edulis syn. *Erythea edulis*
Guadeloupe Fan Palm

Native to Guadeloupe Island off Baja California

A robust palm with a mature height of 12m and a dense spread of 3m. The trunk is stout, and spent fronds fall naturally, cleaning the trunk. Rigid palmate leaves up to 2m across are grassy green and thinly glaucous on both sides. Leaves are borne on leaf stalks 1m long that have stout, curved or hooked teeth along their margins. On mature plants, a long drooping flower stalk appears from among the leaves arching out far beyond them. The fragrant flowers are creamy-yellow in clusters of three and are followed by dark brown to black fruit 2cm in diameter, hanging down in bunches. When ripe, they are edible with a sweet pulp. Grow in full sun in a well-drained, rich soil. This slow-growing palm will take slight frost, beach and desert conditions. A wonderful and dramatic palm that is ideal as a specimen.

BRUNFELSIA
Solanaceae
Native to America

The genus includes about 50 species of shrubs or small trees. Leaves are simple, alternate, glossy and dark green, although some species have lighter-green or greyish leaves. Flowers are tubular or bell-shaped with flaring corolla lobes, ranging from white to shades of blue and purple. All have fragrant flowers to some extent, and some are highly fragrant. Species are never found on calcareous soil.

Brunfelsia americana
Lady of the Night

Native to South America

An evergreen large shrub or small tree growing 2 to 3m high, forming an upright structure with a rounded shape. Leaves are crowded on the stems, often yellowish green, oblong-ovate, 5 to 10cm long, entire, and pointed at both ends. This gives this shrub an attractive, bushy appearance. Tubular creamy white flowers are 5cm long. The five petals are white, soon turning yellowish, oblique, opening to about 5cm in diameter. Flowers are extremely fragrant after dark when the scent floats in the air like a Gardenia but much softer, giving it its common name. These are also mildly fragrant during the day. These attractive flowers attract butterflies and other insects to your garden. It

Brachychiton acerifolius.

Brachychiton bidwillii.

Brachyglottis greyi.

Brahea armata.

Brunfelsia americana.

Brunfelsia pauciflora.

Buddleja davidii.

Buddleja madagascariensis.

prefers full sun to semi-shade, some summer watering and well-draining soil. Frost sensitive. A beautiful and low-maintenance shrub, perfect for any garden, it is also a good container plant. However, caution should be taken when handling the plant, as all parts of it are highly toxic.

Brunfelsia pauciflora
Yesterday Today Tomorrow
Native to Brazil

A beautiful, evergreen, slow-growing shrub 2.5 to 3m tall with a similar spread. Evergreen leathery leaves are oblong 8 to 15cm long, with smooth margins and dark green above and pale green below. Flowers open blue to purple with a white centre then gradually change to white with a corolla tube 2 to 3cm long with lobes spreading to 5cm. These are produced in terminal clusters in leaf axils in early spring. The colour quickly fades, giving it the common name 'Yesterday' purple, 'Today' lavender, 'Tomorrow' white. The plant is covered with sweet-scented flowers, day after day. These shrubs are dense, so thinning to open up the shrub a little improves its health and appearance. While these tropical shrubs do well in warmer climates, they do not enjoy extreme heat, and also thrive in cooler, frost-free areas. They grow better in morning sun and afternoon shade or dappled sunlight all day. Best with some summer water. They enjoy slightly acidic soil and generous feeding. 'Floribunda' is a variety that flowers more freely with flowers that open a rich violet colour, 'Macrantha' has larger flowers up to 8cm across.

BUDDLEJA (*also spelt* Buddleia)
Scrophulariaceae
Butterfly Bush
Native to tropical and subtropical parts of North and South America, Africa and Asia

A genus of over 100 species, nearly all are shrubs less than 5m tall, but a few qualify as trees, the largest reaching 30m. Both evergreen and deciduous species occur in tropical and temperate regions, respectively. Leaves are lance-shaped and opposite in most species, ranging from 1 to 30cm long. Flowers of Asiatic species are mostly produced in terminal panicles 10 to 50cm long, American species more commonly as cymes forming small, globose heads. Each individual flower is tubular and divided into four spreading petals about 3 to 4mm across, in various colours, such as purple, pink, white or yellow. These flowers are typically fragrant and have a sweet scent that attracts butterflies, bees and other insects.

Buddleja alternifolia
Fountain Butterfly Bush
Native to southern China

A deciduous shrub or small tree up to 4m high spreading as wide with slender, arching willow-like branches. Lance-shaped leaves up to 7cm long are dull green above with whitish down underneath. It is enormously generous with its arching sprays of lilac-purple flowers in dense rounded clusters to 4cm long and intensely fragrant. Flowers are produced in spring from the previous year's growth. For best results, grow in full sun or partial shade. Although drought resistant, it grows better with some summer water to maintain growth. Grows well in poor, dry, even gravelly soils. Can be trained to make a fine weeping tree.

Buddleja davidii
Butterfly Bush, Summer Lilac
Native to China and Japan

A vigorous semi-deciduous shrub, which makes fast rank growth up to 3m high with long, arching branches. The pale-brown bark becomes deeply fissured with age. A thick layer of hair covers the younger shoots. Leaves are 7 to 15cm long, tapering, and dark green on the upper side, with a white down underneath. Slender terminal panicles of densely packed honey-scented flowers are 30cm or more long. Smaller panicles appear at the ends of side branches. Flowers vary from pink, lilac, purple or violet to white. The shrub should be cut back hard in early spring to produce the largest flowers. Grow in full sun or partial shade. Although drought resistant, it grows better with some summer water. There are many named cultivars available.

Buddleja madagascariensis
Smokebush, Madagascan Butterfly Bush
Native to Madagascar

A vigorous evergreen straggling shrub to 4m or more high and wide. Young stems and shoots are covered with white felt. Lance-shaped opposite leaves are 5 to 13cm long, dark green above and covered in white felt underneath. During late autumn and winter, it produces 15 to 25cm-long terminal panicles of yellow or orange flowers, with a scent which some people find unpleasant. This large shrub needs room to grow. If given some summer water, it will make an attractive silver-leaved shrub. It can be pruned to keep in shape, which is best carried out in spring after flowering.

Buddleja pikei 'Hever'
Garden origin

A deciduous wide-spreading shrub up to 3m high and wide with slender, arching shoots. Opposite or alternate grey-green leaves are ovate to oblong to 15cm long. Arching panicles, to 30cm long, of fragrant lilac-mauve flowers with their deep orange throat cover the branches in early spring. The shrub should be cut back hard in early spring to produce the largest flowers. Although drought resistant, it grows better with some summer water. Grow in full sun or partial shade in any well-drained soil.

Buddleja salviifolia
South African Sage Wood
Native to southern and eastern Africa, from Kenya to Angola

An evergreen shrub up to 4m high spreading to 3m wide with more or less square stems, which are covered in felt.

Lance-shaped grey-green leaves are 13cm long and conspicuously wrinkled and puckered above, densely covered with whitish or brown hairs below. This gives the appearance of the herb sage. Terminal panicles 15cm long bear many sweetly scented, dull to clear white to almost true purple flowers in autumn and winter. Although drought resistant, grows better with some summer water. It is useful as a framework or background plant and should be cut back hard in early spring to produce the largest flowers. If pruned often, it makes an excellent hedge.

BULBINE
Asphodelaceae
Native to southern Africa

A genus of 30 species of clump-forming, succulent, occasionally slightly woody-stemmed, sometimes bulbous or tuberous perennials. They have linear, to broad lance-shaped, blue-green basal leaves. Dense terminal racemes of small star-shaped to cup-shaped flowers with hairy stamens appear during spring and summer.

Bulbine frutescens
Orange Bulbine

Native to South Africa

A succulent perennial forming a dense rosette of linear, fleshy green leaves to 45cm long. Long racemes 15 to 30cm of small, yellow or pale-orange flowers with frilly stamens are borne above the leaves to 45cm tall. These are popular with bees and butterflies. Easy to grow, tough, heat- and drought-tolerant once established and needing little care. Suitable for xeriscaping. Grow in full sun or light shade in well-drained sandy soil. Tolerates poor rocky soils. A desirable plant for Mediterranean and water-wise gardens. Great in containers or as ground cover.

Bulbine latifolia
Native to eastern South Africa

A stemless aloe-like succulent with rosettes of 20 to 30cm soft, long, bright-green, nearly translucent leaves. Plants are often single headed, but they may sometimes form a clump of several rosettes. The flower stalk is slender and smooth, topped by a narrowly conical raceme, which bears many bright, starry yellow flowers, rising 30 to 60cm, on an unbranched inflorescence opening widely and facing outward (sometimes slightly angled upward). Flowers appear in late winter to spring. Plant in full sun to light shade. Drought tolerant.

BUTIA
Arecaceae
Jelly Palms, Pindo Palms

Native to drier parts of southern Brazil, Paraguay, Uruguay and northern Argentina

A genus of eight to twelve monoecious single-stemmed palms. The trunk varies in height and is often covered with persistent leaf bases, giving it a rough texture. Leaves are pinnate and arranged in a feather-shaped pattern along a central stalk. Leaflets are usually stiff and blue-green or silver-grey. They bear long arching panicles of three-petalled, sweetly scented male and female flowers among the leaves. These are followed by round, grape-like edible fruit, which are orange when ripe. Often found in regions with a Mediterranean or subtropical climate, where they can tolerate a wide range of temperatures and soil conditions. Tolerant of drought, heat and poor soil conditions. They prefer well-draining soil and full sun but can also tolerate partial shade.

Butia capitata
Jelly Palm

Native to Brazil, Uruguay and Argentina

A slow-growing, hardy palm with a stout heavy trunk up to 6m high with leaves spreading to 5m wide. The grey trunk is patterned with stubs of old leaves. Graceful, silver-blue leaf fronds, 2m long, are strongly recurved. Leaf stalks are sometimes as long as the leaf and are edged with 2 to 3cm spines. Small, yellow flowers are borne in large drooping clusters up to 1.5m long in summer. They are not decorative but are followed by gigantic clusters of edible fruit. When ripe, 3cm long, oval fruit turn bright orange to yellow. These are sweet and good for making jelly. Grow in well-drained soil in sun or light shade. Although drought tolerant when established, it grows better with regular summer water. A hardy palm that is excellent in a tub on a hot sunny terrace. This species stands more heat, frost and drought conditions than any of the other feather palms. It stands out well against other green trees or shrubs.

Butia yatay
Yatay Palm

Native to Argentina, Paraguay and Uruguay

A slow-growing palm that is similar in most respects to *Butia capitata*, except the trunk often grows at an incline and is from 3 to 16m high and up to 45cm thick. It has the same beautiful, blue, arching leaves. The flowers and fruit are edible. Although drought tolerant when established, it grows better with regular summer water. This palm is highly recommended.

C

Caesalpinia gilliesii see *Erythrostemon gilliesii*

CALENDULA
Asteraceae
Marigolds

Native to southwestern Asia, the Mediterranean region

A genus of about fifteen to twenty species of fast-growing, annual and woody-based evergreen perennials. Leaves are alternate, simple and aromatic. Daisy-like flowerheads have orange or yellow ray florets with yellow, orange or brown disc florets, blooming throughout summer. Many cultivars have been raised. They make excellent cut flowers.

Calendula officinalis
Pot Marigold

Native to southern Europe

A short-lived, aromatic perennial, growing to 80cm tall, with sparsely-branched lax or erect stems. Leaves are oblong-lanceolate, 5 to 17cm long, aromatic, softly hairy on both sides, and with margins entire or occasionally waved or weakly toothed. Inflorescences are daisy-like, single or double, yellow, orange, cream, or apricot, comprising a thick flowerhead 4 to 7cm diameter surrounded by two rows of hairy bracts. In the wild, plants have a single ring of ray florets surrounding the central disc florets. The disc florets are tubular and bisexual, and of a more intense orange-yellow colour than the female peripheral ray florets. Flowers may appear all year long where conditions are suitable. Easily grown in well-drained, even poor soil in sun or partial shade. Somewhat drought tolerant once established. Avoid excessive water with these plants. Great for borders and containers. Ideal colourful plants for Mediterranean gardens.

CALLIANDRA
Fabaceae
Powder Puff Plant, Fairy Duster

Native to tropical and subtropical regions of America, Africa, India

A large genus of about 150 species of evergreen perennials, shrubs and small trees growing up to 6m with bipinnate foliage. Flowers are produced in cylindrical or round inflorescences, which have 10 to 100 colourful stamens, giving rise to the common names. These plants flower all year round, but the best blooming is usually in spring and summer. They can be easily pruned. Attractive to nectar-feeding birds and butterflies.

Calliandra californica
Baja Fairy Duster, Red Fairy Duster, Flame Bush

Native to California and Baja California, Mexico

A species of evergreen woody shrubs 1.5 to 1.8m high that are known for their striking red puffball flowers 3.5cm long, which bloom from late winter to spring. They are reminiscent of feather dusters, hence its common name. Long-lasting flowers are highly attractive to bees, butterflies and other pollinators. Grow in full sun in well-drained soil. It is heat and drought-tolerant once established, making it a popular choice for water-wise landscaping in arid regions. Makes a great ornamental feature in gardens and landscapes.

Calliandra eriophylla var. *eriophylla*
Fairy Duster

Native to deserts and arid grasslands in California, Arizona, New Mexico, Texas and Mexico

A round, evergreen, slow-growing shrub around 1m high and wide. It produces bipinnate leaves 7 to 12cm long, each pinna subdivided into 1 or 2 pairs of elliptic to ovate, dark-green leaflets, softly hairy beneath. Flowers, which appear in summer, have dense spherical clusters 3cm across from pale to deep pink flowers 1.5cm long with reddish purple stamens, which are the most attractive part of the flower. Although it is a desert plant, its water requirements are higher than most. It is typically found where there is some subsurface water year-round.

Calliandra tweediei
Mexican Flame Bush

Native to northern South America

A large shrub or small tree 2 to 5m high and 1.5 m to 2m wide. It has fine and ferny foliage of bipinnate leaves 10 to 15cm long, each pinna subdivided into ten to twenty pairs of narrowly oblong, often curved leaflets. Striking red or pink flowers to 5mm long with red stamens are borne in axillary spherical powder-puff heads 5 to 7cm across for most of the year, attracting birds and insects. A low-maintenance plant for frost-free areas. Grows best in a sunny position in moist and well-drained soil. Good for coastal areas, it also does well in containers. Perfect for use as a ground cover in rockeries, where the weeping foliage is simply gorgeous grown over embankments. Responds well to hard pruning if needed, but can be left unpruned for low-maintenance gardens. A shrub or tree that grows primarily in the seasonally dry biome.

CALLISTEMON *see* MELALEUCA

CALODENDRUM
Rutaceae

Native to southern Africa

A small genus of just two species of evergreen trees, which are grown for their spectacular flowers. The name comes from the Greek meaning 'beautiful tree'.

Bulbine latifolia.

Butia capitata.

Calendula officinalis.

Calliandra eriophylla.

Calliandra tweediei.

Calodendrum capense.

Camellia japonica.

Campsis grandiflora.

Campsis radicans 'Flava'.

Calodendrum capense
Cape Chestnut
Native to the Cape of South Africa
A broad-crowned tree that slowly grows 8 to 10m high and wide-spreading, often multi-trunked with smooth grey bark. Dark-green oval leaves are ovate 5 to 20cm long, with a paler underside and a slightly wavy margin, either opposite or whorled on the stem. It is deciduous in cold winters. From late spring to midsummer, the entire tree canopy is covered with a wonderful display of lightly fragrant flowers that are clustered in upright panicles to 30cm long at the ends of branches. Each flower has five light pink to rose pink sepals (modified leaves) that look like radiating petals up to 5cm across. In addition, there are five petal-like upright stamens that are pale pink with red or maroon-coloured dots. Trees rarely flower until they reach maturity. Grow in full sun in well-drained slightly acidic soil. Drought tolerant once established. Makes a wonderful shade, specimen or contrast tree.

Calothamnus quadrifidus see *Melaleuca quadrifida*

CAMELLIA
Theaceae
Native to East Asia, primarily China, Japan, Korea and Vietnam
There are over 220 described species in the genus. They are popular ornamental tea and woody-oil plants that have been cultivated throughout the world for centuries. To date, over 26,000 cultivars, with over 51,000 cultivar names including synonyms, have been registered or published. They are cultivated worldwide for their beautiful flowers and, with *Camellia sinensis*, for tea production.

Camellia japonica
Japanese Camellia
Native to China
An evergreen flowering tree or shrub with upright or spreading branches up to 6m tall and 3m wide. The youngest branches are purplish brown, becoming greyish brown as they age. Its beautiful, alternate, glossy leaves are leathery, dark green on top, paler on the underside, usually 5 to 8cm long. Flowers appear towards the ends of branches either alone or in pairs. They come in a vast range of sizes, miniatures 4cm to huge 12cm across. Their colour ranges from white to soft pink to dark red and even yellow. Sometimes single, semi-double, or double. These flowers typically bloom in late winter to early spring, making them a popular choice for adding colour to gardens during the colder months. It prefers acidic, well-draining soil and partial shade, although some varieties can tolerate full sun. It requires average water. Often grown as an ornamental shrub or small tree in gardens, parks and landscapes around the world, providing stunning displays of flowers season after season. Great, when grown in a container on a patio.

CAMPSIS
Bignoniaceae
Trumpet Creeper, Trumpet Vine
Native to North America and East Asia
A genus of just two species and one hybrid of deciduous woody climbers that climb by aerial roots. These plants are renowned for their vigorous growth habit, climbing abilities and vibrant trumpet-shaped flowers, which attract pollinators such as hummingbirds and bees. They are low-maintenance plants, preferring full sun and well-drained soil. However, their aggressive growth can sometimes make them invasive in some regions. Pruning and regular maintenance are often necessary to keep them in check.

Campsis grandiflora
Chinese Trumpet Creeper
Native to China, Japan
A deciduous climber that can grow 6 to 9m high with few aerial roots. Dark green 30cm long pinnate leaves have seven to nine leaflets 8cm long. Leaflets are coarsely toothed and hairy underneath. Terminal clusters of spectacular flame-red, trumpet-shaped, deeply five-lobed flowers flare open to 8cm across and up to 10cm long, adorned with golden yellow throats. These are produced throughout the summer. Not so vigorous or hardy as *Campsis radicans*. The climber can be grown in full sun or partial shade in well-drained soil. Grows best if given moderate summer water but will still grow and flower with little water. Particularly effective when trained through a fence, covering a large wall, or climbing into a tree.

Campsis radicans
Trumpet Creeper
Native to eastern United States
A vigorous, self-clinging woody climber that will grow 6 to 12m high. Dark-green pinnate leaves have nine to eleven leaflets 4 to 6cm long with fine hairs underneath. Spectacular deep-orange or red trumpet-shaped flowers, 8cm long, with flared lobes 5cm wide, are in terminal clusters of six to twelve. These are produced at the ends of branches from summer until late autumn. Grow the climber against a wall, pergola or fence, where its arching sprays of flowers can be seen at their best. It will grow in full sun or shade. This floriferous vine is heat, cold and drought tolerant. Widely grown in Mediterranean gardens.

Campsis radicans 'Flava'
A vigorous deciduous climber that produces splendid, yellow, trumpet-shaped blooms 8cm long. Add a beautiful touch to your patio, pathway, or garden perimeter by installing a trellis, fence or arbour. Once it is established, it flourishes and blooms beautifully with minimal attention, except for regular pruning to keep it in check.

Campsis × tagliabuana 'Madame Galen'
A variable hybrid of *C. grandiflora* and *C. radicans*. A vigorous deciduous climber,

9m or more high. Pinnate dark-green leaves are up to 30cm long with seven to fifteen leaflets that are slightly downy on the veins underneath. Panicles of six to twelve dark salmon-red, funnel-shaped flowers with spreading lobes up to 8cm wide are produced during summer. This floriferous vine is heat, cold and drought tolerant. Excellent choice for walls, trellises and fences.

CANARINA

Campanulaceae

Native to the Canary Islands, Madeira, and the western Mediterranean region

A genus of three species of herbaceous, perennial, scrambling vines forming thick, fleshy, beet-like tubers with bell-shaped flowers. They are grown as ornamental plants for their colourful blooms and lush foliage.

Canarina canariensis

Canary Islands Bellflower

Native to the Canary Islands

A scrambling, deciduous climber with grey-green opposite leaves that are simple and lobed. The shoots are annual, with a marked dormancy during summer. This plant comes out of dormancy in late summer with tiny purple shoots at first, that elongate quickly during autumn and winter, and form an enormous mass of scrambling, branching stems often over 2m long with a flower at each tip. It scrambles through scrub or hangs down cliffs. Flowers are axillary, solitary, bell-shaped, approximately 7cm long and 5cm wide. Its stunning flowers are orange-red and intricately veined in red; they glow amongst the foliage and produce abundant nectar, which makes them attractive to insects. The orange-purple fruits are edible and can be compared to figs. It does not like much heat during summer or frost during winter. After flowering, the foliage dies down until growth resumes again in autumn. This is how it has adapted to survive summer drought in its natural habitat.

CANTUA

Polemoniaceae

Magic Tree, Sacred Flower of the Inca, Sacred Flower of the Andes

Native to South America, particularly the Andean region

The genus comprises about 30 species of flowering shrubs or small trees. Most species typically prefer cool, moist conditions and are often found growing at high elevations in their native habitats. They are cultivated as ornamental plants in gardens and landscapes, particularly in regions with mild climates. However, they may require protection from frost in cooler areas.

Cantua buxifolia

Peruvian Magic Tree

An evergreen shrub growing to 4m tall by 2.5m wide. It has small, lance-shaped, softly hairy, mid-green leaves held on long, arching branches. Most of the year it is not interesting, some would say straggly, but come late spring it produces a wonderful display of tubular flowers 8cm long, held in clusters, mainly in magenta reds, but there is a white variety too. These weigh down the slender branches. Flowers are a magnet for birds, especially hummingbirds. It is the national flower of Peru and is prized for its strikingly beautiful tubular flowers. These flowers are often used in traditional Andean ceremonies and celebrations. It enjoys rich soils with plenty of humus and a sunny sheltered location. Water freely when the plant is actively growing during summer, but winter drought tolerant. Prune after flowering to help keep it more compact and bushy.

CAPPARIS

Capparidaceae

Distributed across tropical and subtropical regions around the world, with the highest diversity found in the Mediterranean region and in arid to semi-arid regions of Africa, Asia and Australia.

A genus of about 300 species of tropical or subtropical shrubs or trees with simple, often succulent leaves and usually large white or yellowish flowers. Well adapted to dry and rocky habitats and are known for their tolerance of drought and poor soil conditions. Only one species is commonly grown.

Capparis spinosa

Caper Bush

Native to dry rocky places in the Mediterranean region

A spiny, essentially glabrous shrub with a habit that varies from a prostrate spreading plant to a dense round shrub to 2m high and wide. Deep-green leaves are nearly round up to 5cm across. Solitary 5 to 8cm-wide flowers are white with showy brushes of lavender stamens. Every leaf base produces long stalks that bear flowers, opening in the morning and closing in the afternoon. They are produced continuously throughout the summer. *Capparis spinosa* is cultivated for its edible flower buds known as capers. Capers are widely used as a seasoning or garnish in various cuisines, particularly in Mediterranean dishes such as salads, pasta and fish recipes. The immature flower buds are harvested by hand and then pickled in vinegar, brine or salt. The shrub needs to be grown in full sun. Tolerates or even prefers poor soil, but needs good drainage. Difficult to establish, but then drought tolerant. Can be grown as a ground cover or planted where it can hang down over a wall. Sometimes can be seen growing from old city walls.

CARAGANA

Fabaceae

Pea Tree

Native to central Asia and Europe

A genus of about 80 to 100 species of hardy, usually spiny shrubs and small trees. The species are valued for their ornamental qualities, drought tolerance and ability to thrive in poor soil conditions. They are often planted for erosion control, windbreaks and as ornamental shrubs in gardens and landscapes. Some species also have nitrogen-fixing abilities, which can improve soil fertility. Grown for their showy pea-like flowers. Species are easy to grow and require minimal maintenance once established. They prefer full sun and well-drained soil but can tolerate a wide range of soil types, including sandy and alkaline soils. These plants are also cold hardy and can withstand harsh winters, making them suitable for temperate and cold climates.

Caragana arborescens
Siberian Pea Shrub
Native to Siberia

A fast-growing shrub 2 to 6m high with a spread of 4m. The four to six pairs of even-pinnate leaves are up to 8cm long, with the terminal leaflet reduced to a spine. Yellow, pea-like fragrant flowers are 1.5cm long, appearing in great profusion during spring in drooping clusters. A nearly indestructible shrub that will grow in the poorest of soils, succeed in the most exposed areas and is completely drought tolerant. Useful as a windbreak or clipped into a hedge. The variety 'Pendula' is a weeping form, while 'Lorbergii' has narrow, almost grass-like leaves and smaller flowers.

CARICA
Caricaceae
Native to tropical and subtropical America

A genus of around 25 species of soft-wooded small trees or, rarely, climbers. Only one species is grown for its fruit. They should be planted in groups, as they are dioecious.

Carica papaya
Pawpaw
Native to Central America

An evergreen, soft-stemmed, sparsely-branched tree that grows with a single straight stem up to 6m high and is topped with a spirally-arranged crown of leaves. The lower trunk is conspicuously scarred where leaves and fruit were borne. Broad fan-like leaves usually have five to seven deep lobes. They are up to 60cm across and borne on a leaf stalk up to 60cm long. Inconspicuous flowers are cream or yellow, followed by fruit. The fruit is oval, 30cm or more long, green when young ripening to yellowish-green or orange, and can weigh from 200 grams to several kilograms. With a ripening period of six to eight months, the fruit has thick, yellow flesh and abundant small black seeds. In order to grow trees effectively, choose a warm, sheltered location with nutrient-rich, well-drained soil, ensuring they receive full sun and ample water in summer. They are susceptible to the roots rotting because of cold wet soil in winter. Grow on the sunny side of a wall or house to take advantage of reflected heat in winter. Fruit can be expected from female trees a few months after planting, but since they do not live long, they should be replaced with easily-raised seedlings.

CARISSA
Apocynaceae
Native to tropical and subtropical Africa, Asia and India

A genus of about 35 species of much-branched, evergreen, often spiny shrubs or small trees. They are often grown for their tart edible fruit. Plants have fragrant flowers, milky sap and spines.

Carissa macrocarpa syn. *Carissa grandiflora*
Natal Plum
Native to South Africa

A dense evergreen shrub 2m or rarely 3m high, which can also be trained into a beautiful small tree. Dark, glossy-green oval leaves are variable up to 8cm long and 5cm wide. They have stiff, mostly forked spines at the base of the leaves. Solitary, 5cm-wide, bright white, star-shaped, five-petalled flowers are richly fragrant with perfumed scent intensifying at night. Ornamental plump, plum-shaped, crimson fruit appears in summer and autumn at the same time as the blooms. In mild coastal areas, fruits appear throughout the year. The fruit can be eaten raw or made into pies, jams, jellies and sauces. To grow well, it needs full sun and some summer water, but it may tolerate some drought once established. As the shrub is so impenetrable, it is often grown on boundaries as a screen or hedge. Also grows well in coastal areas. There are many cultivars, 'Horizontalis', which is exceptionally compact and prostrate, 'Green Carpet', which makes an excellent ground cover, and 'Tuttlei', which grows 1m high and 2m wide with dense compact foliage producing a heavy crop of flowers and fruit.

CARNEGIEA
Cactaceae
Saguaros
Native to Arizona, the Mexican state of Sonora, and areas of California

A single species in this monotypic genus is certainly the most widely recognised and stereotypical cactus of all. A columnar cactus that grows notable branches, usually referred to as arms. Over 50 arms may grow on one plant, with one specimen having 78 arms growing from 3 to 16m tall, and up to 75cm in diameter. They are slow growing, but routinely live 150 to 200 years. They are the largest cactus in the United States.

Carnegiea gigantea

A columnar cactus, which grows slowly to 15m with a spread of 10m determined by the number and length of its arms. Stems can be up to 75cm in diameter and may live for 250 years. Branches form on larger plants at around 2 to 3m high when they are decades old. Its vertical ribs are straight and may be narrow or broad, depending on the amount of moisture stored in the tissue. Spines are golden-brown to grey from 2.5 to 4cm long. Spines are unequal, with one prominent central spine per areole that is distinctly pointed downward – a useful identification key. In late spring, flowers form near the apex of the stem or 15 to

Canarina canariensis.

Cantua buxifolia.

Capparis spinosa.

Caragana arborescens.

Carica papaya.

Carissa macrocarpa.

Carnegiea gigantea.

Carpenteria californica.

Carpobrotus edulis.

30cm below the tip. They are waxy white, bell shaped, 5 to 6cm wide and 13cm long. Flowers are fragrant, mildly sweet-smelling and are open during the day and night, lasting one to two days. It is extremely slow-growing, only adding about 30cm every ten years. Its water demands are minimal, as it is extremely drought tolerant, needing water only in extended periods of drought. Full sun and well-draining soil are essential, sandy or gravelly soil is best. It makes a dramatic vertical silhouette in a dry garden.

CARPENTERIA
Hydrangeaceae

Native to Sierra Nevada in California, United States

A genus of only one species of evergreen shrub, which is grown for its attractive leaves and beautiful cup-shaped white flowers.

Carpenteria californica
Tree Anemone

An evergreen shrub that makes slow growth to 2m high with many basal branches. New branches are purplish while the old bark is light coloured and peeling. Leaves are oblong to 10cm long, green and shiny above, grey underneath. It is prized for its large, fragrant, pure white flowers with prominent yellow stamens. Blooms profusely in late spring to early summer, in clusters at the shoot tips. The flowers resemble those of single-petalled roses and are attractive to pollinators such as bees and butterflies. These are 4 to 8cm wide with five rounded petals and a mass of golden anthers. It is drought tolerant once established but may benefit from occasional deep watering during hot, dry periods. Excess water in winter is especially harmful. Relatively easy to cultivate, it prefers well-drained soil and full sun to partial shade. Prune after flowering to maintain a tidy shape and encourage fresh growth. It can be grown as a freestanding shrub or planted against a wall, making it an excellent choice for ornamental gardens and landscapes. Easily raised from seed.

CARPOBROTUS
Aizoaceae
Pigface, Ice Plant

Native to South Africa, Australia, North and South America

A genus of about 30 species of creeping, perennial succulents and subshrubs. Species are well adapted to coastal habitats and are often used for erosion control and landscaping in sandy or rocky coastal areas. They are valued for their ability to withstand salt spray, drought and poor soil conditions. These plants are characterised by their fleshy, triangular leaves and colourful, daisy-like flowers. Although Carpobrotus species are useful for gardens and landscaping, they are invasive in non-native regions. It is essential to consider the cultivation and management of these to avoid unintended ecological outcomes.

Carpobrotus edulis
Hottentot Fig, Highway Ice Plant

Native to South Africa

One of the most widely-cultivated species is a creeping, branching succulent 15cm high that can spread to many metres wide. Individual stems can grow to 2m or more long and root along their length. The 8 to 12cm-long leaves are three-angled, fleshy and slightly bent inwards. Large yellow, yellowish-pink or purple flowers, 8 to 10cm across with narrow silky petals, open at midday. These are produced continuously from spring to early autumn, often followed by large edible fruit. The fruits may be consumed fresh or used to make jams and jellies. Grow in full sun in sandy or well-drained soil. Drought tolerant once established. Often planted as a sand binder along seashores or covering sunny banks. Can be grown from seed but easily raised from cuttings. Rooted cuttings planted out in spring will quickly cover a large area.

CARYOPTERIS
Lamiaceae

Native to East Asia

A genus of about seven species of aromatic hairy-leaved shrubs or perennials from habitats including dry, hot slopes and woodlands. They have opposite entire or toothed leaves. Small, usually blue flowers are borne in terminal or axillary panicles. Often used as border plants, in mixed shrub borders, or as focal points in garden beds.

Caryopteris × clandonensis
Blue Mist, Bluebeard

Garden origin

A small shrub growing only to about 1m high and wide. Lance-shaped leaves are deciduous, greyish green to 5cm long, often white or grey underneath, aromatic, and coarsely toothed at the edges. Opening from deep indigo blue buds, the clusters of tiny tubular flowers 1cm across appear on the tips of the current season's branches late in summer. These are attractive to butterflies, bees and other beneficial insects. Often followed by attractive seed heads. Grow in full sun in average well-drained soil, drought and heat tolerant once established. Perfect for small gardens or containers. Looks good when planted in bold groups. As it flowers on new wood, it should be cut back nearly to the base of the previous year's growth in spring each year. The variety 'Arthur Simmonds' is more commonly grown. 'Heavenly Blue' is more compact, and 'Kew Blue' is a deeper blue.

CATANANCHE
Asteraceae

Native to dry meadows in the Mediterranean region

These are cultivated for their cornflower-like blooms appearing in summer, in shades of blue, yellow and white. They are suitable for a sunny border, and for dried flower arrangements.

Catananche caerulea
Cupid's Dart
Native to southern Europe

An attractive, short-lived perennial with clumps 45 to 70cm high of linear, grass-like hairy leaves to 30cm long. Leaves are covered in long soft woolly hairs (pilose) lying on the surface, giving both leaf surfaces a greyish-green colour. From the heart of the rosette one or a few, strongly branched, erect, again woolly-haired and greyish green flowering stems rise. These stems carry only a few leaves, similar to the basal leaves, to 30cm long, with up to four lateral lobes. Throughout summer it bears solitary violet-centred blue to lilac-blue daisy-like flowerheads 3 to 5cm across, set individually at the end of a branch up to 30cm long, surrounded by a few small papery bracts. A favourite of flower arrangers. Grow in any well-drained soil. Easy to grow in a sunny spot where you want a bright splash of colour. It may self-sow in good conditions. Drought tolerant. Several cultivars are available, including: 'Bicolor', with white flowers with purple centres; 'Alba', with white flowers; 'Major', with lavender petals and purple centres. Cut back after flowering.

CATHARANTHUS
Apocynaceae
Madagascar Periwinkle
Native to Madagascar

There are about eight known species of annuals and perennials with opposite leaves. Flowers are usually solitary in the leaf axils. Each has a calyx with five long, narrow lobes and a corolla with a tubular throat and five lobes. Several cultivars have been bred to produce flowers in many shades. Only one species is grown as bedding plants.

Catharanthus roseus
Madagascar Periwinkle, Vinca

Typically grows as an evergreen small shrub, reaching a height of about 30 to 60cm with milky sap. Ovate leaves are elliptic to oblanceolate, 3 to 9cm long, glossy green. Flowers are salverform with five spreading rounded lobes 5cm wide, tube 2 to 3cm long, borne in clusters continuously throughout the year. These come in a variety of colours, including white, pink, purple and red, often with a contrasting colour at the centre. Grow in fertile, well-drained soil in full sun or partial shade. A popular choice for gardens, borders and containers, because of its low maintenance requirements and long blooming period. Heat and drought tolerant, making it suitable for various climates. Its form can become unattractive with age and replanting is recommended. Often self-seeding, it may become naturalised.

Centranthus ruber see *Valeriana rubra*

CEANOTHUS
Rhamnaceae
California Lilac
Native to western USA, particularly California, and eastern United States, Mexico

A genus of 50 to 60 species of deciduous and evergreen shrubs or small trees occurring naturally on dry rocky slopes. They have opposite or alternate, usually toothed leaves. These are grown for their often spectacular displays of blue, sometimes white or pink flowers. Dislikes being hard pruned and will not re-sprout from old wood. Not considered long-lived plants – five to ten years is usual – but make rapid growth in early life.

Ceanothus arboreus 'Trewithen Blue'
Garden origin

A vigorous evergreen shrub or tree up to 5m high spreading 5m or more. The broad oval to rounded mid-green leaves 8 to 10cm long are shallowly toothed with fine soft hairs underneath. It is noted for its abundant pyramidal, terminal and lateral panicles, 12cm long, of tiny, fragrant, deep blue flowers in late spring and early summer. The flowers are so abundant they completely engulf the plant, resulting in a breathtaking show. The blooms are borne on arching branches. It is enticing for both birds and butterflies. Grow in average, well-drained soil in full sun. Drought tolerant. Excellent plant for sunny areas, ideal as a specimen plant, or for hedges or screens.

Ceanothus impressus
Santa Barbara Ceanothus
Native to California

A densely-branched, broad-spreading, evergreen shrub up to 2m high and wide. Thickly branched, its dark-brown stems are clad with small, 1cm-long, oval, rigid, wrinkled dark-green leaves that become sweetly fragrant on warm days. It is noted for its abundant clusters 2 to 3cm across of fragrant, dark-blue flowers, which are produced in great profusion during late spring. This stunning shrub is a moderate grower and thrives in both cool coastal climates and hot seasons. It is extremely drought tolerant once established. Excellent for sunny areas, banks and slopes, hedges and screens. Thrives in dry, sandy, well-drained soils.

Ceanothus thyrsiflorus
Blueblossom
Native to California

A large, upright-spreading, evergreen, hardy shrub 4m high and wide, or a small tree to 6m high. Arching branches are covered with alternate, oblong, finely-toothed leaves, 5cm long, which are glossy above. Spring brings about large, fluffy clusters of pale- to dark-blue flowers with yellow stamens, packed tightly in terminal and lateral clusters that can grow up to 20cm long. The shrub is completely engulfed in a sea of blue flowers, creating a breathtaking sight. Grow in average, well-drained soil in full sun. Tolerant of drought, salt spray, poor sandy soil. Great for coastal gardens, borders along walls, and Mediterranean gardens. The prostrate variety 'repens' is low-growing to about 1m high, spreading to 3m wide. Makes an excellent ground cover, as it forms a dense carpet. In spring and early summer, the shrub is covered with a mass of fluffy sky-blue flowers.

ryopteris × clandonensis.

Catananche caerulea.

Catharanthus roseus.

anothus impressus.

Ceiba speciosa.

Cenchrus alopecuroides.

entaurea cineraria.

Cerastium glomeratum.

CEIBA
Malvaceae

Native to northeast Argentina, east Bolivia, Paraguay, Uruguay and southern Brazil

The genus has 28 recognised species of evergreen or deciduous trees with spiny, fleshy trunks and spectacular flowers.

Ceiba speciosa syn. *Chorisia speciosa*
Floss Silk Tree

Native to Brazil and Argentina

A deciduous tree growing 9 to 15m high and 6 to 9m wide, maturing to a broadly conical shape. Its trunk is bottle-shaped, often bulging in its lower third to 2m in girth, and studded with thick, sharp conical spines. Young trees have a green trunk because of abundant chlorophyll, enabling photosynthesis without leaves. As it gets older, it becomes grey. Branches tend to be horizontal and are also covered with spines. Long-stalked, pinnate leaves 8 to 12cm long are composed of five to seven lance-shaped leaflets. Large, showy five-petalled flowers are 8 to 12cm wide, pink to almost red, with white to yellow throats and brown or purple dots. Their nectar attracts insect pollinators and hummingbirds. These spectacular flowers appear in late summer or autumn when the tree may be briefly deciduous. They may be followed by pear-shaped fruits containing silky floss on the seeds, but these are rarely seen in cultivation. Grow the tree in full sun, in neutral to acid soil with good drainage. Give a deep watering once a month when the tree is established. Reducing the watering of established trees in late summer is the key to successful flowering. It is resistant to drought and moderate cold.

CENCHRUS
Poaceae

Native to tropical and warm temperate regions of the world

This genus of 80 to 140 species of grasses includes some ornamental species and others that are among the worst weeds. Some are short while others produce stems up to 8m tall. Species are clump- or mat-forming, annual or perennial grasses spread by rhizomes or stolons to form clumps. Stems are round, hollow, prostrate to erect and tufted with overarching, short-stemmed, narrow to quite broad leaves that often have a prominent midrib. Flower stems usually extend above the foliage clump and carry cylindrical or rounded, feathery, spike-like flowerheads often interspersed with bristles that are often strongly pink-tinted, and usually appear from late summer to autumn. They are among the most graceful of ornamental grasses.

Cenchrus alopecuroides syn. *Pennisetum alopecuroides*
Chinese Fountain Grass

Native to Asia and western Australia

A clump-forming, densely-tufted, perennial grass 90cm to 1.2m high. The flat, linear, pointed, bright-green leaves are 30 to 60cm long, turning yellow in autumn and brown in winter. In summer it produces brown or pinkish, bristly, bottle-brush flower spikes 20cm long on stems 1.2m tall. The plant thrives in full sun or partial shade in most well-drained soil. When established, it withstands some drought, but grows much better with some summer water. An attractive grass that looks good in a mixed border or when covering a bank. Flowers are useful for both fresh and dried arrangements. 'Hameln' is a dwarf, early-flowering form, with greyish-brown spikes to 12cm long.

Cenchrus longisetus syn. *Pennisetum villosum*
Feathertop, Abyssinian Fountain Grass

Native to northeast Africa

A perennial grass with clustered stems to 60cm high and wide. Upright or arching stems bear mid-green leaves 15cm long. In late summer, the plant produces gracefully nodding, softly furry, cylindrical, plume-like flower spikes 5cm long. They start white and become golden when mature. The plant thrives in full sun or partial shade in most well-drained soil. When established, it withstands some drought, but grows much better with some summer water. Although a perennial, it is often treated as an annual. Wonderful for flower arrangements. It has become an invasive weed in parts of Australia.

CENTAUREA
Asteraceae
Knapweeds, Cornflowers

Native mostly in the Mediterranean region, west and central Asia and north Africa

This genus comprises over 700 species, including annuals, biennials, perennials and shrubs. Foliage varies among species, with some having finely divided or fern-like leaves and others having broader, lance-shaped leaves. Plants typically produce flower heads that are composed of many small individual flowers packed closely together. The flower heads are often surrounded by bracts, which can be colourful and showy.

Centaurea cineraria
Dusty Miller, Silver Dust, Silver Ragwort

Native to the Mediterranean region

A subshrub that can be grown as an annual or perennial, growing 80cm or more high and spreading to 45cm wide. It is grown for its dense, downy, grey-green foliage rather than the yellow thistle-like flowers that are usually trimmed to promote foliage growth. Leaves are 10 to 15cm long and deeply divided into many blunt segments and covered with fine matted hairs on both sides, giving them a felt-like or woolly appearance in silver or white. The solitary purple flowers to 3cm across, with dark-brown pointed bracts beneath, appear in summer. Grow in well-drained, moderately rich soil in full sun. It will tolerate poor soils and partial shade but can become leggy. Drought tolerant when established. Use in a container, as an edging plant along paths, for accent, or on slopes. The leaves reflect moonlight, making it a welcome addition to a night-time garden, as well as a cottage or drought-tolerant garden.

CERASTIUM
Carophyllaceae

A genus of about 100 species of low growing or mat forming annuals or perennials found throughout the world. All but a few are too weedy for the garden

Cerastium glomeratum syn. *Cerastium tomentosum*
Snow-In-Summer

Native to Italy, but naturalised in Europe

A hardy, evergreen, low creeping perennial 15 to 25cm high that will spread to 1m or more. Masses of lance-shaped 2cm-long leaves are whitish and tomentose, flat or linear, prolonged, acute and smooth-edged. During spring, the plant is covered with a profusion of snow-white flowers 2cm across with five deeply-notched petals. It will grow in full sun or partial shade. Great for planting in rock gardens or raised beds or edging borders. Good drainage is important, as waterlogged soil causes the roots to rot. Drought-tolerant once established, but grows better with some summer water.

CERATOSTIGMA
Plumbaginaceae
Plumbago, Leadworts

Native to Asia and tropical East Africa

A genus of about eight species of small shrubs or perennials. Often grown as ornamental plants for their long-lasting blooms, attractive foliage and the ability to tolerate a variety of soil conditions. Species typically prefer full sun to partial shade and well-drained soil. Once established, they require minimal maintenance and are commonly used as ground covers or in rock gardens. Often called 'Hardy Plumbago', as they are closely related to *Plumbago auriculata*.

Ceratostigma griffithii
Burmese Plumbago

Native to the Himalayas of Tibet and Bhutan

A multi-stemmed evergreen shrub up to 80cm high and wide, which forms mounds of densely massed spreading stems carrying matt green leaves up to 3cm long, with purple-tinged edges. These turn a rich plum colour as colder autumn weather arrives. Brilliant, deep-blue flowers grow up to 2cm across in clusters from late summer until late autumn. Frost- and drought-tolerant once established, but will grow and flower better with some summer water. Sun-loving, but can also handle some shade in any well-drained soil. Can be hard pruned in spring to remove old wood and encourage fresh growth.

Ceratostigma plumbaginoides
Dwarf Plumbago

Native to western China

A dwarf multi-stemmed deciduous shrub up to 40cm high and wide, spreading by rhizomes. These form an attractive mat of wiry stems clothed with oval, shiny, bronze-green or dark-green leaves 5cm long, which may turn reddish-brown in autumn. Blooming from midsummer until autumn, clusters of rich gentian blue flowers 2cm across are in terminal heads, above the foliage. Performs best in full sun in fertile well-drained soils, but appreciates afternoon shade in hot summer climates. Although drought tolerant, it will grow and flower better with summer water. Suitable for a large rock garden or the front of a shrub border. With age, the old crown may become woody, when it should be replaced with new rooted stems. Hard pruning in spring keeps the bush looking its best.

Ceratostigma willmottianum
Chinese Plumbago

Native to western China and Tibet

A low-spreading, multi-stemmed deciduous shrub to 1.5m high with angled branches. Both sides of the oval to roundish leaves, 5cm long, are covered in bristles and turn red during autumn. Bright blue, salver-shaped flowers, 1 to 2cm across, are in dense terminal or axillary heads in profusion from midsummer until autumn. Culture is like *Ceratostigma griffithii*.

CERCIS
Fabaceae
Redbuds

Native to North America, the Mediterranean and Asia

A genus of about seven species of ornamental deciduous trees or shrubs. These plants are admired for their vibrant, brightly coloured, pea-like, showy flowers that appear in early spring before the foliage emerges. Flowers can range from pink to magenta, depending on the species and cultivar. Blooms appear along the branches before the leaves unfurl. They are versatile plants that can thrive in various soil types and moisture conditions, although preferring well-drained soil. Often cultivated as ornamental trees in gardens, parks and landscapes for their spring flowers and attractive foliage.

Cercis siliquastrum
Judas Tree

Native to the eastern Mediterranean

A deciduous shrub or multi-trunked tree that grows to 10m high with an equal spread and a rounded crown. Emerging bronze-red, the roundish, 7 to 12cm-wide, heart-shaped leaves mature to deep green in summer before turning yellow in autumn. Masses of small, purplish-rose, pea-shaped flowers 1 to 2cm long appear in spring before the leaves. These cover the naked branches and sometimes appear from the limbs and trunk. They are replaced by attractive clusters of reddish, flattened pods, which persist until after the leaves have fallen. Summer drought tolerant once established. Grows best in hot, dry, stony places. Plant when young, as it is likely to die if transplanted when mature. Often seen growing along the sides of roads, making a wonderful sight when in full flower. 'Albida' has white flowers.

CESTRUM
Solanaceae

Native to tropical America and the West Indies

About 150 species of evergreen shrubs and small trees, typically having simple, mostly narrow, alternate leaves. Tubular or trumpet-shaped flowers are produced in terminal or axillary clusters, sometimes with a scent. Typically, the flowers are white, green, or a shade of yellowish green. These are often highly fragrant, especially at night, and are pollinated by moths and other nocturnal insects. Small, fleshy berries are produced after pollination. Some species contain toxic compounds, such as alkaloids that can be harmful if ingested, so caution should be exercised, especially in households with pets or small children.

Cestrum aurantiacum
Orange Cestrum, Orange Jessamine

Native to Nicaragua and Guatemala

An evergreen shrub that when mature can take on a dense, well-branched, upright to arching habit and reaches up 3m tall with a similar spread in tropical climates. Leaves are simple, oblong to elliptic, alternate, dark green and glossy, giving the plant an attractive appearance. Terminal clusters of vibrant, gold-orange, tubular flowers bloom from spring through summer, attracting butterflies and other insect pollinators. Flowers are fragrant, producing a pleasant scent, especially in the evening, often followed by 1cm diameter white berries. Easy to grow, tolerating a range of well-draining soils, in full sun to partial shade. It can be trained to climb an arbour or trellis. Heavy pruning is recommended for smaller garden areas and more formal landscapes. It has escaped cultivation, becoming invasive in some areas of Africa, Asia and Australia.

Cestrum parqui
Palqui, Green Cestrum, Chilean Cestrum, Willow-Leaved Jessamine

Native to Chile

A fast-growing, upright, semi-evergreen shrub up to 3m high and wide with many branches from the base. Alternate bright green willow-like leaves, up to 10cm long, have an unpleasant rubber-like smell when crushed. It produces terminal sprays of star-shaped, pungently-scented, tubular, greenish-yellow 2cm-long flowers. These have an unpleasant odour during the day, but the perfume is incredibly powerful at night. It blooms year-round, especially in warmer climates, with a peak in spring. The small, black fruits are highly attractive to birds. Grow in full sun or partial shade in well-drained soil. Somewhat summer drought tolerant. In some countries, the plant is regarded as a noxious, invasive weed. All parts of the plant are reported to be highly toxic.

CHAENOMELES
Rosaceae
Flowering Quince, Japonica

Native to eastern Asia and Japan

A small genus of four species of deciduous or semi-evergreen spiny shrubs growing 1 to 3m tall. Leaves are alternate, simple, with a serrated margin. Flowers are 3 to 4.5cm in diameter, with five petals, usually bright orange-red, but can be white or pink. They are grown for their attractive flowers, which are produced in late winter or early spring. The fruit is a pome with five carpels and it ripens in late autumn. All species can withstand frost.

Chaenomeles speciosa
Chinese Flowering Quince

Native to eastern Asia

A strong-growing, bushy, deciduous shrub to 1.3m high and 1.8m wide with upright to spreading spiny branches. Oval, glossy, dark green leaves are up to 8cm long. In midwinter or early spring, vibrant clusters of red flowers 5cm across with attractive pale- to bright-yellow anthers appear in profusion. They are followed by fragrant, green-yellow, round to pear-shaped fruits to 6cm across. Grow in full sun or partial shade. Tolerant of most garden soils, but may become chlorotic in highly alkaline soil. Drought-tolerant once established, but does best with some summer water. Prune by one third immediately after flowering to encourage new spring growth. Once buds have formed, stems can be cut for indoor decoration. A tough and practically indestructible shrub that flowers when little else is around. Perfect for informal hedges. Many named varieties have been raised with red, pink or white flowers.

CHAMAECYTISUS
Fabaceae

Native to the Canary Islands and Morocco through mainland southern Europe to eastern Mediterranean

A genus of 43 species of shrubs and small shrubby trees growing to 5m high.

Chamaecytisus elongatus syn. *Cytisus multiflorus*
Portuguese Broom, White Spanish Broom

Native to Spain and Portugal

A deciduous, much-branched, upright to spreading shrub 3m high and 2m or more wide with erect, striped-green, grooved branches. Leaves are in groups of three leaflets on lower branches and a single leaflet on higher branches up to 1cm long, silvery when young. Young stems and leaves are covered with short hairs, which are lost as the plant ages. White

ratostigma plumbaginoides.

Ceratostigma willmottianum.

Cercis siliquastrum.

strum aurantiacum.

Cestrum parqui.

Chaenomeles speciosa.

amaecytisus elongatus.

Chamaerops humilis.

Chamelaucium uncinatum.

flowers with a pink streak at the base 1 to 2cm long are borne in axillary clusters of one to three. Both the flowers and seed pods are pea-like, covering the shrub in spring and early summer. Best grown in full sun. Tolerant of poor rocky soil, drought and pollution. An ideal shrub for the back of a dry garden. Although the flowering season is short, it is spectacular.

CHAMAEROPS
Arecaceae
Native to the western Mediterranean region, particularly Southern Europe and North Africa

The genus contains only one species of hardy palm. It is widely cultivated as an ornamental plant in gardens and parks because of its attractive fan-shaped leaves and tolerance for a range of climates. It is a popular choice for landscaping in the Mediterranean.

Chamaerops humilis
Mediterranean Fan Palm

A slow-growing palm that typically grows in clumps, with multiple stems arising from the base, which only in ideal conditions forms a trunk to 6m high. The trunk is rough and clothed with fibre, but growth is extremely slow. Tough blue-green fan-shaped leaves are stiff and folded, 45cm long and up to 60cm wide, and divided into many narrow segments, which are split nearly to the base. They are carried on flat, prickly leaf stalks up to 90cm long. Small red-brown fruit follows the bunches of greenish-yellow flowers that are produced in spring. Completely drought tolerant, but summer water will improve it. One of the hardiest palms thriving in full sun or partial shade in well-drained, even poor soil. While it can withstand frost, it thrives in hot summers. It is commonly used in landscaping for its ornamental value and ability to thrive in warm dry climates. A versatile palm that can be massed under trees or made into a low informal hedge. Also, a good palm for tubs on a patio.

CHAMELAUCIUM
Myrtaceae
Waxflowers
Native to Western Australia

The genus comprises around 30 species of evergreen shrubs. Leaves are small, narrow and aromatic, with a glossy texture. Small, five-petalled flowers are waxy in texture and have a delicate, star-like appearance, typically white or shades of pink and purple with a sweet, honey-like fragrance. They are long-lasting and often used in floral arrangements. Species are well-suited to the Mediterranean climate and are commonly found in dry sandy or gravelly soils. They are cultivated for their ornamental value and are popular in gardens and landscapes around the world.

Chamelaucium uncinatum

A dense but spreading shrub, 2 to 6m high and wide. Leaves are small, narrow, dark green and glossy. Flowers are small, waxy and star-shaped, with five petals in a variety of colours, including white, pink, purple and shades in between. The flowers are borne in terminal clusters and have a pleasant fragrance. It is well-adapted to sandy, well-drained soils and the Mediterranean climate of its native habitat. Drought tolerant once established, it prefers full sun or partial shade. It is one of the most well-known and widely cultivated species within the genus. Popularly used in floral arrangements, where its long-lasting flowers and attractive foliage add texture and colour. In Australian culture, it is highly regarded as an iconic native plant. It is commonly associated with beauty, resilience, and the natural landscapes of Western Australia. The plant holds cultural significance for Indigenous Australians communities, who have traditional uses for its flowers and foliage.

CHASMANTHE
Iridaceae
Native to South Africa

A genus of about nine species of herbaceous perennials growing from corms. These plants are known for their striking, sword-shaped leaves and vibrant, tubular flowers. They are popular ornamentals in gardens and landscapes, prized for their colourful blooms and ability to naturalise in certain climates. Typically, they produce tall flower spikes adorned with clusters of fiery orange, red or yellow flowers, depending on the species and variety. Species prefer sunny locations and well-drained soil. Plants are easily cultivated and can become invasive.

Chasmanthe floribunda
African Corn Flag

A perennial herbaceous plant sprouting from a corm and producing clumps of long, narrow leaves. Bright green lance-shaped leaves are stiffly erect, 30 to 60cm long, 4cm wide and often branched. It produces one thin, tall flowering stem, which may be 1m high. At the top of the stem is a spike inflorescence, holding 20 to 40 flowers in neat vertical rows. The 8cm-long flower is a curving tube with a long upper lobe curving down over smaller lobes. Protruding from the flower are stamens with large, hanging anthers, and a style. The flower is bright orange-red or scarlet on the upper lobe and yellow to orange in the lower lobes. Flowering stems appear in great profusion during winter and early spring. Easily grown, in both sun and shade, although it prefers full sun. It will grow in most well-drained soils. As it is summer dormant, it requires no water. Chasmanthe emerges from the ground in autumn in the Western Cape, South Africa, after the first winter rains, where it is frequented by sunbirds. One of the most well-known and commonly cultivated species. When clumps have become too large and overcrowded, lift and divide in summer after flowering and the leaves have turned yellow. It has often escaped into the wild and has become an invasive weed in many areas.

CHILOPSIS
Bignoniaceae
Desert Willows, Desert Catalpas

Native to deserts of southwestern North America, Mexico

A monotypic genus of flowering plants. Its willow-like leaves give it the common names.

Chilopsis linearis

A small to medium-sized deciduous tree or shrub to 3m high and spreading to 2m with a graceful, weeping growth habit. It has shaggy bark and green willow-like leaves. Known for its ornamental flowers that are trumpet-shaped and come in various shades of pink, purple or white, depending on the cultivar, often spotted or streaked with purple. These bloom in spring and summer, attracting pollinators such as bees and hummingbirds. It typically grows in arid and semi-arid environments, often along stream banks, washes and in other riparian habitats. This species is valued for its drought tolerance, heat resistance, and ability to thrive in poor, sandy soils. It is commonly used in landscaping to add colour and texture to water-wise gardens and other dry landscapes.

CHLOROPHYTUM
Asparagaceae

Native to tropical and southern Africa and Asia

This genus includes about 200 species of evergreen perennials. They grow to 10 to 60cm tall, with a rosette of long, slender leaves,15 to 75cm long and thick, fleshy tuberous roots. Flowers are small, usually white, produced on sparse panicles up to 120cm long. In some species, the plants also reproduce vegetatively through plantlets, tiny plants that take root on touching the ground.

Chlorophytum comosum
Variegated Spider Plant

An evergreen perennial, which grows to about 60cm tall, with thick, fleshy, tuberous roots. Long, narrow, dark-green leaves are 20 to 45cm long, edged with white stripes. Flowers are produced in a long, branched inflorescence, which can reach to 75cm and eventually bend downward to meet the ground. Flowers initially occur in clusters of one to six at intervals along the stem of the inflorescence. At the bottom of each cluster is a bract that can range in length from 2 to 8cm, with a gradual decrease in size towards the end of the inflorescence. Initially, many of the flowers that are produced wither away, leaving the inflorescences sparsely populated with blooms. Individual flowers are greenish white, borne on stalks some 4 to 8mm long. The inflorescences carry plantlets at the tips of their branches, which eventually droop and touch the soil, developing adventitious roots. Plants are easy to grow and require little maintenance, preferring a well-drained organic soil that is kept slightly moist. Ideal for ground cover in shady beds or borders. They tolerate most light levels, except the harsh afternoon sun.

CHOISYA
Rutaceae

Native to southwestern North America and Mexico

A small genus of around seven species of evergreen shrubs popular in gardens and landscaping for their aromatic foliage and clusters of fragrant white flowers, which resemble orange blossoms. Leaves are typically glossy and divided into three leaflets, giving them a distinctive appearance. Flowers bloom in spring and sometimes again in autumn, attracting pollinators like bees and butterflies. These shrubs prefer well-drained soil and full sun to partial shade. They are relatively low-maintenance and tolerant of dry conditions once established.

Choisya ternata
Mexican Orange Blossom

Native to Mexico

An easily grown, medium-sized shrub that forms a dense rounded mound up to 3m high and perhaps 4m wide. Leaves are trifoliate, shiny dark-green, 8cm long, and form fans, giving the shrub a dense, massive look. They have a strong pungent odour when crushed. Clusters of white sweetly scented flowers, 2 to 3cm across, cover the shrub in early spring and are held conspicuously above the foliage. A few flowers may appear intermittently throughout the summer. While they can tolerate shade, the most beautiful flowers thrive in full sun. Grow in a well-drained soil that is not too alkaline. Drought tolerant, but for good growth and flowering water occasionally and deeply during summer. The leaves can suffer from wind damage. Makes an attractive informal hedge or screen. The variety 'Sundance' has bright golden foliage and is lower growing but may scorch in full sun.

Chorisia speciosa see *Ceiba speciosa*

CHORIZEMA
Fabaceae

Native to Australia, California

A genus of around eighteen species of evergreen shrubs and climbers or subshrubs, usually with simple, opposite leaves. Flowers are usually in racemes, each flower on a short pedicel. These are pea-shaped with five petals in a fixed arrangement. Its main back petal is called a 'standard', two lateral petals called 'wings' and two fused petals at the bottom called the 'keel'. The lobes are more or less equal, the upper pair broader and partly joined, the standard more or

Chasmanthe floribunda.

Chilopsis linearis.

Chlorophytum comosum.

Choisya ternata.

Chorizema cordatum.

Cistus aguilari.

Cistus albidus.

Cistus ladanifer.

less round or kidney-shaped, the wings oblong and much longer than the keel. Fruit is an oval pod containing 4 to 32 seeds.

Chorizema cordatum
Heart-Leaf Flame Pea, Holly Flame Pea

Native of southwest Western Australia

A climbing shrub with many stems that can reach 2m or more, forming clumps up to 1m wide. Leaves are alternate, to 6cm long and 3cm wide, ranging from ovate to oblong to heart-shaped (cordate), light- to dark-green and with small linear stipules at the base of the petioles. Chorizema can have yellow, orange or red flowers or dazzling combinations, to 12mm across, appearing mainly in spring. Flowers are produced on terminal racemes, well beyond the foliage, in clusters of up to twenty or more. Fruit is a pod of about 7mm long by 5mm wide, which contains black seeds. It is typically found in dry sclerophyll woodland, shrub land and forest, on sandy to clay soils with granite and laterite bases. Thrives in areas with well-drained sandy soils, whether in full sun or part shade. It can withstand summer drought, but only for brief periods. Prune lightly after flowering.

CISTUS
Cistaceae

Rock Rose, Sun Rose

Native to the Mediterranean region, Middle East, also Canary Islands

A genus containing about twenty species of small or medium evergreen shrubs found on dry or rocky soils. Many hybrids have arisen in the wild and in cultivation. Leaves are opposite, simple, usually slightly rough-surfaced, 2 to 8cm long. In a few species (notably *C. ladanifer*), the leaves are coated with a highly aromatic resin called labdanum. They have showy, five-petalled flowers ranging from white to purple and dark pink, in a few species with a conspicuous dark red spot at the base of each petal. Being totally drought tolerant, they are excellent for dry gardens in full sun. Thrive in any poor, well-drained soil and can take salt spray and wind. Pinch back young plants to encourage a bushy habit and remove a few old stems from time to time. Excellent on a dry bank, on a large rock garden, or in rough areas along the side of paths and drives.

Cistus aguilari
White Rockrose

Native to Spain and Morocco

An upright-growing shrub to 2m or more spreading to 2m wide. The sticky, narrow ovate, wavy-edged leaves are up to 10cm. Gorgeous crêpe-paper-like fragrant flowers 13cm wide are white with a yellow centre. In spring, they are covered in flowers. Each morning, a whole new batch of buds will break forth and provide a fresh breathtaking display. The buds are attractive with their red outer shell and white flower tips peeking through.

Cistus albidus
White Leaved Rockrose

Native to Portugal to Italy, western north Africa

A conspicuous shrub up to 1m high. The oblong to elliptic leaves are 2 to 5cm long, with three prominent veins and are densely covered with short hairs, producing a greyish white appearance. Large crumpled rose or magenta flowers are in cymes of one to seven individual flowers, 4 to 6cm across with five purple to pink petals and five sepals. The terminal heads of one to four flowers appear in spring. Another flush of flowers may be produced in autumn.

Cistus ladanifer
Gum Cistus, Crimson-Spot Rockrose

Native to Portugal to France, western north Africa

A compact growing shrub up to 1m or more high and wide. Lance-shaped, 10cm-long leaves are dark green above with white, fragrant, sticky cotton hairs underneath. The foliage is strongly resin scented in full sun. In spring, this dense, evergreen shrub is covered with a profusion of large, 5 to 10cm, solitary papery white flowers blotched with dark red spots at the base of each petal. Although each flower only lasts for a day, this vigorous shrub provides a succession of flowers for about a month. Considered one of the most beautiful Cistus and definitely one of the showiest.

Cistus laurifolius
Laurel-Leaf Cistus

Native to Portugal and Italy

A highly-branched, flowering evergreen shrub with stiff, erect growth to 1.5m high and wide. Leaves are larger than in the other species, up to 9cm long, lance-shaped, dark green, sticky and aromatic, while the underside is whitish. It bears white flowers 5 to 7cm wide, with a yellow spot at the base of each petal. These are borne in long stalked clusters of three or more during early summer.

Cistus populifolius

Native from Portugal to southern France

A large aromatic shrub up to 1.5m high with sticky hairless branches, which makes a dense bush of attractive foliage. Heart-shaped, aromatic, pointed leaves are up to 10cm long with deeply ruffled edges. In spring, every tip shoot carries a handsome cluster of large round buds enclosed in red sepals, as attractive as the chalk-white flowers with a yellow centre. They are 4 to 6cm across, opening in late spring through into summer. Bees love this shrub.

Cistus × purpureus
Orchid Rockrose

Garden origin

A small shrub with reddish stems up to 1m high and wide. Lance-shaped, grey-green, downy, 3 to 5cm long leaves have a wavy edge. Flowers with showy, light-rose pink petals appear in spring and summer, like ruffled crêpe. They have a dark red spot at the base of the petal, which contrasts with the cluster of yellow stamens. Petals usually fall within a few hours of opening, forming an attractive carpet on the ground beneath.

Cistus salviifolius
Sage-Leaf Rockrose
Native to southern Europe

This wide-spreading bushy shrub 30 to 60cm high and 1m wide has stems covered by clumpy hairs. Small oval grey-green leaves are 2cm long, opposite, reticulate, tomentose on both sides, with a short petiole, not sticky and hardly aromatic. The inflorescence holds one or more round flowers, long-stalked at the leaf axils. Five white petals have a yellow spot at the base, forming a corolla 4 to 6cm in diameter. The stamens are also yellow, and the anthers shed abundant yellow pollen. Flowers are solitary or in small heads and are produced in great profusion. Its flowering period extends throughout spring. This plant is pollinated by insects, especially bees.

CLEISTOCACTUS
Cactaceae
Native to South America

A genus of about 50 species of slender stem cacti that are tall, often many-branched, up to about 3m high. Stems are typically only 2.5cm in diameter. Typically, they grow as shrubs that branch at the base to form noticeable clumps, although occasionally branching higher and becoming small trees. As the plant matures, shoots first stand upright but later bend over, sometimes hanging. Spines are small and flexible but usually many, even to the point of obscuring its stems. In most species, flowers appear in large numbers individually from the areoles. Flowers are tubular and the tips hardly open with only the style and stamens usually protruding. Flowers range from green to white, yellow, orange and red to violet, with shades of red predominating. A Cleistocactus species may have flowers open in the right conditions every day of the year.

Cleistocactus strausii
Silver Torch, Woolly Torch
Native to Bolivia

A striking, slender, erect, columnar cactus that branches out from the base to create breathtaking huddles, with several upright, grey-green columns growing up to 3m tall, but only about 6cm across. There are 25 to 30 ribs densely covered with areoles, completely covered by dense spines up to 4cm long and twenty shorter white radials. Older cacti, over 45cm tall, produce tubular flowers deep-red to burgundy up to 6cm long, protruding horizontally and radially from the stem of the cactus in late summer. The flower-tube is densely covered with silky hairs. Flowers last four to five days on the whole stem of each plant, but are never fully open with only the style and stamens protruding. Grow in dry rocky soil. It must be kept dry in winter and given minimal water in summer, extremely drought tolerant. It will tolerate frost in winter if kept dry. In hot climates, providing light shade during the afternoon is recommended. Fantastic for potted arrangements, as they will grow extremely slender. Plants will also pup and shoot from the base naturally, so they just look so much better with age.

Cleistocactus winteri
Golden Rat Tail
Native to Bolivia

This columnar cactus forms huge tangled mounds of fairly rapid, hanging or creeping growth. Green shoots reach 90cm on stems 2 to 2.5cm wide with sixteen to seventeen ribs and many spines 1cm long. The brown areoles are close together. It has many short, bristly golden spines that are flexible, thin and straight, covering the surface of the stems. Salmon-pink flowers in spring and summer are 4 to 6cm long and 5cm in diameter. The flowers can bend upwards, outwards, or upright, depending on how the shoots are positioned. The bracts are orange-red, the outer ones radiating to slightly reflexed, the inner ones distinctly shorter and erect with stamens and style protruding from the flower. Each flower survives for only a few days. The plant requires water during summer but to be kept dry in winter or the moist soil combined with dormancy may cause the roots to rot. Great forming a mound in a dry garden or grown in hanging pots or baskets because of its trailing stems, which can grow up to 30cm per year.

CLEMATIS
Ranunculaceae
Native to much of the world except the Americas

A large genus of over 200 species of perennials or mostly deciduous woody climbers. All have attractive flowers, some are spectacular. The choice cultivars prefer cooler conditions, cool soil and more moist air. There are only a few species that grow well in warm dry climates.

Clematis aristata syn. *Clematis indivisa*
Australian Clematis, Wild Clematis, Goat's Beard, Old Man's Beard
Native to dry and wet forests of eastern Australia and New Zealand

A reasonably vigorous, dioecious 'leaf climber', having leaf stems that coil around the branches of other plants or around its own branches, thus enabling it to climb to around 6m. Adult leaves are usually trifoliate, each leaflet being ovate and up to 8cm long, often with toothed margins. Starry, white to cream flowers are relatively large, 3 to 7cm in diameter and have no petals but have four petal-like sepals. Male and female flowers are similar. Flowers are followed on female plants by fluffy seed heads, which give rise to the common name. A popular garden plant, which is hardy in most soils. It prefers a sunny or semi-shaded position and will withstand heavy pruning. It is vigorous but is unlikely to become a problem by smothering other plants.

Clematis cirrhosa
Early Virgin's Bower
Native to the eastern Mediterranean

A climber that is deciduous in summer eventually reaching 6m high, but which can be kept lower by pruning. Attractive small, fern-like, finely cut, dark-green, shiny leathery leaves turn bronze-purple in winter and may die off in the hottest part of summer. Citrus-scented, bell-shaped, creamy-white flowers 6cm across, adorned with reddish-maroon freckles inside, appear during winter and spring. In late spring, the silky, fluffy seed-heads can be as showy as the flowers. It will take drier soils than most Clematis but grows better with some summer water. Thrives in well-drained soil in full sun, preferring 'head in the sun and feet in the shade'. Perfect for covering a wall, trellis, or fence. The variety 'Balearica' has pale yellow flowers spotted reddish purple; 'Freckles' is a larger-flowered form, tinged pink with maroon spots; 'Wisley Cream' has large, creamy white unspotted flowers.

Clematis montana var. *grandiflora* syn. *Clematis grandiflora*
White Virgin's Bower
Native to the Highlands of Ethiopia

A hardy, vigorous, deciduous climber, happily scrambling up to 6m high, as it twines and clings to its own stems or a support. It is ideal for climbing trees, a pergola, shed or fence. While it does no damage to its tree host, it needs a sizeable tree. Single, pristine white flowers 7cm across are adorned with bright-yellow centres. It absolutely covers itself with a mass of snow-white flowers through spring. Blooming is so profuse you can barely see a gap between the blooms. Each bloom is sweetly vanilla scented, so the overall effect of the scent is one joy of spring. Bees and other pollinating insects flock to it for nectar. Plant in sun or half shade. Robust and frost hardy, this is a tough, easily-grown climber. Perfect for a pergola or trellised seating area, as it lets the sun and light in during the winter, but shades effectively during the summer. It can be pruned after flowering or allowed to grow freely.

Clematis urophylla
Native to southern China

A woody evergreen climber about 3 to 4m tall. Dark-green leaves have three leaflets. This superb Clematis bears its delicate, waxy, bell-shaped flowers in the depths of winter. Small, nodding, urn-shaped flowers to 4cm across have downy, creamy-white petals surrounding a prominent boss of cream anthers. They emerge from pale green buds and become paler, and more flared at their tips as they mature. One of the prettiest winter-flowering climbers for a warm garden. Best grown against a warm house wall so that you can appreciate its winter flowers. This sought-after variety will appreciate a sheltered site with some winter protection. Grow in any well-drained soil with a little summer water. Prune hard after flowering.

CLEOME
Cleomaceae
Spider Flowers
Native to regions with warm climates, including Africa, Asia and the Americas

This genus includes about 170 species of annuals, perennials and shrubs. They are popular for their attractive foliage and unusual flowers, which typically have long stamens that resemble spider legs, hence the common name. Flowers range from white and pink to purple.

Cleome spinosa
Native to southern South America in Argentina, Paraguay, Uruguay and southeast Brazil

A fast-growing annual growing to a height of 2m, with spirally arranged leaves. Aromatic leaves are palmately compound, with five or seven leaflets each up to 12cm long and 4cm broad, with a spine at the base of each leaf. Dramatic, large, loose balls of sweetly fragrant flowers have fascinating long stamens that protrude out, giving a spider-like appearance. The scented blooms are sometimes compared to citronella. Fruit is a capsule up to 15cm long, containing several seeds. Flowering lasts from late spring to early autumn. Performs best in full sun or light shade in average, dry to medium moisture, well-drained soils. Drought tolerant once established. May be grown from seed.

CLERETUM syn. *DOROTHEANTHUS*
Aizoaceae
Native to South Africa

A genus of thirteen species of low-growing, basally-branching, succulent annuals. They have opposite or alternate narrowly linear to spoon-shaped leaves, glistening with small crystal-like structures. In summer, they produce many long-stalked, iridescent, many-petalled, daisy-like white, yellow, orange, pink or red flowers that close in dull weather. In temperate areas it is popularly grown as a half-hardy annual and lends itself to mass plantings or as edging plants in summer bedding schemes in parks and gardens. Grow in well-drained, low fertility, sandy soil in full sun. Summer drought tolerant.

Cleretum bellidiforme syn. *Dorotheanthus bellidiforme*
Livingstone Daisy, Crystalline Ice Plant, Ice Plant
Native to the Cape Peninsula in South Africa

This winter-growing, succulent annual forms a low ground cover with several spreading branches. Green or maroon-tinted leaves are tongue-or spoon-shaped and more or less flat, with conspicuous raised, bladder-like surface cells modified for water storage, which glisten in bright

Cleistocactus strausii.

Cleistocactus winteri.

Clematis cirrhosa.

Clematis montana var. *grandiflora.*

Cleome spinosa.

Cleretum bellidiforme.

Clianthus puniceus.

Clivia miniata.

Cobaea scandens.

sunlight. The slender, fleshy, upright or leaning flower stalks up to 2.5cm long emerge from the branch tips. Many large, solitary, brightly-coloured flowers, 2 to 3cm in diameter, each having many narrow petals, open wide in bright sunlight. Petal colour is highly variable, including white, cream-coloured, yellow, salmon-coloured, orange, pink, mauve, magenta or red, sometimes with contrasting white, maroon, yellow or light-orange bases. In the flower's centre, the stamens are clustered together, arranged in two to four rows, and comprise maroon filaments with either purple or yellow anthers. The ripe fruit is a capsule.

CLIANTHUS
Fabaceae
Native to Australia and New Zealand

A small genus of two species of erect or trailing tender shrubs. They have striking clusters of red flowers that resemble the beak of the *kākā*, a New Zealand parrot.

Clianthus puniceus
Lobster Claw, Parrot's Beak

Native to New Zealand

A vigorous, evergreen, upright shrub-like climber growing to 3m high and 3m wide. Spreading branches produce leaf stalks up to 15cm long. Glossy pinnate leaves are 8 to 15cm long and composed of many oblong pairs of leaflets. The peculiar, claw-like, brilliant-red flowers have an 8cm long keel-petal swung downwards in clusters of six to fifteen on a pendulous stalk. These are produced for most of summer or even year-round. The flowers resemble a parrot's beak, hence its common name. Often followed by 8cm-long seed pods. Because of its weak growth, it is best given some support, trained against a wall or allowed to tumble down a bank. Grows well in full sun in warm dry climates with sandy well-drained soils and can be trained as a vine. It can rot in winter if the soil is waterlogged. In their native habitat, they can be found on cliffs, bluffs, or margins of bodies of water. Shoots are typically pruned once flowering is over. A white form 'Albus' is sometimes grown.

CLIVIA
Amaryllidaceae
Native to South Africa

A small genus of four species of large, evergreen, stemless, bulbous perennials, with fleshy roots and swollen, bulb-like leaf bases.

Clivia miniata

An evergreen perennial that makes bold clumps of dark-green, strap-shaped leaves 50cm long, arranged oppositely in a single plane. During winter, stout stems carry brilliant clusters of up to twenty flowers, 8cm long on stems up to 60cm high. Flowers are funnel-shaped, usually orange or scarlet with a yellow throat. These are followed by ornamental berries, which will readily produce seedlings. With multiple garden varieties, the colours can vary. To maintain the best growth, leave plants undisturbed for a few years. If they become overcrowded, separate by lifting and dividing. To thrive, they need a soil that is sandy, well-drained and rich in organic matter, preferably in partial shade. Keep dry during winter, but water during the growing season. Excellent for growing in pots or containers where they flower well. Plants should be kept in the same pot for several years and given generous liquid feeding. Useful on patios and on balconies. They can also be used for edging paths or borders where there is shade from trees. This is the most widely grown species.

COBAEA
Polemoniaceae

A genus of ten or more species of evergreen shrubby and herbaceous climbers native to Mexico and tropical South America. Only one species is grown for its unusual large flowers.

Cobaea scandens
Cup and Saucer Plant

Native to Mexico

A vigorous, evergreen climbing perennial 10m or more high with a wide spread that becomes woody when mature. Climbs by tendrils that cling to any rough surface without support. Rich green leaves are pinnate, composed of four to six ovate leaflets 10cm or more long. The midrib of each leaf ends in a branched tendril. Flowers are borne on long stalks rising from leaf axils. With its lobed and wavy appearance, the calyx is reminiscent of a saucer and is a vibrant shade of green. The central bell-shaped flower 5cm long with prominent stamens opens a creamy green, then ages to violet or rosy-purple. They have a revolting smell at first, which becomes sweeter once the flower changes colour. Flowers are produced mostly in spring and early summer, but may continue throughout most of the year. Grow the climber in full sun in well-drained soil. It needs a little summer water. Use it to clothe a pergola, sunny wall or grow into a tree. Perfect as a fast-growing cover or screen. Although a perennial in warm areas, it soon becomes untidy, therefore is often treated as an annual as seeds germinate easily.

COLCHICUM
Colchicaceae
Autumn Crocus, Naked Ladies

Native to West Asia, Europe, parts of the Mediterranean coast, down the East African coast to South Africa and the Western Cape

A genus of about 50 species of cormous perennials that are grown for their beautiful autumn-blooming flowers. Despite its common names, it is not a true crocus or saffron plant. Colchicum plants typically produce large, cup-shaped flowers in shades of pink, purple or white. They emerge from bulbs in late summer or early autumn, often before the foliage appears. Leaves typically appear in spring and die back before or after flowering. Colchicum plants contain colchicine, a toxic alkaloid, so caution should be exercised when handling. Despite being toxic, they are appreciated for their ornamental qualities and frequently cultivated in gardens for their charming autumn appearance.

Colchicum autumnale

Autumn Crocus, Meadow Saffron

Native to British Isles

An herbaceous perennial with a corm 3 to 5cm long with a blackish sheath. Upright linear leaves are produced in spring in a group of four or more, up to 25cm long. In autumn, it produces flowers 10 to 25cm high, solitary or in groups of up to five with long stalks. These are goblet-shaped and lavender-pink, rose-pink or white, 4 to 7cm across, with six tepals and six stamens with orange anthers and three white styles. Grow in full sun where they are not disturbed. Plants may need lifting and dividing after four or five years. Give water during spring growing season in dry spells and none during summer dormant period. All parts of the plant are highly poisonous.

Colchicum cupanii

Mediterranean Meadow Saffron

Native to southern Europe, north Africa

A cormous perennial with upright linear glossy leaves to 15cm long, which are produced in spring. In autumn, it produces multiple star-shaped pale to deep purplish pink flowers with a heavenly sweet perfume 4 to 5cm high. Flowers over a long period in full sun. Grow in well-drained sandy soil. Only give water during spring growing season in dry spells and none during summer dormant period. Plants may need lifting and dividing after four or five years.

COLQUHOUNIA

Lamiaceae

Native to the Himalayas and southwestern China south to Peninsular Malaysia

A genus of about six species of evergreen or semi-evergreen shrubs or subshrubs. Growing 1 to 3m tall with aromatic leaves that are to 3 to 12cm long and 1 to 6cm wide, finely toothed and borne in opposite pairs on square stems. The flowers are tubular, two-lipped, and carried on terminal spikes.

Colquhounia coccinea

Scarlet Flowered Colquhounia, Himalayan Mint Shrub

Native to China, Bhutan, Nepal, Myanmar, India and Thailand

An evergreen or semi-evergreen shrub growing to 2.5m tall. Large ovate to ovate-lance-shaped leaves, 10 to 15cm long, have serrated margins and felty, greyish white undersides. Leaves are aromatic when bruised. Tubular, orange-red to scarlet or dark-red flowers to 3cm long with yellow insides bloom at the stem tips in dense terminal racemes or in smaller axillary clusters (whorls) from late summer into autumn. Its native habitats include slopes, stony grassy hillsides, thickets and river valleys. It is not entirely hardy and requires a sheltered position in full sun, with protection from winter wet. This shrub should be planted in a protected position that is sheltered from cool winds. Stems may die back to ground level in cold winters. It is best grown in moist, well-composted, well-drained soils in full sun to part shade. May require some summer water. Prune stems back as needed in spring.

COLUTEA

Fabaceae

Bladder Senna, Bladderpod

Native to many regions from southern Europe to northern Africa and the western Himalayas

A genus of about 25 species of hardy deciduous shrubs or small trees with pinnate leaves and showy yellow or orange flowers. The characteristic feature of these plants is their bladder-like seed pods, from which they get their common name. Pea-like flowers are commonly seen in racemes or clusters. Seed pods are often inflated and can be quite ornamental.

Colutea arborescens

Bladder Senna

Native to southern Europe, Mediterranean region

This strong-growing, bushy deciduous shrub to 3m high takes a rounded form and has many branches covered in deciduous leaves. Pinnate pale green leaves 15cm long comprise many pairs of slightly hairy oval-shaped leaflets, each up to 3cm long. During summer, yellow pea-like flowers 2 to 3cm wide are carried in clusters in leaf axils. These are followed by attractive 8cm-long inflated bladder pods 2 to 3cm long, which dry to a papery texture and contain many seeds. A tough shrub that will tolerate drought, poor soil, coastal conditions and pollution. Grow in full sun, ideal for hot dry locations. Prune after flowering to encourage bushiness.

CONICOSIA

Aizoaceae

Narrow Leaved Ice Plants

Native to southern Africa

A genus of relatively short-lived succulent perennials with underground stems. Dull-pointed, triangular leaves are tentacle-shaped. They bear large tubular flowers often exceeding 10cm in width, with up to 250 fringe-like petals in a ring around a centre with hundreds of stamens. The fruit is a capsule, which opens when wet, slowly releasing hundreds of tiny seeds as they fall out of its drying flesh.

Conicosia pugioniformis

Narrow Leaved Iceplant, Pigroot

Native to South Africa

A tufted, fleshy perennial, growing 12 to 40cm tall, with a huge tap root and trailing branches. Fingerlike, fleshy, grey-green, hairless leaves are up to 20cm long and densely arranged. Large, solitary, scented yellow flowers on long pedicels, 5 to 8cm wide, are produced in spring and early summer. Flowers have around 200 to 250 petals, often with long hairs on the lower parts. Several thin, tangled stamens are at the centre of

chicum autumnale.

Colquhounia coccinea.

Colutea arborescens.

nicosia pugioniformis.

Convolvulus cneorum.

Convolvulus sabatius.

prosma × kirkii variegata.

Coprosma repens.

the flower. Stigmas are separate. Grow in full sun open, sandy or light clay soil. Summer drought tolerant but performs best if given some water during winter.

CONVOLVULUS
Convolvulaceae
Bindweed

Distributed around the world

A large genus containing some 250 species of annuals, perennial herbaceous vines and a few species of woody shrubs, growing to 3m or more tall. Many are twining or trailing evergreen shrubs or subshrubs, most of which are too weedy for the garden. Leaves are spirally arranged, and the flowers are trumpet-shaped, mostly white or pink, but also blue, violet, purple, or yellow in some species.

Convolvulus cneorum
Silverbush

Native to central and western Mediterranean

A small, hardy, evergreen, rounded shrub, which makes rapid growth to 40cm high and 60cm wide. The oblong 2 to 6cm silky lance-shaped leaves are covered with velvety silver hairs. During spring and summer, masses of pink buds emerge, followed by large white funnel -shaped flowers 4cm across with yellow centres. Thrives in a sunny position in well-drained soil. Requires little summer water once established. A good shrub for a dry border. Perfect for white- or silver-themed gardens, borders, containers and coastal areas. Light pruning to remove spent flowers will prolong flowering.

Convolvulus sabatius
Ground Morning Glory, Blue Rock Bindweed

Native to Spain, Italy, north Africa

A low-growing evergreen perennial 15cm high that will spread to 1m or more. Although roots are produced as it spreads, it is not considered invasive. The soft, pale grey-green, pubescent roundish leaves are 1 to 3cm long. Bell-shaped, lavender-blue flowers, 3 to 5cm wide, are produced throughout summer and autumn. Easily grown in gritty, well-drained soil with occasional watering in full sun to light shade. Drought tolerant once established. Ideal on sloping banks and scrambling over walls and container edges. Great for beds and borders, Mediterranean gardens, cottage gardens, rock gardens or containers, or as an edging plant.

COPROSMA
Rubiaceae

Native to Australia, New Zealand and Pacific Islands

A genus containing about 90 species of evergreen, usually dioecious shrubs or small trees. Opposite leaves are simple, linear to rounded, often leathery and light to dark green, purple or brown, often variegated. Inconspicuous, tubular or narrowly funnel-shaped flowers are borne singly or in clusters. Grow in neutral or slightly acid, moist but well-drained soil in full sun or partial shade.

Coprosma × kirkii variegata

Garden origin

Variants of this hybrid are of irregular spreading habit 1.5m high and up to 2m wide. Arching branches bear linear-oblong or lance-shaped dark green leaves to 4cm long. 'Variegata' is a spreading shrub with white margined, grey-green leaves with white berries. It grows 75cm high and 1.5m wide. Some summer water is needed.

Coprosma repens
Mirror Bush, Looking Glass Bush, Taupata

Native to New Zealand

A large dioecious shrub or tree up to 2.5m high, much branched, sometimes prostrate with stiff spreading branches. Leaves 2 to 8cm long are ovate-oblong, a deep lustrous green above, paler below, stiffly fleshy. Inconspicuous small flowers give way to small orange/red berries. Grow in full sun or partial shade in light well-drained soil. Somewhat drought tolerant once established, it has a remarkable ability to put up with the harshest seaside gales. Good as a shrubbery accent plant or in a low hedge, in containers and general landscaping. A light pruning will help keep it tidy – otherwise it is easy to maintain. While the green-leafed form is attractive, it is the eye-catching, colourful foliage cultivars that are usually grown, including 'Marginata', 'Marble Queen' with cream mottling, while 'Variegata' has leaves blotched with yellowish green. These grow better in partial shade, as strong sunlight can burn the leaves. Some summer water is needed.

CORDYLINE
Asparagaceae
Cabbage Tree, Cabbage Palm

Native to the western Pacific Ocean region

A genus of about twenty species of sparsely-branched, evergreen, palm-like shrubs or trees. They are valued for their vibrant foliage that ranges from green to purple-red, depending on the species and cultivar. Cordylines are popular choices for landscaping in tropical and subtropical regions because of their striking appearance and relatively low-maintenance requirements. When young, they are great for growing in pots or containers.

Cordyline australis
Cabbage Tree

Native to New Zealand

An upright-growing, palm-like tree, which may eventually grow to 8m high, usually forming a single stout trunk and bearing several stout upright branches. Each branch has narrow sword-shaped leaves clustered at the tips of the branches up to 1m long. Upper leaves are upright, while lower leaves droop. On a young plant, this gives it a fountain-like appearance. In spring and early summer, sweetly-perfumed flowers are produced in large, dense panicles (flower spikes) 60 to 100cm long. Flowers are more crowded along the last branches of the panicles. The bracts that protect the developing flowers often have a distinct pink tinge before the flowers open. Will take any soil, withstand frost and is drought tolerant. Looks good when grown amongst rocks on a bank to give a tropical look. Also suited to coastal areas, as it withstands salt-laden sea breezes. Grow in full sun, as it dislikes shade. It is a characteristic feature of the New Zealand landscape.

The form 'Atropurpurea' has purple leaves and is slower growing, while 'Albertii' has a cream edge to the leaves. Both forms only grow up to 3 to 4m high.

Cordyline indivisa
Mountain Cabbage Tree
Native to New Zealand

A distinctive species, which can be distinguished from all other Cordyline species by its broad blue-grey leaves, and its smaller, tightly compacted inflorescence, which is produced from beneath the foliage. It forms a stout tree up to 8m tall, with a trunk from 40 to 80cm in diameter. The stem is usually unbranched or has few branches. Leaves are 1 to 2m long and from 10 to 30cm wide. The foliage, which droops with age, is blue green and shaped like a broad sword, with a wide and conspicuous midrib that is often tinged red, orange-red or golden. Masses of small white or cream flowers are borne in large drooping panicles that may be 1m or more long. Grow in full sun or partial shade. It tolerates drought and coastal conditions. Looks good near a swimming pool. The variety 'Purpurea' has bronze-purple leaves.

COREOPSIS
Asteraceae
Native to North and South America, southeastern United States and Mexico

A genus of about 40 species that vary in size and growth habit, with some forming compact mounds and others growing tall. Many cultivars and hybrids have been developed, offering a range of flower colours, sizes and foliage characteristics to suit different garden preferences. Daisy-like flowers come in various colours, including shades of yellow, orange, red and pink. These typically bloom from late spring to early autumn, attracting pollinators such as bees and butterflies to the garden. These plants are popular choices for gardens and landscapes because of their long flowering period, low maintenance requirements and ability to thrive in a wide range of growing conditions, from full sun to partial shade. Plants are often used in borders, rock gardens and containers, adding colour and texture to the landscape.

Coreopsis lanceolata
Laceleaf Tickseed
Native to North America

This upright perennial grows 30 to 60cm high and spreads to 45cm wide. Single slender stems rise above a basal tuft of narrow, hairy lance-shaped leaves 5 to 15cm long. A profusion of daisy-like, bright-yellow flowers 5cm across adorned with a flat yellow central disc appears during summer. Grow in dry to medium damp soil in full sun. Tolerant of drought, dry soil and shallow rocky soils. Easy to grow, it makes good cut flowers. Freely self-seeds, and in optimum growing conditions will naturalise to form large colonies. Prompt dead-heading of spent flower stalks encourages additional blooms and prevents unwanted self-seeding. It produces masses of freely germinating seeds and can be an environmental weed even in areas with poor quality soil. Many excellent cultivars of this species are available in commerce.

COROKIA
Argophyllaceae
Native to New Zealand and Pacific Islands

A small genus of about ten species of evergreen shrubs or small trees, known for their distinctive foliage. Species typically have small, leathery leaves that are often silver or grey-green, and some varieties feature interesting zig-zagging or twisted branches. Small, star-shaped flowers that can be white or yellow are followed by small berries. Valued for their ability to tolerate a range of conditions, including coastal exposure and poor soil. Often used in landscaping as hedges, borders or specimen plants.

Corokia buddleioides
Korokio
Native to New Zealand

An evergreen erect shrub up to 3m high and 2m wide with slender stems. Young slender shoots are covered with a close, greyish-white felt which persists into the second year. Glossy, dark green, 6cm-long, linear-lance-shaped leaves taper, usually to a long, finely pointed apex with silvery white felt underneath. Terminal racemes of 1cm-wide, yellow, star-like, fragrant flowers appear in spring, followed by dark red berries. Grow in sun or partial shade, or even in dry shade. A well-drained soil is essential. It can take some drought but grows better if given some summer water. Can also be grown as hedging plants.

Corokia cotoneaster
Wire Netting-Bush Korokio, Korokia-Tarango
Native to New Zealand

A rounded, intricately branched shrub about 3m high and wide, bearing interlacing shoots. Stiff, wiry branches are nearly black. They are contorted and zigzag in all directions, giving it the common name. Small, 2cm-long, oval leaves are dark green above with white felt underneath. In late spring, small fragrant yellow flowers appear singly or in clusters of up to four in leaf axils, followed by small orange-red berries. The shrub tolerates alkaline soil and dry conditions, but grows better if given some summer water. A good shrub for coastal gardens as it withstands salt-laden sea breezes.

Corokia × virgata

Garden origin

A variable, hybrid, upright shrub to 3m high with stems normally covered in white felt. Spoon-shaped or lance-shaped leaves are dark green above and white beneath to 5cm long. Fragrant yellow flowers appear in spring in clusters of three in leaf axils, followed by small orange or red berries. It can take some drought, but grows better if given some summer water. A well-drained soil is essential. Many forms have been raised, including 'Bronze King', with bronze-tinted leaves.

CORONILLA

Fabiaceae

Native to Europe and North Africa

A genus of about eight species of deciduous and evergreen hardy shrubs and herbaceous perennials. Plants have typical pea-shaped flowers.

Coronilla valentina

Native to the Mediterranean region

A dense, evergreen, bushy shrub that grows 1 to 2m high spreading 2m wide. Small, glaucous, silver or grey-green pinnate leaves are 5 to 8cm long with about ten rounded leaflets. In spring, it produces masses of rich yellow pea-shaped flowers 1cm long with the fragrance of ripe peaches. Some flowers appear intermittently throughout the summer. The shrub grows best in full sun and, once established, is drought tolerant. 'Variegata' has leaves with cream or white edges.

Coronilla valentina subsp. *glauca*

Native to the Mediterranean region

A subspecies that is frequently confused with, and misnamed as, the species. More compact, it only grows to about 80cm high and wide. The blue-green leaves have five to seven leaflets. Bright yellow flowers, 1cm long, grow in clusters of up to fourteen. These are larger and showier than the species.

CORREA

Rutaceae

Australian Fuchsia

Native to Australia

A genus of about eleven species, although there are many forms that are difficult to allocate to any species. Botanical revision of the genus is warranted. Evergreen shrubs and small trees have simple, opposite leaves. Plants are grown for their striking pendant, tubular or bell-shaped flowers. Flowers have four sepals, four petals usually fused for most of their length, and eight stamens.

Correa alba

White Correa

A prostrate to erect shrub to 2m high and wide. Leathery, oval, rich green leaves are 1 to 3cm long and grey-woolly underneath. White flowers appear from leaf axils, about 1 to 2cm long. They are not in a bell-shaped tube but are more open with protruding stamens, the floral tube split to give a star-like shape to the flowers. These hang down along branches and are produced throughout most of the winter, but occasional flowers will be seen at other times. The shrub thrives in partial shade but will take full sun. Drought tolerant once established. Grows well in poor rocky soil, which must have good drainage. Over-watering or generous feeding will kill it. Grows well in coastal conditions as it withstands salt-laden sea breezes. Attractive when grown in pots or containers. The variety 'Pinkie' has pale pink flowers.

Correa backhouseana

A rounded shrub that typically grows to 2m with its young branchlets covered with woolly, rust-coloured hairs. Leaves are leathery, elliptical to ovate or round, mostly 3cm long on a short petiole. The upper leaf surface is relatively smooth, while the lower surface is heavily coated with woolly hairs. Usually, the flowers are pendant and either single or in groups of two or three, on short side shoots. Colours range from cream to pale green or red and yellow. Petals are 1.5 to 2.5cm long and create a corolla that is cylindrical or funnel-shaped. The eight stamens are slightly longer than the corolla. Flowers may be produced all winter. Cultural conditions are the same as *Correa alba*.

Correa 'Dusky Bells'

A low-growing shrub up to 90cm high with a broad spread about 2m or more. Slender stems are reddish brown. Deep-green leaves are 3 to 4cm long, narrow elliptic or lance-shaped to ovate. Beautiful clusters of tubular deep red to pink flowers are 2 to 3cm long. The four fused petals are pale carmine-pink, hanging in clusters from the branches from autumn to spring.

Correa 'Mannii'

A good, tough hybrid between *C. reflexa* × *C. pulchella*, that ultimately reaches 2m high and 2 to 3m wide with erect branches. Oval, deep green leaves are 2 to 3cm long with a paler underside. Red tubular flowers 4cm long with reflexed tips hang in small clusters from the branches all winter. Hardy to dry shady conditions.

CORTADERIA

Poaceae

Native to South America and New Zealand

A genus containing about 24 species of large perennial grasses, forming large clumps with leaves crowded at the base, giving them a bold and striking appearance. Plants are known for their tall, feathery flower plumes, which can range from white to pink to purple, depending on the species and cultivar. They are

rosma repens **'Marginata'**.

Cordyline australis **'Purpurea'**.

Coreopsis lanceolata.

rokia × virgata.

Coronilla valentina.

Correa alba.

rtaderia selloana.

Corymbia ficifolia.

Corynabutilon vitifolium.

popular in landscaping for their dramatic appearance and ability to add texture and movement to gardens. However, in some regions, the grass has become invasive, out-competing native plants and disrupting ecosystems.

Cortaderia selloana
Pampas Grass

Native to Brazil, Argentina, Chile

A gigantic tufted grass that normally grows 2 to 3m high but may reach 6m in ideal conditions. Arching, glaucous, mid-green leaves are 2.5 m long and 2 to 3cm wide with sharp teeth along the edges. In late summer, from the centre of the plant, silky, silver, often pink- or purple-flushed plumes are borne in pyramidal to oblong panicles 45 to 90cm long on erect stems. A tough plant that can take the driest soils to the wettest. Grown in full sun in fertile, well-drained soil. The flower plumes can be dried for indoor decoration.

CORYMBIA
Myrtaceae

Bloodwoods

Native to Australia

A genus of about 100 species of tree that, along with Eucalyptus, Angophora and several smaller groups, are referred to as eucalypts. Until 1990, Corymbias were included in the genus Eucalyptus and there is still considerable disagreement among botanists whether separating them is valid. As of January 2020, Corymbia is an accepted name at the Australian Plant Census.

Species in the genus are trees, sometimes growing with multiple stems from the ground, which either have rough, fibrous or flaky bark, or smooth bark that is shed in small flakes or short strips. Young plants and coppice regrowth have leaves that differ from adult leaves. Adult leaves are alternate, with oil glands. Flower buds are in groups on a branching peduncle, each branch usually with seven buds, but with the pedicels of differing lengths, so that the inflorescence is flat-topped or convex. Performs well in most well-drained soils, full sun and is tolerant of coastal conditions and light frosts.

Corymbia citriodora syn. *Eucalyptus citriodora*
Lemon-Scented Gum

Native to northeastern Australia

A beautiful, tall tree that can grow to 20m high, 8m wide with smooth, slender white to pinkish stems and weeping branches. These have distinctive, often powdery white- to grey-coloured bark, which curls and flakes off in spring. Light-green leaves are 8 to 15cm long and lemon scented when crushed. Its aromatic scent is a distinguishing attribute, with the essential oils produced from this variety often being used in fragrances, as well as insect repellents. Small inconspicuous white flowers appear near the top of the tree during summer and autumn. Feathery white flowers make it an excellent source of food for honey bees. The tree makes fast growth, but the trunk is weak so stake it securely. Older specimens make beautiful trees, becoming picturesque with age.

Corymbia ficifolia syn. *Eucalyptus ficifolia*
Red Flowering Gum

Native to southwest of Western Australia

A straggly tree that typically grows to a height of 10m with a rough, fibrous brownish bark on the trunk and branches. When fully grown, leaves become dull to slightly glossy and are paler underneath. They are oval, to broadly lance-shaped, 7 to 13cm and tapering towards the petiole. Flower buds are on the ends of branchlets on a branched peduncle. Mature buds are oval to pear-shaped. Flowering in summer and autumn brings to gardens an explosive display of fiery red flowers, reminiscent of wild flames. This spectacular flowering gum is renowned for its intense colouration, which stands in striking contrast against its deep green foliage. These gorgeous flowers attract neighbourhood attention and nectar-hungry birds. Plant in full sun. Adapts well to most soil types, providing they are well drained. The tree does not grow well in alkaline soil. Tolerates drought and coastal conditions. Young growth can be sensitive to frost. Mulch well to keep moisture and keep weeds at bay. Trim lightly after flowering to keep desired shape. One of the most widely cultivated of all garden eucalypts.

CORYNABUTILON
Malvaceae

Native to southern Chile and Argentina

A genus of about seven species of shrubs and small trees, tropical and tender perennials.

Corynabutilon vitifolium syn. *Abutilon vitifolium*
Chilean Tree Mallow, Flowering Maple

Native to central and south-central Chile

A large, handsome, fast-growing shrub to 4m high and 3m wide with young wood covered in downy shoots. Downy, grey-green, ovate leaves are up to 15cm long and as wide, usually three to five lobed, coarsely and unevenly toothed. Saucer-shaped flowers are borne, three or four together, towards the end of a woolly stalk, 8 to 15cm long, springing from leaf-axils along the stem throughout summer. Each flower, 5 to 8cm across, has five rounded petals of a beautiful pale, purplish blue with long protruding stamens. Plant in full sun to part shade in well drained and well mulched soil. Somewhat drought tolerant. A short-lived shrub that grows quickly and readily from seed. Self-sown seedlings are frequently produced. The variety 'Album' has white flowers, which come true from seed. 'Tennant's White' has large pure white flowers that are produced over a longer period. Great in a pot or container, where its showy handsome leaves and large striking blooms can be seen.

COSMOS
Asteraceae
Native to southern USA and Central America, mostly Mexico

A genus of about 25 species of typically showy annuals or short-lived perennials with feathery, fern-like foliage. These plants are well-loved for their colourful, daisy-like flowers and easy cultivation. Flowers come in white, pink, red, orange and yellow, attracting butterflies, bees and other pollinators. Cosmos blooms from summer to autumn, adding a burst of colour to gardens and landscapes.

Cosmos bipinnatus
Native to Mexico

A fast-growing, much-branched annual to 1m or more high spreading to 45cm wide. The much-divided, fern-like leaves are up to 30cm long. It produces a mass of delightful, solitary, bowl or saucer-shaped flowers 8cm across with yellow centres from midsummer to autumn. These come in shades of crimson, rose and pink, together with white. The fine foliage makes an ideal background for the brilliance of the flowers. Although the plants look delicate, they are easily grown from seed. This colourful annual will often self-seed. They are excellent on poor, well-drained soil in a sunny position, needing little summer water once established. Often grown in borders, containers and wildflower meadows, because of its low-maintenance requirements and long-lasting blooms. It is a favourite among gardeners for its ability to attract beneficial insects and its cheerful appearance.

COTA
Asteraceae
Native to Mediterranean region and southwestern Asia

A genus of about 24 species of clump-forming evergreen perennials. Plants are valued in a border or rock garden for their fine foliage and extended flowering season. The genus was recently split from Anthemis.

Cota tinctoria syn. *Anthemis tinctoria*
Golden Marguerite, Yellow Chamomile

Native to Mediterranean region and parts of southern Asia

A bushy, clump-forming, evergreen perennial usually growing to a height of 20 to 60cm and spreading as wide. The plant has distinctive, erect, reddish, hairy stems 60 to 90cm high. Medium green alternate leaves, sometimes with a greyish tinge, are curly, bipinnate, deeply serrated, giving a feathery appearance. Foliage is aromatic with a chamomile scent. Daisy-like flowers 2 to 4cm across have vibrant yellow centres and radiating petals from lemon yellow to creamy white, blooming throughout summer until autumn. Grow in average well-drained soil in full sun. Drought tolerant once established. One of the lovely bright wildflowers that light up the Mediterranean region and southern Europe in spring and early summer.

COTINUS
Anacardiaceae
Smoke Bush, Smoke Tree

Native to rocky habitat from Mediterranean region to China

A small genus of just three species of deciduous trees and shrubs. These are among the most attractive of the larger summer-flowering shrubs that also have a good autumn colour. Renowned for their unique, billowy inflorescences, which resemble puffs of smoke, hence the name.

Cotinus coggygria
Smoke Bush, Venetian Shumach

Native to southern Europe to Asia

A multiple-branching deciduous shrub growing to 5 to 7m tall with an open, spreading, irregular habit, only rarely forming a small tree. Leaves are 3 to 8cm long, rounded ovals, green with a waxy glaucous sheen. The autumn colour can be strikingly varied, from peach and yellow to scarlet. Inconspicuous flowers are borne in panicles in summer. Most of the flowers in each inflorescence abort, elongating into yellowish-pink to pinkish-purple feathery plumes. When viewed en masse, these have a wispy 'smoke-like' appearance, hence the common name. Grows best in cold winters and dry summers. It thrives in well-drained soil and full sun, and relatively drought tolerant once established. A prime candidate for a dry garden. *Cotinus* 'Purpureus' has large panicles of purplish-grey flowers that resemble puffs of pink smoke from a distance. 'Royal Purple' has deep wine-purple leaves and reddish purple 'smoke'. These versatile plants can be grown as ornamental specimens in gardens or used for hedging. Pruning can help maintain their shape and encourage bushier growth. They are valued for their appearance, colourful foliage and low-maintenance requirements, making them popular choices for landscaping and ornamental gardening.

COTONEASTER
Rosaceae
Native to the temperate regions of Europe, Asia and north Africa

A genus of over 200 species of hardy deciduous and evergreen shrubs and trees. The branches are covered in white or pink flowers in spring and clusters of bright red berries in autumn and winter. All grow vigorously and thrive with little or no maintenance. Grow in moderately fertile, well-drained soil in full sun. Most are drought tolerant, requiring little or no summer water once established. They are ideal in a dry garden as background planting. Also good as ground cover, in hedges and when planted on dry slopes, can reduce erosion.

Cotoneaster coriaceus syn. *Cotoneaster lacteus*
Native to western China

A dense evergreen shrub to 4m high and wide with arching branches. Relatively large, 5 to 8cm long, dark green, oval leaves have sunken veins and whitish undersides. In summer it bears flat-topped

Cosmos bipinnatus.

Cota tinctoria.

Cotinus coggygria.

Cotoneaster lacteus.

Cotyledon orbiculata 'Silver Waves'.

Crassula perfoliata var. *falcata.*

Crassula ovata.

Crinum asiaticum.

clusters of creamy-white flowers, which have an unpleasant smell. These are followed by an abundance of long lasting, showy, hanging bunches 5 to 8cm wide of red berries in autumn and winter. It succeeds in dry soils and any soil that is not marshy or waterlogged. Grows well in full sun or semi-shade but does not fruit so freely in a shady position. Fairly tolerant of maritime exposure. It is a useful plant in difficult sites or as an informal hedge or screen. Flowers are attractive to bees, whilst the fruit is a good winter food source for many species of birds. If kept clipped, the berries will be lost.

Cotoneaster franchetii
Franchet's Cotoneaster, Grey Cotoneaster, Orange Cotoneaster, Silverleaf Cotoneaster, Rockspray Cotoneaster

Native to southwestern China, northern Myanmar and northern Thailand

An upright or arching shrub or small semi-deciduous tree growing from 1 to 3m, occasionally up to 5m. Stems are upright and become spreading or arching as the plant matures. Leaves are elliptical or ovate, 2 to 3cm long, with entire (without teeth or lobes) margins and petioles 1 to 4mm long. The upper leaf surface is usually green, hairless to hairy and shiny, while the lower surface is whitish and densely covered in felty hairs. Pinkish-white flowers appear in midsummer, followed by a splendid display of orange red fruit. It is tolerant is a wide range of environmental conditions of heat, drought, cold, wet, salinity. Makes a good hedge or screen.

Cotoneaster microphyllus
Rockspray Cotoneaster

Native to the Himalayas

An evergreen ground cover or shrub, 30 to 90cm high, densely branched, with creeping, slender, rooting stems, and upright secondary branches. Leaves are only 1.5cm, oval, rounded at apex, margins curling downward, dark green above and woolly beneath. Tiny solitary white flowers are followed by small, deep rosy-red fruit crowded along stems. Effective on rock gardens and banks. Sun to part shade. It succeeds in dry soils. Adaptable, it needs little or no maintenance.

Cotoneaster salicifolius
Willow Leaf Cotoneaster

Native to western China, Tibet

A vigorous, evergreen shrub to 4m high and wide with gracefully arching branches. It is clothed in lance-shaped, leathery, glossy, dark green leaves 10cm long. In late spring to early summer, the branches are studded with flat-topped clusters of white flowers 5cm across, followed by a heavy crop of small, bright-red fruit in autumn. A tall, graceful shrub that is useful as a screening or background plant. Grow in full sun to partial shade in moderately fertile, well-drained soil. It tolerates dry soil. Excellent for coastal gardens and cottage gardens.

COTYLEDON
Crassulaceae

Native to southern Africa

A genus of about twenty species of clump-forming succulents or small shrubs. These plants are characterised by their fleshy leaves and stems, which help them keep water in arid environments. Plants are grown for both their foliage and flowers. All make excellent subjects for a dry or succulent garden. They typically have thick, rounded leaves that may be various shades of green, often with unusual patterns or markings. Some species produce colourful flowers in clusters atop tall stems.

Cotyledon orbiculata 'Silver Waves'
Silver Waves Pig's Ear

Native to South Africa

An attractive succulent that can grow 30cm high and 70cm wide with stout stems and erect branches with leaves densely packed on the stems. Fleshy, oval, greyish-white, wavy leaves are concave, up to 10cm long. Clusters of orange to red bell-like flowers up to 2cm long sit on stalks above the foliage during winter. Grow in full sun or partial shade in well-drained soil. Keep on a dry side most of the time, particularly during winter. It will take the extremes of summer heat and winter cold of an inland climate, whilst never looking tired. This ground cover is as tough as they come. Makes a good pot or large container plant. Great feature plant in the garden. Outstanding for the cactus or succulent garden.

CRASSULA
Crassulaceae

Native mostly in South Africa and Madagascar

A large genus of about 200 succulents or shrub-like plants, with a wide range of growth habits, leaf shapes and sizes. Some species form low-growing rosettes close to the ground, while others develop tall, branching stems. Leaves are typically fleshy, often with unusual textures, colours or patterns. Crassulas are easy to care for, requiring plenty of sunlight and well-draining soil. Drought tolerant but will benefit from occasional watering during the growing season. These versatile plants can be grown indoors as houseplants, in containers, or outdoors in rock gardens, succulent beds, or as ground cover in suitable climates. They are also commonly used in succulent arrangements and terrariums because of their interesting shapes and textures.

Crassula arborescens
Silver Jade Plant, Chinese Jade Tree

Native to South Africa

A heavily-branching evergreen succulent, growing treelike to 1.2m high and 1.5m wide with a thick trunk. Stems are covered with fleshy, round, silver-grey leaves, 4 to 8cm long, adorned with reddish spots and often with reddish edges. The tips' colouration is more intense in full sun. Terminal clusters of small, starry, five-petalled white flowers, ageing to pink, appear during spring and summer. Flowers are not usually produced until the plant is many years old. Thrives in average to poor, rocky or sandy well-drained soil. Full sun is best but can take light shade. Drought tolerant, indeed excessive moisture will cause root and stem rot. Perfect for rock gardens, succulent gardens, Mediterranean gardens. A slow-growing succulent that makes an ideal pot or container plant.

Crassula perfoliata var. *falcata*

Airplane Plant, Propeller Plant, Scarlet Paintbrush

Native to southern Africa

A lovely clump- or low-growing shrub that usually grows less than 60cm tall. Stem is usually unbranched above, but forms new shoots at the base, becoming woody in age. Grey to green, fleshy foliage resembles miniature airplane propellers. It has peculiar, grey-green, sickle-shaped leaves that are in overlapping pairs along a usually unbranched stem. Its crowning glory, however, are the showy dense clusters that rise above foliage of brilliant orange-red or scarlet-red, five-petalled flowers with contrasting yellow stamens. Accented flower heads grow 8 to 12cm wide. Flowers open slowly and last for nearly a month when in full bloom. Flowers starts to develop in summer and are in full bloom in late summer. Apart from adding colour to rockeries, they also attract birds and bees. Open and well-drained soils are best. As with many succulents, they are drought tolerant and are particularly suited to xeriscape gardening or can also be grown indoors.

Crassula sarmentosa syn. *Crassula ovata*

Jade Plant, Jade Tree

Native to Cape Province and Natal, South Africa

This evergreen, freely-branching, succulent shrub with shiny stems may eventually make a small tree 2m high and 1m wide. Thick oblong leaves 2 to 4cm long, bright jade-green usually with a red margin, turn reddish in the sun. With age, it produces clusters of small starry white or pink flowers 2cm across in winter. Easily grown in gritty, well-drained soil in full sun. Tolerant of summer drought, it should be kept on a dry side, particularly during winter. Makes a good pot or large container plant. The variegated form 'Tricolor' has beautiful green foliage with golden yellow margins. Grows quickly and can rapidly develop a trailing habit. Excellent in hanging baskets or cascading over container edges.

CRINUM

Amaryllidaceae

Seashore Lily, Poison Bulb, Crinum Lily, Asiatic Poison Lily

Native to tropical and subtropical regions of Africa, Asia and the Americas

A large and diverse genus, comprising around 180 species of perennial bulbous plants, known for their attractive and often fragrant flowers. Plants typically have long, strap-like leaves that arise from a bulbous underground stem or rhizome. Lance-shaped leaves can be flat or slightly twisted and can grow up to a metre or so long. Bulbs are large and fleshy and serve as an energy storage organ for the plant. Flowers are borne on long, erect stalks. Showy inflorescence comprises a cluster of large funnel, trumpet, or bell-shaped flowers with six petals in two whorls. They come in various colours, including white, pink, red or a combination of these. Some species produce fragrant flowers, particularly in the evening or at night, to attract pollinators. Crinum plants are adaptable and can grow in a range of environments, from dry to wet soils, preferring full or partial sun. Some species can tolerate brackish water or even thrive in aquatic habitats. Commonly cultivated as ornamental plants in gardens and parks because of their beautiful flowers and foliage.

Crinum asiaticum

Giant Crinum, Poison Bulb

Native to various tropical and subtropical regions, including parts of Asia, Africa and the Pacific Islands

A deciduous clump-forming perennial 1 to 1.5m high. Long, strap-like, dark-green leaves can grow 1 to 1.5m long with a slightly wavy or undulating edge. Umbels of 20 or more showy, white, pleasantly fragrant, narrow petalled flowers 10cm long appear from spring to summer. Grow in well-drained rich soil in full to partial shade. It has a wide distribution and is adaptable to dry subtropical climates, particularly in coastal regions. Often used in landscaping to add a tropical or exotic touch to gardens. The common name 'poison bulb' reflects the fact that various parts of the bulbs contain toxic alkaloids that can lead to poisoning.

Crinum moorei

Natal Lilly, Moore's Crinum Lilly, Lily of the Orinoco

Native to South Africa

A deciduous bulbous perennial. Resting just below the soil's surface, the bulb can grow up to 20cm in diameter, while its elongated neck protrudes 20 to 30cm above the ground. Broadly arching, strap-like, dark-green leaves are 1 to 1.5m long. Flower stalks, up to 1.2m long, bear umbels of six to twelve white to pale pink fragrant, striking, trumpet-shaped, scented flowers 8cm long during late summer. They can withstand damp and marshy soils, though also do well in dry, well-drained soils too. Avoid extended periods of full sun, which will scorch the leaves, as these plants prefer open, dappled shade. They will die back over winter and emerge again in spring. A clump under trees can make a spectacular sight. Excellent in beds, borders and containers.

CROCOSMIA

Iridaceae

Montbretia

Native to tropical and southern Africa

A small genus of about seven species of perennials with corms. These plants are known for their vibrant, funnel-shaped flowers and sword-like leaves. Crocosmia species are commonly cultivated in gardens and landscapes, with various hybrids and cultivars available. These typically bloom in summer, producing clusters of brightly-coloured flowers ranging from shades of yellow and orange to red. Plants prefer full sun to partial shade and well-drained soil.

Crocosmia crocosmiiflora

Native to South Africa

A cormous perennial quickly forming large clumps with sword-shaped leaves 60 to 80cm long. Thin, slightly arching, one-sided, branched spikes of orange or orange-red curved funnel-shaped flowers 4 to 5cm long appear from late summer until autumn, lasting a long time. Although drought tolerant, they benefit from some summer water. Prefers some shade but will take full sun. Widely grown in mild climate gardens for their brilliant flowers. Divide clumps every three to four years when they become overcrowded, replanting the corms 10cm deep. A popular hybrid that is much cultivated for cut flowers.

Crocosmia hybrids

Garden origin

There is a wide range of garden hybrids available in a range of flower colours and heights ranging from 45cm to 1.2m high. 'Canary Bird' has small yellow flowers. 'Emberglow' has dark red flowers on deep reddish-brown stems. 'Lucifer' has flame-red flowers on stems 1m high, while 'Solfatare' features attractive sprays of soft, apricot-yellow flowers floating atop a nicely contrasting foliage of erect, sword-shaped, bronze-green leaves. Cultivation is the same as *C. crocosmiiflora*.

Crocosmia masoniorum

Golden Swan Tritonia, Giant Montbretia

Native to South Africa

A magnificent cormous, clump-forming, deciduous perennial, which has wonderful, narrow-ribbed, mid-green leaves 60cm to 1m long. Branched arching stems 60 to 90cm high have two-tiered spikes of bright-orange to red, funnel-shaped, upward-facing 4cm long flowers hovering high above the foliage. The buds open slowly from the base to the tip and are produced from mid- to late summer. These make excellent cut flowers. A brilliant all-round garden plant, often planted in flower beds and at the edge of shrub borders, wall side planting and can be grown in containers. Cultivation is the same as *C. crocosmiiflora*.

CROCUS
Iridaceae

Native to a wide range of habitats, including central and southern Europe, North Africa and parts of Asia

A genus comprising about 80 species of dwarf, cormous perennials, many widely grown for their blooms in early spring or autumn. They emerge from an underground corm and die back shortly after flowering. The corm is covered in a dry sheath, known as a tunic, and many species have contractile roots that can pull the corm deeper into the soil. Each corm typically produces one or two low-growing, relatively large, white, yellow, orange or purple and even striped or bi-coloured flowers. Flowers have six tepals (petals and sepals that look similar) arranged in a cup-shaped structure. Often found growing in dry stony places with well-drained soil in full sun to partial shade. Crocuses are often used in gardens, rockeries and naturalised in grassy areas to add early-season colour.

Crocus chrysanthus

Golden Crocus

Native to the Balkans and Turkey

This perennial corm has many cultivars or hybrids whose flowers vary from yellow or white to blue, sometimes striped on the back. Leaves are narrow with a silver central stripe 7 to 10cm high. In early spring, it bears up to four rounded scented flowers 1.5 to 4cm long. Grow in full sun and gritty, poor to moderately fertile well-drained soil. It needs water during the growing season. Tolerant of summer drought.

Crocus suaveolens

Native to western Italy from Naples to Rome

A late winter- and early spring-flowering crocus with one or two flowers 3 to 4.5cm long, with long perianth tubes. Flowers are a rich violet-purple inside and biscuit-brown outside, with pronounced violet stripes. These open during winter in sunshine. Leaves are shiny and dark green. It needs fertile sandy soil and water during winter and spring. Tolerant of summer drought.

CUPHEA
Lythraceae

Native to tropical regions of Mexico, Central and South America

A large and variable genus of about 250 species, some annuals, perennials and subshrubs. All have more or less hairy stems, and leaves that are opposite or whorled on the stems. The genus is characterised by showy flowers, which are typically tubular or funnel-shaped and have brightly-coloured petals. Flowers are often produced in clusters at the ends of stems. Many species have an extended flowering period, making them popular ornamental plants. A terrific addition to sunny garden beds and containers, where they create a dazzling display through the summer and beyond. The plants are also valued for their ability to attract pollinators, such as butterflies, to the garden.

Cuphea hyssopifolia

Mexican Heather, False Heather

Native to Mexico, Guatemala and Honduras

A small evergreen shrub that grows to 60cm high with an equal spread. Leaves are opposite, pinnately veined, oblong to narrow lance-shaped, to 2cm long, densely packed on the hairy stems. Small flowers appear singly in leaf axis along the stem and bloom profusely. They are tiny cylinders with six expanded lobes of blue to lavender purple. It tolerates high summer heat and some drought. Grows best in full sun in well-drained soil. Moderately salt-tolerant. Use as a border plant, along walkways or as a container plant on patios or indoors. The plant can set seed and become invasive.

Cuphea ignea
Cigar Plant, Cigar Flower, Firecracker Plant, Mexican Cigar

Native to Mexico and Central America

A spreading, freely-branching, soft-stemmed shrub to about 1m high. Opposite lance-shaped leaves, 8cm long, are a medium green with a prominent and lighter-coloured midrib. Flowers are produced continuously throughout the year, singly in leaf axils. Each flower is a 3cm-long cylinder of scarlet with a dark purple-red ring near the end, tipped with white and yellow, giving it the common name. These plants are ideal for adding beauty to beds and borders in full sun or partial shade. They flourish in average, well-drained soil with additional moisture in dry spells.

Cuphea llavea
Bat Faced Cuphea

Native to Mexico

A fast-growing, densely-branched, evergreen subshrub 45 to 75cm tall and up to 60cm wide. Small, opposite, linear to lance-shaped deep-green leaves with distinct pinnate veins, 2 to 5cm long, are pubescent with smooth margins. It boasts masses of tubular flowers 2.5cm long, adorned with a pair of red ear-like petals and a purple calyx for most of the year. These are said to resemble the face of a bat, hence its common name. It is best-grown in average, medium moisture, well-drained soil in full sun. Plants tolerate high heat and some part shade. Although they are tolerant of dry conditions, they thrive when provided with consistent moisture. Their growth can become elongated as the season progresses, so it is important to pinch the stem tips as necessary to keep the plant looking good. It is a terrific addition to sunny garden beds, along edges of borders or paths, or in containers and hanging baskets, a real conversation piece. They attract pollinating insects and butterflies.

CUPRESSUS
Cupressaceae

Cypress

Native to Europe and the Mediterranean

A genus of about ten mostly tender monoecious, coniferous, evergreen trees. Cypress trees are known for their tall, slender forms, with scale-like or needle-like leaves arranged in spirals along the branches. They typically have small, round cones that contain seeds. Besides their ornamental value, cypress trees have been historically significant both culturally and symbolically. They are often associated with longevity, resilience and mourning in various cultures. They are excellent specimen trees, which tolerate dry conditions.

Cupressus sempervirens
Mediterranean Cypress, Italian Cypress

Native to the eastern Mediterranean region and Iran

A coniferous tree up to 20m high spreading to 6m wide, which can vary in shape from narrow columnar to broad and spreading. It is long-lived, with some trees reported to be over 1,000 years old. The species itself has almost horizontal branches but is highly variable in habit and texture. Trees bear upright sprays of tiny, dark-green leaves, which are scale-like, 2 to 5mm long, and produced on rounded (not flattened) shoots. Pollen from the female flowers is produced in vast quantities in early spring, which can fill the air when the tree is shaken. Round female cones to 4cm across hang from branches almost indefinitely. Probably the best known and most typical conifer of the Mediterranean region. Exceedingly drought tolerant, needing no water once established. A light dry soil suits it best. Useful as hedges, windbreaks and specimen trees. Grows best in full sun and well away from a wall, as this will cause leaves on that side to die. 'Stricta', the columnar form most typically seen in the Mediterranean region growing to 20m high and only 3m wide, results from a clone originally selected in Italy. Its tall dark columns stand guard by many houses, cemeteries and villages. 'Glauca' grows similarly but has blue-green foliage.

CURIO
Asteraceae

Native to South Africa

A genus containing over twenty species, all formerly belonging to the genus Senecio. In the wild, they mostly scramble over rocks and bushes, often emerging out of cracks in rock in search of the right microclimate. Their oddly shaped, succulent leaves are an evolutionary adaptation to the tough conditions in which they evolved.

Curio repens syn. *Senecio serpens*
Blue Chalksticks, Blue Chalk Fingers

Native to South Africa

A semi-trailing, low-growing, dwarf succulent that forms a dense mat to about 30cm high, spreading to 90cm wide. Ascending at first, the stems become prostrate, suckering at the base and rooting as the nodes touch the ground. Silvery-bluish, cylindrical, finger-like fleshy leaves 3 to 5cm long are borne on prostrate stems. From spring to autumn, it produces small, round, pompom-like flowers held in corymbs that rise above the foliage. These are creamy white but have yellow and pink tinges on the stamens. Drought and heat tolerant, this succulent has great ornamental appeal as a ground cover, border plant or in a rock garden. Easily

num moorei.

Crocosmia crocosmiiflora **'Solfatare'.**

Crocus chrysanthus.

phea hyssopifolia.

Cuphea ignea.

Cuphea llavea.

pressus sempervirens.

Curio repens.

Curio rowleyanus.

grown in sandy dry to medium moisture, well-drained soil in full sun or light shade. Quickly forming a dense blue mat with its upward-curving leaves, it provides extraordinary form and colour contrast in the landscape.

Curio rowleyanus syn. *Senecio rowleyanus, Kleinia rowleyana*

String of Beads

An evergreen perennial succulent with thin creeping or pendant stems to 60cm long. Stems have adventitious roots, and the plant can form a dense mat. It receives its common name from specialised leaves, which are the size and shape of small peas, about 6mm in diameter. Its trailing stems can grow from 60 to 90cm. There is a small tip at the distal point of each leaf and a thin band of dark-green tissue on the side known as a 'window'. A compound bloom comprising clusters of small, white, trumpet-shaped flowers with protruding brown stamens, measuring about 13mm in diameter, appear in summer. The flower's fragrance, reminiscent of cinnamon and other spices, will linger for approximately one month. This succulent can be grown in the sun but prefers some shade. Like most succulents, it requires infrequent watering (about once a month), a few hours of direct sunlight and is not affected by humidity. Good soil drainage is essential to prevent root rot, so sandy soil is recommended. This plant is commonly found in hanging baskets, with its leaves gracefully flowing over the container's edge. Looks good when hanging over the top of a wall.

CYATHEA

Cyatheaceae

Found throughout the world in tropical and subtropical areas

A genus of over 470 species of tree ferns. Most species have rather slender, scaly trunks. Rarely, the trunk may be branched or creeping. Many species also develop a fibrous mass of roots at the base of the trunk. They grow in habitats ranging from tropical rain forests to temperate woodlands.

Cyathea capensis syn. *Gymnosphaera capensis*

Native to southern Africa, South America

A tree fern with a slender, erect trunk up to 6m high and about 15cm in diameter. Leaf stems are mostly smooth, with only sparse, dark-brown or black scales. Fronds are tripinnate, born on long stalks, and 2 to 3m long. The main stem of the leaf (rachis) is smooth to slightly warty and covered in scales that range from tan to brown or dark brown. The frond stalks are covered with dark brown or black scales. It is cultivated as an ornamental plant that is relatively easy to grow if provided with a semi-shady, moist and sheltered environment, and can likely tolerate several degrees of frost. Thrives in peaty soil, in shade. Tolerant of summer drought.

Cyathea dealbata

Silver Fern, Silver Tree-Fern, Ponga, Punga

Native to New Zealand

A slow growing, single-trunked tree fern characterised by silvery-green frond stalks (stipes) and soft fronds up to 3m long held horizontally that are distinctly silvery on the underside. Old fronds shed by breaking their stipes some distance above the attachment point, resulting in persistent stipe bases covering the surface. An understorey tree in native and mixed plantings. Plant with other ferns to enhance subtropical and woodland gardens. Prefers moist, sheltered conditions but will tolerate full sun and dry conditions once established. Grows best in well-drained soil. It is marginally frost hardy and needs shelter from strong winds.

CYCAS

Cycadaceae

Cycads, Sago Palms

Native to the Asia-Pacific, East Africa and Madagascar

A genus of about 30 species of dioecious cycads characterised by their large, palm-like, pinnate leaves that grow in a rosette pattern from a central stem or trunk. Leaves are typically stiff and leathery, with a glossy surface and a waxy coating that helps to prevent water loss. New leaves are soft upon emergence, and the leaflets are coiled. With age they produce a trunk of varying heights, trunks of a few species being subterranean. Many species sucker and produce offshoots from the base of the parent trunk. Male reproductive structures are cone-like structures that produce pollen. Female reproductive structures are larger and bear seeds. They are prized for their ornamental value and are commonly grown as landscape plants, particularly in warmer regions. Cycads are among the oldest group of seed plants on earth, surviving unchanged for millions of years.

Cycas circinalis

Queen Sago

Widely spread throughout Asia, from India to the South Pacific Islands

A medium-sized suckering cycad, growing 3 to 5m tall. With a rather palm-like appearance, it produces one or more usually unbranched stems around 25 to 45cm in diameter, topped with a crown of large, bright-green, glossy leaves. Usually evergreen, the plant can lose its leaves in extremely dry seasons. Feathery leaves of this species arranged in a rosette pattern add a sense of the tropics to the landscape. Leaves are bright green, semi-glossy, 1.5 to 2.5m long, flat (not keeled) in section (opposing leaflets inserted at 180° on rachis), with around 170 leaflets, tomentum shedding as leaf expands. Male sago plants develop a cone approximately 30cm tall from the centre of the top. The cone is white or yellow, rounded and produces abundant pollen. It prefers a warm, sunny position with plenty of water in summer, and a dryish winter. A good all-around species that deserves its popularity.

Cycas revoluta

Sago Palm, King Sago Palm, Japanese Sago Palm

Native to southern Japan

A robust evergreen cycad that forms an attractive rosette of shiny, arching, pinnate leaves 60 to 150cm long, atop a rugged upright trunk. Each leaf is divided into many narrow, leathery, spiny-tipped, deep-green leaflets adorned with revolute edges. It is slow growing, and can take many years to reach full size, typically 1 to 3m tall. Some plants live 100 years or more. Easily grown in good, well-draining, slightly acidic soil, and tolerant of summer drought and coastal conditions in Mediterranean climates. The plants can create a stunning tropical look in garden beds and borders, working well as a focal point, or can be planted in groups to create a dramatic effect. They can also be planted in large pots or containers and placed on patios or in entryways. They require little maintenance.

CYCLAMEN
Primulaceae
Sowbread, Swinebread

Native from the Mediterranean region to Iran and north Africa

A genus of 23 species of tuberous perennials valued for their flowers with unswept petals and variably patterned leaves. In most species, leaves appear in autumn, grow through winter and then die in spring, remaining dormant through a dry Mediterranean summer. Flowering time may be any month of the year, depending on the species.

Cyclamen hederifolium
Ivy Leaved Cyclamen

Native to the Mediterranean region

A hardy tuberous perennial that blooms and sprouts leaves in autumn, grows through winter, and goes dormant before summer, when the seed capsules ripen and open. Leaves are variably shaped and coloured 5 to 15cm long, delicate silver-lined dark green reminiscent of ivy. Pale to deep pink flowers 2cm long, sometimes scented, are produced in late summer and autumn before the leaves, on stems 8 to 10cm high. Grow in full sun or partial shade in well-drained soil. Keep soil moist during the growing season, but summer drought tolerant. A vigorous and easy plant to grow, it thrives almost anywhere that is not baked in summer. It is perfect for growing at the base of small shrubs and trees, and naturalising in grass. Self-seeds with enormous generosity, often on top of the mother corm. Baby corms often reach flowering size in as little as two years.

Cyclamen persicum

Native to rocky hillsides, from south-central Turkey to Lebanon, Syria and the Palestine region

A tuberous perennial, to about 20cm high with heart-shaped, fleshy leaves, 2.5 to 14cm long, usually deep green with lighter markings on the upper surface. Leaf underside may be pale green or reddish, with margins slightly thickened and usually serrated. The rounded, slightly flattened tuber is about 4 to 15cm or more in diameter. Sweet-scented white, pink, mauve, purple or red flowers 1 to 2cm or more long have five small sepals and five upswept petals and are produced on tall slender stems with the leaves from early winter to spring. At its best, when grown in light shade, it flourishes underneath deciduous trees. Give water during the winter growing season. Summer dormant, needing no water, then grows again at the beginning of the colder season. When mass planted, this beautiful miniature makes a wonderful sight.

Cyclamen repandum

Native to southern Europe and some Mediterranean islands

A spring-flowering tuberous perennial. Leaves are heart-shaped to 13cm long, marbled with silver and lightly toothed edges. Fragrant, bright-crimson flowers to 2cm long, with long narrow petals, are borne on stems 13 to 16cm long in spring with the leaves. Easily grown in leafy, stony soil, in shade in hot areas, and away from spring frosts in cold areas. As the leaves die in the early summer, it is tolerant of summer drought. Cultivation is like other cyclamen species.

CYDONIA
Rosaceae
Quince

Native to northern Iran and eastern Turkey

A genus of just one species of thornless deciduous shrubs or small trees. Attractive pale pink flowers are followed by edible fruit and attractive autumn foliage.

Cydonia oblonga
Common Quince

A tree or shrub, often with crowded branches to 6m high, spreading almost as wide. With age, branches can become gnarled and twisted. Leaves ovate to oblong are simple, alternate, 6 to 10cm long, with an entire margin and densely pubescent with fine white hairs. Flowers are produced in spring after the leaves, white or pink, 5cm across, with five petals. These appear singly in leaf axils at the ends of the current season's growth. Yellow pear or apple-shaped fruit, 8 to 10cm or more in diameter, are wrinkled and covered with light brown felt, ripening in autumn. The fruit is incdible when raw but is used for making jams, jellies and in cooking. Grow in full sun in fertile, well-drained soil. Give it little summer water. Prune only enough to stimulate fresh growth and remove any suckers from the base. Several improved varieties have been raised, including 'Lusitanica', which has larger, dark-yellow fruit, and 'Vranja', which has fragrant, pale-green fruit that ripen to golden yellow.

Cyphomandra betacea see *Solanum betaceum*

CYRTANTHUS
Amaryllidaceae

Native to South Africa

A genus of about 60 species of perennial bulbs growing in tropical and temperate zones, with their habitats ranging from

Cyathea dealbata.

Cycas revoluta.

Cyclamen hederifolium.

Cydonia oblonga.

Cyrtanthus elatus.

Cytisus praecox albus.

Cytisus scoparius.

Dais cotinifolia.

along streams to dry desert. Within the genus, there are summer growing and winter growing varieties with heights from 10cm to a spectacular 75cm. Its leafless stems emerge from a partially to fully exposed bulb. Individual bulbs can produce one to several stems, with each stem boasting one or more flowers. Variety specific, white, yellow, orange, red and pink flowers can be scented or unscented and stand erect or hang in a pendent form. After flowering, leaves will emerge.

Cyrtanthus elatus
George Lily, Scarborough Lily

This evergreen, summer-growing bulb reaches 40 to 65cm high in flower. It grows from a bulb up to 4cm long, which reproduces by formation of offsets and bulblets. Erect or arching deep-green leaves are broadly strap-shaped and produced in two opposite rows with rounded tips. One to several hollow flower stems emerge per bulb. The flower head (umbel) produces two to ten widely funnel-shaped, slightly irregular, unscented blooms, each with a long, straight, perianth tube 15 to 20cm long, on dull-green flower stalks. Each flower comprises six oblong or oval scarlet, deep-red, rose-pink or, rarely, white tepals. Stamens are in a single row, with bright yellow, ripe anthers. Flowers appear during late summer and autumn. Easy to grow in a mild to warm climate in sun or dappled shade. Bury bulbs up to their necks. Grow in well-drained soil with plenty of organic matter. Water well in spring and summer and reduce watering over winter. Great, either in borders or in pots.

CYTISUS
Fabaceae

Broom

Native to Europe, west Asia and north Africa

A genus of about 50 species of deciduous and evergreen shrubs producing masses of brightly-coloured, pea-like flowers, often highly fragrant, that cover the plant.

Cytisus multiflorus see *Chamaecytisus elongatus*

Cytisus × praecox
Warminster Broom

Garden origin

A hardy, deciduous, compact-growing shrub up to 2m high and almost as wide, with many slender, grey-green arching stems. Small silky grey-green simple leaves to 2cm long drop early in summer. In spring, the stems boast a profusion of pale yellow to creamy white pea-like 1 to 2cm-long flowers held in clusters. Incredibly showy, these cover the plant. One of the most eye-catching sights in spring. A fine choice for mass planting along slopes or hillsides. A tough shrub that grows in full sun. It tolerates drought, dry and poor soils and salt.

Cytisus scoparius
Common Broom, Scotch Broom

Native to west Europe

This dense evergreen shrub up to 3m high has slender, bright-green shoots with small deciduous trifoliate leaves 1 to 2cm long. During spring and early summer, it becomes completely covered in 2 to 3cm-long golden yellow flowers, either alone or in pairs. With its hardy, easy-to-maintain nature and resistance to droughts, this plant will bring you seasons of joy with no hassle. Grow in any soil type that is extremely well-drained. Prune back after flowering. As it sets seed readily, it can become invasive, which has earned the genus a bad name. More hardy and even tougher than *Cytisus × praecox*.

D

DAIS
Thymelaeaceae

African Button-Flower

Native to South Africa, Madagascar

A genus comprising just two species of deciduous shrubs. They have tough fibres under the bark, which can be made into string.

Dais cotinifolia
South African Tree Daphne, Pompon Tree

An attractive, slow-growing shrub or small tree that forms a rounded bushy habit to 4 to 5m high and wide. Leaves are shiny, dark green, narrowly ovate 8cm long. Evergreen in warmer climates but deciduous in cold climates. Lilac-pink flower heads, about 10cm across, are a distinctive feature, as they are borne in terminal spherical clusters, appearing as balls of pink, hence the common name. These sweet-scented flowers appear abundantly during summer. It makes an excellent specimen that adds a mass of colour to the garden. Prefers light to medium well-drained soil in a protected sunny position. Drought and frost resistant. Provides cool, beautiful shade in gardens where the branches drape over a path and waft the gorgeous perfume as you walk under it.

DAPHNE
Thymelaeaceae

Native to Asia, Europe and North Africa

The genus contains around 50 species, typically small to medium-sized shrubs with glossy green leaves. They are grown mainly for their clusters of delicate, four-lobed, often highly-scented flowers generally blooming in late winter or early spring when few other plants are in flower. Species require well-drained acid soil and prefer partial shade or dappled sunlight. Many require cool conditions. Most species are toxic if ingested, so caution should be exercised when planting them, especially in areas frequented by children or pets.

Daphne collina syn. *Daphne sericea*

Native to southern Italy, Sicily, Malta, Greece, Crete, Turkey, Syria and Lebanon

A compact or open, rounded evergreen shrub to 30 to 50cm or more high. Lance-shaped, dark-green leaves to 5cm long are glossy above, hairy beneath. Flowers are in terminal or axillary clusters of up to fifteen. Fragrant flowers to 1cm across open a rich pink and fade to a pale yellowish-brown when they get older. A shrub can be entirely one colour or mix several flowering stages and are produced from late spring to early summer. Fertilised flowers produce fleshy fruits, orange-red to orange-brown. Grow in a sunny to half-shady situation in moderately moist well-drained soil. The soil should be gritty loam.

Daphne oleoides syn. *Daphne jasminea*

Jasmine Daphne

Native to southeast Greece, Crete, Lybia

This upright, many-branched, evergreen shrub grows 10 to 30cm tall and wide, often found on limestone rocks. Oblong-obovate, hairless, grey-green or blue-green leaves are 1cm long. These provide an attractive backdrop to the clusters of small, star-shaped, fragrant, white, sometimes pink-flushed flowers that appear in late winter to early spring. These resemble those of jasmine, hence its common name. Prefers well-drained soil and full sun to partial shade with little summer water. It adds beauty and fragrance to gardens, particularly during the cooler months when its blooms stand out against the winter landscape.

Daphne pontica

Native to southeast Bulgaria through Turkey to the Caucasus

A spreading evergreen shrub 1 to 1.5m high, with glabrous branchlets and leaves. Leaves obovate, 2 to 8cm long and glossy green. Clusters of up to ten fragrant, yellowish green, flowers to 2cm across with slender pointed lobes are borne during spring in pairs from the axils of bracts at the base of recent shoots. It forms a dense mass of blossom crowned by the tips of young twigs. Although the flowers of this Daphne have no bright colour, they are fragrant and profuse, and the shrub is a cheerful evergreen. It likes a moist, loamy or peaty soil in a sheltered, partially shaded spot. Useful for grouping near woodland walks.

DASYLIRION

Asparagaceae

Native to dry areas of Texas and Arizona, USA and Mexico

A genus of about eighteen species of evergreen, stemless, yucca-like, dioecious shrubs. In most species, rosettes of long, narrow, stiff leaves arise from woody underground stems, often with sharp spines along the margins. Valued for their resilience and ability to thrive in hot, dry climates with well-drained soil. They are often used in xeriscaping and desert landscaping, where their architectural form adds interest. Plants make striking shrubs, which are ideal for dry cactus and succulent gardens.

Dasylirion acrotrichum

Green Sotol or Coahuila Sotol

Native to northeastern Mexico

This species typically forms compact rosettes of narrow, stiff, green leaves, which may have serrated edges and sharp tips. Long, slender leaves grow up to 1m, radiating from a central point to form an attractive, symmetrical shape. There is also a tuft of fibres at the point of each leaf. It may produce a tall flower spike 3 to 4m high in spring or summer, topped with clusters of small, creamy-white bell-shaped flowers. It does well in dry rocky places in full sun and can thrive in arid environments, often found in desert scrublands and grasslands in its native range. In cultivation, it is valued for its drought tolerance and low maintenance requirements.

Dasylirion wheeleri

Bear Grass, Spoon Flower, Desert Spoon

Native to southern USA and Mexico

A small ornamental evergreen succulent that makes a striking symmetrical rosette 1 to 2m round with leaves radiating in all directions from a central stem. Long, narrow, rigid leaves with sharp points along the margins are silvery blue-green, up to 1.5m long. Older shrubs may develop multiple trunks 1 to 1.5m tall. A flowering spike 3 to 4m high may appear in spring with many small bell-shaped whitish flowers. Easily grown in well-drained soils in full sun. Well-adapted to arid and semi-arid environments, thriving in hot, dry conditions. Ideal as specimen plants in Mediterranean and xeriscape gardens. Slow-growing and carefree.

DATURA

Solanaceae

Thornapples, Moonflowers

Native to the Americas, Asia, Africa and Australia

A small genus of about eight species of annuals or short-lived perennials. Leaves of the species are typically large, lobed, and alternate along the stems. Species are known for their showy, trumpet-shaped flowers that may be white, yellow, purple or pink. Flowers are often fragrant and may bloom at night, attracting nocturnal pollinators such as moths and bats. All species are poisonous, some deadly. In certain areas, they can become invasive. Many species formerly listed under Datura are now listed as Brugmansia. There is still much taxonomic confusion over this genus.

Datura metel

Native to southwest China

A glabrous bushy annual or short-lived shrubby perennial herb usually 1 to 1.5m high. Stems are hollow, green or purple-black, somewhat woody, and have a strong odour. It is slightly pubescent, with green to dark-violet shoots and oval to broad oval leaves that are often dark violet as well. Broadly oval greyish-green leaves are simple, alternate, petiolate, with entire or deeply-lobed margins to 20cm long with a strong odour when crushed. The plant boasts upward-facing trumpets up to 20cm long, in shades of white, yellow, lilac and dark purple, both single and double. Noted for their over-powering honeysuckle fragrance, these are produced from mid- to late summer. The ravishing single or double blossoms open in the evening and last until noon the next day, giving way to seed capsules that split open, releasing seeds. A full sun lover, this plant is best grown in rich moist well-drained soils. Almost drought tolerant but grows better with some summer water. Makes an attractive pot or container plant for the patio. Perfect for beds and borders in Mediterranean gardens. Naturalised in all warm parts of the world.

Datura innoxia

Angels' Trumpet, Downy Thorn-Apple, Indian Apple, Moonflower

Native to southern USA and Mexico

A tuberous rooted subshrub that typically reaches a height of 0.6 to 1.5m. Stems and leaves are covered with short, soft greyish hairs, giving the whole plant a greyish appearance. It has elliptic smooth-edged leaves with pinnate venation. All parts of the plant emit a foul odour when crushed or bruised. Flowers are fragrant, white, trumpet-shaped, 12 to 19cm long, growing upright at first, and later incline downward. These open in the evening, bloom at night but only last to late after-noon of the next day. Flowers will bloom intermittently from midsummer to frost. Often followed by green oval fruit to 5cm long, which are covered in spines. Easy to grow in dry, well-drained average alkaline or sandy soil in full sun to partial shade. Drought tolerant. Makes an attractive pot or container plant for the patio. Beware that all parts of the plant are poi-sonous, particularly the fruit. Several places now consider the plant to be invasive.

DELAIREA

Asteraceae

Native to southern Africa, southern Brazil

The genus currently only contains two species: *Delairea odorata* and the recently discovered *Delairea aparadensis*.

Delairea odorata syn. *Senecio mikanioides*

German Ivy

Native to South Africa

A fast-growing vine that can climb 2 to 4m high. Alternate glossy semi-succulent leaves are evergreen or nearly so, triangu-lar with five to seven sharp lobes 8 to 10cm across, giving it an ivy-like appear-ance. In winter to early spring, it produces clusters to 8cm across of small, sweet-scented, yellow, daisy-like flowers. Stems and leaves die between late summer and early autumn, being superseded by fresh shoots that employ the old stems as climbing support. Grow in full sun or par-tial shade. Drought tolerant once estab-lished. This tough plant is useful for growing up old trees or covering fences. Also useful as a ground cover, but it can become weedy.

DELONIX

Fabaceae

Flamboyant Tree, Royal Poinciana

Native to tropical regions of Africa, Madagascar and the Indian subcontinent

A genus of ten species of trees character-ised by their strikingly beautiful and flam-boyant display of flowers, giving the common names. Only one species is commonly planted in gardens.

Delonix regia

Native to Madagascar

It is among the world's most beautiful flowering trees, deciduous or semi-evergreen, reaching to 12m or more. The trunk is typically stout, with a spreading, umbrella-like crown. If pruned while still young, it can be trained to a height of 3 or 4m with a flat top and a spread of 4m or more. Leaves are up to 60cm long, fern-like and bipinnate, giving the foliage a delicate and airy appearance. Leaflets are typi-cally small and opposite. Renowned for its large, showy, five-petalled, 10cm-wide, bright-red or orange-red flowers with long, claw-like petals. One of the five petals is larger than the other four and is sometimes pinkish, speckled red and bearing a streak of yellow in its centre. Dense terminal clusters create a stunning spectacle when in full bloom, a breathtaking flush that covers the entire tree, leafless or not appearing during early summer. Fruit is a long, flattened pod that develops after the flowers have faded, initially green and then turning brown as it matures. Thrives in full sun and well-drained soil. Drought tolerant once established. The trees are well-suited to warm tropical and subtropical climates. They are com-monly planted in parks, large gardens and along broad streets to provide shade and create a visually dramatic landscape.

DENDROMECON

Papaveraceae

Tree Poppy

Native to dry, rocky areas of California and Mexico

This genus comprises only two species of evergreen shrubs, which are grown for their glaucous foliage and brilliant yellow flowers.

Daphne collina syn.
Daphne sericea.

Daphne pontica.

Dasylirion wheeleri.

Datura innoxia.

Delairea odorata.

Delonix regia.

Dendromecon rigida.

Dianella tasmanica variegata.

Dianthus caryophyllus.

Dendromecon rigida
Bush Poppy, Tree Poppy
Native to California

A stiff, rounded, much-branched, evergreen shrub up to 3m high and wide with shedding bark. Grey-green or bluish, leathery, lance-shaped leaves are up to 10cm long. Solitary, fragrant, brilliant yellow four-petalled flowers, to 7cm across with many stamens, are poppy-like. These appear terminally on short branchlets or on long stalks in leaf axils in great profusion from spring to autumn. Grow in full sun in well-drained sandy soil. As it has a brittle taproot, it does not transplant well. Although tolerant of summer drought, some water is beneficial. It can also be trained against a wall. For best results, prune back after the flowers have finished. A good shrub for a dry garden or for covering banks.

DIANELLA
Asphodelaceae
Flax Lilies
Native to Australia, New Zealand

A genus of 25 to 30 species of variable, evergreen, rhizomatous perennials. Grass-like or lance-shaped leaves are borne on stems 40 to 80cm high. These are grown for their loose panicles of slightly pendant star-shaped, usually blue flowers followed by round berries. Plants are considered drought tolerant once established. They can go for long periods of time without water and still maintain their healthy appearance.

Dianella caerulea
Blue Flax Lily
Native to eastern Australia, Tasmania

A hardy clumping perennial, growing up to 1m high and wide. Bright-green, grass-like strappy leaves have straight or toothed margins and may reach 75cm long. Sprays of small blue flowers in spring and summer are followed by indigo-coloured berries. The berries have small black seeds inside. Grows in full sun to shady spots. Frost- and drought-tolerant once established. It grows from an underground rhizome, so it can be cut back to tidy up if needed and it will resprout. It adapts readily to cultivation and is commonly seen in gardens and amenities' plantings. A good plant for stabilising sand, it will grow well on coastal sites.

Dianella tasmanica
Flax Lily
Native to Tasmania, southeast Australia

This tufted perennial forms clumps of strap-shaped, stiff, rough-margined leaves to 1.2m long. It sometimes also produces tall, cane-like stems with tufts of leaves at the top. Branching panicles to 60cm long of star-shaped, lavender-blue to violet flowers 2cm across are borne in early summer, followed by dark blue berries, which are poisonous. Once established, it is drought and frost tolerant. It prefers some shade but can also grow in heavy shade. It is a splendid choice for poolside, containers or mass planted in borders and also for planting in dry shade under large trees.

Dianella tasmanica variegata
Variegated Flax Lily, Variegated Dianella, Tasman Flax Lily

A lovely, drought-resistant, perennial compact form of Dianella growing to 50cm high and wide. Leaves have variegated white margins. Foliage is complemented by stalks of shiny, turquoise blue berries from autumn into winter. Ideal for adding light and colour to shaded areas of the garden, impressive in mass plantings. For best results, water regularly to moisten soil in the first growing season for a stronger deep root system. In second and following seasons, it only needs watering during drought. Likes shady areas but does better when it receives full or partial sun for most of the day. Grow in well-drained soils, tolerates clay, and sand. Great for mass planting near pools or in garden beds and borders.

DIANTHUS
Caryophyllaceae
Native mainly in Europe and Asia

A genus of about 340 species of mostly herbaceous perennials, a few annuals or biennials, and some low subshrubs with woody basal stems. Leaves are opposite, simple, mostly linear and often strongly glaucous grey green to blue green. Flowers have five petals, typically with a frilled or pink margin, and are in almost all species pale to dark pink. Some species, particularly the perennial pinks, are noted for their strong spicy fragrance.

Dianthus caryophyllus
Wild Carnation, Clove Pink
Native to the Mediterranean region

A loosely-tufted, woody perennial with flattened, soft mid-green leaves to 15cm long with conspicuous sheaths. Bears loose cymes 5cm across, of one to five strongly-fragrant, single, toothed flowers to 1.5cm across on stiff stems to 80cm in summer. They come in a variety of colours, including white, pink, red, yellow and purple. Carnations are prized for their vibrant colours, delicate fringed petals, and enchanting fragrance. The scent of carnations is often described as spicy, clove-like, or reminiscent of a combination of cinnamon and nutmeg, hence the common name. This delightful aroma has made carnations a popular choice for perfumes, pot-pourri and scented products. Carnations require excellent drainage and alkaline soil. If your soil is acidic, adding some lime when planting will get them off to a good start. Although they have moderate drought tolerance, they require adequate water during spring to support the formation of flower buds. In summer droughts, additional watering might be required. These like a warm environment but wilt in extreme heat. They do best in low humidity. However, an occasional light spray of cool water during hot weather may help.

DICLIPTERA
Acanthaceae

Native to tropical and temperate parts of the world

A genus of about 223 species of annuals, evergreen subshrubs, perennials and climbers with angled stems. They are grown for their opposite, lance-shaped, velvety leaves and slender, tubular, two-lipped, brightly-coloured flowers.

Dicliptera squarrosa syn. *Dicliptera suberecta*
Firecracker Plant

Native to central South America

A tender herbaceous perennial or evergreen subshrub with erect or arching slender stems more or less hexagonal in section. It typically forms a shrubby mound, 45 to 65cm tall and as wide. Opposite, dull grey-green leaves are 4 to 8cm long with the whole plant covered in fine velvety grey hairs. Bright orange/red tubular flowers, 4cm long, with protruding stamens, bloom in compact terminal clusters rising above the foliage throughout summer and into autumn. The show lasts well into autumn when the plant goes somewhat dormant through winter. Grow in full sun in a well-draining soil and water only occasionally, as it is tough and drought tolerant. This is a great small showy plant for the front of a border, with attractive foliage even before flowers appear above, attracting hummingbirds and bees to the garden. As the seeds germinate readily in favourable locations, it can become invasive.

DIERAMA
Iridaceae

Hairbells, Angel's Fishing Rod, Fairybells, Wandflowers

Native to Africa

A genus of around 44 species of evergreen perennial corms. Most are clump forming and have tough, flat, narrow leaves. The thin, wiry, branching stem may bend and droop when in flower. It is lined with leaves that have linear blades with thick longitudinal veins and often no midrib. The inflorescence is a panicle of several spikes of bell-shaped flowers hanging from arching stems. Flowers of most wild species are pink but there are many cultivars in a range of colours, sometimes with spots of yellow or blue.

Dierama pulcherrimum
Angel's Fishing Rod

Native to South Africa

An elegant, evergreen perennial growing to 1.2 to 1.5m high. Clumps of long, narrow, grass-like leaves are evergreen in mild winter climates. It features dense arching stems of tubular bell-shaped, pale to magenta-pink, occasionally purple-red or white flowers 3.5 to 6cm long. These open in sequence along its wiry stems as the season progresses, making a beautiful display from early to late summer. Striking when sited above a low wall, or near a pool. Easily grown in full sun in humus-rich, well-drained soil. Tolerant of summer drought. Great for beds and borders, banks and slopes, coastal gardens, Mediterranean gardens. Resents being moved.

DIETES
Iridaceae

Wild Iris, Butterfly Iris, Fairy Iris, Spanish Iris

Native to southern and central Africa

A genus of six clump-forming, rhizomatous species with erect, dark green, sword-like, leathery, basal leaves. Branching stems bear a succession of flat, individually short-lived iris-like flowers from spring to summer. The open-faced, white flowers streaked with yellow and mauve are held above the foliage on tall stems.

Dietes bicolor
African Iris, Fortnight Lily, Yellow Wild Iris

Native to the Eastern Cape, South Africa

This evergreen, rhizomatous perennial forms clumps from 60 to 80cm tall with long sword-like evergreen pale-green leaves, which grow from multiple fans at the base. Flowers, appearing in spring and summer, are pale yellow with three dark purple spots, which may be so dark as to appear black. Each is surrounded by an orange outline. These are followed by a capsule that may bend the flower stalks to the ground. It can form large clumps if left undisturbed for years. Easy to grow in well-drained soil, tolerates poor dry soils, drought tolerant. Plants thrive in dappled shade rather than direct sunlight, resulting in abundant flowering. Flower stalks are perennial and should never be cut, as they make new flowers year after year. A hardy, low-maintenance plant, with a long flowering season. Ideal for landscaping, weed suppressing, creating a natural border and erosion control, commonly used in mass plantings.

Dietes grandiflora

Native to eastern and southern Africa

An evergreen, rhizomatous perennial with sword-shaped leaves. Large iris-like flowers 10cm across are borne on erect, slender stalks 90 to 120cm high. Each waxy white flower comprises three outer petals with a stripe of rich yellow near the base and three inner segments flecked with brown at the heart. Radiating from the blooms' centres are three pale-violet style arms. Flowers appear in spring and summer in flushes. Easy to grow in full sun in well-drained soil, tolerates poor dry soils. It is a popular garden plant as it is drought tolerant, ideal for Mediterranean gardens and cottage gardens. Spectacular when mass planted. Flower stalks are perennial and should never be cut, as they make new flowers year after year.

DIGITALIS
Plantaginaceae

Foxgloves

Native to Europe, western Asia, and northwestern Africa

A genus of about twenty species of herbaceous perennials, shrubs and biennials. Flowers are tubular, produced on a tall spike, and vary in colour with species, from purple to pink, white and yellow. The scientific name means 'finger'. The genus was traditionally placed in the figwort family, Scrophulariaceae, but phylogenetic research led taxonomists to move it to Veronicaceae in 2001. More recent phylogenetic work has placed it in the much-enlarged family Plantaginaceae.

Digitalis canariensis syn. *Isoplexis canariensis*
Canary Islands Foxglove

Native to Canary Islands and Madeira

An evergreen, sparsely branched, rounded shrub to 1.5m high and 1m wide with stems that become woody with age, and glossy, serrated, oval, dark-green leaves. The inflorescence is a cluster of orange-reddish, 3cm-large flowers with short petals and noticeable upper and lower lips. These are foxglove-like with a flattened appearance, held on upright spikes to 30cm. Highly distinctive blooms can last from spring to late autumn, with the biggest show during summer. Flowers stay open for a long time and are pollinated by birds and bees. Grow in well-draining soil that is kept moist, but it can take some summer drought. It enjoys a mix of sun and shade, with protection from scorching afternoon sun. It is reportedly hardy but does best when kept from freezing. The plant's flowering vigour declines after several years, but you may propagate it by seeds or cuttings. It grows well in a pot or container and is best clipped back annually to around 50cm.

DIMORPHOTHECA
Asteraceae

Native to southern Africa

A genus of about 21 species of low-branching erect annuals, or evergreen shrubby perennials. Closely related to Osteospermum, some species can hybridise with them, and crosses are sold as cultivated ornamentals. Leaves are alternate, lance-shaped, entire to pinnatisect with wavy margins and toothed edges. Daisy-like flowerheads appear on stiff stems that close in dull weather. They are attractive container, bedding or border plants flowering during summer. Grow in light well-drained soil in full sun. Tolerant of summer drought.

Dimorphotheca hybrids

Garden origin

A lovely, thick-growing annual or perennial to 20cm high and 30cm wide, often grown in borders. It comes in a variety of colours, including yellow, cream, apricot and orange, but can also be mauve or purple. Flowers emerge in spring and summer and need full sun to be their best, though they tend to close up when it is cloudy and overcast. These are excellent border plants, providing plenty of strong colour with little maintenance required. Grow in almost any well-drained soil. Drought tolerant but flowers better with water in dry conditions. Deadhead spent flowers to encourage further flushes. If you grow them as a perennial, trim back the foliage after flowers have finished.

Dimorphotheca jucunda syn. *Osteospermum jucundum*
Trailing Mauve Daisy

Native to South Africa

A straggling, somewhat shrubby, evergreen perennial 60cm or more high and wide. Lush green, sparsely-toothed, linear to oblong leaves are up to 8cm long. Leaves and stems are covered with small white hairs. Almost flat daisy-like flower heads are 5 to 8cm across and are held erect above the leaves, a single daisy at the tip of a long, strong, flowering stem up to 20cm long. Petals are pure white, almost shiny, above and mauve with blue lines beneath. Disc-florets in the centre of the flower are tipped with black and open to bright yellow. Each flower lasts for a few days and remains open during the evenings and on cloudy days. Flowering starts in early spring and continues through summer to autumn. The plant hybridises easily, and many colours have been raised.

Dimorphotheca sinuata syn. *Dimorphotheca aurantiaca*

Native to southern Africa

An upright to sprawling annual that grows up to 30cm tall. Leaves are slender, oblanceolate, light green when mature, reaching up to 8cm long, with shallowly lobed or toothed margins. Larger indented narrow leaves are present close to the base of the plant. The reddish stems are frequently concealed by the surrounding masses of leaves. Flowerheads are impressively large and can be orange or yellow with centres that match, depending on where they are found. Each centre of the ray florets has a slender ring that is greenish purple. Flowerheads are deeply cup-shaped, up to 8cm across, and borne singly at the tip of a branch. Flowering is mainly from mid-winter to mid-spring. A wonderful choice for hot, sunny, dry areas.

Dimorphotheca spectabilis syn. *Dimorphotheca ecklonis*
Cape Marguerite, African Daisy, Van Staden's River Daisy

Native to South Africa

An evergreen, perennial, dwarf shrub growing 25 to 50cm high and becoming woody with age. Leaves are 5 to 8cm long, alternate, sessile, simple, elliptic, slightly succulent, with entire to conspicuously dentate margins. These are crowded at the ends of branches, while lower branches are quite bare. Large flower heads are solitary or in loose corymbs, up to 8cm in diameter and borne singly or in a few groups at the end of branches on short stalks (peduncles). The ray florets are long, bright white on the upper side and light blue or violet on the lower side. The disc florets are dark blue or purple. It thrives best in full sun, in poor, sandy soil. It is widely used as an ornamental plant in pots, summer borders and balcony boxes. There are many hybrids and varieties, including upright, up to 1.5m high, and low forms.

Dicliptera squarrosa.

Dierama pulcherrimum.

Dietes bicolor.

Dietes grandiflora.

Digitalis canariensis.

Dimorphotheca sinuata.

Dimorphotheca spectabilis.

Dioon edule.

Dodonaea viscosa purpurea.

DIOON
Zamiaceae
Native to dry exposed sites in Mexico and Central America

A genus of about ten species of slow-growing dioecious cycads with stout trunks. Leaf pinnae are all the same width, and do not narrow to their base, so they have an ancient, underdeveloped appearance. These magnificent architectural plants should be placed carefully so that their form can be seen to an advantage.

Dioon edule
Virgin's Palm, Chestnut Dioon

An extremely slow-growing cycad which eventually forms a single stout trunk to 2m high. A terminal rosette of stiff, glossy, bright green pinnate leaves 1 to 2m long are upright at first, then incline with age. The many lance-shaped, sharp-tipped leaflets are a beautiful, shiny light green to bluish green, while the lower ones are almost spine-like. Cones are rarely produced in cultivation. Grow this cycad in partial shade in a humus-rich, neutral to acid soil. It is fairly drought tolerant once established, only needing moderate summer water. Needs good drainage, as it is intolerant of waterlogged soil. A staple for xeriscaping, it can be grown in the ground, where it will stay for hundreds of years, or planted in containers.

DISTICTIS *see* AMPHILOPHIUM

DODONAEA
Sapindaceae
Native to the tropics and subtropics of both hemispheres, but mostly in Australia

A genus containing about 70 species of evergreen shrubs or small trees growing to 1 to 5m tall. Leaves are alternate, simple, or pinnate. Flowers are produced in short racemes. Fruit is a capsule, often with two or three wings. Some have medicinal properties and most of them have resinous, sticky excretions.

Dodonaea viscosa 'Purpurea'
Purple Hopseed Bush

Possibly introduced from New Zealand but grown in warm regions worldwide

The most popular and arguably the most beautiful type of *Dodonaea viscosa* is the purple form. It is an evergreen shrub that makes fast growth to 3m high and 2m wide, with many upright branches. Leathery leaves are oblong to lance-shaped, 10 to 13cm long, an attractive copper-purple turning an even deeper colour in winter. Leaves are green in the type. Insignificant flowers appear in short racemes. In late summer, these are followed by showy, winged seed pods that are also purplish-red and long lasting, which attract birds. Once established, it is hardy and will tolerate drought, pollution and coastal, salty winds. It is not fussy about soil conditions but should be well drained. To keep good leaf colour, plant in full sun. It is an ideal hedging or screening plant, also useful for stabilising soil in areas in need of erosion control. Prune lightly in spring for bushy growth, do not prune into old wood. Can be clipped to form a hedge or left to grow into an informal screen.

DORONICUM
Asteraceae
Leopard's Bane

Native to Europe, southwest Asia

A genus of about 35 species of rhizomatous or tuberous perennials with alternate elliptic to ovate basal leaves with heart-shaped bases. Daisy-shaped flower heads are borne singly or in corymbs. Grow in humus-rich soil in partial or dappled shade. The flowers are also good for cutting.

Doronicum columnae syn. *Doronicum orientale*
Native to southeastern Europe, Turkey, Lebanon

A slow-spreading, clump-forming perennial herb that grows to approximately 60cm tall. Basal foliage is bright green with cordate leaves that have scalloped margins. Daisy-like, yellow flower heads up to 5cm across on long, slender, branched stems, bloom in early spring and attract nectar-eating insects. Its native habitats include moist, rocky outcrops and woodland areas. It likes both shade and sun and is easily grown in fertile soil. Summer drought tolerant but prefers some moisture. There are many named varieties.

DOROTHEANTHUS *see* CLERETUM

DRACAENA
Asparagaceae (formerly Agavaceae)
Native to tropical and subtropical regions of Africa, Asia and the Americas

A genus of around 120 species of stiff, erect, evergreen clumping perennials, trees and shrubs that are known for their long, strap-like leaves usually growing in a rosette pattern. Leaves can be green, variegated, or striped with various shades of green, yellow, white and red. Some species produce fragrant flowers or fruits, but they are not as showy as the foliage.

Dracaena draco
Canary Islands Dragon Tree, Drago

Native to the Canary Islands, Cape Verde, Madeira, western Morocco

An evergreen, long-lived tree up to 15m or more high with a trunk 5m or more in circumference. It starts with a smooth bark that develops to a rougher texture as it ages. When young, it has a single stem. At about ten to fifteen years of age, the main stem stops growing. Soon a crown of terminal buds appears, and the plant branches. Each branch later branches again, so that a mature plant has an umbrella-like habit. Clusters of mid-green, sword-shaped leaves are up to 60cm long. Greenish-white, lily-like perfumed flowers are borne in erect terminal panicles up to 1m long in summer, followed by coral berries. Dark resin that seeps from the trunk looks similar to blood. Grow in any dry rocky soil in full sun. Tolerant of summer drought.

Dracaena marginata
Madagascar Dragon Tree
Native to Madagascar

A tree with a slender, branching trunk up to 4m high and spreading 1 to 2m wide. Each branch is topped with a dense rosette of sword-shaped leaves, up to 45cm long and 3cm wide, rigidly spreading horizontally. They are a shiny, deep olive-green with narrow red margins. Trees do not flower in cultivation until they reach maturity. Terminal panicles 40 to 50cm across are produced in summer, containing many small white flowers. The flexible stems have a tendency to branch and twist, giving an artistic appearance. Grow where its beautiful form can be seen, preferably in full sun. It is easily grown, slow and durable, requiring little summer water. If the plant becomes too tall, cut the top off and root it, the old stem will shoot out again. The variety 'Tricolor' has leaves with creamy white stripes with red edges. 'Magenta' has attractive maroon leaves.

Dracaena trifasciata syn. *Sansevieria trifasciata*
Mother-In-Law's Tongue, Bowstring Hemp
Native to tropical West Africa from Nigeria east to the Congo

The name was changed in 2017.

An erect, evergreen perennial that forms a clump of leaves up to 1m high. Leathery, linear, lance-shaped, flat to concave leaves are marked with light-green to grey-white cross bands. Fleshy rhizomes bear an average of six to eight leaves. Tiny greenish-white flowers that are fragrant at night are produced in loose racemes 30 to 75cm high at any time of the year. Ideal for pots or containers on the patio or for planting in a courtyard garden. It makes a novel edging to a pathway. Grows best when given some shelter from the hot midday sun. A tough plant that is tolerant of neglect as it is drought tolerant, only needing deep, infrequent watering, but good winter drainage is essential. 'Laurentii' is the leading commercial variety, because of its elegant leaves with yellow bands on either side of the deep-green banded centre.

DRACUNCULUS
Araceae
Native to the Mediterranean, Madeira and the Canary Islands

A genus of two species of rounded tuberous perennials. They are characterised by a large purple spathe and spadix, often produced before the dark-green leaves with radiating lobes, each deeply cleft or divided often with white mottling. The open spathe is usually accompanied by a foul smell, attracting carrion and blowflies.

Dracunculus vulgaris
Dragon Lily, Dragon Arum, Black Arum, Vampire Lily
Native to central and eastern Mediterranean

A tuberous, herbaceous perennial with large palmate lobed leaves that have occasional cream flecks along the veins. Leaves up to 30cm long appear in clusters on a purple pseudo-stem. In late spring to early summer, a large flower spike called a spadix appears, surrounded by a spathe up to 50cm tall and 20cm wide. The spadix comprises small flowers with male flowers on top and female flowers below. This can be as tall or taller than the spathe. Flies and beetles are drawn to the flower's foul odour to assist with pollination. It is hard for insects to escape the spadix until pollination is done, usually within a day, after which the flower withers. Berries are then formed that mature to red-orange and attract birds. Drought tolerant but prefers full sun to partial shade in fertile, moist loam. It spreads by seeding and bulb offsets that can be divided. Use this plant as an accent or specimen but be aware of the foul odour from its flower and plant away from windows, doors or seating areas. The genus name means 'small dragon', referring to the shape of the leaves resembling dragons' feet.

DRIMIA syn. URGINEA
Asparagaceae
Native to tropical Africa, the Mediterranean region

A genus of about twenty species of bulbous perennials found on dry rocky hillsides with white to yellowish green or brown short-lived flowers.

Drimia maritima syn. *Urginea maritima*
Sea Onion, Squills
Native to the Mediterranean region

A bulbous perennial that forms a huge, reddish-brown bulb 10 to 15cm thick, partially above ground. In late autumn, strap-shaped leaves appear, remaining until spring, then it is summer dormant. Leaves are shiny, rather fleshy, and 30 to 40cm long. Before the leaves appear, it sends up a stout erect stem 30 to 90cm long, at the top of which is a spike up to 60cm long containing many tiny star-shaped white flowers that open in succession. Grow in full sun in sandy or stony, free-draining soil with the neck of the bulb exposed. Ideal for autumn colour in hot, dry gardens as the bulb needs no summer water. A clump will make a striking effect. Ideal for coastal gardens, as it withstands salt-laden sea breezes.

DROSANTHEMUM
Aizoaceae
Native to southern Africa

A genus of about 95 species of succulent shrubs, mostly low to creeping and wide spreading. Fleshy leaves are adapted for storing water, which is crucial for survival in arid environments. Many species are appreciated for their colourful flowers, in shades of pink, purple, orange and

ronicum columnae.

Dracaena draco.

Dracaena marginata.

acaena trifasciata.

Dracunculus vulgaris.

Drimia maritima.

osanthemum floribundum.

Dudleya pulverulenta.

yellow. These often open during the day and close at night, a trait common in many plants in the Aizoaceae family. In cultivation, the species are valued for their drought tolerance, making them suitable for xeriscaping and rock gardens in regions with dry climates, requiring well-draining soil and plenty of sunlight to thrive. Like many succulents, they are relatively low-maintenance plants, making them popular choices for gardeners looking to add some unusual flair to their landscapes.

Drosanthemum floribundum

Dew Flower, Ice Plant

Native to South Africa

An evergreen succulent that creates a dazzling carpet less than 15cm high but spreading 1 to 2m or more with stems rooting along the length. Leaves are tiny, fleshy, cylindrical and dark green. In late spring to early summer, it is covered in a profusion of 2cm-wide pink or mauve flowers that are attractive to bees. Flowers usually open about midday and close in the evenings. On dull, cool days they remain closed. Ideal for covering a dry slope with a dense mat that blocks the growth of weeds and stabilises soil. It looks great tumbling over rocks or hanging down over a wall from a raised bed. Grows best in full sun with little or no summer water once established. Heat, drought and salt tolerant. It is ideal for containers and rock gardens.

Drosanthemum hispidum

Miniature Pig Face, Hairy Dewflower

Native to South Africa

An evergreen succulent perennial up to 60cm high, spreading to about 1m wide with small, finger-shaped, light-green, succulent leaves that create a dense mat. Leaves 2cm long are cylindrical, incurved, light green to reddish and covered in glistening dots. Rough hairs cover the rooting branches. In summer, it produces a profusion of solitary, magenta, daisy-like, shiny petalled flowers up to 3cm wide with contrasting yellow centres. Well-drained soils are important, as they dislike sitting in overly moist soils at all. These can handle poor, sandy and rocky soils, but respond well to soils that have added organic matter. These hardy plants will grow in difficult locations, like sand dunes, but also grow well in domestic gardens as ground covers, or in hanging baskets where they will spill over the edge to great effect. An excellent addition to gravel gardens and rockeries and for an extremely low-maintenance or desert garden. Choose a sunny location – the more sun, the more they will bloom.

The two species listed are often confused.

DUDLEYA

Crassulaceae

Native to the western coast of North America, California, Baja California and parts of Arizona

This genus comprises about 40 species of succulents, characterised by their rosette-forming growth habit. Usually fleshy, wax-covered leaves range from green to various shades of blue, grey or red. Species are popular among succulent enthusiasts for their unusual appearance and ability to thrive in arid environments.

Dudleya pulverulenta

Chalk Lettuce, Chalk Dudleya, Chalk Liveforever

Native to California

A rosette-forming, succulent species, covered in a distinctive chalky and mealy wax, known as a farina, or more technically, epicuticular wax. It is one of the largest species. As it grows older, stems gradually become decumbent and are densely clothed with old, dried leaves. At the top of this stem is a solitary rosette, as the stem does not form axillary branches. The rosette 7 to 60cm wide is composed of 40 to 60 wide, flat, fleshy, chalky-white leaves, which age to a pinkish papery texture. Leaves are 8 to 25cm long by 3 to 10cm wide. In late spring to early summer, the rosette sends up arching flower spikes up to 1.5m long. All parts of the inflorescence are covered in a chalky wax. Clusters of long, red flowers hang downward, an adaptation to hummingbird pollinators. After flowering, fruits are turned erect by a sharp turn of the branchlet, known as a pedicel, connecting the flower to the inflorescence. Drought tolerant, easily grown in sandy, dry to medium moisture, well-drained soil in full sun. In summer, the rosettes close up to protect themselves from sunburn and dessication. Do not water them, even if they appear crisp. They are dormant and unused to summer rain.

DUVALIA

Apocynaceae

Native to southern Africa

The genus comprises about nineteen species of prostrate or semi-erect, mainly leafless, clump-forming, perennial succulents. They have toothed stems, each with four to six blunt, watery ribs separated by transverse furrows. Star-shaped, stalked flowers have five fleshy lobes, recurved at the tips. Solitary or in clusters, they are found at the base of the stems. Frost tender.

Duvalia corderoyi

Carrion Plant, Starfish Flower

Native to southwestern and central regions of southern Africa

A ground cover, clump-forming perennial succulent to 5cm high and an indefinite spread, with short, somewhat rounded six-ribbed, leafless, green or purple stems. Despite being small, the plant readily clumps. In brighter light, they develop purple highlights but remain green in shade. Soft purple hairs adorn the two to four dull olive-green, star-shaped, unscented flowers, 5cm across. Flowers are abundant during late summer and autumn, but may bloom at any time. They can take some direct sun, but prefer partial shade, especially on scorching afternoons. Grow in well-drained soil and keep dry in the winter, unless you have good growing conditions then.

DYCKIA

Bromeliaceae

Native to the rocky terrain of Brazil, South America

A genus of over 100 species of rosette-forming, stemless, evergreen succulent terrestrial perennials, usually found in rocky areas. Some species are even saxicolous (meaning they live attached to rocks), though most grow in the ground. They have linear to lance-shaped or short triangular, spiny margined, stiff, often grey, scaly leaves. Long stalks with multiple red, yellow, or orange flowers appear in spring. Many species develop a trunk-like stem while some form mats. These can endure warm areas with abundant rain for six months and arid conditions for the remaining period. Maintaining the perfect moisture balance for Dyckia care can be challenging. They are used to rather poor soil when they grow in the ground and should be planted in a gritty mixture. They need full sun to thrive.

Dyckia fosteriana

Native to central South America, primarily eastern Brazil

A spiny, stemless bromeliad resembling prickly succulents. It has shiny, stiffly-arching, dull-grey leaves up to 22cm long and 1 to 2cm wide, viciously armed with tiny, hooked spines along the edges, growing in a tight rosette. In bright sunlight, the colour changes to rich metallic bronze. In spring, bell-shaped, orange-yellow flowers 2cm long appear on slender flower stalks 22 to 30cm long. These flower stalks rise from a side of a mature rosette, not from the centre, as on other bromeliads. This means that the plant does not die after flowering like most other bromeliads. It forms new rosettes rapidly, building up into a relatively large cluster, spreading a little over 30cm.

E

ECCREMOCARPUS

Bignoniaceae

Native to Peru and Chile

A small genus of about five species of evergreen or nearly evergreen perennials, climbing by coiling leaf tendrils. Species are known for their vigorous growth habits and showy, tubular flowers that attract hummingbirds and other pollinators. They typically have pinnate leaves and produce clusters of colourful flowers in shades of orange, red or yellow. The vines are often grown along fences, trellises or pergolas, where they can add a splash of colour and attract wildlife.

Eccremocarpus scaber

Chilean Glory Flower, Trumpet Vine

Native to Chile

A semi-woody, fast-growing climber up to 4m high. Leaves have two lobes 3cm wide with tendrils at the end of the main stalk. From late spring to autumn, flowers appear in terminal clusters. Flowers are narrowly tubular, contracted at the mouth and 2 to 3cm long. Several colour variations are now widely available, with the old scarlet red being replaced by pale pink, lavender, mauve, almost orange, yellow and several shades in between. All have a yellow mouth to the flower. Somewhat drought tolerant, but flower better with some summer water. They thrive in partial shade or full sun in colder regions. Easily raised from seed, indeed, they readily seed themselves in the garden in favourable conditions. Grow as short-lived perennials to clothe an arch, wall, or climb into a tree. A problem is their tendency to form untidy masses of stems and foliage, so it is better to raise new plants from seed each year.

ECHEVERIA

Crassulaceae

Native to dry desert areas from Texas to Argentina, but especially in Mexico

A genus of over 150 species of evergreen or deciduous succulents and sub-shrubs, usually around 10 to 20cm tall and 10 to 30cm wide. Plants are prized for their rosettes of fleshy, succulent, often brightly-coloured leaves, usually in rosettes often covered in powdery wax or tiny hairs. Flowers on short stalks (cymes) arise from compact rosettes of leaves, usually during summer. These are bell-shaped or star-shaped, orange, red, pink, yellow or white, and usually vibrant and attractive. Plants are drought tolerant, because of their succulent leaves that store water. Perfect for xeriscaping or for areas with water restrictions.

Echeveria agavoides 'Red Tip'

Native to rocky areas of Mexico

This stunning succulent features sharply-pointed, fleshy, succulent leaves in a distinctive rosette with vivid red margins. Enchanting bell-shaped coral flowers with yellow, star-shaped tips atop coral stalks grace it in summer. Thrives with well-drained soil and optimal drainage. Prolonged sun exposure, as well as cooler weather, will intensify the colour.

Echeveria elegans

Native to Mexico

A stemless succulent that forms clusters of tight greyish-white rosettes each 5 to 10cm across, mounding up with time. Silvery-blue, waxy, spoon-shaped leaves are 3 to 6cm long and 2 to 3cm wide, sometimes with a red or white translucent margin. Arching flower stems are a delicate pink with pink and yellow flowers 1cm long. These are striking against the pale grey-white rosettes. A good container plant. When grown in the ground, they need excellent drainage and must not become waterlogged. They rarely send roots deep into the soil, growing instead on their own leaf-litter. Depending upon location, they may prefer some shade from hot and dry sun, which can scorch the pearly-white leaves. Easily propagated by separating any rosette from its clump.

Echeveria minima

Native to northeast Mexico

This plant typically forms small, tight rosettes with densely-packed, thick, fleshy leaves. The rosettes are often flat or slightly cup-shaped and range from 3 to 8cm in diameter. Drought tolerant, it prefers well-draining soil. Thriving in bright sunlight it can tolerate some direct sunlight, especially in cooler climates. In warmer regions, it may benefit from partial shade during the hottest part of the day. When mature and under the right conditions, it produces slender, upright flower stalks with bell-shaped flowers. This succulent's small size makes it a perfect choice for container gardens, rock gardens, or as a delightful accent in miniature landscapes.

Echeveria 'Perle von Nurnberg'

Garden origin

A beautiful succulent that forms a symmetrical rosette around 20cm of curved, thick, fleshy leaves that change colour from gorgeous shades of pink, red and purple through the cooler months, to shades of greyish pink during summer. Leaves are rounded, tapering to a point, and covered with a powdery bloom. Coral-pink flowers with yellow interiors appear on reddish inflorescences up to 30cm long in summer. A popular hybrid, it is one of the most beautiful Echeverias. An ideal plant for containers, borders and rockeries, preferring a mostly sunny position in well-draining soil with protection from frost.

ECHINACEA
Asteraceae
Coneflowers

Native to central and North America

A genus of about ten species of bold stiff perennials, usually with thick, black rootstock and short rhizomes. Leaves are normally hairy with a rough texture. Basal lance-shaped leaves and lower stem leaves have petioles, while as leaves progress up the stem, the petioles often decrease. Solitary, daisy-like, purple, red or pink flowerheads with pointed stiff scales on the undersides and prominent cone-shaped brownish yellow to orange central discs appear during summer.

Echinacea purpurea
Coneflower

Native to United States

An erect perennial to 1.5m high and 45cm wide with smooth, sometimes rough-hairy, red-tinted green stems. Basal leaves are rough hairy, toothed 15cm long. Flowers appear during summer to autumn, raised on long single stems. Flowers are daisy-like, with raised cone-like centres that vary from green to yellow and brown. Depending on variety, the flowers are usually purple, pink or white, but hybrids range from fiery red to sunset pinks, pale yellows and oranges. Easy to grow in full sun to partial shade in well-drained, humus-rich soil. Drought and frost tolerant once established. Ideal for borders, rock gardens, garden beds, pots and containers, and in large groups. They attract birds and butterflies to the garden. They can be used fresh or dried for flower arranging.

ECHINOPS
Asteraceae
Globe Thistles

Native to Europe, east to central Asia, and south to the mountains of tropical Africa

A genus of about 120 species of perennials, biennials and annuals found on hot gravelly slopes and dry grasslands. They have simple, entire or pinnate spiny foliage, usually greyish white or woolly. They bear spherical white, grey or blue terminal flower-heads with bristly bracts. Best grown in poor well-drained soil in full sun. Drought tolerant once established.

Echinops ritro
Southern Globe Thistle

Native to southern and eastern Europe, central Asia

A compact, bushy herbaceous perennial thistle, growing to 60cm tall. Grey-green, deeply-cut, prickly leaves are covered in down beneath. Abundant, dark violet-blue flowers appear at the end of gracefully curving, branched silvery stems. These bear perfect spherical globes of steel-blue flowers 2.5cm to 4.5cm in diameter from midsummer well into autumn. These can be used fresh as a cut flower or dried to use later. A spectacular garden plant and cut flower, adding both texture and colour. This hardy beauty copes in a wide range of soils, including sandy, gravel and poorer soils, but it requires good drainage, and will become miserable in waterlogged, heavy soil. It relishes full sun and is undaunted by heat but also frost hardy.

ECHINOPSIS
Cactaceae
Hedgehog Cacti

Native to South America

As of October 2023, there are about twenty accepted species, ranging from large, tree-like types to small globose cacti. They are remarkable for the great size, length of tube and beauty of their flowers, borne upon small and dumpy stems. These flowers are all similar in structure – funnel shaped, with hairy or woolly-scaled floral tubes, which give rise to hairy, globular fruit filled with a soft, mushy pulp. Flowers seldom last more than a single day and may be diurnal or nocturnal, depending on the species. These species hybridise easily and have resulted in a tremendous number of hybrids. There are certainly enough hybrids to keep even ardent hobbyists busy.

valia corderoyi.

Dyckia fosteriana.

Eccremocarpus scaber.

heveria agavoides 'Red
o'.

Echeveria 'Perle Von Nurnberg'.

Echinacea purpurea.

hinops ritro.

Echinopsis oxygona.

Echium candicans.

Echinopsis aurea
Golden Easter Lily Cactus
Native to northern Argentina

A small, globose cactus with fierce spines. The dark-green stem is lined with fourteen to fifteen prominent sharp-edged ribs separated by deep grooves. It is covered in fine, white radial spines and has long, stout central spines. It usually grows solitarily or sometimes with many basal and lateral offshoots. Stems can reach up to 15cm high and 10cm in diameter. Funnel-shaped flowers are usually lemon yellow and bright yellow inside but can also be white, pink, or red. These are 10cm long and appear in late spring and occasionally in summer. These open during the day and close at night. Easily grown in extremely well-drained, sandy or gritty soil. It grows well in the sun or partial shade. Keep lightly moist in summer but allow to dry out in winter.

Echinopsis oxygona
Easter Lily Cactus
Native to South America

A small, spherical, mat-forming cactus with densely-clustered, globose or cylindrical, ribbed stems reaching around 30cm high featuring short, black spines. From late spring to summer, it produces large, sweetly scented, funnel-shaped, white or lavender flowers around 20cm across. Flowers are its chief attraction, spectacular as they stand aloft on elongated tubes from the rest of the cactus. Each flower lasts for less than 24 hours, opening in late afternoon and fading by the middle of the next day. Easily grown in extremely well-drained, sandy or gritty soil. It grows well in the sun or partial shade. Frost and heat tolerant. Keep lightly moist in summer but allow to dry out in winter.

ECHIUM
Boraginaceae
Native to Europe, especially the Mediterranean region, South Africa

A genus of about 70 species of annuals, biennials or shrubby perennials from stony hillsides, cliffs, open woodlands and grassy steppes in Europe. They are grown for their often one-sided panicles or their spiky clusters of flowers, which range from blue and purple to pink and white. Often cultivated in gardens because of their striking appearance and ability to attract pollinators like bees and butterflies. Grow in moderately fertile, well-drained soil in full sun. Tolerant of summer drought.

Echium candicans
Pride of Madeira
Native to Madeira and Canary Islands

A shrubby perennial with many branches to 2m high, spreading to 2m wide. The 15 to 20cm-long, rough, lance-shaped, prominently veined leaves, which form rosettes around the stem, have a coating of silver hairs. Towering above the foliage, large terminal spikes to 30cm long of many 1cm blue narrowly funnel-shaped flowers appear during spring and summer. Drought and frost tolerant. Echium lasts only 3 to 5 years before looking ragged, but usually leaves a few self-sown seedlings behind. To maintain shape, remove dead flower heads and prune lightly. Grow in full sun. When established, it withstands drought but grows and flowers better with some summer water. Makes a bold plant against a wall or on a dry slope amongst rocks.

Echium pininana
Tree Echium, Pine Echium, Giant Viper's-Bugloss, Tower of Jewels
Native to the island of La Palma in the Canary Islands

A biennial or short-lived perennial with a dense rosette of leaves to 90cm wide. They are lance-shaped, 8cm long, and deep green with rough silver hairs. During its first year in the garden, it makes a large bristly leaved basal rosette, some 90cm across. After two or three years, a massive flower spike appears up to 5m high in spring to early summer. It contains many mauve or blue tubular flowers 1 to 2cm wide and small leaves. It dies after flowering, but usually leaves a few self-sown seedlings behind. Grow in full sun in well-drained soil. When established, it withstands drought but grows and flowers better with some summer water. Frost tolerant once established. Makes a bold and dramatic plant that is rarely seen.

Echium wildpretii
Native to the Canary Islands

A soft, much-branched biennial up to 2m high spreading to about 60cm wide. The dense, silver tufts of hairy, lance-shaped leaves are up to 20cm long. It is a biennial, producing a dense rosette of leaves during the first year, flowers from late spring to early summer in the second year, and then dies. The many tiny, soft, brick-red, funnel-shaped flowers are borne on an erect inflorescence, 1 to 3m high. Plenty of seed is produced, and it self-seeds readily. Grow in a sandy, well-drained soil in full sun in a sheltered position. It tends to die suddenly for no apparent reason.

ELAEAGNUS
Elaeagnaceae
Oleasters, Silverberries
Native to Asia, southern Europe and North America

A genus of about 45 species of evergreen or deciduous shrubs or small trees. Most have silvery scales or dots on the leaves, particularly on the undersides. Plants are cultivated for their attractive, often coloured or variegated leaves. Many produce deliciously-scented flowers followed by small edible fruit. They are primarily seashore plants as they are excellent wind resisters. Valuable for hedges and shelter belts in exposed areas.

Elaeagnus angustifolia
Oleaster, Russian Olive
Native to southern Europe, central Asia and China

A small, vigorous, fast-growing, usually thorny, deciduous tree or large shrub up to 6m high and wide with spiny silver branches. Branches and trunk are covered with exfoliating brown bark that is attractive in winter. Leaves are silver grey, lance-shaped up to 10cm long. Small fragrant greenish-yellow flowers to 1cm long appear in early summer. These are followed by berry-like fruit that are silver-yellow, resembling small olives. The fruits are edible and sweet, though with a dryish, mealy texture. Easily grown in average, dry to medium, well-drained soil in full sun to part shade. Best in light, sandy loam in full sun. Drought tolerant once established. Can be clipped to make a medium-sized hedge.

Elaeagnus × ebbingei
Silverberry
Garden origin

This hybrid makes a large, hardy, fast-growing, dense, evergreen shrub up to 3m high with a wide spread. Dark green leathery leaves 5 to 10cm long are silver on both sides when young. Small fragrant white flowers are produced in autumn and followed by small red fruit. Thrives in sunny, partial shaded locations in well-drained soil. Fast growing, it is perfect for group planting to form a hedge, even near the sea. It requires occasional pruning, including a light prune in autumn, to encourage and shape the shrub, but more to encourage a healthy growth.

The variegated form 'Gilt Edge' has leaves margined yellow, drought resistant, perfect for growing in well-drained soils as a hedge or screen or trained as a climber against a wall.

'Limelight' foliage has a silvery colour when young and matures into irregular slashes of dark green, lime green and gold. It tolerates all soil types, even overly dry, although it prefers well-drained soil. Once established, it is drought tolerant. It will grow well in both full sun and partial shade. The plant is also resistant to salt-laden winds and does beautifully planted near the coast as a windbreak.

Elaeagnus macrophylla
Native to Korea and Japan

An evergreen spreading shrub up to 4m high and 8m wide with branches covered in white scales when young. Broad leaves are 10cm long, silvery on both surfaces, becoming dark glossy green above with age. Small fragrant flowers appear in autumn. As young leaves are especially pleasing, the shrub can be pruned to encourage them. This hardy shrub tolerates dry, windy areas in sun and part-shade. Drought tolerant, it prefers free-draining soil but tolerates most soil types. On shallow chalky soils, it may become chlorotic.

ENCEPHALARTOS
Zamiaceae
Native to central and southern Africa

A genus of about 30 species of slow-growing, dioecious cycads, which are sometimes tuberous or have stout trunks. They come from open dry forests and scrub and rocky slopes. Most species are clustering, many palm-like. These magnificent architectural plants should be placed carefully so that their form can be seen to advantage. All are drought tolerant once established and withstand only light frost.

Encephalartos altensteinii
Prickly Cycad, Bread Tree
Native to South Africa

A variable, suckering, palm-like cycad with trunks either branched or unbranched eventually to 5m high with an equal spread. The straight to arching, pinnate, dark-green leaves are 2 to 3.5m long. These are composed of many narrowly oblong stiff leaflets about 15cm long, 2 to 3cm wide and sparsely toothed at the margins. Leaflets arise at an angle, giving a trough to the leaf. In summer, mature plants produce yellowish brown cones, mostly in clusters of two to five. The male is cylindrical and 30 to 40cm long, while the female is broadly oval to 45cm long. Grow in partial or light shade in well-drained, humus-rich, neutral to slightly acid soil. Drought tolerant but grows better with some summer water. A wonderful architectural plant for a sheltered, shady situation.

Encephalartos horridus
Ferocious Blue Cycad
Native to Eastern Cape South Africa

A suckering, showy cycad, which slowly forms a stem underground or to only 30cm high. The trunk is crowded with a cluster of stiff prickly pinnate leaves, which are a glaucous green, 60 to 90cm long. Leaves are upright at first, then arch with age comprising many lance-shaped leaflets 10cm long, curled and deeply cut along the lower margin into one to three spine-tipped lobes. They open a beautiful silvery blue to almost purple and slowly change to an icy blue or bluish green. In summer, mature plants produce reddish-brown cones. The male is cylindrical and 10cm long, while the female is broadly oval to 35cm long. For the best colour, grow it in full sun in average garden soil, but it needs excellent drainage with little or no summer water. A spectacular and dramatic plant for a sunny border.

Encephalartos lehmannii
Blue Leaved Cycad, Karoo Cycad
Native to South Africa

This low-growing, small to medium cycad with an erect grey trunk up to 2m tall and 40cm across forms clumps of up to ten stems, with suckers produced from the base. Old leaf bases form ring patterns on the stem, the surface of which is papery and dry. Its trunk is crowned with a rosette of elegant stiff and erect pinnate leaves that are recurved at their ends. It has beautiful blue leaves 1m or more long, with many glaucous blue-green leaflets to 20cm long with a spiny tip. Leaflets arise at an angle, giving a V shape to the leaf. Solitary bluish-green cones are produced in summer, the male up to 35cm long, the fatter female cone to 40cm long. This cycad has been described as the hardiest, most drought resistant of the South African species, easy to cultivate. It needs neutral to alkaline soil with excellent drainage. If grown in shade or with too much moisture, the leaves will lose their metallic blue colour and will turn green, so grow it in full sun. It is suited to temperate regions, including those with a semi-arid climate. Do not over-water.

Echium wildpretii.

Elaeagnus angustifolia.

Elaeagnus × ebbingei.

Encephalartos altensteinii.

Epacris longiflora.

Epilobium canum.

Eremophila nivea.

Eremurus isabellinus 'Cleopatra'.

EPACRIS
Ericaceae

Native to eastern and southern Australia, New Caledonia and New Zealand

A genus of about 40 species of evergreen heather-like shrubs with simple leaves found on open slopes and scrublands. They are cultivated for their often showy, tubular, cylindrical to bell-shaped, five-lobed flowers, which are freely produced for many months. These are arranged singly in leaf axils near the ends of the branches, sometimes extending along the branches.

Epacris impressa
Pink or Common Heath

Native to eastern and southeastern Australia

Erect to spreading, often slender, evergreen shrub 1 to 1.5m tall with narrowly ovate, deep-green, rigid, alternate leaves 1.5cm long tapering to a point at the end. Pendant cylindrical red, pink or white flowers 2cm long are borne on slender erect terminal racemes. Flowers can form a stem-packing cluster or can be sparse and one-sided. Flowering lasts from late autumn to late spring, with a peak in winter. This long flowering time is the reason this plant is often sought after in gardens. Grow in well-drained soil in partial shade, or full sun provided the roots are shaded and kept moist. It prefers a slightly acidic soil. It makes an excellent container plant. A bushier habit can be encouraged by pruning. Well-established plants tolerate drought for a short while.

Epacris longiflora
Fuchsia Heath, Cigarette Flower

Native to southern west Australia

This erect or spreading shrub grows to a height of 0.5 to 2m and has stems with prominent short, broad leaf scars and tiny egg-shaped, pointed leaves. Flowers are red with a white tip, sometimes all red, tubular, which gives the plant its name *longiflora*, and are usually present throughout the year. These attract nectar-eating birds. There are distinct colour forms, from red or pink tipped with white to all white varieties. It naturally grows in well-drained acid sandy soils with dappled shade, with a regular supply of moisture. Hard to grow if moist sandy soils are not present. They dislike root disturbance. Can be grown in containers if you do not have a well-drained spot. Good for protected coastal gardens and can tolerate only light frost once established. Trimming the tips after blooming encourages a more compact habit, as it grows with an open structure.

EPILOBIUM
Onagraceae

Willowherbs

Worldwide distribution in the subtropics and tropics

A genus of about 197 species of mostly herbaceous annuals or perennials, while a few are subshrubs. They are typically quick to carpet large swathes of the ground and may become the dominant species of local ecosystems. Annual varieties are more common in cool regions but occur occasionally as a cool season weed in warmer areas. The plants are sometimes cultivated but must be carefully confined. Soil preference depends on the species as some invade wet areas and some prefer dry sites.

Epilobium canum syn. *Zauschneria californica*
California Fuchsia

Native to southwest United States

A woody-based, semi-evergreen perennial with upright or arching slender stems 30 to 60cm high, spreading 60 to 90cm wide. The spreading underground stems may become invasive. Lance-shaped leaves are grey-green and hairy up to 4cm long and velvety to the touch. Terminal clusters of beautiful, rich scarlet, trumpet-shaped flowers with protruding stamens 4 to 5cm long make an attractive show from summer to autumn. It thrives in hot, dry summers. Grow in full sun in well-draining sandy or gritty soil. Drought tolerant once established. The plant can be killed by waterlogged winter soil. Looks good when grown at the front of a border, scrambling over banks or in a rock garden. Cut back in spring to renovate. 'Carmen's Grey' is a grey-leafed form.

EREMOPHILA
Scrophulariaceae

Emu Bush

Native in widespread arid areas of Australia

A genus of over 270 species of evergreen perennials, shrubs and trees. Leaves are simple, entire, linear to rounded, alternate or opposite. They are grown for their tubular-based two-lipped flowers, produced singly from the uppermost leaf axils. The beauty and abundance of their flowers, variety of foliage and habit, and extended flowering period make them attractive garden plants. They are mostly drought resistant, and many are also tolerant of frost, allowing them to be grown in most situations. In nature, most Eremophila grow where rainfall is infrequent and are adapted to dealing with long dry spells, even droughts lasting years. They are therefore suited to low-maintenance gardens, those where water supply is limited or where gardeners want a garden that does not require large volumes of water. In fact, excessive water can kill many species.

Eremophila nivea
Silky Eremophila

Native to Western Australia

An erect shrub, which grows to 1.5 to 2m. Branches, leaves and sepals are covered with a layer of soft white to greyish matted hairs, giving the plant a silvery-greyish appearance. Leaves are alternate, linear, mostly 8 to 18mm long, with a covering of woolly hairs. Flowering begins in late winter with masses of vibrant clusters of showy lilac bell-shaped blooms, with spot flowering throughout the year. Flowers are borne singly or in pairs in leaf axils on short woolly stalks.

This eye-catching shrub is a visual feast, whether or not in flower. Will thrive in full sun in heavier, well-drained soil. This sun-loving plant is quite hardy and will tolerate mild frosts and drought once established. Suitable for coastal gardens. For best results, prune after flowering to maintain compact growth.

EREMURUS
Scrophulariaceae

Native to southern Europe, temperate Asia, Turkey

A genus comprising 40 to 50 species of clump-forming, fleshy-rooted perennials found in dry grasslands and semi-desert. Grey-green, straplike leaves grow in a tuft from the succulent root crown. Eremurus is known for its thick, finger-like roots, which grow from a central growth point. Leafless flowering stems, usually one per crown, each produce a dense raceme of star-shaped flowers usually pink, white, yellow or red-orange. The blooming spike is notably tall and relatively narrow, rising from 1 to 3m above the foliage.

Eremurus × isabellinus 'Cleopatra'
Foxtail Lilies

Garden origin, species native to drier regions of western and central Asia

A robust tufted perennial that bears clumps of sword-like, blue-green leaves 15 to 30cm long. Produces a huge tapering spire of flowers, which open gradually from the base upwards. The spire comprising hundreds of flowers, in a glowing burnt orange, can reach 3m high, creating a stunning effect. It is extremely attractive to bees and other insects. One of the most colourful tall flowers available, foxtail lilies are also excellent in cut-flower displays. The lilies need to be planted in fertile but well-drained soil with the crown not far below soil level in a sunny, sheltered site in well-drained soil. Ideally, the tubers bake in the sun, as shade can decrease the number of flowering spikes produced. They start to grow in late winter and spring, gathering their strength before producing their towering flower spikes in summer. After flowering, the plant dies back and lies dormant: a survival strategy to cope with the scorching temperatures and drought in its native homeland. They can bloom for ten to fifteen years without dividing.

ERICA
Ericaceae
Heather

Native to Europe, west and central Asia, mostly South Africa

A large genus of over 500 species of usually evergreen dwarf shrubs to small trees. Most of the species are small shrubs from 20 to 150cm high, though some are taller, some even up to 7m. All are evergreen, with minute, needle-like leaves 2 to 15mm long. Flowers are sometimes axillary, sometimes borne in terminal umbels or spikes, and usually outward or downward facing. The seeds are tiny, and in some species may survive in the soil for decades. Most species need acid soil.

Erica arborea
Tree Heath, Tree Heather

Native to southern Europe, north Africa

A dense, upright, feathery-looking shrub 2 to 3m high but which can occasionally grow to 5m high spreading to 3m wide, with one or many closely upright trunks. Upper branches are soft and covered with whitish woolly hairs. It has tiny narrow 3 to 4mm long dark green leaves in whorls of three to four. Tiny fragrant bell-shaped white flowers 3mm long are produced profusely in large terminal pyramidal heads in early spring. When in full flower, it looks quite stunning. Grow in full sun or partial shade. It needs acid soil with excellent drainage and lots of humus to grow well. A sandy soil with added humus is ideal, while heavy clay soil can be fatal. Several cultivars and hybrids have been developed for garden use. Tolerant of summer drought.

Erica australis
Spanish Heath

Native to Spain, Portugal

A slender upright open shrub to 2m high and 1m wide. The tiny, linear, dark-green leaves are in whorls of four. Striking reddish-pink to purple bell-shaped flowers 1cm long are borne in terminal clusters from spring to early summer. One of the showiest of the tree heathers. Culture is the same as *E. arborea*. 'Mr. Robert' is a beautiful white form.

Erica lusitanica
Portuguese Heath

Native to Portugal

An upright feathery shrub to 3m high spreading to only 1m wide. Tiny linear leaves are light green. Pinkish white, tubular to bell-shaped slightly fragrant flowers 5mm long, are borne in branched racemes in early spring. When in flower, it makes a spectacular sight. Culture is the same as *E. arborea*.

ERIOBOTRYA
Rosaceae

Native to the Himalayas and east Asia

A genus of about 30 species of mostly evergreen shrubs and small trees. They all have large leathery leaves with prominent veining. One species grown for its edible fruit.

Eriobotrya japonica
Loquat

Native to central China and southern Japan

A vigorous tree or shrub that grows to 5 to 10m tall but in cultivation is often smaller, about 3 to 4m, with a rounded crown, short trunk and woolly new twigs. Leaves are dark green, tough and leathery, 10 to 25cm long, with a serrated margin. Underneath they are densely velvety-hairy with thick yellow-brown pubescence, often rust coloured. Flowers are produced in autumn or winter in pyramidal terminal clusters up to 15cm high. Each small white single flower is sweetly scented. These are followed by clusters of orange to yellow small round fruit 2 to 4cm across, with a soft downy skin, in early spring. These are edible with a pleasant aromatic, slightly sweet taste and can be eaten fresh or used in pies or jam but contain several often large seeds. The shrubs are often grown from seeds, but to obtain good fruit buy a named grafted variety. Needs little or no summer water once established. Makes a good ornamental specimen tree on a patio where it casts good summer shade. Easily grown in fertile, well-drained soil in a sheltered site in full sun. Tolerant of summer drought.

ERIOCAPITELLA
Ranunculaceae

Native to East and Southeast Asia

This genus has recently been separated from Anemone. They are low-growing herbaceous perennials, which bloom in late summer to autumn. Many hybrids are available, with long-lasting flowers in white, pink or purple.

Eriocapitella hupehensis syn. *Anemone hupehensis*
Japanese Anemone

This species is a clump-forming perennial with fibrous roots. It has three to five basal leaves, each with a petiole from 5 to 35cm long. Leaves have three blades with a central leaflet 4 to 10cm long and 3 to 10cm wide and smaller lateral leaflets. The stem is 30 to 120cm long, with a whorl of three bracts wrapped around the stem with smaller leaves. Tall, branching flower stems bear clusters of white or mauve to pink, simple, poppy-like flowers 5cm across during summer and autumn. Grow in well-drained, rich, neutral to slightly alkaline, friable loam with plenty of organic matter added. Summer drought tolerant; avoid waterlogged soils, especially in winter. Select a semi-shaded location, as the flowerheads will be more erect with plenty of direct sun. Best planted in drifts for the maximum effect of their delicate flowers. An ideal choice for growing in woodland locations or beneath trees, also in pots and containers.

ERIOCEPHALUS
Asteraceae

Native to South Africa

A genus of about 30 species of aromatic, usually silvery or silky shrubs. They are fairly woody with evergreen, alternate or subopposite leaves that are tough and thick in order to reduce water loss. Some species have thorny, silky-greyish leaves, while most have finely soft or woolly hairs, and some are glabrous. They have a characteristic, rather spicy aroma, especially when bruised, similar to the aroma of rosemary, though not convincingly so. Leaves may be used similarly in cooking. Small flowering heads with short stems become woolly after flowering. In a few species, the flowers are solitary.

Eriocephalus africanus
Wild Rosemary, Kapokbossie, Cape Snow Bush

A much-branched shrub up to 1m high and wide. Narrow, 2cm-long, almost round, rosemary-like leaves are silky white in clusters along the stem. From late autumn to spring, terminal clusters of 6 to 8cm long flowers are produced. Each white disc-shaped flower is 1cm wide, with a cluster of dark red stamens with a slight scent. Grow in full sun in well-drained soil. Drought resistant once established. A useful shrub for filling in the background of a dry garden with its mass of grey foliage. Also useful for coastal gardens as it withstands salt-laden sea breezes.

ERYNGIUM
Apiaceae

Native to Europe, Mediterranean, central Asia and China, mainly South America

A genus of over 250 species of annuals, biennials and perennial herbs with hairless and usually spiny leaves. Dome-shaped umbels of steely blue or white flowers have whorls of spiny basal bracts. Some species are native to rocky and coastal areas, but the majority are grassland plants. Striking plants for naturalising, some providing long-lasting displays for a border. Eryngiums revel in the hottest, driest, most exposed, sunny position you have. Well adapted to long periods of summer heat and drought, it has low water needs. Prefers soils that are rich in calcium. Great for dried flower arrangements.

Eryngium amethystinum
Amethyst Eryngo, Italian Eryngo, Amethyst Sea Holly

Native to Italy, Sicily and the Balkans

A clump-forming, evergreen hardy perennial with tap roots. Its stem is 30 to 50cm long and light blue to purple with a basal circle of dark green, deeply cut, leathery, spiny toothed leaves 10 to 15cm long with oblong leaflets. The upper leaves are three-lobed. It flowers in mid to late summer with striking cylindrical umbels, 2 to 3cm long atop silvery blue bracts surrounded by spiky, darker-blue bracts on branched stems. These are ideal for cutting either dried or fresh. The plant is tap rooted, making it difficult to move or divide, so it is best to grow from seed, which must be fresh. It will often self-seed.

Eryngium maritimum
Sea Holly, Sea Eryngo, Sea Eryngium

Native to most European coastlines

A glabrous, evergreen, intensely glaucous, clump-forming hardy perennial growing to around 60cm tall and 50cm wide with a deep, well-developed root

Erica arborea.

Erica australis.

Eriobotrya japonica.

Eriocapitella hupehensis.

Eriocephalus africanus.

Eryngium amethystinum.

Eryngium maritimum.

Erythrina caffra.

Erythrina crista-galli.

system. The leathery, three-lobed, intensely glaucous blue basal leaves are 10 to 15cm long with coarse spiny teeth and rolled when young. All leaves have thick margins, often with purplish veins. In summer, stiff branched flower heads 2 to 3cm across are surrounded by spiny bracts the same intense glaucous blue as the leaves. Its small flowers are pale blue. This highly ornamental plant should be grown in full sun. Thrives in poor to moderately fertile, free-draining, sandy soil. Drought tolerant once established, it needs little summer water. Ideal for coastal gardens as it occurs naturally in coastal sands. Attractive in a rock garden.

Eryngium × tripartitum
Tripartite Eryngo

Probably Mediterranean origin

A clump-forming, evergreen, hardy perennial about 60 to 90cm tall, spreading to 50cm wide that forms a long tap-root. Basal rosettes of three-lobed deep grey-green leaves 6 to 12cm long are coarsely toothed. In summer to early autumn, the small, erect, much-branched, cylindrical, violet-blue flower heads 1 to 2cm across are surrounded by spiny grey-blue bracts. These appear on wiry stems, which are ideal for cutting either dried or fresh. Prefers good, well-drained poor to moderately fertile soil in full sun. A neat plant suitable for the front of a border. Drought tolerant once established, it needs little summer water, and dislikes winter wet.

Erythea edulis see *Brahea edulis*

ERYTHRINA
Fabaceae

Coral Tree

Native to tropical and temperate regions worldwide

A large genus of over 100 species of mostly deciduous or semi-evergreen trees and shrubs grown for their brilliant flowers. Stems are usually thorny, with leaves divided into three leaflets. Larger species grow up to 30m high.

Erythrina caffra
Coral Tree, Lucky Bean Tree

Native to eastern South Africa

A slow-growing, multi-trunked, usually deciduous tree up to 10m high with wide-spreading angular branches forming a round-headed canopy. The trunk and branches are grey, sometimes with short, sharp hooked thorns. Leaves are typically trifoliate (three leaflets), broadly ovate to elliptic, the terminal leaflet being the largest, 8 to 16cm. Lateral leaves are slightly smaller and without hairs or prickles. Before the leaves emerge in spring, bare branches produce spectacular, brilliant red, tubular flowers with five petals that are 5cm long. Thick, fleshy stalks hold large terminal clusters of flowers 30 to 60cm long. Each flower has a short, broad, standard petal, the lower half of which curves upward to expose the stamens, giving the flower a whiskered appearance. Superficially, they are shaped like cockscombs. Flowering starts from winter and carries on throughout spring. This beautiful tree should be planted in full sun in well-drained soil. It can tolerate quite moist soils, as it often grows on the banks of rivers and streams; however, it will also tolerate summer drought and poor soils. They do not respond well to cold conditions. It makes an excellent shade tree, and also provides an ideal filtered shade for a host of herbaceous and perennial shrubs.

Erythrina crista-galli
Cockscomb, Common Coral Tree

Native to southern Brazil, Uruguay and northern Argentina

A deciduous tree 3 to 4m high or many-stemmed shrub with branches that have vicious, stout thorns with an open habit. Trifoliate leathery leaves are up to 30cm long, each leaflet 5 to 8cm long and 2 to 5cm wide with a backward pointing thorn. It produces masses of terminal racemes 30 to 60cm or more long of brilliant scarlet 4cm long flowers. These appear in flushes throughout spring, giving a dazzling effect. The tree grows best in full sun in well-drained soil, but needs protection from wind. Drought tolerant once established. Remove old flower stems to encourage fresh growth. During winter, stems may die back, but once fresh growth has started in spring, the dead stems should be cut away. The tree is a popular ornamental plant and is widely grown in tropical and subtropical regions for its striking red flowers.

ERYTHROSTEMON
Fabaceae

Native to tropical and subtropical regions around the world, including parts of Africa, Asia, the Americas and Australia

A genus of about 150 species that vary widely in size, shape and growth habit. They can be evergreen or deciduous small shrubs, large trees, or even climbing vines. Leaves are usually compound and alternate, composed of several leaflets. Plants typically produce vibrant, showy flowers, often in clusters or spikes that can range from yellow and orange to red and purple. Some species are grown in gardens and landscapes because of their attractive flowers and foliage.

Erythrostemon gilliesii syn. *Caesalpinia gilliesii*
Bird of Paradise Bush

Native to Argentina and Uruguay

An upright or spreading shrub or small tree, which quickly reaches 3 to 4m high, spreading 1 to 2m wide, with rather open, lax branches. The bipinnate 20cm-long leaves contain many small leaflets, which may drop in a cold winter. Spectacular flowers are borne in upright terminal pyramidal racemes containing 30 to 40 flowers for most of summer. Each bright yellow cup-shaped flower 3 to 4cm across has tassels of bright red, 10cm-long stamens. Flowers are usually followed by 10cm-long seed pods. Grow in full sun in well-drained soil. Drought tolerant once established.

ESCALLONIA
Escalloniaceae
Native to temperate South America
A genus of 50 to 60 species of mainly evergreen shrubs and small trees known for their attractive foliage and showy clusters of small flowers. They are popular ornamental plants in gardens and landscapes, valued for their ability to withstand various growing conditions and their low maintenance requirements. They typically prefer full sun to partial shade and well-drained soil. There are many named varieties with flowers from red to pink and white.

Escallonia bifida
White Escallonia
Native to Brazil and Uruguay
A vigorous, tall, broad, evergreen shrub up to 3m high spreading almost as wide. Dark-green, glossy, narrowly oval leaves are 8 to 10cm long and finely toothed, glabrous and bright green above, furnished with small resinous dots beneath. Flowers, pure white, 1 to 3cm across, appear from late summer to autumn in rounded terminal panicles, the largest of which are as much as 20cm long and 13cm wide, but usually much smaller. The shrub can take full sun, but in hot gardens it grows better with some shade. When established, it is drought tolerant but grows better with some summer water. Useful as a large screening shrub. Particularly good for coastal gardens, as it withstands salt-laden sea breezes.

Escallonia rubra
Native to Chile and Argentina
A vigorous upright evergreen shrub 2 to 5m high spreading almost as wide, with peeling brown bark. It features glossy, elliptical, serrate evergreen leaves up to 6cm long, which are aromatic when bruised. The upper side is glossy and dark green, while the lower side is much lighter. Loose clusters of deep pink to crimson flowers, 1cm long, bloom abundantly from summer to autumn in clusters up to 10cm long. The shrub is much used for hedging and as windbreaks, especially near the coast where it withstands salt-laden sea breezes and other tough locations. When established, it is drought, wind and frost tolerant but grows better with some summer water. Grows almost anywhere. The variety 'Macrantha' is probably the best variety for hot dry conditions. Its bell-shaped, sweetly honey-scented flowers are produced throughout summer. Foliage is denser and darker.

ESCHSCHOLZIA
Papaveraceae
Native to western North America, Mexico
A genus of about twelve species of branching annuals, biennials or perennials, known for their bright, cup-shaped flowers in shades of yellow, orange or pink. Species are often grown because of their showy and brightly coloured flowers and the ability to thrive in dry, sunny conditions. The California poppy is the state flower of California and is celebrated for its vibrant blooms that blanket hillsides during the springtime.

Eschscholzia californica
California Poppy
Native to the western United States
An annual or perennial that flowers in its first year to 30cm tall with many-branched stems often forming a mat. Waxy, pale blue-grey leaves are much dissected into fine segments. Flowers are solitary on long stems, silky-textured, with four petals, each petal 1 to 5cm long and broad, carried well above the leaves. Flowering is from early summer to mid-autumn. The petals close at night or in cold, windy weather and in shade. These open again the following morning, although they may remain closed in cloudy weather. Flowers are followed by long, curved seed pods. Garden seed strains are offered in a wide range of colours but mainly yellow, orange and white. An easily grown plant that flourishes in light well-drained soil. Tolerant of summer drought, but flowering can be extended by giving it extra water. Flowers at its best in full sun. The plants commonly self-seed. As they do not transplant well, sow seeds where they are to grow. A glorious sight when naturalised on a sunny hillside or in informal areas of the garden.

EUCALYPTUS
Myrtaceae
Eucalypt, Gum Tree, Ironbark
Native mainly in Australia
Some authorities now place some species of Eucalyptus in the genus Corymbia. Although the term 'eucalypt' is usually regarded as applying to the genus Eucalyptus, it also includes the closely related Angophora and the genus Corymbia. This contains 113 species, 80 of which were formerly within Eucalyptus. Angophora comprises about thirteen species.

A huge genus of over 1,000 species of evergreen trees making fast growth, particularly in the early stages. Some seedlings can grow to 2m in the first year. Most have two types of foliage, soft juvenile leaves on young trees and new branches, and tougher adult leaves. Nearly all eucalyptus leaves have some fragrance and are rich in oils. They are well suited to warm dry conditions, needing to be grown in full sun with little or no summer water once established. If possible, grow from seed, because containerised plants, especially when older, do not transplant well. A valuable source of timber as the wood is durable and resistant to damp, but splits easily. The term 'gum tree' is derived from the habit of some eucalypt species to exude a sticky, gum-like substance from the trunk. This is not a general characteristic, but 'gum tree' has become a common generic term for most eucalypts.

Eucalyptus citriodora see *Corymbia citriodora*

Eucalyptus ficifolia see *Corymbia ficifolia*

Eucalyptus nicholii
Narrow Leaved Peppermint
Native to New South Wales
This particularly beautiful small to medium-sized tree grows fast but rarely

reaches over 15 to 18m high with thick, rough, fibrous, reddish brown bark that is deeply furrowed. The tree has fine weeping branches and pendulous foliage on an upright main trunk. Juvenile leaves are blue-green, narrow and willow-like, 7 to 13cm long. Adult leaves are the same dull greyish green on both sides, narrow lance-shaped, 6 to 14cm long. When the leaves are crushed, they smell of peppermint. Young trees keep their foliage to ground level. Flower buds are in groups of seven. Small white inconspicuous flowers are produced from late summer to early autumn. A splendid garden or street tree. The billowing fine-textured foliage gives it a willow-like form.

Eucalyptus perriniana
Spinning Gum

Native to southeastern Australia and Tasmania

A small straggly tree up to 15m high with smooth, copper-coloured bark, which often turns white, grey or greenish as it ages before being shed in short ribbons each year. Blue-grey or green juvenile leaves are opposite, more or less circular and lack a stalk. When the leaves release their grasp, they rotate on the stem in the breeze. Lance-shaped adult leaves are greyish green, pendant 8 to 12cm long. The silver foliage is useful for flower arranging. Creamy flowers are in small clusters of three, appearing during summer. Usually treated as a shrub by cutting it back to produce its attractive new leaves. Makes an attractive grey-leaved plant for a border.

Eucalyptus polyanthemos
Silver Dollar Gum

Native to New South Wales

A fairly fast-growing, broadly conical evergreen tree 10 to 15m high and 5m wide, which may be single or multi-stemmed. The fibrous bark is reddish brown, and the trunk may be sculptured whilst the bark is quite smooth. Juvenile leaves are grey green, oval or round 5 to 8cm long. Mature leaves are lance-shaped, 9cm long and grey-green. Creamy-white flowers appear in small clusters in spring and summer. It is a particularly hardy tree, which will thrive in dry, shallow, infertile soils, and tolerates difficult, dry, stony soils. Will grow almost anywhere but dislikes wet conditions. It has become quite popular in recent years as a tree for street planting and for amenity plantings in public areas because of its aesthetic appeal and small size. The foliage is useful for flower arranging.

Eucalyptus torquata
Coral Gum

Native to West Australia

A small, slender, upright, aromatic tree to 6m high and 4m wide with rough grey to black bark on the trunk and larger branches. Its bark flakes rather than peels. Slender, light brown stems frequently bend under the weight of blossoms. Lance-shaped, bluish-green leaves are up to 10cm long. It is a stunning ornamental tree choice because of the dazzling usually red flowers that appear in spring and summer, and the intricate detail of the tree's flower buds and gumnuts. Its spectacular flowering panicles contain many 3 to 4cm long scarlet or crimson flowers. The flower buds are like small Japanese lanterns appearing mainly from summer to autumn, but may be produced at any time of the year. Flowers appear at an early age. Attractive to birds and much wildlife, it is drought resistant and low maintenance. It can tolerate light frosts but prefers a sunny, dry environment to thrive. A spectacular flowering tree that makes a good specimen tree in a small area. The foliage is useful for flower arranging.

EUCOMIS
Asparagaceae

Pineapple Flowers, Pineapple Lilies

Native to seasonally damp meadows of South Africa

A genus containing fifteen species of large, bulbous perennials with long basal rosettes of lance-shaped to strap-shaped leaves, which may be green or burgundy. They are grown for their unusual racemes of flowers borne in late summer and autumn. Stout stems are sometimes freckled with purple and bear a tight raceme of star-shaped flowers 2.5cm across with a tuft of green bracts at the top, superficially resembling a pineapple – hence the common names. Often used as a cut flower by florists.

Eucomis comosa
Native to South Africa

A deciduous, summer-growing bulb up to 1.2m tall, including the flower stalk. Semi-erect, lance-shaped, bright-green leaves to 90cm long have purple streaks underneath. Sweet-scented, cream-coloured flowers with a purple ovary are carried on a stout, green, hollow stalk in mid- to late summer. The inflorescence to 30cm long is topped by a tuft of leaf-like bracts, which are relatively small in this species. Flowers are usually white, or greenish yellow, but sometimes pink, or purplish. Most plants have a pleasant coconut-like scent. It has many forms in cultivation, and the leaves can be quite variable, from light green to a dark burgundy. Tolerates some shade, however, the best colour is produced when planted in well-drained soil and full sun. Somewhat drought tolerant once established, but do not allow to dry out over extended periods of heat. No pruning required other than removal of spent flower stems to encourage further flushes. In cold climates, foliage will recede during winter with colourful fresh growth reappearing in spring. Hardy and easy to grow, tolerating dry conditions and small or narrow spaces in gardens or courtyards. Last well as a cut flower in floral arrangements.

Eudianthe coeli-rosa see *Silene coeli-rosa*

EUONYMUS
Celastraceae

Spindle Tree

Native mainly in Asia but also found in the rest of the world

A genus of about 130 species of deciduous and evergreen dwarf shrubs, climbers

Erythrostemon gilliesii.

Escallonia bifida.

Eschscholzia californica.

Eucalyptus perriniana.

Eucalyptus polyanthemos.

Eucalyptus torquata.

Eucomis comosa.

Euonymus fortunei 'Emerald 'n' Gold'.

and small trees. Leaves are opposite (rarely alternate) and simple ovoid, typically 2 to 15cm long, and usually with a finely serrated margin. Inconspicuous flowers occur in small groups, and can be green, yellow, pink or maroon. These garden shrubs are popular because of their attractive leaves, especially the deciduous ones that display dazzling red autumn colours, and their decorative berries.

Euonymus fortunei
Wintercreeper

Native to east Asia, including China, Korea, the Philippines and Japan

An evergreen shrub that will trail, form a mound or climb by rootlets with support. Will grow to 60cm high as a mound or to 5m as a climber, spreading almost indefinitely. Its long stems will root at intervals. Leaves in opposite pairs are elliptic 2 to 6cm long, veined underneath, with finely serrated margins and often variegated with white or gold. Flowers are inconspicuous, 5mm in diameter, with four small greenish-yellow petals and produced in loose clusters in summer. Small round, white fruit appears in autumn. Grow in full sun or partial shade. Although frost hardy, it also takes heat well and grows well even in dry areas with little or no summer water. The coloured leafed forms are normally grown.

Euonymus fortunei 'Coloratus'

A trailing or climbing evergreen form up to 8m high with dark-green leaves that turn purple-red in late autumn. A full sun to full shade lover. Easily grown in average well-drained soil.

Euonymus fortunei 'Emerald 'n' Gold'

A dense, evergreen dwarf bush 30 to 60cm high, spreading to 120cm wide. Leaves are deep green with a broad, bright gold margin, which becomes cream flushed with pink in winter. Grow in full sun.

Euonymus fortunei 'Silver Queen'

A compact evergreen shrub 1.5 to 3m high or up to 6m as a climber. Young leaves in spring are glossy, dark green, ovate to elliptic, edged with white margins. In cold weather, the leathery foliage becomes tinged with purplish pink. Its variegated colouring does not fade in full sun. Good when massed to control soil erosion.

Euonymus japonicus
Japanese Spindle

Native to China, Japan and Korea

A large, densely-branched evergreen shrub or small tree 2 to 8m high with a 2m spread. Opposite, dark glossy green, oval, toothed, leathery leaves are up to 6cm long, with finely serrated margins. Flowers are inconspicuous, greenish white, 5mm in diameter. The more interesting variegated forms are normally grown. A valuable shrub where heat tolerance is important, and soil conditions are poor. Fairly resistant to frost and summer drought. Grows well in full sun or partial shade. A good windbreak shrub for coastal gardens with salt spray or for planting as a hedge. A popular ornamental plant for parks and gardens. Many cultivars have been selected with beautiful foliage (often with variegated or yellow leaves).

Euonymus japonicus 'Albomarginatus'

A bushy, medium-sized, evergreen shrub 2.5 to 4m high with variegated oval leaves 3 to 5cm long, dark bluish green in the centre with conspicuous creamy white edges. Well-drained soil in full sun or partial shade.

Euonymus japonicus 'Aureus'

A wonderfully colourful shrub 1.5m high and about 1m wide with golden yellow and green evergreen foliage. Deep green leaf edges make a striking contrast with the golden centres. This shrub has a tendency to revert to all green leaves, so care should be taken to remove all green shoots as they are vigorous, quickly taking over.

Euonymus japonicus 'Ovatus Aureus'

A striking bushy, erect, evergreen shrub 2m high and 1.5m wide, with leaves tinged with green and yellow margins. It provides all-year interest with its evergreen foliage. This shrub is a great all rounder, able to be planted in almost any location in full sunlight or an area with dappled shade, in well-drained soil. Recommended planting locations include banks, slopes, ground cover or cottage and informal schemes. Makes a beautiful golden mound with little tendency to revert to green. This also makes a great container plant, or if planted close together, creates a thick, bushy evergreen hedge or screen.

EUPHORBIA
Euphorbiaceae

Milkweed, Spurge

Native to temperate, subtropical and tropical regions of the world

This vast genus contains a wide range of around 2,000 species, including annuals, herbaceous perennials, subshrubs, shrubs, trees and cactus-like plants. Leaves are usually small and simple and often fall off early in the growing season. Flowers are small and inconspicuous, usually surrounded by showy bracts that may be brightly coloured, giving the impression of a single, large flower. Most have an acrid milky sap that can be poisonous.

Euphorbia characias subsp. *wulfenii*
Mediterranean Spurge, Albanian Spurge

Native to Portugal and the western Mediterranean

An evergreen subshrub with many upright stems to 1m high spreading as wide. Stems have spirally arranged, narrow, blue-grey leaves, each one about 13cm long. They are decoratively topped with flowers produced on the previous season's growth. Greenish-yellow flowers are contained in dense masses of glowing, lime-yellow, paper-like bracts 10 to 20cm long with purple nectar glands. These are borne in large terminal heads in spring and early summer. After flowering, the stems should be removed. A full sun lover, it thrives in dry to medium, well-drained soils. The plant grows well in fairly poor soil conditions, in sun or partial shade. While it can withstand drought once established, it benefits from some watering in dry summers, yet it does not thrive in hot and humid summers. The subspecies *wulfenii* is the most often seen form, with yellow-green flowers. Valued in Mediterranean or desert gardens.

Euphorbia ingens

Giant Spurge, Candelabra Tree, Candelabra Euphorbia

Native to southern Africa, particularly parts of South Africa, Zimbabwe and Mozambique

This striking succulent typically has a massive, tree-like, candelabra-like, freely branching, thick, upright trunk that can reach impressive heights, often exceeding 6m and 3m wide in cultivated specimens. Its trunk is covered with greyish-green bark and is studded with prominent, vertical ribs. A broad, rounded crown is formed by the branches, which are yellowish-green to dark green and have four or five angles. Stems are constricted into oblong segments, which are wavy toothed and set with spines. It produces small, greenish-yellow flowers in clusters along the upper portions of the branches. Flowering typically occurs in late winter to early spring. A strong architectural plant for a dry garden. Grow the succulent in well-drained soil in full sun. It is a drought-tolerant plant that can withstand dry conditions, making it suitable for arid gardens.

Euphorbia marginata

Snow on the Mountain

Native to temperate parts of North America

This easily grown, single-stemmed, summer annual grows to 60 to 80cm high, spreading to 30cm wide. Oblong 3 to 8cm long grey-green leaves become striped and margined with white on the upper parts of the plant, giving it a dazzling effect. From late summer to autumn, it bears a terminal inflorescence in umbels with showy bract-leaves with edges trimmed by wide white bands 6 to 8cm long. Small white flowers are long lasting. Stems are often used in floral arrangements. One of the few variegated plants that grows well in full sun. Sow seeds directly in the flowering position in spring. Performs well in pots, rockeries and a wide range of gardens, and like all succulents, is drought tolerant. Looks better if given moderate summer water, but will survive on little. This succulent shrub is a great addition to any garden, as the plant provides great texture and can be used effectively in softening hard surfaces, such as steps, edging or a fence-line. The sap is highly corrosive to the skin and can cause dermatitis or burns.

Euphorbia milii

Crown of Thorns

Native to Madagascar

A woody, slow-growing, evergreen succulent shrub with stems that are irregularly branched to 1.8 m or more long and covered in long spines. Straight, slender spines, up to 3cm long, help it scramble over other plants. Fleshy, oval, light green, 4 to 5cm-long leaves are found mainly on fresh growth near the tips of the stems. Clusters of brilliant scarlet flowering bracts appear nearly all year containing tiny, fleshy, yellowish-green, red, pink or white flowers up to 12mm broad. It thrives best on dry rocky soil in full sun. Drought tolerant once established but grows better with some summer water. Ideal for coastal planting, especially as a hedge. Many varieties and hybrids have been raised that vary in form, size and colour of the bracts, including a purple leaved form. 'Splendens' is semi-prostrate to scrambling, looking effective when grown on the tops of walls or banks and allowed to tumble down. 'Dwarf Cream' is a dwarf variety with cream-coloured flowers and growing to 1m high and 65cm wide.

Euphorbia pulcherrima

Poinsettia

Native to Central America and tropical Mexico

An evergreen, branching shrub 1 to 3m high and wide with a woody trunk and milky sap. Dark-green, coarse, ovate leaves are 10 to 15cm long, sometimes lobed or toothed. In winter, the terminal petal-like bracts to 30cm wide appear, which are normally flaming red, with cultivars in orange, pale green, cream, pink, white or marbled. These are often mistaken for flower petals because of their groupings and colours, but are actually leaves. True flowers on the tips of the stems are greenish yellow and inconspicuous. They hold their colour for several weeks. Grow in a well-drained, slightly acid soil with average to little water during summer. Will take full sun but prefers some shade. Prune occasionally to prevent it from becoming too leggy. The dwarf form 'Paul Mikkelsen' is often used as a pot plant as the bracts are extra large. A popular pot plant seen in many homes in midwinter.

EURYOPS

Asteraceae

Native to southern Africa

A genus of about 100 species of evergreen shrubs, herbaceous perennials and annuals. The species are appreciated for their attractive daisy-like flowers, which can range from yellow to white, and sometimes a hint of blue or purple. These

onymus japonicus 'Ovatus Aureus'.

Euphorbia characias Wulfenii.

Euphorbia milii var. *splendens.*

phorbia milii 'Dwarf Cream'.

Euphorbia pulcherrima.

Euryops acraeus.

yops pectinatus.

Evolvulus pilosus.

Fargesia murielae.

typically bloom from spring to autumn. These plants are often grown for their showy flowers and their ability to tolerate dry conditions. Species are low-maintenance and can thrive in a variety of soil types, as long as they have good drainage. They prefer full sun and are relatively drought tolerant once established.

Euryops acraeus

Native to the Drakensberg Mountains of South Africa

A much-branched, dome-shaped shrub to 30cm high and wide spreading by underground stems. Stems are covered with beautiful, leathery, oblong, silver-grey leaves 2 to 3cm long, borne in dense clusters near the ends of branches. From autumn to early summer many canary-yellow flower heads 2 to 3cm across appear singly or in clusters of two to three on strong stems covering the shrub, making a brilliant display. Requires full sun, any well-drained soil. Hardier than other species, it will withstand frost. Makes an attractive shrub for rock gardens. Thrives in coastal gardens as it withstands salt-laden sea breezes.

Euryops chrysanthemoides

African Bush Daisy, Bull's-Eye

Native to Cape Province of South Africa

A compact, densely-branched, leafy, evergreen shrub, 0.5 to 2m in height, rapidly forming a low mound early in life. Leaves are attractive, shaped rather like an oak leaf, up to 10cm long, deeply indented lobes, close set, particularly on young growth. A wealth of brilliant yellow, single, narrow petalled daisy-like flowers, each 3 to 4cm across, with 15 to 30 bright yellow ray-florets and deep golden yellow disc-florets are carried well above the leaves on thin, wiry stalks 10 to 15cm long, some distance above the foliage. These appear mostly in autumn to early summer, but can cover plants for most of the year. Grows best in full sun in any soil but needs excellent drainage. This astonishingly free-flowering shrub is ideal for a dry garden in the front of a border, or even in larger rock gardens, where it will enjoy nestling between boulders. It looks most impressive in pots on a sunny terrace.

Euryops pectinatus

Native to Western Cape of South Africa

A vigorous shrub growing 1.5m high and wide with strongly upright branches. All parts of the shrub are covered in soft, whitish hairs. Deeply divided, silvery green, hairy leaves are up to 10cm long. Bright yellow daisy-like flowers 5 to 6cm wide are borne singly or in small clusters on stems 15cm long, appearing mostly in autumn to early summer but can cover the plant for most of the year and into winter in areas with mild climates. Grows best in full sun in well-drained deep soil. It must be grown in a sheltered location, away from frost-prone areas. Widely used in urban areas because of its almost perpetual flowering. An easily maintained shrub that is a good filler and useful for a dry garden. It makes a most attractive pot plant for a sunny terrace.

EVOLVULUS

Convolvulaceae

Dwarf Morning Glories, Bindweeds

Native to tropical and subtropical regions worldwide, with the highest diversity in the Americas

A genus of about 100 species, mostly herbaceous annuals or perennials, a few woody species. They typically have trailing or creeping stems with small, funnel-shaped flowers that often resemble those of their close relatives, the morning glories (genus Ipomoea). Flowers come in shades of blue, purple, pink and white. Species are often grown for their attractive flowers and the ability to thrive in a variety of conditions, from full sun to partial shade. They are commonly used as ground covers, in hanging baskets, or as edging plants in gardens and landscapes. However, some species can be invasive in certain regions because of their vigorous growth habits.

Evolvulus pilosus

Shaggy Dwarf Morning-Glory

Native to central United States

This easily grown ground cover subshrub grows to 10cm high in a semi-prostrate manner to 30cm wide with slender, trailing stems. It bears lovely green-grey spoon-shaped leaves that have a silky surface, creating an attractive silver effect. Blue funnel-shaped flowers 1.5 to 2cm across appear in summer through to autumn. These close up and re-open the following morning. Will tolerate poorer soils, in most well-drained sites in full sun to part shade. Drought tolerant once established. A heat-loving plant, it thrives in the middle of a hot summer and continues to impress all the way until autumn. A great option for neglected areas of the garden or even for containers that receive infrequent water. It does not tolerate wet soil, which kills the plant. Ideal for rockeries and sloping sites.

F

FARGESIA

Poaceae

Umbrella Bamboo, Fountain Bamboo

Native to North America, east and south Asia

There is much confusion over the naming of these plants, as many species that were formerly in the genus Arundinaria have now been reclassified.

A genus of about 80 to 90 species of woody, evergreen, small to medium clumping bamboos that form rhizomes. Grown for their attractive linear to lance-shaped, slightly tessellated, bright mid- or dark-green leaves, and erect canes 2 to 5m tall with yellow-brown or dark-purple nodes. Inflorescences are terminal panicles or racemes. They are some of the world's hardiest bamboos that do not spread vigorously. Because of their increasing popularity for their dense clumping behaviour, these plants are now more affordable and can be found at a wider range of nurseries.

Fargesia murielae syn. *Arundinaria murieliae*

Native to China

A vigorous-growing bamboo that forms large clumps with evergreen arching stems 2.5 to 4m high. Fresh shoots are light blue with tan culm sheaths, aging to a yellowish-green. Stems have many slender branches growing from nodes. Bright-green leaves are tapered, reaching 6 to 10cm long and 1 to 2cm wide. Requires some water in spring when in growth but needs less or none during summer. It looks best when planted in an area that gets afternoon shade or dappled sunlight throughout the day. Like all other Fargesias, it does not have running rhizomes and needs no containment to prevent it from spreading. It will keep its pastel green foliage throughout the winter, though it usually sheds a few leaves in late autumn. The canes, which are correctly known as culms, make quick growth in spring. Individual culms live for many years but should be removed when they die. Excellent as an isolated specimen plant, or to give shade to a pathway.

FEIJOA

Myrtaceae

Native to South America

A small genus containing two or three species of evergreen shrubs or small trees. One species is planted in warm countries for its edible fruit and ornamental flowers.

Feijoa sellowiana syn. *Acca sellowiana*

Pineapple Guava

Native to southern Brazil and Argentina

A large shrub or small tree up to 2m high with an equal spread, normally having many stems, often picturesquely twisted with a reddish-brown trunk. Opposite, oval, leathery leaves are 5 to 8cm long, grey-green above with a white felt underneath. In late spring, 4cm wide showy flowers appear in leaf axils, with fleshy crimson and white petals and a central bunch of long crimson stamens. Flower buds are often covered with a layer of pinkish-red sepals, creating an attractive contrast. The petals are edible, making an unusual addition to a fruit salad. These are followed by 5 to 8cm oval fruit, which is greyish green, commonly known as feijoa. Drought tolerant but grows better with some summer water. They prefer a subtropical to mild temperate climate and well-drained, slightly acidic soil. After flowering, the shrub can be pruned hard to keep it in shape. Can be trained to form an espalier, screen, hedge or small tree.

FELICIA

Asteraceae

Blue Daisy

Native to southern Africa

A genus of about 80 species of annuals, shrubby perennials or subshrubs grown for their daisy-like flowers. Individual flowers are small and clustered in typical heads. The centre of the head is yellow, seldom whitish or blackish-blue disc florets, and is almost always surrounded by a single whorl of mostly purple, sometimes blue, pink, white or yellow petals.

Felicia amelloides

Blue Marguerite

Native to South Africa

A shrubby perennial that rarely grows over 50cm high, forming a dense mound up to 60cm wide. Roughish, slightly aromatic, oval green leaves are 3cm long. During summer it is covered in 3 to 4cm-wide pale blue daisy-like flowers, which have a yellow centre. Some flowers may be produced at any time of the year. It is best grown in full sun in well-drained soil. Tolerant of summer drought, but a moderate amount of water during summer is required to keep it flowering. Looks good when grown in pots or containers, and when planted on the top of a wall or raised bed where it can tumble down. This is a vigorous plant that becomes untidy after a few years, but it can be trimmed at any time of the year to encourage more flowers or cut back hard in autumn to give it a good shape. There are many named forms including 'Reads Blue', which is more compact with blue flowers, 'Reads White', which has white flowers, 'Santa Anita' with large rich blue flowers, and a lovely, variegated form with cream splashed leaves.

FEROCACTUS

Cactaceae

Native to Mexico and southwestern United States

A genus of about 25 to 30 species of slow-growing, large, barrel-shaped cacti to 3.5 m tall, mostly with large spines and small flowers. Young specimens are columnar, but as they grow older, ribs form, and they take on a barrel shape. They are typically up to 30cm in diameter with a green waxy skin and clusters of spines on the outer ridges. Most species are solitary, but some have clustering habits. Flowers are pink, yellow, red or purple from spring to autumn, and the petals sometimes have a darker stripe. They are desert dwellers and can cope with some frost and intense heat. Typically grown in areas where water flows irregularly, or depressions where water can accumulate for short periods of time.

Ferocactus acanthodes syn. *Ferocactus cylindraceus*

California Barrel Cactus, Desert Barrel Cactus, Compass Barrel Cactus

Native to the southwestern United States and northwestern Mexico

This cylindrical or spherical cactus is usually found in clusters, with some older specimens forming columns that can grow up to 50cm in diameter and 3m tall. The stem has 18 to 27 distinct ribs and is covered in many straight spines 17cm long, which are red, white, pink or yellow when new and become curved and grey as they age. Each areole typically contains four to seven central spines as well as 15 to 25 radial spines resembling strong hairs. In spring it bears funnel-shaped flowers 3 to 6cm long that are maroon outside, bright yellow inside, with red tints and yellow centres on the sides that face the sun. Easily grown in full sun in well-drained sandy or rocky soil. Summer drought tolerant.

Ferocactus glaucescens

Blue Barrel Cactus, Glaucous Barrel Cactus

Native to Mexico

A solitary or branching cactus, globular when young, gradually becoming cylindrical as it matures, with spherical or cylindrical blue-green frosted shoots, growing up to 45cm high and 60cm wide. It has eleven to fifteen prominent ribs with areoles spaced evenly along them. Its yellow spines, which are difficult to distinguish between central and peripheral, reach up to 3.5cm long, with one central spine and six to seven radial spines. Bell-shaped, yellow flowers are up to 4.5cm long and 2.5 to 3.5cm wide. Thrives in full sun, which enhances its blue-green colouration and promotes flowering. Requires well-draining soil, to prevent root rot. Water moderately during the growing season, allowing soil to dry out completely between waterings. Reduce watering significantly in winter. Perfect for xeriscapes, rock gardens and desert-themed landscapes. Can be grown in containers, making it suitable for patios, balconies or indoors with ample sunlight. Its unique colour and form make it a striking focal point in any dry garden.

Ferocactus pilifer syn. *Ferocactus pilosus*

Mexican Lime Cactus

Native to Mexico

A clumping or simple, deep-green, barrel-shaped to columnar cactus to 2.4m high and 30 to 45cm wide, with prominent ribs adorned with areoles sprouting bright red spines. Bright red to orange flowers 2.5cm wide appear in spring to summer on mature plants, forming a ring at the top of the plant. Over time, plants can form groups. Easily grown in full sun in well-drained soil. Only water if needed when in growth and keep dry in winter. Regarded as one of the most spectacular species in the genus. Great for adding texture, colour and shape to desert, rock or Mediterranean gardens.

FERULA

Apiaceae

Native from the Mediterranean region to central Asia

A genus of over 150 species of herbaceous perennials with large tap roots and aromatic foliage. Only one species is usually grown in gardens.

Ferula communis

Giant Fennel

Native to the Mediterranean region

A robust perennial up to 3m high and about 60cm wide with thick, often branched and hollow stems. During late winter, it produces a mound of intricately cut lacy leaves some 90cm across by 90cm tall, each many times divided into narrow linear segments. During spring a strong shoot, like a thick asparagus spear, pushes through the centre of the foliage mound and soon makes a 2m tall stem carrying dozens of 15cm wide umbrellas of sulphur-yellow flowers. After flowering, the whole plant dies to the ground as if it was a spring flowered summer dormant bulb. In late summer, the seed heads appear containing a mass of small brown seeds. Grow the plant in full sun in well-drained soil. When established, it withstands summer drought. Makes an effective foliage plant for a dry garden. As the roots have one or more long taproots, it is impossible to transplant once established. The bronze- and purple-leaved forms are particularly attractive. The giant fennel should not be confused with the culinary herb called fennel, which is Foeniculum.

FESTUCA

Poaceae

Fescue

Widely distributed throughout the temperate regions of the world

A genus of around 400 to 650 species of evergreen or deciduous herbaceous perennial tufted grasses ranging from 10 to 200cm high. Some species are used for lawns, others as ornamental grasses.

Festuca glauca

Blue Fescue

Native to northern and southern temperate regions

A low, densely-tufted, evergreen ornamental grass. Threadlike linear leaves are rolled inwards or circular and are 15 to 20cm long. They are erect or arching,

ioa sellowiana.

Felicia amelloides.

Ferocactus acanthodes.

rocactus pilifer.

Ferula communis.

Festuca glauca.

us pumila.

Foeniculum vulgare.

smooth and silver blue. In early summer, it produces short, branched panicles of violet flushed, blue-green flowers up to 30cm high. This tufted grass is commonly used in rockeries, for border planting or as a ground cover for sunny or partially shady areas. It is frost and drought tolerant as it requires little summer water once established. The blue fescue is perfect for a low maintenance dry garden. Divide and replant every three to four years to maintain foliage colour. It is not a grass that can be walked on. There are many named varieties that vary in intensity of blue coloured leaves and in height from 15 to 40cm.

FICUS
Moraceae
Fig, Fig Tree

Native throughout the tropics with a few species extending into the warm temperate zone

A huge genus of around 850 species of mainly evergreen or deciduous large trees, shrubs and woody, root-clinging climbers. Most have a milky sap and insignificant flowers. One important member is grown for its fruit (*Ficus carica*) while others are grown for shade or ornament, some as pot plants.

Ficus carica
Common Fig

Native to the eastern Mediterranean and west Asia

A much-branched, deciduous tree, growing about 5 to 6m high and 5m wide with smooth white bark. Heavy, thick branches appear from ground level, forming a dense mass. Young shoots also appear from underground. Thick leaves have three to five deep lobes, 10 to 20cm long and nearly as wide, dark green and rough to touch. This important Ficus is grown for its edible fruit, which can be eaten fresh, cooked or dried. The figs are 5cm long, pear-shaped, green when young ripening to yellow-green or purple depending on the variety. Fruit appears singly in leaf axils in early summer and ripens from midsummer onwards. Dried fruit is often seen in shops and markets. The tree needs to be grown in full sun in free draining soil. Drought tolerant once established. They tolerate moderate seasonal frost and can be grown even in hot-summer continental climates. There are many named varieties raised to suit local conditions, some with green skinned, others with purple or black-skinned fruit. The milky sap of the green parts is an irritant to human skin.

Ficus pumilla
Creeping Rubber Plant

Native to China, Vietnam and Japan

A vigorous, root clinging, evergreen climber that will grow 2.5 to 4m or more and branches freely. When young, it is sometimes slow to climb. Bright-green, 4cm-long juvenile leaves, which are heart-shaped at first, are restricted to a thin mat covering the surface onto which stems cling. In maturity, leaves develop into large leathery adult ones 10cm long. Drought tolerant once established. It does not tolerate frost. It is one of the best climbers that can scale walls effortlessly, whether in the sun or shade. Given the right conditions, there is no limit to its size. Plant in well-draining soil. The plant has a creeping/vining habit and is often used in gardens and landscapes where it covers the ground and climbs up trees and walls. Buildings constructed with delicate materials can suffer structural damage from the secondary roots or tendrils. It can be invasive when environmental conditions are favourable. It is fast growing and requires little in the way of care.

FOENICULUM
Moraceae
Fennel

Native to coastal areas of the Mediterranean region

A small genus of just two or three species of aromatic perennials. One species is grown for the leaves and aromatic seeds, which are used in flavouring food.

Foeniculum vulgare
Common Fennel

Native to southern Europe

A robust, deep-rooting, herbaceous perennial with stems that are thick, often branched and hollow, usually growing to 3m high. Glaucous leaves are soft, many times divided into narrow linear segments to 30cm long. Leaves die down in summer and reappear in autumn. In mid- to late summer, the plant produces central, flat terminal umbels 10cm wide of tiny yellow flowers, which are followed by aromatic seeds. Young leaves and seeds have a liquorice taste. Grow in full sun in well-drained soil. Ideal for a dry garden as it is drought tolerant, needing no summer water. Easily raised from seed, indeed it can become invasive, often seen growing on roadsides. The form 'Purpureum' is more attractive, with its bronze-purple foliage.

FREESIA
Iridaceae

Native to South Africa

A genus of about nineteen species of cormous perennials, known for their fragrant, colourful flowers and popular as ornamentals in gardens and floral arrangements. Freesias typically have long, narrow leaves and tubular flowers that grow on slender stems in a variety of colours. They require well-drained soil with plenty of sunlight to thrive. They have been much hybridised to produce the florist's types that are normally grown.

Freesia corymbosa × hybrids

Native to South Africa

A cormous perennial with sword-shaped linear leaves up to 30cm long. Slender, usually branched and bent wiry stems grow to 30cm or more long and, unless supported, will lie on the ground. Tubular 5cm flowers are produced in early spring, irregularly spaced along the stem. Hybrids have flowers that come in a wide range of colours, including pink, red, yellow, orange, white and bicolours. All are powerfully scented, making wonderful cut flowers. They will seed themselves if old flowers are not removed. Plant corms 8cm deep in autumn in a sunny position in well-drained soil. Water only during the growing and flowering period, then allow to rest and bake in summer by reducing the water. Great in pots or containers sited near the home where the scent can be enjoyed.

Freesia refracta
Grandma's Freesias

Native to the winter rainfall region of South Africa

These herbaceous plants grow from a corm, which sends up a tuft of narrow, strap-like leaves 10 to 30cm long and a sparsely branched stem 10 to 40cm tall bearing a few leaves and a loose one-sided spike of flowers with six tepals. These have fragrant, narrowly funnel-shaped flowers that bloom facing upwards because their stems have the unusual habit of turning at right angles just below the bottom flower. As a result, the top part of the stem grows nearly parallel to the ground. Flowers bloom in succession from the base to the top of the inflorescence. Flowers are cream with a gold throat. This is the most sweetly scented and has cultivars in pink, red, purple, beige, gold and pure white. It is found growing in sandy or stony soils amongst dune scrub or at forest edges, usually in light shade. Summer drought tolerant. A relatively common species of dry interior valleys in the Western Cape. Widely naturalised in mild climates when introduced as a garden plant.

FREMONTODENDRON
Malvaceae

Flannel Bush

Native to the southwestern United States and northwest Mexico

A genus of just three species of evergreen or semi-evergreen large shrubs. Leaves have a leathery and fuzzy texture reminiscent of flannel (hence the name), and the yellow to orange flowers are large and showy. The leaves and young shoots can cause skin and eye irritation.

Fremontodendron californicum
California Flannelbush

Native to California

A fast-growing, upright, eye-catching, large evergreen shrub up to 5m high and 3m wide. Leathery dark-green leaves have three, five or seven lobes up to 10cm long. These are crinkled, and the underneath is covered with dense pale brown hairs. In early summer, the shrub is covered with lemon-yellow, saucer-shaped flowers up to 6cm wide. These are followed by conical seed capsules that are covered with rust-coloured hairs. The vibrant blooms attract bees and butterflies. In its natural environment, it grows in sandy or chalky soil. Grow in full sun in soil with excellent drainage. When established, it is drought tolerant. It is notably intolerant of summer water and should stay dry, even when it looks like it needs water. Supplemental irrigation that is too close to it can kill it. This plant depends on its long roots to reach moisture at a distance, so be sure to plant it near other low-moisture plants. As it makes shallow roots, do not disturb the soil around the plant, and stake carefully when young. It is usually a short-lived shrub.

FRITILLARIA
Liliaceae

Native to the Mediterranean, North Africa, Eurasia, southwest Asia and western North America

A genus of about 130 to 140 species of perennial herbaceous bulbs. They die back after flowering in spring or early summer to underground storage bulbs, which then regrow in the following year. Leaves are usually lance-shaped with one or two basal leaves. Flowers are usually solitary, nodding and bell-shaped with erect segments in the upper part. Bulbs have fleshy scales resembling those of lilies.

Fritillaria imperialis
Crown Imperial

Native to Turkey, Iran, Pakistan

These beautiful perennial bulbs are native to a harsh environment, which has helped to create this majestic and truly unique flower. With a single stem, it bears lance-shaped, glossy leaves at intervals along the stem. Growing to a statuesque height of up to 1m tall, it shows off a cluster of impressive, downward-facing, bell-shaped flowers topped with a perfect whorl of small leaves looking like a crown, hence its name. Whilst the flower itself is not fragrant, the whole plant emits a musky odour. While the wild form is usually orange-red, various colours are found in cultivation, ranging from scarlet through oranges to yellow. Its pendulous flowers make a bold statement in the late spring garden. Easy to grow in well-drained soil in a sunny site. Drought tolerant. Plant bulbs sideways about 10 to 15cm deep into a well-fertilised soil in autumn, and ensure they remain sheltered and dry until foliage emerges in late winter or early spring. Once foliage has emerged, plants need a sunny position with regular watering, but ensure soil does not become too wet.

FURCRAEA
Asparagaceae

Native to tropical regions of Mexico, the Caribbean, Central America and northern South America

A genus of about 30 species that are characterised by their large, rosette-forming leaves, which are often stiff and sharp-tipped. Some species can produce flower spikes that are as tall as 10m. Greenish-white, tubular flowers are usually produced in large clusters at the top of the flower spike. Some species are grown as ornamental plants, particularly in arid and semi-arid regions.

Furcraea foetida 'Variegata'
Variegated Mauritius Hemp

Native to the Caribbean, northern South America

A large, evergreen, succulent shrub growing approximately 2m tall by 2m wide. The variegated foliage forms a fountain of upright, long, sword-shaped leaves with slightly wavy margins, resembling undulating ribbons. With broad, decorative creamy yellow stripes along its centre, the luminous green leaves are soft and lack serrations. Usually stemless, this plant produces strongly scented, greenish-white flowers at the top of a 5m spike that are attractive to bees. They open in succession over several weeks. This plant is monocarpic and dies after flowering. While it does not offset and form pups, it produces abundant plantlets along the bloom spike that you may want to plant. Makes a fantastic feature plant in full sun, or semi-shade, average well-drained soil. Requires minimal watering during a dry season.

G

GAILLARDIA
Asteraceae

Blanket Flower

Native to United States and South America

A genus of about 30 species of annuals, perennial herbs or subshrubs, sometimes with rhizomes. Stems are usually branching and erect up to 80cm high. Leaves are alternate. Some species have only basal leaves that vary in shape and are glandular in most species. The inflorescence is a solitary flower head which usually has fifteen or more ray florets, while some species lack any ray florets. These can be almost any shade of yellow, orange, red, purple, brown, white, or bicoloured. There are many tubular disc florets at the centre of the head in a similar range of colours, and usually tipped with hairs. Flowers are produced over a long period.

Gaillardia grandiflora
Garden origin

A bushy perennial to 90cm high and 45cm wide. Grey-green, lance-shaped leaves to 30cm long are entire or lobed with a roughish texture. Flower heads 8 to 10cm across are single or double. There is much variation in colour, mostly warm shades of red, yellow and orange, with blood red towards the blackish centre cushion. Flowers are produced throughout most of summer. Plants grow and flower best in full sun, thriving in heat in any well-drained soil. Drought tolerant, they need only occasional watering during the hottest months. Effective in sunny borders, they also make good cut flowers. Plants are not long-lived but are easily raised from seed. If sown early, they will flower the first year. Seed companies list many varieties, including 'Dazzler' with bright, orange-red flowers tipped with yellow and 'Kobold' (syn. 'Goblin'), a compact variety with large, deep-red flowers tipped with yellow.

GARDENIA
Rubiaceae

Native to tropical and subtropical regions of Africa, Asia, Australia and the Pacific Islands

A genus of approximately 250 species of evergreen shrubs and small trees. The spectacular fragrant flowers are usually solitary or in small terminal clusters, typically white or creamy yellow, although some species may have pink or yellow flowers. Gardenias are revered for their fragrance, which is highly valued in perfumery and aromatherapy. The scent of the flowers is often described as rich, sweet and reminiscent of jasmine or orange blossoms. They require well-drained, acidic soil and thrive in locations with partial shade or filtered sunlight. Popular ornamental plants in gardens in warm climates.

Gardenia thunbergia
Forest Gardenia, Tree Gardenia, White Gardenia, Wild Gardenia

Native to southern and eastern regions of South Africa

This sturdy large shrub or small tree grows largely in forests or on forest margins up to 5m high. It is densely twiggy and rigid with smooth light-grey bark. Leaves are smooth, veined, shiny, whorled and entire, to 14cm long, clustered at the ends of branchlets. Abundant, spectacular, fragrant, open-faced flowers appear in spring and early summer. These are creamy white with tubular corolla about 7cm in diameter, perhaps the most hardy and fragrant of all gardenias. Fairly drought tolerant in winter but likes to be kept moist over the warmer months. Prefers well-drained, acidic soils that contain plenty of organic matter. Best suited to medium to larger gardens, it brings a heady perfume and a sturdy shape, providing an excellent background when not in flower.

esia corymbosa × hybrids.

Fremontodendron californicum.

Fritilaria imperialis.

rcraea foetida 'Variegata'.

Gaillardia grandiflora.

Gardenia thunbergia.

arrya elliptica.

Gazania rigens.

Gelsemium sempervirens.

GARRYA
Garryaceae

Native to Mexico, the western United States, Central America

A genus of about eighteen species of evergreen, dioecious, wind-pollinated shrubs or small trees growing 1 to 5m tall. Leaves are opposite, simple, leathery, dark green to grey-green, ovate, 3 to 15cm long, with an entire margin and a short petiole. Flowers are grey-green catkins, short and spreading when first produced in late summer.

Garrya elliptica
Coast Silk-Tassel, Silk Tassel Bush, Wavyleaf Silktassel

Native to the coastal ranges of California and southern Oregon

An erect, bushy, evergreen shrub reaching a height of 2 to 5m high with dense, upright branching. Opposite leaves are 6 to 8cm long, with a tough leathery feel, glossy green on top, but paler and duller on the underside with wavy leaf margins. Flowers are concentrated in inflorescences that cascade downward in separate male and female plants. Pendant male catkins are much more showy and are grey-green and up to 30cm long, while female ones are shorter and silver-grey. Although the flowers bloom in late winter and early spring, dried bracts remain on the plant well into summer as light grey decorations. Grow in moderately fertile well-drained soil in full sun or partial shade. Tolerant of summer drought and frost. Prune in spring, as soon as the old catkins have faded, shortening each shoot to encourage fresh growth.

GAZANIA
Asteraceae
African Daisies

Native to southern Africa

A genus of about sixteen species of low-growing perennials or annuals with dazzling daisy-like flowers. These are often planted as drought-tolerant ground cover. Species are grown for the brilliant colour of their flowerheads, which appear in late spring and are often in bloom throughout the summer into autumn. They prefer a sunny position and are tolerant of dryness and poor soils. There are basically two types, those that form clumps and those that trail.

Gazania hybrids
Treasure Flower

Garden origin

A spreading evergreen perennial, which may grow to 30cm high and wide. Leaves are typically 15cm long, narrow, and dark green, with lance-shaped or lobed structures and silver undersides. Flowers, 8 to 10cm wide, grow on stems 15 to 20cm long, in white, yellow, orange, pink or red, either single colours or with dark centres. These are produced continuously throughout summer, at their best in full sun. Flowers will close up temporarily when clouds come over or when it rains. Drought tolerant, needing little summer water. Well adapted to the Mediterranean climate. Excellent for planting on dry banks where they help to prevent erosion or for edging along sunny paths. Good as temporary fillers in between young shrubs or as ground cover. There is a host of hybrids available, all with similar attributes but varying in petal colour and patterns.

Gazania rigens
Trailing Gazania

Native to South Africa

A half-hardy, evergreen perennial that will grow 30cm high spreading rapidly to 40cm or more wide. Its many leaves are all basal, narrow and more or less lance-shaped, 15cm long, usually entire and silver grey. Many brilliant, daisy-like, composite flowerheads appear throughout summer. Large-flowered hybrids are available in white, orange and yellow, mostly with a black eye. A sun lover with the flowers only opening up in full sun. Drought tolerant, it still requires some summer water. Grows well in light sandy well-drained soil. Useful for planting on banks or on the tops of walls where their stems can trail down, creating a dazzling effect over a long period. Also attractive in hanging baskets if given enough summer water.

GELSEMIUM
Gelsemiaceae

Native to Asia and North America

A small genus of three species of twining or straggling shrubs producing attractive fragrant flowers. One species is commonly grown as a garden flower worldwide.

Gelsemium sempervirens
Carolina Jasmine, Evening Trumpet Flower, Yellow Jessamine

Native to southeast United States and Mexico

A vigorous, evergreen, twining perennial with thin stems 3 to 6m long when given suitable climbing support in trees. Oblong, glossy, dark-green, evergreen, lance-shaped leaves are 5 to 10cm long in pairs along the stems. Flowers are borne in clusters from late winter to spring, the individual flowers yellow, sometimes with an orange centre, trumpet-shaped, 3cm long and 2.5 to 3cm wide. These are strongly scented and produce nectar that attracts a range of pollinators. It requires a sheltered position in full sun or light shade. It is best grown in richly organic, moderately fertile, well-drained soil in full sun with some summer water. If the soil is too alkaline, the plant might develop chlorosis. Ideal to cover arbours, walls or sunny porches, on banks, or against a wall. Prune severely if it becomes top heavy. All parts of the plant are poisonous.

GENISTA
Fabaceae
Broom

Native to Europe, Mediterranean region and west Asia

A genus of about 90 species of mainly deciduous or evergreen shrubs or trees that are sometimes spiny, often with brush-like foliage. They bear masses of small, pea-like yellow blooms, which are sometimes fragrant. Many species have flowers that open explosively when alighted on by an insect, producing a shower of pollen that coats the insect.

Genista aetnensis
Mount Etna Broom
Native to Italy

A small tree or large shrub 4.5 to 6m high of erect, sparse habit, with little foliage, but many slender, bright green, rush-like branches, which are pendulous when young. Tiny narrow leaves are almost absent and soon fall. Fragrant golden-yellow flowers are produced in great profusion from mid- to late summer, scattered singly towards the end of recent shoots, each about 1cm across. Petals are golden yellow, the calyx green, angular-toothed, bell-shaped. Flowers are followed by seed pods containing two to three seeds. Ideal for poor, stony soil in a sunny dry garden as it is drought tolerant once established. Its tall habit makes it useful for planting at the back of shrubberies, where it can grow without unduly shading other plants. Although practically devoid of foliage, the bright-green young branchlets give the plant almost the quality of an evergreen. With its graceful habit, it makes an excellent specimen. When pruning, do not cut into old wood.

Genista hispanica
Spanish Broom
Native to southwest Europe

A dense, spiny, deciduous shrub 60cm high spreading to 1m wide, forming a dense, cushion-like mass. Branches are interlacing, spiny and hairy, the spines much branched. Tiny leaves are confined to the flowering twigs, linear-lance shaped, hairy beneath. Small golden yellow flowers appear profusely on terminal racemes up to 4cm long. It flowers in early summer, producing a gorgeous display of golden yellow blossom, more than probably any other dwarf shrub. Healthy plants are completely covered with bloom, producing a brilliant colour effect. Tolerant of dry sunny sites with poor but well-drained soil. Good for rock gardens and for planting on sunny banks.

Genista monosperma see *Retama monosperma*

GERANIUM
Geraniaceae
Cranesbill
Found throughout temperate regions of the world and mountains of the tropics, with the greatest diversity in the eastern Mediterranean region

A genus of over 300 species of tuberous, tufted or creeping annuals, herbaceous perennials, or seldom shrubs. About 40 species are native to Europe. True Geraniums should not be confused with the genus Pelargonium, which has the common name Geranium.

Geranium incanum
Native to South Africa

This hardy, fast-growing, undemanding, evergreen ground cover spreads and forms a dense carpet approximately 30cm thick with branching stems. Filigree, grey-green, basal leaves to 8cm long are each deeply cut into five segments, which are each lobed and toothed. Masses of roundish, deep pink or mauve flowers to 3.5cm long are produced throughout the year, with a peak in summer. The leaves and flowers are edible and make a refreshing tea. Drought tolerant but requires rich soil. Grow in full sun or semi-shade, although it flowers better and forms a tighter carpet in full sun. Can be used effectively on banks or as a colourful border plant. Attractive when allowed to trail over retaining walls or garden pathways and steps. Also equally useful in mixed borders, pots or hanging baskets. Valuable for a wildlife-friendly garden, as it attracts a host of insect pollinators.

Geranium maderense
Madeira Stork's Bill, Giant Herb-Robert
Native to Madeira

A mound-forming, much-branched, evergreen perennial growing 1.2 to 1.5m high and wide with many upright stems. Shiny green leaves up to 20cm long are deeply divided, giving a fern-like appearance. They are carried on long brownish-red stalks. In spring, an enormous bouquet of showy, purplish-pink flowers, adorned with dark centres and illuminated by pale veins, rise well above the attractive foliage. Its flowering stems and sepals are covered with brilliant hairs. Tolerant of summer drought. It performs best in full sun or part shade, not fussy about soil provided it is well drained. The plant is short-lived, usually dying after flowering, but it self-sows profusely. A plant in full flower makes a wonderful sight in beds and borders in Mediterranean gardens. This is a desirable plant for mild winter gardens.

GERBERA
Asteraceae
Native to temperate regions of Africa, Madagascar, Asia and Indonesia

A genus of over 40 species of tufted, hairy perennials, often with a woolly crown, up to 80cm high with a rosette of basal leaves. Leaves are elliptical with entire or toothed margin, pinnately veined, often leathery and felted beneath. Single to several flowering stems from each rosette bear a simple, one-headed inflorescence. A dense, flat cluster of small flowers or florets radiates, with several rows of bracts. Plants are grown for their striking flowerheads, which are often used by florists.

Gerbera jamesonii
Transvaal Daisy, Barberton Daisy
Native to southeastern Africa

An herbaceous, tufted perennial that forms a clump 60cm wide growing to

45cm high. Deeply lobed leaves, 25cm or more long, are dark green above with a paler underneath, which is densely woolly. Spectacular flowers are produced 12cm in diameter with normally orange-red (rarely yellow, orange, white or pink) ray florets. Double forms are also available. These rise directly from the crowns on stalks 45cm long, appearing mainly from late spring to late summer, but may appear at any time. Grow in full sun but give partial shade in the hottest areas. Thrives in open sandy, well-drained soils. Prefers regular watering but fairly drought tolerant once established. Let the plants grow into large clumps before dividing during winter as it resents transplanting. Good for growing in pots or containers on a sunny terrace. Fresh seed germinates readily. Flowers are excellent for arrangements.

Giandrisis setifolia see *Moraea setifolia*

GLADIOLUS

Iridaceae

Native mainly in South Africa but also in the Mediterranean region, Africa, Madagascar and west Asia

A genus of 250 to 300 species of cormous perennials. Stems are unbranched, producing one to nine narrow, sword-shaped, longitudinal grooved leaves, enclosed in a sheath. Flowers of unmodified wild species vary from tiny to perhaps 4cm across, in inflorescences bearing anything from one to several flowers. The spectacular giant flower spikes in commerce are the products of centuries of hybridisation and selection. Flower spikes are large and one-sided, each subtended by two leathery, green bracts.

Gladiolus communis subsp. *byzantinus*

Corn Flag, Byzantine Gladiolus

Native to the Mediterranean region

This cormous perennial is one of the showiest plants in a dry garden during its mid-spring flowering season when 80cm tall, sword-like stems carry large, intensely purple-red flowers. Its dense spikes of up to twenty funnel-shaped flowers 4 to 5cm across are marked with cream flashes on the lower segment. A tough plant that is drought tolerant and frost hardy. It grows happily in full sun, as well as light shade. The cormlets spread quickly, soon forming a colony. Ideal for a dry garden to give a bold splash of colour in spring. This Gladiolus grows during winter and is summer dormant.

Gladiolus grandiflorus hybrids

Garden origin

A strong, showy, cormous perennial that is a descendant of many South African species. Corms are 5cm or more wide with a flattened base. Upright sword-shaped leaves are borne in basal fans, mid to dark green, 24 to 60cm long. Spectacular flower spikes of large showy funnel-shaped flowers 10 to 18cm or more are borne in profusion on stiff fleshy spikes 60 to 90cm long. Flowers open from the bottom of the spike upwards, with many flowers open at a time. The flowers appear from midsummer to early autumn, adding dramatic splashes of colour to the garden. For the best effect, plant in full sun in rich soil that is well-drained with plenty of added humus. Winter dormant but needs regular summer water. A wide range of colours have been bred including white, cream, yellow, orange, salmon red, rose, purple and many bicolours. Spectacular in clumps, drifts or rows along garden borders or in larger pots or tubs on a patio. They also make wonderful long-lasting cut flowers.

Gladiolus italicus

Mediterranean Field Gladiolus, Italian Gladiolus

Native to southern Europe

A cormous perennial with sword-shaped leaves 5 to 50cm long. In late spring to early summer, it produces loose spikes of up to twenty pink to magenta funnel-shaped flowers 4cm across. Flowers are loosely arranged and face various directions, pale pink, as well as purple-pink to magenta with a pale blotch outlined in purple on the lower lobes. A tough plant that needs no summer water, flowering best with dry summer dormancy. The cormlets spread quickly, soon forming a colony. Ideal for a dry garden, they will give a bold splash of colour in spring.

GLANDORA

Boraginaceae

Native to the western and central Mediterranean region

The genus Glandora was split from Lithodora in 2008.

Now a genus of eight species of low-growing or upright evergreen shrubs. Leaves are linear, lance-shaped, elliptic and hairy, 1 to 4cm long. They are cultivated for their five-lobed, funnel-shaped blue or white flowers produced in leafy terminal cymes. Species are often cultivated in rock gardens or raised beds.

Glandora diffusa syn. *Lithodora diffusa*

A hardy, evergreen, low-growing, prostrate, much-branched shrub growing to 15cm high and 60cm wide with dense green foliage. Deep green leaves are 1 to 4cm long and hairy. It bears a profusion of small, bright-blue star flowers 1cm across from late spring through summer. Grows well in most soil types, does not mind poor soils that are well-draining. Easily grown in full sun or partial shade and tolerates summer drought. Mounding and trailing for easy colourful arrangements in pots, containers, rockeries and garden beds. Ideal for softening edges or for the front of mixed borders. Good for filling small or narrow spaces. Frost hardy.

GLEDITSIA

Fabaceae

Native to North America, Asia and tropical Africa

A genus of about twelve species of deciduous spiny trees, grown for their beautiful

enista hispanica.

Geranium maderense.

Gerbera jamesonii.

adiolus grandiflorus.

Gladiolus italicus.

Glandora diffusa.

editsia triacanthos.

Gloriosa modesta.

foliage. An elegant form in the landscape, species have deeply cut, fern-like leaves that cast dappled shade. Flowers are inconspicuous but are followed by large, pendant seed pods. Trunks and branches are thorny. They make attractive specimen trees. Tolerant of most fertile, well-drained soil in full sun.

Gleditsia triacanthos
Honey Locust, Thorny Locust

Native to central and eastern United States

An elegant spreading tree up to 20 to 30m high with a spiny trunk and shoots. The spines are branched and can be 8 to 15cm long. Glossy, dark-green leaves to 25cm long turn yellow in autumn. They are pinnate with fourteen to twenty leaflets or two-pinnate with four to sixteen pairs of oblong lance-shaped leaflets. Inconspicuous flowers are followed by 45cm long shining brown seed pods. This resilient tree is hardy to the cold. Tolerates acid or alkaline soil, drought or generous watering, great heat or wind, and atmospheric pollution. Its feathery foliage casts light shade, which makes it a magnificent specimen in a lawn. 'Sunburst' is fast growing, with golden yellow foliage, to 12m and 10m wide.

GLORIOSA
Colchicaceae (Formerly: Colchicaceae / Liliaceae)

Gloriosa Lily, Climbing Lily, Fire Lily, Flame Lily, Glory Lily

Native to tropical and subtropical regions of Africa, Asia and naturalised in Australia and the Pacific

A genus of twelve species of tuberous, climbing, herbaceous perennials that climb or scramble over other plants, reaching 3m high. Alternate opposite or whorled leaves have a coiled tendril-like tip. Plants have showy flowers on long pedicels from upper leaf axils. Many have distinctive and pronouncedly reflexed petals, like a Turk's cap lily. These range from a greenish yellow through yellow, orange, red and sometimes even a deep pinkish-red.

Gloriosa modesta syn. *Littonia modesta*
Climbing Lily, Climbing Bell

Native to Natal, South Africa

A summer growing, deciduous climber, about 1m high. The green stems are adorned with stunning leaves of a fresh, soft green, with leaves in alternating, opposite and whorled patterns on the same stem. Leaves are linear to ovate-lance shape to 15cm long with tendrils at their tips. Unlike lilies, the stems of this plant continue to grow after the flowers have completed their cycle, sometimes reaching 1.8m. The plant climbs by attaching its tendrils at the end of its leaves, which then wrap around plants or climbing frames. Usually there are five flowers per stem, a true waxy, golden yellow, bell shaped, with hanging pointed petals about 5cm across, solitary in leaf axils. They are summer flowering. Easily grown in normal well-drained garden soil. As growth begins water freely, reduce water as growth fades, then leave dry and dormant during summer. A dainty little creeper that is often found in the semi-shade of shrubs where it scrambles for sunlight. Excellent for flower arrangements.

Gloriosa superba 'Rothschildiana'
Glory Lilies, Flame Lilies

Native to tropical Africa and southern Asia

This climbing, deciduous, summer-growing tuberous perennial has one to four slender stems growing 1 to 2m long, emerging from a fleshy, red brown, elongated, often forked tuberous rhizome. Stems produce oval to spear-shaped, glossy, emerald green leaves that grow alternately, sometimes opposite or whorled. It uses tendrils at the ends of its leaves to climb surrounding plants or structures. Showy, solitary claw-shaped flowers with prominent stamens appear from midsummer onwards on flower stalks to 15cm long in leaf axils. Each single flower has six widely separated, reflexed tepals, which are three petals and three sepals 6 to 8cm long, all similar. The tepal margins may be wavy or curling, and are most often bright red to orange, sometimes with yellowish bases. In their native habitat, flowers are likely pollinated by butterflies and sunbirds. Flowers are followed by fleshy, oblong fruits. It requires full sun or semi-shade for optimal growth and likes a moderate amount of water during its growing season, then drought tolerant. An easy-care plant that is sure to draw attention with its eye-catching colourful flowers. Ideal for pots or used against a trellis or other structure suitable for climbing. These plants can easily be divided after a few years. The flowers are often used in floral arrangements and make long-lasting corsages.

GOMPHOCARPUS
Apocynaceae

Native to southern Africa

A genus of twenty species of erect perennial herbs or sometimes shrubs found on dry slopes and in scrub. Stems are thin, stiff, sometimes woody, often with milky sap. Leaves are variable, opposite, alternate or whorled. Flowers are pale or white, in loose pedunculate umbels beside upper leaf axils, followed by large inflated seed pods.

Gomphocarpus fruticosus syn. *Asclepias fruticosus*
Wild Cotton, Milk Bush, Milkweed

Native to southern Africa

A dense, multi-stemmed, evergreen, bushy shrub 1 to 2m high and 1m wide. Light-brown stems branch higher up to form the crown. When cut, the stem exudes a milky latex. Narrow, linear, opposite, pale to mid-green leaves are up to 12cm long. Axillary clusters 5cm across of attractive, creamy yellow flowers are carried in pendulous clusters. Usually grown for its fat, inflated, pale-green seed pods covered with bristle-like hairs and containing dark seeds, which are up to 8cm long, borne in autumn. Seeds are attached with cotton-like, silky hairs that aid in their dispersal. Drought tolerant, grow in ordinary soil in full sun. It will self-seed readily, often becoming invasive. Because of their deep roots, they do not transplant readily. When stems are cut and dried, they are good for flower arrangements.

GRAPTOPETALUM
Crassulaceae

Native to Rocky Mountains of southern Arizona into central Mexico

A genus of about nineteen species of small perennial rosetted succulents with fleshy, smooth leaves varying from silvery-grey or pink to waxy green with a surface that may be speckled. In many species, the petals are also speckled. Stamens characteristically curve outwards between the petals when the stigmas become receptive, presumably to avoid self-pollination. Grow in moderately fertile, sharply-drained soil in full sun or partial shade. Tolerant of summer drought.

Graptopetalum amethystinum

Native to mountains in Mexico

A beautiful, slow-growing succulent with erect to decumbent or pendant, sometimes basally branched brownish stems, up to 30cm long. Each stem bears a rosette up to 15cm in diameter of thick, fleshy, rounded leaves with a powdery white coating at its end. The branching flower stem carries clusters of flowers in spring and summer. Flowers have five rounded grey-green sepals and five lance-shaped red petals with a basal grey-green band spotted with red and a grey-green outer surface. Stamens are lemon yellow. These plants need plenty of sunlight to look their best. They require a gritty, porous soil with excellent drainage. Over-watering causes root rot. A low-maintenance, drought-tolerant plant that is perfect for those looking for an easy-care addition to their home or garden. They are frost tolerant, so can thrive in cooler climates. New plants can be propagated from stem or leaf cuttings.

Graptopetalum paraguayense syn. *Sedum weinbergii*
Ghost Plant, Mother of Pearl Plant

Native to Mexico

A beautiful, much-branching succulent with thick, fleshy stems that form rosettes of thick, fleshy leaves at the tips up to 20cm high. Stems can grow up to 30cm long, while the rosettes can reach up to 10cm in diameter. Leaves are greyish white, warm to pinkish yellow in hot and dry conditions, and turn blue grey in partial shade. They are flat, shortly pointed, 7cm long and 3cm wide. The foliage has a subtle opalescent blending of colours and is brittle and easily breaks when handled. In spring, the plant produces white star-shaped 1 to 2cm white flowers with small red spots on branched stalks up to 15cm long. Prefers full sun but will grow in partial shade. A drought-tolerant succulent, preferring well-draining soil. Commonly used in succulent gardens, rock gardens, containers and hanging baskets. It can be grown indoors as a houseplant, provided it receives sufficient light. A succulent that can easily be divided, even a leaf will quickly root.

GREVILLEA
Protaceae

Native to Australasia

A large genus containing some 350 species of evergreen trees and shrubs with simple or compound, alternate leaves. Flowers are typically in pairs along a sometimes branched raceme at the ends of branchlets. Flowers usually have four tepals in a single whorl. Some species are grown as street trees while others are used as pot plants when young. Most have beautiful flowers and many new hybrids are appearing with red, pink or yellow flowers. They are well suited to dry climates.

Grevillea robusta
Silky Oak, Southern Silky Oak, Silver Oak, Australian Silver Oak

Native to Australia

A fast-growing tree with a single main trunk, growing from 5 to 30m high, spreading to 10m wide with dark grey and furrowed bark. It forms a pyramid when young but becomes broader topped when old. Delicate, pinnate, fern-like leaves are 15 to 30cm long, divided with many main lobes, pale green above and silvery underneath. There is usually a heavy fall of leaves in spring before flowering. Orange or yellow flowers appear in densely-packed horizontal one-sided clusters 5 to 10cm long in late spring. The tree grows in most soil, even poor compacted soil, if not over watered. Summer drought tolerant. The branches are brittle so they can be damaged by wind. Young plants should be staked securely. Thrives in heat but when young can be damaged by frost. Easily raised from seed, growing to 30cm high in less than a year. Often used as a decorative pot and florists' plant when young.

Grevillea rosmarinifolia
Rosemary Grevillea

Native to New South Wales, Australia

A many-branched, compact shrub that typically grows to a height of 2m and 1 to 5m wide, with silky hairy young growth. Deep green, needle-like leaves are 1 to 4cm long and silky underneath, similar to rosemary. Flowers are on the ends of branches, usually in groups of four to twelve. They are rosy-red, white or pink and produced in spider-like terminal racemes 4 to 8cm long from late autumn to summer. The shrub tolerates heat and is drought tolerant but needs an acid or neutral soil that is well drained. Can be used as an informal hedge in dryish places. 'Canberra Gem', which has pinkish-red flowers from late winter to late summer, is outstanding and undemanding.

Gymnosphaera capensis see *Cyathea capensis*

Gloriosa superba **'Rothschildiana'.**

Gomphocarpus fruticosus.

Graptopetalum paraguayense.

Grevillea robusta.

Grevillea rosmarinifolia.

Haemanthus coccineus.

Hakea laurina.

Hardenbergia violacea.

Hedera canariensis **'Gloire de Marengo'.**

H

HAEMANTHUS

Amaryllidaceae

Blood Lily

Native to South Africa

Now a genus of 21 species of tender, evergreen or deciduous, bulbous perennials found in grassy, rocky hillsides. About fifteen species occur in the winter rainfall region of Namaqualand and the Western Cape, the rest in the summer rainfall region, with one species, *Haemanthus albiflos*, occurring in both regions. Many species formerly included here have been moved to the genus Scadoxus.

Haemanthus albiflos

Paintbrush

A variable plant growing to about 20 to 30cm tall by 15cm wide when in flower. The upper half of the bulb is usually exposed and bright green. Oblong leaves, up to 40cm long vary from pale to dark green or greyish green and are usually smooth and sometimes shiny. They may have a covering of short, soft hairs, and occasionally yellow spots on the upper surface. In late autumn and winter, brush-like umbels comprising multiple tiny white florets are borne on stout stems, followed by fleshy red oval fruits that have white seeds. The flowers produce abundant nectar and pollen and a faint smell unattractive to humans. Once established, it is drought tolerant. It requires a dappled shade and likes to remain undisturbed for many years in well-drained soil. Flowers are better if restricted in a small pot. Prized for its unusual appearance and extreme tolerance of neglect. It also makes an excellent subject for containers, which need not be deep as the roots naturally spread out horizontally. Pots can be grown successfully on a shady veranda. It likes to become pot-bound, and mature bulbs flower reliably yearly.

Haemanthus coccineus

Shaving Brush Plant, Blood Flower, Blood Lily

A large bulb that produces pairs of thick, fleshy leaves, which can be up to 60cm long and 15cm wide. There are usually two large leaves per bulb, occasionally three, which appear after flowering. Leaves are elliptic or broad, often barred with red or dark green on the underside, which may also be prostrate or recurved. The bare flower stalk emerges just before the leaves in late summer with a short green flower stem that is spotted with red. At the top is a cluster of bright red stamens with yellow anthers that are packed into a 5 to 8cm wide flower which is enclosed by red bracts. It usually grows in winter and spring and goes dormant for the summer. Grow in a lightly shaded spot in well-drained soil. Give it ample water during the growing season to keep the leaves green and healthy so they can produce food for the bulb. Do not remove the leaves until they naturally turn yellow. Like most bulbs, it needs a rest after flowering by drying off.

Haemanthus multiflorus see *Scadoxus multiflorus*

HAKEA

Proteaceae

Native to Australia

A genus of over 150 species of evergreen small trees and shrubs with leaves that are sometimes flat, otherwise circular in cross-section, sometimes divided. Small tubular flowers are usually in groups in leaf axils. They are found in every state of Australia with the highest species diversity being found in the southwest of Western Australia. All need to be grown in acid soil.

Hakea laurina

Pincushion Tree

Native to southwestern Australia

A dense, rounded tree or shrub to 6m high and 5m wide. Narrow, shiny, grey-green leathery leaves are up to 15cm long, often with a red margin and have a tendency to wave and curl. Stunning showy flower clusters are produced along the branches in winter. Fascinating, cherry red, ball-like flowers appear from autumn to late winter, adorned with long, white pin-like stamens, earning its common name. Budding starts in late summer, with flowers opening from late autumn through winter. It is tolerant of drought, salt winds and poor soil, but it needs good drainage. Best grown in full sun but can take part shade. Frost tolerant, but fresh growth can sustain some frost damage. A shallow-rooted plant, so it can be affected in windy weather. Attracts birds into the garden and can also be useful as a cut flower.

HARDENBERGIA

Fabaceae

Coral Pea

Native to Australia

A small genus containing three species of strikingly attractive twining climbers or creeping ground covers. Alternate leaves are simple or pinnate with three or five leaflets, with stipules at the base. They are grown for their colourful pea-like flowers, which are produced in great profusion. Flowers are usually in pairs or small clusters in leaf axils and are medium-sized, violet, white or pinkish, the standard petal with a yellowish or greenish centre.

Hardenbergia comptoniana

Lilac Vine

Native to Western Australia

An evergreen, twining climber that makes moderate growth to 3m high or more with an equal spread. Dark green, narrow lance-shaped leaves are divided into three or five leaflets, each one up to 15cm long. The brilliant 1 to 2cm-long pea-shaped flowers appear on 15cm long pendant racemes from late winter to spring. These range from mauve to purple or dark blue, with pink and white forms also known. A reliable and attractive climber that can be grown in full sun or partial shade. Grows best in a light, well-drained soil. Drought tolerant but flowers better with some summer water. Cut back after flowering to prevent tangling. 'Rosea' has pink flowers.

Hardenbergia violacea
Purple Coral Pea

Native to eastern Queensland, eastern New South Wales, south-eastern Victoria and southern South Australia

An evergreen, prostrate or twining, strong-growing subshrub with wiry stems that grows to 3m high or more with an equal spread. Leaves are simple, lance-shaped, usually undivided, 3 to 10cm long and 1 to 5cm wide on a petiole about 1cm long. They are leathery, glabrous and paler on the lower surface. Axillary clusters of between 20 and 40 small flowers, often in pairs, are purple to violet, sometimes white, pink or lilac with a yellow basal spot. They are borne in pendant racemes 10 to 13cm long during winter and spring. Grow the climber in full sun or partial shade. Drought tolerant, but flowers better with some summer water in well-drained soil. Grows well in subtropical, warm temperate and Mediterranean climates. Cut back after flowering to prevent tangling. Use it to cover a pergola wall or grow it through a small tree. Can also be pegged down as a ground cover. 'Pink Cascade' has pink flowers. 'White Crystals' has pure white flowers in winter.

HEDERA
Araliaceae

Ivy

Native to Europe, north Africa, west Asia

A genus of about ten species of evergreen, woody, trailing or self-clinging climbers. On level ground they remain creeping, not exceeding 5 to 20cm in height, but on surfaces suitable for climbing, including trees or masonry, they can climb to at least 30m above the ground. Ivies have two leaf types, with palmately-lobed, juvenile leaves on creeping and climbing stems and unlobed cordate adult leaves on fertile flowering stems exposed to full sun. The flowers are greenish yellow with five small petals, produced in umbels from autumn to early winter and rich in nectar. They are trouble-free plants that have many uses, ideal for covering eye-sores, climbing on walls, fences, or arches. Useful as soil binders to discourage soil erosion. Especially good in shady places. There are many cultivars with leaves boldly marked with yellow, cream or white.

Hedera canariensis
Algerian Ivy, Canary Islands Ivy, Canary Ivy

Native to the Azores, Canary Islands and north Africa

A vigorous evergreen perennial climber that quickly reaches 20 to 30m or more high with a wide spread and can also be grown as ground cover where there are no vertical surfaces. Leathery, shiny, rich green, triangular leaves are 5 to 20cm wide with one to five shallow lobes. Leaves become more heart-shaped as they mature. These are carried on wine-red stalks and often have reddish hairs on the underneath of the leaf. Flowers are greenish and the fruits globular and black when ripe. Drought tolerant but grows better with some summer water. Grow in well-drained soil in full sun or even deep shade. An attractive, strong growing climber that needs to be sited with care. 'Gloire de Marengo' has long been cultivated in Europe. It has silvery green leaves variegated with yellow and cream.

Hedera colchica
Persian Ivy

Native from the Caucasus to Iran

A bold, vigorous, woody climber easily growing to 10m or more high with a huge spread. The largest of the ivies. Leaves are alternate, of two types, with palmately five-lobed juvenile leaves on creeping and climbing stems, and unlobed cordate adult leaves. Entire, leathery, dark green, somewhat heart-shaped leaves are up to 15cm across and 25cm long. Flowers are produced from late summer until late autumn, individually small, greenish, in large numbers in umbels. These are rich in nectar, an important food source for bees and other insects. Drought tolerant when established but grows better with some summer water, growing well in full sun or deep shade in well-drained soil. 'Dentata Variegata' is a striking plant with bright-green leaves splashed with grey and broadly margined in creamy yellow that ages to white. 'Sulphur Heart' has bright-gold and lime-green variegations, while some are entirely yellow, and are invaluable for bringing splashes of light to a dark shady wall.

HELIANTHEMUM
Cistaceae

Rock Rose, Sun Rose

Native to Northern Hemisphere, especially the Mediterranean

A large genus containing about 110 species of evergreen shrubs or subshrubs and some herbaceous annuals or perennials. Leaves are opposite, but some plants may have alternate leaves along the upper stems. Flowers are solitary or borne in an array of inflorescence types, such as panicles, racemes, or headlike clusters. They are ideal for rock gardens or raised beds. Many colourful named hybrids between several species have been raised with red, orange, pink and yellow flowers.

Helianthemum nummularium
Common Rock Rose, Sunrose

Native to Europe

A dwarf trailing subshrub that spreads widely to about 1m only growing to 20cm high, usually forming a mat. Grey-green, lance-shaped leaves are up to 5cm long. The one-sided clusters of single or double saucer-shaped flowers are 2cm across. In the centre is a tight cluster of orange stamens, which are sensitive to touch, and spread outwards to reveal the tall stigma in the middle. The wild species has yellow flowers, but garden varieties range from white through yellow to deep red. Though the individual blooms are short-lived, the plant produces a mass of flowers through the summer. Grow in full sun in a rock garden with poor dry soil or in the front of a border. Summer drought tolerant. Good drainage is essential as over watering will kill it. After flowering trim off all the dead flower heads and lanky growth to keep bushy. Looks good in a container on a sunny patio.

HELICHRYSUM
Asteraceae
Native to Europe, Asia, Australasia, and particularly South Africa

A large genus of about 600 species of annuals, herbaceous perennials, evergreen subshrubs or shrubs growing to a height of 0.6 to 1m. Their leaves are oblong to lance-shaped, flat and pubescent on both sides. These shrubby plants are usually low growing, often with attractive aromatic foliage and commonly found in dry sunny sites.

Helichrysum italicum
Curry Plant, Italian Strawflower, Immortelle

Native to southern Europe

A hardy, variable, bushy subshrub that grows up to 1m high and 60cm wide with silvery-grey, woolly stems that are woody at the base, found on dry, rocky or sandy ground around the Mediterranean. It is sometimes called the curry plant because of the strong fragrance of its narrow, grey leaves, 3cm long. Terminal, long-stalked clusters of many tiny bright yellow flowers, 1cm wide, appear during summer. They keep their colour after picking and are used in dried flower arrangements. When established, it withstands drought but grows better with some summer water. Grow in full sun in well-drained soil. Probably one of the best silver plants in the Mediterranean region. It looks best when grown in groups.

Helichrysum petiolare
Liquorice Plant

Native to South Africa

An evergreen subshrub with white, woolly, trailing, branching stems 50cm or more high, that will eventually form a huge mound 3m or more round. It is grown for its felt-like, silvery-green, oval leaves 4cm across and stems covered with cobwebby white hairs. Terminal clusters of small creamy-white to yellow flowers 5cm across appear in late summer. Drought, heat and frost tolerant once established. Grows well in most well-drained soils, including dry gravel. Tolerating some shade, it is at its best in full sun. The silvery foliage also makes it a popular choice for mixed borders, where it complements the colourful blooms of perennials. It is strong growing and needs to be controlled by constant clipping. The variety 'Limelight' has lime-green leaves and 'Variegatum' has cream-edged leaves. Both varieties are less strong growing and need some shade to keep the colour in the leaves.

Helichrysum serpyllifolium see *Plecostachys serpyllifolia*

HELIOTROPIUM
Boraginaceae
Heliotrope

Native to North and South America, the Pacific Islands and the Canary Islands

A genus of about 325 species of tender annuals, evergreen subshrubs and shrubs. They have simple, mostly entire, roughly hairy, usually alternate leaves. Grown for their small, sweetly scented tubular flowers, which are produced in summer.

Heliotropium arborescens
Heliotrope, Cherry Pie

Native to Peru, Chile

A bushy evergreen shrubby perennial to 1m high, spreading to 45cm wide that is often grown as an annual. The whole plant is covered in fine hairs. Oval to lance-shaped greenish-purple leaves are up to 10cm long and 5cm wide with prominent veins. Dense clusters 8 to 10cm across of tiny tubular flowers are from darkest violet through to silvery mauve. These are sweetly scented and produced mostly in spring, but some appear in summer. Grow in a rich well-drained soil in partial shade and give some summer water. Often grown as a pot plant where it looks good on a patio or terrace. Many named varieties have been raised with a powerful scent. 'Marine' has rich foliage and profuse blooms with flower heads to 15cm across, making it a superb choice for summer bedding or window boxes. In warmer climates, grow in the front of a border or in containers outdoors.

HESPEROYUCCA
Asparagaceae
Native to southern North America

A small genus of two recognised species of flowering plants closely related to, and recently split from, Yucca. It has taken recent DNA analysis to confirm that they are indeed genetically distinct from Yucca.

The splitting of Hesperoyucca from Yucca is still not widely reflected in available literature.

Hesperoyucca whipplei syn. *Yucca whipplei*
Our Lord's Candle

Native from California to Mexico

An evergreen shrub forming a dense, trunkless rosette of long, rigid, grey-green leaves 20 to 90cm long, which end in a sharp point with finely saw-toothed leaf edges. In summer, mature plants are topped with a striking flower stalk 1.8 to 4m high, bearing hundreds of bell-shaped, white to purplish, scented flowers 3cm in diameter on a densely branched panicle up to 70cm broad, covering the upper half of the inflorescence. The fruit is a dry winged capsule, which splits open at maturity to release the seeds. The plant takes several (usually five or more) years to reach maturity and flower, at which point it usually dies.

Helianthemum nummularium.

Helichrysum italicum.

Helichrysum petiolare.

Heliotropium arborescens.

Hesperoyucca whipplei.

Hibbertia scandens.

Hibiscus insularis.

Hibiscus syriacus.

Hippeastrum aulicum.

Most subspecies produce offshoots from the base, so that although the parent plant flowers and dies, a cluster of clones around its base continues to grow and reproduce. It may also grow back from its base after much of its foliage has been scorched off by wildfires that frequent its range. Easily grown in full sun in well-drained soil. Highly tolerant of drought, heat and frost. Also of architectural appeal, as it does spectacularly well in pots beside or inside buildings, in foyer areas or out in the open near a pool or perhaps a courtyard. Provides a spectacular focal point in Mediterranean gardens, gravel gardens and xeriscape gardens.

HIBBERTIA
Dilleniaceae
Native mostly in Australia and Tasmania

A genus of 400 species of evergreen trees, shrubs, rarely climbers, that often form mats. Leaves are usually alternate, clustered on short side-branches, with smooth, rarely toothed or lobed edges. Flowers are usually arranged singly in leaf axils or on the ends of stems.

Hibbertia scandens
Guinea Gold Flower, Snake Vine, Climbing Guinea Flower

Native to eastern Australia

A fast-growing shrub that will climb by twining stems 3 to 6m high, spreading to 3m wide. Young stems are a reddish-brown with silky hairy shoots. Leaves are typically glossy, leathery, and either lance-shaped or oval, 8cm long. They are smooth on top and silky-hairy underneath. Solitary, terminal, 5cm wide, bright yellow flowers have over 30 stamens around between three and seven glabrous carpels. Flowers are produced throughout the year, but mostly during summer. While unpleasantly scented, it makes a spectacular sight when in full bloom. Grows best in light shade but will also grow in full sun where it will not be so rampant. Good for training on a trellis or over a low wall. As it is native to sand dunes, good drainage is important. Drought tolerant, needing little summer water. Often used as a ground cover. Grows well in containers on a shaded patio or terrace.

HIBISCUS
Malvaceae
Native to warm temperate and tropical regions of the world

This large genus has perhaps 250 species of deciduous and evergreen trees, shrubs, annuals and herbaceous perennials. Leaves are alternate, ovate to lance-shaped. Most have large undivided leaves, although some have deeply dissected leaves, often with toothed or lobed margins. They are grown mainly for their usually large and spectacular flowers, which are produced over a long season. The conspicuous flowers are trumpet-shaped, with five or more petals. Colour ranges from white to pink, red, orange, peach, yellow or purple. One species is often used as pot plants in cooler climates.

Hibiscus huegelii see *Alyogyne huegelii*

Hibiscus insularis
Phillip Island Hibiscus

Native to Phillip Island, a small island to the south of Norfolk Island, Australia

A large, fast-growing evergreen shrub up to 3m high and about 5m wide with dense, leathery, shiny, dark-green leaves with crenulate margins. It has small leaves and short internodes, which makes it good for a dense hedge, but left unpruned it will create a low, domed shape of neatly layered branches. Showy, greenish-yellow flowers are cream to light green with a dark magenta centre, turning to dark rose at maturity, and with a reddish violet eye. Flowers are produced in abundance for most of the year. Most plants in cultivation are from cuttings from the last two wild specimens, thus the genetic variation is extremely low in this species. Well-drained, humus-rich soils in a sunny spot are best. Drought tolerant but some summer water encourages more flowering.

Hibiscus mutabilis
Confederate Rose

Native to southern China

A fast-growing, upright to spreading, evergreen shrub or small tree to 3m or more high and 2m or more wide with soft green stems covered with hairs becoming woody with age. Large three- to seven-lobed leaves are 10 to 20cm long and wide, a dull green and covered with hairs. Flowers are produced in leaf axils near the end of branches and can be double or single, 10 to 15cm in diameter, opening white or pink and change to deep red by evening. This gives the shrub a dramatic effect with many shades of colour at the same time. Flowers are produced continuously throughout the summer. This dramatic shrub is easily grown in well-drained soil, requiring little attention with only a moderate amount of summer water. Often seen in municipal gardens trained into standards.

Hibiscus syriacus
Rose of Sharon

Native to east Asia

A hardy deciduous shrub with upright-growing branches 2 to 4m high, with a compact habit when young but sometimes more open with age. The usually three-lobed, coarsely-toothed, dark-green leaves are 5 to 8cm long. It bears large 7cm-wide, open trumpet-shaped flowers with prominent, yellow-tipped white stamens. Flowers are often pink but can also be dark pink (almost purple), light pink or white. Individual flowers are usually single, but occasionally double, are short-lived, lasting only a day, but blooming continues until autumn. Grow in full sun or light shade, in well-drained, organically rich soil. Once established, it is drought tolerant but grows better with some summer water. It is highly tolerant of air pollution, heat, humidity, poor soil and the only Hibiscus that is frost hardy. For larger flowers prune severely in winter. The species has naturalised well in many suburban areas and might even be termed slightly invasive. The variety 'Blue Bird' has single deep blue-mauve flowers with a crimson blotch at the base. 'Diana' has single white flowers. 'Woodbridge' has large rosy-pink flowers with a maroon patch at the base.

HIPPEASTRUM
Amaryllidaceae
Amaryllis

Native to Central and South America

A genus of about 90 species and many hybrids and cultivars of perennial, herbaceous and bulbous perennials. The majority have large, fleshy bulbs from 5 to 12cm in diameter. Bulbs produce two to seven long-lasting evergreen or deciduous leaves 30 to 90cm long and 2.5 to 5cm wide. Leaves usually develop after flowering. In the species, the flowers are large red or purple but many colours and cultivars have been created over the past hundred years. Generally, the spectacular large-flowered hybrids are grown. They are often wrongly referred to as Amaryllis, which is a separate genus.

Hippeastrum aulicum syn. *H. morelianum*
Lily of the Palace

Native to the Atlantic Forest and Cercado ecoregions from Brazil to Paraguay

A bulbous, perennial epiphyte, growing on rocks and trees with four or more mid- to deep-green strap-shaped leaves 30 to 50cm long and 5cm wide. The plant is almost evergreen, shedding its leaves each summer, and replacing them shortly after. Even without blooms, it is highly ornamental, with lush, full foliage, and doesn't have a long dormancy. In spring, large funnel-shaped flowers are carried on robust hollow stems to 50cm high. Each bold flower is scarlet with a green throat, up to 15cm across, usually with four flowers to a stem. They are overlaid with intricate, crimson veins, and have a lime-green star in the centre. This is a true species, not a cultivated hybrid. It makes offsets fairly readily, which you may separate. The bulb is normally grown in pots or containers but can be grown outdoors in well-drained soil in sun or partial shade. Once the flowering has finished, remove the flower stem, keep watering and feeding until the leaves turn yellow, which may be in late autumn. Only then withhold water, letting the bulbs dry out. A beautiful bulb which looks attractive when planted in groups in a border.

Hippeastrum hybrids
Fire Lily

Garden origin

A splendidly vigorous, bulbous perennial with four or more mid- to deep-green strap-shaped leaves up to 60cm long. Up to six large funnel-shaped flowers are carried atop robust hollow stems to 60cm high. Each flower can be 20 to 25cm wide, white, pink, salmon, orange to red, some with stripes, others with delicate shading. They are usually single, but there are some double forms. Flowers are usually produced in late spring but can be forced to appear much earlier. Bulbs are normally grown in pots or containers, but also make excellent border plants and can be placed in groups in warmer climates in a warm but not hot, semi-shady spot in the garden in well-drained soil. Remove the flower stem once blooming is over and keep watering and feeding the plant until the leaves turn yellow, which can occur in late autumn. Only then withhold water, letting the bulbs dry out. When planting, the top third of the bulb should be left exposed. When growing in pots, choose a smaller one where the bulbs will fit rather tightly. Pots can be brought inside when the bulbs are blooming, for a week or so. Flowers can be cut for vases.

HIPPOPHAE
Elaeagnaceae
Sandthorn, Sallowthorn, Seaberry

Native to Europe and Asia

A genus of only two or three species of dioecious spiny shrubs or trees covered with silvery scales. Shrubs reach 0.5 to 6m tall, with alternate or opposite leaves. Attractive orange berries are produced on female plants. They are exceptionally hardy plants. Because species develop an aggressive and extensive root system, they are planted to inhibit soil erosion and used in land reclamation for their nitrogen fixing properties.

Hippophae rhamnoides
Sea Buckthorn

Native to northern Europe across to northern China

A hardy, tall deciduous shrub or small tree 2 to 4m high and wide, with a rough, brown or black bark and a thick, greyish-green crown. Alternate, slender, silver or silvery green willow-like leaves are up to 5cm long. Inconspicuous yellow flowers appear before the leaves. The sex of seedlings can only be determined at the first flowering, which mostly occurs after three years. The male inflorescence comprises four to six flowers, whereas the female inflorescence typically has just one flower. Female plants bear many 1cm deep-orange berries along the branches. Therefore, grow the shrub in groups to contain both sexes. Berries contain an acrid juice, so birds avoid them. Particularly good on light sandy soils where they make excellent wind resisters in coastal areas. When established, it withstands summer drought, but grows better with some water. The silver leaves and stems make a good background to other plants.

HOMERIA *see* MORAEA

HORDEUM
Poaceae

Native throughout temperate regions of Africa, Eurasia and the Americas

A genus of 33 species of annual and perennial plants. One species, *H. vulgare* (barley), has become of major commercial importance as a cereal grain, used as fodder crop and for malting in the production of beer and whisky. Many species are grown for their ornamental flowerheads.

Hordeum jubatum
Foxtail Barley, Bobtail Barley, Squirrel-tail Barley
Native to northern North America, Asia

A hardy grass species that is usually grown as an annual or short-lived perennial 30 to 60cm high. It has clumps of light-green, arching, strap-like leaves to 15cm long. Distinctive nodding feathery flower spikes are 13cm long, green, flushed with pale pink or purple and fade to tan as they mature. For best results, grow in full sun and well-drained soil. Reasonably tolerant of summer drought. The pale pink flowers create a beautiful and harmonious sight when planted together in a large area, gently moving with the wind. It is easy to grow from seed and will also self-seed readily. Good for coastal gardens, as it can tolerate saline conditions. Use your fingers to comb out tatty leaves or flowers and cut back hard in spring. Useful for dried flower arrangements. Cut flowerheads for drying before fully mature.

HYACINTHUS
Asparagaceae
Native to eastern Mediterranean, Iran

A small genus of three species of bulbous herbs, each producing around four to six narrow, untoothed leaves and one to three spikes or racemes of flowers, usually growing to a height of 15 to 20cm. In the wild species, flowers are widely spaced, with as few as two per raceme. Cultivars have much denser flower spikes and are more robust.

Hyacinthus orientalis
Common Hyacinth, Garden Hyacinth, Dutch Hyacinth
Native to southwestern Asia, southern and central Turkey

This bulbous perennial with a 3 to 7cm-diameter bulb produces leaves in a basal whorl. Leaves are linear to lance-shaped, channelled, bright green 15 to 35cm long and 1 to 3cm wide, with a soft, succulent texture. In spring, erect racemes appear of up to 40 tubular, bell-shaped, waxy, fragrant flowers 2 to 3.5cm long with a tubular, six-lobed perianth. Each flower is pale violet-blue at the base and almost white above, with spreading, then recurving lobes. The flowering stem grows to 20 to 35cm. Grows best in full sun to part shade in well-drained, but not dry, soil. Requires a winter dormancy period of drought. The bulb was introduced into Europe in the sixteenth century and is now widely cultivated everywhere in the temperate world for its strongly-fragrant flowers. These appear exceptionally early in the season, frequently forced to flower at Christmas time. Over 2,000 cultivars have been selected and named, with flower colour in shades of blue, white, pale yellow, pink, red or purple. Most cultivars have also been selected for denser flower spikes than the wild type, bearing 40 to 100 or more flowers on each spike.

HYLOTELEPHIUM
Crassulaceae
Sedum, Stonecrop, Live-For-Ever
Native to Asia, Europe and North America

A genus of about 33 species of succulent plants formerly included in Sedum. They are mainly tall, perennial plants with usually thick and sometimes tuberous roots. These popular garden plants are undemanding, not aggressive, with fleshy, drought-resistant foliage and lovely domed flower heads packed with a profusion of tiny, star-shaped, white, pink, or red flowers that appear in late summer or early autumn. All species have more or less edible leaves and roots.

Hylotelephium spectabile syn. *Sedum spectabile*
Iceplant
Native to China and Korea

An herbaceous perennial growing to 45cm tall and broad. It has alternate, simple leaves on erect, unbranched succulent stems and a tuberous root rhizome. Leaves are usually opposite or in threes, more or less wedge-shaped at the base, frosted blue above, 3 to 10cm long. Leaf margins are smooth or serrated towards the tip. Star-shaped pink flowers are borne in flat cymes 15cm across from summer until first frost. The many-flowered inflorescence is about 7 to 11cm wide. These popular garden plants are easy to grow in full sun. Tolerating light to partial shade in hot summer climates but producing weak, floppy growth when grown in deep shade or overly rich soils. These succulents do not need rich soil but require excellent drainage. They are heat tolerant, drought resistant and frost hardy, making them popular outdoor plants. Great in containers.

Hylotelephium telephium 'Purple Emperor' syn. *Sedum telephium* 'Purple Emperor'
Stonecrop
Garden origin

A semi-upright, clump-forming perennial that forms a clump of thick, fleshy purple foliage 45 to 60cm high. Foliage starts out the most delicate grey-purple, before intensifying to a rich shade of purple from late spring through to autumn. Masses of rosy-pink flowers open to white, densely packed in large umbrella-shaped flowerheads, atop bright reddish-purple stems clad with dark purple, fleshy leaves. A magnet for bees and butterflies. For best results, grow in well-drained dry to medium moisture soil in full sun, which is ideal for the front of a border. Thrives in sandy or gravelly soils. This outstanding heat and drought tolerant plant is useful in a dry garden.

Hymenocallis narcissiflora see *Ismene narcissiflora*

Hymenocallis × festalis see *Ismene × deflexa*

HYMENOSPORUM
Pittosporaceae
Australian Frangipani
Native to eastern Australia and New Guinea

A genus containing just one species of evergreen tree that is closely related to

Hippeastrum hybrid.

Hippophae rhamnoides.

Hordeum jubatum.

Hyacinthus orientalis.

Hylotelephium spectabile.

Hylotelephium telephium 'Purple Emperor'.

Hymenosporum flavum.

Hyophorbe lagenicaulis.

Pittosporum. It is grown as an attractive tree with a showy clusters of flowers.

Hymenosporum flavum

Native Frangipani, Sweetshade

A small evergreen tree or large shrub up to 6m high with a spread of 5m, native to coastal brush forests. Growth may be slow at first, but moderate once established. An attractively shaped tree is formed with well-spaced, slender, bushy branches. Bark is grey and roughish, and the branches sparse, radiating in whorls from the main stem. Shiny, dark-green, smooth, oval to oblong leaves 5 to 15cm long are alternately grouped at the ends of twiggy branchlets. Fragrant, open, tubular flowers are quite large, about 4cm in diameter with a floral tube up to 3cm long. They are initially functionally male, and coloured white with lemon tinges. Over a period of about five days, the stigma develops and stamens curl away. The colour deepens until the fully functioning female flower is golden yellow with red or purple track lines in the throat. These appear in loose terminal panicles to 20cm across and 3cm long, often completely covering the crown of the tree from spring to summer. This hardy tree grows well in full sun but can take some shade. Summer drought tolerant, if some water is available. Grow in well-drained soil, preferably with a high organic content. The cultivar 'Gold nugget' is a compact perfumed beauty, growing to only 0.5 to 0.7m high and wide. Because of its compact habit, this cultivar is recommended for small gardens. It can also be grown in pots both outdoors and indoors.

HYOPHORBE

Arecaceae

Bottle Palm

Native to the Mascarene Islands east of Madagascar

A small genus of five species of single-stemmed, pinnate-leafed palms. All five species can reach over 6m, and two of the species develop swollen trunks that have made them popular as ornamentals, but all are endangered in the wild.

Hyophorbe lagenicaulis

Bottle Palm, Palmiste Gargoulette

Native to Round Island, Mauritius

This dwarf palm will grow slowly to 3 to 4m high. The palm has a large swollen (sometimes bizarrely so) trunk. Its trunk is smooth, light grey to almost white when young with a rounded bulge and gradually elongates and flattens somewhat as the palm matures. Palms have only four to six pinnate leaves open at any time. Leaves of young palms have a red or orange tint, but are deep green at maturity. Pinnately compound leaves or fronds can grow to 3.5m long and are attached to a 25cm petiole or stem. Its slender, lance-shaped leaflets are dark green, approximately 60cm long, and grow oppositely to form a 'V' shape on the rachis or middle of the frond. The palm produces beautiful, heavily-branched inflorescences that encircle the trunk just below the crown-shaft on 75cm stalks. Male and female small white flowers occur on the same inflorescence and are white or cream coloured. Grow in moderately fertile, well-drained soil, where it can take some summer drought. It grows best in full sunlight but can tolerate moderate shade. Bottle palms are killed by frost for any appreciable length of time. They may survive a brief, light frost, but will have foliage damage. It makes a fine container-grown palm, as long as it is protected from the cold and not overwatered. Makes a great feature palm.

Hyophorbe verschaffeltii

Spindle Palm

Native to Mauritius

A single stemmed palm to 6m high with a trunk that is narrow at the base, becoming wider in the middle and then tapering again to the swollen crown-shaft, which has rings left by the old leaves. This spindle shape gives it the common name. The crown shaft is fairly short, bright green with 8 to 10 pinnate fronds arching outward and down at the end, forming a 'V' shape, growing 2.5m long. Leaves are held somewhat erect and hang gracefully, giving it an attractive appearance. Horn-like flower spikes emerge from below the crown-shaft on mature specimens. Easily grown in any soil in full sun, it tolerates summer drought. Ideal for coastal gardens as it withstands salt laden sea breezes. A showy and unusual palm, with even large plants taking up little space. They make good container plants. Elegant looking and prized in tropical and subtropical areas of the world.

HYPHAENE

Arecaceae

Native to Africa, Madagascar, the Arabian Peninsula and India

A genus of about ten species of doecious palmate-leafed palms usually found in poor or exhausted soil in hot, dry areas. They are unusual among palms in having regular, naturally branched trunks, when most other palms are single stemmed. Some species are stemless, some have creeping stems, others tree-like.

Hyphaene coriacea

Doum Palm

Native to South Africa, east Africa and Madagascar

This slow-growing palm has a trunk up to about 6m high and 10 to 20cm in diameter, which occasionally branches, but may also occur as a short-stemmed cluster of plants. Trunks are scored horizontally and prominently with the scars from old leaf bases. Older and longer stems tend to recline. Suckering occurs from the base to allow clump development. Leaves are robust, thick, fan-shaped, up to 1.5m in diameter on a 1.5m long leaf stalk that is armed with thick, black, recurved thorns along its margins. The foliage is an attractive grey-green with a whitish bloom on the leaf undersurfaces. Although relatively slow growing, it is an ideal palm for a dramatic effect. Will do well in any sunny well-drained site in a frost-free garden. It needs little or no summer water but grows better with an occasional deep soaking. The somewhat limited garden use of this palm may be because of difficulties in germinating its seed.

Hyphaene thebaica
Gingerbread Palm
Native to north Africa

A medium-sized palm that is one of the few truly branching palms. It grows 6 to 10m high and spreads to 6m wide. The bole appears smooth overall, but bears the scars of fallen leaves and features bunches of large leaves at the ends of the branches. Old trees have trunks that are blackish. Petioles (leaf stalks) are about a metre long, sheathing the branch at the base and armed with stout upward-curving claws. Leaves are fan shaped and measure about 1.2 by 1.8m. The inflorescences of male and female plants are similar in appearance, up to about 1.2m long, branching irregularly and with two or three spikes arising from each branchlet. The tree bears an irregular oval fruit about the size of an apple. Fruit has a red outer skin and a thick, spongy, and rather sweet inner substance that tastes like gingerbread, giving it the common name. When established, it withstands drought, but grows better with some summer water. Will do well in any sunny well-drained site in a frost-free garden. A dramatic and unusual palm.

I

IBERIS
Brassicaceae
Candytuft
Native to central Europe and the Mediterranean region

A genus of 30 to 40 species of small annuals, perennials and evergreen subshrubs with white, pink, purple or red four-petalled flowers that are sometimes fragrant. These are grown for their showy flowers, often planted in rock gardens or in sunny borders. These plants are native to chalky, open areas.

Iberis saxatilis
Native to the Mediterranean

A small evergreen subshrub 10 to 15cm high spreading to 30cm wide. It can spread via adventitious rooting of stems that contact soil. Many narrow, fleshy, almost cylindrical dark green leaves to 2cm long are carried on the upright stems. Small, white, four-petalled, snowflake-like flowers in dense, flattened clusters (corymbs) appear profusely from spring to summer. These flattened heads, 3 to 4cm across of small white flowers, are often tinged pink with age. They are borne at the ends of short branches, so dense that they often totally obscure the foliage beneath. It thrives and flowers best in full sun with well-drained soil that is neutral to alkaline but will tolerate partial shade. Drought tolerant. It is typically grown in gardens that simulate the rocky conditions of the plant's natural habitat, particularly if placed to drape over the rocks. A bright, cheerful plant for the garden that is easily raised from seed.

Iberis sempervirens
Evergreen Candytuft
Native to southern Europe

An evergreen, spreading subshrub growing to 30cm high spreading to 40cm wide forming neat leafy mats of foliage. Narrow, shiny, dark green, slightly fleshy leaves 2 to 6cm long form a billowing mound. Many tight clusters of fragrant white flowers 5cm across are borne on long stalks, which rise above the foliage from winter to spring. These cover the plant making a wonderful show. As an ornamental plant, it is a spring-blooming favourite, often seen cascading over rocks and walls, or used as ground cover. Grow in ordinary well-drained soil in a dry sunny place. When established, it withstands drought, but grows better with some summer water. Ideal for the rockery, front of a border or admirable for the top of a wall. It is easily raised from seed. 'Little Gem' grows 10 to 15cm high. 'Snowflake' grows 10 to 30cm high with wider leaves and larger flowers.

Iberis umbellata
Garden Candytuft, Globe Candytuft
Native to the Mediterranean region

A mound-forming, hardy annual 30 to 40cm high and spreading to 25cm wide. Lance-shaped leaves are up to 1.5 to 2.5cm long with the lower leaves toothed. Flowers are in umbel-shaped corymbs to 5cm across. The calyx is violet, and the corolla is composed of four white, pink or purple petals. Abundant throughout summer, these flowers are both brilliant and sweet-smelling. It requires well-drained soil but tolerates a wide range of soil types, including poor and highly alkaline soil. Summer drought tolerant, it may decline with excessive rain. Grow in a sunny position as it does not tolerate shade. It can become untidy looking once flowering is over, so planting some more later season flowers in the same area is a good idea. A beautiful plant for the border and splendid for cutting. They also make attractive pot plants.

IBOZA *see* TETRADENIA

IPHEION
Amaryllidaceae
Native to Argentina, Uruguay and southern Brazil

A genus of about ten species of small bulbous perennials from meadows and rocky sites with narrow grass-like leaves. They are grown for their honey-scented, star-shaped spring flowers, usually white or blue.

Ipheion uniflorum
Spring Star Flower

Native to Argentina

A bulbous perennial that quickly multiplies to form a clump. During autumn the flattish, bluish-green strap-shaped leaves to 25cm long appear. They smell like onions when crushed. In spring solitary upward-facing flowers 4cm across appear on stems 15 to 20cm high. Each honey-scented, star-shaped flower has six pointed lobes up to 3cm long, pale to deep purple blue, often with a deeper mid-vein. Grow the bulbs in full sun or light shade. Summer dormant so they need no water, indeed they like to be baked during summer. Easy to grow in any soil, as they will quickly multiply. Ideal for planting in drifts under deciduous trees or large shrubs. They also make a bright and cheerful edging to a border or a ground cover in semi-wild areas. 'Album' has white flowers, 'Wisley Blue' has lilac-blue flowers.

IPOMOEA
Convolvulaceae
Morning Glory

Native to tropical and warm temperate regions worldwide

A large genus of about 500 species of twining annual and perennial herbaceous to woody vines and a few erect-growing shrubs. Leaves are usually cordate (heart-shaped) but may be deeply divided into lobes or even thread-like segments. Flowers are solitary or in clusters, trumpet, funnel or bell-shaped, in a variety of colours. The sap is often milky. All species grow fast, some rampantly so and need at least some sun. They are mostly grown for their large flowers, but some have outstandingly beautiful leaves or fruit. One is an important food crop, the sweet potato.

Ipomoea alba
Moonflower, Tropical White Morning-Glory

Native to tropical America

This fascinating, sweetly-scented perennial vine earns its name from its pure white flowers, which open in the evening and close when touched by the morning sun. At dusk, densely packed buds pop open, and the flower petals unfold within a few minutes. They reveal a pale green star extending from the throat and send their sweet fragrance into the night air. At dawn, the large, flat flowers, 8 to 15cm, close by rolling up. The flowers attract night-flying moths. The plant is noted for its milky sap, and somewhat prickly, twining stems. Its foliage comprises large, rounded, broad-ovate, deep green leaves that are 10 to 15cm long with cordate bases. These provide a dense leafy cover. Highly valued for its fast growth, reaching 3 to 5m in height and width, it is an excellent choice for hiding fences, scaling walls, or scrambling through arbours and trellises. New flowers are produced daily, so the plant blooms continuously most of the summer. Thrives in full sun in average, well-drained soil. Tolerant of summer drought once established.

Ipomoea lobata syn. *Mina lobata*
Spanish Flag Vine, Firecracker Vine

Native to Mexico and parts of South America

An herbaceous, perennial vine, widely grown around the world as an ornamental. Mature vines reach up to 5m tall and spread as wide. Leaves reach between 5 and 15cm long and have three distinct lobes. Single-sided, 15cm long racemes of tubular flowers are held on slender stems that gently arc upward and outward away from the vine. The flowers mature from red to pale yellow, creating a gradient from the top of the raceme to the base. Blooms freely from mid- to late summer. Flowers are highly attractive to hummingbirds, butterflies and other pollinators. It does best in organically rich, well-draining soil in a sheltered spot with full sun. It will tolerate some shade, but the colourful floral display will suffer. Somewhat drought tolerant, but flowers best with some water. Requires a trellis, arbour, or other structure to climb in full sun. Use as a vertical accent in sunny mixed borders or patio plantings. Plant several next to each other to create a quick privacy screen. Can also be grown in a large container. The common name Spanish flag vine refers to the gradient of red to yellow flowers on each raceme. The common name Firecracker vine gets its name from its blooms that look like colourful fireworks shooting out of the vine. Easily grown from seed.

Ipomoea purpurea
Common Morning-Glory, Tall Morning-Glory, Purple Morning Glory

Native to Mexico

An annual climber with hairy stems that trail or twine. It wraps itself around structures, growing to a height of 2 to 3m. Heart-shaped leaves are entire or three-lobed, and stems are covered with brown hairs. It produces an abundance of large, funnel-shaped flowers 3 to 6cm in diameter in solitary or few-flowered cymes. Flowers are large, funnel-shaped, deep purple, white, pink or magenta, with a red star and white throat, and white below. Flowers open in the morning and last only one day. Adaptable to most well-drained soils from poor to rich. Tolerant of summer drought but give some water for the best performance. Perfect for growing on trellises, arbours, lattice or chain-link fences, or as a ground cover.

Hyphaene coriacea.

Iberis sempervirens.

Ipheion uniflorum.

Ipomoea alba.

Ipomoea lobata.

Ipomoea purpurea.

Iris palla.

Iris xiphium.

Ismene × deflexa.

IRIS

Iridaceae

Native to the Northern Hemisphere

A large and remarkably diverse genus of 200 to 300 species of rhizomatous or bulbous perennials found in a wide range of habitats. Some species are found in marshes and wet areas, but most inhabit dry ground and become dormant or semi-dormant during summer. They vary in flower colour and form, cultural needs and flowering times. Most produce their colourful, even spectacular flowers during spring and summer. A few are evergreen but most are deciduous, some being summer dormant. Leaves are sword-like or grass-like. Flowers are usually complex with three inner petals called 'standards', which may be upright, arching or horizontal. The three outer petal-like segments, the sepals, called the 'falls', may be horizontal or drooping. Botanically, iris are divided into several subgenera and sections, but in horticulture they are divided into bulbous iris and rhizomatous iris.

The rhizomatous iris has sword-like leaves that overlap to form flat fans and flowers that are bearded, beardless or crested. Bearded are the most commonly grown. Many years of hybridising has produced a vast number of beautiful hybrids in a wide range of colours. They range from dwarf, growing 20cm, up to 1m or more high. All need excellent drainage and full sun.

Iris × germanica

Bearded Iris, German Bearded Iris

Originating from Europe, probably the Mediterranean region

A robust, rhizomatous, bearded iris that grows 60 to 120cm high and 30cm wide. The flat fans of glaucous grey-green leaves are up to 45cm long. Tall branched stems bear many fragrant flowers 10cm across in late spring. There are hundreds of cultivars, representing nearly every colour, from jet black to sparkling white and red. Some cultivars are known to re-bloom in autumn. An easily grown, drought-tolerant plant that needs no summer water. Grow in full sun in well-drained soil. The rhizomes should be planted to lie on the surface of the soil. Clumps become overcrowded over time, reducing flowering after three to four years, so divide in late summer so that autumn rains settle them in. There are many cultivated varieties that have escaped from cultivation and are naturalised in various parts of the world.

Iris histrio

Native to Israel, southern Turkey, Syria and Lebanon

A small, bulbous member of the reticulata group of irises characterised by a fibrous net surrounding the bulb. It only grows to 20cm high with narrow, square-sectioned leaves up to 10cm long. They appear shortly before flowering time. In late winter and early spring, it bears beautiful solitary flowers 6 to 8cm across. These are pale blue with intricate markings, shading to purplish blue at the base with the falls deep blue at the margins, and creamy white with blue blotches in the centre. The standards are also blue. Grow the bulbs in full sun in well-drained soil. They are best planted in large drifts and left undisturbed for several years. As they are summer dormant, no water is required.

Iris lutescens

Crimean Iris

Native to northeast Spain, southern France, Italy

A variable, rhizomatous perennial with nearly straight leaves, 30cm long and 2.5cm wide. It is found on rocky or sandy hillsides and in woodlands. It produces a branched stem with one or two purple, claret, yellow, white or violet flowers 5 to 7cm across in spring. Prefers full sun, a slightly acid soil, and dry conditions during its summer dormancy. It is frost hardy. Easily grown in dry sandy soil, preferably up on a bank.

Iris pallida

Dalmatian Iris, Sweet Iris

Native to the Mediterranean

A rhizomatous, bearded iris that prefers rocky places. Its evergreen grey-green leaves are sword-shaped, 20 to 60cm long, much shorter than the flower stem. The inflorescence, produced in May or June, is fan-shaped and contains two to six flowers 10cm across. These are silky, crinkled, a clear, light lavender-blue with golden imperials, and deliciously scented. Grow in well-drained soil in full sun. Tolerant of summer drought. Unlike modern bearded iris, it can be left undivided for many years and still flower well. The cultivar 'Variegata' has pale green leaves with silver white stripes and is less vigorous.

Iris xiphium

Dutch Iris, Spanish Iris

Native to Spain and Portugal

A vigorous, bulbous iris with a flowering stem to 60cm high. The channelled, lance-shaped, greyish-green leaves emerge in autumn 20 to 70cm long and die after the flowers fade. In late spring, the bulb produces a slender stem with two flowers 12cm across on the top. Its standards are narrow and upright, while the oval to circular falls project downwards. The species colour is violet-purple, pale or deep blue, but hybrids come in a wide range of colours including white, mauve, brown, orange, yellow and bicolours. Plant the bulbs during autumn in well-drained soil in full sun. Only needs water during any dry spell in winter while the plant is in growth. After flowering, allow the foliage to continue growing to replenish the bulb, then let them dry off during summer. Excellent as cut flowers and good in containers. Spanish iris is favoured by florists for its striking colour combinations. This species has several varieties popular in horticulture, among them *Iris xiphium* var. Lusitanica, whose flowers are yellow all over.

ISMENE

Amaryllidaceae

Native to Peru, Ecuador

A genus of ten species of tender perennial bulbs bearing a strong resemblance to those of Hymenocallis, a genus into which Ismene was often grouped in the past. However, its morphology differs from Hymenocallis in several significant ways: its vegetative parts, natural range and chromosome number are all distinct.

Ismene × deflexa syn. *Hymenocallis × festalis*
Peruvian Daffodil

Garden origin

A broadleaf, semi-evergreen or deciduous bulbous perennial with strap-shaped leaves up to 90cm long and 5cm wide. In spring and summer, clusters of two to five white or cream, long flared trumpet-shaped, heavily fragrant flowers, 8 to 12cm across appear on long stems. Each has a white daffodil-like cup, surrounded by six slender, curled petals (tepals). Plant the bulbs in a rich well-drained soil in sun or partial shade. Water during the growing and flowering period, then allow them to dry out once the leaves have turned yellow. An exotic-looking addition to a mixed border. When grown in containers, move near the house to enjoy the scent.

Ismene narcissiflora syn. *Hymenocallis narcissiflora*
Ismene Lily

Native to Peru and Bolivia

A bulbous plant with a star-shaped array of strap-shaped leaves to 60cm long and 5cm wide. These are joined at the base to form a false stem foliage surrounding the central flower spikes that hold the flower head 60cm aloft. Clusters of two to five fragrant flowers appear in early summer. These are extremely showy, being pure white, with a green stripe, 10cm long, funnel-shaped with fringed lobes that fold elegantly backwards. The stamens are even longer, surrounded by six slender segments, spidery and most ornate. Plant bulbs in a rich, well-drained soil in autumn with the tips 3 or 4cm below the surface. Grow in sun or partial shade; added humus is appreciated. Water during the growing and flowering period, then allow them to dry out once the leaves have turned yellow. A good summer-flowering plant for borders or in containers. For cultivation, do nothing, do not even lift and divide – they will do the work themselves.

Isoplexis canariensis see *Digitalis canariensis*

ISOPOGON
Proteaceae

Conesticks, Cone Bush, Coneflowers

Native to Australia

A genus of over 35 species of mainly small evergreen shrubs, usually found in woodland and drought-prone forests. They are erect or prostrate shrubs with rigid, usually compound, rarely simple leaves. Compound leaves are deeply divided with flat or cylindrical lobes. The flowers are usually on the ends of branches, surrounded by bracts, in a more or less conical or spherical spike. Each flower is symmetrical, the tepals spreading as the flower develops, the lower part persisting until the fruit expands.

Isopogon anethifolius
Narrow Leaved Drumsticks

Native to the east coast of New South Wales, Australia

A tall thin shrub with mostly vertical stems, usually standing from 1 to 3m high. Stems are reddish, and fresh growth in winter is tinged with reddish and tan tones. Their 16cm length allows them to branch either once or twice. Leaves are simple, or heavily dissected into segments (appearing compound), alternate, up to 15cm long by about 4cm wide. Inflorescences are typically globular terminal heads, around 4cm in diameter, conspicuously displayed on the ends of the branches and surrounded by the erect foliage. These comprise many bright-yellow flowers with styles turning a darker shade of yellow-orange. Each head has 50 to 100 flowers with each flower about 2cm long. They are produced in late spring and early summer. Best grown in a well-draining neutral to acid, sandy, poor to moderately fertile soil in dappled shade with some sunny periods. Summer drought tolerant. Shelter from cold drying winds.

Isopogon dubius
Pincushion Coneflower

Native to southwest of Western Australia

A shrub that typically grows 0.5 to 1.5m high with hairy, reddish brown branchlets of young leaves. Leaves are deeply three-lobed or pinnate, 2.5 to 6cm long on a petiole about 2cm long. The tips of the lobes or leaflets are sharply pointed. Deep-pink flowers appear in winter and spring, conspicuously displayed on the ends of the branches. Flowers are in sessile, more or less spherical heads of pink to reddish pink flowers, 4 to 5cm diameter with many hairy, egg-shaped rosettes of bracts at the base. They are followed by round (barrel-shaped) seed pods, which remain on the plant for an indefinite period. This is a spectacular species, which is well known in cultivation. It performs best in well-drained soils in areas with dry summers, as it is drought tolerant. A sunny position will produce the best flowering, but some shade is tolerated. It withstands light to moderate frosts.

Isopogon formosus
Rose Coneflower

Native to the coast of Western Australia

An erect or spreading shrub that typically grows to a height of 1.5 to 2m with pale to reddish brown young branchlets. Leaves are up to 3.5cm long on a petiole up to 2.5cm long, and divided with grooved cylindrical segments that have a sharply pointed tip. Flowers are on the ends of branchlets or in upper leaf axils, in sessile, spherical to oval heads about 6cm in diameter with oval to lance-shaped bracts at the base. The flowers are red or mauve-pink and more or less glabrous, appearing in winter and spring. Makes for an excellent and unusual feature plant. Plant in full sun to part shade in well-drained soil, ideally sandy-gravelly soils. Summer drought tolerant. Protect from strong winds and harsh frosts.

IXIA
Iridaceae
African Corn Lily
Native to South Africa

A genus of about 40 species of cormous perennials. They have sword-shaped leaves and long, wiry stems with star-shaped, brightly-coloured flowers, which often have conspicuous dark centres. There are many named varieties with colours ranging from white, creamy white with purple centres, to red and pink flowers. They have a specific, mild fragrance.

Ixia maculata
African Corn Lily
Native to the Cape Provinces of South Africa

A cormous perennial with flowering stems up to 60cm high with an erect, unbranched stem. There are a few twisting sword-shaped basal leaves up to 35cm long and strongly ribbed. In spring, thin, wiry, flowering stalks bear a series of twelve to eighteen charming cup-shaped flowers 3 to 6cm across. These are usually orange or yellow, sometimes with areas of dark purple or black centres. Plant bulbs in drifts in full sun in well-drained soil and leave undisturbed for several years. As the bulbs are summer dormant, they are drought tolerant and need no water. Ideal for floral arrangements as cut flowers are long lasting.

Ixia viridiflora
Duck Egg Blue Ixia, Turquoise Ixia

A cormous perennial 30 to 60cm high with erect linear leaves 40 to 55cm long. From spring to early summer, it bears spikes of twelve or more cup-shaped flowers 5cm across that are a beautiful metallic turquoise with a dark purple centre. Well suited to warmer climates. Their late flowering season bridges the gap between spring flowering bulbs and summer flowering perennials, making bright accent points in the garden. Prefers full sun in well-drained soil. Summer drought tolerant. Ideal for pots and containers. Makes a perfect cut flower as they last well in a vase.

J

JACARANDA
Bignoniaceae
Native to tropical America

A genus of about 49 species of deciduous and evergreen shrubs to large trees ranging from 20 to 30m high. Leaves are bipinnate in most species, pinnate or simple in a few. Flowers are produced in conspicuous large panicles, each flower with a five-lobed blue to purple-blue corolla. A few species have white flowers. One species is widely planted as a specimen or street tree in tropical and subtropical regions. The wood is durable and often used for carpentry work.

Jacaranda mimosifolia
Jacaranda, Blue Jacaranda
Native to Argentina and Bolivia

A deciduous tree that will quickly reach 15m high, forming an open broad head 7 to 10m wide. Its bark is thin and grey-brown, smooth when the tree is young but eventually becoming finely scaly. Light reddish-brown twigs are slender and slightly zigzag. Finely divided, bipinnate leaves 25 to 45cm long are fern-like and only deciduous in early spring. Flowers are up to 5cm long, trumpet-shaped, white-throated with five lobes. These are grouped in 30cm loose pyramidal panicles containing many glowing, pure blue to lavender flowers. These magnificent showy flowers appear during late spring, often entirely covering the bare trees and last for up to two months covering the ground once flowering is finished. Trees may produce a few flowers during autumn in warm areas, although not so profusely. Large, flattened, curved, red-brown seed pods eventually dry and open. Grow in moderately fertile light or sandy, well-drained soil in full sun. When established, it withstands drought. The tree can be pruned hard in late winter if it becomes too big for the space. A popular and impressive specimen tree, often used as a street tree. Easily raised from seed, it makes an attractive pot plant in its early years.

JACOBAEA
Asteraceae
Native to northern Eurasia, the Mediterranean region

A genus of about 120 species that used to be in the genus Senecio but have been separated because of molecular phylogenetics in order to maintain genera that are monophyletic.

Jacobaea maritima syn. *Senecio cineraria*
Dusty Miller
Native to the Mediterranean region

An evergreen bushy subshrub that forms a mound 15 to 45cm high, spreading as wide with silver stems. Grown mainly for its striking white leaves, 10 to 15cm long. The silvery, finely textured, dissected leaves, often lace-like, are covered with fine matted hairs, giving them a woolly, silvery appearance. Clustered heads of small, daisy-like, cream to yellow flowers 2cm across appear on beautiful white felted stalks in summer, flowering the second year. Often used as striking ground cover, in which case it should be kept short and bushy by cutting back in spring. Striking in the night garden. Easily grown in average well-drained soil in full sun. Drought and heat tolerant, needing only light watering in summer. Easily grown from seed.

JARAVA
Poaceae
Native to Central and South America

A genus of about ten species of tufted grass perennials (most species are not yet transferred from Stipa or Achnatherum). They have linear, pleated, inrolled, sometimes flat leaves and bear narrow panicles of flat spikelets, often with long feathery or bristly awns from summer to autumn. They are grown for their beautiful inflorescences, which may be dried and dyed in flower arrangements.

Jarava ichu syn. *Stipa ichu*
Peruvian Feather Grass

A gorgeous, and impressive, perennial grass forming dense clumps 60 to 90cm

Isopogon anethifolius.

Isopogon formosus.

Ixia maculata.

Ixia viridiflora.

Jacaranda mimosifolia.

Jacobaea maritima.

Jarava ichu.

Jasminum mesnyi.

high, of upright to slightly arching, slender bright green leaves. During autumn, they change to attractive shades of golden mustard, staying vibrant for months. In summer, the foliage is topped with stunning masses of long, slender, silvery white, feathery plumes that persist through the winter. It is these flowers that add glorious movement and an ethereal softness to the display. Easily grown in full sun or partial shade in moderately fertile well-drained soil. Drought and heat tolerant once established. If too moist, it rots. Goes well with other drought tolerant Mediterranean plants and looks good in cottage gardens, in mass plantings as a ground cover or makes an easy accent or backdrop plant.

JASMINUM
Oleaceae

Native to Europe, Asia and Africa

A large genus containing about 300 species of deciduous and evergreen shrubs and climbers, which are cultivated for their terminal auxiliary flowers, typically around 2cm in diameter. These are white or yellow, although in rare instances they can be slightly reddish. The flowers are borne in cymose clusters with a minimum of three flowers, though they can also be solitary on the ends of branchlets. Each flower has about four to nine petals.

Jasminum azoricum
Jasmine, Lemon-Scented Jasmine

Native to the Portuguese island of Madeira

A large, evergreen, twining climber that makes rapid growth to 5m high and wide. Glossy, rich-green leaves have three oval leaflets, each 5cm long. White, fragrant flowers 2cm across emerge from pink buds in terminal clusters in late summer and continue throughout autumn. Be prepared to be overwhelmed at sunset when the fragrance is released at its highest levels. Sweet and musky, it is an experience no one should miss. It can be grown as a shrub with some support or as a climber on wires or a trellis. Plant in a warm and sunny aspect and avoid frosts. Does best in full sun in well-drained soil, with some summer water. Quickly covering a large area, it needs pruning occasionally after flowering to keep in shape. Ideal for covering large fences, walls or a house where the scent and flowers can be appreciated.

Jasminum grandiflorum
Poet's Jasmine, Spanish Jasmine

A semi-deciduous, twining vine that grows to 4m tall with arching square stems spreading to 2m, bearing leaves composed of five or seven small leaflets. At the branch tips, spectacular 4cm-wide flowers are produced for most of summer. The individual flowers, 1 to 2cm wide, are held on unequal-length pedicels. The buds and undersides of the petals are tinged pink. They are also powerfully fragrant with a pinkish outside of the buds. The flowers contain an essential oil used in perfumery, for which the variety 'De Grasse' is often used. It is frost hardy. Plant in full sun with average soil. Drought tolerant but grows better with some summer water.

Jasminum mesnyi
Primrose Jasmine

Native to southwest China

An evergreen, rambling, weeping shrub that can be treated as a climber, where it will grow 2 to 3m tall, with square stems and long arching branches 3 to 4m long. Opposite, glossy, dark-green leaves have three lance-shaped leaflets up to 7cm long. Fragrant semi-double or double bright primrose-yellow flowers, 5cm across, are scattered singly throughout the plant during spring and well into summer. Fairly drought tolerant, it is best grown in a sunny or lightly shaded spot. A strong-growing shrub that needs space but may need occasional severe pruning. It can be trained on a fence, allowed to spill down banks and slopes, or used to cover pergolas, or large walls.

Jasminum officinale
Common White Jasmine

Native to Iran to west China

A strong-growing, trailing or twining deciduous climber that can reach 10m high and wide. Leaves are pinnate with five to nine leaflets, 6 to 7cm long and sharply pointed. Exceptionally pretty, five-petalled, white flowers have a long flowering season from summer to early autumn. Star-shaped flowers 2 to 3cm wide are deliciously fragrant, borne in terminal clusters of up to five flowers. Grow in full sun in any well-drained soil. It can tolerate some drought but needs water to flower well. Good for twining around garden fences and climbing over walls, or into trees filling the air with its perfume, especially in the evening. Easily propagated, as the long trailing stems root into the ground as they go.

Jasminum polyanthum
White Jasmine

Native to west China

A beautiful, vigorous, deciduous or sometimes evergreen, twining climber, up to 6m high and wide. Opposite, deep green, pinnate leaves have five to seven leathery lance shaped leaflets, up to 9cm long. Its masses of intensely fragrant white flowers up to 2cm wide open from crimson-pink long pointed buds, which develop best when plants are grown in the open. These are borne in dense clusters up to 10cm long throughout summer and autumn. Grow in full sun to flower well but keep the roots in shade. Drought tolerant but grows better with summer water and feeding. Use as a climber or ground cover. Also grows well in containers on sunny patios and terraces. It grows well in the Mediterranean, California and in London. Often sold as a pot plant.

JUBAEA
Arecaceae

Native to southwestern South America

A monotypic genus containing just one species of palm.

Jubaea chilensis
Chilean Wine Palm, Chile Cocopalm

This palm grows slowly, taking over twenty years to become a medium tree. Its immense dark-grey trunk grows up to 30m, with a diameter of 1m or more, and often has a swollen region that tapers towards the crown. Its dense crown supports 40 to 50 green or blue-grey, pinnate leaves 3 to 5m long, which on dying fall cleanly to the ground rather than persisting on the stem. Borne amongst the leaves, large inflorescences hang down with both male and female three-petalled flowers in early winter, with fruits ripening from late winter onwards. Spherical fruits are yellow or brown, and, like a mini-coconut, have a nut-like shell with three 'eyes' through which the root emerges at germination. Grow in fertile, well-drained soil in full sun. Summer drought tolerant. It prefers mild winters, but will tolerate frost as well as relatively cool summers, making it one of the hardiest of pinnate-leaved palms. In the wild, the tree lives almost only on steep slopes of ravines. Many consider it one of the most impressive palms in the world. In warm, dry regions, grow as a majestic specimen or avenue palm. The lifespan of this species is not known, but there are reports of large specimens in Chile living for several hundred years.

JUNIPERUS
Cupressaceae
Juniper

Widely distributed throughout the Northern Hemisphere

A genus of about 60 species of evergreen, coniferous trees and shrubs, with a wealth of marvellous forms ranging from prostrate or creeping alpines to dense bushy shrubs and tall, conical or columnar trees. Leaves of juvenile plants are usually needle-like or narrowly wedge-shaped and usually pointed up to 1.5cm long. The colour ranges from green to yellow, grey and steel-blue. Adult leaves are usually scale-like, overlapping and crowded, either lying flat along the shoots or spreading and 2 to 6mm long. Sometimes they keep the juvenile form. Fruits are usually roundish, fleshy, berry-like, 4 to 10mm across, and persistent, often taking two to three years to ripen. Junipers are a versatile genus, containing plants that tolerate a wide range of soils and conditions, particularly chalky soils. They are ideal for hot, sunny sites with little or no summer water. Prostrate forms are excellent as ground cover, while the upright forms make attractive specimens. They look good near a swimming pool. Nurseries offer a vast number of named varieties.

Juniperus chinensis
Chinese Juniper

Native to China, Japan

An extremely variable, spreading shrub to conical tree growing to 20m high with brown bark, which peels in long strips. Pungently scented leaves grow in two forms, juvenile needle-like leaves 5 to 10mm long, and adult scale-leaves 1.5 to 3mm long. Mature trees usually continue to bear some juvenile foliage as well as adult, particularly on shaded shoots low in the crown. This species is often dioecious, but some individual plants produce both sexes of flowers. Rounded fruits 5 to 7mm across ripen in the second year. This is a popular ornamental tree or shrub for gardens, parks, and in tough coastal conditions of scorching sun and sandy fast-draining soils. Drought tolerant. A wide range of named cultivars are available from prostrate shrubs to tall trees.

Juniperus communis
Common Juniper

Native to Northern Hemisphere

This is highly variable in form, ranging from 10m tall to a low, often prostrate spreading shrub in exposed locations. Leaves are needle pointed, glossy green, in whorls of three, 1 to 5cm long, marked with a broad white lengthways stripe. Yellow male and female cones are usually on separate plants, so requiring wind pollination. They are berry-like, 6mm in diameter, turning to bluish-black when ripe in the second year. Oil of Juniper is distilled from the green fruits and used to flavour gin. A wide range of named cultivars is available from prostrate shrubs to small trees. Performs best in full sun in any well-drained soil. Tolerates a wide range of soils, including poor soils. Drought tolerant once established. Low maintenance, as no pruning is required.

Juniperus horizontalis
Creeping Juniper

Native to North America

A dwarf or prostrate shrub growing only 10 to 30cm high with long, often horizontal branches with an indefinite spread. Leaves are in opposite criss-cross pairs, or occasionally in whorls of three. Adult leaf blades are scale-like, 1 to 2mm long with long, sharp points. They are glaucous green, grey-green or blue but vary in intensity, often turning plum-purple in winter. Fruits are rarely produced in cultivation. This is one of the best species for ground cover. Usually found growing in rocky or sandy soils from rocky outcrops to streams, this shrub is fairly adaptable to various soil types and pH as long as the soil is well drained. It is drought tolerant, fairly salt tolerant, and grows well in coastal conditions. It prefers full sun and tolerates hot weather, moderately poor soils, and many air pollutants found in urban areas. Many named cultivars have been selected for use as ornamental plants in gardens, their strictly prostrate growth habit being valued for ground cover.

Juniperus oxycedrus
Prickly Juniper

Native to the Mediterranean region

A large shrub or tree up to 10 to 15m high with an open, drooping habit. The trunk has fibrous grey to brown-red bark peeling in longitudinal stripes. Leaves are needle-like in alternating whorls of three. Needles are 1 to 2.5cm long, awl-shaped, sharp pointed, green above with two white bands underneath. Roundish fruits 3 to 9mm long turn a shining red-brown when they ripen in the second year. It is suitable for cultivation as an ornamental shrub in Mediterranean climates, where several cultivars, especially with more pendulous foliage, are commonly planted in gardens and parks. Its wood is resistant and hard, highly valued for making furniture and other carpentry items. Essential oils are extracted from the branches and leaves.

Juniperus sabina

Savin Juniper, Savin

Native to central and southern Europe, west Asia

An extremely variable, usually spreading or occasionally upright shrub with flaking reddish-brown bark. It can grow from 1 to 4m high and can spread to 6m or more wide. Leaves are of two forms, juvenile needle-like leaves are 5 to 10mm long, and adult scale-leaves 1 to 2mm long on slender shoots. Adult leaves are green or grey green with a pungent, disagreeable smell when crushed. It is largely dioecious, but some individual plants produce both sexes. Roundish fruit, 5 to 7mm across, is bluish black with a whitish bloom and ripens over the first winter. A spreading juniper that withstands tough conditions, often used in rockeries and roadside planting. Its silver-green, flat-growing foliage is perfect for sprawling over retaining walls, erosion control or blocking out weeds in low-maintenance areas. Many cultivars have been raised.

K

KALANCHOE

Crassuliaceae

Native to Africa and Madagascar, Asia, Australia

A genus of about 125 species of shrubs or perennials, a few annuals or biennials. The largest can reach 6m tall, but most species are less than 1m. Kalanchoes open their flowers by growing new cells on the inner surface of the petals to force them outwards, and on the outside of the petals to close them. Flowers are divided into four sections with eight stamens. The petals are fused into a tube. Some are grown as pot plants for their attractive leaves or flowers, while others grow well in a dry garden.

Kalanchoe beharensis

Felt Plant, Velvet Elephant Ear

Native to Madagascar

An often tree-like perennial succulent up to 3m high and 2m wide. Stems are covered in fine hairs that give them a soft and velvety texture and are usually unbranched with leaves crowded at the ends. Leaves are usually in six to eight pairs at the tips. Leaves are triangular, 10 to 20cm long, borne on long stalks, and strikingly waved and crimped at the edges, giving a dramatic effect. These are covered with a dense felt-like coating of minute, fine silver or golden hairs. The upper leaves are bronze while the undersides are silvery-grey, a stunning mix of colours. In winter, older plants bear panicles of greenish-yellow, bell-shaped flowers 7mm long, which are not showy. This spectacular succulent prefers full sun but can take considerable shade. Grow in well-drained soil with little or no summer water. Ideal for larger rock gardens or raised beds.

Kalanchoe blossfeldiana

Christmas Kalanchoe, Flaming Katy, Florist Kalanchoe

Native to Madagascar

A compact, glabrous, branching succulent to 30cm high and 10 to 50cm wide. Oval, dark glossy green, ovate, opposite leaves are 6cm long, 2 to 4cm wide, fleshy, often edged with red and scalloped. Flowers appear in late autumn to early winter. Each flower is 1cm long, tubular and has four petals borne in large, branched clusters held well above the leaves. They can be one of a wide variety of colours, from dark red or pink to orange, gold or white. It is a short-day plant, meaning that its blooming cycle is regulated by the amount of sunlight it receives each day. The plant will bloom when it is receiving approximately ten hours of daylight and fourteen hours of darkness for six to eight weeks. The plant should be grown in partial shade or shade. A common pot plant that is valued for its winter flowers, which remain fresh for almost a month. Drought tolerant so it needs little summer water. It makes an attractive addition to dry gardens. There are many hybrids and named varieties that can be raised from seed.

Kalanchoe daigremontiana

Maternity Plant, Mexican Hat Plant, Devil's Backbone

Native to Madagascar

An upright, single-stemmed succulent up to 1m high and 30 to 60cm wide. The foliage of this plant is one of its most distinctive features. Fleshy, alternate, lance-shaped, waxy, brownish-green leaves are 15 to 20cm long and 3 to 4cm wide, green above, often spotted with red or purple underneath. The most remarkable aspect of the leaves is their ability to generate new plantlets on the notches of their toothed edges, that drop off and grow into new plants where they land. In winter, clusters of pendant, small, tubular, pink or orange flowers to 2cm long are produced on tall stalks. Highly drought tolerant, needing minimal watering. Grows well in sandy well-drained soil. Prefers bright indirect sunlight, not midday sun. A useful pot or container plant. It can be grown in a dry garden, where it will quickly form a clump as the plantlets drop to the ground and root, often becoming invasive.

Jasminum officinale.

Jubaea chilensis.

Juniperus horizontalis.

Kalanchoe beharensis.

Kalanchoe blossfeldiana.

Kennedia rubicunda.

Kleinia fulgens.

Kniphofia uvaria.

Koelreuteria paniculata.

Kalanchoe fedtschenkoi 'Marginata'

Aurora Borealis Plant

Native to Madagascar

A succulent subshrub with glossy, erect branches growing to 60cm high. When it gets tall, it will bend to touch the soil where it can grow new roots. It can also occasionally produce new plantlets along its leaf edges. Rather crowded, scalloped-edge leaves are oval, 5 to 8cm long, fleshy and softly toothed, pale blue-green at the base with a variegation of cream and pink. Flowers on this variety are quite stunning, particularly in large groups. Many coral, tubular blooms 2cm long of purple or yellow flowers hang like bells and attract pollinators. Clusters are produced on stalks held well above the plant in winter or early spring. Thrives outdoors in part sun, or indoors near a sunny window. Extremely easy to grow as it is drought tolerant, needing little summer water. It makes an attractive pot or container plant or can be planted in beds or borders in a dry garden. Easily rooted from cuttings.

Kalanchoe tomentosa

Pussy Ears, Panda Plant

Native to Madagascar

An attractive succulent that has branching, woody stems with an upright habit up to 60cm high and wide. It has a woody stem with an open rosette of pale grey-green oval leaves. Leaves are covered in a grey felt and the margins are dotted with a rich chocolate brown edge. Its dense covering of hairs performs a vital function for water conservation. In a dry environment in which it lives, it must conserve what little water it can absorb from the soil. In addition, the white-silver appearance of the leaves reflects light, lessening the chances of the leaves overheating. The plant develops small, pale-green flowers that are held aloft on spikes. Incredibly easy to care for, it thrives with minimal attention as it is drought tolerant, needing little summer water. Makes a superb contrast to mix in between rockery gardens or looks good as a feature in a decorative pot.

KENNEDIA

Fabaceae

Coral Pea

Native to Australia

A genus of about fifteen species of prostrate or climbing perennials that usually have softly hairy foliage and a stem that is woody at the base. Leaves are alternate and are usually trifoliate with stipules at the base of the petiole. Their pea-like flowers are in leaf axils, relatively large and showy, red, blue, violet or almost black with stipule-like bracts at the base, which sometimes fall off as the flowers open.

Kennedia rubicunda

Dusky Coral Pea

Native to eastern Australia

A vigorous evergreen twining shrub 4 to 6m high with the young growth covered in silky brown hair. Its branches twist around the stems of other plants. Leaves are alternate, glossy green, 10 to 15cm long and divided into three to five oval hairy leaflets. Dark-red, pea-shaped flowers 4cm long appear in pairs in leaf axils during spring and summer. These are followed by 10cm-long flat seed pods. Once established, it is drought tolerant. Grow in full sun or in partial shade. A vigorous climber that will quickly cover a large area, so restrictive pruning may be necessary. It can also be used as a ground cover. The species deserves to be more widely grown and, if given room to spread, will be a long-lasting addition to gardens in temperate to tropical areas. It tolerates dry conditions and is a useful plant for growing on a trellis or pergola.

KLEINIA

Asteraceae

Native to the Canary Islands, throughout tropical Africa to India and Arabia

A genus of around 50 species of succulent perennial herbs that were previously included in the genus Senecio. Leaves are often glaucous alternate, usually entire. It is closely related to Senecio, but is distinguished primarily by having succulent stems or leaves.

Kleinia fulgens syn. *Senecio fulgens*

Native to southern Africa

A hardy, attractive, evergreen succulent with a creeping tuberous rootstock growing up to 60cm tall with a rather soft stem. It has broad, flattened, slightly fleshy stalkless grey-green leaves to 15cm, with a purple margin that arises directly from a fleshy stem. Clusters of bright-orange or scarlet flowers are carried on long, flowering stems from late autumn to winter. The flowers attract pollinating insects to the garden. This long-flowering plant will brighten up a rockery or mixed flowerbed. Easy to grow in well-drained soil in full sun or light shade. It is ideal for hot, dry spots in a garden as it is drought tolerant. Ideal for planting in rockeries or other dry, sunny spots, as the scarlet flower heads add a splash of colour in mid-winter.

Kleinia rowleyana see *Curio rowleyanus*

KNIPHOFIA

Asphodelaceae

Red Hot Poker, Torch-Lily

Native to Madagascar, tropical and southern Africa

A genus of about 60 to 70 species of evergreen or deciduous, grass-like, perennials from 50cm to 1.8m high with cord-like roots and thick basal leaves. Most have narrow, grass-like leaves 10 to 100cm long, while evergreen species have broader, strap-shaped foliage up to 1.5m long. All plants produce upright spikes that come in a variety of colours well above the foliage. The flowers produce copious nectar while blooming and are attractive to bees and insects. They have been in cultivation for long enough for many hybrids to have been raised in a wide range of colours, from red, orange, yellow, greenish to white, some opening red then turning to yellow. Some varieties are evergreen while others are deciduous. Kniphofia requires full sun and humus-rich, preferably sandy, well-drained soil. Most species are frost tolerant, though none will tolerate heavy frosts.

Kniphofia uvaria
Red Hot Poker, Torch-Lily, Poker Plant

Native to South Africa

An evergreen perennial that forms a large dense clump about 1.2m high, spreading to 60cm wide. The grey-green, grass-like leaves are 1m long. During spring and summer, it sends up flower spikes that can be up to 2m high. These are topped with clusters up to 30cm long of drooping bright orange-red or yellow tubular 5cm long flowers. Plants can be grown in full sun but will take some shade. They are good for a dry garden as they are drought tolerant and require little summer water once established. Cut old leaves to the ground in autumn. Nurseries offer many named hybrid varieties.

KOELREUTERIA
Sapindaceae

Native to Japan, China and Korea

A genus of about four species of deciduous trees or shrubs found in dry woodlands. They have alternate pinnate leaves, and large pyramidal panicles 10 to 35cm long of shallowly bowl-shaped flowers. All are fine specimen trees with fragrant flowers that are attractive to bees. They grow best in areas with hot summers.

Koelreuteria paniculata
Golden Rain Tree, Pride of India

Native to China and Korea

A small to medium-sized deciduous tree growing to 7m tall, with a broad, dome-shaped crown and branches that droop at the ends, creating a slight weeping effect. Branches are rather open, giving light shade. It has serrated, green, pinnate leaves 15 to 40cm long, with seven to fifteen leaflets 3 to 8cm long. They open pinkish red, become green, then turn a beautiful bronze to gold in autumn, staying on the tree until late in the season before dropping. In summer, large pyramidal showy panicles of small yellow 1cm-wide flowers 20 to 30cm long are produced, followed by papery lantern-like seed pods which hang from the tree in large clusters. They resemble clusters of Chinese lanterns and vary in colour from dull red to brown. Easily grown in all soils. It will withstand cold, heat, drought and wind once established, although it needs regular watering when young. This is the hardiest and most widely cultivated species. The cultivar 'Fastigiata' has a narrow columnar habit, growing 8m high and only 1m wide.

KUMARA
Asphodeloideae

Native to South Africa

A small genus of just two species. Phylogenetic studies showed that two species that were traditionally classed as members of the genus Aloe were genetically distinct and comprised an entirely separate clade. The species were accordingly split off as a separate genus Kumara. Both species bear characteristically strap-shaped leaves in a two-ranked arrangement. They have a unique fan arrangement with their grey, strap-shaped leaves. Both are also indigenous to roughly the same range of mountains in the southwestern corner of the Western Cape, however the tall tree-like *Kumara plicatilis* is found on the lower slopes of the mountains, while the tiny stemless *Kumara haemanthifolia* inhabits the high peaks.

Kumara plicatilis syn. *Aloe plicatilis*
Fan Aloe

This many-branched shrub or tree may with age reach 3m or more high, spreading to 1.8m wide. Strap-shaped leaves are 30cm long, pale glaucous blue with a pale edge and completely spineless. They are closely packed on the tips of the stems in one plane, like a fan. In spring, 60cm high spikes of scarlet to orange 6cm long flowers appear. Eventually it develops an attractive gnarled trunk but makes a good container plant when young. Easily grown in sandy, well-drained soil in full sun or light shade. Drought tolerant. Great in rock gardens, coastal gardens, Mediterranean and succulent gardens.

KUNZEA
Myrtaceae

Native to Australia

A genus of about 60 species (as at writing but under revision) of evergreen shrubs or small trees, from sandy soil areas of mostly coastal habitats. Usually their leaves are alternate. The flowers are in clusters near the ends of branches, which in some species, continue to grow after flowering. Flowers of most species lack a stalk, but those that have one are usually solitary or in groups of two or three. In some species, the flowers are surrounded by enlarged bracts. There are five petals, five sepals and many stamens, which are always longer than the petals.

Kunzea ambigua
White Kunzea, Poverty Bush, Tick Bush

Native to eastern Australia

A small- to medium-sized spreading shrub that may reach 5m both in height and width, though usually much smaller, is about 1m. Its bark is fibrous and furrowed. Simple and alternate, heavily clustered leaves are 12mm long and 1.5mm wide with an acute point and sometimes with hairs. Leaves are aromatic and mid- to dark green. White, conspicuously staminate flowers, like many of their myrtle-relatives, are 1.2cm in diameter and sweetly fragrant. Each flower has many stamens, which are longer than the petals. Flowers are usually produced in high numbers in terminal or sub-terminal clusters from spring to summer. Drought tolerant. This plant is easily cultivated and tolerant of many well-drained soils. It needs some room to spread out and it can get leggy, but regular pruning should keep its shape. A favourite for insects when it is flowering. It is also used in amenities planting and sand-dune stabilisation.

Kunzea pulchella

Native to southwest of Western Australia

An erect or spreading shrub to about 1 to 3m high and 1.5m wide, with grey-green, ovoid leaves to about 15mm long. Flower clusters are profuse and conspicuous, usually bright red with gold-tipped stamens. White- and cream-flowered forms are also known. Flowers usually appear in late winter to spring, followed by small single-celled fruits that release many small seeds when ripe, popular with wildlife. This hardy plant is particularly suited to Mediterranean climates (dry summer, wet winter) as it is drought and frost tolerant, but will also grow in more humid climates. It requires excellent drainage and a sunny or lightly shaded position. An attractive feature shrub or screening plant, the silver foliage is the perfect backdrop for the deep red bottlebrush flowers. Prune after flowering to keep in shape.

L

LAGERSTROEMIA

Lythraceae

Native to the warmer parts of Asia, Pacific islands and Australia

A genus of about 50 species of evergreen and deciduous trees and shrubs. Most species have sinewy, fluted stems. Branches have a mottled appearance that arises from having bark that sheds throughout the year. While all species are woody, they can range from under 30cm to over 30m tall. Most, however, are small to medium, multiple-trunked trees and shrubs. Leaves are opposite and simple, with entire margins, and vary from 5 to 20cm. They are chiefly known for their colourful and long-lasting panicles of crinkled flowers with a crêpe-like texture, which appear in summer and autumn. Colours vary from deep purple to red to white, with almost every shade in between. They make showy ornamentals, which are easily cultivated. Sometimes grown as attractive pot plants.

Lagerstroemia indica

Crepe Myrtle

Native to China

A beautiful deciduous shrub or small tree rarely reaching 6m high and wide. With age, it develops a smooth trunk with mottled pealing bark that reveals a smooth grey or pink inner bark. Leaves 3 to 6cm long are oblong, dark glossy green, tinged with bronze when young, opposite, alternate, or in whorls of three. In autumn, these turn a lovely yellow or orange red. From summer to autumn 15 to 30cm long terminal panicles of white, pink, red or mauve flowers with crumpled petals 2 to 3cm across are produced, making a dazzling display, even on young plants. Easily grown in areas with warm summers. It requires full sun and well-drained soil. Drought tolerant once established, though it will tolerate occasionally wet soil. Place in a sheltered location protected from winter winds and mulch the soil to protect roots. There are many named hybrids varying in height and flower colour.

LAGUNARIA

Malvaceae

Native to Australia and nearby islands

A small genus of two species: *L. patersonia*, which occurs on Norfolk and Lord Howe Islands; and *L. queenslandica* from northeast Queensland. The latter was previously regarded as *L. patersonia* subsp. *bracteata* but has been raised to species status based on morphological and ecological differences. *L. patersonia* also is more robust in habit and has larger, scaly leaves. The two species also differ in their habitats, with *L. patersonia* occurring in rainforest, while *L. queenslandica* is found in non-rainforest areas, often along rivers and creeks.

Lagunaria patersonia

Norfolk Island Hibiscus, Cow Itch Tree, Primrose Tree

A handsome, easily-grown, hardwood tree that will quickly reach 10 to 15m or more high and 2m or more wide, forming a distinct pyramidal shape with dense foliage. Thick, leathery, oval, dark green leaves are 5 to 10cm long and whitish underneath. They become narrower as the plant flowers. It bears a succession of cup to trumpet-shaped flowers with five pink to rosy-pink recurved petals, 4 to 6cm wide, singly in upper leaf axils, rather like Hibiscus. These are produced during summer and followed by brown seed capsules which hang on the tree for a long time. Handle these with care, as the seed pods contain short stiff hairs which can easily cause skin irritation. Grow in full sun with little summer water once established, as it is drought tolerant. It is not fussy about soil conditions. As it resists ocean winds and salt sprays, it is good for coastal gardens. A fine accent, windbreak, or a showy specimen tree.

Koelreuteria paniculata seed pods.

Kumara plicatilis.

Kunzea ambigua.

Kunzea pulchella.

Lagerstroemia indica.

Lagunaria patersonia.

Lagurus ovatus.

Lampranthus glaucoides.

inland species occur in open grassland or woodland. All species grow in well-drained, sandy soil.

Leschenaultia biloba syn. *Lechenaultia biloba*

Blue Leschenaultia

Native of south Western Australia

This spreading shrub typically grows 30cm or less and has a similar width, and often forms suckers. Branches are twiggy with linear, narrow grey-green to green fleshy leaves around 6 to 10mm long. Flowers are in compact clusters, produced in summer. These are five-petalled, about 2 to 3cm in diameter, quite large given the small size of the plant. Usually flowers are a vivid blue, but pale forms are known as are pure white forms. A popular and spectacular small shrub, it is an ideal rockery plant in suitable climates, tolerating exposed, hot, sunny positions despite its delicate appearance. Drought tolerant. It is fairly short-lived, about four to six years in ideal conditions is about average, but it is easily propagated. The cultivar 'White Flash' has blue flowers with white streaks.

LEUCADENDRON

Proteaceae

Cone Bush

Native to a small area of the Cape Peninsula, South Africa

A genus containing about 83 species of dioecious evergreen small trees or shrubs that are erect or creeping. Most species are shrubs to 1m, some to 2 or 3m high. A few grow into moderate-sized trees up to 16m tall. Leaves are elliptical, sometimes needle-like, spirally arranged, simple, entire and usually green, often covered with a waxy bloom. They have small flowerheads surrounded by stiff, often brightly-coloured bracts. Seed heads are woody, cone-like structures, containing many seeds, giving rise to their generic common name. Several species store seeds in fireproof cones and release them only after a fire has killed the plant or at least the branch bearing the cone. Many such species hardly reproduce naturally except after fires.

Leucadendron argenteum

Silver Tree

Native to a tiny area in and around the city of Cape Town

An erect, well-proportioned, large shrub or small ornamental tree, growing 7 to 10m tall, with a stout trunk and thick, grey bark. Upright branches are densely covered with large silvery-grey, silky, narrow lance-shaped leaves, 10 to 15cm long, which overlap each other up the stem, concealing the thick branches. They are more silver in hot dryer weather. From spring to summer spherical flowerheads to 4cm across appear, yellowish green on male trees, silver on female trees. These are surrounded by leaf-like but boarded and more lustrous bracts to 2cm long. The silvery cones often persist on trees for several years. It needs fast-draining soil that is slightly acid and low in nutrients. Like most Protea relatives, it dislikes high phosphorous fertiliser. Give it mostly sunny conditions and regular watering during the growing season, but it is summer drought tolerant. Prefers a sheltered position, although it needs good air circulation. It can be grown in a large pot or container, if you give it good air circulation. The roots are prone to Phytophthora rot, especially if overwatered in warm weather.

LEUCANTHEMUM

Asteraceae

Shasta Daisies

Native to southern and central Europe

A genus of about 42 species of perennials growing from red-tipped rhizomes. It produces one erect stem, branching or unbranched, and hairy to hairless, usually reaching 40 to 130cm tall. Some species have mainly basal leaves, while some have leaves along the stem as well. Some leaves are borne on petioles, and others are sessile, varying in shape, some lobed or toothed. Each flower head is solitary, paired, or in a group of three on the stem. The head has about 13 to 34 ray florets of various widths, occasionally more, and rarely none. The ray florets are always white but fade pink with age. Each head has over 100 yellow disc florets at the centre.

Leucanthemum × superbum

Shasta Daisy

Garden origin

A free-flowering perennial growing 60 to 90cm tall, spreading 45cm wide, with dark, shiny, toothed basal leaves. It produces wonderful displays of classic, single, yellow-centred, white daisy-like flowers up to 8cm across held aloft on slender stalks. In warmer climates, the foliage remains after flowers have died back, making a useful herbaceous fill-in. Flowers can be singles or gorgeous doubles. Many varieties have been bred for improved performance, such as flowering for longer periods, different flower shapes and a greater range of plant sizes, including compact varieties suitable for pots. Grow in average to dry well-drained reasonably fertile soil in full sun to partial shade. Tolerant of summer drought, but flower better with some water. Good for informal perennial borders and cottage style gardens, and for attracting pollinating insects. Stake tall-growing varieties in spring. It makes an excellent cut flower. Cut back dead growth to the ground anytime during autumn to early spring.

Leucanthemum vulgare

Marguerite, Ox-Eye Daisy

Native to most of Europe and temperate Asia

A hardy, extremely variable rhizomatous perennial to 60cm high and 30cm wide. Dark-green basal leaves up to 10cm long are spoon-shaped on long stalks, while the stem leaves are smaller and sometimes lobed. It produces a sea of large, pure white, single daisy-like flowers with golden yellow centres, 8cm wide on upright stems, in profusion during spring to late summer. Grow in full sun or partial shade in any well-drained soil. When established, it withstands drought, but flowers are better with some summer water. Remove fading flowers and cut old stems to ground level in autumn. The plant is valued for its abundant floral display. Excellent choice for cottage gardens. Makes excellent and long-lasting cut flowers. It is invasive in some places.

LEUCOJUM
Amaryllidaceae
Snowflake
Native to Europe, Turkey to Iran

Until 2004, the genus Leucojum was treated as including species now placed in Acis. Leucojum now comprises only two species, *Leucojum aestivum* and *Leucojum vernum*.

Leucojum aestivum
Summer Snowflake
Native to central and southern Europe

A hardy, bulbous perennial with strap-shaped upright leaves to 45cm long. Its leaves, which are well developed at the time of flowering, are narrow, reaching to about the same height as the flowers. The flowering stem is hollow and has wings with translucent margins. Pendant bell-shaped, faintly-scented, 2cm-long flowers appear in late spring and are borne in umbels of usually three to five, sometimes as many as seven. The flower stalks are of different lengths, 2.5 to 7cm long. Flowers about 3 to 4cm in diameter have six white tepals, each with a greenish mark just below the tip. Bulbs are best planted in large drifts under deciduous trees or shrubs where they can naturalise. They prefer partial shade in summer and sun during the flowering period. Summer dormant, so give no water to allow the bulbs to become dry. They should remain undisturbed for many years.

Leucojum autumnale see *Acis autumnalis*

Leucojum trichophyllum see *Acis longifolia*

LEUCOSPERMUM
Proteaceae
Native to South Africa

A genus of 48 species of evergreen shrubs and small trees. Alternate, leathery, simple, entire or toothed leaves may be linear to elliptic, inversely lance-shaped oval or oblong. Most species have rounded heads tightly packed with bright red, orange or yellow flowers with long prominent styles. These give the flower a 'pincushion' effect. Grow in well-drained neutral to acid soils in full sun.

Leucospermum cordifolium
Ornamental Pincushion, Nodding Pincushion
Native to south coast of the Western Cape province of South Africa

A rounded and spreading shrub up to 1.5m high and 2m wide. It has a single trunk at its base from which branches spread horizontally and often bend towards the ground. Hard, vibrant green leaves are set alternately along the branches, more or less directed upwards. Up to 8cm long, they are stalkless, leathery and spirally arranged, sometimes with three to six teeth at the tips. Large flowerheads to 12cm across vary from pinkish-yellow through brilliant orange to crimson-red. These appear from early spring to midsummer, on horizontal to downwards arching stems, which bend sharply upwards at their tips. This is the best known and most cultivated species of the genus, along with many hybrids. Grows best in sandy acid, well-drained soil, in full sun. Tolerant of summer drought, but give water during the growing season. Great for xeriscaping. Tolerates coastal conditions with salt laden air. Excellent as cut flowers.

LILIUM
Liliaceae
Lily
Native to Europe, the Mediterranean region, Asia and North America

A genus of about 100 species of bulbous perennials, mainly from wooded habitats and scrubs. Most species are summer flowering, with tall stems and many scaled bulbs. They are grown for their showy, often trumpet-shaped, sometimes extremely fragrant flowers. Most lilies prefer an acid or neutral soil. There are also a vast number of hybrids and cultivars listed by specialist nurseries.

Lilium candidum
Madonna Lily
Native to southeast Europe to eastern Mediterranean

A bulbous perennial that forms bulbs at ground level, and, unlike other lilies, grows a basal rosette of leaves during winter, which dies the following summer. It grows a single stiffly erect stem to 1m high. Broad, glossy, lance-shaped basal leaves are up to 20cm long, becoming progressively shorter up the stem. The flowering stem with many narrow leaves emerges in early spring with blooms opening in late spring. Clusters of five to ten wide, open trumpet-shaped flowers are pure waxy white 5 to 8cm long and tinted yellow in their throats, sweetly scented, the upper ones erect, the lower ones drooping. The plant grows with the first rain in autumn and dies down soon after flowering. Grow plant with the top in full sun while the roots prefer some shade. It requires a neutral to alkaline soil. As it is summer dormant, no water is needed. Looks best when grown in groups near a path or house where the scent can be appreciated.

Lilium formosanum
Formosa Lily, Taiwanese Lily
Native to Taiwan

An elegant, subtropical, stem-rooting, rhizomatous bulb that has naturalised in many subtropical areas. In late spring or at

eucadendron argenteum.

Leucanthemum × superbum.

Leucojum aestivum.

eucospermum cordifolium.

Lilium candidum.

Lilium formosanum.

monium perezii.

Limonium sinuatum.

the start of the summer rainy season, it forms green stems that are purplish brown towards its base. Many dark-green, linear to narrowly oblong lance-shaped leaves, 8 to 20cm long, are scattered and sparse towards the stem top. These bear many white, slender, fragrant, trumpet-shaped flowers 12 to 20cm long. They are flushed reddish purple outside, with flared and somewhat recurved tips, borne singly or in umbels of up to ten. Easily grown in cool tropical areas in leafy well-drained soil. Tolerant of winter drought, water well in summer.

Lilium longiflorum syn. *Lilium wallichianum*

Easter Lily

Native to southern Japan and Taiwan

A vigorous, warmer-climate, stem-rooting bulbous perennial with a single stiffly erect stem 50 to 80cm high. Lance-shaped, shiny, deep-green leaves are up to 18cm long. In early summer, each stem carries up to ten extremely fragrant, pure white, trumpet-shaped flowers up to 20cm long that are tinged green at the base and have golden yellow anthers. After flowering, stems will ripen and die down. As it is summer dormant, it needs no summer water. Mulch well to keep the roots cool. It likes a sunny location, though a little shade throughout the day will be tolerated. Water well when coming into flower, allow to die right off before cutting back. Plant in autumn in well-drained, friable soil that is rich in organic matter. It is lime tolerant, which is unusual for lilies. They are best when planted in groups of a minimum of four plants, for best effect. The flowers are excellent for cutting with their powerful scent. Outstanding performers in pots and containers.

LIMONIUM

Plumbaginaceae

Sea Lavender, Statice

The genus is found in most of the world except South America. The highest diversity, with over 100 species, is found in the region from the Canary Islands to central Asia.

A vast genus of about 600 flowering species of annuals, biannuals, evergreen perennials and subshrubs, growing 10 to 70cm tall from a rhizome. A few (mainly from the Canary Islands) are woody shrubs up to 2m tall. Many species flourish in saline soils and are therefore common near coasts and in salt marshes, and also on saline, gypsum and alkaline soils in continental interiors. Leaves are simple, entire to lobed, and from 1 to 30cm long. Most leaves are produced in a dense basal rosette, with flowering stems bearing only small brown scale-leaves (bracts). Flowers are produced on a branched panicle or corymb, individual flowers are small 4 to 10mm long, with a five-lobed calyx and corolla, and five stamens. They are pink or violet to purple in most species, white or yellow in a few. Many produce flowers that are suitable for cutting and for drying.

Limonium arborescens

Native to the Canary Islands

This is a tough perennial herb growing from a woody rhizome. Thick leaves are oval and up to about 30cm long, including the petioles, in a basal rosette around the stem. The inflorescence is a stiff, branching panicle often exceeding 1m tall, bearing large clusters of flowers with lavender sepals and smaller white petals. These usually appear during winter. Grow in well-drained soil in full sun. Drought and frost tolerant. Great for cut flowers.

Limonium perezii

Native to the Canary Islands

An evergreen, tough perennial herb growing up to 60cm high from a woody rhizome. Rich green leaves are up to 30cm long and 15cm wide in a basal rosette around the stem. The inflorescence is a stiff, branching panicle 15 to 45cm tall, topped with bushy clusters of deep indigo blue, white-flecked flowers throughout most of summer. Flowers are long lasting and good for drying. Ideal for coastal gardens, as it often naturalises on the coast. Grows well in full sun and tolerates heat and most soils, but needs good drainage. Drought tolerant once established, needing little summer water.

Limonium platyphyllum syn. *L. latifolium*

Sea Lavender, Broad-Leaved Statice, Florist's Sea Lavender

Native to Black Sea region

A rosette-forming, evergreen perennial with a woody base growing 60cm or more high and 45cm wide. Basal leaves are oblong to spoon-shaped and smooth edged, up to 25cm long with a long leaf stalk that lies nearly flat against the ground. A much-branched, wiry flowering stem appears up to 30cm high in summer, covered with many tiny, tubular, lavender-blue flowers. Their dry, papery petals keep their colour well, making them an excellent choice for cut-flower or dried arrangements. Attractive to bees and other pollinators. Grow in full sun in well-drained soil. Ideal for dry coastal gardens, drought tolerant once established. The lavender-blue flowers associate well with silver-leaved plants.

Limonium sinuatum

Statice, Wavyleaf Sea Lavender, Sea Lavender, Notch Leaf Marsh Rosemary, Sea Pink

Native to the Mediterranean region

This is a short-lived perennial, often treated as an annual, up to 40cm high and rough hairy throughout. Basal rosettes of oblong to lance-shaped leaves up to 10cm long are deeply lobed with wavy edges. All parts are downy. Upright, branched, bright-green, winged flower stems about 70cm tall also carry leaves. These stems carry short, papery clusters of tiny funnel-shaped flowers that are blue, pink, red, white or yellow in summer and early autumn. Grows well in full sun in well-drained soil. Drought tolerant once established. They are grown for their bright flowers that can be cut fresh or used when dried. Seed is available in single colours and in mixtures. It can become invasive.

LINNAEA syn. ABELIA
Caprifoliaceae
Native to Asia, Mexico

In 2013, to maintain each genus as a set of closely-related plants descended from a single common ancestor, Maarten Christenhusz proposed merging Abelia into Linnaea. World Flora Online now has Linnaea as the accepted genus. Naming is unresolved at the time of writing in 2024.

This genus of about 30 species and hybrids of shrubs ranges from low-growing varieties of 1m tall to larger shrubs up to 3m. Plants typically have opposite, simple leaves that are usually glossy and dark green. Evergreen or deciduous leaves may be oval or lance-shaped, often with serrated edges. In some species, leaves turn bronze or purplish in autumn. They typically have a compact, rounded, or arching growth habit. A profusion of tubular, fragrant flowers, white, pink, or pale lavender, is usually bell or funnel shaped. Flowers are produced in clusters or small cymes and can attract pollinators like bees and butterflies. After flowering, plants may produce small, rounded or elongated fruit that varies from pink to red or dark purple.

Linnaea chinensis syn. *Abelia × grandiflora*
Glossy Abelia

Native to China

This semi-evergreen shrub is the most popularly grown Chinese species. Dainty arching stems may reach 2m high and spread 2 to 3m wide. Leaves are opposite or in whorls of three, ovate, glossy, dark green, 1.5 to 8cm long, turning purplish-bronze to red in autumn. Flowers appear in upper leaf axils and stem ends in loose terminal panicles over most of the summer and autumn. These are pendulous, white flushed pink, bell shaped, 2cm long and usually scented. It needs average summer water, growing best in a well-drained rich soil. It is suitable for growing in the sun or in part shade. The variety 'Francis Mason', which has gold variegated leaves, needs shade. 'Prostrata' is a prostrate form that can spread up to 1m and is useful as a ground cover plant.

Linnaea chinensis 'Kaleidoscope' syn. *Abelia x grandiflora* 'Kaleidoscope'
Kaleidoscope Abelia, Glossy Abelia

Garden origin

This dense, semi-evergreen, compact shrub grows to about 60cm tall and 1m wide. It has reddish-purple stems and foliage that emerges green and yellow. New variegated growth emerges bright yellow with a light green centre throughout spring, and then gradually turns to a golden yellow with a deep-green centre in summer. By autumn, this combination turns to bright orange to fiery red throughout winter, extending until early spring. Colouration is most vibrant when grown in full sun. Its pink buds open into dainty white fragrant flowers. This is an exceptionally tough garden variety, which can tolerate extended periods of drought and grow in a wide range of climatic conditions. Select a sunny location in well-draining soil. It naturally has a compact dense habit, and unlike others within the genus, rarely forms long branching runaway shoots from the base. It looks fantastic as a small hedge and also looks great in large tubs and containers. Ideal to brighten up any garden, it will reward you with colour interest all year round.

Linnaea floribunda syn. *Abelia floribunda*
Mexican Abelia

Native to Mexico

A medium- to low-growing shrub to 4m tall with arching branches that bear small, glossy, semi-evergreen or evergreen ovate leaves. It produces clusters of pendant, tubular, pink flowers throughout summer. It is only slightly frost hardy and prefers a sheltered position. This is the most striking species, with outstanding flower colour and size, producing blooms in profusion for a fabulous display. When not in bloom, this plant decorates quietly with its attractive, glossy foliage. Grows best in a well-drained, rich soil in full sun and can tolerate a fair amount of shade. It needs average summer water. Prune back in autumn to promote strong flushes of fresh growth in spring, to keep it looking its best.

Linnaea parvifolia syn. *Abelia schumannii*
Native to western China

A deciduous slender shrub to 1.5m or more with pendulous arching branches. Small oval leaves are 3cm long with a sharp tip, which first emerges bronze. Rosy-pink 3cm-long flowers are blotched with orange and slightly fragrant. These make a continuous display during summer and autumn. Thrives in well-drained soil enriched with leaf-mould in a sunny protected site. Needs a moderate amount of summer water. Easy to maintain, it can grow in patio pots. More hardy than other Linnaea.

LIQUIDAMBAR
Altingiaceae
Sweetgum, Star Gum, Gum, Redgum, Satin-Walnut

Native to southeast and east Asia, the eastern Mediterranean and eastern North America

A genus of fifteen species of large, deciduous trees. Palmately three- to seven-lobed leaves are arranged spirally on the stems 12 to 20cm long, having a pleasant aroma when crushed. Leaves can be bright red, orange, yellow or even purple. Mature bark is greyish and vertically grooved. Small flowers are produced in a dense globular inflorescence of 1 to 2cm in diameter, pendulous on a 3 to 7cm stem.

Liquidambar formosana
Formosa Sweet Gum

Native to central and southern China, Taiwan and Indochina

A medium, deciduous tree that grows up to 12m tall. Leaves are 10 to 15cm wide and three-lobed, unlike the five- to seven-lobed leaves of most American Liquidambar species. Leaves are alternate, simple, palmately veined, with serrated margins. The foliage turns an attractive red in autumn. Roots can be aggressive, and branches are usually covered with corky projections. Individual flowers are unisexual. However, both sexes can be found in the same plant (monoecious). Male flowers are in catkins, while female flowers form dense spherical heads. Easily grown in full sun in well-drained fertile soil. Tolerant of summer drought, harsh conditions and frost. A hardy tree once established that tolerates many growing locations, including wet soil. It is often planted as a street tree for its beautiful autumn colour.

LIRIOPE
Asparagaceae
Lilyturfs

Native to East and Southeast Asia

A genus of five or six species of tufted rhizomatous and tuberous, evergreen and semi-evergreen perennials. They have arching, linear, grass-like leaves, which form dense clumps. Tiny violet-blue flowers, which only open slightly, are clustered in short spikes in late summer. These are more prolific with a dose or two of fertiliser early in the season. Several variegated varieties are now available to add golden or silver flashes of colour to shady situations.

Liriope muscari

Native to China, Taiwan, Japan

This stout, tufted, evergreen perennial 30 to 45cm tall features clumps of strap-like, arching, glossy, dark-green leaves. Clumps slowly expand by short stolons to a width of about 30cm, but plants do not spread aggressively. Roots are fibrous, often with terminal tubers. Erect spikes with tiered whorls of small, showy, dense, white to violet-purple flowers rise above the leaves in late summer. Flowers resemble those of grape hyacinth (Muscari), which is the origin of the specific epithet. Flowers develop into blackish berries, which often persist into winter. There is considerable variation in leaf colour and size among several recognised cultivars. Grow in light, moderately fertile, acidic, well-drained soil in partial to full shade, sheltered from cold drying winds. Drought tolerant.

Liriope muscari 'John Burch'

This has 1cm-wide, variegated leaf blades, green with yellowish-white margins. It blooms with full, lavender, coxcomb shaped, flower spikes in midsummer. It stays in clump form as it does not spread by rhizomes. Perfect for borders, edging and mixed beds. Also used for erosion control on banks, slopes, large bed plantings and in woodland gardens. Mature height is 30 to 40cm, spreading 30 to 40cm.

Lithodora diffusa see *Glandora diffusa*

Littonia modesta see *Gloriosa modesta*

LOBULARIA
Brassicaceae

Native to Asia, Macronesia and the Mediterranean region

A genus of five species closely related to (and formerly often included in) the genus Alyssum. The genus comprises annuals and perennials growing to 10 to 40cm tall, with hairy oblong-oval leaves and clusters of cross-shaped (cruciform), fragrant white flowers.

Lobularia maritima syn. *Alyssum maritimum*
Alyssum

Native to Europe, Asia, and northern Africa

Widely cultivated as an ornamental annual (rarely a short-lived perennial) 5 to 30cm tall and 20 to 30cm wide, with highly branched stems. Lance-shaped leaves are 1 to 4cm long and 3 to 5mm wide, alternate, sessile, quite hairy, with an entire margin. It is mainly grown for its masses of small sweet-smelling flowers, with an aroma like honey. It blooms profusely in spring and early summer. Flowers are typically white, pink, or purple and are arranged in dense clusters atop trailing stems. It thrives in full sun to partial shade in well-drained soil, and it is relatively low maintenance. This plant is valued for its ability to attract pollinators such as bees and butterflies. It is often used as a ground cover, in containers, or as an edging plant because of its low-growing nature. A popular choice for gardeners looking to add charm and fragrance to their landscapes, especially in spring and early summer.

LOMANDRA
Asparagaceae
Mat Rushes

Native to eastern Australia

A genus of over 50 species of tufted dioecious perennials with long, narrow blade-like leaves that arise from a central stemless base and have thick woody rhizomes and fibrous roots. An enormous range of cultivars has increased the diversity of this exciting plant and offers a wealth of variation in colour, form and size to suit any garden. They are typically hardy and will tolerate most growing conditions from extreme wet to drought. Happy in full sun or shade and will cope with a wide range of soil types and pH levels. Typically, their dense root systems penetrate deep into the soil, making them ideal for erosion control and steep banks. The striking form of typical varieties is good for accent plantings, mass plantings and as a special feature.

Lomandra longifolia
Spiny-Head Mat-Rush, Spiky-Headed Mat-Rush, Basket Grass

Native to New South Wales, Australia

A rhizomatous perennial with linear or nearly flat, yellow-green to dark-green leaves 40 to 80cm long and 8 to 12mm wide. In spring to early summer, it bears cylindrical or tubular, purple-flushed yellow, slightly fragrant flowers 5mm long. It grows in a variety of soil types and is frost, heat and drought tolerant.

naea chinensis.

Linnaea chinensis **'Kaleidoscope'.**

Liquidambar formosana.

iope muscari **'John Burch'.**

Lobularia maritima.

Lomandra longifolia.

nicera etrusca.

Lonicera japonica.

Loropetalum chinense.

Lomandra longifolia 'Great White'

A variegated form with bigger flowers and a more compact and dense form that is welcomed amongst growers and landscapers. It grows to 50cm high and wide with strikingly striped foliage and many chunky, perfumed, yellow flowers appearing in spring. They live on natural rainfall in most areas, but an occasional top up of water is required in extreme drought. Growing uniformly, they are excellent when planted in a large group, and also dotted amongst other plants for contrast interest. Good in locations such as roadsides, factories, offices and other areas that require low-maintenance plants.

Lomelosia graminifolia see *Scabiosa graminifolia*

LONICERA

Caprifoliaceae

Honeysuckle

Widespread in the Northern Hemisphere

A genus of over 158 species of usually hardy, deciduous, sometimes evergreen erect or twining climbers, a few with a shrubby habit. Leaves are opposite, simple, oval, 1 to 10cm long. Many species have sweetly-scented, bilaterally-symmetrical flowers that produce a sweet, edible nectar, borne in pairs. They are grown for their usually tubular flowers that are often fragrant. Some species have become invasive in some areas.

Lonicera etrusca

Etruscan Honeysuckle

Native to the Mediterranean region

A deciduous or semi-evergreen vigorous twining climber up to 4m or more high and wide. Pairs of oval or obovate, mid-green leaves, up to 10cm long, are joined at the base and hairy underneath. Tubular two-lipped, sweetly-scented yellowish flowers, 5cm long, become flushed with red and darken with age. Stamens and style protrude from the flower's mouth. Flowers are produced in terminal and axillary whorls from summer to autumn and are usually followed by red berries. Easily grown in any well-drained soil in a warm position. Thriving in full sun, it is drought tolerant once established, but grows better with some summer water. Good for covering large walls or fences. Prune severely once a year to restrict size.

Lonicera japonica

Japanese Honeysuckle

Native to Japan

A vigorous twining vine up to 10m or more high that spreads as wide. Normally evergreen but can be deciduous in cold regions. Opposite, simple, oval leaves are 3 to 8cm long and 2 to 3cm wide. When its stems are young, they are slightly red and may be fuzzy. Older stems are brown with peeling bark and often hollow on the inside. Strongly-fragrant, 4cm-long, tubular, two-lipped, white flowers that age to yellow are produced in pairs in leaf axils from spring to autumn. Thriving in full sun it is drought tolerant once established, but grows better with some summer water. Easily grown in any well-drained soil in a warm position. The climber is good for covering large walls or fences but can become invasive. Prune severely once a year to restrict size. While the nectar from the flowers can be safely consumed by humans, all other parts of the plant have the potential to be toxic.

'Aureoreticulata' has leaves with yellow and green veins. Grow in partial shade as the leaves burn in full sun.

'Purpurea' has leaves tinged with purple and purple veins. The young shoots are also purple. The bright red flower buds open cream fading to white.

'Halliana' Hall's Honeysuckle

A vigorous, evergreen twining climber up to 10m or more high that spreads as wide. Young leaves 8cm long are lightly hairy. Flowers are produced in profusion in spring and continue through to autumn with a few at other times. They are in pairs, creamy white, aging to yellow, and fragrant. Drought tolerant once established but grows and flowers better if given some summer water. A tough climber for difficult situations such as poor soil, hot winds and hot walls in full sun. It will quickly cover fences, pergolas or climb into trees, easily enveloping a small tree with its twining stems. Often used as a bank or ground cover, where it will soon cover a large area smothering other plants. Prune severely once a year to restrict size.

Lonicera pilosa

Mexican Honeysuckle

Native to central and southern Mexico

A smallish, evergreen or deciduous vine to about 3m, with ovate pale-green, 2 to 3cm-long leaves. In summer, unscented clusters of about ten to twenty tubular, orange-red flowers each about 5cm long appear. While they are orange overall, they have multiple hues ranging from yellow to red. The clusters are hairy on the outside and capped with an umbrella-like bract that protects the blooms from rain. It comes from a climate with mild daytime temperatures and cool nights, so it probably cannot survive more than a light frost. It prefers part sun, with protection from strong afternoon sun. Easily grown in any well-drained soil in a warm position. Tolerant of summer drought. Give it something to climb through, like a trellis or a shrub.

LOROPETALUM

Hamamelidaceae

Chinese Fringe Flower

Native to China, Japan and Southeast Asia

A genus of about three species of evergreen to semi-evergreen shrubs to 3m high found in warm winter areas on rocky hills and dry open woods. They typically have glossy, elliptical to lance-shaped leaves that can range from deep green to reddish-purple, depending on the cultivar. They are prized for their attractive foliage and vibrant, often spidery flowers that appear in clusters, resemble small, spidery blooms and come in shades of white, pink, or red.

Loropetalum chinense
Chinese Witch Hazel

A bushy, evergreen shrub with branches forming horizontal layers. Leaves are alternate, ovate, 2.5 to 5cm long by 2.5cm wide and have a slightly abrasive feel. In late winter or early spring, it bears sweetly-scented flowers 2cm wide with strap-like petals in small, crowded cymes of three to six. Grows best in fertile, slightly acidic soil in full sun for deepest foliage colour and is hardy. Drought tolerant but prefers some summer water. It is a popular ornamental plant, grown for its prolific clusters of flowers and (with the pink flowering variety) deeply coloured foliage that may contain various green, copper, purple and red tones. Great as a hedge, specimen plant or in containers. Pruning can help maintain its shape and promote flowering. There are several popular cultivars, such as 'Ruby' with deep burgundy foliage and pink flowers, 'Burgundy' with dark purple leaves and fuchsia pink flowers, and 'Sizzling Pink' with bright pink blooms and bronze foliage.

LOTUS
Fabaceae

Distributed in warmer regions of the world, excluding the Americas

A large genus of over 150 species of annuals, perennials, evergreen and deciduous subshrubs. The genus Lotus is currently undergoing extensive taxonomic revision. Species native to the Americas have been moved into other genera. They are grown for their attractive pea-like flowers that come in a range of colours.

Lotus berthelotii
Parrot's Beak, Canary Island Bird of Paradise

Native to the Canary Islands

A much-branched subshrub only growing to 20cm high with trailing stems 1m or more long, covered in silver hairs. Small 1cm-long, semi-evergreen leaves are silver grey and narrow. It is known for its distinctive, bird-like flowers that resemble a parrot's beak, hence its common name. Flowers 2 to 3cm long are bright orange-red and curved, with elongated petals. These form a startling contrast to the grey foliage. They are produced abundantly in waves during spring and summer, at their best in spring. In its native habitat, it grows in rocky, coastal areas with well-drained soil. It is adapted to a Mediterranean climate and thrives in full sun. Drought tolerant once established. It is suitable for rock gardens, containers, on banks, or on the tops of walls where its striking silver-grey foliage can be seen at its best, and in hanging baskets. A short-lived plant, as after four or five years it can become untidy or exhausted and should be replaced. It is also important to protect it from frost in colder climates.

Lotus maculatus

Native to the Canary Islands

A low-growing, evergreen subshrub up to 20cm high with prostrate silver hairy branches. Alternate tiny grey leaves are divided into needle-like segments. Flowers are winged, 4 to 5cm long and bright yellow tipped with a slender brown beak, resembling lobster claws. These are produced singly or in groups of two to five in spring and early summer. The plant is similar in most respects to *L. berthelotii*, as are the cultural conditions.

LUPINUS
Fabaceae

Native to the Mediterranean, North Africa, North and South America

The genus comprises about 200 species of annuals, perennials and evergreen shrubs found in dry, hilly grassland and open woodland. Most have short-stemmed, palmate, often hairy, mid-green, mainly basal leaves with lance-shaped leaflets. Widely known for their tall spikes of colourful pea-like flowers. Flowers come in blue, purple, pink, red, yellow and white. Some species also have bi-coloured or multi-coloured flowers. They have specialised root nodules that contain nitrogen-fixing bacteria, which convert atmospheric nitrogen into a form that can be used by plants. Many species are cultivated as ornamentals in gardens. These are valued for their showy flowers, which attract pollinators such as bees and butterflies.

Lupinus albifrons
Silver Lupine, White-Leaf Bush Lupine, Evergreen Lupine

Native to western North America, particularly California and Oregon

An herbaceous perennial typically growing 1m tall, though it can reach up to 2m. It forms a large, round, bushy mound of silky, silvery-grey to dark green, palmately compound leaves with five to nine leaflets. In spring and early summer, it produces showy, fragrant, erect spikes 10 to 13cm long, of pea-shaped flowers in shades of yellow, blue, purple or sometimes white. The blossoms are borne at the tips of short branches well above the foliage. They are attractive to bees, butterflies and other pollinators. Often cultivated as an ornamental plant in gardens and landscapes, particularly in regions with a Mediterranean climate. It is valued for its drought tolerance, attractive foliage and showy flowers. It can be grown from seed and prefers well-drained soil and full sun.

Lupinus arboreus
Yellow Bush Lupine, Tree Lupin

Native to California

An evergreen shrub growing to 2m tall in sheltered situations, but more typically 1 to 1.5m tall. It has green to grey-green palmate leaves, with five to twelve leaflets per leaf. Leaflets are 2 to 6cm long, often sparsely covered with fine, silky hairs. In spring it bears many racemes, 30cm long, of fragrant, soft yellow, pea-like flowers. Both yellow and lilac to purple flowering forms are known, but the yellow form is more common. Summer drought tolerant. Widely grown as an ornamental plant, for its attractive flowers in traditional, native plant and wildlife gardens, also used to bind drifting sand dunes. It can be seen growing in cracks in vertical stone walls, because of the sharp drainage. Also cultivated on balconies or patios in pots.

LYCIANTHES
Solanaceae
Native mainly in the Americas

A genus containing roughly 150 species, mostly from tropical America, with 35 to 40 species in Asia and the Pacific. Only one species is usually grown in gardens for its spectacular flowers.

Lycianthes rantonnetii syn. *Solanum rantonnetii*
Blue Potato Bush

Native to Argentina and Paraguay

An evergreen, spreading shrub with arching branches, which in the open will grow to 2m high and wide, but if trained against a wall may reach 3m or more high. Bright-green, oval to lance-shaped leaves are 6 to 10cm long, often wavy margined. Although evergreen it may drop its leaves in severe cold. It boasts a nearly non-stop display of lightly-fragrant, violet-blue or pale-blue flowers adorned with a bright yellow centre, trumpet-shaped, 2 to 3cm across. These appear in loose axillary clusters to 6cm across from early spring until autumn, and often throughout the year. Thrives in full sun in well-drained soil. Tolerant of frost and summer drought. An easily-grown attractive shrub, which may need severe pruning to keep in shape. Often seen in nurseries as a short-stemmed standard grown in a container, which looks most attractive on a terrace, patio or by a swimming pool. 'Royal Robe' is more compact, with a longer flowering season and fragrant, deep violet-blue flowers with yellow centres.

LYCORIS
Amaryllidaceae
Spider Lily, Surprise Lilies

Native to eastern and southern Asia

A genus of about twelve species of bulbous perennials. These plants are well-known for their striking tubular flowers with protruding stamens that appear on leafless stems in late summer or autumn, giving them their surprise element. Bulbs are easy to grow and require well-drained soil and in full to partial sunlight. After flowering, they often produce strap-like leaves that persist through the winter and then die back in spring, making them suitable for naturalising in garden borders or woodland areas.

Lycoris aurea
Golden Spider Lily

Native to China, Japan

A bulbous perennial with a clumping habit. Its strap-shaped leaves remain green all winter long and at the first hint of warm weather the following spring they die. Leaves are 60cm long, mid-green, shiny and held semi-erect. These hardy bulbs are dormant during the summer and bear their beautiful flowers during autumn before growing foliage in the cooler months. Flowers are presented on a tall stem with eye-catching umbels up to 20cm across, of five or six wavy-margined, golden-yellow flowers adorned with elegantly curled petals and protruding stamens. Grow in a border in full sun or partial shade, in fertile well-drained soil that dries out. Summer dormant, needing water during the flowering and growing period only. Leave plants undivided until a thick clump forms after several years. Plant bulbs with the tip just below the surface. The bulbs rot in waterlogged soil. They make attractive pot or container plants when in flower and excellent cut flowers.

Lycoris radiata
Red Spider Lily, Red Magic Lily

Native to Japan

A bulbous perennial with strap-shaped leaves 30 to 60cm long. Greyish-green leaves emerge in autumn, parallel-sided, with a paler central stripe. The plant keeps its leaves throughout winter but will shed them as temperatures warm in late spring before flowers appear. Showy, bright-red flowers have spindly stamens, likened to the image of spider legs extending slightly upward and outward from the flower's centre. Flowers appear around late summer, before the leaves fully develop, on scapes rising 30 to 70cm from the ground. Four to six 5cm-long flowers in umbels sit atop each plant stalk. Individual flowers are irregular, with narrow segments that curve backwards. Cultural requirements are the same as *L. aurea*. This is the best-known species, and easiest to grow.

tus berthelotii.

Lupinus arboreus.

Lupinus albifrons.

cianthes rantonnetii.

Lycoris aurea.

Lycoris radiata.

acrozamia communis.

Magnolia grandiflora.

M

MACROZAMIA

Zamiaceae

Native to Australia

A genus of around 40 species of cycads with partially submerged bole or tree, small to medium height, bearing a crown of palm-like fronds. Dioecious plants bear large cones, becoming even larger when ripening on the female, containing reproductive parts of great size. Male and female plants are needed to produce seed. Many parts of the plant have been utilised for food and material, most of which are toxic if not processed correctly.

Macrozamia communis

Native to east coast of Australia

A medium-sized cycad with large, fern-like leaves arising from a short or subterranean trunk. Leaves are 1 to 2m long with glossy green, linear leaflets 10 to 30cm long. Male cones are cylindrical up to 45cm long by about 15cm wide, aging to a greyish brown. Female cones are barrel shaped to about 45cm by 20cm. When ripe, the cone on female plants breaks apart to release large, bright red seeds, which are about 5cm long by 2.5cm wide. Extremely hardy and drought tolerant, withstanding extended dry periods. It naturally grows in dappled shade under trees in the wild, but can also be grown in sunny spots. A good landscaping and garden specimen plant, it will also do well in a large container. However, the plant is slow growing and may take five years or more to be noticed as a feature plant and many more years to reach anything like a reasonable size. Cones should not be expected for at least ten years. The seeds contain toxic compounds that have caused fatalities to both humans and livestock.

MAGNOLIA

Magnoliaceae

Native to North and Central America, Asia including China, Japan

A genus of about 125 species of deciduous and evergreen trees and shrubs. Leaves are large, leathery and glossy, typically alternate, simple, ovate or elliptical, with smooth or serrated edges. Trees are renowned for their large, showy flowers that come in various shapes, sizes and colours. Beautiful and often fragrant flowers are typically solitary or in clusters at the ends of branches. They can be cup, star or saucer shaped, and include white, cream, pink, purple and yellow. These are popular ornamental plants in gardens and landscapes around the world.

Magnolia grandiflora

Southern Magnolia, Bull Bay

Native to southeast United States, North Carolina to Florida and Texas

An evergreen tree growing slowly to about 6m high, making a pyramidal or rounded crown with a straight trunk. It has smooth, greyish-brown bark that becomes rough and furrowed with age. Leaves are large and leathery, around 12 to 20cm long, oblong or elliptical with a glossy upper surface, while the underside is covered with a brownish or reddish felt-like coating. The truly remarkable cup-shaped flowers, 25cm in diameter, with a waxy texture, are pure white and emit a delightful fragrance, often described as lemony or citrus-like. These are composed of nine to twelve petals, which are thick and showy. The flowers appear in late spring to early summer and continue to bloom sporadically throughout the summer. Drought tolerant once established. Prefers well-drained soil and full sun to partial shade for optimal growth. It is often used as a shade tree or as a specimen tree in larger gardens. It can take several years to flower, so buy named grafted cultivars, some of which have more compact growth habits and usually flower younger. The tree produces strong shallow surface roots, so do not plant underneath it.

MALCOLMIA

Brassicaceae

Native to Mediterranean region to Afganistan

A genus of about 35 species of bushy, sometimes prostrate annuals and perennials with elliptical to lance-shaped and green-grey leaves. They are grown for their short racemes of narrow cross-shaped, four-petalled white, purple or red flowers, which appear from spring to autumn.

Malcolmia maritima

Virginian Stock, French Forget-Me-Not

Native to the Mediterranean

Semi-prostrate or erect, woody based annual 20 to 40cm high, 10 to 15cm wide. It has elliptical, hairy-toothed or entire, blunt-tipped, green-grey leaves 5cm long. Flowers are small at 1cm, and fragrant in white, red, mauve and pink. These are borne in slender terminal racemes, sweetly fragrant. Plants have a long flowering season from late spring to early autumn. Grow in moderately fertile soil in full sun or light shade. Fairly tolerant of summer drought, but they flower better with some water. Flowering is poorer in regions with hot, humid summers. They can flower quickly from seeding – so plant out throughout the season for a continuing display. Great for path edges, rockeries and combining with other plants in tubs and planters. They self-seed easily, so may be sown directly into the ground.

MALEPHORA

Aizoaceae

Mesembs

Native to southern Africa

A genus of thirteen to seventeen species of perennial bushy, prostrate to erect and woody-based succulents. Stems have prominent internodes. Leaves are opposite, about 6cm long, fleshy, smooth, bright, to bluish green, fleshy (succulent), soft and usually covered with a thick, waxy bloom that is easily rubbed off. Short-stalked, showy, star-shaped terminal or axillary flowers are golden yellow, deep orange or reddish purple, and occur singly or in small clusters. The undersurfaces of petals are often a rich purple, differing from the orange or yellow upper surfaces. Plants grow with ease and flower within the first year. Drought tolerant, preferring direct sunlight and well-drained, sandy soil.

Malephora crocea

Coppery Mesemb, Red Ice Plant

Native to the Western Cape of South Africa

A perennial herb with a creeping corky to woody stem, which roots where nodes come in contact with soil. Succulent leaves are triangular in cross-section, 5cm long, pale green to reddish, and somewhat waxy in texture. Solitary golden yellow flowers 3cm across with red-backed petals are produced in late summer. It is grown as an ornamental plant and a ground cover in landscaping for its low water needs, as it is drought tolerant. Grow in full sun in poor or moderately fertile soil. It has been recommended as a ground cover in areas prone to wildfire, because of its low flammability.

MALOPE

Malvaceae

Annual Mallow

Native to the Mediterranean region

A small genus of three species of tall bushy annuals or perennials. One species is often used as an ornamental plant grown for its showy trumpet-shaped flowers.

Malope trifida

Native to the western Mediterranean region

An upright, stout-stemmed annual to 1m high, whose upright bushy branches have stems and leaves covered in hairs. The rounded deep green leaves have three to five pointed lobes. In summer it is covered in broad trumpet-shaped white to pale pink to dark purple-red flowers 5 to 8cm across with five heavily-veined petals. Drought tolerant once established, but flowers are better with some summer water. Grow in well-drained soil in full sun. An easily-grown and free-flowering annual that is attractive in a sunny border. Flowers are produced over a long period and are suitable for cutting. 'Alba' has white flowers. 'Grandiflora' has large, deep rose-red flowers. Seed of mixed colours are available with pink, red, purple and white flowers.

MALVA syn. LAVATERA

Malvaceae

Mallow

Native mostly in the Mediterranean region, central Asia, Australia, California

The genus Lavatera no longer exists, taxonomically speaking at least, as its species have been transferred to Malva, commonly called 'Mallow'. Genetic and morphological studies published in 1998 by botanist Martin Forbes Ray show that the two genera showed so many common characteristics there was no reason to separate them.

The combined genus now contains some 50 species, including annuals, biennials, perennials and soft-wooded shrubs.

Malva alcea

Cut Leaved Mallow, Hollyhock Mallow

Native to southern Europe

A variable, bushy, erect, woody-based perennial up to 1m or more high spreading to 60cm wide. Stems and leaves are covered in hairs. Upper leaves, to 15cm long, are usually deeply five-lobed with further lobes or teeth, while the lower leaves, to 30cm long, are more heart-shaped. Saucer-shaped bright pink flowers with notched petals are 2 to 5cm wide, covering the plant from early spring through to autumn. Easily grown in full sun in average soil with good drainage and some summer water. When raised from seed sown in early spring, it will flower the first year. With long-lasting and showy flowers, it is suitable for a border or wildflower garden. 'Fastigiata' grows narrower and more upright to 80cm high with pink flowers.

Malva arborea syn. *Lavatera arborea*

Tree Mallow

Native to the Mediterranean region, north Africa

An almost tree-like, short-lived, evergreen perennial with stout stems, woody at the base, up to 3m high spreading to 1.5m wide. Leaves are a rounded heart-shape, hairy, up to 20cm in diameter, broad, grey-woolly underneath, and have coarsely serrated margins. Large funnel-shaped rose-purple flowers are veined with deeper purple 3 to 5cm across in terminal clusters. These are produced profusely throughout summer. It is well suited to poor, dry, coastal gardens. It needs little summer water as it is drought tolerant. Grows and flowers are best in the full sun. Easily raised from seed, usually flowering the first year. Often used as a quick and easy screen or as a windbreak.

Malva subovata syn. *Lavatera maritima*

Mediterranean Shrub Mallow

Native to the shores of the western and central Mediterranean

An upright, soft-wooded, fast-growing, evergreen shrub up to 1.5m high and 1m wide. Grey-green leaves are almost rounded, shallowly lobed or toothed, up to 6cm long, densely covered with soft whitish hairs. Throughout summer and autumn, it produces solitary, axillary, pale-pink flowers 4 to 8cm across, with dark-rose veining and crimson-purple centres on long stalks. This attractive shrub is easily cultivated and is ideal for coastal gardens as it withstands salt-laden sea breezes. It prefers rich, well-drained soil in a sunny spot throughout the year. Needs little summer water, as it is drought tolerant. Not frost tolerant. A Mediterranean species from coastal areas, which has become rather rare because of the destruction of its habitat.

Malva trimestris syn. *Lavatera trimestris*

Annual Mallow, Rose Mallow, Royal Mallow, Regal Mallow

Native to the Mediterranean region

A fast-growing, softly hairy, herbaceous and shrubby annual 1.2m or more high and 45cm wide. It has attractive heart-shaped mid-green leaves, 3 to 6cm in diameter, with five to seven shallow lobes or toothed. Lovely, solitary, silken, open bell-shaped flowers are produced in shades of rose and pink with some white varieties as well. Many named varieties have been raised with more intense colours. These striking flowers are up to 8cm wide and appear in summer and autumn in great profusion. Easily raised from seed sown in spring in any well drained and fertile soil. Useful as a colourful summer hedge, also makes good cut flowers. Ideal for coastal gardens. Many cultivars have been developed for garden use, all of which are annuals to be sown in spring for flowering the same year.

MATTHIOLA
Brassicaceae
Stocks

Native to west Europe, South Africa, central and southwest Asia

The genus contains about 50 species of bushy, erect annuals, biennials and perennials. Most species have simple, often grey-green leaves that are sometimes toothed. Heavily scented, colourful flowers, which appear from spring through to summer, are four-petalled and grow on upright, often branching stems. They range from pink to mauve and purple, and some species can make lovely cut flowers, as well as being suitable for garden bedding. There are also many garden strains in a wide range of flower forms and colours.

Matthiola incana

Native to Arabia, west Europe, Mediterranean region

A woody-based perennial or subshrub, sometimes short-lived, to 80cm high and 40cm wide. It has grey-green to white, hairy, lance-shaped leaves 5 to 10cm long. Upright racemes of sweetly scented, mauve, purple, pink or white flowers 2 to 3cm across appear in early summer. There are many cultivars that produce single or fully double, almost rosette-like, highly-scented flowers. Grow in full sun in average to moderately rich, well-draining, sandy, nearly neutral to slightly alkaline soil. Tolerant of summer drought.

MAURANDELLA
Plantaginaceae

Native to California

A genus of just one species of herbaceous perennial climber from dry desert riverbeds.

Maurandella antirrhiniflora
Violet Climbing Snapdragon

A delicate, wiry climber 1 to 2m high with shallowly three- to five-lobed triangular bright to mid-green leaves 2 to 10cm long. Produces bright-purple, pinkish or red snapdragon-shaped flowers 2 to 3cm long, with a yellow throat. The sepals are narrow and curve outwards. Flowers appear from summer to autumn. Easily grown in well-drained soil in full sun with some midday shade. Tolerant of summer drought. Not frost hardy. Used to cover a pergola, arch, or trellis.

MAURANDYA
Plantaginaceae

Native to Mexico, Central America

A genus comprising two species of twining, woody-based, herbaceous, perennial climbers. Leaves are triangular to broadly ovate, sometimes heart-shaped at the base. Solitary trumpet-shaped blooms are borne in leaf axils during summer and autumn.

Maurandya barclayana
Angels Trumpet, Mexican Viper

Native to Mexico

A medium-sized, erect, free-flowering, perennial climber growing 2 to 5m high. In its native habitat, it scrambles through shrubs and hangs down on cliffs in dry areas. Angular to shallowly lobed, mid- to light green leaves are 3 to 5cm long with heart-shaped bases. It flowers for most of the summer. Flowers are from 4 to 7cm long with white or green tinted tubes and white, pink or deep purple lobes. Easily grown in any moderately fertile, well-drained soil in full sun. Tolerant of summer drought. Not frost hardy. Used to clothe a pergola, arch, or trellis.

MELALEUCA
Myrtaceae
Bottlebrush, Paperbark

Native to Australia, New Caledonia, Indonesia and Papua New Guinea

The genus comprises approximately 34 species of evergreen shrubs and trees, including all formerly known as Callistemon. They are characterised by their distinctive inflorescence, which resembles a bottlebrush, hence the common name. The inflorescence comprises cylindrical spikes of many small, colourful flowers with long, prominent stamens. These stamens give the flower spikes their brush-like appearance and can be in shades of red, pink, purple, yellow or white. The foliage is dense and composed of narrow lance-shaped leaves, usually dark green, glossy and aromatic, exuding a pleasant scent when crushed. There is much confusion among nurseries, as many kinds are still sold under their old name Callistemon.

Melaleuca citrina syn. *Callistemon citrinus*
Lemon Bottlebrush, Crimson Bottlebrush

Native to eastern Australia

This vigorous spreading shrub will reach 4 to 5m high, or can be trained into a tree when young, reaching perhaps 6 to 7m. It has a dense and bushy spreading growth habit, forming a rounded or oval shape. Narrow, rigid lance-shaped leaves are 8cm long, dark green, leathery, and have a slight lemon scent when crushed. New growth is a copper colour turning a vivid green with age. A distinctive feature is its 15cm long cylindrical bright crimson inflorescence, composed of many small individual flowers. These are squeezed together at the ends of stiff stems during summer. There are cultivars with variations in shades, including pink and crimson. Do not remove the old flower heads, as fresh growth and flowers are produced

alcolmia maritima.

Malephora crocea.

Malope trifida.

alva trimestris.

Matthiola incana.

Maurandella antirrhiniflora.

aurandya barclayana.

Melaleuca citrina.

Melaleuca nesophila.

from the tips of the old flower. It usually flowers in spring or early summer. Flowers are nectar rich and attract birds, bees and butterflies. Drought and heat tolerant once established, preferring full sun but can tolerate partial shade. Grow in well-draining soil. It needs little maintenance and rarely requires extensive pruning.

Melaleuca linearis var. *linearis* syn. *Callistemon rigidus*
Stiff Bottlebrush, Rigid Bottlebrush

Native to eastern Australia

A large shrub with erect, sparse, arching branches, which can form a small tree 6m high with a 3m spread. Rigid, sharply-pointed, lance-shaped leaves up to 13cm long clothe the branches. These are fragrant when bruised. Dense spikes of deep red flowers 8 to 10cm long appear during spring and summer. They will bloom intermittently throughout the year in frost-free areas, providing a copious source of nectar for birds and insects. The seed capsules are prominent and remain on the shrub for at least a year. It is valued for its striking flowers, drought tolerance and low maintenance requirements. Prefers well-drained soils and full sun. It is suitable for planting in a variety of garden settings, including borders, hedges and containers.

Melaleuca nesophila
Pink Melaleuca, Showy Honey-Myrtle, Mindiyet

Native to Western Australia

A large shrub or tree that makes fast growth to 3 to 6m spreading to 3m wide with freely branching stems and greyish white, papery, peeling, spongy bark. Alternate greyish green obovate leaves are 1 to 3cm long. Lavender to rose pink 'pom-pom' flowers appear over a long period from spring to midsummer. Flowers are in heads or short spikes on the ends of branches, which continue to grow after flowering and sometimes also in upper leaf axils. The heads are up to 3cm in diameter and contain between two and twenty groups of three flowers fading to white with yellow tips. A useful shrub, as it withstands heat, sea breezes and poor soil. It is extremely drought tolerant once established. Can be clipped into a hedge or trained into a tree with striking branch structures or used as an informal screen.

Melaleuca quadrifida syn. *Calothamnus quadrifidus*
One-sided Bottlebrush, Common Net Bush

Native to the southwest region of Western Australia

An upright, compact or spreading, heavily-branched, evergreen shrub that grows to about 1.5 to 2.5m high and wide. Grey-green or green needle-like leaves are about 3cm long and usually hairy, giving the foliage a lovely soft appearance. Showy flowers, clustered in one-sided spikes, are produced during spring and well into summer. Its brightly-coloured stamens, usually red, are the conspicuous parts of the flower and are fused together in bundles, known as staminal claws. Fruits are woody capsules that remain on the plant throughout its life and can contain seeds for many years. It grows naturally in a dry summer climate, so it is drought tolerant, but will also grow in more humid conditions. Grows well in either full sun or part shade, though it favours a warm, open and sunny position. Moderately hardy, tolerating windy and coastal situations.

Melaleuca viminalis syn. *Callistemon viminalis*
Weeping Bottlebrush

A beautiful evergreen shrub or small tree fast growing up to 7m high with a 4m spread. Spreading to weeping branches are adorned with narrow lance-shaped leaves 10cm long, bronze when young then turning a light green. Dense spikes of bright-red, 15cm-long flower spikes are produced two or three times a year. It grows best in sheltered areas, as it is easily damaged by wind. Requires more summer water than other species. May also be damaged by cold in some winters. Some branches may need removal to improve the shape and preventing it becoming top heavy. Useful as a screen plant, foundations, hedges, especially in Mediterranean gardens.

MELIA
Meliaceae

Native to Asia and Australia

A genus containing three to five species of deciduous trees or large shrubs, some having scented wood. Only one species is cultivated in gardens for its attractive flowers and berries.

Melia azedarach
Chinaberry, Indian Bead Tree, Persian Lilac

Native to northern India, central and western China

A deciduous fast-growing tree 9 to 15m high spreading to 5 to 8m wide. It forms a many-branched, round, open-headed tree with attractive rough bark. Beautiful, dark-green, large 30 to 90cm long doubly pinnate leaves have many 2 to 5cm oval toothed leaflets. Clusters of small, star-shaped, fragrant, lilac flowers 2cm across appear on branches during spring. These are followed by clusters of pea-sized, yellow bead-like fruit, which hang from the bare branches long after the leaves have fallen, often until the following spring. The poisonous fruit is plump when ripe, becoming wrinkled with age. Seed of the fruit is used as beads for rosaries in Asia, giving it the common name. The tree grows easily from seed and makes fast growth. Commonly grown as a street tree or a patio shade tree in many warm countries. Grows well in full sun. Resistant to drought, needing no summer water. A good tree for difficult sites, as it tolerates poor alkaline soils and is wind resistant.

MELIANTHUS
Francoaceae
Honey Flower
Native to southern Africa

A small genus containing about six species of tender evergreen shrubs with attractive foliage and unusual flowers. They have large pinnate leaves with prominent stipules, and erect racemes of nectar-rich flowers. The vegetative parts are toxic. Only one species is grown in gardens.

Melianthus major
Honey Bush
Native to South Africa

A handsome, evergreen, suckering, semi-woody shrub. Upright, hollow, grey or green stems with few branches make fast growth 2 to 3m high with leaves in terminal clusters. Most of the stems appear from ground level. Deeply-toothed pinnate leaves are 30 to 45cm long with nine to seventeen leaflets in pairs, a glaucous blue-green above with a paler underneath and has a distinctive musky odour. Boldly-patterned leaves give it a striking sub-tropical effect. Dark-red, nectar-laden flowers 6cm long in terminal erect racemes 30 to 80cm appear in spring, followed by green pods. Grows well in fertile, leafy, well-drained soil in full sun or partial shade. Drought tolerant once established. As the fresh growth is most attractive, it responds well to cutting back after flowering. It is chiefly grown as a foliage shrub. It makes a good silhouette plant for a raised bed or a striking accent plant. Also good near swimming pools. All parts of the plants are poisonous.

MELOCACTUS
Cactaceae
Turk's Cap Cactus
Native to tropical and subtropical regions of the Americas, including the Caribbean, Central and South America

A genus of around 50 known species of cactus. They have globose, green stems with multiple ribs. Spines are stout and usually feature a distinct central spine surrounded by radial spines resembling an asterisk. Mature plants begin to develop a cephalium (elongated stalk at top of cactus where flowers emerge). The red, wool-coated cephalium, resembling a Fez worn by Turkish men during the late Ottoman Empire, gives the plant its common name. After the cap is formed, the stem stops growing, but the cephalium keeps growing until the plant dies. The underside of most cephaliums is white while the top is orange, but they can also be entirely white. It is in this mass of areoles that the flowers are formed. These are quite small, typically ranging from pink to red to yellow, and come out of the top of the cephalium sporadically or in rings in late spring or early summer. These cacti have adapted to thrive in harsh desert environments where water is scarce.

Melocactus intortus
Native to the Caribbean

A spiny, evergreen, solitary, succulent cactus with a stem that becomes barrel-shaped, growing as an unbranched, almost cylindrical, succulent shrub to 75cm high. The trunk is up 35cm in diameter, with up to twenty ridges. On the ridges, areoles, 1 to 2cm apart, have ten to twenty radiating spines each, 1 to 6cm long. It is crowned by a cylindrical cephalium (sometimes more than one) densely covered with whitish, cottony fibres and spirally-arranged clusters of reddish spines. Flowers are reddish pink, to 1cm wide, with many stamens, spirally arranged on cephalium, surrounded by a cluster of reddish spines. A slow-growing plant requiring a sunny position in a well-drained acid soil. Established plants are extremely drought tolerant. Plants are tender and can be damaged by cold. Overall, plants are easy to grow and care for, making them a great addition to any collection or garden. With the right conditions and proper care, they can thrive for many years.

MERWILLA
Asparagaceae
Native to southern Africa, from Zimbabwe to South Africa

A genus of about five species of bulbous perennials. Species grow from relatively large bulbs, the upper part usually above ground, producing broad lance-shaped leaves. The bulbs have light-yellow to grey coverings. Flowers are borne in a raceme with each flower having six blue tepals, forming a star shape. Stamens have white filaments that are joined at the base and small anthers. The oblong seeds are brownish when dry, paler when fresh, which distinguishes Merwilla from related genera with glossy black or dark-brown seeds.

Merwilla plumbea syn. *Scilla natalensis*
Native to eastern South Africa

A deciduous, tall, perennial flowering bulb 10 to 15cm in diameter growing during summer and dormant in winter. The bulb produces a basal rosette of six to fifteen broad, light-green, semi-erect, lance-shaped leaves 40 to 60cm in summer as the flowers fade. In early summer, it produces tall conical racemes usually about 1m tall, of 50 to 100 star-shaped bright violet, pale blue, or blue and white flowers 1.5cm across. Flowers have a honey-like scent towards evening and are visited by bees during the day. An easy bulb to grow in full sun in any soil. This bulb is relatively drought tolerant but prefers moisture in summer when in growth and drying out in winter. It looks wonderful when grown in large drifts between shrubs and deciduous trees. Also looks attractive when grown in pots. All parts of this plant are highly toxic.

MESEMBRYANTHEMUM
Aizoaceae
Native to southern Africa

A genus of about two species of prostrate, shrubby, short-lived perennial suc-

Melaleuca quadrifida.

Melaleuca viminalis.

Melia azedarach.

Melianthus major.

Melocactus intortus.

Merwilla plumbea.

Mesembryanthemum cordifolium.

Metrosideros kermadecensis variegata.

Mirabilis jalapa.

culents, characterised by fleshy, succulent leaves that help them adapt to arid conditions. Leaves often have a distinctive appearance and may be cylindrical, triangular, or flattened, depending on the species. Flowers are typically solitary and have a daisy-like appearance, coming in shades of pink, purple, orange, yellow and white. They are well adapted to arid and semi-arid environments, often growing in sandy or rocky soils. Some are also known for their ability to tolerate salty conditions. Some are low-growing and form dense mats or ground covers. This growth habit makes them suitable for landscaping, especially in areas with poor soil and low water availability. Often cultivated as ornamental plants, particularly in rock gardens, containers or landscapes with well-drained soil. They are appreciated for their drought tolerance and vibrant flowers.

Mesembryanthemum cordifolium
Dew Plant

A much-branched succulent with trailing stems 60cm, only growing 5cm high. Cylindrical soft fleshy stems are greenish with fleshy ovate bright green leaves 2 to 3cm long. Small, 1cm-wide, solitary, red or purple flowers are produced continuously throughout summer. The succulents need little summer water, as they are drought tolerant and are also tolerant of heat and poor soil. When grown on the tops of walls or on banks in full sun, it will flower profusely. Also makes excellent ground cover. Easily propagated from cuttings. The variety 'Variegata' has leaves attractively edged with white.

METROSIDEROS
Myrtaceae
Pohutukawa
Native to the Pacific region

A genus of about 60 species of evergreen shrubs, trees and woody climbers. Most tree forms are small, but some are exceptionally large, the New Zealand species in particular. They are grown for their showy flowers that are like the Melaleuca species. Often cultivated for their showy flowers, as street trees or in home gardens. Flowers are usually red, but some cultivars have orange, yellow or white flowers.

Metrosideros excelsa
Pōhutukawa, New Zealand Christmas Tree
Native to New Zealand

A handsome tree 10 to 20m high with spreading dome-like form to 10m wide. It usually grows as a multi-trunked, spreading tree. Trunks and branches are sometimes festooned with matted, fibrous aerial roots. Oval, pointed, leathery, shiny green leaves are 5 to 10cm long with dense white felt underneath. The tree flowers throughout summer with a peak in early summer, covered in brilliant crimson flowers, hence the common name. Flowers are in terminal branched clusters up to 10cm across. These consist mainly of showy, brilliant scarlet stamens up to 4cm long, which extend beyond the small petals. Easily grown in humus-rich, well-drained neutral to acid soil in full sun. Excellent for coastal planting in frost-free areas as it is tolerant of salt-laden wind. Moderate water is needed for the first two to three years to establish, then little summer water. Makes a beautiful specimen tree. Sometimes used as a street tree. 'Aurea' has rich yellow filaments.

Metrosideros kermadecensis
Native to New Zealand

A bushy spreading tree 15m or more tall in its native habitat, but usually seen as a bushy shrub 2 to 3m high in cultivation. The trunk is up to 1m or more in diameter. Leaves are broadly ovate to 5cm long, dark green above and densely white felted underneath. Spectacular flowers are in broad, branched, terminal clusters to 10cm wide with crimson filaments and yellow anthers. They are produced abundantly, mainly in spring and early summer. Cultivation is the same as for *M. excelsa*, with which it is often confused.

Metrosideros kermadecensis 'Variegata'
Garden origin

Extremely attractive and showy with dark-green leaves edged with broad, irregular creamy-white to yellow margins. Beautiful red pin-cushion flowers can cover a young plant only 50cm high. Flowers appear from spring through to winter. A slow-growing shrub, 8m high and 5m wide after five years. It needs a frost-free site. A great screen choice. Ideal for coastal landscaping.

Mina lobata see *Ipomoea lobata*

MIRABILIS
Nyctaginaceae
Four O'Clocks, Umbrellaworts
Native to the southern United States and South America

A genus of about 60 species of annuals and herbaceous perennials. Branched stems bear opposite ovate leaves. Large, trumpet-shaped, often fragrant flowers are borne in axillary panicles during summer.

Mirabilis jalapa
Marvel of Peru, Four O'Clock Plant
Native to Peru

A deep-rooted, much branched, herbaceous perennial about 1m high and wide, quickly forming large clumps. The roots form large tubers that can in ideal conditions weigh up to 20kg. Leaves are deep green, oval, 5 to 10cm long and shiny above. Clusters of fragrant trumpet-shaped flowers, 3 to 5cm wide, are red, pink, white or yellow, often striped or mottled, with several colours on the same plant. Flowers appear continuously from summer until late autumn, opening in late afternoon and dying by morning, hence the common name. The flowers are followed by small green fruit, which contain one black seed when ripe. Grows best in full sun in any well-drained soil. Drought tolerant, requiring no summer water once established. Often seen in beds or borders as it is easily raised from seed.

MISCANTHUS

Poaceae

Silvergrass

Native from Africa to east Asia

A genus of about twenty species of deciduous or evergreen tufted or rhizomatous perennial grasses. Reed-like stems 2 to 4m tall bear linear or narrow lance-shaped, arching, mid-green, blue-green or purplish-green leaves. Dense, arching, terminal plumes are typically produced in late summer. They range from pale silver to buff and deep purplish red. Shining in the summer sun, they fade to silver, then soft and fluffy. Grow in full sun or partial shade in average well-drained soil. Summer drought tolerant. Stems are ideal for flower arrangements. Some species can become widely invasive even in northern climes. It is lovely to look at, but it displaces native plants. In dry conditions, its flammability creates a fire hazard. Before planting, check to see if your variety is listed as invasive in your area.

Miscanthus sinensis

Native to Japan, Korea and China

A clump-forming, warm-season grass that typically grows to 1 to 2m tall. It has a dense clump of upward-arching stems and leaves that give it a rounded, fountain-like appearance. Linear leaves 1 to 1.2m long have tapered tips, serrated margins and whitish to silvery midribs. Foliage often turns attractive shades of yellow to orange by autumn before gradually fading as the seeds ripen to beige-tan for winter. Pink to red flowers in feathery, whisk-like, loose terminal panicles 20 to 25cm long bloom above the foliage from late summer. The arching shape and ornamental interest of the foliage remains intact throughout winter. Easily grown in average, medium moisture, well-drained soil in full sun to part shade. Tolerant of a wide range of soils, from well-drained sandy to heavy clay soils. Performs best in full sun, as in shade it is less vigorous with decreased flowering and a tendency to flop. Tolerant of summer heat and humidity. Clumps maintain their tight shape while slowly expanding in circumference through short rhizomes. Throughout winter, it is recommended to leave the foliage standing to enhance visual interest and protect the crown. Cut foliage close to the ground in early spring just before fresh shoots appear.

Miscanthus sinensis 'Dixieland'

Garden origin

This cultivar is a dwarf form of the popular *Miscanthus sinensis* 'Variegatus', but has a more erect habit and less inclination to flop in late season because of its small size. Its graceful arching leaves 1 to 1.5m long and 2cm wide are variegated with green-and-white vertical stripes. Showy, tiny, reddish-tinged flowers in tassel-like inflorescences appear in late summer, maturing to silvery white plumes. After seed sets, the continuing flower effect of the plumes lasts well into the winter. This variety should not need staking like its taller cousin. It provides a strong white element to the landscape, which is especially pronounced when planted in front of larger shrubs or evergreens. It can be used as a specimen for massing or screening, in large containers, or at the edge of a pond. Drought tolerant once it is established. Plant this grass where its wonderful winter interest can be enjoyed.

Miscanthus sinensis 'Zebrinus'

Garden origin

A dramatic, clump-forming perennial grass to 1.3m high and 1m wide with broad, bright-green foliage and striking yellow horizontal bands in variable patterns. Some leaves sport more stripes than others. Although its foliage is its major attraction, it may also bear silky, slender plumes of pink flowers on the end of tall stalks in summer, lasting well into winter. Drought and salt tolerant once established, plants need some moisture to thrive in warm and temperate climates, but avoid boggy conditions. Plant in full sun and allow a couple of years for young plants to amass the clump of foliage that they are known for. The perfect foil for more colourful plants. Grow it as a specimen plant at the back of a floral border to contrast with brightly coloured blooms. It will also provide interest and structure throughout autumn and winter, when little else is growing. For best growth, cut back in early spring before fresh growth appears.

MONTANOA

Asteraceae

Native to Central America

A genus of about 35 species of pithy-stemmed, small shrubs or small trees or vines, which are grown for their showy winter flowers. Stems are minutely pubescent on herbaceous parts. Leaves are opposite, petiolate, with three main veins, entire to deeply three- to five-lobed or coarsely divided, but not to the central axis.

Montanoa bipinnatifida

Daisy Tree

Native to Mexico

An open growing shrub to 3m high with grey woody stems. Large, 40cm or more-long opposite leaves are deeply indented or lobed, dull green and roughly hairy on both sides. Large, terminal, branched flower clusters contain many white flowers with protruding yellow stamens up to 8cm across. Flowers are daisy-like, giving it the common name. Flowers are produced from autumn but are usually at their best in midwinter. Prune hard after flowering to encourage new stems, which will grow quickly. Grows well in full sun when given regular summer water, but will survive periods of drought. Grow in regular well-drained soil. It is attractive with large, bold leaves and showy winter flowerheads. Tropical looking as a background plant.

Montbretia crocata see *Tritonia crocata*

MORAEA syn. HOMERIA
Iridaceae

Native to Africa, the Mediterranean, central and southwestern Asia

In 1998, Moraea was merged by taxonomists with several other genera.

A genus of about 220 species of cormous perennials. While some species thrive during summer, the majority are winter-growing and feature purple or yellow flowers resembling miniature beardless irises. Certain species are referred to as 'Peacock Flowers', because of their vibrant flowers and contrasting centres. They are grown for their scented, showy flowers that are produced in succession.

Moraea collina syn. *Homeria breyniana, Moraea grandiflora*

Native to the Western Cape, South Africa

A cormous perennial with branched or unbranched stems to 45cm high. In late autumn or winter, one or two narrow, sword-shaped leaves 45cm long emerge on the lower part of the flowering stem. Ranging from golden yellow to peach or pink, the cup-shaped flowers are scented and 6 to 8cm wide with tepals enclosing a narrow cup. They are borne in succession over several weeks during spring. The plant is summer dormant, so drought tolerant, only needing water if winter rains are insufficient. Good drainage is essential. It is a good filler, growing where many other plants will not grow, including in the full sun. Plant the corms during autumn.

Moraea macrocarpa
Bigseed Tulp

Native to the northwest Cape, South Africa

A cormous, deciduous perennial growing to about 12cm high with linear, sword-shaped or rolled leaves. Flowers are violet or blue with conspicuous yellow and white nectar guides on the outer three tepals. Dark-blue or violet lines radiate out beyond these nectar guides. The inner tepals are smaller and unmarked, also with rounded tips. The style is branched and erect, coloured like the tepals, covering the stamens. Flowers in spring with individual flowers short-lived. This species is found in the Northern Cape, where it grows in sandy soil among arid fynbos. Drought tolerant.

Moraea setifolia syn. *Giandrisis setifolia*

Native to South Africa

This cormous, deciduous perennial has narrow-linear, single, 20 to 60cm long leaves. It produces stems to 30cm of small blue or lavender flowers with many per stem. Flowers open in early afternoon and close by late afternoon. It makes up for the short bloom by producing many flowers over a long period. It makes a striking display in the garden or in pots. A sunny, well-drained situation suits best or a well-drained gritty mix if grown in pots. It is found on sandy and gravelly flats and slopes in a wide distribution area, including winter rainfall and year-round rainfall areas. This species is winter growing in its native habitat.

Moraea tricolor

Native to southwestern Cape, South Africa

A cormous, deciduous perennial growing 5 to 15cm tall with linear, sword-shaped or rolled leaves. It is best known for having bright pink flowers, but in the wild they can have a wide range of colours, including red, purple, orange, yellow, white, green and terracotta. They have yellow nectar guides on the outer tepals and are fragrant. It has specialised style branches in the centre of the flowers, which are flattened. Each of the segments of the corolla of the flower is modified leaves and is typically coloured. They are fragrant, with a perfume reminiscent of 'Old Spice' aftershave – you have to be quick, each flower only lasting a few hours, but appearing over a period of several weeks. Flowering in late winter to early spring in the wild, where it is summer dormant. Best grown in a well-drained, fairly heavy soil.

MUSCARI
Asparagaceae

Grape Hyacinth

Native to the Mediterranean region, southwest Asia

A genus of about 79 species of small, bulbous perennials, often with a coating of powdery white crystals. There are usually two or three mid-green basal leaves with prominent strands of fibre. The inflorescences comprise short spikes (racemes) of small tubular flowers, each with six short lobes, ranging from pale blue to deep violet. Heights vary from about 5cm to 25cm, depending on the species. They grow in rocky habitats, such as hillsides, which are hot and dry in summer. Some species are among the earliest garden flowers to bloom in spring. They multiply quickly when planted in good soils. Prefers well-drained sandy soil, acid to neutral and not too rich. Naturally found in woodlands or meadows, they are commonly cultivated in lawns, borders, rock gardens and containers. Requiring little feeding or watering in summer. Grow in sun or light shade.

Muscari armeniacum
Garden Grape Hyacinth, Armenian Grape Hyacinth

Native to eastern Mediterranean

A bulbous perennial that produces narrow, channelled basal leaves to 30cm long, which are semi-erect appearing in autumn. In spring tubular, nodding, bright-blue flowers with constricted white mouths are borne in tight, unbranched tapering spikes. Spikes are up to 8cm long on stems and 20cm high. They are best grown in a sunny, well-drained position. No summer watering is necessary because they are dormant. For the best look, plant the bulbs in clusters under trees, shrubs, or along pathways. Ideal for the rock garden. The bulbs are long lived, usually becoming overcrowded, so lift and divide congested clumps when dormant in summer. 'Blue Spike' is a double form with large heads of dark blue flowers.

Miscanthus sinensis 'Dixieland'.

Miscanthus sinensis 'Zebrinus'.

Montanoa bipinnatifida.

Moraea setifolia.

Moraea tricolor.

Muscari armeniacum.

Muscari macrocarpum.

Mutisia decurrens.

Muscari macrocarpum
Yellow Grape Hyacinth
Native to Crete, southwest Turkey
A robust plant with large bulbs that have thick fleshy roots. Each bulb produces several greyish-green leaves. In spring, flowers are borne in a spike or raceme on a stem 10 to 15cm high. Dense heads of wax-textured, yellow flowers open from purplish buds, becoming yellow when fully open, wonderfully scented. Individual flowers may be over 1cm long. Prefers a warm spot and a well-drained soil. Summer drought tolerant. Cultivars include 'Golden Fragrance'.

MUTISIA
Asteraceae
Native to South America
A genus of about 60 species of upright or climbing shrubs. Leaves are alternate or simple, varying from broadly elliptical to linear and from deeply toothed to entire. The midrib is frequently prolonged into a tendril, sometimes branched. Flowers are terminal, their beauty depending mainly on the ray-florets, which are often attractively and brilliantly coloured. These are produced throughout summer and autumn.

Mutisia decurrens
Native to Chile and Argentina
A much-branched, glabrous, suckering climber to 3m high and wide. Oblong to lance-shaped dark green leaves to 12cm long are entire or toothed, ending in a two-lobed tendril. Graceful, pure, glowing orange daisy-like flowers 10 to 12cm across are borne singly from leaf axils throughout summer. Grows best in partial shade, although it will take full sun. Grow in moderately fertile well-drained soil. It needs to be kept moist during the growing season, not in winter. Attractive when planted in a small courtyard garden or grown into trees. Also useful for covering fences or a trellis. Trim back untidy growth during spring. Easily propagated from suckers.

Mutisia ilicifolia
Native to Chile and Argentina
A slender-stemmed evergreen climbing plant to 3m high. Young shoots have toothed ridges (wings) and are clothed with a whitish or pale-brown wool, as are the leaves and flower-stalks. Leaves are holly-like, leathery, simple, stalkless, ovate-oblong, deeply heart-shaped at the base, 1 to 3cm long, the margins strongly spiny-toothed. The prolonged midrib forms a slender curling tendril, 2 to 10cm long, its upper-surface dark green. Solitary, terminal, pink flowers with a yellow centre 7cm across are borne on long stalks singly from leaf axils throughout summer and autumn. Best in full sun, although it will take partial shade. Grow in moderately fertile well-drained soil. Ensure the roots are kept dry in winter. A delicate plant that needs the support of a wall or trellis.

MYOPORUM
Scrophulariaceae
Native mostly to Australia, a few to New Zealand, Hawaii, China and Japan
A genus of about 30 species of evergreen shrubs and trees, mostly glabrous with simple alternate leaves and often lacking a petiole. Flowers are adapted for pollination by insects and have white, or sometimes pinkish, petals and usually four stamens. They are tough, fast-growing plants that are often used for hedging.

Myoporum laetum
Mousehole Tree
Native to New Zealand
A vigorous evergreen shrub or tree of exceptionally fast growth to 10m high spreading to 6m wide, with a trunk up to 30cm in diameter, which forms a dense, billowing mass of dark green. Older growth is stiff and woody while young growth is flexible. Fleshy, glossy, bright-green leaves are lance-shaped up to 10cm long with translucent oil glands. In summer, clusters of two to six bell-shaped, 1cm-wide flowers appear. These are white with purple markings and may be followed by deep reddish-purple berries. It grows well in full sun when given moderate summer water, but can take some drought. Good for coastal gardens, as it withstands salt-laden sea breezes. Makes a good background shrub that will block sound, wind and sun. If left unpruned, it will form an attractive multi-stemmed tree, or it can be clipped into an informal hedge. A greedy plant with invasive roots, so do not grow choice plants nearby.

MYRTUS
Myrtaceae
Myrtle
Native to the Mediterranean region, north Africa
A small genus that has been much changed by taxonomists. It is now recognised as having just two species. *Myrtus communis* grows wild all around the Mediterranean basin and *Myrtus nivellei*, known as Saharan myrtle, is found in north Africa.

Myrtus communis
Common Myrtle
Native to the Mediterranean region
An evergreen, bushy shrub that normally grows 3 to 5m high and 6m across. Pairs of glossy, bright-green, oval, pointed leaves are 2 to 3cm long and strongly scented when crushed, because they contain a fragrant essential oil. White or pink-tinged, sweetly-scented, 2 to 3cm wide flowers have many creamy-white protruding stamens. Flowers appear on the axils of upper leaves in spring and summer. They are followed by bluish-black berries. The shrub is not fussy about soil conditions but needs good drainage. Grows well in full sun but will also take partial shade. Drought tolerant, so needs no summer water once established. May be grown as a free-standing specimen or in a hedge. There are several compact and variegated forms.

N

NANDINA

Berberidaceae

Native to eastern Asia from the Himalayas to Japan

A monotypic genus of just one species, a frost-hardy, evergreen shrub. Widely grown in gardens for its attractive flowers, fruit and elegant foliage. There are several cultivars that display bright-red autumn foliage in the cool months, and attractive new foliage growth in spring. Although a popular ornamental shrub, the berries are toxic to birds, especially towards the end of the winter when other food sources become scarce.

Nandina domestica

Heavenly Bamboo, Sacred Bamboo

An evergreen shrub that forms a clump of slender, upright, cane-like shoots to 1.6m high, spreading to 1.2m wide. Leaves to 30cm long are divided into two or three lance-shaped, pointed leaflets 3 to 6cm long. New leaves open pinkish to reddish-purple, turn a soft green as they mature, then become bronze in autumn, often bright red in winter. In late spring or summer, large, branched sprays to 30cm long of star-shaped, creamy white flowers, each 1cm wide with large yellow anthers appear at the tips of the stems. These are followed by masses of large, long-lasting, glossy, bright-red berries displayed during autumn, winter and early spring. The shrub is best grown in groups, as single plants seldom fruit heavily. It grows happily in the most difficult of shaded spots, even dry shade, but for the best colour grow in full sun. Thrives in a rich well-drained soil, needs water to establish, then little water as it can withstand some drought. Good as a hedge or screen and as a pot or container plant. Despite its common name, it is not a bamboo at all. There are many named dwarf cultivars.

NARCISSUS

Amaryllidaceae

Daffodil

Native to the Mediterranean region, from Greece to Portugal, north Africa

A genus of over 50 species of bulbous perennials. Many thousands of cultivars have been developed. Most daffodils need a cold spell to initiate flower production, so are unsuitable for growing in warm areas.

Narcissus papyraceus

Paper White Narcissus

Native to southern Spain, southern Portugal and north Africa

A bulbous perennial with broad upright leaves to 1cm wide and 30cm long. Each bulb can produce three or four upright flower stems, to 30cm high, carrying clusters of five to ten strongly-fragrant pure white flowers, which are the strongest-scented narcissus. They are small, cupped 1 to 2cm across, appearing in midwinter and early spring. When planted in drifts underneath deciduous trees or shrubs, they make a wonderful sight with their snowy-white flowers. They will seed and naturalise well. Because they are dormant in summer, they can withstand drought and do not require any water. As with other bulbs, allow the leaves to grow until they turn yellow and die naturally before removing.

NASSELLA

Poaceae

Native to North and South America

As of 2001, there were about 116 species in this genus of frost-hardy, evergreen or deciduous feather or needle grasses. Many species formerly assigned to Stipa have been reclassified into new genera. They are grown for their form or for the large open inflorescences.

Nassella tenuissima syn. *Stipa tenuissima*

Mexican Feather Grass

Native to southern United States, Mexico, Argentina

A densely-tufted, evergreen perennial to 60cm high and 30cm wide. Bright-green, narrowly linear leaves to 30cm or more long, form erect clumps that arch outwards at the top. Throughout summer it bears many thin flowering stems up to 30cm long. They divide and redivide into almost hair-like fineness, green at first, ripening to golden. The whole plant billows in the slightest breeze. Grow in full sun in any well-drained soil. When established it withstands drought, but grows better with some summer water. When planted among ground cover or boulders, single or scattered clumps can look most effective. Can self-sow in irrigated gardens.

NEMESIA

Scrophulariaceae

Native to sandy coasts or disturbed ground in South Africa

A genus of 50 or more species of annuals, perennials and subshrubs. Leaves are opposite, simple, usually linear to lance-shaped, frequently toothed. Flowers are two-lipped, with the upper lip comprising four lobes and the lower lip two lobes, borne singly in leaf axils in summer. Many hybrids have been selected, and the annual cultivars are popular with gardeners as bedding plants. In temperate regions they are usually treated as half-hardy, grown from seed in heat, and planted out after all the danger of frost has passed.

Nemesia strumosa

Cape Jewels, Pouch Nemesia

Native to the southwestern Cape Provinces of South Africa

This basely-branching annual 18 to 30cm high has lance-shaped, entire to

voporum laetum.

Myrtus communis.

Nandina domestica.

rcissus papyraceus.

Nassella tenuissima.

Nemesia strumosa.

epeta grandiflora
ummer Magic'.

Nerine bowdenii.

Nerium oleander.

coarsely-toothed, slightly hairy leaves to 7cm long. Flowers appear in a compact cluster in spring and summer. They are two-lipped and pouched at the base. The colour combination is striking and broad, with cream, yellow, blue, orange, crimson, pink and bicolours – almost every colour of the rainbow – with orange being the most prominent. Flowers are long lasting, so they make excellent cut flowers. Flowering can be prolonged with regular dead-heading. Plants like full sun and regular moisture for the best flowering but can take some drought. Grow in well-drained, fertile and slightly acidic soil. They are frost tender and dislike sudden environmental changes, preferring cool to moderate climates, so in hotter areas they will need light shading.

NEOMARICA see TRIMEZIA

NEPETA
Lamiaceae
Catnips

Native to Europe, Asia and Africa

A genus of about 250 species of perennials native to various habitats. They have sturdy stems with opposite, lance-shaped, green to grey-green, sometimes hairy leaves, with usually aromatic foliage and flowers. The spike-like cymes or panicles of tubular flowers, lavender, blue, white, pink or lilac, are borne in interrupted axillary whorls towards the tip of the stems, often over long periods. Some species attract cats, most are attractive to bees.

Nepeta grandiflora
Catnip, Catmint

Native to the Caucasus

A clump-forming perennial with erect, sparsely-branched stems, growing to 75cm tall by 30cm wide. Leaves are grey green, 10cm long, ovate, scalloped, softly hairy and aromatic. Spike-like whorls of purple or blue flowers to 2cm long are produced during summer. Grow in any well-drained soil in full sun. Summer drought tolerant once established. Appreciates afternoon shade in hot areas. An excellent plant to provide contrast in borders or for edging or rock gardens, gravel gardens, coastal gardens and Mediterranean gardens. The cultivar 'Summer magic' is an outstanding selection that blooms all summer. The upright, deep-lavender blooms are held high above the grass-green foliage and never flop. This plant looks great in a container.

NERINE
Amaryllidaceae

Native to southern Africa

A genus of 20 to 30 species of bulbous perennials, some evergreen, associated with rocky and arid habitats. They bear spherical umbels of lily-like flowers in shades from white through pink to crimson. Large, colourful flowers appear before the leaves in autumn in most species. Many cultivars have been developed.

Nerine bowdenii

Native to South Africa

An elegant, variable, clump-forming, hardy perennial bulb. It produces glossy green, strap-shaped leaves 3cm wide and 30 to 45cm long, which emerge in late winter after the flowers have faded and die down in summer. In autumn, umbels of eight to twelve funnel-shaped, faintly-scented flowers appear on stems 45cm high. Each flower up to 8cm across is deep rose pink with a darker line on each segment and a wavy edge recurving at the tips. The blooms last for several weeks. Grow the bulbs in a border in full sun or partial shade in well-drained soil. Give water during the growing and flowering period. Summer drought tolerant, so ensure bulbs dry out as the bulbs can rot in waterlogged soil. They are attractive when grown as pot or container plants. For best flowering, leave undisturbed until a thick clump forms after several years. Plant bulbs with the tip just below the surface.

Nerine sarniensis
Guernsey Lily

Native to the mountainous regions of the Cape in South Africa

The bulb produces upright, slightly glossy, strap-shaped basal leaves 30cm long and 2cm wide. Leaves appear after the flowers have faded. In autumn, the flower stalk up to 45cm high appears with large clusters of ten to twenty trumpet-shaped, 4cm-long, crimson flowers with wavy-edged petals and conspicuous stamens. Many varieties have been bred with pink, orange, scarlet and white flowers. Culture is the same as *N. bowdenii*, but it is more hardy. Good for coastal conditions.

NERIUM
Apocynaceae

Native from the Mediterranean region to China

A genus of a single species of upright, evergreen shrubs or small trees, cultivated worldwide in temperate and subtropical areas as an ornamental and landscaping plant. They are grown for their wonderful show of flowers, which are produced for most of summer. Many cultivars have been developed. **Caution:** all parts of the plant are poisonous!

Nerium oleander
Oleander, Rosebay

An evergreen shrub or small tree growing 2 to 6m high and nearly as wide. Leathery, dark-green, lance-shaped leaves are usually in opposite pairs or whorls of three on short leaf stalks and 10 to 30cm long. From summer to autumn, it bears large terminal clusters of funnel-shaped flowers 5 to 8cm across, with some varieties having a distinct fragrance. The colours range from white, yellow, pink, salmon and crimson to purple with some double as well as single forms. It needs to be grown in full sun or it will not flower freely. Grows in any well-drained soil. When established, it is drought and heat tolerant, even when flowering. It is grown extensively in the Mediterranean region and in other hot and dry regions, as it is adaptable to a wide range of situations. Often used as roadside screens, as hedges, specimens or as pot plants. Ideal for coastal gardens, as it withstands salt-laden sea breezes. 'Variegata' has beautifully variegated leaves with bold cream edges and pink flowers, which are slower growing, and will take some shade.

NICOTIANA
Solanaceae
Tobacco Plant

Native to Australia, North America and tropical South America

About 70 species of annuals, perennials or shrubs with alternate linear or oblong-lance-shaped hairy leaves. Flowers are tubular to trumpet shaped, sometimes scented and borne in racemes or panicles during summer and autumn. Flowers often open in the evening and at night, while some cultivars stay open during the day. All parts of the plant are poisonous if eaten.

Nicotiana alata
Flowering Tobacco, Jasmine Tobacco, Sweet Tobacco, Winged Tobacco

Native to southern Brazil, northern Argentina

A tender perennial often treated as an annual, which grows to 1.5m high and 30cm wide. Coarse, ovate, rosette-forming leaves are 10 to 25cm long. Branched stems are topped with a raceme of tubular 5 to 10cm long, greenish-yellow flowers that flare at the mouth into five pointed lobes. They normally open towards evening and are strongly fragrant in the evening to night. It has been much hybridised and there is now a wide range of colours from white to pink and red including lime-green, which stay open during the day. They are easily raised from seed and will self-seed. A good plant for beds and borders near the house where the scent can be enjoyed. Grow in fertile, well-drained soil in full sun or partial shade. To grow well, they need regular summer water, but can take some drought. Deadhead spent flower stalks for the best blooming results.

Nicotiana glauca
Tree Tobacco

Native to South America

A small tree or shrub with many branches that normally grows to over 2m but can reach as high as 7m, with arching, sticky stems. Bluish-green ovate to lance-shaped leaves are up to 15cm long. Stems are topped with large loose panicles of strongly evening-scented, funnel-shaped, greenish-yellow flowers about 10cm long, which cover the entire shrub for most of summer. The flowers are followed by small pods containing many seeds, which will readily germinate. A good plant for a dry garden, as it is drought tolerant and requires only occasional watering. Grow in fertile, well-drained soil in full sun. The leaves are toxic to animals.

NIGELLA
Ranunculaceae

Native to the Mediterranean region, north Africa

A genus of about twenty species of erect, bushy annuals growing to 50cm high and spreading to 30cm wide, often found on rocky slopes. Leaves are alternate, often feathery. Solitary, sometimes paired, terminal flowers are borne mainly in summer. They come in shades of pink, blue, yellow or white, sometimes nestled in a showy ruff-like surround of strongly veined leaves with hair-like divisions at the tip.

Nigella damascena
Love-in-a-Mist

Native to southern Europe, north Africa and southwest Asia

A single-stemmed or branching annual that grows to 20 to 50cm tall, with pinnately divided, thread-like, alternate leaves. Terminal saucer-shaped flowers, to 4.5cm across, appear in early summer and are most commonly different shades of blue, but can be white, pink or pale purple, with 5 to 25 sepals. They are surrounded by a ruff of filigree, finely divided at the tips. These are followed by horned seed pods. Self-seeding may occur. Easily grown in fertile, well-drained soil in full sun or partial shade. They provide long-lasting cut flowers. It is the source of many cultivars.

O

OENOTHERA

Onagraceae

Evening Primrose, Suncups, Sundrops

Native to Mexico, southern North America

A genus of about 145 species of annuals, biennials and perennials varying from small alpines 10cm tall, to vigorous lowland species growing to 3m tall. They grow in well-drained, sunny sites such as mountain slopes. Lance-shaped leaves form a basal rosette at ground level and spiral up to the flowering stems. The blades are dentate or deeply lobed (pinnatifid). Flowers of many species open in the evening, hence the name 'evening primrose', often opening in under a minute. Most species have yellow flowers, but some have white, purple, pink or red. Most native desert species are white. One of the most distinctive features of the flower is the stigma, which has four branches in an X shape.

Oenothera macrocarpa

Evening Primrose, Missouri Evening Primrose

Native to southern central United States

This herbaceous, prostrate perennial can sprawl along the ground up to 60cm and produce a red stem up to 45cm high with a woody base. Leaves are soft, hairy, lance-shaped, up to 15cm long, densely crowded alternately along the stem. Large, lemon yellow, funnel-shaped flowers open from slightly red spotted buds, flaring to nearly 10cm wide. These are produced in great numbers almost continuously from late spring throughout summer. The flowers last for one day, opening in the evening and closing the following morning. A useful perennial for a dry garden, which makes a glorious show needing little summer water as it is drought tolerant. Grow in a well-drained soil in sun or light shade. Easily propagated by seed.

Oenothera deltoides

Birdcage Evening Primrose, Basket Evening Primrose

Native to the southwestern United States and northern Mexico

An erect, spreading annual or perennial with a short central stem and spreading branches from the base. Lance-shaped, entire or pinnatifid, mid-green leaves are 5 to 10cm long. Large, solitary, bowl-shaped flowers 4 to 8cm across, initially white then pink, opening around sunset and wilting by mid-morning, appear from spring to summer. Thrives in dry sandy, really well-drained soil. Tolerant of summer drought.

Oenothera speciosa

Pink Ladies, Pink Evening Primrose, Mexican Primrose

Native to southwest United States, Mexico

An upright to sprawling, herbaceous perennial, which spreads to form extensive colonies. It has glabrous (smooth) to pubescent stems that grow to 50cm high. The pubescent leaves are variable, from linear to obovate, alternate to 10cm long and toothed or wavy edged. Nodding buds open into large, four-petalled, pink or white delicate-textured, cup-shaped 4 to 5cm wide flowers in upper leaf axils on slender, downy stems. Flowers are lined with pink or red veins. They bloom throughout summer into early autumn, both day and night, but typically in pre-dawn hours, closing when the full sun hits them. A hardy and drought-resistant species. Grow as ground cover in well-drained soil in full sun. Frequently grown in gardens, but can escape from cultivation.

OLEA

Oleaceae

Olive

Native to the warm dry areas of the Mediterranean region, Africa, Asia and Australasia

A genus of about twelve species of evergreen trees and shrubs with small opposite, leathery, entire leaves. Along with figs and almonds, the olive tree typifies a Mediterranean region.

Olea europaea

Olive Tree

Native to the eastern Mediterranean region

A slow-growing, evergreen tree to 6m or more high with an equal spread. Young trees grow fairly fast, then slow with maturity. The trunk is typically gnarled and twisted. Lance-shaped leaves 4 to 10cm long are a silvery grey-green above with a silvery underside. Insignificant yellowish flowers are produced in axillary racemes on the previous year's wood in early summer. The fruit is a small drupe 1 to 2.5cm long when ripe, thinner-fleshed and smaller in wild plants than in orchard cultivars. Olives are harvested in the green to purple stage. Olive oil of commerce is extracted from these fruits. They can also be eaten if treated by soaking in brine. Drought tolerant once established. Grown in full sun in a well-drained soil. They can withstand hard pruning, indeed old trees can be reduced to stumps and will shoot out well, completely rejuvenating themselves. Old trees with gnarled trunks can, with care, be lifted and transplanted into large crates, adding maturity to a young garden. Cultivated since time immemorial.

OLEARIA

Asteraceae

Daisy Bush, Tree Daisies

Native chiefly to New Zealand, Australia

A genus of almost 200 species of evergreen shrubs, of which 130 are distributed throughout Australia. They are characterised by a composite flower head with single-row ray florets enclosed by small overlapping bracts arranged in rows appearing during summer. Most species come from areas where the humidity is relatively high. Suitable for coastal gardens and grow well in chalky soils.

cotiana glauca.

Nigella.

Oenothera macrocarpa.

enothera speciosa.

Olea europaea.

Olearia 'Henry Travers'.

puntia basilaris.

Opuntia gosseliniana.

Olearia haastii

A natural hybrid from New Zealand

A rounded, dense, much-branched shrub to 2m high and wide. Alternate, oval leaves to 3cm long are white felted underneath. They open glossy dark green, aging to a dull grey green. Fragrant daisy-like white flowers appear in dense clusters to 8cm across. In early summer, they smother the shrub. Grow in full sun in any well-drained soil. When established, it withstands drought, but grows better with some summer water. An excellent, well-proven hedging plant. Tolerates pollution, so useful for town gardens. Ideal as a windbreak in coastal gardens. Moderately frost hardy.

Olearia 'Henry Travers'

A natural hybrid from New Zealand

A rounded, much-branched shrub to 3m high and 2m wide with slender shoots covered in white felt. Slightly toothed, lance-shaped, grey-green leaves to 10cm long are silvery underneath. In early summer, it bears solitary daisy-like flowerheads 5cm across, which are lilac with purple centres. Not hardy, but otherwise cultivation is the same as *O. haastii*.

Olearia traversii

Native to New Zealand

A fast-growing, evergreen shrub or small tree 6 to 10m high spreading to 5m wide with stout, four-angled shoots covered in white felt. Opposite leaves to 6cm long are broadly oval to oblong, leathery, glossy dark green above with white felt underneath. Daisy-like white flowerheads produced in summer are insignificant. An ideal evergreen windbreak for coastal gardens. Grows well even in poor sandy soils. Cultivation is the same as *O. haastii*.

OPUNTIA

Cactaceae

Prickly Pear Cactus

Native to the Americas

A vast genus containing perhaps 300 or more species of prostrate forms to 60cm high to tree-like cacti 5m high. They have become naturalised all over the world in arid or semi-arid regions. Some species are cold tolerant, all drought tolerant. They usually fall into two groups: those with flat pads and those with round joints. Some species have edible fruit.

Opuntia basilaris

Beavertail Prickly Pear

Native to southwestern United States

This species reaches about 30cm tall and grows in clumps, sporting hundreds of striking 10cm blue, red-purple or bronze pads. Pads may have spines, though often not, but they have glochids (a barbed bristle on the areole). Its brilliant flowers steal the show, featuring 8cm ruffled violet or magenta petals with bright yellow and red filaments at the centre. Red fruits are pretty, but inedible, while birds love them. In cold or arid environments, the pads can turn purple. Its common name comes from the grey-blue pads, which resemble the tails of beavers.

Opuntia engelmannii var. *lindheimeri* syn. *Opuntia cantabrigiensis*

Prickly Pear

Native to southwestern United States and Mexico

This species was identified as *Opuntia cantabrigiensis* by the Cambridge University Botanic Garden's Curator, Richard Lynch, in 1903. In recent years, it has been re-identified as *O. engelmannii* var. *lindheimeri*.

A sprawling cactus with bluish-green flattened pads about 20cm long and 15cm wide with whitish spines. Pale-yellow flowers 7cm wide appear during summer. Grow in well-drained sandy soil in full sun. Summer drought tolerant and frost tolerant. Keep dry during wet seasons.

Opuntia ficus-indica

Prickly Pear, Indian Fig

Origin unknown, probably native to Mexico

A large, flat-jointed cactus that makes a bush to 4m high and wide. Large, smooth-green or glaucous, bluish pads are from 30 to 60cm long. Some forms are spineless or nearly so, but with clusters of irritating yellow bristles. Luminous yellow, cup-shaped flowers 10cm across appear in spring or early summer. These are followed by pear-shaped, juicy, red or yellow fruit, which are 6 to 8cm long. These are edible but not delicious and, like the plant, are covered in irritating hairs. Any segment of the plant that falls to the ground will root quickly, so that it has become invasive in many warm countries. It can make an impenetrable barrier requiring no attention and no summer water. Ideal for coastal gardens, as it withstands salt-laden sea breezes. Widely cultivated, possibly the world's most widely grown cactus.

Opuntia gosseliniana

Violet Pricklypear

Native to Arizona and Mexico

A shrubby or tree-like cactus with a short trunk and branches that comprise flattened, almost circular pads, 20cm long and 18cm wide. It can grow up to 1m tall with needle-like spines on older trunks and branches. Pads are grey-green to bluish-green and turn lavender to red purple under stress. Spines are up to 10cm long and can be short and stiff or long and flexible. They vary from cream or bright yellow through shades of orange, red and brown to nearly black. The areoles bear a tuft of yellow to tan glochids that age to brown. In late spring and early summer, it produces yellow flowers 7cm in diameter. Fruits are purplish, elliptical to cylindrical, and contain tan seeds. Easily grown in well-drained sandy soil in full sun. Summer drought tolerant.

ORNITHOGALUM

Asparagaceae

Star of Bethlehem

Native to Europe, the Mediterranean region, Asia and South Africa

A genus of about 150 species of bulbous perennials grown for their showy spring flowers. They are usually trouble free, grow in any soil and naturalise easily. Ideal for woodland gardens and borders. All parts of the plant are poisonous.

Ornithogalum arabicum

Native to the Mediterranean region

A bulbous perennial with bluish-green, rather floppy, lance-shaped basal leaves up to 60cm long, sometimes with a white longitudinal band on the upper side. In late spring, stems up to 60cm high are topped with luminous racemes of up to fifteen cup-shaped, sweetly fragrant, waxy white flowers 3 to 6cm across with a contrasting bead-like black eye. Grow the bulbs in full sun in any well-drained soil. As leaves are produced in the wet winter months, they are drought tolerant, needing no summer water. Best where summers are warm and dry. Ideal for planting in drifts under trees where the bulblets will naturalise well. They make excellent long-lasting cut flowers.

Ornithogalum dubium

Sun Star, Star of Bethlehem, Yellow Chincherinchee

Native to South Africa

A bulbous perennial growing 20 to 30cm high. The nearly prostrate foliage comprises narrow lance-shaped, dark green to lime green leaves 10 to 25cm long. Flowers are borne in winter or spring, boasting brilliant clusters of 5 to 25 yellow to orange flowers, 2cm across, adorned with a contrasting black eye. Drought tolerant during the dormant season, but requires ample water when in growth. Soil needs excellent drainage. It should be grown in a sheltered spot in full sun. Frost-tender. Mostly grown for cut-flower and flowering pot plant production. Makes an excellent rock plant where it will happily naturalise.

Ornithogalum narbonense

Narbonne Star-of-Bethlehem, Pyramidal Star-of-Bethlehem, Southern Star-of-Bethlehem

Native to the Mediterranean region

A bulbous perennial with three to six semi-erect, grey-green, lance-shaped leaves, up to 60cm long, all spreading in a rosette on the ground, remaining green during flowering. In late spring, stems 10 to 30cm high are produced with a long, pyramidal, many-flowered spike of small white flowers. Each star-shaped flower 2cm across has petals with a narrow green band. Grow the bulbs in full sun in any free-draining soil. Drought tolerant, needing no summer water.

Ornithogalum umbellatum

Garden Star of Bethlehem

Native to the Mediterranean region and north Africa

A bulbous perennial with grass-like leaves up to 30cm long adorned with a broad white mid-vein that fades as the flowers emerge. Clusters of 2 to 3cm-wide star-shaped white flowers striped green on the outside are produced on the top of a stem 30cm high in spring. The flowers only open if enough sunlight is present. Thrives in moderately fertile, well-drained soil in full sun or partial shade. Drought tolerant once established. If conditions are right, it will naturalise and may become weedy, spreading by offsets. Best planted where they will not disturb other plants. They make excellent cut flowers, but they close at night.

ORTHROSANTHUS

Iridaceae

Native to southwestern Australia

A genus of about ten species of rhizomatous perennial herbs. The linear to sword-shaped leaves are in a layered fan. Flowers are usually blue, except in one white-flowered species. This genus is closely related to the genus Libertia. The flowers are similar, but Libertia flowers are usually white.

Orthrosanthus multiflorus

Morning Iris

A clumping perennial forming neat tufts to around 30 to 60cm high. Grass-like, glabrous leaves grow from 10 to 45cm long and 2 to 6mm wide. From mid-spring through summer, few-branched inflorescences to 70cm tall appear just above the foliage and open to reveal lovely sky-blue to mauve and, rarely, white flowers. Each cluster has three to eight flowers. Flowers only last a day each but are produced in profusion, such that the plant is rarely out of flower in spring and early summer. Prefers semi-shade but will tolerate full sun. Grows in a wide variety of soils, often moist for a period, preferring free-draining soil. Drought tolerant and frost tender. A lovely, iris-like plant ideal for rockeries, garden edging and informal borders. Attracts bees and butterflies. Remove spent flowers as required and apply a slow-release fertiliser annually.

OSTEOSPERMUM

Asteraceae

African Daisy

Native to southern Africa

A genus of about 74 species of perennials and evergreen subshrubs. Daisy-like, composite flowers comprise disc florets and ray florets, growing singly at the end of branches or sometimes in terminal clusters in many colours. Many species flower a second time in late summer, stimulated by cooler night temperatures. Hardy types show profuse flowering in the spring, but they do not get a second flush of flowers. They have been much hybridised, and many named cultivars have been raised.

Osteospermum ecklonis

Native to South Africa

A variable evergreen, upright or prostrate subshrub 30 to 90cm high and wide. Leaves are up to 10cm long, lance-shaped, slightly fuzzy or smooth, depending on the cultivar. Daisy-like flowers 6 to 8cm across have a central dark disc surrounded by petals, ranging from white to pink, purple, blue and yellow, which close at night. Solitary flowers are borne on long stalks. In warm climates, plants are covered in flowers from early spring to early summer. In cooler climates, plants flower until frost. Grow in any well-drained soil in full sun. Drought tolerant once established but for better flowering, give moderate summer water. A tough plant, as it will withstand neglect. Ideal for planting in large groups on slopes or along the edges of paths.

Osteospermum fruticosum
Trailing African Daisy

Native to South Africa

A low, woody perennial spreading rapidly by trailing rooting branches, spreading 30cm wide and growing to 30cm high. Semi-succulent, 10cm-long ovate to spoon-shaped, sparsely-toothed, mid-green leaves are hairy and almost sticky to touch. Daisy-like flowers are up to 6cm across, white above and violet, lilac or rosy-lilac underneath, with a dark purple centre and large ray florets. Flowers are produced from early autumn until late spring. Grow in full sun in a well-drained soil. Summer drought tolerant, it will grow and flower better if given moderate water. Grows well in coastal gardens, as it withstands salt-laden sea breezes. The plant makes an excellent ground cover or looks attractive when tumbling over rocks. Can become weedy and tired after a few years, when it should be replaced. Many cultivars are available with an assortment of flower colours and sizes. Used as an annual or perennial.

Osteospermum hybrids

Garden origin

Osteospermums seed and hybridise easily, with many named hybrids raised. The range includes 'Buttermilk' with pale-yellow flowers with a dark centre, 'Cannington John' with pink spoon-shaped petals and a white centre, 'Port Wine' with dark-purple flowers, and 'Weetwood' with white petals with deep mauve underneath and a yellow centre. Cultivation is the same as *O. ecklonis*.

Osteospermum jucundum see *Dimorphotheca jucunda*

P

PAEONIA
Paeoniaceae

Peony

Native mostly in the Mediterranean, others in eastern Asia

The only genus in the family with about 33 species of herbaceous perennials or shrubs. The herbaceous perennials are clump-forming, 30 to 90cm tall, rhizomatous with thickened tuberous roots. All have large compound, deeply-lobed leaves and large, often fragrant flowers, ranging from purple and pink to red, white or yellow, appearing in late spring and early summer, usually upright and solitary, sometimes several to a stem. Flowers close at night or when the sky is overcast. Each flower usually lasts only seven to ten days. Plants may take one to two years to become established and may not reach their full size for about five years. As they resent disturbance, they are best left undisturbed for many years. These grow well in any fertile soil with plenty of organic matter. Grow in full sun, but the flowers will last longer with some shade. Give regular water in summer. Specialist nurseries list a vast number of named hybrids with beautiful, large, brightly coloured, showy, single, semi-double or fully double flowers. Most of these are scented and flower more profusely than the species.

Paeonia broteri

Native to Portugal, southern and western Spain

An herbaceous perennial to 50cm high and wide with glossy pinnate leaves divided into nine leaflets. It bears single cup-shaped, highly fragrant, rose-pink flowers 10 to 13cm across with a boss of yellow stamens.

Paeonia cambessedesii
Majorcan Peony, Balearic Peony

Native to the Balearic Islands

An herbaceous perennial up to 45cm high and wide. Stems, major veins and undersides of the leaves remain purple-red, while the upper surface of the leaves turns into a metallic bluish-green when fully grown. Lower leaves comprise nine leaflets. Beautiful, single, deep rose-pink flowers, 10cm across, have wavy margined petals and yellow stamens and smell like roses.

Paeonia mascula
Wild Peony

Native to the Mediterranean Region

An herbaceous perennial up to 1m high and wide with pinnate leaves divided into nine leaflets. The red, pink or occasionally white flowers 12cm across with a central mass of yellow stamens appear in late spring and early summer.

Paeonia officinalis
Common Peony

Native to southern Europe

An herbaceous perennial 60 to 70cm high and wide with upright stems that are slightly hairy at first. Deep-green, pinnate leaves are divided into nine leaflets. Single, fragrant, bowl-shaped deep-pink or deep-red flowers, 10 to 13cm across with yellow stamens, appear in late spring. This is the parent of the traditional cottage-garden peonies.

Paeonia officinalis ssp. *humilis*

Native to southwest Europe

An herbaceous perennial up to 80cm high and wide with hairy stems and leaf stalks. It forms a compact mound of pinnate leaves divided into nine leaflets deeply cut into oblong lobes. Single purple-red flowers are 10 to 13cm across, with a tuft of yellow stamens appearing in mid-spring.

PALLENIS
Asteraceae

Native to the Mediterranean region, Canary Islands and the Middle East

The genus comprises annual or biennial herbaceous plants with white, sub-silky

nithogalum arabicum.

Ornithogalum dubium.

Orthrosanthus multiflorus.

teospermum ecklonis.

Paeonia cambessedesii.

Paeonia officinalis.

llenis maritima.

Pancratium maritimum.

Panicum virgatum 'Heavy Metal'.

hairs on soft stems, growing to a height of 20 to 50cm. Often found growing on uncultivated or disturbed land and roadsides, they are hardy, surviving in dry environments and cold spells. Small, alternate, entire leaves are elliptic to obovate, having short petioles at the base of the stem. Its solitary inflorescence grows at the tops of branches. The large, slightly convex receptacle has many yellowish-orange, bisexual disc florets and two whorls of yellow ray florets. These are produced from spring to early summer. Only one species is in common cultivation.

Pallenis maritima syn. *Asteriscus maritimus*

Gold Coin Daisy, Sea Aster, Tunisian Carpet, Mediterranean Beach Daisy

Native to the Mediterranean region

This low-growing, evergreen perennial grows up to 30cm high and 45cm wide to form dense mats. Leaves are small, to 6cm long, lance-shaped, often slightly hairy, grey green. Solitary deep yellow flowers, 4cm across, have finely-toothed, yellow daisy-like petals, with bright-yellow, button-like centres. These bloom profusely from spring to early summer, adding cheerful colour to coastal landscapes. Grows in most well-drained soils in full sun and is drought tolerant, needing little summer water once established, but dislikes cold wet conditions. Valued as a ground cover for its ability to stabilise sandy soils and prevent erosion in coastal areas as it is tolerant of salt spray and wind. Looks good in a sunny rock garden or Mediterranean-style garden, and other low-maintenance landscaping schemes.

PANCRATIUM

Amaryllidaceae

Native to the Canary Islands, Africa and the Mediterranean region

A genus of about sixteen species of bulbous perennials that are grown for their showy large, white, fragrant flowers.

Pancratium maritimum

Sea Daffodil

Native to southwest Europe, the Mediterranean region

A perennial, long-necked bulb with strap-shaped, glaucous, broadly linear basal leaves up to 50cm long. They are produced in autumn and grow through winter, dying in the heat of summer. In late summer, terminal umbels of three to fifteen showy white flowers on stalks to 30cm high are produced. Each fragrant flower has six spreading outer petals and a central cup up to 10cm across with prominent stamens. These flowers have a pleasing, exotic and subtle lily scent, which only becomes apparent during still, windless summer nights that allow the delicate fragrance to become perceptible. Grow the bulbs in sandy soil with excellent drainage in full sun. Drought tolerant in summer when dormant but needing water during the growing season. Ideal for sandy coastal gardens. They can often be seen growing naturally in coastal sand dunes.

PANICUM

Poaceae

Panicgrass

Native throughout the tropical and temperate regions of the world

A large genus of about 450 species of grasses, often large, annual or perennial, growing 1 to 3m tall. Leaves are thread-like in bud, usually becoming flat and linear, and mid-green, grey-green or purple. In late summer and autumn, they bear finely branching panicles of two-flowered spikelets up to 60cm long with many seeds.

Panicum virgatum

Switchgrass

Native to the United States, Mexico

A narrowly upright, rhizomatous, deciduous, warm-season, perennial grass to 1m high and 75cm wide, forming clumps of purple to glaucous mid-green stems that bear upright, flat, linear, mid-green leaves up to 60cm. Leaves turn yellow in autumn and light brown in winter. It bears broad, diffuse weeping panicles to 50cm long of tiny purple-green spikelets in early autumn. Most of its growth occurs from late spring to early autumn, when it becomes dormant during colder months. Grow in full sun in moderately fertile well-drained soil. Drought tolerant.

Panicum virgatum 'Heavy Metal'

Garden origin

This attractive cultivar makes clumps of dramatic, stiff, upright stems around 1.4m high and 80cm wide, clothed in glaucous, blue leaves. Later in autumn, the foliage turns a lovely golden-yellow. Autumn flowers, held above the stems, are bluish at first and then turn to oat gold, highlighting the colour of its blue leaves. It looks fabulous, planted in bold clumps that can sway in the breeze. A splendid choice for meadows and naturalised areas. This variety makes a colourful backdrop to other grasses, as its hazy flowers create a curtaining effect to separate blocks of other flowering perennials. Looks stunning in drifts, as well as a single specimen. Leave the seed heads and foliage alone to provide winter interest, then cut right back to make way for fresh growth.

PAPAVER

Papaveraceae

Native to central and southern Europe, west Asia, South Africa, western North America

A genus of 70 to 100 species of frost-tolerant annuals, biennials and perennials. The usually unbranched, wiry, sometimes hairy stems grow to 45cm high. Leaves are simple and toothed or pinnate to three-pinnate, bristly or smooth, light or dark green. The whole plant has a milky sap. Flower buds are often nodding and borne on solitary stalks. Flowers have four to six petals with many stamens surrounding the ovary. The two sepals usually drop off as the petals unfold and the ovary develops into a spherical capsule topped by a disc formed by the stigmas. Many small seeds escape from pores beneath the disc when the capsule is shaken by the wind.

Papaver atlanticum
Moroccan Poppy, Spanish Poppy, Atlas Poppy
Native to hot, dry areas of Spain and Morocco

An erect, clump-forming, short-lived perennial 30cm high and 15cm wide. Leaves are oblong to lance-shaped, coarsely toothed, mid-green, to 15cm long and hairy. In summer soft apricot-orange, single or occasionally semi-double blooms appear continuously on long upright stems above the leaves. It is almost never out of bloom and is incredibly tough – almost indestructible – growing almost anywhere, and will even self-sow in the cracks of a dry rock wall. They are an excellent addition to a sunny mixed border, for best effect plant in groups. These are hardy poppies being both drought and cold resistant, though they dislike waterlogged soils. Great as cut flowers, but with hairy-stemmed flowers use only a small amount of water in the vase, as they do not like their stems sitting in water.

Papaver commutatum syn. *Papaver rhoeas*
Caucasian Scarlet Poppy, Ladybird Poppy
Native to northern Turkey, north-western Iran, the Caucasus

An erect annual growing to 45cm tall by 15cm wide, with hairy stalks and regularly-lobed leaves with lance-shaped segments to 15cm long. It bears large, brilliant crimson bowl-shaped flowers, 8cm wide, with a large black spot at the base of each petal. A prolific bloomer from late spring to early summer, each plant may bear 24 or more flowers at a time. Flowers give way to ornamental seed pods. Adaptable to most well-drained garden soils in an open sunny position. Tolerant of poor sandy soils, and drought and frost resistant. It is more dramatic when planted in a large group – a must for every spring garden. Self-sows freely.

PARASERIANTHES
Fabaceae
Native to Australia

A genus of a single species.

Paraserianthes lophantha syn. *Albizia lophantha, Albizia distachya*
Plume Albizia, Cape Leeuwin Wattle, Bicol Wattle, Cape Wattle, Crested Wattle

A fast-growing semi-evergreen tree that quickly reaches up to 10m high spreading to 3m wide. Beautiful pinnate or doubly pinnate leaves are dark velvety green, up to 30cm long. Yellow or greenish yellow 'bottle brush' cylindrical racemes of flowers, 5cm long, are produced in axillary spikes in early spring. This fast-growing tree soon ages, which makes it perfect for providing quick cover for shade while other plants become established, or as a screen or windbreak. Grows best in a sunny position. Succeeds in a wide range of soils, preferably well-drained, though it can tolerate wetter conditions. Drought tolerant, it often naturalises. Also good for erosion control, even for dune stabilisation. This species has a symbiotic relationship with certain soil bacteria, which form nodules on the roots and fix atmospheric nitrogen. Some of this nitrogen is utilised by the growing plant, but some can also be used by other plants growing nearby.

PELARGONIUM
Geraniaceae
Geraniums
Native mostly in South Africa

A large genus of about 280 species in many growth forms, including evergreen perennials, annuals, succulents, sub-shrubs and shrubs. Leaves are usually alternate, palmately lobed or pinnate, often on long stalks, sometimes with light or dark patterns. Erect stems bear five-petalled flowers in umbel-like clusters, which are occasionally branched. Because not all flowers appear simultaneously, but open from the centre outwards, this is a form of inflorescence referred to as 'pseudoumbels'. Countless cultivars have been raised from about twenty species to give the popular garden plants we have today. Many authoritative books have been written about Pelargoniums. In frost-free areas, grow in a sunny border in rich well-drained soil. They all can survive periods of drought and neglect, but flower better if given some summer water.

Pelargonium domesticum
Regal Pelargonium, Lady Washington Geranium
Garden origin

A bushy evergreen perennial with erect or spreading short-jointed stems to 1m high on somewhat woody stems. The crinkled, medium-green, heart-shaped leaves are 5 to 10cm wide with irregular teeth. Large, showy clusters of usually single but sometimes double flowers are up to 5cm across. These come in single or combined shades of white, pink, red, orange, lavender or purple, often speckled with unusual markings and splotches. Flowers usually only appear for about a month in spring, although some may appear throughout summer. 'Grand Slam' is one of the most widely grown. It has red satiny flowers to 5cm across, with dark purple internal markings. It makes an excellent pot plant.

Pelargonium graveolens
Lemon Geranium, Sweet Scented Geranium

A vigorous, evergreen, erect, multi-branched shrub that grows up to 1.5m spreading to 1m. Leaves are strongly rose-scented, some leaves are deeply incised, others less so, with a central bronze marking, to 10cm long. They are velvety and

Papaver atlanticum.

Papaver commutatum.

Paraserianthes lophantha.

Pelargonium domesticum.

Pelargonium peltatum.

Penstemon barbatus.

Penstemon heterophyllus.

Phaenocoma prolifera.

soft to the touch, because of glandular hairs. Showy, star-like, white to pinkish flowers 2cm across are borne in an umbel-like inflorescence from late winter to summer, peaking in spring. It grows well in most semi-shaded positions in the garden, where it can be used as filler. Its velvety leaves add texture to the planting. Also grows well in a good container or hanging basket, provided it is kept in semi-shade.

Pelargonium hortorum
Common Geranium, Zonal Geranium

An erect, shrubby, succulent-stemmed, evergreen perennial up to 1m or more, with older plants becoming woody. Leaves are rounded, 8 to 14cm wide, velvety hairy and soft to touch. These are deep green but often zoned with dark bronze-green, bi-coloured or multicoloured. Flowers are produced in showy umbel-like clusters 3 to 5cm across on a long petiole. The brightly-coloured flowers vary from white or shades of pink, lavender, purple, orange, apricot, to red and burgundy or bi-colours, both single and double. There is a vast number of named varieties. Grow in full sun to partial sun in well-drained soil, with a light mulch covering the soil to cool the root zone. Dead-heading of spent inflorescences allows for continuous bloom throughout the summer. Frequently used as a bedding plant for group or mass plantings, foundations, entranceways, pathways and borders throughout the summer. Commonly used as a bold-textured accent in urns, hanging baskets, window boxes, planters and even as an indoor plant in winter.

Pelargonium odoratissimum
Apple Geranium

An aromatic, bushy, evergreen, tender perennial up to 30cm high and 60cm wide, with a short main stem and trailing flowering branches. Pale-green leaves are rounded, apple scented, 4 to 5cm across, with crinkled edges. They are covered with fine short hairs, making them soft to touch. Blooming from spring to summer, the plant is covered in clusters of star-shaped white flowers 1 to 2cm across. Their two upper petals are adorned with red veins. Growth is best in fertile, neutral to alkaline, well-drained soil in full sun, although some shade is appreciated in hot climates. Drought tolerant once established. Ideal for beds and borders, Mediterranean gardens. They look great in containers.

Pelargonium peltatum
Ivy Leaved Geranium

A bushy, evergreen perennial with trailing, slender, smooth, brittle stems to 1m or more long. The stiff, glossy 5 to 8cm wide bright green leaves are alternate or sometimes opposite, often adorned with pointed lobes. Rounded clusters of single or double 2 to 3cm wide flowers are produced throughout summer to autumn. They are white, pink, rose, red to lavender and many combinations. Growth is best in fertile, well-drained, organically rich soil in full sun, although some shade is appreciated in hot climates. Drought tolerant once established. Often used as ground cover or as climbers, but mostly grown as hanging plants in window boxes and raised beds. They look best when seen tumbling down over a wall or hanging from pots or containers. Ideal for beds and borders and Mediterranean gardens. The cultivar 'L'Elegante' has bluish-green leaves with a silver-white edging that turns purple, as if parched in full sun. It bears white or lilac single flowers in clusters to 8cm across.

PENNISETUM see CENCHRUS

PENSTEMON
Plantaginaceae

Native to North and Central America

A large genus of about 250 species of deciduous and evergreen perennials or subshrubs. Leaves are usually lance-shaped to ovate with entire or serrated margins. Some are evergreen and others deciduous. Species are recognised for their striking tubular flowers, each with a distinct, often bearded fifth stamen. They range from blue, purple, red, to pink, often with contrasting colours. Specialist nurseries have produced many bushy, free-flowering hybrids that come in a wide range of colours.

Penstemon barbatus
Scarlet Beard-Tongue

Native to western United States to Mexico

A hardy, erect, clump-forming perennial with an open rather sprawling habit to 1m high, evergreen basal leaves and deciduous stems. Opposite, lance-shaped, bright-green leaves are 15cm long. Loose panicles of pendant, tubular, brilliant scarlet flowers 2 to 4cm long are borne in profusion throughout summer. Many colourful named varieties have been raised from this species. Thrives in full sun or partial shade in most well-drained soils, dislikes damp conditions. Drought tolerant once established. Usually a fairly short-lived plant of between three and four years. Ideal for beds, borders and rock gardens. Looks good hanging over a low wall.

Penstemon centranthifolius
Scarlet Bugler

Native to California and parts of Mexico

A perennial herb that has many straight, hairless, erect branches, which may exceed 1m high spreading to 45cm wide. Thick, untoothed leaves are up to 10cm long, opposite, with some pairs fused together about the stem. The top of the stem is occupied by a long inflorescence bearing narrow tubular flowers with small projecting lobes at the lips, the longest flowers being 3cm long. Flowers are bright red to orange-red and hairless all over. This perennial has gorgeous, red flowers that are an absolute favourite with hummingbirds. Grow in full sun to partial shade in well-drained soil. Drought tolerant once established. Great for beds and borders, it looks terrific in rock gardens and is cold tolerant. Creates an impact in Mediterranean gardens. Summer deciduous.

Penstemon heterophyllus

Bunchleaf Penstemon, Foothill Penstemon, Foothill Beardtongue

Native to California

A species of clump-forming, evergreen perennial herb that produces upright, branching stems over 1m high, becoming woody at the bases. Leaves are dark green up to 10cm long. The large flower cluster produces several wide-mouthed tubular flowers up to 4cm long in shimmering shades of blue or purple to nearly magenta. In spring and summer, the profuse blossoms are borne on upright, branching stems well above the foliage. A second flowering can be induced by trimming after flowering. Performs best in fertile well-drained soil in full sun. Drought tolerant. If conditions are right, can be long-lived. Several cultivars have been developed for Mediterranean climate and other low-water-use gardens, including 'Heavenly Blue,' 'Margarita BOP' and 'Blue Springs.'

Penstemon hybrids

Border or Garden Penstemon

Garden origin

Many bushy, free-flowering cultivars have been raised, mostly semi-evergreen with basal growths and upright stems up to 1m or more high. Leaf and flower characteristics are variable. They come in a wide range of colours, predominately blue, red or purple. All easy to grow, and if cut back after the main flush of flowers fade, they will flower again. They thrive in full sun or partial shade in most well-drained soil. Drought tolerant once established.

Perovskia atriplicifolia see *Salvia yangii*

PHAENOCOMA

Asteraceae

Cape strawflower

Native to Western Cape, South Africa

There is only one known species, native to cool, well-drained, sandy, mineral soils, often on slopes. It occurs in full sun, in mountain and valley fynbos shrublands.

Phaenocoma prolifera

A rigid, erect, woody shrub up to 1.2m high and wide, tapering at its top, often forming a conical shape that has a single stem with tightly upright branches, so that they seem rather top heavy. Branches have many short leafy stalks at right angles to the main branches. These have many tiny, rounded, grey-green leaves densely covering the purely grey stems. Its unusual foliage becomes a fantastic back drop to straw flowers that open magenta-red, purple or pink to 5cm wide, appearing in spring on the tips of upper branches, where they remain for most of the year. The colour gradually fades through pink as summer progresses. What look like petals are actually bracts, which are rigid, papery, dry and do not wilt. When cut as ornamentals, the flowers last for years, provided they are kept dry. For this reason, it is one of several species which is given the nickname 'Everlasting'. Grow in full sun or light shade, it is more dense and blooms better in full sun. Grow in sandy acid soil that is damp in spring. Tolerates summer drought. It also excels in mixed containers where it will grow smaller.

PHLOMIS

Lamiaceae

Native to the Mediterranean region, central Asia to China

A genus of about 100 species of mainly low-growing shrubs, subshrubs and sage-like herbaceous perennials. The overall size varies from 30cm up to 2m tall. Leaves are entire and opposite, with each leaf pair at right angles to the next and rugose or reticulate veined. The bracts (floral leaves) are similar or different from the lower leaves. All parts are frequently covered with hairs. Flowers are in whorls, which encircle the stems. Stems are usually square in section with rounded corners, although woolly down on the stems can make them appear round. The flowers vary from yellow to pink, purple and white.

Phlomis chrysophylla

Native to southwest Asia

A rounded evergreen shrub up to 1m high and wide with stiff, spreading branches. Elliptic to broadly ovate, woolly-textured, sage-like leaves to 8cm long are grey green when young, taking on a golden tinge after midsummer. Whorls of hooded, golden-yellow, tubular flowers up to 5cm long in spikes or pairs along the stem adorn this golden-hued shrub from midsummer to frost. Attractive to bees and butterflies. To grow well, it prefers full sun and to be dry in summer. Grows happily in well-drained, average, gritty or clay soil, adaptable to various soil conditions. Effective when massed in a border, making good foliage plants even when not in flower.

Phlomis fruticosa

Jerusalem Sage

Native to the Mediterranean region

A much-branched, semi-evergreen shrub with grey-green stems 60 to 120cm high spreading to 1.5m wide. Grey-green, ovate lance-shaped, woolly, grey-green leaves are 12cm long, with wrinkled edges. Whorls containing 20 to 30 bright-yellow, hooded flowers 3 to 4cm long are borne along the upper half and at the tips of erect stems in spring and early summer. It grows best in full sun in fertile, well-drained soil. Drought tolerant once established. Excellent for dry sunny borders and coastal gardens. Cut back after flowering to encourage additional blooming.

Phlomis italica

Balearic Islands Sage

Native to the Balearic Islands of Spain

A stiffly-upright, soft-wooded shrub with white hairy stems up to 1m high and 60cm wide. Evergreen, grey woolly, dull-green, lance-shaped leaves are up to 10cm long. Whorls of two-lipped, soft, dull purple or pink tubular flowers are produced at the ends of branches in summer. It grows best in full sun in fertile, well-drained soil. Drought tolerant once established. Excellent for dry sunny borders and coastal gardens. Cut back after flowering to encourage additional blooming, as it can become a rather untidy plant.

PHOENIX
Arecaceae
Native from Canary Islands and Mediterranean region across to China

An important genus of seventeen species of dioecious palms, which are mostly medium to robust, but also includes a few dwarf species. Trunks are solitary in some species, suckering and clumped in others. Many of the trunked species do not form above-ground stems for several years. Pinnate leaves can be 1 to 6m long. Flowers are inconspicuous, yellowish brown and about 1cm wide, but grouped on conspicuously large, multi-branched panicles 30 to 90cm long, forming large, pendant clusters. Many species are widely planted as ornamentals and one, the date palm, is of major commercial significance. These palms are used to give a tropical look to a garden, are easy to move even when mature, giving immediate effect.

Phoenix canariensis
Canary Islands Palm
Native to the Canary Islands

A solitary, stout, heavy-trunked palm 15m or more high, growing slowly until it forms a trunk, then speeding up. Its trunk can become 1m wide with age, grey-brown and embossed with diamond-shaped leaf bases. It is crowned with many arching leaf fronds that may reach 6m. Leaves are pinnate with 80 to 100 leaflets on each side of the central rachis. Deep-green leaflets, to 30cm long, grow off the central rib, almost meeting, with a sharp point at the tip. Each leaflet is folded lengthways to form a V shape. Older trees produce clusters of small, creamy-yellow, bowl-shaped flowers in large drooping panicles to 1m long in summer. These are followed by large clusters of small, round fruit, which ripen to orange. Easy to grow in full sun, drought and salt tolerant, and tolerant of significant winter cold. Thrives in poor soils but requires good drainage. Ideal for coastal gardens. Lower leaves need to be removed to keep this palm looking neat. One of the most popular palms in temperate, subtropical and tropical regions, used extensively for avenues or as street trees, where they make a truly impressive sight.

Phoenix dactylifera
Date Palm
Probably native to north Africa and the Near East

A tall, slender-trunked palm that with age may reach to 15 to 25m high. Feather-like fronds can reach 3 to 5m long with leaflets to 30cm long. They are grey green to almost silvery or bluish and the bases are armed with stout spines. Bowl-shaped creamy-yellow flowers appear in drooping panicles to 2m long in summer. Flowers on female palms give way to showy clusters of large, edible, sweet cylindrical fruits, which are green when unripe, ripening to brown. The trees have been grown for their fruit for thousands of years. Although frost hardy, fruit is only produced in areas with a hot, dry climate. As it is indigenous to desert areas, it withstands drought once established. It is an excellent tree for coastal gardens tolerating salt-laden winds. If fruit is required, both male and female plants are needed. As it has been cultivated for so long, its origin is obscure.

Phoenix roebelenii
Pygmy Date Palm, Miniature Date Palm
Native to southeastern Asia

A beautiful, solitary-trunked palm slowly growing to only 3m high. It has a slender trunk with a rounded crown of 50 or more fine-textured, lustrous-green, arching fronds. Each compound pinnate leaf is 1m long and is divided into many leaflets to 20cm long. Leaves are unusual in being lightweight and soft in texture. Mature trees produce bowl-shaped cream or yellow flowers in panicles to 45cm long in summer. Grow in moist, well-drained soil in full sun or part shade. Frost hardy. When young, it makes an excellent pot or container plant for the terrace.

PHORMIUM
Asphodelaceae
Flax Lily
Native to New Zealand and Norfolk Island

A genus of just two species of large evergreen perennials. One species is native to New Zealand, while the other is native to New Zealand and Norfolk Island.

Phormium tenax
New Zealand Flax

A large, bold, clump-forming, evergreen perennial 1.2 to 1.8m high and 2m or more wide. It is grown mainly for its basal rosette of attractive strap-shaped leaves, which may be 2m long and up to 15cm wide, often with a V-shape. They are dark or brownish-green above and bluish-green underneath with reddish margins, often splitting at the tip. Leaves grow stiffly upright from the base, giving a bold appearance. In early summer, a dramatic flowering stalk, to 3m high, bears panicles of red tubular flowers 3 to 5cm long, which are attractive to nectar-seeking birds. Easily grown in well-drained soil in full sun to part shade and drought tolerant. With their tolerance for salt-laden sea breezes, they are ideal for coastal gardens. Adds architectural height to the garden, a splendid choice for beds and borders. They look good when grown in containers or near a swimming pool. Ideal for Mediterranean gardens. Many cultivars have been raised with bronze, purple-red, dark-purple to bronze leaves. Many are dwarf forms only growing up to 1m high. 'Variegatum' has creamy white or yellow markings along leaf edges, making a bold and dramatic plant in a garden. The paler forms may burn in full summer sun, so are best grown in partial shade and given more water.

PHOTINIA
Rosaceae
Native from the Himalayas to south and east Asia

A genus of about 60 species of large, mainly evergreen or deciduous shrubs and small trees. They are grown for their brilliant new leaves and attractive flower clusters.

Photinia × fraseri
Red Tip Photinia, Christmas Berry
Garden origin

A variable hybrid making an upright, vigorous, evergreen shrub or tree 3 to 4m high and 2m wide. Evergreen, lance-shaped leaves 10 to 20cm long are dark green but a showy crimson red when young, especially in early spring. Flowers are small, with five petals united in large white inflorescences up to 15cm wide, blooming at the end of spring. Grow in well-drained soil in full sun to part shade, but in full sun the red foliage is more prominent. It is tolerant of frost once established, and dry periods, but grows best with a layer of mulch and regular deep watering. It can be used to create a dense hedge or screen, and with regular clipping, will display brilliant red foliage highlights throughout the year. Prune back quite hard after the foliage has faded to a dull bronze to encourage this spectacular foliage. This will ensure a further 'crop' of fresh growth. It is best to prune during the growing season. 'Red Robin', a spectacular clone raised in New Zealand, is more compact, has sharply toothed leaves that are brilliant red when young.

PHYGELIUS
Scrophulariaceae
Cape Fuchsia, Cape Figwort
Native to South Africa

A small genus of two species of evergreen or semi-evergreen subshrubs grown for their large clusters of fuchsia-like flowers.

Phygelius aequalis
Cape Fuchsia

An upright, suckering, semi-evergreen, bushy shrub to 1m high and wide with four-angled stems. Ovate, dark-green leaves are up to 10cm long. Throughout summer it produces upright pyramidal spikes, to 25cm long, of dusky pink-red tubular flowers, up to 6cm long with an attractive yellow throat. These short-lived shrubs will tolerate drought but prefer moist, fertile, free-draining soil. It will grow in full sun but prefers some shade. Remove dead flower heads to encourage further flowering. 'Yellow Trumpet' is a striking form with pale creamy-yellow flowers and pale green leaves.

Phygelius capensis
Cape Figwort, Cape Fuchsia

An upright, suckering, semi-evergreen, bushy shrub to 1.2m high with a more sprawling habit than *P. aequalis*. The young branches have a purple tint. Opposite, ovate, dark-green leaves are up to 9cm long. Throughout summer, it produces upright panicles, 60cm long, of narrow tubular flowers, 5cm long, orange-pink along the outline of the petals and yellow throated. The plant has an exceptionally long blooming season of roughly six months, throughout summer. Grow in full sun or part shade in a fertile, well-drained soil. Although it will survive some summer drought, it grows and flowers better with moderate water.

Phygelius × rectus

A hybrid between the two above species, which has produced many interesting named varieties. 'African Queen' has pendant pale red flowers, 'Devil's Tears' has deep-pink flowers with yellow throats, 'Moonraker' has pale creamy-yellow flowers, 'Salmon Leap' has orange flowers. All require similar conditions to the above.

PHYLLOSTACHYS
Poaceae
Native to east Asia and the Himalayas

A genus of about 80 species of tall, graceful, medium to large, evergreen, hardy bamboos. All have creeping rhizomes that send up fresh shoots some distance from the plant each year, in time forming large clumps that can be invasive. Leaves are yellow green, light green, or dark green and arise from hollow, grooved culms that often zigzag from node to node. Their elegant form looks great in containers, as specimens, or in a border. They love a woodland setting in full sun or dappled shade. Provide protection from harsh, desiccating winds if not frost-resistant.

Phyllostachys aurea
Golden Bamboo, Fishpole Bamboo
Native to Fujian and Zhejiang in China

A vigorous running bamboo that forms clumps with stiffly upright canes growing from 2 to 4m high with wide-growing rhizomes, so it has an indefinite spread. Smooth, brilliant-yellow culms 3cm thick feature prominent nodes that are often crowded at the base of canes and are hard when mature. Leaves are narrowly lance-shaped, 10cm long, and yellowish to golden green. Young shoots that are produced in spring are edible. The dense foliage makes it a good plant for a screen. Grow in full sun or partial shade. Tough, cold hardy and summer drought tolerant. Ideal as a specimen plant or a tall screen.

Phyllostachys nigra
Black Bamboo
Native to east and central China

A vigorous, running, clump-forming bamboo with arching slender canes growing to 25m high. Clumps of slender, arching canes are green at first, becoming speckled with dark brown or black, then an even jet black in the second or third year. Slim branchlets carry abundant lance-shaped leaves that are 4 to 13cm

lomis fruticosa.

Phoenix canariensis.

Phoenix roebelenii.

ormium tenax
urpureum'.

Photinia × fraseri.

Phygelius × rectus 'Moonraker'.

yllostachys aurea.

Physalis peruviana.

Phytolacca dioica.

long. Young shoots produced in spring are edible. This attractive bamboo enjoys a sunny position but grows best with some afternoon shade where summers are hot. Grow in full sun or partial shade in well-drained soil. Can withstand summer drought but grows better if given water during spring. Best planted in an open position. May remain in a clump in poor or dry soils but can become invasive in warm, moist conditions.

PHYSALIS
Solanaceae
Ground Cherry

Native to Chile and Peru

A genus of approximately 75 to 90 species of herbaceous bushy annuals or perennials that sometimes form rhizomes. Species grow from 30cm to 3m tall, similar to the common tomato, a plant in the same family. Most require full sun and fairly warm to hot temperatures. Some species are sensitive to frost, but others tolerate cold when dormant in winter.

Physalis peruviana
Cape Gooseberry

Native to tropical South America

An annual in temperate locations, but a perennial in warm regions. As a perennial, it develops into a much-branched shrub, reaching 1 to 1.6m, with spreading branches and velvety, hairy soft stems. Heart-shaped leaves are 5 to 10cm long and slightly toothed. In spring the flowers are bell-shaped and drooping, 15 to 20mm across, yellow with purple-brown spots internally. As the flower drops, the calyx expands and eventually forms a beige husk that envelops the fruit. Its small, bright-yellow to orange fruit is edible, rather sweet with a characteristic, mildly tart grape-like flavour. It can be eaten fresh or cooked in pies, preserves and pickles. The plant grows best in a warm position in full sun or partial shade. Productive in long, hot summers if given a rich well-drained soil in a protected partially shaded position, and frost tender. Moderately drought tolerant but grows better with some summer water. As the fruit contains many seeds that germinate readily, seedlings can appear anywhere in the garden.

PHYTOLACCA
Phytolaccaceae
Pokeweed

Native to tropical and subtropical regions of Africa, Asia and the Americas

A genus of 35 species of perennials, shrubs and trees growing from 1 to 25m tall. They have large, alternate, simple leaves, pointed at the end, with entire or crinkled margins. Leaves can be deciduous or evergreen. Stems are green, pink or red. Spikes of tiny, greenish-white to pink flowers are produced in long racemes at the ends of the stems. They develop into globose berries 4 to 12mm in diameter, green at first, ripening dark purple to black.

Phytolacca dioica
Tree Poke, Umbra Tree

Native to South America but widely grown in the Mediterranean region

A massive, vigorous, evergreen, soft-wooded dioecious, heavy-limbed tree 15 to 20m high with a thick trunk and a huge swollen base. It has an umbrella-like canopy that spreads to a diameter of 12 to 15m. Leaves are elliptic or ovate, glabrous, 7 to 15cm long, with veins obvious on the lower surface, dark green at first, turning yellow and then purple with a petiole to 8cm long. Small flowers, which are white or greenish in pendant terminal racemes 10cm long, appear in early spring. They are followed by dark-purple, berry-like fruit on female plants. Grow the tree in full sun in a position where the enormous base can develop, as with age this can be up to 18m wide. This is formed by the extraordinary lower trunk and surface roots, which are massive. Drought tolerant, as water is stored in its fleshy trunk. This outstanding plant makes a wonderful shade tree for a larger garden. The canopy is massive, open and graceful. Parts of the plant, including the leaves and fruit, are likely to be poisonous.

PINUS
Pinaceae
Pine Tree

Native throughout the Northern Hemisphere

A genus of about 120 often tall, evergreen, coniferous, valuable timber trees, which produce edible nuts and include many ornamental and shade trees. Many naturally grow on rocky slopes or in pure sand, so well-drained soil in full sun is important. These pioneer trees are well suited for challenging, arid landscapes, but are easily affected by pollution.

Pinus halepensis
Aleppo Pine

Native to the Mediterranean region

A conical tree 10 to 20m high with silver-grey bark when young. With age it becomes more or less umbrella-shaped to 6m wide. Bright, yellowish-green needle-shaped leaves are in pairs, distant, sparse and slightly twisted to 10cm long. Brown cones 5 to 12cm long are pendulous or with downward curved stalks remaining on trees for three years before opening. This important and widespread tree is extremely drought tolerant and will grow on dry, shallow chalky soils in full sun.

Pinus pinaster
Maritime Pine

Native to the western Mediterranean region

A tall, pyramidal tree 20 to 30m high with spreading branches 6 to 8m wide, distinguished by its reddish trunk and brown shoots. Leaves are in pairs, thick, stiff and slightly twisted, 10 to 20cm long. Large cones are 8 to 18cm long, in clusters, bright, shining brown when ripe and more or less sharply pointed. The cones remain on trees for several years. Extremely drought tolerant, it will grow on sandy soil in coastal conditions. Often grown for reclaiming sand dunes. A valuable source of resin, turpentine and timber.

Pinus pinea
Stone Pine, Umbrella Pine
Native to southern Europe and Turkey
A conical tree when young, but becoming a tall tree to 25m or more high spreading to 20m wide. With age it develops a characteristic dense, flat-topped or umbrella-shaped head. Dark-green needle leaves are in pairs up to 15cm long, well-spaced, stiff and slightly twisted with sharp points. Shining, nut-brown female cones are up to 15cm long and contain large edible seed kernels, the 'pignolia' or pine nuts of commerce. This tree is suitable for sandy soils in coastal areas, as it withstands heat and drought. Careful staking is needed when young. Also useful as a container plant when young.

PISTACIA
Anarcardiaceae
Pistachio
Native to warm and semi-desert areas across the world
A small genus of ten to twenty species of dioecious shrubs and trees growing to 5 to 15m tall, grown for their attractive foliage, autumn berries or nuts. Leaves are alternate, pinnately compound, and evergreen or deciduous, depending on species.

Pistacia lentiscus
Lentisc, Mastic Tree
Native to the Mediterranean region
An evergreen, dense shrub or small bushy tree 1 to 5m high and wide. Leathery, pinnate leaves have six to eight ovate glossy green leaflets, to 10cm long with winged stalks and midribs. Panicles of inconspicuous male and female flowers are produced in spring. These are followed by small red fruit, which ripens to black. It prefers full sun in well-drained soil, but also thrives in poor soil. Established shrubs are summer drought tolerant and can take great heat. Useful as screening in hot dry gardens. The sap yields mastic, an aromatic resin used in medicine and varnish.

Pistacia terebinthus
Terebinth, Turpentine Tree
Native to the Mediterranean region
A deciduous, freely-branching shrub or tree to 10m high and wide. Pinnate leaves, 10 to 20cm long, are aromatic with three to six pairs of dark, glossy-green leaflets. They are oval or lance-shaped with untoothed margins and a terminal leaflet. In spring, greenish-red flower clusters appear on the previous year's growth. These are followed by small reddish fruits, which turn purplish brown. It prefers full sun in well-drained soil, but also thrives in poor soil. Established shrubs are summer drought tolerant and can take great heat. The sap yields a sweet-scented gum used in tanning and formerly in turpentine.

Pistacia vera
Pistachio
Native to regions of central Asia
A spreading deciduous tree to 10m high and wide. It has deciduous, pinnate leaves 10 to 20cm long. Dense panicles of inconspicuous brownish-green flowers are produced in spring. These are followed by clusters of oblong reddish fruit 2 to 3cm long. Inside the husk is the pistachio nut of commerce. Trees are summer drought tolerant once established. Thriving under long hot summers with low humidity, but needs moderately cold winters to satisfy their chilling requirements. Grow in full sun in well-drained soil. Often seen where olives and almonds grow.

PITTOSPORUM
Pittosporaceae
Cheesewood
Native to Australasia, southern Africa and Asia
A large genus of about 200 species of evergreen trees and shrubs growing between 2 to 30m tall. Leaves are spirally arranged or whorled, simple, with an entire or waved (rarely lobed) margin. Flowers are produced singly or in umbels or corymbs, each flower with five sepals and five petals, and often sweetly scented. They make attractive ornamental garden plants, thriving especially near the sea. Several have small fragrant flowers, but are chiefly grown for their foliage.

Pittosporum crassifolium
Karo
Native to New Zealand
A relatively fast-growing, evergreen shrub or small tree 5 to 10m high spreading to 5m wide with bark that is smooth, dark grey. It can be pruned annually to keep it smaller. Upright stems are covered in white felt when young. Oval leaves are 5 to 7cm long, thick, leathery, deep green above and covered in white felt underneath. This provides protection against coastal winds by preventing salt damage and moisture loss. Terminal clusters of small dark crimson or purple 1cm wide flowers appear in spring. Female plants produce pale-green seed pods. An excellent, tough plant for dry or windy sites, making a dense screen. The shrub is fairly drought resistant but responds well to some summer water. 'Compactum' is a smaller, denser shrub growing to 2m high.

Pittosporum tenuifolium
Kohuhu
Native to New Zealand
An evergreen shrub or small tree to 10m high with a 2 to 5m spread. Alternate, pale-green leaves are 2 to 4cm long, with undulating edges ranging from oval to almost circular, and attractively set on

black twigs. Small, dark reddish-purple, bell-shaped flowers usually go unnoticed. These appear in spring and are filled with nectar and exude a honey scented fragrance in the evenings, its scent being more obvious in slightly damp conditions. This attracts moths and night-flying insects. Grow in full sun or partial shade in well-drained soil. Fairly tolerant of summer drought, but grows better with some water. Good for coastal gardens, as hedging, or can be trained to form a small tree. A good foliage plant for cutting for floral arrangements. There are many variegated and coloured-leaved forms with silver, yellow or bronze-purple leaves.

Pittosporum tenuifolium 'Silver Sheen'

A reasonably fast-growing evergreen shrub with magnificent silvery-green foliage. Ideal for formal hedging or screening along paths and driveways. Responds well to pruning to maintain the desired shape. Prefers full sun to part shade, will tolerate light frost and requires little water once established. Also suitable for container planting.

Pittosporum tobira
Japanese Mock Orange, Japanese Cheesewood

Native to eastern Asia

A rather slow-growing, evergreen, broad, dense shrub up to 10m high and 3m wide that can become tree-like. The dark grey, smooth trunk is rarely straight, giving it a picturesque look. Leaves are oval with edges that curl under, up to 10cm long. These are leathery, hairless and darker and shinier on the upper surfaces with lighter-coloured midribs. They are clustered near the ends of branches in whorls. Spectacular clusters of creamy-white, strongly-scented flowers 2 to 3cm wide appear on branch tips in spring. These age to a deep yellow, filling the air with its fragrance of orange blossom. Grows well in full sun but will tolerate partial shade. Drought resistant once established in well-drained soil. It is especially useful for coastal gardens, as it withstands salt-laden sea breezes. It can also be trimmed into a good hedge or screen. Many cultivars have been developed, including dwarf forms.

Pittosporum tobira 'Variegata'

A beautiful plant with grey-green leaves, having an irregular creamy-white margin, that only grows to 1.5m high. Makes a most attractive hedge that will grow in partial shade. It is used for hedges, living privacy screens and indoor and outdoor planter boxes. Stems, leaves and dried fruits are used in flower arrangements.

Pittosporum undulatum
Victorian Box, Australian Mock Orange

Native to eastern Australia

An evergreen tree that makes moderately fast growth 8 to 15m, spreading 3 to 7m wide. Dark, shiny green undulated leaves are 7 to 15cm long. They are fairly thin, oblong-lance-shaped and paler underneath, with a paler-coloured midrib. Leaves are sticky when handled and pruned and have a sickly-sweet smell when crushed. Terminal clusters of up to ten flowers per cluster, of creamy-white, bell-shaped, 1 to 2cm-wide, sweetly-scented flowers fill the air with their scent, which is like an orange blossom in early spring. They are followed by small, yellow or orange fruit. Grow in full sun or partial shade in well-drained soil. Drought resistant once established, requiring little summer water. Almost no maintenance is needed. It makes a useful shade tree, or an excellent specimen or background tree. The variety 'Variegata' is a beautiful silver-variegated form. Leaves are larger than those of the species and with white variegations, chiefly along its leaf margin. The species has become invasive in parts of Australia where it is not indigenous. It is also highly invasive in many other warm regions.

PLECOSTACHYS
Asteraceae

Native to South Africa

A genus of just two species of shrubby perennials grown for their attractive foliage. Formerly included in Helichrysum.

Plecostachys serpyllifolia syn. *Helichrysum serpyllifolium*

An evergreen, rather dense, shrub-like herb with white woolly, trailing or climbing, branching stems to 1m or more high, spreading 1.2m wide. Tiny, alternate, woolly, broad-elliptic leaves are 3 to 6mm wide, greyish-green above and silver underneath. Terminal woolly clusters of flowers 2 to 4cm across appear from summer into autumn and are composed of small yarrow-like composite flowers with cream-coloured rays and pink disc centres. Grows well along the beach and in coastal areas, where it is extremely drought resistant, even to where it may spread into non-irrigated areas. As it is grown mainly for its silver foliage, it should be grown in full sun to be seen at its best. The trailing branches can hang down over the edges of beds and borders, used as ground cover or climb through trees and shrubs.

PLECTRANTHUS
Lamiaceae

Native to southern and tropical Africa and Madagascar

Formerly a genus of 350 species, now containing around 85 species of aromatic herbs, annuals, evergreen perennials, semi-succulents and shrubs with a wide range of growth habits, often upright at first becoming sprawling with growth. Leaves are typically opposite, varying in shape from rounded to elliptical or serrated, green, grey green, variegated, or even purple. Flowers are typically tubular or bell-shaped and in whorls around a terminal spike ranging from white and pink to shades of lavender and blue, sometimes fragrant. Often used in a shady garden as

us pinaster.

Pistacia vera.

Pittosporum tenuifolium variegatum.

tosporum tobira.

Plecostachys serpyllifolia.

Plectranthus plepalila **'Mona Lavender'**.

ımbago auriculata.

Podranea ricasoliana.

bedding plants and especially as ground cover or trailing in hanging baskets.

Plectranthus ecklonii
Cockspur Flower, Blue Spur Flower

Native to South Africa

An aromatic, semi-succulent, fast-growing, erect shrub to 1.8m high and 1.5m wide with ascending branches that are covered with short, multi-cellular hairs pointed upward. Ovate to elliptical, leaves are 7cm to 20cm long in opposite pairs on square-shaped stems, with clumps of purplish hairs on the nodes. Leaves make a nicotine-like smudge on the skin if crushed or rubbed. The inflorescence comprises a terminal panicle 40cm long. Double-lipped petals are 1.5 to 2.5cm long, ranging from bluish-purple to pink or white. Flowers top each straight stem in a fluffy whorl. It produces flowers in autumn, although sporadic blooming can occur at any time of the year. A drought-tolerant plant that can survive when in close competition with other plants. Grow in any reasonably well-drained soil. An easy-care perennial that flowers reliably even in a deep shade. They also thrive in that difficult dry spot under established trees. Cut back fairly hard after flowering to keep them bushy.

Plectranthus glabratus syn. *Plectranthus coleoides*
White-Edged Swedish Ivy, Coleus

A small subshrub to about 1m high, with many stems of up to 1m or more, creating a lush and full appearance. Leaves are opposite to 5cm long, ovate with scalloped margins densely held on purplish stems with a velvety texture, commonly a rich greyish-green with a creamy-white margin. Mainly grown for its leaves, it also produces small, inconspicuous flowers that come in different shades of white, lavender or purple. Thrives in partial to full shade, though it can tolerate some morning sun or filtered light. Grow in well-draining soil. Drought tolerant, it performs better with regular watering. In its native habitat it can be found growing in shady and humid areas, often along forest margins or under the canopy of trees. This fast-growing plant can trail or cascade, making it a popular choice for hanging baskets or as a trailing plant in container gardens. Despite its common names, it is not a true ivy or a coleus.

Plectranthus plepalila 'Mona Lavender'

Garden origin

A hybrid of two South African parents: *Plectranthus saccatus* and *Plectranthus hilliardiae*. An attractive, neat, low shrub to 75cm high with an upright habit that does not spread like other species. It has highly ornamental leaves, green on top and dark purple on the undersides, with serrated edges. From late summer through to autumn it produces spikes of lovely delicate, lavender flowers dashed with purple markings and protruding stamens. Thrives in partial shade to full shade, though it can tolerate some morning sun or filtered light. Grow in well-draining soil. Drought tolerant but performs better with regular watering. Will take a light frost only. This is a useful plant to fill shady corners while providing colour close to patios and around water features. Also goes well as edging to borders, paths and driveways.

PLUMBAGO
Plumbaginaceae

Leadwort

Native to warm-temperate to tropical regions worldwide

A genus of ten to twenty species of herbaceous plants and shrubs growing to 0.5 to 2m tall, some of which are climbers. Leaves are spirally arranged, simple, entire, 0.5 to 12cm long, with a tapered base and often with a hairy margin. Mature plumbago leaves often have a whitish residue on their undersides, a feature that can confuse gardeners. While this white material resembles a powdery mildew disease or a chemical spray deposit, it is actually a natural exudate from 'chalk' glands that are found on the species. Flowers are white, blue, purple, red or pink, with a tubular corolla with five petal-like lobes and are produced in racemes. One species is extremely popular for its attractive blue summer flowers.

Plumbago auriculata syn. *P. capensis*
Cape Plumbago

Native to South Africa

A slender-stemmed, rambling, evergreen shrub with brownish arching stems. In nature, it can become a sprawling bush 6m high and 3m wide, but in cultivation can be kept 3 to 4m high. Alternate leaves are light green, oblong 5cm long. Large terminal racemes of slender-tubed flowers are 15cm wide. Each flower is usually sky blue, 4cm long, with five spreading lobes and sticky calyces. These cover the plant almost continuously in warm weather, making a brilliant show. The shrub is a great favourite for subtropical gardens where it clambers over other plants, makes attractive hedges, sprawls down banks, or becomes a good wall shrub. Easily grown in full sun or in semi-shade in fertile, well-drained soil, it even grows well in poor soil. Drought tolerant once established, needing little summer water. The cultivar 'Alba' has white flowers and 'Royal Cape', a recent introduction from South Africa, has richer blue flowers, which in the right conditions can bloom year-round.

PODRANEA
Bignoniaceae

Native to tropical and southern Africa

A small genus of about two species of climbing shrubs grown for their showy foxglove-like flowers.

Podranea ricasoliana
Pink Trumpet Vine

Native to South Africa

A vigorous, woody, rambling, evergreen climber without tendrils, which sends up many tall, strong stems. If left unchecked, these can grow up to 10m high, with long, spreading branches with a graceful arching habit. Pinnate leaves up to 25cm long contain seven to eleven serrated leaflets, dark green above and pale green underneath. From spring through to autumn, it bears fragrant lilac-pink, funnel-shaped, foxglove-like flowers 5cm long, usually striped with red, opening into five rounded lobes. These appear in profusion in loose terminal panicles of about twelve at the branch tips of the fresh growth and are held above the foliage. After flowering, new side branches develop behind the spent flowers, making a spectacular show. It does best in full sun, in nutrient-rich, well-drained soil. An established plant is tolerant of periods of drought, heat, light frost, strong sunlight and wind. With regular summer water, it will become too vigorous. Prune severely in spring to keep a reasonable size. Excellent for arbours, pergolas and carports, and a valuable shade-giving plant in a hot climate. Ideal for planting against a wall or a fence to create a screen. Can be used as ground cover for an embankment, as the stems root wherever they touch the soil. It even tolerates coastal sea spray. Also looks good in a large container.

POLYGALA
Polygalaceae
Milkwort

Distributed widely throughout much of the world in temperate zones and the tropics

A large genus of about 660 species of annuals, evergreen perennials, shrubs and trees. The leaf blades are undivided, smooth edged and alternate in most species. Plants are grown for their colourful, pea-like flowers.

Polygala myrtifolia
Sweet Pea Shrub

Native to South Africa

An erect, much-branched, evergreen shrub up to 2.5m high and spreading with age to 2m wide. Leathery, obovate, mid- to deep-green leaves are 3cm long. In spring to autumn, short terminal clusters of greenish-white flowers 2cm long are veined with purple, the lower petal having a fringed crest. Grow in full sun or light shade in humus-rich, well-drained soil, as it does not like wet feet. It can take some drought but does better with some summer water. Makes a good temporary filler, as it is not a long-lived plant. A light trimming between flowering times will keep it dense. Hardy in most garden positions, including coastal settings. Great as a container specimen or garden shrub. 'Grandiflora' has larger, deep violet-purple flowers with a white-crested lip, but is weedy and likely to become invasive. Seeds are easily spread, can live a long time and will germinate in sun and shade in moist soil.

Polygala virgata

Native to eastern and southern Africa, from Congo and Tanzania to South Africa and Namibia

This upright or arching semi-evergreen shrub grows to 1.5 to 2.5m high. A single stem is formed at the base of the plant, and slender hairless branches occur at the top. Alternate simple leaves usually drop before flowering. Leaves are narrow, dark green with a velvety texture and 1cm long. Drooping racemes of deep reddish-purple, pea-like flowers are borne at the ends of branches. The flower is enclosed by two large, purple, bonnet-like bracts and streaked with darker veins. When open, these flowers display a purple tuft of small hairs on the top of the lower-keeled petal. The outermost petals encircle the bottom petal, resembling a bonnet. Peak flowering time is from spring onwards. Grow in fertile, well-drained soil in full sun or partial shade. Tolerant of summer drought, wind and some frost. Ideal for coastal conditions. With its beautiful sprays of flowers, it makes an accent plant in a shrubby garden or rockery. Ideal for cut-flower arrangements.

PORTULACA
Portulacaceae
Purslanes

Found in the tropics and warm temperate regions worldwide

A genus of over 100 species of flowering, succulent, prostrate to decumbent or erect, annual or perennial herbs, found in dry sandy soils in warm temperate and tropical regions, often with thickened tap roots. Thin, fleshy, succulent leaves about 2cm long cluster at stem tips and joints. Leaves may take on a reddish tinge if grown in direct sunlight. Flowers have heart-shaped petals, usually five per flower, though double-flowered cultivars and hybrids exist. Flowers are usually 3cm across and come in ranges of yellow, orange, red, pink and white. They close at night and on cloudy days.

Portulaca grandiflora
Rose Moss, Eleven O'clock, Mexican Rose, Moss Rose, Sun Rose, Rock Rose

Native to hot, dry plains in southern Brazil, Argentina and Uruguay

A small but fast-growing annual to 30cm tall, though often less. Upright or ascending long shoots branch, usually near the base. Leaves are thick and fleshy, up to 2.5cm long, alternate or in small clusters. The compressed inflorescences are surrounded by eight to ten leaves. In summer it bears flowers 2.5 to 3cm diameter with five petals, variably red, orange, pink, white and yellow. Many cultivars have been selected for double flowers with additional petals, and for variation in flower colour, plain or variegated. This plant does best in full sun or bright, direct light and well-drained sandy soil. Drought tolerant once established. It is widely grown in temperate climates as an ornamental plant for annual bedding or as a container plant. Remove the spent blooms if growing outside to prevent self-seeding. Needs little attention and spreads itself easily. It can grow between stones in the road or paths in a frost-free climate. Seeds are often sold as mixtures.

PROSTANTHERA
Lamiaceae
Mint Bush
Native to Australia

A genus of about 100 species of strongly-aromatic evergreen shrubs or subshrubs, rarely trees. Leaves are simple, entire or toothed, opposite, mostly square in the cross-section. They are grown for their abundant tubular cup or bell-shaped flowers arranged in panicles in leaf axils or on the ends of branchlets, usually white, blue or purple, occasionally red, yellow or green.

Prostanthera rotundifolia
Round Leaved Mint Bush
Native to southeast Australia, including Tasmania

An upright bushy shrub up to 2m high spreading 1m wide with slender pubescent stems. Simple, small roundish leaves are 1 to 2cm long, green above and pale green underneath, often with lobed margins and aromatic with a minty scent. In late spring and early summer, the plant is covered in a profusion of small, bell-shaped flowers, purple or white tinged with lilac, 1cm across. Each flower has an upper lip with two lobes and a lower lip with three lobes. Pink-flowered forms are sometimes seen. Grow with some shelter from direct summer sun. It prefers partial shade in fertile, acid or neutral, humus-rich, well-drained soil. Summer drought tolerant. It is short-lived but grows quickly, and flowers well. A showy plant for frost-free gardens. It looks great when cultivated in shrubberies or planted beside a path where you brush against the plant so its perfume is released from the foliage. Prune annually after flowering by about one third to keep its shape, but avoid cutting into old wood.

PROTEA
Proteaceae
Sugarbushes
Native to Cape Province South Africa

A genus of around 115 species of evergreen shrubs found on rocky hillside and dry scrub. They range in stature, from tiny shrubs to tall trees of 7m or more. Leaves are in a spiral around the stem, usually tough and leathery, and may be rounded, oval, paddle-shaped, or needle-like. These can be light to dark green, blue-green or grey-green. Unusually, they can absorb water to take advantage of accumulating moisture from coastal fog, an adaptation to their often-dry environment. Usually flowering during spring, the flowers have large heads made of small florets packed on a woody receptacle, each floret reddish or pinkish and between 3 and 5cm. The flowers are long lasting and often sold as cut flowers. Grow in poor, neutral to acid, well-drained soil in full sun. Plants are moderately frost hardy and drought tolerant once established.

Protea cynaroides
King Protea, Giant Protea, Honeypot, King Sugar Bush

A robust-stemmed, woody, sparsely to moderately branched shrub 1 to 2m high and wide. Elliptic, dark-green, glossy, leathery leaves 8 to 14cm long are on petioles 8 to 14cm long. From late spring to summer, it produces goblet or bowl-shaped inflorescences, the largest of all proteas, to 30cm wide. The inflorescences have a collection of flowers in the centre, surrounded by large colourful bracts, from about 12 to 30cm in diameter. The bracts vary from a creamy white to a deep crimson, but soft pale pink bracts with a silvery sheen are the most prized. In a single season, large, healthy plants can produce six to ten inflorescences, while outstanding plants have the potential to produce up to 40. The flowers are visited by nectar-feeding birds, bees and beetles. It is valued worldwide as a magnificent cut flower. Ideal for Mediterranean gardens, coastal conditions and containers.

Protea eximia

A large, upright shrub or small tree 2 to 5m tall, 2 to 3m wide with a single main trunk and a rather lanky, sparsely-branched growth habit. Ovate leaves are greyish green to purplish green, coated with a whitish bloom, 6 to 10cm long, heart-shaped at the base, sometimes with a red margin. Flower heads are large, 10 to 14cm long, and up to 12cm across when fully opened. Fine, silky hairs cover the outer surfaces of the floral bracts, with fringed hairs along the margins. Its outer floral bracts are typically greenish or yellowish white, with a touch of pink and a brown border. The inner series of floral bracts are long and spoon-shaped, and usually deep pink, although colour varies in wild populations from pink to orange-brown. When the flower head opens, there is a central dark purple ring in the centre.

PRUNUS
Rosaceae
Found mainly in northern temperate regions

A large genus of over 400 species of mainly deciduous, but some evergreen, trees and shrubs. It includes many common fruit and nut trees, plums, cherries, peaches, nectarines, apricots and almonds. It also includes many beautiful flowering trees suitable for temperate regions, some of which are grown for their foliage.

Prunus cerasifera 'Pissardii'
Purple-Leaved Plum
Garden origin

A small, deciduous, rounded tree to 10m high and wide with fresh shoots of purple-red. Ovate leaves on blackish stems are 6 to 8cm long, dark red-purple and shiny above, becoming greenish bronze in late summer. The foliage also makes an excellent foil to other plants. Solitary bowl-shaped pinkish white flowers 2 to 3cm wide appear in great profusion in early spring, making a beautiful contrast. These are followed by a heavy crop of small, red plums 3cm across, which are not edible. A popular form plant that is easy to grow in most soils. Grow in full

lygala myrtifolia.

Portulaca grandiflora.

Prostanthera rotundifolia.

otea cynaroides.

Protea eximia.

Prunus cerasifera pissardii.

unus lusitanica.

Pultenaea stipularis.

Punica granatum.

sun or partial shade in reasonably fertile soil. Survives summer drought but will grow better if given some water. It is low maintenance, requiring little in the way of pruning. 'Nigra' has darker, purple leaves, which are red when young.

Prunus dulcis
Common Almond

Native to north Africa and Asia but naturalised in the Mediterranean region

An upright deciduous tree 3 to 5m high. Young twigs are green at first, becoming purplish where exposed to sunlight, then grey in their second year. Lance-shaped, long pointed, finely-toothed leaves up to 12cm long appear in spring and drop in late summer. Fragrant flowers up to 5cm across with five petals are solitary or in pairs, white or pale pink, appearing before the leaves in late winter. These are followed by velvety-covered green fruit to 6cm long, which split open when ripe to reveal the edible nut. Grow in full sun in any well-drained soil. Drought tolerant, needing no summer water once established. Widely grown in the Mediterranean region as the source of the important almond nut.

Prunus lusitanica
Portugal Laurel

Native to Spain and Portugal

A beautiful, large, dense, bushy evergreen shrub or small tree to 6m high spreading to 4.5m with dark-brown bark. Dark green, lance-shaped leaves are up to 12cm long and glossy above. Small, to 2cm wide, cup-shaped, strongly-fragrant white flowers appear in slender racemes in early summer. These may be followed by small, red fruits that ripen to black. Makes a beautiful specimen tree if allowed to develop naturally, or a good hedging plant. Can be grown in full sun or partial shade. Drought tolerant, needing no summer water once established. Grows in most soils, even shallow chalky soils. 'Variegata' is an attractive form, which has leaves conspicuously margined with white.

Pseudodictamnus acetabulosus see *Ballota acetabulosa*

PULTENAEA
Fabaceae

Native to Australia

A genus of about 100 species of erect to low-lying or prostrate shrubs with simple, usually alternate leaves, often with papery stipules. Flowers have a main back petal called the 'standard', two lateral petals called 'wings' and two fused petals at the bottom called the 'keel'. These appear in leaf axils, often in a condensed raceme near the ends of branchlets. Several species are cultivated for their spring flower display. Most of these are fast-growing and adaptable to diverse growing conditions.

Pultenaea daphnoides
Large Leaf Bush Pea

Native to southern Australia

A soft, spreading shrub 1 to 2m high, with pubescent stems that are often golden. Alternate, elliptic to round leaves are 1 to 3mm long, the upper surface usually pubescent and paler than the lower surface, which has spreading hairs. The stipules are lance-shaped, 1 to 2mm long. Flowers are solitary, pea shaped, with five petals, two joined to form the keel. The standard petal is 6 to 10mm long, yellow to orange on the front, rarely with red-brown stripes, wings yellow to orange, keel is red brown. Flowers appear in leafy clusters in axils towards tips of short lateral branches from winter to summer in terminal umbel-like heads, about 3cm wide. Useful as a feature or stand-alone gap filler, especially in gardens with sandstone outcrops. It attracts insects. Prune lightly after flowering. Grow in well-drained soil. Frost and drought tolerant but give some water in extra dry periods.

Pultenaea stipularis
Handsome Bush-Pea

Native to New South Wales, Australia

An erect shrub that typically grows to a height of 0.8 to 2m with glabrous stems. Dark-green to blue-green leaves are alternate and clustered heavily on stems. They are linear to narrowly elliptic, 1.5 to 3cm long and 1 to 2mm wide, with stipules at the base. The brown stipules, up to 1cm long, stand out among the leaves. Flowers are to 1.5cm long, in dense terminal heads, the same colours as *P. daphnoides*, appearing from winter to summer. Grow in full sun to semi-shade in well-drained soil. It grows on free-draining sandstone soils in the wild, and so may need these conditions replicated in a garden. Summer drought tolerant and winter hardy. It is one of the most attractive and showy in the genus, with dazzling conspicuous flowers and soft but stiff foliage that is a pleasure to run through the hand. A beautiful addition to any garden if it can be established.

PUNICA
Lythraceae

Native to southeast Europe, south and western Asia

A small single genus with just two species of fruit-bearing deciduous shrubs or small trees. The pomegranate is extensively grown throughout the Mediterranean region where it has become naturalised.

Punica granatum
Pomegranate

Native to southeast Europe to Himalayas

This long-lived, shrubby tree growing 4 to 5m high and almost as wide is often seen as a dense, many-stemmed thicket with spiny stems. Opposite, narrow, glossy, oblong 8cm long leaves are bright green while the fresh growth is often bronze. Flowers are 4 to 5cm across, brilliant scarlet with three to seven crinkled petals and a red calyx. These appear solitary or clustered at the ends of branches for most of summer. Fruit is up to 13cm in diameter with a thick skin, which is brownish yellow to purplish red. It contains many seeds, each enclosed in a juicy edible red pulp which has a refreshing taste. The tree has been cultivated for its fruit since ancient times. Pomegranates should be grown in full sun for the fruit to ripen. They will grow in highly alkaline soil that would kill most plants. Drought tolerant, but the fruit is better if given regular watering during summer. There are several double-flowered forms, including 'Flore Pleno' orange red, 'Alba Plena' white, and a dwarf form 'Nana', which can be used as a pot plant. Some fruitless varieties are grown for the flowers alone.

PYRACANTHA
Rosaceae
Firethorn
Native to south Europe, southwest Asia to China

A small genus of about seven species of evergreen, usually thorny, upright or spreading shrubs up to 5m tall. Plants are grown for their leaves, small white flowers and showy red, orange or yellow clusters of fruit. Flowers are produced during late spring and early summer, with fruit developing in late summer and maturing in late autumn.

Pyracantha coccinea
Native to south Europe

A dense, thorny, bushy, rounded shrub up to 3m high and wide, which will grow much taller if trained against a wall. Oval to lance-shaped, finely-toothed, dark-green leaves are up to 4cm long and recent growth has greyish hairs. Small creamy-white flowers are borne in dense clusters on spurs of last year's growth, appearing in late spring to early summer. These are followed by clusters of small, bright-red berries that usually cover the plant and persist well into winter. Easily grown in average dry to medium well-drained soil in full sun but able to take some shade. Drought tolerant, needing little summer water. Great as a specimen plant, in shrub borders, or as a barrier hedge. Looks good alone among rocks where little else will grow. They are also good shrubs for a wildlife garden, providing summer flowers for bees and an abundance of berries as a food source. Many cultivars have been raised, including 'Golden Charmer', which has bright yellowish-orange berries. 'Mohave' produces a heavy crop of orange-red fruit. 'Orange Charmer' has dark-orange berries, while 'Soleil d'Or' has golden-yellow berries.

PYROSTEGIA
Bignoniaceae
Native to South America

As of May 2020, Plants of the World Online recognises two species of evergreen, tendril-climbing shrubs. Only one species is widely grown.

Pyrostegia venusta
Flame Vine, Golden Shower
Native to Bolivia, southern Brazil, northern Argentina

An evergreen, vigorously growing, woody climber that makes fast growth to 10m or more with many slender stems, The foliage comprises opposite, pinnate, rich-green leaves with two or three, 4 to 8cm leaflets, and a three-branched tendril, which all arise together from the end of the leaf petiole. One of the most spectacular winter and early spring-flowering climbers you can find, its profusion of flowers appears on dense terminal racemes that often form a curtain hanging with the weight, making an impressive sight. Each tubular, waxy, deep-orange flower 8cm long flares open into five reflexed lobes. Easily grown in any well-drained soil. Whilst fairly drought tolerant, it will appreciate some watering during the hottest summer months, especially in its first year. This hardy plant will tolerate coastal conditions and even neglect. This vigorous, strong-twining vine will cling to almost anything, including bare brick walls, though a strong trellis or fence is best. Perfect for creating shade in a hurry, trained along slanting wires or outstanding over a pergola or arch, or over a fence. Pruning should be carried out in spring once flowering has finished, which may be necessary often to keep the plant a manageable size.

Q

QUERCUS

Fagaceae

Oak

Native to most of the Northern Hemisphere

A large genus of over 600 species of small to huge evergreen or deciduous trees and shrubs with spirally arranged leaves, often with lobed edges. The nut is called an acorn, borne within a cup. They are grown as ornamentals or for timber. One species is an important source of cork.

Quercus coccifera

Kermes Oak

Native to Portugal and the Mediterranean region

Usually an extremely slow-growing, bushy, evergreen shrub up to 2m high that forms a dense thicket but may become a small tree. The variable, leathery, holly-like leaves are 3 to 5cm long and persist for two to three years. They may be spiny margined or flat and smooth, bright green and shiny, usually on both surfaces. It blooms in spring when the weather is still wet and may be followed by solitary acorns with prickly cups. An ideal backcloth for a dry rock garden. Thrives in full sun, and can survive drought without needing water in the summer. Often seen growing in arid stony ground. An exceedingly tough plant that will re-sprout after fire, cutting to the ground or browsing by animals.

Quercus ilex

Holm Oak, Evergreen Oak, Holly Oak

Native to Portugal and the Mediterranean region

A large, slow-growing tree with a rounded shape 20 to 28m high, developing in open situations an enormous head of densely leafy branches as much across. Terminal portions of branches are usually pendulous in old trees. Its trunk is sometimes over 6m in girth, having attractive corrugated bark. Young shoots are clothed with a close grey felt. Leathery leaves vary in size and shape, most frequently 4 to 8cm long and 2 to 3cm wide, persisting for two to three years. Dark glossy-green above and pale green to white underneath, entire or toothed. The shape and size of the leaves varies with the age of the tree and the growing conditions. Bears acorns either solitarily or in groups of two to three. Although it can grow into a large tree, it is also often seen as a shrub that forms a thicket similar to *Q. coccifera*, with which it will happily grow. Thrives on poor rocky soils with no summer water. Valuable for coastal plantings.

Quercus suber

Cork Oak

Native to southern Europe and north Africa

A slow-growing evergreen tree 10 to 15m high with a round top that can spread almost as wide. Young twigs are densely hairy, light grey or whitish. Older branches are strong and knotty. Older trees only form short shoots between 7 and 15cm long. Shining dark green leathery leaves are up to 8cm long, have toothed margins and are greenish-grey with felt underneath. It grows best in hot regions away from the coast, where established trees can take considerable drought. Tolerates most soils but needs good drainage. A mature specimen in a garden makes an impressive sight and makes a splendid shade tree. The heavy trunk and larger limbs are covered with a thick, deeply furrowed and spongy bark, which can be 15cm thick and is used for the cork of commerce. It is removed down to the cambium layer every seven to ten years, and then regrows without seriously harming the tree. An important tree of commerce in Portugal and Spain.

R

RESEDA

Resedaceae

Native to Europe, North Africa and parts of Asia

A genus of 41 species of fragrant-flowered, herbaceous annuals, biennials and perennials growing 40 to 130cm tall. Leaves form a basal rosette at ground level, then grow spirally up the stem. These can be entire, toothed or pinnate, and range from 1 to 15cm long. Flowers are produced in a slender spike, each flower small, 4 to 6mm in diameter, white, yellow, orange or green, with four to six petals. Several species have become popular garden flowers.

Reseda odorata

Garden Mignonette, Common Mignonette

Native to the Mediterranean region, North Africa

An annual herb, producing branching erect stems to 80cm high. Blooms are carried in dense, spike-like racemes of many flowers from midsummer until frost. Small and fringed creamy-white to yellowish or greenish flowers deliver a wonderful spicy-sweet perfume. Plants like rich well-drained soil, and mild temperatures. Somewhat drought tolerant, but they flower better with regular water. These make excellent cut flowers and even keep their fragrance. Plants look good in a large group, or a few in scentless plantings provide fragrance. The essential oil has been used in perfumes.

RETAMA

Fabaceae

Native to the Mediterranean region and west Asia

A genus of just four species of deciduous shrubs found on rocky and sandy soils. They are closely related to and often sold as Genista.

racantha coccinea.

Pyrostegia venusta.

Quercus coccifera.

uercus suber.

Reseda odorata.

Retama monosperma.

etama sphaerocarpa.

Rhamnus alaternus.

Retama monosperma syn. *Genista monosperma*
Bridal Veil Broom, Spanish Broom

Native to the Mediterranean region

An upright growing, deciduous shrub to 2.5m tall and 2m wide with slender, arching, silky grey-green, almost leafless stems that droop like a weeping willow. Small linear leaves to 2cm long appear in winter and soon fall. In early spring, the shrub is covered with small, fragrant, pea-like milky-white flowers in dense axillary racemes to 4cm long. An ideal shrub for a dry garden, as it prefers full sun, is heat and drought tolerant, requiring no summer water once established. It grows best in a sandy soil but will grow in any sharply-drained soil. A useful shrub with its elegant, arching habit that will certainly become the talking point of any garden when in flower.

Retama sphaerocarpa

Native to the Iberian Peninsula and North Africa

An upright, deciduous shrub with a deep root system. Its flexible stems are greyish green and much branched, growing 1 to 4m tall. Alternate leaves, when they appear, are lineal or lance-shaped, deciduous and grouped in three leaflets and quickly drop. The plant remains leafless for most of the year, photosynthesis being carried out by its green stems. Flowers are yellow, tiny at 5 to 8mm long, releasing a pleasant aroma, and grouped into many hanging clusters on the tip of branches during spring and early summer. Drought tolerant. Thrives in full sun in any well-drained soil but prefers most dry and poor ones. It is sometimes grown as an ornamental, especially in Mediterranean climates. A multi-purpose plant, it has been widely used for a variety of purposes as a medicine and source of various materials.

RHAMNUS
Rhaminaceae

Buckthorn

Native to temperate regions of the Northern Hemisphere and a few in Brazil and South Africa

A genus of about 150 species of deciduous and evergreen shrubs and small trees, ranging from 1 to 10m tall. Leaves are simple, 3 to 15cm long. Many buckthorns have an unusual characteristic where the leaf veins curve upwards towards the tip. Fruit is black or red berry-like drupes. These are grown for their form and foliage effect.

Rhamnus alaternus
Italian Buckthorn

Native to the Mediterranean region, Portugal, Spain and Morocco

A bushy, evergreen shrub 1 to 5m high spreading to 4m wide. Stems have reddish bark and pubescent young branches. Small, alternate, ovate, lance-shaped leaves are 2 to 6cm long, dark glossy green above, yellowish-green underneath. Tiny, fragrant, yellowish-green flowers appear in spring in short axillary racemes. These are followed by bluish-black 1cm-long fruits. Grows well in full sun or partial shade. Takes great heat, is drought tolerant, surviving with little summer water once established. A tough plant that can withstand coastal conditions and industrial pollution. The shrub is valuable as a fast-growing screen or can be clipped into a hedge. In Spain a small-leaved, creeping form can be found covering rocks.

Rhamnus alaternus 'Argenteovariegata'

Garden origin

A variegated cultivar with silver-green leaves edged with cream, bushy and fast growing to 6m high with an equal spread. In late spring and early summer, small, fragrant, golden flowers are produced, followed by glossy red berries in autumn. For best results, grow in full sun or partial shade in well-drained soil. It is not reliably hardy, so should not be planted in cold, exposed locations. It makes a good hedging plant and also looks good as part of a coastal border. A striking plant that makes a brilliant splash against a dark background. One of the best variegated shrubs that will take great heat and survive with little summer water. Sometimes plain green shoots appear, which should be removed.

RHAPHIOLEPIS
Rosaceae

Native to southern and eastern Asia

A small genus of about fifteen species of dense glossy evergreen shrubs. Species vary in size, some only reaching 1 to 1.5m, while others can reach 10m. Leaves are alternate, leathery, glossy dark green, simple, 3 to 9cm long, with an entire or serrated margin. The flowers are white or pink, 1 to 2cm in diameter, produced in small to large corymbs with a panicle structure. They are grown for their attractive dense foliage, compact growth and their fragrant apple-like flowers.

Rhaphiolepis indica
Indian Hawthorn

Native to southern China

A small bushy shrub growing about 1.2m high, although it may become taller in deep shade. Lance-shaped, glossy, dark-green, toothed, leathery leaves are 4 to 6cm long, emerging with bronze tints. During winter and early spring, fragrant white or pink flowers about 1 to 2cm across are produced in loose terminal clusters 8 to 10cm across. These cover the plant in fragrant blossom. The shrub's leaves and flowers usually emerge concurrently, adding to its interest. Easily grown in full sun in a well-drained fertile soil. Drought tolerant once established. Ideal for large-scale ground cover or for low hedges. They make dense shrubs that are attractive throughout the year and look good when planted near swimming pools.

RHODANTHE
Asteraceae

Native to the arid areas of Australia

A genus of 46 species of erect annuals, perennials and subshrubs. Leaves are usually alternate, linear to oblong, simple and grey-green. Plants are cultivated for solitary or corymb-like clusters of daisy-like straw-textured 'everlasting' single to double yellow, white or pink flowerheads borne mainly in summer.

Rhodanthe chlorocephala ssp. *rosea*
Everlasting Daisy

Native to southwest Australia

A fast-growing annual with linear, pointed, stem-clasping, grey-green leaves to 4cm long. In summer it bears solitary, daisy-like flowerheads 2 to 8cm across, with yellow disc florets surrounded by spreading papery white or rose-pink bracts and contrasting bright yellow or deep black centres often with white bases. Growth and flowers are best in sandy, open, well-drained soil in full sun to part shade. Drought tolerant. Each stem is topped with a flower, and pinching out will encourage more stems and thus flowers. These can be used for floristry work and can be dried. Flowers should be picked in bud and hung upside down so that they will open as they dry and keep their colour. Sow seed from autumn to spring, so that they will germinate in two to three weeks and flower from ten to twelve weeks after germinating. Cut back old flowers, so that they will reshoot and flower again. Ideal for courtyard, container growing, cottage garden, flower garden, wildflower meadows.

Rhodanthe manglesii
Pink Sunray, Mangles' Everlasting

Native to southwest Australia

A beautiful, erect, bushy annual to 60cm high and spreading to 15cm wide. Leaves are oblong to heart-shaped, pointed, grey-green 10cm long. The everlasting daisy-like flower heads, which comprise papery bracts in pink or white around a yellow centre, appear mainly in spring and summer, up to 3cm in diameter. Silvery flower buds are also attractive in their own right. It can thrive in most temperate areas but prefers well-drained soils and a sunny location. Drought tolerant. It can also often germinate from seeds produced from the previous season's plantings. This is an easily-grown plant that looks stunning when mass planted for a wildflower meadow look, attracting bees, butterflies and other pollinators. They make great cut flowers as well as long lasting dried flowers. Pick them in bud and hang upside down to dry. Ideal for container growing, cottage garden, flower garden, wildflower meadows. Great in a Mediterranean climate.

RHODANTHEMUM
Asteraceae

Native to north Africa, Spain

A genus of ten to fifteen species of rhizomatous, mat-forming, prostrate perennials or subshrubs. Some are cultivated for their solitary large, composite, daisy-like flowerheads, surrounded by prominent, usually green bracts borne on erect branched or unbranched stems mainly in spring and summer.

Rhodanthemum atlanticum
Moroccan Daisy

Native to Morocco

A rhizomatous, mat-forming, prostrate perennial to 8cm high, spreading to 30cm wide. Rosettes, 5cm tall, are composed of finely textured grey-green, bird-foot-like foliage, topped in summer by 10cm tall spikes, ending in small 5cm wide, white, aster-like flowerheads. Cream ray-florets, each with a maroon stripe, surround a small centre of deep yellow. Easy to grow in moderately fertile, well-drained gravelly soil in full sun. Summer drought tolerant.

Rhodanthemum hosmariense

Native to Morocco, Algeria

A perennial or subshrub that grows to 20cm tall and about 60cm wide with silvery, finely-cut foliage. It bears white, 5cm wide, ray flowers with large yellow centres, which rise above the foliage over a long period, the peak being in winter. Plant in full sun in a well-drained soil and irrigate occasionally. It is drought tolerant and hardy. This plant grows well in the Mediterranean climate, but only tolerates winter rainfall if planted in a sunny location on a mound or in well-drained soil.

RHODOMYRTUS
Myrtaceae

Native to China, southeast Asia, Australia

Described as a genus in 1841 comprising eleven species of evergreen shrubs and trees. However, DNA sequence data and morphological data indicate the genus is artificial. Additional studies are needed before it can be split into two or more, smaller genera.

Rhodomyrtus tomentosa
Rose Myrtle

Native to China, southeast Asia

An evergreen shrub growing up to 4m tall. Leaves are opposite, oval, with a leathery texture, 5 to 7cm long and 2 to 3.5cm wide, with three veins starting from the base, a wide petiole and a smooth edge. These are glossy green on top, while the underside is dense grey or sometimes yellowish hairy. Abundant flowers borne in early summer are solitary or in clusters of two or three, 3cm diameter, with five petals, which are purplish-pink or all pink, tinged white on the outside. The sweet, edible fruit is round, purple, and ranges from 10 to 15 mm. It can be made into pies and jams or used in salads. The shrub is best grown in lime-free, well-drained soil in a sheltered place. Tolerant of an occasional frost and of summer drought. A popular ornamen-

Rhamnus alaternus 'Argenteovariegata'.

Rhaphiolepis indica.

Rhodanthe chlorocephala ssp. *rosea*.

Rhodanthemum hosmariense.

Rhodomyrtus tomentosa.

Rhus typhina.

Ricinus communis.

Robinia hispida.

Roldana petasitis.

tal plant in gardens in tropical and subtropical areas. An invasive species in some countries.

Rhoeo discolor see *Tradescantia spathacea*

RHUS
Anacardiaceae
Sumach

Native to North America, South Africa, Asia and Australia

A genus of about 200 species of dioecious, usually deciduous or evergreen shrubs, trees and climbers supported by clinging roots. They are mainly grown for their striking foliage, often with brilliant autumn colour.

Rhus typhina
Stag's Horn Sumach

Native to China, Japan and Korea

A deciduous tree up to 5m high and wide with soft, hairy young shoots. Large, pinnately compound leaves 25 to 50cm long are divided into 9 to 30 downy pointed serrated leaflets 6 to 11cm long. Leaf petioles and stems are densely covered in rust-coloured hairs. The velvety texture and forking pattern of the branches, reminiscent of antlers, have led to the common name. Small, greenish white to yellowish flowers occur in dense terminal panicles during summer. Yellow to red bristly fruits 10 to 20cm long are borne on drooping clusters on female plants in autumn. Its vigorous, suckering habit makes it unsuitable for smaller gardens. It can grow in full sun in dry and poor soil on which other plants cannot survive. Drought tolerant, needing no summer water. Autumn foliage is brilliant shades of red, orange and yellow. Fruit can remain on plants from late summer to spring and is eaten by many birds in winter. It may produce suckers if the roots are disturbed. With its large leaves, this tree will bring a tropical feel to any garden.

RICINUS
Euphorbiaceae

Native to northeast Africa, western Asia

This genus contains just one variable species of fast-growing tropical shrub, which probably originated in tropical Africa but has become naturalised in many warm regions of the world. Often grown as an annual in cooler climates for its large, palmately-lobed leaves and spikes of small flowers and deep-red or brown seed capsules.

Ricinus communis
Castor Oil Plant

A large, fast-growing, suckering shrub or small tree up to 6m high, varying in its growth habit and appearance. Given good conditions, it can grow 2 or 3m in one season. Often grown as an annual in cooler climates, where it is not cold hardy. Glossy leaves are 15 to 45cm long, long-stalked, alternate and palmate with five to twelve deep lobes with coarsely toothed segments. In some varieties, they start off dark reddish-purple or bronze when young, fading to a dark green, sometimes with a reddish tinge, as they mature. Small, unimpressive greenish-yellow flowers appear in terminal spikes to 15cm long from early spring until late autumn. These are followed by 3cm-wide, attractive, deep-red or brown seed capsules that are covered in soft spines. The seeds are poisonous. Easily grown in an open sunny position in any well-drained soil. Drought tolerant, requiring no summer water once established. Makes a magnificent bold shrub quickly, which can be used as a screen or hedge. Easily raised from seed. Many named cultivars have been raised.

ROBINIA
Fabaceae
Locusts

Native to the United States and northern Mexico

A small genus of up to ten species of fast-growing, deciduous trees and shrubs that grow 4 to 25m tall. Leaves are pinnate with 7 to 21 oval leaflets. Pea-shaped flowers are white or pink, in usually pendulous racemes in spring or summer, sometimes fragrant. Many species have thorny shoots, and several have sticky hairs on the shoots. They make good specimen trees or additions to a shrub border. All parts of Robinia can cause severe discomfort if eaten.

Robinia hispida
Rose Acacia, Moss Locust

Native to southeast United States

An often suckering, deciduous shrub 2 to 3m high and wide, often with red glandular, bristly stems. Compound, alternate, densely hairy, dark green leaves, up to 30cm long, are pinnate with up to thirteen pairs of oblong leaflets. Most leaves have a pair of long spines at their base. Dark to light pink, pea-shaped flowers 2 to 4cm long are borne on showy pendant racemes to 5 to 12cm long during spring or early summer. These may be followed by bristly, brown seed pods. Performs best in full sun in moderately fertile, dry to medium well-drained soil, tolerating even poor dry soils. Extremely drought tolerant once established, needing no summer water. Looks effective when trained against a wall. Can make a good hedge or screen.

Robinia pseudoacacia
Black Locust, False Acacia

Native to eastern United States

A deciduous, upright tree with a straight trunk that quickly grows to 12 to 30m high spreading to 15m wide with open branches and spiny shoots. With age, the bark becomes deeply furrowed and grooved, so that an old tree can become gnarled, giving it an ancient, rather picturesque appearance. Branches are typically zigzag and may have ridges and grooves or may be rounded. When young, the branches are at first coated with white silvery down. Pinnate leaves up to 30cm long have seven to nineteen soft, green, lance-shaped leaflets 2 to

5cm long. In spring and midsummer, it bears racemes 10 to 20cm long of fragrant white flowers 1 to 2cm long in pendant racemes. These may be followed by 10cm long pods, which can remain on the tree until winter. Suckering may be a problem. Easily grown in well-drained dry or sandy soils. Drought tolerant once established.

Robinia pseudoacacia 'Frisia'

A deciduous tree 15m high with a broad canopy to 10m that often has an irregular outline. Lovely, compound leaves with oval leaflets are a chartreuse green in spring with the colour intensifying during summer. White and yellow, perfumed, pea-shaped flowers are borne on pendulous racemes in spring and are followed by reddish brown pods. Great for year-round colour, it makes a wonderful street or shade tree because of its drought and pollution tolerance. Leaves are more delicate than the species and may be scorched by the sun. All cultivars are equally drought tolerant but may require some protection from strong winds.

ROLDANA
Asteraceae
Groundsel
Native to the extreme southwestern United States, Mexico and Central America

This genus was redefined in 2008 to include some 54 species. Other authors include as few as 48 and as many as 64 in the genus, most of which used to belong to Senecio.

Roldana petasitis syn. *Senecio petasitis*
California Geranium, Velvet Groundsel
Native to southern Mexico

A large, sprawling, evergreen shrub that forms a mound up to 3m high, spreading as wide, with many branches from the base. The stems and leaves are covered in velvety hair. Ovate leaves are up to 20cm across, with nine to thirteen large lobes, giving it a tropical look. During late winter or early spring, it produces its large, terminal flowering heads, which contain a mass of small bright yellow daisy-like flowers that stand well above the foliage. A spectacular sight when in full flower. Following a brief period of blooming, an abundance of white hairs of seed emerges. Grow in full sun to part shade in a wide range of well-drained soils. Somewhat drought tolerant, requiring minimal summer watering. It can be pruned hard after flowering to remove the seed heads and to keep tidy. Will tolerate light frost. A good filler shrub with its large sculptural leaves and overall size. Will create a lush tropical look without the watering requirements. Use as a large shrubby perennial in mass planting to create an informal screen or border.

ROMNEYA
Papaveraceae
Matilija Poppy, Tree Poppy
Native to southern California and northern Mexico

A small genus containing just two species of erect glaucous sub-shrubby perennials with woody bases and colourless sap that are grown for their attractive foliage and large showy white flowers.

Romneya coulteri
California Tree Poppy, Fried Egg Plant

An herbaceous or sub-shrubby perennial with tall glaucous grey-green stems up to 2.5m high that will spread almost indefinitely from a network of rhizomes and can appear several metres away from the original plant. Grey-green, deeply-cut leaves are 8 to 10cm long with five to nine lance-shaped lobes to 20cm long. The inflorescence is a large, solitary poppy-like fragrant flower with six crinkly white petals, each up to 10cm long. At the centre of the flower is a cluster of many yellow stamens, which stresses the whiteness. Flowers are produced throughout most of the summer. Grow in full sun in light well-drained soil. Drought tolerant once established, indeed, this may restrict its rampant spread. It is sometimes difficult to establish but can become invasive. Can be used on hillsides as a soil binder.

ROMULEA
Iridaceae
Native to the Mediterranean region, north Africa and South Africa

A genus of about 90 species of small, cormous perennials. These are grown for their charming spring flowers, which are reminiscent of Crocus, usually opening at midday and closing in the evening. Many are quite striking, especially the South African species, where there is significant variation in colour and markings of the flowers.

Romulea bulbocodium
Native to the Mediterranean region

A small, cormous perennial with grooved, thread-like, linear, basal leaves to 10cm long. In spring, a short stem 2 to 3cm long bears one to five funnel-shaped flowers 2 to 3cm long. The flowers are among the largest of the genus. These are usually bluish-lilac with a yellow centre and shaded purple or green on the outside, but vary in colour and size. Individual flowers are short-lived, lasting about three days and only opening from midday to early evening. They require a well-drained, sandy soil in full sun, as they are summer drought tolerant and enjoy being baked. It is native to dunes and sandy places by the sea. Plants are fairly hardy. This bulb is ideal for a dry rock garden in full sun.

Romulea monadelpha
Native to South Africa

This species grows from a small, rounded corm with a toothed tunic. Plants reach from 10 to 20cm tall with narrow, channelled foliage. Each of the three to five leaves is just 1 or 2mm across. An amazing species with scentless, intense claret to burgundy flowers. Each oval petal bears a black (or navy blue) basal blotch, outlined with a thin band of gold. The filaments (which carry the anthers) are fused into a short, stout, shiny-black column. Culture as *Romulea bulbocodium*.

Romulea obscura

Native to the Western and Southern Cape of South Africa

It grows from corms that are rounded at the base. Gorgeous flowers are 18 to 25mm wide, yellow or apricot to deep rosy-pink or dark old-rose with small, purplish-blue or greyish-blue blotches. These are held on short wiry stems 10 to 20cm high above narrow wiry leaves. Culture as *Romulea bulbocodium*.

Romulea sabulosa

Native to the Northern Cape province of South Africa

A low- to medium-height, cormous perennial growing 10 to 20cm high, with a rounded base that is wrapped in a brown tunic with curved pointed teeth. Three to five mid-green, thread-like leaves emerge directly from the soil, about 1mm in diameter with four grooves along their lengths. In early spring or summer, stems bear up to four funnel-shaped, shining scarlet to ruby red, bell-shaped flowers 5cm long, with black blotches within a creamy green cup and free filaments. It is one of the most spectacular species. Culture as *Romulea bulbocodium*.

ROSA

Rosaceae

Rose

Native to Asia, Europe, north Africa and North America

A genus of over 300 species and tens of thousands of cultivars of evergreen or deciduous shrubs and climbers, some trailing. Their flowers vary in size and shape and are usually large and showy, in colours ranging from white through yellows and reds. The rose has been in cultivation for centuries and is probably the best-loved flower and most widely-grown shrub in temperate regions. Many authoritative books have been written about roses. While many will grow and flower spectacularly in hot dry gardens, others will have their delicate petals scorched by the sun. It is best to take local expert advice on the types and varieties to grow. Roses can be rested during the hot summer months by reducing the water and pruning where necessary, so that they will then grow and flower well during the next spring and early summer.

Rosa banksiae 'Lutea'

Banksian Rose

Native to China

A tall-growing, scrambling, evergreen climber to 6m or more high, spreading as wide. Unlike most roses, it is practically thornless, though it may bear some prickles up to 5mm long, particularly on stout, strong shoots. Glossy, pale-green leaves have three to five lance-shaped leaflets 3 to 6cm long with a serrated margin. The large clusters of scented, fully double, yellow flowers are small, 1.5 to 2cm across, appearing in early spring and covering the plant, giving a wonderful show. Thrives in moderately fertile, well-drained soil in full sun. Drought tolerant, needing no summer water, but flowers are better with some water. Grows easily, and is good for covering large banks, walls or growing into trees. Needs little pruning other than removing old, weak or dead growth.

Rosa gigantea

Native to east Asia – southern China, Myanmar, northern Thailand, northern Vietnam

Closely related to *Rosa odorata* and considered as only a subspecies of that plant by some botanists. A vigorous, deciduous to evergreen shrub with long, spiny branches that can be 15m long in cooler climates and up to 25m long in warm climates. Branches scramble over the ground, climbing into the surrounding vegetation and attaching themselves by means of their stout, hooked thorns. Leaves are semi-evergreen, 15 to 25cm long, pinnate, with usually seven leaflets, each leaflet 4 to 8cm long. The plant can be more or less deciduous in cold winters. Flowers are white, creamy or yellow, the largest of any wild rose, 10 to 14cm in diameter. The hips are yellow or orange, about 3cm diameter, hard, and often lasting through the winter into the following spring, sometimes still present at the same time as the next year's flowers. A plant mainly of the subtropics, but it can also be grown in the tropics. Grow in any well-drained soil in a warm climate to flower well. Drought tolerant once established. As its name suggests, it is the largest species of rose.

Rosa laevigata

Cherokee Rose

Native to east and southern China

A vigorous, semi-evergreen, rambling rose to 6m high with large prickles and arching stems. Attractive, glossy, dark-green leaves have three or five lance-shaped finely toothed leaflets 3 to 6cm long. A profusion of large, open-faced, single, fragrant, crisp white flowers, 10cm across, adorned with a conspicuous bouquet of golden stamens, only last for a few weeks during late spring and early summer. Orange to red, hairy hips follow the flowers. Plants do not offer repeat flowering. They can tolerate some shade but flower best in full sun. Grow in well-drained, rich, loamy soil with plenty of added compost or other organic matter, which can be slightly acid or neutral. Best in a warm climate to flower well. Tolerant of summer drought once established. Ideal for Mediterranean gardens. It will quickly cover arbours, arches and pergolas. Can be pruned to 2m to keep it a reasonable size.

ROSMARINUS

Lamiaceae

Rosemary

Native to the Mediterranean region

A genus of just two species of evergreen aromatic shrubs cultivated for their aromatic foliage and flowers. The dried leaves are used in cooking while oil from the fresh flowering tips is distilled for perfumery.

Romneya coulteri.

Romulea bulbocodium.

Romulea monadelpha.

Romulea sabulosa.

Rosa banksiae.

Rosa laevigata.

Rosmarinus officinalis.

Ruscus aculeatus.

Russelia equisetiformis.

Rosmarinus officinalis
Common Rosemary

A dense shrub with forms ranging from upright to trailing. The upright forms can reach up to 1.8m tall. Leaves are glossy, linear, evergreen, 2 to 4cm long, green above, silver-grey underneath. Axillary clusters of tubular two-lipped flowers appear in spring and autumn on the ends of last year's branches. They range from pale to dark blue, occasionally white or pink to 1cm long. One of the best low-growing plants for dry climates, as it is drought tolerant once established, requiring little or no summer water. It endures scorching sun and poor soil, so long as it has good drainage. The shrub makes an attractive informal hedge. Many named varieties have been raised including 'Lady in White' with white flowers, 'Miss Jessup's Upright' a fastigiate form, and 'Prostratus', which makes a large dense prostrate mat that will trail over a wall or raised bed.

RUSCUS
Asparagaceae

Broom

Native to the Azores and Madeira through western Europe and the Mediterranean region

A small genus of about six species of evergreen subshrubs about 1m high. They have branched stems that bear many cladodes (flattened, leaf-like stem tissue, also known as phylloclades) 2 to 18cm long. The true leaves are minute, scale-like and non-photosynthetic. Flowers are small, white with a dark-violet centre, and situated on the middle of the cladodes. The fruit is a small red berry. Some species are dioecious. They spread by underground stems.

Ruscus aculeatus
Butcher's Broom

Native to southern Europe, north Africa

A small, evergreen shrub that forms thick clumps to 1m wide of stout, erect, green branched stems up to 75cm high. Flattened leaf-like branches (cladodes) do the work of leaves. They are spine tipped, dark glossy green, 2 to 3cm long and densely borne on the upper part of the stems. On their underside, a tiny greenish flower on female plants will form in the axil of a papery bract, which is the true leaf of the plant. In autumn, showy scarlet berries, huge in proportion to the little leaf, will appear if male plants are present. They are at their showiest in mid-winter. A plant of woodlands, scrub and old forests, it flourishes in deepest shade where few plants will grow, but will also take full sun. Easily grown in most soils. Drought tolerant but can also take regular summer water. Individual shoots are short-lived, but new ones are produced each year. Dead shoots should be removed at the base in spring. When dried, the shoots with their berries are good for floral arrangements. They are worthy of being grown far more in dry gardens than they are today.

RUSSELIA
Plantaginaceae

Coral Plant, Firecracker Plant

Native to Central America, Cuba

The genus comprises approximately 50 known species of subshrubs or shrubs. Stems are slender, often arching or drooping, creating a graceful appearance with usually small, slender, needle-like leaves. The foliage is typically light to dark green in opposite or whorled patterns along the stems. Abundant, vibrant, tubular flowers are usually trumpet-shaped or elongated, with flared lobes at the opening, varying in colour including red, orange, coral, pink or yellow. Blooms are borne in dense clusters or racemes, and often hang or droop from branches.

Russelia equisetiformis
Fountain Plant, Fountain Bush, Firecracker Fern

Native to Mexico

A glabrous, low-growing, much-branched, dwarf shrub with rush-like, green, nearly leafless stems, which can trail down by 1m or more. Elliptic, scale-like, mid-green leaves grow to 1.5cm long. Drooping clusters of small, tubular, usually scarlet flowers are produced throughout most of the year. Grow in well-drained soil in full sun or partial shade. Each plant produces many branches and is effective when grown in a raised bed, rock garden, on top of a wall or bank, so that the flower-laden stems hang down. When planted in the garden, it is moderately tolerant of summer drought. It also looks good in large containers, but do not allow the roots to dry out. Flowers are attractive to butterflies and small birds. 'Aurea' is a popular yellow-flowered form.

RUTA
Rutaceae

Rue

Native to the Mediterranean region to west Asia

A small genus of ten species of strongly-scented, evergreen subshrubs, up to 1m tall. The leaves are bipinnate or tripinnate, with a feathery appearance, and green to strongly glaucous blue green. Flowers are yellow, with four to five petals, about 1cm in diameter, borne in cymes. They are sometimes used as medicinal or culinary herbs. Only one species is usually grown.

Ruta graveolens
Common Rue

Native to the Balkan Peninsula

An evergreen shrub 60cm to 1m high and wide with blue-green stems. Glaucous, much-divided, blue-metallic, fern-like leaves are up to 15cm long with many obovate lobes that release a powerful aroma when bruised. Terminal clusters of small, mustard-yellow flowers to 2cm across with four to five dull-yellow petals appear in midsummer. Grow in full sun in any well-drained soil, even on dry slopes or in poor chalky soil. Summer drought tolerant. An attractive shrub for a mixed border or for a herb garden. It has long been cultivated for its medicinal properties. 'Jackman's Blue' is a striking form with intensely glaucous-blue foliage and a more compact habit. 'Variegata' has leaves variegated with creamy-white but is a much more delicate shrub that needs some shade and water during summer.

S

SALVIA

Lamiaceae

Sage

A vast genus of perhaps 1,000 species of annuals, biennials, herbaceous perennials and shrubs. They are widely distributed throughout large parts of temperate and warmer regions of the world, usually growing in dry or stony sites. Leaves are typically entire, but sometimes toothed or pinnate. Flowering stems bear small bracts, dissimilar to the basal leaves. In some species, the bracts are ornamental and showy. Flowers are in racemes or panicles, and usually produce a showy display ranging from blue to red, with white and yellow less common. Included are many showy ornamentals and some that are used for culinary or medical purposes. Most have stems with a square cross-section.

Salvia cacaliifolia

Native to Mexico, Guatemala

A bushy, herbaceous perennial that has upright hairy stems to 1m high and wide. The creeping rootstock spreads easily, forming clumps that are easily divided. Shiny, mid-green, almost triangular leaves to 8cm wide and long are covered in soft hairs. In early summer, branched stems bear branching narrow clusters of pure gentian-blue, slightly hairy flowers 2cm long with small green calyces. It grows well in a temperate climate in full sun or partial shade. Somewhat drought tolerant but grows and flowers better with some summer water. However, it does not tolerate frost, so must be given protection in cold wet winters. For best flowering, cut old stems down to ground level each winter. A beautiful and striking plant for a border.

Salvia candidissima syn. *Salvia argentea*

Blazing White Sage

Native to southern Europe, and parts of Turkey, Iraq and Iran

An herbaceous perennial to 60cm high, forming beautiful rosettes of silver, velvety leaves to 20cm long and 10cm wide that sit flat on the ground. Its foliage rosette is decorative and attractive in its own right, even when not in flower. Several small stems grow almost horizontally from the roots before bearing strong upright inflorescences in midsummer. These are 20 to 30cm long, branched, with 1 to 2cm flowers in whorls that are creamy white and sometimes tipped with a yellow lip. Grow in full sun, as it is perfectly adapted to sunny, exposed, or dry positions. It grows on rocky hillsides and shrugs off winter frosts, as well as summer heat. It withstands drought and is happy to exist on minimal extra water. Requires a well-drained position, particularly in winter. An attractive, short-lived perennial for a dry border, ideal for smaller gardens, front edges, perfect for banks, areas with poorer soil, sandy or gravel conditions.

Salvia coccinea

Native to Mexico, tropical South America

A small perennial or bushy annual growing 60 to 90cm high. Leaves are 3 to 5cm long, dark green, heart-shaped, hairy and toothed. Terminal, loose, widely spaced spikes to 30cm long of brilliant scarlet flowers to 2cm long appear during summer and autumn. Thrives in full sun in moderately fertile, light, slightly acid sandy soil. Appreciates some afternoon shade in hot summer climates. Drought tolerant once established. For best flowering, cut old stems down to ground level each winter.

Salvia darcyi

Darcy's Mexican Sage

Native to eastern Mexico

This upright, bushy, herbaceous perennial makes a clump 1.2m high to 2m wide. Leaves are heart-shaped, light green. Throughout summer, the clump is topped by spikes of bright orange-red, vermilion or even crimson flowers with a broad lower lip, at the end of long stems. Flowers can either be opposite or form a simple whorl of four flowers, regularly spaced along the flowering stem. Although winter dormant, it is a hardy perennial for a sunny position in any well-drained soil. Drought tolerant once established. It is best planted behind small shrubs or shrubby ground cover, so a mass of colour appears behind the edge of the bed. Flowers are attractive to bees, butterflies and other insects.

Salvia farinacea

Mealy-Cup Sage

Native to southern United States, Mexico

A bushy perennial with an upright habit 60 to 90cm high, often grown as an annual. Stems have a white covering, giving it the common name. Narrow, lance-shaped, glossy, wavy-edged leaves up to 10cm long are white and hairy underneath. It features elongated spikes of tubular flowers with a mealy or powdery appearance on the flower bract. Flowers come in shades of blue, purple or white, some bicoloured, blooming from spring to autumn. Grow in full sun or partial shade in most well-drained soils. Drought tolerant, making it an excellent choice for xeriscaping or low water gardening. It does not require much care to thrive. Ideal for rock gardens, cottage or wildflower gardens. Great in mixed borders. A showy plant that is easily raised from seed. It can also be used as a cut flower.

Salvia greggii

Autumn Sage

Native to United States, Mexico

An upright evergreen bushy subshrub 60 to 90cm high and wide, branching freely from the base with hairy stems. The minty aromatic foliage of narrow oblong leaves is softly hairy, deep green and 3 to 5cm long. Brilliant racemes of pairs of two-lipped flowers 2cm long are usually red, but may also be purple, pink, yellow or violet. These appear on thin wiry stems in summer and autumn and are long lasting. Easy to grow as it is drought tolerant once established, thrives in full sun or partial shade in light well-drained soil.

uta graveolens.

Salvia candidissima.

Salvia darcyi.

lvia farinacea.

Salvia leucantha.

Salvia officinalis.

lvia yangii.

Santolina chamaecyparissus.

Salvia leucantha
Mexican Sage Bush
Native to Mexico, Central America

A bushy, evergreen shrub or herbaceous perennial 1.2 to 1.8cm high with graceful, arching stems. Leaves, stems and flowers are covered in a dense white wool. Mid-green, lance-shaped leaves are up to 15cm long. Attractive bicolour flowers comprise soft purple sepals in contrast to fuzzy white flowers 1 to 2cm long, appearing from late summer to autumn on spikes up to 50cm long. Easy to grow as it is drought tolerant once established but grows better if given some summer water. Thrives in full sun or partial shade in light well-drained soil. Great for beds, borders or containers. Outstanding as cut flowers. Remove old, flowered stems to encourage fresh growth.

Salvia officinalis
Common Sage
Native to the Mediterranean region

An evergreen subshrub up to 80cm high spreading to 1m wide, grown mainly for its attractive 3 to 8cm-long aromatic oval to oblong leaves. These are grey-green, wrinkled on the upper side, and nearly white underneath because of many short soft hairs. Modern cultivars include leaves with purple, rose, cream and yellow in many variegated combinations. In early summer it sends up terminal upright spikes of camphor-scented, two-lipped violet-blue flowers 1 to 2cm long that are attractive to bees. For best flowering, grow in full sun in well-drained soil. Fairly drought tolerant, needing little summer water once established. Avoid excessive winter wet. If grown in groups, it makes an excellent ground cover. Long cultivated as a culinary herb but also makes an attractive garden plant. 'Purpurascens' has purple leaves that darken through summer. 'Tricolor' has leaves edged with cream with the young leaves tinged pink or purple. 'Icterina' has aromatic, oblong, 1 to 2cm-long leaves that are variegated with pale green and golden yellow. It produces two-lipped purplish-blue flowers on terminal racemes in late spring to early summer.

Salvia yangii syn. *Perovskia atriplicifolia*
Russian Sage
Native to grassland areas in western China, Pakistan and Afghanistan

A subshrub or herbaceous perennial, previously known as Perovskia. Although not originally classified as part of the sage genus Salvia, it has been included in it since 2017.

A hardy, woody-based, multi-stemmed subshrub with stiff, upright growing, greyish-white stems up to 1m high, spreading as wide. Aromatic, deeply cut, grey-green, narrow leaves are up to 6cm long. From midsummer to autumn, small tubular violet-blue flowers appear on many branched terminal panicles, reaching up to 30cm. These form a haze above the foliage. Thrives in full sun in well-drained soil. Drought tolerant, needing no summer water once established. An ideal plant for the Mediterranean climate garden, as it is hardy and likes summer heat. It is useful for coastal gardens, as it withstands salt-laden sea breezes. Excellent for xeriscaping. Cut down to ground level in early spring before the fresh shoots appear. 'Blue Spire' has larger spikes of flowers up to 30cm long and richer-coloured flowers.

Sansevieria trifasciata see *Dracaena trifasciata*

SANTOLINA
Asteraceae
Native to dry, rocky areas of the Mediterranean region

A genus of about eighteen species of small evergreen shrubs growing 10 to 60cm tall. Leaves are simple and minute in some species, or pinnate, finely divided in other species, often densely silvery, hairy and usually aromatic. Composite flowerheads are yellow or white, produced in dense globose heads 1 to 2cm in diameter, on top of slender stems held 10 to 25cm above the foliage. They are frost hardy but short-lived.

Santolina chamaecyparissus
Cotton Lavender
Native to the western and central Mediterranean

A low-growing, mound-forming, evergreen shrub up to 50cm high and spreading to 1m wide with young branches covered in white felt. It is noted for its dense, fine, silver-grey foliage. Small, grey or silver, aromatic, pinnate leaves are finely divided. In summer, it produces masses of button-like composite flowerheads, which are globular, 2cm across, bright lemon-yellow and held on slender stems above the foliage. Thrives in dry to medium well-drained poor soil in full sun. Drought tolerant once established. This plant is valued in cultivation as ground cover or as an edging plant for a hot, sunny, well-drained spot, though it may be short-lived. To keep a compact shape, cut back hard during winter. Some of the low-growing stems may root themselves. Great for beds and borders, coastal gardens, Mediterranean gardens.

SCABIOSA
Caprifoliaceae
Pincushion Flowers
Native to the Mediterranean region, Africa and Asia

A genus of about 80 species of annuals, biennials and perennials from sunny sites in dry meadows and rocky slopes. Leaves of most species are hairy and partly divided into lobes, but a few are smooth, and some have simple leaves. Compound or solitary soft lavender blue, lilac, pink or creamy white flowerheads have domed pincushion-like central florets and larger marginal florets. After flowers have dropped, the calyces together with the bracts form a spiky ball that may be a reason for the 'pincushion' common name. Some species have been developed into attractive cultivars for gardeners.

Scabiosa atropurpurea
Mediterranean Sweet Scabious
Native to southern Europe
An erect, branching, wiry-stemmed, short-lived perennial or biennial up to 90cm high and 25cm wide. Mid-green leaves are 3 to 12cm long. Basal leaves are spoon-shaped and entire or coarsely toothed. Stem leaves are pinnatifid with toothed segments. Wiry flower stems to 90cm high bear solitary, fragrant, purple to dark red flowerheads 5cm across, domed to globular with prominent white stamens, providing a striking contrast. These are borne from summer through to autumn. Grow in moderately fertile, well-drained, slightly alkaline soil in full sun. Summer drought tolerant but protect from excessive winter wet. These frost-hardy plants are great for cottage and perennial gardens and make attractive potted specimens. Remove spent flower heads and trim back old foliage in late autumn. Many varieties have been raised including 'Pincushion Formula Mix', sturdy tall plants suitable for garden display or cut flowers in black, blue, lemon, bright red, salmon rose and white. 'Summer Fruits' has pretty pincushion flowers in berry shades, each of the blooms sweetly fragrant.

Scabiosa columbaria
Small Scabious
Native to Europe, west Asia
A branched, clump-forming, hairy perennial 30 to 50cm tall and wide with long stalked lance-shaped simple or pinnatifid basal leaves 5 to 15cm long. Its profusion of violet-blue or pink, pincushion-like flowers 7cm across atop wiry stems, hovers over the foliage in summer. It thrives in full sun or partial shade in average, well-drained soil. Soil should be moist during the growing season, protected from winter wet. Ideal for coastal gardens, cottage gardens or containers. Great for cut flowers.

Scabiosa graminifolia syn. *Lomelosia graminifolia*
Pincushion Flower, Grass-Leaved Scabiosa
Native to the Mediterranean region
A clump-forming, evergreen perennial to 25cm high and 30cm wide, with tufts of silver-green, grass-like leaves 15cm long covered with tufts of silvery hairs. Summer-borne flowers are solitary, light purple, up to 4cm wide, and held on strong, narrow stalks to 25cm high. Flowers have a slightly domed, pincushion appearance and they come in shades of purples and blues. With its rounded shape, the flower is aptly named pincushion. Easily grown in full sun in average slightly alkaline well-drained soil. Drought tolerant. These plants can flower almost continuously throughout the year in the right conditions. They are great for cottage and perennial gardens and make attractive potted specimens. Bees and butterflies love this plant.

SCADOXUS
Amaryllidaceae
Blood Lily, Paintbrush Lily
Native to southern Africa
A genus of about nine species of perennials, with a bulbous underground structure from which emerge one or more fleshy leaves and flowering stalks. Broad, leathery leaves arranged in a whorl are sometimes spotted or marbled. They are renowned for their spectacular inflorescences, composed of many small flowers with six spreading or erect tepals in a spherical cluster held above the foliage on a leafless stem. Individual flowers are usually small and tubular, with brightly coloured petals, in shades of red, orange or pink. Flowers emerge before the leaves. Plants may take several years to reach maturity and produce flowers.

Scadoxus multiflorus syn. *Haemanthus multiflorus*
Blood Lily, Paintbrush Lily
Native to tropical Africa
This herbaceous perennial growing from a bulb is characterised by its large, fleshy, dark-green leaves that grow in a basal rosette. Leaves are typically broad, leathery, with a glossy texture, 30 to 60cm long. The foliage remains attractive even when it is not in bloom. Its inflorescence emerges from the centre of the leaf rosette, on a sturdy stalk, bearing large spherical flower heads about 10 to 15cm across. Each flower head comprises many individual flowers in a dense cluster. Flowers are vibrant bright red or orange red with prominent stamens. Blooming typically occurs during late winter or early spring, with flowers lasting for several weeks. Flowers exude a faint, pleasant fragrance. The bright red of the blooms gives rise to its common name. Grow in well-draining soil to prevent bulb rot. They prefer partial or full shade, as direct sunlight can scorch its leaves. Water regularly when growing, but none during the summer when they go dormant. They make good container plants.

SCAEVOLA
Goodeniaceae
Native mostly in New South Wales, South Australia and Victoria, Australia
A genus of over 130 species of mainly evergreen perennials but also climbers, shrubs and small trees. Leaves usually alternate, mostly with a tuft of axillary hairs. While they are cultivated for their beautiful flowers, only the perennial varieties are grown in gardens, despite their short lifespan.

Scaevola aemula
Fairy Fan Flower
A tender, mat-forming, evergreen perennial up to 50cm high and wide, with thick, short, jointed stems that sprawl across the ground. It has bright-green,

oval leaves 9cm long with toothed edges. It bears leafy racemes of blue, purple or white flowers 2 to 3cm across. Each flower has five lobes that radiate outwards on one side to form a fan shape. These are borne mainly in spring and summer but often appear almost continuously. Grow in full sun or partial shade in rich, well-drained soil. Drought and heat tolerant once established. A good plant for the front of a border, or attractive hanging down over a wall. Attracts butterflies, bees and other pollinating insects. 'Blue Wonder' has lilac-blue flowers produced in great profusion almost continuously.

SCHINUS
Anacardiaceae
Native to Central and South America

A genus of about 30 species of usually evergreen, dioecious shrubs and trees. The inflorescences are typically panicles, with moderate to considerable branching. Individual flowers are many but unimpressive. Often grown as street trees in the Mediterranean and warm temperate areas where they look spectacular when covered in berries. Resin in the stems and leaves causes allergic reactions in some people.

Schinus molle
Pepper Tree

An evergreen, dioecious tree, which makes rapid growth 8 to 15m high, spreading to 5m or more wide and much branched. With age, it develops a rough, gnarled trunk with knots that frequently sprout leaves or shoots. Branches are pendulous, slender, brown and glabrous, where weeping feathery foliage makes it a highly decorative tree. Bright evergreen, pinnate leaves 10 to 30cm long have many 4 to 5cm narrow leaflets. Many inconspicuous, yellowish-white flowers appear in short, drooping clusters 10 to 15cm long in spring. These are followed on female trees by small rosy-red berries that hang in pendant clusters in autumn. Easy to grow in full sun, drought resistant once established, grows in any soil, and thrives in heat. A tender tree, which can be damaged by cold. It makes a beautiful shade tree. Roots are invasive and greedy, so nothing can be grown underneath; do not plant near house foundations or drains.

SCHOTIA
Fabaceae
Native to southern Africa

A small genus of four or five species of deciduous or semi-evergreen trees with a single trunk and a dense, rounded crown up to 20m, spreading up to 15m, or multi-stemmed shrubs to 3m. Smooth brown to grey bark becomes dark brown with age. Small green branches have lenticels. One species grows by scrambling. Alternate pinnate leaves grow up to 17cm long on petioles. There are masses of inflorescences on old, often leafless wood along the branches. Each one is a small, branched cluster. Flowers are mostly bright red but can be pink. Some have a red stalk or pedicel.

Schotia brachypetala
African Walnut, Tree Fuchsia

Native to South Africa

A large shrub or wide-spreading, semi-evergreen tree to 10m high and up to 6m wide with reddish-brown bark, whose young shoots are grey. Pinnate leaves emerge a rose-red turning to copper, then to bright green. These are up to 18cm long with four to five pairs of oblong leaflets 1 to 2cm long. Throughout summer and autumn, it is covered with crowded clusters to 13cm long, of glowing deep-red, fragrant flowers. The tree briefly drops its leaves during its spectacular flowering period. Each flower has a prominent red calyx to 1cm wide, minute petals and protruding red stamens. These are followed by long bean-like pods to 18cm long containing many seeds that are edible when roasted. A highly ornamental, slow-growing tree with flowers that are attractive to bees. Grow in moderately fertile well-drained soil in full sun. Drought tolerant once established. Useful as a windbreak near the coast. Easily propagated by seed.

SCILLA
Asparagaceae
Native to the Mediterranean, South Africa, southwest Asia and the Middle East

A genus of about 80 to 90 species of bulbous perennials. All species grow from true bulbs that are either submerged under the soil or project above the surface. They are easily grown for their small starry or bell-shaped flowers, usually in shades of blue, sometimes white or pink, with six anthers. Some are winter growing and some are summer growing. Some prefer part shade that does not dry out in summer and others prefer sun with summer dry.

Scilla bifolia
Native to central and southern Europe, the Caucasus and Asia Minor

This small perennial grows from a bulb 1 to 2cm across. There are two or rarely three lance-shaped, curved, fleshy, shiny leaves 5 to 20cm long. The leaf bases clasp around half of the stem. Flowering stems are erect and unbranched, 10 to 20cm high. Slightly one-sided racemes of up to ten star-shaped blue to blue-purple flowers each 1cm across are upward facing, blooming from early to late spring. Excellent for naturalising.

Scilla natalensis see *Merwilla plumbea*

Scilla peruviana
Peruvian Scilla

Native to the Mediterranean region

A clump-forming, bulbous perennial with a basal cluster of almost upright leaves to 30cm long. They appear during autumn and die down during summer. During spring, large dome-shaped clusters of flowers appear on 30cm stems,

'abiosa columbaria.

Scadoxus multiflorus.

Scaevola aemula.

'hinus molle.

Schotia brachypetala.

Scilla peruviana.

'edum acre.

Sedum morganianum.

Senecio macroglossus **'Variegatus'**.

often containing 50 to 100 blue-violet, purple or white star-shaped flowers 2cm across. Strap-shaped leaves die down soon after flowering and the bulb remains dormant during summer. An easy bulb to grow in full sun in any soil. As it grows during autumn and winter, it needs no summer water. It looks wonderful when grown in large drifts between shrubs and deciduous trees. Also looks attractive when grown in pots. Despite its name, it is native to the Mediterranean region.

SEDUM
Crassulaceae
Stonecrop
Native to most parts of the Northern Hemisphere and South America

A genus of perhaps 400 to 500 species of succulent annuals, biennials, evergreen and deciduous perennials. They are characterised by succulent leaves and stems and have water-storing leaves. Flowers usually have five petals, seldom four or six. There are typically twice as many stamens as petals. Various species formerly classified as Sedum are now in the separate genera: Hylotelephium and Rhodiola.

Sedum acre
Goldmoss Stonecrop, Mossy Stonecrop, Goldmoss Sedum, Biting Stonecrop

Native to Mediterranean region

A tufted, evergreen perennial that forms mat-like stands some 5 to 12cm high. For much of the year, stems are short, semi-prostrate and densely clad in pale green leaves to 6mm long. Leaves are alternate, fleshy and shortly cylindrical with a rounded tip. At flowering in summer, the stems lengthen to become erect, somewhat limp and often pinkish brown with leaves further apart, sometimes tinged with red. Starry yellow-green flowers 1.5cm across form a flat-topped cyme 2.5 to 4cm across. These are produced in abundance over long periods during summer. It spreads as a creeping ground cover when allowed to do so, but is easily controlled, being shallow rooted. Drought tolerant. It grows well in poor soils, sand, rock gardens, also in the cracks of masonry and rich garden soil, in full sun or partial shade. Protect from excessive winter wet. Leaves contain an acrid fluid that can cause skin rashes.

Sedum caeruleum
Native to the western-central Mediterranean region

An erect, annual, succulent shrub, which is much branched from the base, 10 to 15cm high to 15cm wide, with slender branches. Leaves are thick, fleshy, ovate to narrowly oblong or almost linear, pale green 1 to 2cm long, shiny green, often suffused with red. In summer it bears star-shaped, usually seven-petalled, blue, pale blue or white, rarely pinkish flowers 6mm across in cymes to 2.5cm across. Leaves and stems gradually flush with red during flowering. It seeds readily. Little attention or care is needed for these plants, as they can thrive in both favourable and unfavourable conditions. With their ability to withstand summer drought conditions, they are perfect for the sunny, dry spots in a garden.

Sedum morganianum
Donkey Tail

Native to Mexico

A lovely, evergreen, succulent perennial with fleshy stems hanging to 1m long. Thick, fleshy, greenish-blue, nearly cylindrical leaves to 2cm long with a silver-blue bloom overlap each other along the stems to give a braided or rope-like effect. They are plump when the plant is well watered, then shrivel when dry. In spring and summer, pale-pink to deep-scarlet, star-shaped flowers to 1cm across are produced in clusters. A beautiful succulent that should be grown in shade. Give generous water and feed during summer but keep dry in winter. Drought and heat tolerant once established. Fast-draining soil is essential. Grow in a hanging wall pot, in a container, or hanging over the top of a wall in a shady place.

Sedum rubrotinctum
Native to Mexico

Pork and Beans

A small, evergreen succulent with sprawling, freely-branching stems up to 20cm high that readily root in the ground. Alternate, thickly clustered, fleshy club-shaped 2cm leaves are glossy green, turning coppery-red in sunshine. Yellow flowers are star-shaped to 1cm across and are produced in winter. A drought-tolerant plant that needs little summer water. Ideal for a rock garden, where it will gradually form a dense mat. It is grown easily and tolerates all types of soil except for those that are poorly drained. It grows well in summer, can take variations in climate, although it is not frost-tolerant. New plants may be grown from leaves (or beans) that drop off or are separated from the stem and laid on soil. It also makes a good pot plant.

Sedum spectabile see *Hylotelephium spectabile*

Sedum telephium 'Purple Emperor' see *Hylotelephium telephium* 'Purple Emperor'

Sedum weinbergii see *Graptopetalum paraguayense*

SENECIO
Asteraceae
Found in all parts of the world

It is one of the few genera occurring in all five regions with a Mediterranean climate. Some species are found in mountainous regions, including tropical alpine-like areas. A vast genus containing about 1,250 species ranging from annuals, biennials, herbaceous perennials, shrubs, to climbers and succulents, while a few from east Africa are tree-like. The flower heads are normally rayed with the heads borne in branched clusters, and usually completely yellow, but green, purple, white and blue flowers are known as well.

Many species formally included in Senecio have been moved to other genera.

Senecio cineraria see *Jacobaea maritima*

Senecio fulgens see *Kleinia fulgens*

Senecio greyi see *Brachyglottis greyi*

Senecio macroglossus

Cape Ivy, Natal Ivy

Native to South Africa

An evergreen, twining, but not tendril-climbing, herbaceous perennial up to 3m high with purple-toned, semi-succulent stems that become woody with age. It has smooth, thin, flexible branches bearing ivy-like leaves, bright glossy green up to 8cm long, with three to five lobes. When broken, both leaves and stems release a fresh, lemony scent. When creeping along the ground, branches sometimes develop roots at the nodes. Solitary, white to pale-yellow, daisy-like flowers to 6cm across with darker centres appear during summer and autumn. Grow in moderately fertile well-drained soil. Drought tolerant, needing little summer water. It needs a well-drained soil, as waterlogged winter soil will kill it. Can be grown in full sun but prefers some shade. Plant in sheltered areas along rockery walls or garden edges, or in hanging pots, wherever it may hang or cascade, to appreciate its delicate beauty.

Senecio macroglossus 'Variegatus' has leaves green to milky green and glossy with an irregular creamy-white to yellow margin, while other leaves are entirely cream. A tender climber that is more suited as a pot or container plant, where it can make an attractive creeper for a shady patio or terrace.

Senecio mikanioides see *Delairea odorata*

Senecio petasitis see *Roldana petasitis*

Senecio rowleyanus see *Curio rowleyanus*

Senecio serpens see *Curio repens*

SENNA

Fabaceae

Native to tropical and temperate regions of the world

A genus of 260 to 350 species of evergreen or deciduous shrubs, sometimes small trees or perennial herbs. Alternate pinnate leaves have up to 25 pairs of leaflets, each leaf with a stipule at the base, that often falls off as the leaves mature. Flowers are in racemes in leaf axils with bracts at the base in shades of orange or red. The fruit is a leathery pod containing several seeds.

Senna alata

Candle Bush, Emperor's Candlesticks, Christmas Candles, Empress Candle Plant

Native from Mexico and the West Indies to Paraguay

A large, short-lived, deciduous, spreading shrub usually growing 2 to 3m tall, but occasionally reaching up to 4m. Pinnate bright green leaves are 45 to 80cm long and 12 to 25cm wide, with eight to fourteen pairs of large smooth or slightly hairy leaflets, each 5 to 17cm long. Leaves close at night. Many beautiful, golden-yellow flowers 3cm long are borne in tall, upright candle-like spikes during late summer and early autumn. Flowers are protected by yellowish-green bracts when in bud. These are fragrant and attract pollinators like bees and butterflies. Easily grown in any type of well-drained soil in full sun. Tolerant of summer drought and occasional frost. Prune hard after flowering to encourage fresh growth.

Senna artemisioides

Feathery Cassia

Native to Australia

An evergreen shrub 2 to 3m high spreading to 3m wide with a light airy appearance. Grey-green or silvery, mostly pinnate leaves have thickly downy leaflets in pairs of one to eight, 2 to 4cm long. The leaves and stems are covered in fine grey silky hair. Small, sulphur-yellow, fragrant flowers are carried in 2cm wide unbranched clusters of five to eight, mainly in spring, but also intermittently throughout the year. Grow in any type of well-drained soil in full sun. Tolerant of summer drought tolerant once established, but grows better with some summer water. Easily raised from seed.

Senna corymbosa

Flowering Senna, Argentine Senna

Native to northern Argentina and Uruguay

A lax evergreen shrub up to 1.5m high and wide, which can be trained into a small tree. Light yellowish-green pinnate leaves, to 60cm long, comprise six to eight narrow lance-shaped leaflets 3 to 5cm long. Gorgeous showy clusters of small, golden-yellow, cup-shaped flowers to 2cm across are held in clusters up to 15cm long, in summer or autumn. These are followed by green bean-like pods that may be straight or curved, up to 12cm long, turning black when ripe. Drought and heat tolerant, needing little summer water. Frost tolerant. If you have a spot with reflected heat where nothing else seems to grow, this may be a good choice. To keep in shape, it should be pruned after flowering.

Senna didymobotrya

Popcorn-Bush

Native to Africa

An evergreen, upright or spreading shrub or small tree up to 3m high and 2m wide with arching branches. Young shoots and leaves are finely downy. Pinnate leaves up to 50cm long comprise eight to sixteen oblong leaflets 6cm long. It produces large clusters of golden-yellow flowers 3cm wide in dense upright clusters 20 to

30cm long. These open from brown buds with a distinct scent of peanut butter in late summer and autumn, making an impressive sight. Easily grown in any type of well-drained soil in full sun. Tolerant of heat and summer drought once established. Makes a large, bold, impressive shrub for the back of a border that is frost free. After flowering, especially when young, it should be pruned to keep in shape, forming a dense bush.

Senna spectabilis

Native to tropical America

A deciduous, fast-growing and spreading tree 4 to 5m high with young branchlets that are softly hairy. Pinnate, bright-green leaves 30cm or more long have ten to fifteen pairs of ovate to lance-shape leaflets 5 to 6cm long, which are softly hairy on the underneath. On the ends of branches, spectacular erect racemes 30 to 60cm long contain many beautiful cup-shaped, golden-yellow flowers 3 to 4cm in diameter, like shining lamps. These are followed by round seed pods 10 to 30cm long that ripen to dark brown, each containing many seeds. Grow in full sun in a warm, sheltered spot that is frost free. Drought tolerant, requiring little summer water once established. Grows best in fertile, neutral to acid soil. Makes a spectacular specimen or street tree. Easily raised from seed.

SILENE
Caryophyllaceae

Widely distributed in the Northern Hemisphere, particularly the Mediterranean region

A genus of about 700 species of annuals, biennials, perennials and some subshrubs. Leaves are opposite, varying from linear to obovate, and entire. Flowers often have notched or split, clawed petals and a tubular inflated calyx borne in panicle-like terminal leafy cymes.

Silene armeria
Sweet William Catchfly

Native to central and southern Europe

A sticky-hairy annual or biennial with upright stems 20 to 30cm high and 15cm wide. Leaves are grey-green, 1 to 5cm long, elliptic, oval or narrowly oval, smooth. Stems are glabrous or slightly hairy with sticky areas, especially just below the flowers. In late summer, it bears broad, dense, rounded panicles of deep carmine-pink flowers to 1.5cm across with shallowly notched petals. Easily grown in well-drained soil in full sun as an annual. Reasonably drought tolerant, it resents winter wet. Often seeds freely. Excellent for the front of borders or wild garden.

Silene coeli-rosa syn. *Eudianthe coeli-rosa*

Native to northern Africa and southern Europe

A hardy annual that grows in a neat mound and has erect, slender, hairless stems with lance-shaped, mid-green leaves 1 to 5cm long. From summer to autumn, it produces beautiful loose, long-stalked clusters of spreading, white-centred, rose-pink flowers to 2.5cm across with deeply notched petals. They make good cut flowers. Grows best in full sun in well-drained soil and will grow in the poorest of soils. Summer drought tolerant but performs better with some water. Apart from growing well in borders and rockeries, they are also good at attracting birds and bees to your garden. It can be invasive.

SOLANUM
Solanaceae

Native to most temperate parts of the world

A vast genus containing perhaps 1,500 species of annuals, biennials, herbaceous perennials, evergreen and deciduous shrubs, sometimes climbing, some spiny, rarely trees. Leaves are typically alternate and simple. Flowers are typically star or wheel-shaped, usually in clusters or racemes in white, yellow, purple or blue. After pollination, plants produce fruits, which are often berries. It includes many of the world's most important edible plants, such as the potato, tomato and aubergine or eggplant. Many species are cultivated as ornamentals. Some are poisonous, such as nightshade.

Solanum aviculare
Kangaroo Apple

Native to New Zealand and Australia

An upright to spreading evergreen shrub, which makes fast growth to 3m high and 2m wide. Lance-shaped to ovate, deep-green leaves 8 to 30cm long are entire or irregularly lobed. In spring and summer, it bears clusters of mauve to blue-violet or white, 2 to 3cm wide, shallowly-lobed flowers. These are followed by 2 to 3cm ovoid green fruit that is poisonous while green. Grow in full sun or partial shade in a fertile, well-drained neutral to alkaline soil. Moderately drought tolerant but performs better with some summer water.

Solanum betaceum syn. *Cyphomandra betacea*
Tamarillo, Tree Tomato

Native to Peru

A tree-like shrub that makes fast growth to 4m high or more spreading to 2m wide, with a life expectancy of about five to twelve years. Pointed oval leaves are soft, downy, 20cm long and 10cm wide, and have a strong pungent smell. Small pinkish white flowers, 2 to 3cm wide, form clusters of 10 to 50 flowers, which are fragrant and attract insects. These appear in spring and summer and are followed by 5 to 8cm long orange-red plum-like fruit, one to six fruits per cluster. These are edible only when fully ripe, with a sharp taste and may be eaten fresh but are usually stewed or made into a jelly. They are produced from late summer to winter. Grow in full sun or in partial shade. It thrives best in deep, fertile soil with some water during summer. The roots are shallow and not pronounced, therefore can be damaged by strong winds.

Solanum crispum
Chilean Potato Tree

Native to Chile and Peru

This vigorous, deciduous or semi-evergreen shrub annually produces scrambling downy stems 2 to 5m long. Ovate,

enna alata.

Senna corymbosa.

Senna spectabilis.

lene armeria.

Solanum betaceum.

Solanum laxum 'Album'.

olanum wendlandii.

Sparaxis tricolor.

downy with crisped margins. In summer it bears slightly fragrant lilac to purple-blue flowers 2.5cm across with a bright yellow centre, in loose terminal clusters 15cm across. Grows well in full sun or partial shade with moderate summer water. Ideal for growing against a wall, as it withstands hard pruning. This shrub is well suited for alkaline soils. It will withstand a few degrees of frost. 'Glasnevin', an Irish cultivar, is an improved form with a longer flowering season and richer flower colour.

Solanum laxum syn. *Solanum jasminoides*

Potato Vine

Native to eastern Brazil

This vigorous, evergreen shrub with twining stems 2 to 5m high climbs by winding leaf stalks around supports. Glossy, dark-green, lance-shaped leaves are 4 to 8cm long, while older leaves, sometimes three to five lobed, have a purplish tinge. In summer and autumn, it bears fragrant, pale bluish-white flowers 2cm across with yellow anthers in terminal and axillary clusters. Grows well in full sun or partial shade with moderate summer water. Can be cut back severely at any time of year to prevent becoming tangled. Ideal for covering walls or pergolas for light summer shade. 'Album' is a more beautiful pure white variety, the one more often seen growing in gardens. 'Aureovariegatum' is less strong, growing with beautiful golden yellow edges to its leaves.

Solanum mauritianum

Mauritius Nightshade, Tree Tobacco

Native to South America

A soft-stemmed, multi-branched shrub or small tree 2 to 4m high and 2m wide, with a strong odour. Young branches are green and densely covered in felt. Large, softly hairy, dark-green, lance-shaped leaves are up to 30cm long and silver-green underneath. During winter and spring, stiff terminal flower stems are produced to 20cm long. They are topped with 15cm-wide clusters of star-like, white-striped, slightly-scented, violet flowers to 2cm wide. These are followed by 1cm-round green or yellow ornamental fruit that is attractive to birds. Grow in full sun in any well-drained garden soil. Grows best with moderate summer water, but will survive with little water. An interesting and attractive tree for the back of a border with its shimmering silver-green leaves and violet flowers. Grows well as a pot or container plant that flowers when small. Easily raised from seed but naturalised in many tropical countries where it has become invasive.

Solanum rantonnetii see *Lycianthes rantonnetii*

Solanum wendlandii

Costa Rican Nightshade, Giant Potato Vine, Giant Tuberose

Native to Costa Rica, Panama, Nicaragua

A beautiful, deciduous, shrubby climber with stout woody stems to 5m or more high with hooked spines on the stems and leaves. Bright-green, 10 to 25cm-long leaves on the upper parts of stems are three lobed, while they are pinnate on the lower parts. Big, showy, branched clusters of lilac-blue flowers are 15cm across, containing many 4 to 6cm wide, shallow trumpet-shaped flowers with a distinctive star shape and yellow stamens. These weigh branches down in late summer. It can be trimmed to maintain a desired shape and size, which makes it perfect for arbours, pergolas or to clamber into trees. This is a beautiful plant but extremely tender, so should only be grown in sheltered locations in full sun or partial shade with a fairly rich, well-drained soil. Tolerant of summer drought but does better with summer rain and rich, balanced feeding.

SOLLYA *see* BILLARDIERA

Sophora japonica see Styphnolobium japonicum

SPARAXIS

Iridaceae

Harlequin Flowers

Native to Cape Province of South Africa

A small genus of about thirteen species of cormous perennials. With exceptionally hot and dry summers in some parts of South Africa, the plants have adapted by remaining dormant during these times, only to bloom when conditions are cool and moist. They are grown for their brightly-coloured, upright flowers.

Sparaxis tricolor

Wandflower, Harlequin Flower

A cormous perennial with a basal fan of upright sword-shaped leaves 30 to 40cm long, which are produced in autumn and die down during summer. Over a long period in spring, wiry stems carry loose heads of up to five brightly-multicoloured, open star-shaped flowers 5 to 8cm across. Flowers range over shades of red, orange, yellow, lavender or white, with a bright yellow throat outlined in black, giving it the common name. Grow in full sun in any well-drained soil. Water freely while growing, but it is then drought tolerant in summer. In frost-free areas, grow in large drifts around deciduous trees and shrubs. Excellent for adding a splash of colour in beds and borders in Mediterranean gardens or containers. Can be left in the ground for several seasons, when crowded lift in summer and replant in autumn. Easily propagated by seed.

SPARTIUM

Fabaceae

Native to the Mediterranean region

A genus comprising just a single species of deciduous shrub.

Spartium junceum
Spanish Broom

A hardy, ornamental shrub with many green, upright, cylindrical, almost leafless stems up to 3m high and wide. Inconspicuous, dark-green, deciduous, narrow leaves, 1 to 3cm long, are silky-hairy underneath. Many large, bright-yellow, honey-vanilla scented, pea-like flowers 2.5cm long are borne in clusters at the ends of the flexible, erect, green broom-like stems in spring and early summer. They are followed by flattened hairy seed pods to 8cm long. Grows best in full sun. Ideal for a dry garden, as it needs no summer water. Thrives on neglect and grows in poor, chalky, well-drained soil in full sun. Excellent for coastal conditions as it withstands salt-laden sea breezes. Makes a showy bank cover. Ideal for beds and borders in Mediterranean gardens. Easily raised from seed. It can become an invasive weed.

SPHAERALCEA
Malvaceae

Globe Mallows, False Mallows

Native to the drier regions of North America, South America

A genus of about 40 to 60 species of annuals, perennials and shrubs. Leaves are spirally arranged, and usually palmate or toothed. Both stems and leaves are downy. Like other Malvaceae species, the flowers are saucer- or cup-shaped, with the stamens joined into a column in the centre.

Sphaeralcea ambigua
Apricot mallow, Desert Hollyhock

Native to the deserts of Mexico and the southwest United States

A shrubby perennial that forms a rounded mound about 1m high and 90cm wide. Upright or decumbent stems bear spirally arranged, linear lance-shaped to rounded toothed leaves covered in white felt. It bears orange or pinkish cup-shaped mallow-like flowers for most of summer, with the stamens joined into a column around the styles. Flowers are rich in nectar and provide a long season of feasting for bees and butterflies. Tolerant of summer drought and hot dry positions. Also, mildly frost tolerant, a truly hardy desert survivor. Grow in well-drained, sandy or rocky soil with low fertility. It is usually considered a short-lived perennial, as it can flower itself to a standstill after a few years, but it is easy to raise from seed, and can even self-seed in a dry garden.

SPIREA
Rosaceae

Native to temperate regions of Europe, Asia, North America

A genus of about 80 species of hardy, evergreen or deciduous shrubs. Leaves are simple and usually short stalked, arranged in a spiralling, alternate fashion. In most species, leaves are lance-shaped and about 2.5 to 10cm long. Leaf margins are usually toothed, occasionally cut or lobed, and rarely smooth. Many small flowers are clustered together in inflorescences, usually in dense panicles, umbrella-like corymbs, or grape-like clusters. The radial symmetry of each flower is fivefold, with flowers usually bisexual, rarely unisexual. These flowers have five sepals and five white, pink, or reddish petals that are usually longer than the sepals. Each flower has many stamens. They are mainly sun-loving plants.

Spirea cantoniensis
Bridal Wreath, Reeve's Spiraea

Native to China

An upright to spreading, semi-evergreen shrub to 2m high and wide with arching branches that give it a rounded and spreading appearance. Lance-shaped, 4cm-long, dark-green leaves are toothed. White flowers are small, pompom-like and grow in umbel-like clusters 5 to 6cm wide on short branchlets along the length of arching stems. The overall effect for a few weeks in spring is one of a white waterfall and absolutely stunning. Grows best in full sun but will take partial shade. Drought tolerant once established, but flowers are better with some summer water. Easy to grow in most well-drained soils. It will grow in coastal gardens and, once established, it tolerates frost and neglect. It makes a great informal hedge or screen. Of the species, this is the most suited to warmer climates. Prune after flowering by removing old weak growth. 'Flore Pleno' has double white flowers.

SPREKELIA
Amaryllidaceae

Native to Mexico, Central and South America

A small genus of only two species of frost-tender, bulbous perennials. Only one species is usually grown. The species are characterised by flamboyant red flowers with somewhat narrowed petals, long anthers and large stamens with yellow pollen.

Sprekelia formosissima
Aztec Lily, Jacobean Lily, St. James Lily

A tender, bulbous perennial whose lance-shaped, basal leaves to 50cm long appear in spring just before the spectacular flowers. Several leaves are produced from each bulb growing upright at first, then flopping over as they get longer. It produces a single short, sturdy stem to 30cm tall, which bears orchid-like dark crimson flowers 12cm across with one erect upper segment, two lower horizontal segments, and three narrow, pendant segments rolled together into a tube at the base, then separating into individual pendant segments. The flower has long prominent stamens. Blooming in late spring to early summer and often again in autumn, these elegant flowers only last a few days. Grow in well-drained, slightly alkaline soil in full sun. Give water while in growth, reduce water as leaves fade, keep dry while dormant. Excessive moisture may cause the bulbs to rot or not flower. It is most effective when planted in groups, but as the roots resent disturbance, do not lift the bulbs until necessary. Looks good in a sunny border or especially in pots.

STACHYS
Lamiaceae
Widely distributed throughout northern temperate regions

A genus of 300 to 400 species of shrubs and annual or perennial herbs, one of the largest in the mint family. The precise extent of the genus and its relationship to other genera in its subfamily are poorly known. Growing from 50cm to 3m tall, with simple, opposite, triangular leaves with serrate margins. In most species, leaves are softly hairy. Flowers are clustered in the axils of leaves on the upper part of the stem.

Stachys byzantina
Lambs' Ears

Native to the Middle East

A mat-forming, herbaceous perennial up to 45cm high and spreading to 60cm wide. Stems and rosettes of leaves are usually densely covered with grey or silver-white, silky-lanate hairs. Soft, thick, white-woolly lance-shaped leaves are up to 10cm long, resembling the ears of a lamb, giving it the common name. Flowering stems are erect, often branched, and tend to be four-angled, growing 40 to 80cm tall. Upright woolly flower stalks bear many whorls of small purplish flowers in summer and autumn. This perennial grows in low, spreading clumps of attractive silver leaves and is often used for its texture and foliage rather than flowers. Grow in full sun or partial shade in well-drained soil. Drought tolerant once established, making it a good choice for xeriscaping and low water gardens. 'Silver Carpet' has intensely silvered, white leaves.

STERNBERGIA
Amaryllidaceae
Autumn Daffodil

Native to the Mediterranean region

A small genus of about eight species of frost-hardy, bulbous perennials. Often growing in rocky places, they look a bit like Crocus, although they are more closely related to Narcissus. Mostly flowers are yellow and bloom in autumn, but there are two spring-flowering species and one that is white. They are winter growing and summer dormant. Many of the autumn-blooming species bloom after the first rains and before their leaves are produced.

Sternbergia candida
Native to southwest Turkey

A tender, bulbous perennial with lance- to strap-shaped leaves 15cm long. Long grey-green leaves to 1cm wide appear in late winter to early spring with the flowers. It is the largest-flowered species in the genus, and the only one that produces pure white flowers, that are glistening and crystalline, and emits a fragrance similar to that of Freesia on stems up to 20cm high. It thrives in full sun in most moderately fertile, dry to medium, well-drained soils in order to develop into a large bulb. Once the mother bulbs are established, it will grow freely and offset naturally.

Sternbergia lutea
Native to Mediterranean region

A clump-forming bulbous perennial with narrow, lance-shaped, deep-green leaves to 30cm long. These are produced in autumn and remain green for several months, then die down with summer heat. Solitary, beautiful, goblet-shaped, waxy golden-yellow flowers 5cm across appear during autumn on stems 15 to 20cm high. Leaves and flowers usually appear at the same time. Easily grown in full sun in most moderately fertile, dry to medium, well-drained soils. Bulbs are intolerant of winter wet, so they need soil with excellent drainage. Summer dormant, so no water is needed. Good for growing in sunny borders, rock gardens, Mediterranean gardens or near pools. Good for cut flowers. When bulbs become crowded, lift, divide and replant in the summer dormant period.

STIPA
Poaceae
Feather Grass, Needle Grass

Native to temperate and warm temperate areas worldwide

A large genus of perhaps 300 species of frost-hardy, evergreen or deciduous feather or needle grasses. Many species formerly assigned to Stipa have been reclassified into new genera. They are grown for their form or for the large open inflorescences.

Stipa calamagrostis see *Achnatherum calamagrostis*

Stipa ichu see *Jarava ichu*

Stipa lagascae* syn. *Stipa gigantea
Giant Feather Grass, Spanish Oats, Golden Oats

Native to Portugal, southern and central Spain

A densely tufted evergreen perennial to 2m high and 1.2m wide. Clumps of narrow, linear, arching leaves grow 60 to 90cm high. Large golden oat-like plumes up to 50cm long appear in the early summer on stems to 2m high. These shimmer in an attractive broad cloud. Easy to grow in full sun in any well drained, even poor, soil. Drought tolerant after flowering and during the heat of summer as the plant becomes dormant.

partium junceum.

Sphaeralcea ambigua.

Spirea cantoniensis.

prekelia formosissima.

Stachys byzantina.

Sternbergia lutea.

ipa lagascae.

Strelitzia nicolai.

Strelitzia juncea.

Stipa tenuissima see *Nassella tenuissima*

STRELITZIA
Strelitziaceae
Bird of Paradise

Native to Madagascar, southern Africa

A genus of about four rhizomatous and tree-like herbaceous perennials that grow in clumps and have thick, fleshy roots. They are characterised by their large, paddle-shaped leaves arranged in a fan-like manner on long petioles. These provide an attractive display even when not in bloom. Flowers grow from boat-shaped bracts, with three upright petals and three colourful, often contrasting sepals. These flowers closely resemble the plumage of tropical birds, hence the common name. Flowers produce copious amounts of nectar to attract nectar-feeding birds, which play a crucial role in the plant's reproductive cycle. These plants are popular in tropical and subtropical landscapes because of their bold and exotic look.

Strelitzia juncea
Narrow Leaved Bird of Paradise

Native to South Africa

An evergreen perennial, which forms a large clump, 1 to 2m high and about 1m wide with upright, cylindrical, blue-green, narrow stalks 1.2 to 1.5m long, which are actually leafless petioles. The most striking feature is its extraordinary flowers, which arise from tall stems up to 1.8m just above the foliage. They emerge from boat-shaped bracts and are composed of three upright petals and three sepals. The outer-most petal is bright orange, while the inner petals are blue and purple. Typically, the plant blooms in autumn to late spring, but under perfect conditions it can blossom all year round. The flowers are long-lasting and can remain on the plant for several weeks. Grow in full sun to partial shade in fertile well-drained soil. Drought tolerant once established. A popular ornamental plant in gardens and landscapes worldwide. Looks great when massed in beds and borders. Ideal for Mediterranean or subtropical gardens. This species is the most frost-resistant of the genus. Makes excellent cut flowers.

Strelitzia nicolai
White Bird of Paradise

Native to South Africa

Grown primarily for its dramatic foliage, it brings a sensational tropical accent to the garden. This massive, evergreen species of banana-like plants with erect woody stems can reach a height of 7 to 8m, and the clumps formed can spread as far as 3.5m. Leaves are enormous at 1.5 to 3m, oblong, shiny grey-green with long, thick leaf stalks. They are arranged fanwise on the stems, often tearing in the wind, and can come to resemble giant feathers. Blooms throughout the year with a peak in spring and summer. Large, blue and white flowers up to 50cm long are produced in succession from purplish-grey, beak-like spathes. Spectacular blooms resemble the head of a bird, with a white crest and purple beak. Since one flower spathe sprouts out of another, this gives them a double-decker appearance. This plant is highly sought after for its striking appearance and is grown as an ornamental for its beautiful flowers and lush, tropical foliage. Performs best in full sun to partial shade in fertile, well-drained soils. Reasonably drought tolerant once established.

STREPTOSOLEN
Solanaceae

Native to Colombia, Venezuela, Ecuador, Peru

A monotypic genus of an evergreen shrub.

Streptosolen jamesonii
Marmalade Bush

A tender, evergreen, rambling shrub that without support can grow to 1.5m high and spread 1.5m wide. If it is trained against a wall or trellis, it may reach to 3m or more high. Stems are clothed in rough, hairy, wrinkled, oval leaves 3 to 5cm long that are sticky to touch. Long, flexible branches arch under the weight of panicles of tubular, striking orange flowers 3 to 5cm across from early spring to late autumn, though a few may be seen throughout the year. They bloom in large terminal corymbs to 15cm across. The flowers emerge with yellow-orange petals that are often slightly reflexed and age to deep orange-red, which give the plant the multi-coloured look that reminds one of marmalade. Easily grown in fertile, well-drained soil in full sun or partial shade. Summer drought tolerant once established. It also looks good in a hanging basket. Butterflies and birds regularly visit.

STYPHNOLOBIUM
Fabaceae
Necklacepod

Native to China and to the Americas

A genus of only three or four species of small trees and shrubs. Previously, it was included within the genus Sophora. The deciduous leaves are pinnate, with 9 to 21 leaflets. Species are cultivated for their panicles of pea-shaped flowers in axillary pendulous racemes, but need long hot summers to flower well.

Styphnolobium japonicum syn. *Sophora japonica*
Japanese Pagoda Tree, Chinese Scholar Tree, Pagoda Tree

Native to China, Korea

A large, deciduous tree to 15m high spreading to 15m with a rounded crown. With age, the bark of this tree is an attractive feature, having a grey, corrugated appearance. Glossy, light-green, 30cm long, compound leaves have up to seventeen leaflets each 1 to 5cm long, with hairy undersides, that turn yellow in autumn. Loose, 30cm long panicles of small, creamy-white, pea-shaped, sweetly-perfumed flowers appear in late summer. Unusual pods that resemble a string of beads follow the flowers. This tree thrives in warm, dry conditions. Drought tolerant once established but needs moderate summer water when young. Easily grown in most well-drained soil in full sun but can take partial shade. Train to a single leader when young and remove any irregular growth in late winter or early spring. With age can make a refreshing shade tree.

SWAINSONA
Fabaceae

Native to Australia

A genus of 85 species of prostrate to erect annual or perennial herbs or sub-shrubs, often with many stems at the base. Flowers are borne in a raceme in leaf axils on an erect stalk with bracts at the base, which are joined to form a bell-shaped tube with five equal lobes, or the upper two lobes shorter. Pea flowers comprise four petals, the 'standard', the 'keel' and two 'wings'. The standard petal is kidney-shaped to more or less round, usually longer than the wings and often longer than the keel.

Swainsona formosa

Native to southern and western Australia

A prostrate annual or short-lived perennial herb, with several dense, softly-hairy stems growing to about 2m high. Grey-green pinnate leaves are mostly 10 to 15cm long with about fifteen elliptic to ovate leaflets 10 to 30cm long, the end leaflet slightly longer. There are broad, densely hairy stipules, sometimes 1.5cm or more, at the base of each petiole. The classic desert pea flower has deep scarlet or red petals with a black or dark red boss. These are about 9cm long, borne in groups of five or six, ranging from red through pinks to yellow and even albino forms. The petals are considerably distorted from the 'typical' pea shape to be almost unrecognisable as a member of the pea family. Flowering occurs from winter through to summer. Grow in moderately fertile well-drained soil in full sun. Drought and frost tolerant once established. Also good in a large tub or a terracotta drainage pipe stood upright and filled with gritty, free draining soil, or in a hanging basket. Usually treated as an annual, it should flower four months after sowing from seed.

Swainsona galegifolia
Darling Pea

Native to New South Wales and Queensland, Australia

A long-lived shrubby perennial growing to 60cm high. Branches 1m long grow annually from the crown, the outer ones pushed outward and leading to a more spreading shape. Branches are well clothed to ground level with fine pinnate leaves about 10cm long, smooth and sometimes greyish, forming a bold, graceful outline, even without flowers. Flower spikes up to 15cm long are held well on long stems. They open to sturdy pea flowers about 2.5cm across, from pure white through clear pinks and mauves to magenta and crimson, followed by balloon-like pods often tinted pink. Easy to cultivate with a long flowering season, the best display in late spring. Grow in moderately fertile, well-drained soil in full sun. Drought and frost tolerant once established. The old, flowered branches should be cut out each year at the end of winter, or in warmer climates after the main flowering season in autumn, to maintain a strong plant. Useful for quick cover in a difficult situation and excellent as a single specimen.

SYAGRUS
Arecaceae

Native to South America

A complex genus of 65 species of pinnate-leaved palms. Most are solitary trunked, but a few have clustering trunks. The stems are normally spineless, but some species have spiny leaf sheaths or spines. Those species that have upright trunks grow 2 to 36m tall. Many are relatively cold tolerant and will grow in warm temperate and subtropical regions.

Syagrus romanzoffiana
Queen Palm

A solitary, straight, slender-trunked palm quickly reaching to 18m high and 6 to 10m wide. Can grow up to 60cm per year. The smooth, light-grey trunk is ringed with old leaf bases. A high canopy of arching, deep-green leaves can be up to 6m long with 1m-long pendulous leaflets. The inflorescence to 1m long contains many small creamy-white flowers and usually appears during spring and summer. These give way to showy, hanging clusters of yellow edible dates. Easily grown in full sun in well-drained, slightly acidic soil. Drought tolerant once established, but grows better with some summer water. Grows well in coastal gardens, as it withstands salt-laden sea breezes. A mature palm is moderately frost hardy. A beautiful specimen tree.

SYZYGIUM
Myrtaceae

Native to tropical and subtropical regions of the world

A large genus of about 1,200 species of aromatic evergreen shrubs and trees. They have opposite leathery leaves and terminal or axillary cymes or panicles of saucer-shaped four- or five-petalled flowers, each with a prominent boss of stamens.

Syzygium paniculatum
Australian Brush Cherry, Brush Cherry

Native to southeastern Australia

An evergreen, hardy small tree, which can grow to 10m or more tall and 5m wide. As a shrub, it lends itself to shearing into

Streptosolen jamesonii.

Styphnolobium japonicum.

Swainsona formosa.

Syagrus romanzoffiana.

Syzygium paniculatum.

Tamarix parviflora.

Tanacetum densum ssp. amani.

Tecoma stans.

a pyramid, formal shape or hedge. Slender branches are dense with nearly stalkless leaves 8 to 10cm long. These are elliptic to lance-shaped, reddish-bronze when young, becoming dark glossy green. In summer it bears white flowers 2 to 3cm wide with many yellow stamens in small axillary and terminal clusters. Fruit is pink to rose purple, showy, 1 to 2cm long, edible but insipid. Easily grown in full sun or partial shade in well-drained soil. Drought tolerant once established but grows better with some summer water. Prune to encourage a desired shape and denser foliage. They can get leggy with gaps in the foliage if not pruned. Hedges need frequent clipping to stay neat. As a specimen tree in a large lawn or park, it is beautiful but formal in appearance. With its new, red foliage and showy fruit, it makes a most useful plant in a garden. Flowers and fruits more prolifically after pruning.

T

TAMARIX
Tamaricaceae
Tamarisk

Native to drier areas of west Europe, the Mediterranean region

A genus of 50 to 60 species of frost-hardy, evergreen or deciduous shrubs or trees growing 1 to 18m high and forming dense thickets. They are characterised by slender branches and grey-green foliage. Bark of young branches is smooth and reddish-brown. As they age, the bark becomes grey brown, ridged and furrowed. Leaves are scale-like, almost like that of junipers. Pink to white flowers appear in dense masses on 5 to 10cm long spikes at branch tips in summer.

Tamarix parviflora
Smallflower Tamarisk

Native to southeast Europe

A spreading shrub 2 to 5m high with graceful brown or purple arching branches and pale-green, scale-like foliage. Flowers are rose-pink, appearing towards the ends of branches in plumes up to 5cm long in spring on last year's growth. Easily grown in full sun in well-drained, light sandy soil and saline soils that would be toxic to other plants. Summer drought tolerant once established. As it is resistant to salt-laden sea breezes and wind, it is ideal for planting in coastal gardens. Often used as a windbreak or hedge in exposed areas.

TANACETUM
Asteraceae

Native to dry slopes of northern temperate regions

A genus of about 160 species of mainly perennial herbs, some annuals and subshrubs. Some are a few centimetres tall, while others reach 1.5m high. They vary in form, with one or more branching stems growing erect or prostrate, usually from rhizomes. They are hairy to hairless in texture, and most are aromatic. Leaves are alternate, sometimes borne on petioles, usually deeply lobed and may have toothed edges. Most species have flowers in loose or dense inflorescences. Flowers have layers of distinct bracts around the base and may be flat to hemispherical. These have many disc florets, sometimes over 300, in shades of yellow or white with yellowish bases. Some species lack true ray florets but have flat, yellowish disc florets that look like rays.

Tanacetum argenteum
Feverfew

Native to eastern Mediterranean

A mound-forming, usually evergreen, woody perennial 15cm high, with a stout woody rootstock to 40cm or more across. Silvery-downy stems have intricate, laced, soft, silver foliage 2 to 7cm long, which may be toothed. In summer, daisy-like yellow flowerheads 3 to 4mm across are borne singly or in corymbs. The trailing and prostrate habit of this plant brings a wealth of silver foliage to the garden. Drought tolerant, perfect for dry areas in sun or semi-shade, fully hardy. Grow in well-drained soil. Ideal for coastal gardens, as it is mildly salt-tolerant. Adds spreading silver foliage to borders, cottage gardens, Mediterranean and rock gardens, in containers, amongst limestone rocks and on cliffs.

Tanacetum densum ssp. *amani*

Native to southeastern Turkey

A mound-forming, usually evergreen, woody perennial with white downy stems and ovate to broadly elliptic two-pinnatisect downy, grey-white leaves. They are around 8 to 13cm tall, creating a ground cover that becomes a foundation for clusters of small, golden-yellow, button-like flowers appearing on stems slightly above the foliage in late spring and early summer. The yellow and white make an appealing contrast, particularly in a large colony. These clusters on slightly fuzzy, prostrate stems form a frilly mound radiating a silvery white to almost blue cast. Easily grown in full sun in well-drained soil. Drought tolerant once established. The contrast of silvery white against the greens of other leaves is striking. Its habit of crawling over stones and inching its way up and down slopes makes it ideal for a rock garden. Can be pruned back hard regularly, as it will come back on woody stems following pruning. Cut back any thinning spots close to ground level for dense re-sprouting.

TECOMA
Bignoniaceae
Trumpetbush

Native to the Americas

A genus of about six species of frost-tender, evergreen climbers, shrubs or small trees. Only one species is usually grown.

Tecoma capensis see *Tecomaria capensis*

Tecoma stans
Yellow Bells, Trumpet Bush, Yellow Elder

Native to tropical America

An evergreen shrub or small tree that quickly reaches 5m or more high and 3m or more wide with open, upright branches. Pale-green, pinnate leaves up to 35cm long are divided into five to thirteen oblong-ovate to lance-shaped, toothed leaflets 5 to 10cm long. Dense, many-flowered, pendulous clusters, up to 15cm long, contain showy bright-yellow, funnel-shaped flowers 3 to 5cm wide. They are produced in great profusion during summer and autumn. Easily grown in deep, well-drained soil in full sun. Drought tolerant once established. Requires heat to grow well. Makes an excellent windbreak for coastal gardens.

TECOMARIA
Bignoniaceae

Native to southern Africa

The genus Tecomaria was absorbed into Tecoma because the leading botanists working on the family considered that the differences in the flowers between Tecomaria and Tecoma were not enough to justify keeping them apart and they should be treated as one. Hence *Tecomaria capensis* became *Tecoma capensis*. However, recent molecular studies show that Tecomaria is in fact more closely related to Podranea than Tecoma, so it can no longer be lumped together with Tecoma, and the genus Tecomaria is reinstated. This is a case where DNA evidence overturns decisions made on genetic relationships that are based just on morphology (how the plants look).

Tecomaria capensis syn. *Tecoma capensis*
Cape Honeysuckle

A fast-growing, scrambling, multi-stemmed shrub, which may grow up to 2 to 3m high and spread over 2.5m. It is evergreen in warm regions. It has pinnately compound, glossy leaves that have oval leaflets with blunt teeth. Flowering time for this shrub is highly erratic, and it often flowers all year round. Flowers are tubular in showy, many-flowered heads and vary from red, deep orange, yellow to salmon. Grow in full sun or partial shade in well-drained soil, but it can become chlorotic if the soil is alkaline. Drought tolerant once established, well suited to water-wise gardens. Also withstands hot dry conditions. To keep compact, it requires regular severe pruning, which induces fresh growth where the flowers are produced. Can make a low hedge, cover banks or may be trained as a wall shrub. Makes a most striking shrub when in flower. The cultivar 'Aurea' has yellow flowers with paler-green leaves. This is much smaller growing, and more tender, requiring a warm sheltered position to grow well.

TELOPEA
Proteaceae
Waratah

Native to southeastern Australia

A genus of five species of tender evergreen shrubs or small trees. Alternate leaves are simple, leathery and sometime toothed or lobed. Tubular flowers 2cm long are in pairs, which are split on the lower side. Each flower has four short lobes with the margins rolled under and a prominent stigma. The inflorescence is in dense, terminal, umbel-like heads surrounded by red or pink bracts. These appear during spring and summer.

Telopea speciosissima

Native to New South Wales, Australia

An upright shrub to about 3m tall, but often shorter. It usually grows as a single- or few-stemmed plant until it is cut back by fire. It then regenerates from an underground woody growth and may become multi-stemmed. Leaves up to 25cm long are large, leathery and may be irregularly serrated. Flowers occur from mid-spring to early summer in a tight cluster at the ends of erect stems. The inflorescence is 15cm or more in diameter, usually a brilliant red, with large, leafy bracts at the base. Grow in well-drained sandy, slightly acidic soil in full sun or partial shade. Water during hot or dry spells, never letting the soil dry out completely. Over-watering in heavy soils will cause waterlogging. Plants are tolerant of at least moderate frost. The species is widely cultivated for the cut-flower market both in Australia and overseas, being long-lasting. Several selected forms are being brought into cultivation and hybrids with other Telopea species, with variations in the colour of flowers and bracts.

TETRADENIA syn. IBOZA
Lamiaceae

Native to tropical and southern Africa

A small genus of about twenty species of perennials and shrubs with stems normally square in the cross-section.

Tetradenia riparia syn. *Iboza riparia*

Misty Plume Bush, Nutmeg Bush

Native to South Africa

A small, semi-deciduous, strongly aromatic shrub that grows 3 to 5m high. It is slightly succulent and has an irregular branch pattern. Stems are brown and smooth, except for the younger portions, which are covered with glandular hairs and have a ruby tinge. Glandular hairs also cover both surfaces of the leaves, making them slightly sticky to the touch. Broad, velvety, heart-shaped leaves are 10cm long with toothed edges. The spectacular, large, upright, terminal, branched inflorescence, 20cm or more long, comprises many tiny, creamy-white to purple fragrant flowers produced throughout winter and spring, completely covering the plant, providing colour in cooler months. Easily damaged by frost and cold wind. Grow in full sun or partial shade. It prefers water in summer but not as much in winter, thus making it a good waterwise plant for summer rainfall areas. As it can become tall or untidy, cut back after flowering.

TEUCRIUM

Lamiaceae

Germander

Native to the Mediterranean region

A genus of about 300 species of perennial herbs or shrubs with four-cornered stems, often with simple hairs. Leaves are opposite, simple or with three leaflets, sometimes with lobed or serrated edges. Whorled clusters of two to six tubular to bell-shaped, sometimes two-lipped flowers are white, blue or cream coloured.

Teucrium fruticans

Bush Germander

A bushy evergreen shrub with loosely-growing, silver stems up to 2m high and wide. Aromatic, grey-green, lance-shaped leaves up to 3cm long are white woolly underneath. Tiny, pale blue, tubular to bell-shaped flowers 3cm long, in terminal spikes 10cm long, appear in summer. Easily grown in full sun in well-drained neutral to alkaline soil. Drought tolerant once established, it is easily damaged by wet, poorly drained soil. Good for informal hedging as it tolerates shearing. Makes a tough, grey-leaved plant as a specimen or mass planted in a dry garden. Great for coastal gardens, Mediterranean gardens in beds and borders.

THUNBERGIA

Acanthaceae

Native to Africa, Madagascar, tropical Asia

A genus of about 100 species of typically vigorous, climbing vines with tendrils that can reach up to several metres long. Leaves are simple, alternate, usually heart-shaped or oval. Flowers are trumpet-shaped, in many colours. These are in clusters at the ends of stems and typically appear during summer. Several species are great favourites in tropical and subtropical landscaping.

Thunbergia natalensis

Natal Blue Thunbergia, Dwarf Blue Thunbergia

Native to southern Africa

A soft-wooded shrub growing to around 1m high that comes from areas with high summer rainfall and dry winters. It is one of the few Thunbergia species that is not a climber. Stems grow from a woody base and tend to be unbranched with dense, attractive, opposite, rich-green, heart-shaped leaves growing along the stem. Conspicuously displayed outside the foliage, plentiful good-sized 8cm lavender-blue trumpet-like flowers highlighted by a bright golden-yellow throat appear in mid-spring to summer. Grow in well-drained, humus-rich soil in partial shade. In areas with dry or cold winters the stems die down, and the plant becomes dormant with stems emerging again in spring. However, in warmer areas with regular rainfall, stems may not die back in winter and will need to be cut back to encourage new spring growth and keep the shape tidy. It is useful as a filler plant or ground cover under trees or amongst shrubs. It can become invasive.

THYMUS

Lamicaeae

Thyme

Native to temperate regions in Europe, North Africa and Asia

A genus of over 300 species of aromatic, herbaceous perennials and subshrubs to 40cm tall, with narrow or even wiry stems. Leaves are evergreen in most species, in opposite pairs, oval, entire and small, 4 to 20mm long, usually aromatic. Thyme flowers are in dense terminal heads with an uneven calyx, with the upper lip three-lobed, and are yellow, white or purple. Cultivated for its fragrant leaves and used as a culinary herb in Mediterranean cooking.

Thymus × citriodorus

Lemon Thyme

Garden origin

A bushy, rounded, evergreen shrub to 30cm high and 25cm wide, with many branching stems. Oval to lance-shaped, dark-green leaves may have a creamy variegation. It produces small, tubular, lavender-pink flowers in terminal clusters in early summer, which are attractive to bees and butterflies. Grown primarily as a culinary herb with a bonus of colourful leaves. Easily grown in full sun in well-drained soil. Tolerant of poor soil and drought. Perfect for edging or border fronts in rock gardens, herb gardens and Mediterranean gardens.

Thymus serpyllum

Breckland Thyme

Native to most of Europe and North Africa

A dwarf, evergreen shrub growing to 8cm tall with woody, creeping stems to

Tecomaria capensis.

Telopea speciosissima.

Tetradenia riparia.

Teucrium fruticans.

Thunbergia natalensis.

Thymus × citriodorus.

Thymus serpyllum.

Tigridia pavonia.

Tipuana tipu.

30cm long and a tap root. It forms mat-like plants that root from the nodes of the squarish, limp stems. Oval blue-green leaves are 3 to 8mm long in opposite pairs, nearly stalkless. The plant sends up erect flowering shoots in summer bearing strongly scented flowers that are lilac, pink-purple, magenta, or rarely white, 4 to 6mm long, produced in clusters. This hardy plant tolerates some pedestrian traffic and produces odours ranging from heavily herbal to light lemon, depending on the variety. Easily grown in full sun in a well-drained average to dry, alkaline to neutral soil. Drought tolerant. Excellent ground cover or filler between stepping stones where it releases its fragrance when trodden on. Cut back as necessary to maintain appearance.

Thymus vulgaris
Garden Thyme
Native to Mediterranean region

A cushion-forming, bushy subshrub 8cm high spreading to 30cm wide. A highly aromatic plant with densely-branched, woody stems, covered with tiny, narrow to oval, finely hairy, dark grey-green leaves up to 1.5cm long. Terminal spikes of tiny pink, white or lilac flowers appear in late spring and early summer. They attract bees and butterflies with rich nectar. Easily grown in full sun in a well-drained average to dry, alkaline to neutral soil. Drought tolerant once established. Perfect for edging or border fronts in rock gardens, herb gardens and Mediterranean gardens or containers. Cut back occasionally to keep compact. Use the aromatic leaves fresh or dried in cooking.

TIGRIDIA
Iridaceae
Peacock Flowers, Tiger-Flowers, Shell Flowers
Native to Central America, Mexico to Chile

A genus of about 60 species of bulbous or cormous perennials, 45 to 60cm tall. Each flower is short-lived, often blooming for only one day, but often several flowers will bloom from the same stalk. Usually dormant during the winter dry season.

Tigridia pavonia
Mexican Shell Flower
Native to Mexico

A bulbous perennial with narrow, lance-shaped leaves 20 to 50cm long borne in a basal fan, forming a clump from which a slender, erect stem appears. Each stem can produce several striking flowers to 15cm in diameter successively in mid- to late summer. The three-petalled blooms may be red, orange, yellow, pink or white, with strongly contrasting central markings. These open early in the morning and close before dusk. Easily grown in full sun in well-drained soil. Drought tolerant once established, making them a good choice for water-wise gardens, Mediterranean gardens. Great for containers. Fantastic as cut flowers.

TIPUANA
Fabaceae
Tipu Tree
Native to southern Brazil to Bolivia

A genus containing just a single species of frost-tender, fast-growing tree. Grown for its beautiful, showy pea-like flowers and attractive foliage, often seen as a street or shade tree.

Tipuana tipu
Pride of Bolivia

A deciduous or semi-evergreen tree that makes rapid growth to 10m high, eventually a gracefully spreading tree with a flattened crown 8m wide. Old trees become picturesque with their massive low branches, which may be horizontal or contorted. Light-green, pinnate leaves are up to 45cm long and divided into nine to twenty-five leaflets, each 4cm long with notched tips. Clusters up to 30cm long of pea-shaped flowers 2 to 3cm across appear in spring and summer. They are golden yellow or apricot with crumpled petals and red veins, appearing in great profusion like small butterflies. Flowers are followed by 6cm-long woody pods. Easily grown in full sun in well-drained soil. It grows well in poor soil but may become chlorotic in strongly alkaline soil. Drought tolerant once established. When grown in a lawn or near a patio or terrace, it can provide a useful shade canopy. An avenue planted with these trees in full flower is a spectacular sight. The tree does not grow well in coastal conditions. The timber is the source of rosewood.

TITHONIA
Asteraceae
Mexican Sunflower
Native to Mexico and Central America

A small genus of about ten species of stout annuals, perennials and shrubs. Leaves are usually alternate, entire or lobed. The large, showy flowers are usually solitary. One species is sometimes grown as a summer annual.

Tithonia rotundifolia

A shrubby, fast-growing, upright annual that forms a bush 1 to 2m high and 60 to 90cm wide with dark-green, hairy stems. Mid-green, heart-shaped or three-lobed leaves, up to 30cm long, are hairy underneath and carried on hairy, stout blackish stalks. Spectacular, daisy-like, mostly solitary 8 to 10cm-wide flower heads have bright orange or yellow petals surrounding a central disc. These are borne from late summer to autumn on long hollow stems. Flowers serve as a nectar source for insects and butterflies. Grows well in full sun in well-drained soil. Drought tolerant once established, making it a colourful annual for a dry garden or xeriscaping. Provides long-lasting cut flowers.

TRACHELOSPERMUM
Apocynaceae

Native to southern and eastern Asia and Australia

The genus includes about ten species of evergreen vines and shrubs known for their attractive foliage and fragrant flowers. Only two species are usually grown, with long stems climbing to 12m or more high. Leaves are opposite, simple, broad lanceolate to ovate, 2 to 8cm long and up to 4cm wide. Flowers are salverform (like those of Phlox), simple, 2 to 7cm broad, with five white, pale-yellow or purple petals joined at the base to form a tube. These plants are popular choices for gardens and landscapes, often used as ornamental vines or ground covers. They typically prefer warm climates and well-drained soil, thriving in full sun to partial shade.

Trachelospermum jasminoides 'Tricolor'

Variegated Chinese Star Jasmine, Star Jasmine, Star Jessamine

Native to southern and eastern Asia

This variegated form of the popular Trachelospermum, used widely as a ground cover or twining climber, grows 15 to 30cm high, spreading and rooting later when not climbing. Its beautiful foliage is a remarkable blend of green, creamy-white and pink shades on leaves. Flowers are 2cm wide, white, and exude a sweet, heavenly fragrance in summer, reminiscent of jasmine, which is how this plant earned its name. These appear in clusters and contrast beautifully against the variegated foliage. This low-maintenance climber thrives in well-draining soil and is drought and coastal tolerant once established. For the best-looking plant, grow in shade or semi-shade, but it can also take full sun. Excellent under trees, shrubs, dense enough to discourage weeds. Slow-growing, its dense, low growth makes it a fantastic ground cover. It will also climb, making it suitable for trellises and fences. Tricolor adds a burst of colour to gardens and vertical structures with its stunning foliage. Great in containers or hanging baskets.

TRADESCANTIA
Commelinaceae

Spiderworts, Wandering Jews

Native to tropical to warm temperate North and South America

A genus of 85 species of perennials that includes both climbing and trailing species growing 30 to 60cm tall. Stems are usually succulent or semi-succulent, often rooting at the nodes. Leaves are alternate, sometimes semi-succulent, often purple-flushed or variegated. Saucer-shaped flowers can be white, pink, purple or blue, with three petals and six yellow anthers. Several species have flowers that last for only a day, opening in the morning and closing by evening.

Tradescantia pallida 'Purpurea'

Purple Heart, Purple Queen

Native to Mexico

A popular, ornamental, evergreen perennial known for its striking purple foliage with a scrambling, climbing growth habit and vine-like stature. It is distinguished by vivid purple, elongated and slightly pointed leaves, 5 to 12cm long. Alternate leaves on thick, yet fragile, purple stems are deep purple on top and even more vibrant underneath, especially in bright light. It bears small clusters of bright pink, three-petalled flowers 2.5cm emerging from stem tips. The foliage creates a dense, cascading effect, making it suitable as a ground cover or for hanging baskets. Easily grown in full sun to partial shade in well-drained soil. The best colour occurs in the full sun. Drought tolerant once established but water freely in extreme dry weather. Over-watering should be avoided, as it can lead to root rot. Great for border fronts, ground cover, rock gardens, Mediterranean gardens or containers.

Tradescantia sillamontana

Native to northeastern Mexico

An evergreen, almost succulent, erect perennial with shoots and stems reaching 30 to 40cm high, first erect, then later prostrate and rooting at the soil surface. White hairs almost completely cover all parts of the plant, leaves, shoots and even the buds, protecting the plant from direct sunlight and excessive evaporation. Stem-clasping leaves are arranged in a precise geometric shape. They are fleshy, ovate, 3 to 7cm long, covered with greyish-white short hairs. In summer, flower clusters of small, bright purple-pink petals and three small sepals appear. This species is one of the most succulent and xerophytic, also one of the most attractive, with its recognisable and distinctive appearance. The more sun and less water the plant gets, the more silver and compact it remains. Soil should allow good drainage, with at least a third made up of coarse sand and gravel. Moderate watering is required during its growing season, but it should be kept almost dry in winter. In the subtropical zone, this is one of the most popular garden plants.

Tradescantia spathacea syn. *Rhoeo discolor*

Moses-In-The-Cradle, Oyster Plant

Native to Mexico and Central America

A clump-forming perennial to 30cm high and wide with fleshy rhizomes. Rosettes of semi-erect, waxy, sword-shaped leaves to 30cm long, are dark to metallic green above, with glossy purple beneath. Flowers are relatively small and inconspicuous, white, tubular and nestled within boat-shaped purple bracts 2 to 4cm long. Flowers bloom throughout the year. It is tough and adaptable, suitable for full sun or part shade. Plants will spread to form a dense ground cover over time. Grow in well-drained or rocky soil. Drought tolerant once established. This is a common border or edging plant

honia rotundifolia.

Trachelospermum jasminoides 'Tricolor'.

Tradescantia pallida purpurea.

descantia sillamontana.

Tradescantia spathacea.

Tradescantia spathacea 'Stripe Me Pink'.

nezia caerulea.

Tritonia crocata.

in tropical or subtropical gardens. Its colourful foliage makes it a useful plant for adding foliage contrast around the garden.

Tradescantia spathacea 'Stripe Me Pink'

A dwarf form of evergreen, semi-succulent, clump-forming perennials growing to a height and width of 30cm. Attractive, fleshy, dark-green leaves with striped, pink variegation and purple undersides make it an ideal addition to any garden. Plant in full sun to part-shaded position, in a moderately fertile soil, where it will tolerate periods of dryness. Keep moist during growth periods.

TRIMEZIA syn. NEOMARICA

Iridaceae

Walking Iris

Native to Central and South America

As of May 2019, the World Checklist of Selected Plant Families accepted about 80 species of Trimezia. It grows and spreads from underground rhizomes, and plantlets form at the ends of the flower stems after blooming. Erect, sword-shaped leaves are ribbed or heavily veined in basal fans. Species vary in height from about 7cm to 1.6m. As the plantlets grow, the stems bend down to touch the ground and take root, hence the common name. They have orchid-like flowers and have now been hybridised into new colour combinations.

Trimezia caerulea syn. *Neomarica caerulea*

Native to southern to southeast Brazil

An evergreen perennial with short rhizomes that form large clumps. Stiff, dark grey-green, sword-like leaves grow to 1.6m long. In late spring and early summer, it bears strikingly beautiful flowers that appear well above the foliage on a stout, leaf-like winged inflorescence. Fragrant flowers 8 to 10cm wide, with bright violet-blue petals, purplish-brown bases and upright white and blue inner perianth segments, open only for a day, but succeed each other in flushes so that it gives a good show of colour over a long period. It will grow in full sun, but foliage colour is best in light shade. Give regular to occasional water in summer, but it is drought tolerant in shady locations. A rich, well-drained soil produces the best results, but plants also tolerate clay soils. Cold hardy for a short duration.

TRITONIA

Iridaceae

Native to South Africa

A genus of up to 30 species of cormous perennials up to 80cm high, with fan-shaped leaves. Flowers are funnel- or cup-shaped in shades of yellow, orange or brown, sweet-smelling, giving off a strong fragrance, especially at night. They are closely related to Crocosmia.

Tritonia crocata syn. *Montbretia crocata*

A deciduous, winter-growing geophyte (a plant with a subterranean storage organ). It produces a fan of short, lance-shaped leaves in autumn up to 35cm high, which die down during summer. Over a long period in spring, wiry arching stems carry spikes of up to ten bright, fiery, orange or reddish-orange, almost regular, cup-shaped flowers 1.5cm long. Grow in light, well-drained, preferably sandy soil in a sheltered site in full sun. Summer dormant, so needs no water. It is free-flowering, makes an ideal container and rock garden subject, and multiplies rapidly. In frost-free areas, grow in large drifts around deciduous trees and shrubs. Can be left in the ground for several seasons, when crowded lift in summer and replant in autumn. They also look attractive when grown in pots. 'Princess Beatrix' has deep-orange flowers with dark markings.

TULBAGHIA

Amaryllidaceae

Native to Eastern Cape Province of South Africa

A genus of about 26 species of clump-forming, mainly deciduous tuberous or cormous perennials. Basal, strap-shaped to linear, grey-green leaves have a smell similar to onions. They are grown for their many flowered umbels of purple or white star-like flowers.

Tulbaghia violaceae

Society Garlic

A clump-forming bulb with narrow bluish-green leaves to 30cm long, which grow from a central point. They are evergreen in mild climates. Terminal umbels of eight to twenty tubular, lilac-pink to purplish-pink, six-petalled fragrant flowers, up to 3cm wide, spread to an open star with six points, from midsummer to early autumn. They rise above the leaves on 30cm or more long stalks. The dainty flowers emit a lovely fragrance, but the leaves smell of garlic, hence the common name. Easily grown in full sun or partial shade in well-drained soil. Good heat and drought tolerance but require moisture during the growing season. Ideal for planting in drifts where they will soon naturalise to form ground cover. Stunning in sunny borders, beds, rock gardens or as edging plants. Perfect for Mediterranean gardens. 'Silver Lace' has leaves edged in white and larger flowers.

U

URGINEA see DRIMIA

URSINIA

Asteraceae

Native to southern Africa

A genus of annuals and evergreen perennials and subshrubs to 45cm high from dry savannah. Leaves are usually alternate with toothed margins, simple or finely divided, often hairy or downy, frequently aromatic. Daisy-like, 5cm flowerheads are solitary on a long stalk held above the rich green mound of ferny foliage.

Ursinia anthemoides

Solar Fire

Native to the Cape Provinces of South Africa

A bushy, evergreen perennial, usually grown as an annual, to 45cm high, spreading to 35cm. Finely-divided, often hairy or hairless leaves are 2.5 to 4cm long, with linear, almost cylindrical lobes. In summer, it explodes into a mass of sunny, eye-catching golden-yellow flowerheads 2.5cm across. Its golden blooms last for months. Easy to grow in full sun in well-drained, sandy, fertile soil. Heat and drought tolerant once established. Will easily self-sow. Can be planted at any time of the year and makes a good winter bloomer too. Good for cut flowers and containers.

V

VALERIANA

Caprifoliaceae

Valerian

Native to dry sunny areas of Europe, the Mediterranean region, Africa and southwest Asia

A genus of about twelve species of annuals or perennials. Only one species is in common cultivation, grown for its attractive flowers that appear over a long season.

Valeriana rubra syn. *Centranthus ruber*

Red Valerian

Native to southern Europe, north Africa and Turkey

A compact bushy perennial to about 1m high and 45 to 60cm wide with glaucous stems. Oval to lance-shaped, fleshy, shiny leaves are 10cm long. Dense, terminal clusters of small deep-crimson to pale-pink or white, star-shaped, fragrant flowers are produced during spring and summer. A tough perennial that will grow in difficult situations in full sun or in shade. Makes a wonderful sight when mass planted. As it sets seed easily, it can become invasive. Drought tolerant, it thrives in the poorest of soils. In richer soils with more water, it can become softer and lax. Attracts birds and butterflies. Removing the old flowering stems will encourage a second crop of flowers and reduce seed distribution. Butterflies are drawn to the attractive flowers. The variety 'Albus' has white flowers.

VELTHEIMIA

Asparagaceae

Native to South Africa

A small genus of only two species of frost-tender, bulbous perennials. They are grown for their terminal spikes of pendant flowers.

Veltheimia bracteata

Forest Lily

A winter-growing bulbous plant. Leaves die back in summer, and new leaves appear in late summer to autumn after a short period of dormancy. Handsome, broad, lance-shaped, bright-green leaves are up to 30cm long and 10cm wide with distinct wavy edges. These form an approximately 25cm high by 35cm wide rosette from the top of the scaly brown bulb. In winter or early spring, a long reddish or purple flower stalk appears from the centre of its rosette. This bears a densely-packed flower spike up to 10cm long, of tubular, nodding flowers 4cm long. Flower colour is variable, and can be pale-pink, dusky-pink, orange-pink or deep rose-pink, or occasionally greenish yellow. Flowers are held upright when in tight bud and are pendant when open, with tips of the flowers sometimes green or spotted with green. The flower spikes can last for several weeks. Its bold leaves make it attractive even when not in flower. Keep the bulb moist while in leaf and flower, allowing it to rest by drying out in summer. It prefers a partly-shaded position and requires protection from extremes of weather. Looks most attractive when grown in a pot or container, but care needs to be taken to keep it dry during the dormant period.

VERBASCUM
Scrophulariaceae
Mullein

A genus of about 300 species of hardy biennials with a few annuals, perennials and subshrubs, native to Asia and Europe, chiefly the Mediterranean region. Most produce tall upright flower spikes in summer.

Verbascum bombyciferum
Giant Silver Mullein, Turkish Mullein, Broussa Mullein
Native to Turkey

A tall, upright, biennial or short-lived evergreen perennial up to 2m high, forming a rosette with silky white hairs covering the stems. Oval silvery leaves are up to 60cm across in its first year. In the second year, it bears an impressive, upright, sparsely-branched silvery flower spike, 60 to 120cm long, with a succession of yellow, saucer-shaped lemon flowers 4cm wide from early to late summer. Easily grown in full sun in average well-drained soil, even tolerates poor soils. Completely drought tolerant once established and frost tolerant. Topped with magnificent clusters of bright-yellow flowers, this statement plant will really stand out. Grow in a sunny border where its columnar habit and grey-green leaves will give a pleasing effect. Excellent for hot sunny sites, it is well suited to gravel gardens, garden beds or containers.

Verbascum olympicum
Greek Mullein, Olympian Mullein, Olympic Mullein
Native to southern Greece

A tall, upright, evergreen, short-lived perennial up to 2m high. Silvery-grey, felted evergreen leaves grow in wide rosettes in an attractive, succulent-like basal pattern. Each leaf can be 30cm long and nearly half as wide. These lie flat on the ground, like an open fan. Blooming in succession over a long period from early to late summer, it forms a tall and spectacular candelabra of flowering spikes, 75cm or more long, smothered with bright-yellow, saucer-shaped flowers 3cm across, with yellowish-white and woolly filaments. These appear in the second or third year, the plant generally dying after flowering. Easily grown in full sun in average well-drained soil, even tolerates poor soils. Drought tolerant, ideal for a dry garden as it requires no summer water. Suitable for costal planting. It attracts a wide variety of pollinators, including bees and butterflies. Spectacular and easily grown from seed.

VERBENA
Verbenaceae
Vervain, Verveine
Native to North, Central and South America, southern Europe

A genus of 150 species of mostly annuals or perennials, many prostrate. Leaves are usually opposite, simple and in many species hairy, often densely so. Flowers are small, with five petals, and borne in dense spikes. They are grown for their brightly coloured flowers. All need heat to thrive.

Verbena bonariensis
Native to South America

A tall, slender-stemmed, rough hairy annual or perennial with airy, branching stems up to 1.8m high, spreading to 90cm wide. Its stem is square with long internodes. At maturity, it will develop a woody base. Leaves are mostly basal, dark green, elliptic to 10cm long and often toothed. Stems carry many branched clusters on terminal and axillary stems, to 5cm across, of tiny lavender-blue to purple flowers from summer to autumn. Easily grown in average well-drained soil in full sun or partial shade. Drought tolerant once established. The light, airy effect of the plant gives it a quality that is useful for the front of a border. Great for mass planting in beds and borders. Ideal as cut flowers.

Verbena × hybrida
Garden Verbena
Garden origin

A much-branched, short-lived herbaceous perennial that is normally treated as an annual, growing 15 to 45cm high and spreading to 60cm wide. Its spreading stems often root near the base. Leaves are oblong 5 to 10cm long, conspicuously veined and toothed. Flowers are borne in flat compact clusters 5 to 8cm wide in a range of colours and combinations, which include white, salmon, pink, bright red or purple-blue, often with a white eye. An ideal plant to give a splash of summer colour to beds or borders. It thrives in full sun but requires a moderate amount of summer water. Easily raised from seed.

Verbena rigida
Slender Vervain, Tuberous Vervain
Native to southern Brazil, Argentina

An evergreen perennial with stiff stems growing 60cm high with a spreading habit. Rough, oblong, dark-green leaves are 5 to 10cm long and strongly toothed. Clusters to 5cm across of fragrant, intense purple flowers to 1cm across are carried on terminal branched stems gradually becoming spike-like with age. Easily grown in average well-drained soil in full sun or partial shade. Drought and heat tolerant once established. Plants make underground stems that, if given generous water, can become invasive. An ideal plant for edging, beds and borders or containers in Mediterranean style, low-maintenance gardens. It can be clipped in winter to maintain its size. It is a colourful perennial that grows best for three to five years for its floral impact. Easily raised from seed.

VERTICORDIA
Myrtaceae
Featherflowers
Native to southwest Australia

A genus of about 100 species ranging from tiny shrubs to trees, some spindly,

lbaghia violacea.

Ursinia anthemoides.

Valeriana rubra.

ltheimia bracteata.

Verbascum bombyciferum.

Verbena bonariensis.

rticordia grandis.

Viburnum tinus.

Vinca major 'Variegata'.

others dense and bushy, but the majority are woody shrubs about 2m tall. Flowers are variously described as 'feathery', 'woolly' or 'hairy' and are found in most colours except blue. They often appear to be in rounded groups or spikes but, in fact, are always single, each flower borne on a separate stalk in a leaf axil. Each flower has five sepals and five petals all of a similar size, with the sepals often having feathery or hairy lobes.

Verticordia grandis
Scarlet Feather Flower

A small to medium shrub, usually about 1 to 3m high with one or several sparsely branched main stems that branch out. It has small, stem-clasping, rounded grey-green leaves 0.8 to 1.5cm long. These are aromatic when crushed, a substitute for a floral scent. An oil is contained in prominent glands on the leaf surface, which may become a shade of purple when a plant is stressed. Plumose, five-petalled flowers appear in compact groups that spike out from the upper branch, beginning white and turning to a deep scarlet. The style extends out from the centre of the flower 20 to 25mm, slightly curving at the end. Petals are fused to form a tube, and the sepals are feathery in appearance. In a genus with so many spectacular flowering plants, this must rate as one of the most spectacular. Flowering may occur throughout the year, but mainly in spring and early summer. Grow in moderately fertile neutral to acid soil in full sun. Summer drought tolerant. Excellent for Mediterranean climate of dry summers and wet winters.

VIBURNUM
Viburnaceae

Native to America, Europe and Asia

A large genus of 150 to 170 species of frost-hardy, evergreen and deciduous shrubs or occasionally small trees. Leaves are opposite, simple and entire, toothed or lobed. Cool temperate species are deciduous, while most warm temperate species are evergreen. Some species are densely hairy on the shoots and leaves, with star-shaped hairs. Most species have clusters of white flowers, some highly fragrant, which are often followed by brightly coloured fruits.

Viburnum suspensum
Sandankwa Viburnum

Native to southwestern Japan

An evergreen shrub up to 3m high and wide. Leathery, ovate, glossy, deep green, toothed leaves are up to 10cm long with a paler underneath. In late winter to early spring it produces flat, loose, pendulous clusters of small, tubular flowers to 10cm across that are white or pale pink. These flowers are highly fragrant, attracting bees and butterflies, and are followed by fruits that are bright red berries that turn black with age. Easily grown in full sun or partial shade in well-draining soil that is rich in organic matter. It can tolerate a range of soil types, including sandy and clay soils. Moderately drought tolerant once established. Ideal for hedges, containers, mixed shrubberies, borders or as a feature plant. Good for coastal regions, as it is salt resistant.

Viburnum tinus
Laurestinus

Native to the Mediterranean region

A dense, compact, evergreen, bushy shrub 2 to 7m high spreading 3m wide with a dense, rounded crown. Masses of dark, glossy-green, oval leaves in opposite pairs are leathery, slightly folded under at the edges, 5 to 8cm long with fine hairs persisting on the underside. Pale pink buds open to reveal masses of tiny, fragrant white flowers, forming clusters 5 to 10cm wide that gracefully appear above the foliage from winter to mid-spring. These are followed by bright, metallic-blue berries, which often last throughout summer. Best grown in full sun but tolerates deep shade. Easily grown in most well-drained soils. Moderately drought tolerant once established. With its dense foliage to the ground, it makes an attractive hedge or screening shrub.

Viburnum tinus 'Eve Price'

A dwarf, compact form with smaller leaves and flattened clusters of deep-pink buds opening to small, starry white-pink flowers.

Viburnum tinus 'Variegatum'

A beautiful form with edges of evergreen leaves margined in cream with an interior of soft green, growing to 2.4m tall and 1.5m wide in six years. In autumn, clusters of pink buds form and hold until mid-winter. Then, as the days lengthen, it opens these clusters, which are lightly fragrant and white. Full sun to part shade to high overhead shade. Requires little water once established. This attractive-looking, strong-growing, tough shrub native to the Mediterranean glows year-round and can lighten up dark corners. It is easy to grow and long-lived.

VINCA
Apocynaceae

Periwinkle

Native to Europe, north Africa, central Asia

A genus of about twelve species of trailing, slender-stemmed, evergreen subshrubs to 70cm high with slender trailing stems 1 to 3m long. When stems touch the ground, they often develop roots and help the plant spread extensively. Flowers, produced through most of the growing season, are simple and salverform (like those of Phlox), with petals joined at the base to form a tube.

Vinca major
Greater Periwinkle

Native to western Mediterranean region

A rampant evergreen subshrub up to 40cm high with soft stems 3m or more long which trail along the ground, rooting at the tips as they go. Opposite, ovate to lance-shaped leaves 7cm long are dark glossy green. Erect shoots 30 to 50cm high bear solitary flowers in axils of leaves during winter. The corolla is funnel-shaped with broad spreading lobes 5cm across, bright blue with a white centre. Grows well in full sun or shade. Drought tolerant but grows and flowers better with some water. A tough plant that is easy to grow. Excellent for covering unsightly banks, or to prevent erosion on waste ground. Cut back to ground level in early spring if the growth becomes too tangled, in order to promote strong young growth.

Vinca major 'Variegata'

A rampant, evergreen subshrub 20 to 40cm high with prostrate rooting stems covered with leaves blotched and margined creamy white, forming a dense carpet of rich foliage. Borne on arching shoots over a long season, large, violet-blue, 5cm-across flowers appear for most of the summer. Excellent as ground cover in full sun or partial shade in average, well-drained soil. Drought tolerant. Great in hanging baskets and containers.

Vinca minor

Lesser Periwinkle

Native to southern Europe to Asia

This trailing subshrub spreads along the ground, rooting along the stems to create extensive colonies and sometimes scrambling up to 40cm in height, but it never twines or climbs. Leaves are evergreen, opposite, 2 to 4cm long, glossy dark-green with a leathery texture and an entire margin. Flowers are solitary in leaf axils and borne mainly from early spring to midsummer, but with a few flowers still produced in autumn. They are violet-purple, pale-purple or white, 2 to 3cm in diameter, with a five-lobed corolla. Easily grown in full sun or partial shade in average, well-drained soil. Drought tolerant but looks much better with some summer water. Cut back to ground level in early spring, in order to promote strong young growth, especially if it has become tangled. Makes an excellent ground cover for shady spots. There are many named cultivars, 'Alba' with white flowers, 'Argenteovariegata' with variegated leaves, and 'Multiplex' with double plum-purple flowers.

VIOLA

Violaceae

Pansy, Violet

Native to the temperate Northern Hemisphere

A large genus of about 680 species of hardy annuals, biennials or perennials. Simple heart-shaped or kidney-shaped, often scalloped leaves are alternate, though several have linear or palmate leaves. Stemless species produce basal rosettes. All leaves have stipules that are often leaf-like. They are grown primarily for their solitary five-petalled flowers in many colours on long stalks. Flowers have a spurred lower petal, two upper petals, and two lateral petals. Most cultivars are classified as garden pansies, violas, or violettas, differing in habit, flower characteristics and cultivation requirements. Great in containers, as bedding, in a rock garden, or in a border.

Viola odorata

English Violet, Sweet Violet

Native to west and southern Europe

A stemless, tufted perennial that grows 15 to 25cm high, spreading to 30cm wide with long runners that root at the joints. Dark-green, heart-shaped to rounded leaves, up to 6cm long, are toothed on the margins. Sweetly-scented flowers are 2cm across, with a short spur, usually deep violet, but may be pink or white. They bloom in late winter and early spring. Easily grown in part shade for best flowering but will tolerate sun. Grow in fertile, well-drained soil. Drought tolerant once established. Ideal for planting at the base of a shady wall or terrace. Makes an excellent ground cover and in containers. Many colours and larger-flowered forms, including doubles, have been bred. The violet has long been important as the source of perfume and in the florist trade. Flowers are excellent for cutting and are edible, either fresh or candied. Seed is produced freely, so will naturalise in a shady spot in the wild garden.

VITEX

Lamiaceae

Native to tropical and subtropical regions

A genus of about 270 species of deciduous and evergreen trees and shrubs from 1 to 10m tall. Some species have whitish bark that is characteristically furrowed. Leaves are opposite, usually compound. Most of the cultivated species are grown for their attractive foliage and autumn flowers.

Vitex agnus-castus

Chaste Tree

Native to southern Europe

A deciduous, aromatic shrub or small tree, usually multi-trunked, with a broad, spreading habit 3 to 6m high and wide with grey downy young shoots. Leaves are dark green above and grey underneath and are divided into five to seven narrow oval to lance-shaped leaflets 12cm long, arranged fanwise. Slender racemes of fragrant, tubular lavender-blue or violet flowers up to 30cm long cover the plant in late summer and autumn, attracting butterflies. Grows well in full sun in well-drained soil. It requires high summer heat and is drought tolerant for the best flowering. If given a rich soil and ample summer water, it will produce vigorous growth at the expense of flower. Good for coastal gardens, as it tolerates salt. Cold and wet weather results in dieback and losses. It can be trained to make a small shade tree. 'Alba' has white flowers, 'Rosea' pink flowers.

W

WASHINGTONIA

Cupressaceae

Native to the arid regions of California, Arizona and northern Mexico

A genus of only two species of massive fan palms, usually single-stemmed. Its petioles are armed with sharp thorns, ending in a rounded fan of many leaflets. Both have bisexual flowers in a dense inflorescence, with the fruits maturing into a small blackish-brown drupe 6 to 10mm diameter with a thin layer of sweet flesh over the single seed. Both species hybridise freely when grown together, so they are difficult to distinguish from each other when young, as the trunks and leaves look almost identical.

Washingtonia filifera

California Fan Palm, Petticoat Palm

Native to southern California, southern Arizona

A medium to tall palm that grows slowly at first, then once fully established, grows fast to 12 to 18m and 3 to 6m wide. Its massive, sturdy, greyish trunk can be up to 60cm in diameter. Its crown is open and broad. Showy, palmate, greyish-green fronds are 1m or more across and divided more than halfway to the base with many long threads attached to the segments. Fronds are carried on long, thorny leaf stalks, which hold the leaf upright at first, then droop with age. In nature, it is usually covered in a dense thatch of old leaves that folds down against the trunk rather than dropping off, giving it the common name. Wind or fire often removes these leaves unless they are pruned off to reveal its attractive trunk. In summer, creamy-white, tubular flowers are produced in huge sprays, to 5m long. They are followed by black, pea-sized fruits. Easy to grow in well-drained soil in full sun. Drought tolerant once established. Young trees make good container plants. Popular as street trees and as bold groups in extensive gardens.

Washingtonia robusta

Mexican Fan Palm

Native to northern Mexico

A tall, fast-growing upright palm to 24m high spreading to 3m wide with a slender trunk, usually about 30cm in diameter, that gradually tapers from ground level. The leaf stalk is short with a reddish streak on the underside and is sharply toothed along the entire length. Bright green leaf blade to 1m long is stiff, lightly cut with slender points and no filaments. Unlike other palms, the dead leaves fold down against the trunk rather than dropping off, so the trunk is usually covered in a dense thatch of old leaves forming a shaggy skirt. Older palms have a compact crown on a tall trunk. In summer it produces panicles up to 3m long of tubular, creamy-white, slightly fragrant flowers, which are followed by dark-brown fruit. A spectacular palm, which will grow in poorer soil conditions but grows fast in good soil. Easy to grow in well-drained soil in full sun. Drought tolerant once established. Ideal for coastal gardens, as it withstands salt-laden sea breezes. Often grown in warm-dry climates in avenues to give a tropical effect. Less hardy than *Washingtonia filifera*.

WATSONIA

Iridaceae

Native to South Africa

A genus of about 60 species with two varieties and about 112 names either unresolved or regarded as synonyms. All are perennial herbs growing from corms and producing erect spikes of showy flowers. Most are fynbos plants, adapted to a Mediterranean-type climate, but some occur along the eastern and inland areas of South Africa, adapted to a wider range of conditions, mainly continental climate with summer rainfall. Many species occur mainly in mountainous regions, others in sandy flats and marshy areas. They are grown for their showy spikes of tubular flowers.

Watsonia borbonica

Cape Bugle Lily

A cormous perennial 1 to 1.5m high that is dormant in summer and grows in winter, which is the rainy season in its native habitat. In autumn it produces tall, sword-like, basal leaves to 75cm long growing in a fan. In late spring and early summer, it bears a branched flower spike carrying up to twenty showy, fragrant, rose-pink, funnel-shaped flowers 5cm long with a curved tube and lobes spreading out to a star shape. Grow in full sun in a well-drained soil. Summer drought tolerant. Give water as necessary during the growing season. Clumps are best left undisturbed for several years. Great as pot or container plants. There are many excellent hybrids in colours from scarlet, pink, white to lavender. Excellent for cut flowers.

WESTRINGIA

Laminaceae

Native to dry areas of Australia

A small genus of around 33 species of tender evergreen shrubs with leaves in whorls of three or four. As with other members of the mint family, their upper petal (or lip) is divided into two lobes. There are four stamens – the upper two are fertile while the lower two are reduced to staminodes. Grown for their attractive foliage and flowers.

Westringia fruticosa

Coastal Rosemary, Coastal Westringia

A delicate, rather loose shrub to 2m high and 3m wide, often forming a regular dome with its lower branches covering the ground. Whorls of deep-green to grey-green, narrow, 1 to 2cm long leaves are densely white felted underneath, giving a silvery tint, which adds to its attractiveness. These give it a similar appearance to rosemary but with a finer texture. White, pale blue or lilac flowers 1cm across are borne in axillary clusters throughout most of the summer. Easily grown in full sun in well-drained soil. Drought and frost tolerant once established. Grows well near the coast as it is wind tolerant. A hardy and naturally compact plant that responds beautifully to clipping and shaping, so makes a good

'iola odorata.

Vitex agnus-castus.

Washingtonia filifera.

Vatsonia borbonica.

Westringia fruticosa.

Wigandia urens.

'anthoceras sorbifolium.

Xanthorrhoea australis.

hedge and topiary specimen for formal native gardens. Ideal for warm temperate and Mediterranean gardens. 'Variegata' is more compact with cream edging to the leaves, softer growth and white flowers.

WIGANDIA
Boraginaceae
Native to Central America and South America

A genus containing around twenty species of large evergreen perennials, shrubs or small trees. Only one species is grown for its beautiful, large heads of blue flowers and foliage in subtropical gardens.

Wigandia urens syn. *Wigandia caracasana*
Caracus Wigandia

Native to Mexico, Venezuela and Colombia

A large, robust, evergreen shrub up to 3m or more high and wide with open, soft stems. Stems and leaves are covered in fine silky hairs. Primarily grown for its dramatic foliage and superb form, the large oval leaves are up to 40cm long, deep green above and bronze underneath with coarse teeth along the margins and a fine covering of tiny hairs. Violet or blue flowers 2cm wide with a white tube are borne in large terminal panicles to 30cm or more across in great profusion throughout summer. When in full flower, it makes an impressive sight. Grow in full sun in well-drained soil. Drought and frost tolerant once established. Useful as a background plant where the bold foliage will provide contrast for other plants. Ideal for the back of beds and large borders in Mediterranean gardens. Can be severely pruned after flowering. Suckers readily and can become invasive but is good for a large garden. Always wear gloves and protective clothing when pruning to avoid unwanted stings and skin irritation.

X

XANTHOCERAS
Sapindaceae
Native to northern China

A genus comprising just two species of frost-hardy, deciduous shrubs or small trees. They are related to Koelruteria but are different in appearance. Only one species is grown, for its upright spikes of fragrant flowers.

Xanthoceras sorbifolium
Chinese Flowering Chestnut, Flowering Yellowhorn, Tree Goldenhorn, Popcorn Shrub, Shiny Leaf Yellowhorn

A beautiful, large, deciduous shrub, or more commonly a small tree, to 4m high and 3m wide with a rounded habit. Pinnate leaves, to 30cm long, have nine to seventeen lance-shaped, glossy, toothed leaflets. In spring white flowers appear, up to 3cm across, as the flower matures the yellow throat turns to a deep maroon. Flowers are borne in terminal upright panicles to 20cm long on shoots of the previous year. These combine beautifully with the young fresh green leaves. Ideal conditions for this plant to thrive include dry springs and hot summers, resulting in matured wood and abundant flowering. Thriving in full sun with moderate summer water in most well-drained, even chalky soils. Although frost hardy, buds are easily damaged by frost. Plant as a specimen or in small groups, at the back of a border, or near a patio. As it blooms on old wood, it should be pruned after the spring blooming period. An excellent choice for a small landscape, where light pruning can control its size. Flowers, foliage and seeds are edible and are usually boiled.

XANTHORRHOEA
Asphodelaceae
Grass Tree

Native to Australia

A genus of about 30 species of slow-growing, long-lived, woody perennials. Its stem may take up to twenty years to emerge. Plants begin as a crown of rigid grass-like leaves, with the caudex slowly growing beneath. The main stem or branches continue to develop beneath the crown. This is rough-surfaced, built from accumulated leaf-bases around a secondarily thickened trunk. The trunk is sometimes unbranched, while others naturally grow many branches. Flowers are borne on a long spike above a bare section called a 'scape', which can be over 3 to 4m long in some species. These strange grass trees are ideal for the desert or dry garden. They appear to be dense clumps of grass borne on tree trunks.

Xanthorrhoea australis
Australian Grasstree

Probably the most widely distributed species. It usually develops a rough trunk which may be branched. It is extremely slow-growing, and trunks only start appearing after many years of growth. The trunk can grow up to over 3m high with a width of up to 1m and may be branched. Leaves crown the trunk in a crowded whorl of long, wiry leaves almost spherical. These are arranged in a spiral, forming an erect tuft when young and spreading as they mature, with the oldest leaves dying and forming a hanging skirt around the trunk. Blue-green, needle-like leaves are typically 15 to 40cm long and have a waxy coating. It takes several years to flower, and it does not always flower annually. Its tiny individual flowers are white or cream. They are clustered together in a spear-like spike, which can tower 2m or more above the top of the trunk. The flowers contain considerable nectar, which attracts honey-eating birds. Flowering occurs in spring and is followed by fruits containing a few hard, black seeds. Grow in full sun in well-drained soil, sandy soil is ideal. Drought tolerant once established, ideal for a dry garden.

Xanthorrhoea preissii
Balga, Grass Gum-Tree, Kangaroo Tail

Native to Western Australia

A slow-growing, woody perennial that will eventually form a trunk to 3m high. With great age, the massive black trunks can become 60cm or more thick. At the top of the trunk is a tuft of hard, leathery, reed-like leaves to 1m long and less than 1cm wide, which radiate in all directions. Old leaf bases may be glued together by a black resinous gum. The magnificent inflorescence arises from among the leaves to 1m long on a stem of 1m. Dense spikes contain many small, white flowers which open on the sunny side first. Spikes can be produced at almost any time of the year, but mostly in summer or autumn. Grow in full sun in well-drained soil – sandy soil is ideal. Drought tolerant once established, ideal for a dry garden. These unusual and spectacular plants look good when associated with other drought-tolerant plants.

XERANTHEMUM
Asteraceae
Native to the Mediterranean region

A genus of about six species of erect, white, woolly, branching annuals to 75cm high with linear to linear-elliptic entire leaves. They are cultivated for their alternate, daisy-like, crimson, pink, white, lilac-blue or mauve flowerheads enclosed within papery bracts, borne during summer and autumn.

Xeranthemum annuum
Paper Daisy

Native to eastern Europe and western Asia

A slender, upright annual, which is branched at the bases of wiry stems, bearing linear, entire, woolly silver-green leaves 2 to 6cm long. It bears branched heads of fifteen to twenty delicate, daisy-like, single or double flowerheads to 5cm across in many colours from summer to autumn. Prefers a sunny position and a well-drained soil. Will thrive even in poor soil. Drought tolerant once established. A hardy annual, it makes fascinating border subjects. Ideal for dried flower decorations. Cut the flowers for drying before they have fully opened, and hang upside down in a cool, dark, well-ventilated area.

XEROCHRYSUM syn. BRACTEANTHA
Asteraceae
Native to Australia

A genus of about seven species of perennials. Stalkless ovate to broadly, lance-shaped, glandular hairy leaves 5 to 15cm long are borne on erect branching stems. Daisy-like flower heads have papery white, yellow or pink bracts with central corollas. Great for cut flowers.

Xerochrysum bracteatum syn. *Bracteantha bracteata*
Golden Everlasting, Paper Daisies, Straw Flower

Erect annual or short-lived perennial varying in habit from prostrate to a shrub 1 to 1.5m high. Broadly lance-shaped, green to grey-green leaves are 12cm long. Golden-yellow or white, pink or red solitary flower heads 2.5 to 8cm wide are produced from spring to autumn. Their distinctive feature is the papery bracts that resemble petals. This is a drought-tolerant plant, but dry soil conditions will reduce the flowering. Flowers are best in full sun but will tolerate light shade and light frost. To dry the flowers, pick while in bud and hang upside down until dry. Suitable for subtropical, warm temperate, cool temperate and Mediterranean gardens. It has been cultivated for many years and several forms have been selected for cultivation.

Y

YUCCA
Asparagaceae
Native to the southern United States, Central America, the Caribbean

A genus of 40 to 50 species of evergreen perennials, shrubs or small trees. They are notable for their rosettes of evergreen, tough, sword-shaped leaves rising directly from the ground or on short woody stems. Large, terminal panicles of showy white or whitish flowers emit a scent at night, which attracts insects that act as pollinators. They are native to a wide range of habitats, from humid rainforest and wet subtropical ecosystems to the hot and dry (arid) deserts and savannah.

Yucca aloifolia
Spanish Bayonet

Native to southeast United States

A slow-growing, evergreen shrub or small tree that forms a stiff rosette of leaves, eventually up to 6m high and spreading to 4m wide. Usually it has a single trunk, but it may branch and sprawl along the ground. The trunk is armed with thick, fleshy, sharp-pointed, dagger-like deep green leaves up to 75cm long and 6cm wide. These are set close together spirally around the stem. Eventually the tip of the trunk develops a 60cm-long spike of white, purplish-tinged cup-shaped flowers, each about 10cm across. They appear in dense erect clusters held well above the foliage during summer. Easily grown in full sun in well-drained soil. Tolerant of drought, frost and salt-laden sea breezes, so is good for coastal gardens, even by the beach. Ideal as an accent plant for a dry garden. With age, they take on a picturesque appearance, especially if grown in groups. Remove old dead leaves with care, as the edges can easily cut. Sharp points are a hazard if grown close to paths. 'Marginata' has glaucous green leaves with creamy yellow margins, and 'Tricolor' has a central yellow stripe on its leaves.

Yucca filamentosa
Adam's Needle and Thread

Native to southeastern North America

A usually trunkless, ornamental evergreen shrub with a basal rosette of rigid, sword-shaped, spine tipped, mid-green leaves up to 75cm long edged with curly filaments. Dramatic, pendulous, bell-shaped creamy-white flowers, tinged with green or cream, 5 to 8cm long, appear in tall dense panicles up to 2m high in summer. Easily grown in full sun in well-drained soil. Tolerant of drought, frost, even partial shade and salt-laden sea breezes, it is good for coastal gardens, even by the beach. Ideal as an accent plant for a dry garden. Great for beds and borders in Mediterranean gardens. The variety 'Variegata' has bluish-green leaves with a contrasting creamy-white margin.

Yucca gigantea syn. *Yucca elephantipes*
Spineless Yucca

Native to southern Mexico and Guatemala

A fast-growing upright shrub or small tree usually with several trunks that forms a magnificent, many-branched clump up to 10m high spreading 4 to 8m wide. Many sparsely-branched trunks with a corky texture rise from a swollen base. Bright-green, spineless leaves with a slightly glaucous tinge, up to 1.2m long and 10cm wide, are held semi-erect. On mature shrubs, large, stout flower spikes up to 1m long rise above the foliage in spring. They are densely packed with large, pendant, creamy white, edible flowers 3 to 4cm long, shaded almost indiscernibly with green. Easily grown in full sun in well-drained dry to medium soil. Tolerant of drought, frost, even a few hours of shade and salt-laden sea breezes, it is good for coastal gardens. A great specimen plant for xeriscape gardens, Mediterranean gardens, beds and borders. A decorative and durable pot or container plant. 'Jewel' is a beautiful form with leaves striped with shades of green and cream. 'Variegata' has glaucous green leaves with creamy-white margins.

Yucca gloriosa
Spanish Dagger, Adam's Needle, Lord's Candlestick

Native to southern United States and northern Mexico

An upright shrub with stout, semi-woody stems that is often seen as a many-stemmed rosette growing up to 2m high and wide. The stem is usually branched, covered in dead leaves, topped with a rosette of young leaves. Spine-tipped leaves, 30 to 50cm long, are flat, sword-shaped and glaucous grey-green. During late summer, from the centre of the rosette arises an erect flower panicle up to 2.5m high. Pendulous, bell-shaped, creamy-white flowers are sometimes purple-tinged and open 8 to 10cm wide. Easily grown in full sun in well-drained soil. Tolerant of drought, frost, even a few hours of shade. Occurs naturally along the coast, so is ideal for coastal gardens. 'Variegata' has ornamental leaves margined and striped creamy-yellow.

Yucca gloriosa var. *tristis* syn. *Yucca recurvifolia*
Curve-Leaf Yucca, Curved-Leaved Spanish Dagger, Pendulous Yucca

Native to southeastern United States

A stem-forming, tree-like shrub, usually with a single unbranching trunk 1.2 to 1.8m high that can lightly branch with age. Thick, leathery leaves 5cm wide are 60 to 90cm long, a soft blue-grey green and all but the central crown are gracefully arching to strongly recurving. They are lance-shaped, entire to slightly toothed, with a pliable but sharp point. Pendant, bell-shaped, creamy flowers 6 to 8cm long are borne in dense erect panicles up to 1m or more high in midsummer. Easily grown in full sun or some shade in well-drained soil. Tolerant of drought, frost, even a few hours of shade and salt-laden sea breezes, it is good for coastal gardens. Grows fast by spreading suckers to make a large clump in time. This is the least dangerous yucca, as the leaves are softer and bend to touch. There are variegated forms: 'Marginata' with yellow margins; and 'Variegata', which has a central yellow stripe to its leaves.

Yucca whipplei see *Hesperoyucca whipplei*

eranthemum annuum.

Xerochrysum bracteatum.

Yucca aloifolia
'Marginata'.

ucca filamentosa.

Yucca gigantea.

Zaluzianskya affinis.

aluzianskya divaricata.

Zaluzianskya violacea.

Zinnia elegans

Z

ZALUZIANSKYA

Scrophulariaceae

Native to South Africa

A genus of about 60 species of compact, sticky, low-growing annuals, perennials and subshrubs. By day, the flowers remain tightly curled up, but by evening, uncurl into scented star-shaped white flowers blooming from mid- to late summer. Although it may not be widely seen, the plant has a long-standing tradition as a container plant in Europe. Easily raised from seed.

Zaluzianskya affinis

Sandveld Drumsticks

A short-lived, evergreen perennial with slightly sticky leaves growing to 50cm tall and broad. Leaves are long, narrow, about 4cm long, sessile (stalkless), toothed, covered with hairs and opposite or alternate. Daisy-like flowers have red backs and notched white petals with a red centre. It is valued in cultivation for its intense fragrance, especially at night. Once established, the plant will tolerate drought, but the best blooms come with regular watering. Grow in full sun in sharply-drained soil. Water freely during the summer growing season, but not in the winter dry season. Plant near an outdoor seating area to take full advantage of the wonderful fragrance emitted from this night-blooming plant. It is a suitable subject for container growing, preferring a position in full sun.

Zaluzianskya capensis

Drumsticks, Night Phlox

Native to Namaqualand to the Eastern Cape, South Africa

An annual that grows to about 50cm high. Leaves are long, narrow, about 4cm long, sessile (stalkless), toothed, covered with hairs and opposite or alternate. Stems have clusters of flowers at their tips. When closed, the flower buds are a deep maroon, but open in the evening to reveal a white and scented interior. The five petals are deeply lobed with a noticeable deep yellow centre. When closed, the flowers resemble drumsticks, giving it the common name. The shape of the flowers also appears to be phlox-like. Cultivation as above.

Zaluzianskya divaricata

Creeping Night Phlox, Spreading Night Phlox

An erect, hairy, annual herb growing to 35cm tall. Stems are erect and often single but may be branched into a candelabra-type structure up to 35cm tall. Leaves are lance-shaped, 10 to 20mm long, toothed, hairy with the lower ones opposite and the upper ones alternate, tip pointed to round. Bears distinctive, single, yellow five-petalled tubular flowers with a red streak on tiny stalks arising from the leaf axils during summer. Cultivation as above.

Zaluzianskya violacea

Violet drumsticks

A branched annual or perennial to 25cm high and 60cm wide, with hairs bending backwards. Leaves are narrow, hairy, about 3.5cm long. Flowers crowded at ends of branches are white or lilac, often yellow-eyed with a purple reverse, and have five deeply-notched petals with only two stamens. Blooms from mid- to late summer. Cultivation as above.

Zauschneria californica see *Epilobium canum*

ZINNIA

Asteraceae

Native to southwestern United States to Mexico

A genus of about eleven species of annuals, shrubs and subshrubs. Most species have upright stems, but some have a lax habit of spreading stems that mound over the surface of the ground. They range from 10cm to 1m tall. Pale- to medium-green, stalkless leaves are opposite, ranging from linear to ovate. Solitary, long-stemmed, twelve-petal, composite flowers comprise ray florets that surround disc florets, which may be a different colour from the ray florets and mature from the periphery inwards in a variety of bright colours.

Zinnia elegans

Mexican Zinnia, Common Zinnia

Native to Mexico

A stout-stemmed, upright annual 30 to 120cm high, with bristly stems and ovate to lance-shaped, hairy leaves to 8cm long. Flowers can be single with one row of petals, semi-double with several rows of petals, also with the centre exposed, fully double with several rows of petals hiding the centre of the flower, or cactus-like with long spiky petals. These are large, from 5 to 10cm wide. From spring to late summer, it bears flowers in a wide range of vibrant colours. Grow in rich well-drained soil in full sun, preferably in warm conditions, as it is not hardy. Tolerant of summer drought. Easy to grow and care for, making a perfect addition to any garden, as a colourful edge around a garden bed, in annual displays, herb and cottage gardens, in mixed borders and as cut flowers. Smaller-flowered cultivars are perfect for edging and naturalised areas. Sow seed where it is to grow in late spring.

GLOSSARY OF TERMS

This glossary gives definitions of terms used in this book and in gardening generally.

Accent plant – Plant used in a formal bed or border to emphasise contrasts of height, colour or texture.
Acid (soils) – Which has a pH value of below 7.
Acute – Ending in a short, sharp point.
Adventitious – A plant organ that occurs other than the usual place.
Aerial root – A root formed on the stem or trunk of a plant.
Alkaline (soils) – With a pH value above 7.
Annual – A plant that grows to maturity, flowers and fruits in one growing season and then dies.
Anther – Part of the stamen that releases the pollen usually borne on a filament.
Apex – The tip or growing point of an organ (as a leaf).
Areole – A small area bearing spines or hairs on a cactus.
Arrow shaped – With a narrow-pointed tip widening at the base with two downward-pointing lobes.
Axil – The upper angle at which a leaf or other organ joins its stem.
Axillary – Originating from the leaf axil.

Basal – At the base of an organ.
Basal leaf – A leaf that grows from the lowest part of the stem.
Bicoloured – With two distinct colours.
Biennial – A plant that completes its life cycle in two years. Usually growing in the first year, then flowering and fruiting in the second and then dies.
Bipinnate leaves – Pinnately-divided leaves, each leaflet of which is pinnately divided, with or without a terminal leaflet.
Bisexual – (hermaphrodite) Flowers having both stamens and pistils.
Blade – The expanded portion of a leaf.
Botanical name – The Latin scientific name of a plant.
Bract – Modified leaves below a flower or an inflorescence, intermediate between flower and the normal leaves, frequently coloured.
Bulb – A modified subterranean growth bud with fleshy scales serving as a storage organ and comprising overlapping leaf and often flower buds.
Bulbil – A small, bulb-like organ produced above ground on stems or in inflorescence and serving the same function as subterranean bulbs.

Calcareous – Soil with a high chalk content.
Calyx – A collective term for a flower's sepals, which form the outer circle or cup of floral parts (usually green).
Capsule – A non-fleshy fruit that opens naturally to disperse ripe seed.
Carpel – Female parts of a flower comprising a style, stigma and an ovary.
Cephalium – A flower-bearing, woolly and densely-bristled outgrowth at the top of the stem of some cacti.
Chlorophyll – The green pigment of plant cells, which absorbs light energy in photosynthesis.
Chlorosis – The loss of green colour in a leaf (chlorophyll) is usually because of a nutrient deficiency, usually of iron, disease or insect attack.
Clade – A group of organisms that includes a single common ancestor and all of its descendants.
Clone – A plant that is derived by vegetative propagation from one individual plant and has the identical genetic material.
Cluster – An arrangement of several leaves, stems, roots or flowers that arise from a single point.
Compound leaf – A leaf of two or more leaflets.
Concave – Hollowed out.
Convex – Umbrella-like.
Cordate – Heart-shaped.
Corm – Thickened underground stem, bulb-like but solid, with food stored in the centre from which it produces a whole plant each year.
Corolla – A collective term for the complete circle of petals of a flower.
Corona – A crown or cup-shaped appendage inside a flower comprising united stamens or other flower parts.
Corymb – A flat-topped, open flower-cluster with the individual flowers opening from the outside inward.
Creeper – A trailing shoot rooting at intervals.
Crown – 1 The growing point of a plant, usually at soil level from which roots and shoots, grow. 2 The crown of a tree or shrub is its entire branch structure, including the leaves.
Culm – The peculiar hollow stem or stalk of grasses and bamboo.
Cultivar (cv.) – A variety or form of a species that originates in cultivation and is not found naturally and keeps its distinct uniform characteristics when propagated.
Cyme – A broad, usually flat-topped, branched flower cluster with centre flowers opening first.

Deciduous – The shedding of leaves annually at the end of the growing season.
Decumbent – Growing close to the ground, reclining, but tip upward growing.
Dentate – Describes a leaf margin with coarse teeth, usually directed outward.
Dioecious – The male and female flowers are on different plants.
Diurnal – A term used to describe flowers that open only during the day.
Double flower – A flower that has or seems to have more petals than in the wild state, and with few, if any, stamens.
Downy – Clothed with soft short hairs.
Drought tolerant/drought resistant – Plants that can withstand long periods with little of no water or plants that have low water requirements.
Drupe – A fruit whose hard seed, or seeds, is surrounded by a fleshy area.

Elliptic – An elongated oval with the middle part the widest and both ends tapering.
Elongate – Drawn out in length.
Entire – Describes the margin of a leaf that is smooth and unlobed and lacks any sort of indentation.
Epiphyte – A plant that grows upon another plant without taking food from its host.
Etiolated – Growth that has become long, thin and pallid because of lack of light.
Even-pinnate – An even number of leaflets in a pinnate leaf. The leaf usually ends in a pair of leaflets rather than in a terminal (final) leaflet.
Evergreen – Keeping leaves for more than one growing season An evergreen plant never loses all of its leaves at one time.
Eye – 1 Immature growth bud often on a tuber. 2 The differently-coloured centre of a flower.

F1 hybrid – First generation hybrid derived from artificial cross-pollination between two distinct pure-bred lines, usually giving greater vigour and uniformity.
Family – The primary category in plant classification.
Fan-shaped – Wedge-shaped or semi-circular, often with a pleated or boldly-veined surface.
Fastigiate – Erect habit of growth, often narrow or columnar.
Filament – Thread-like stalk of a stamen attached to an anther.
Frond – Leaf of a fern. Also used to describe large leaves such as palm leaves.

Garden origin – A plant that has been bred or selected and does not occur in the wild.
Genus – The primary grouping of different closely related species (plural: genera; adjective: generic).
Glabrous – Smooth and not hairy.
Glaucous – Covered with a blue-green, blue-grey, grey, whitish or bluish bloom or a waxy and powdery substance that is easily rubbed away.
Globose – Round or almost round, spherical.
Glochid – Fine, hairy spines tipped with barbs.
Glutinous – Sticky.
Ground cover – Usually low-growing plants that are selected to grow over and cover an area of soil and create a uniform appearance.
Growing point – Tip of a shoot from which the recent growth appears.

Habit – The characteristic appearance of a mature plant.
Habitat – The kind of locality in which a plant grows in the wild.
Head – A short dense cluster of flowers.
Herbaceous – Any plant that does not form a persistent woody stem, dies back to the ground each year.
Humus – A dark-brown, decomposing, organic matter in the soil; may also refer to rotted garden compost. It is extremely water-retentive, and an ideal medium for soil life.
Hybrid – The result of crossing two distinct species, subspecies, varieties, cultivars or from two different genera.

Incised – The margins of a leaf, stipule or bract that is deeply, irregularly and sharply cut or slashed.
Incurved – Bending inwards.
Inflorescence – The arrangement of flowers originating from a single point on the stem, branch or trunk, often referred to as a flower head.
Internode – The area on a stem between one leaf node and the next.

Keel – The two lower-most petals of a pea-like flower.

Lanceolate (**Lance-shaped**) – A leaf shape that is longer than wide, with the widest part of the blade near the point of attachment, tapering toward the tip.
Lateral – A stem or shoot that branches off from a bud in the leaf axil of a larger stem.
Latex – Milky-white sap or fluid that bleeds from some plants when the stem is cut.
Lax – Loose, widely spaced, not compact.
Layering – A method of propagation in which a branch will make roots while placed in close contact with the soil surface.
Leader – The main, usually central, stem of a tree or shrub.
Leaf axil – The angle formed between a leaf or leaf stalk and the stem of the plant.
Leaf-blade – The part of the leaf that excludes the leaf stalk.
Leaflet – Single, distinct division (blade) of a compound leaf.
Leaf node – The point where a leaf arises from a stem.
Leaf stalk – The stalk of a leaf.

Lenticels – Raised pores on bark, which provides access for air to the inner tissues.
Linear – Long, narrow and flat margins are more or less parallel, usually used to describe a leaf.
Lip – A petal or modified stamen that is usually larger than the other petals.
Lobe – Any projection of a leaf, rounded or pointed.
Lobed – Leaf cut less than halfway to the base.

Microclimate – The climate of a small area or locality as opposed to that of a larger area.
Midrib (Midvein) – The central main vein of a leaf or leaflet, it is usually the largest and most visually prominent vein in the leaf.
Monocarpic – Refers to a plant that flowers only once, sets fruit, and then dies.
Monoecious – The stamens and pistils in separate flowers but borne on the same plant.
Monophyletic – Forming a clade.
Monotypic – A genus or family of plants that comprises only one species.
Mulch – A layer of organic matter that is spread on the soil around plants.

Native – A species that naturally grows wild in a particular area.
Naturalised – Describes a species that apparently grows wild in a particular area, but is introduced and not native.
Needle-shaped – Long, slender and rigid.
Nocturnal – A term used to describe flowers that open at night and close during the day.
Node – The place on a stem, sometimes swollen, from which a leaf or single group of leaves and side-shoots emerges.

Oblanceolate – Having a lanceolate shape, but broadest in the upper third.
Oblique – Slanting, with unequal sides.
Oblong – Longer than wide with sides more or less parallel for most of their length.
Obovate – A reversed ovate shape, the narrower part being near the point of attachment.
Obtuse – Blunt or rounded at the end.
Odd-pinnate – An uneven number of leaflets in a pinnate leaf.
Offset – A young plant that arises naturally on the parent or on short lateral stems.
Ovary – The basal ovule, bearing part of the pistil, which contains the future seed.
Ovate – Egg-shaped with the broadest part being near the middle and more or less rounded at both ends.

Palmate – Describes a compound or segmented leaf with three or more lobes or leaflets radiating fan-shaped from a common basal point of attachment.
Palmately lobed – Palmately-divided leaf not cut to base.
Panicle – A branched and elongated flower cluster.
Pedicel – The stalk of an individual flower.
Peduncle – The stalk of an inflorescence.
Peltate – Leaf-blade attached to stalk inside its margin; the stalk is usually attached to the centre of the leaf's underside. The leaf is usually rounded in outline.
Pendant – Hanging down from its support.
Perennial – A plant that lives for at least two years. The term is usually used to denote an herbaceous plant or a soft shrubby plant.
Perianth – A collective term for the calyx and corolla.
Petal – Modified leaf of the corolla, usually coloured and showy.
Petiole – The primary stalk of a leaf.
pH – Measure of acidity or alkalinity.
Photosynthesis – A complex series of chemical reactions in green plants with the conversion of carbon dioxide and water into carbohydrates, taking the energy from light, helped by chlorophyll.
Pinnae – Primary division of a pinnate leaf, its leaflets.
Pinnate leaf – A compound leaf whose leaflets are arranged alternately or in pairs on opposite sides of a central axis and comprise over three leaflets, with or without a terminal leaflet.
Pinnatifid – Pinnately divided, but not to the central axis.
Pistil – The female reproductive organ of a flower comprising the ovary, style and the stigma.
Plumose – Radiating at different angles.
Pollen – The grains in the anther containing the male element necessary for fertilisation.
Pollination – The transfer of pollen from an anther to a receptive stigma.
Pubescent – Covered with soft short fine hairs, downy.

Raceme – An unbranched, elongated, simple inflorescence with stalked flowers – the youngest flowers near the tip.
Recurved – Curved backwards or downwards.
Reflexed – Abruptly recurved or bent sharply back upon itself.
Reticulate – Forming a network; for example, veins that join one another at more than one point.
Rhizomatous – Provided with rhizomes.
Rhizome – An underground, horizontal, creeping modified stem, which acts as a storage organ and gives rise to roots, stems and leaves at its nodes or growing tips.
Rosette – 1 A cluster of leaves radiating in a circle from a central point, or crown of a plant, usually near the ground. 2 A cluster of leaves on a trunk or branch. 3 Whorled arrangement of petals.
Runner – A slender, prostrate shoot, rooting at the end or at joints where plantlets are produced.

Salverform – A flower with a corolla that is tubular, long and slim that ends in a more or less flat disc.
Scandent – Climbing, in whatever manner.
Sepal – Each segment of a calyx, or outer floral envelopes.
Serrate – A leaf whose margin is finely toothed. The points curve towards the leaf's apex, like a saw blade.
Serrulate – Minutely serrate.
Sessile – Without a stalk.

Sheath – A leaf whose base is constricted into an almost tubular shape clasping and surrounding a part of a plant, such as the basal part of a palm leaf that surrounds the stem.
Shoot – Main upright growth of a seedling. Also applied to side-growths, or branches.
Shrub – A branched perennial plant with persistent woody growth.
Silky – Having a covering of soft fine hairs.
Simple – Not compound, a leaf that has a single blade and is not divided into separate leaflets, it may, however, be deeply lobed or partially segmented.
Single – A flower with one set of petals.
Solitary – Flowers that are borne singly, alone and not in clusters.
Spadix (plural: **Spadices**) – A usually thick and fleshy cylindrical flower spike of tiny densely set flowers, usually surrounded by a spathe.
Spathe – A relatively large and often coloured bract surrounding or found at the base of an inflorescence.
Species (sp.) – Individuals with the same character and which can be bred with each other.
Spike – An elongated flower stem, with flowers not stalked.
Sport – A plant that differs significantly from its parents because of mutation, such as a variegated shoot.
Spray – A cluster of flowers arranged on a single-branched stem.
Spur – A tubular projection from the base of a petal or sepal.
Stamen – The pollen-bearing or 'male' organ of a seed plant comprising the filament and the anther.
Standard – A shrub that has been trained and pruned to form a rounded head of branches with a single clear stem.
Stem – The main leaf-bearing and flower-bearing axis of a plant.
Sterile – Any flower that is incapable of producing seed.
Stigma – The terminal part of the pistil or style, which receives the pollen to fertilise the ovules.
Stipule – A leaf-like appendage at the base of a petiole.
Stolon – A shoot that creeps along the surface of the soil and roots at specific nodes, creating new plants.
Stoloniferous – Sending out, or propagating itself by stolons.
Style – The connecting stalk between the ovary and stigma.
Subshrub – A low-growing shrub, or one with soft stems and a woody base.
Subspecies (ssp.) – A subdivision of a species.
Succulent – Plant with thick fleshy leaves or stems adapted to life under arid conditions.
Sucker – Arises from the plant's roots, sometimes distant from the mother plant and, with time, will develop into an identical plant.
Synonym (syn.) – A name rejected in favour of another.

Tap root – Goes straight down into the ground from the embryonic root.
Tender – Sensitive to frost, as opposed to hardy.
Tendril – A thread-shaped shoot used for climbing.
Tepal – A sepal or petal that is intermediate in form and not readily distinguished from either.
Terrestrial – Plants growing in the ground or soil rather than epiphytically.
Throat – The opening part of the tubular part of a flower.
Tomentose – Covered in dense short hairs.
Trifoliate – A term used to describe a leaf with three leaflets.
Trumpet-shaped – A flower with a long narrow tube flaring at the throat into lobes, often arching backwards.
Tuber – A thickened fleshy root, or an underground stem that stores food.
Turgid – Inflated; swollen with fluid contents.

Umbel – Flat or round-topped inflorescence in which flower stalks or cluster arise from the same point.
Unarmed – Without spines, prickles or other sharp points.
Underplant – To surround and interplant larger plants with smaller ones.
Undulate – Leaf, sepal or petals are wavy-margined or crimpled.
Unifoliate – Having compound leaves that are reduced to one leaflet.

Variegated – Leaves that are striped, edged, or otherwise marked with a colour different from the primary colour of the leaf.
Variety (var.) – A naturally occurring variant of a species whose distinct character does not justify classification as a separate species.
Vegetative – Propagation by cuttings, division, layering or grafting, as distinct from seeds.

Weeping – Describes a tree or shrub of a pendulous habit.
Whorl – A circular arrangement of leaves, flowers or bracts, around a single point or node.

Xerophyte – A plant adapted to an arid environment.

BIBLIOGRAPHY

Barron, P., *Create a Mediterranean Garden* (Anness Publishing Ltd, 1999)

Brickell, C. (editor) *The Royal Horticultural Society A-Z Encyclopedia of Garden Plants* (Dorling Kindersley, 1996)

de Noailles, V. and Lancaster, R., *Mediterranean Plants and Gardens* (Floraprint, 1977)

Gildemeister, H., *Mediterranean Gardening a Waterwise Approach* (1995)

Kirsten, K., *South African Garden Manual* (WGC Pretoria)

Latymer, H., *The Mediterranean Gardener* (Frances Lincoln, 1990)

Nottle, T., *Gardens of the Sun* (Timber Press, 1996)

Payne, G., *Garden Plants for Mediterranean Climates* (The Crowood Press, 2002)

Rix, M., *Subtropical and Dry Climate Plants* (Cameron House, 2006)

Scott-Macnab, J. (editor), *New Encyclopedia of Garden Plants and Flowers* (Reader's Digest, 1997)

Smithen, J., *Sun Drenched Gardens* (Harry N. Abrams Inc., 2002)

Taylor, J., *Plants for Dry Gardens* (Frances Lincoln, 1993)

Walker, J., *The Subtropical Garden* (Timber Press, 1992)

Some useful websites used in writing this book.:

https://www.gardenia.net/ – An impressive list of plants with lots of information.

https://www.gardensonline.com.au/ – Useful plant descriptions.

https://www.wikipedia.org/ – A vast amount of information about plants.

https://www.worldfloraonline.org/ – An online database of all known plants.

PHOTO CREDITS

The following images are from www.dreamstime.com:

Chapter 1

A beautiful garden can be created with little water. – 322666396 © Anna Chaplygina.

Chapter 2

Trees provide shade for both you and your plants. – 135817276 © Andreistanesc.
Steps between different levels add interest on a sloping site. – 135817030 © Andreistanesc
The gentle sound of running water adds a soothing touch. – 44870509 © Mariusz Jurgielewic
Potted plants soften a high wall in a small space. – 56104362 © Inge Hogenbij
It is a pleasure to walk under a leafy pergola on a hot day. – 75971178 © Guo Amrei

Chapter 4

Acacia saligna - 273501333 © Irina Opachevsk
Acanthus spinosus - 251320436 © Dav Maddoc
Achillea filipendulina - 227919084 © Mykola Ohorodny
Achnatherum calamagrostis - 136295973 © Simona Pava
Acis autumnalis - 292842202 © Tom Meake
Adenocarpus hispanicus - 119090756 © Angel Luis MartÃn Ojed
Aesculus californica - 141501968 © Andreistanesc
Aesculus pavia - 40047414 © Dagobert162
Agapetes serpens - 116558109 © pisces238
Agave americana - 131203709 © Sbhos
Alcea rosea - 67272939 © Hoang Long Nguye
Allium caeruleum - 94984375 © Aleks22
Allium giganteum - 118195872 © Elenarostunov
Allium moly - 184428941 © Hana Richterov
Aloysia triphylla - 220415092 © Mohamed Hadda
Alstroemeria aurea - 149994674 © Yorozu Kitamur
Alyogyne huegelii - 117702740 © InesPorad
Anemone coronaria - 30343590 © Debu55
Anemonoides blanda - 246689541 © Tom Meake
Anigozanthos bicolor - 303808916 © Faithiecannois
Arbutus unedo - 191397170 © Wirestoc
Arctotis hybrids - 327555396 © Maryna Andriichu
Argyranthemum frutescens - 152492038 © Cpimage
Armeria maritima - 152783753 © Kristyna Henkeov
Artemisia schmidtiana - 256353542 © Naeto
Arum italicum - 288209788 © Robert Buche
Arundo donax - 88836731 © Sagegardenherb
Asphodeline lutea - 202220207 © Orest Lyzhechk
Asphodelus albus - 251313393 © Sigur
Aucuba japonica - 109768037 © Simona Pava
Ballota pseudodictamnus - 122630839 © Simona Pava
Banksia coccinea - 123384152 © Orawan Atth
Beschorneria yuccoides - 220259044 © Marinodenisenk
Billardiera heterophylla - 195437450 © John Cale
Billbergia nutans - 44071591 © Werner
Borago officinalis - 91101648 © Tverkhovinet
Bougainvillea hybrid - 5285874 © Duncan Noake
Bougainvillea spectabilis - 76205275 © Rostislav Agee
Brachychiton bidwillii - 124037473 © Karen Blac
Brachyglottis greyi - 272070121 © Simona Pava
Brahea armata - 247726673 © Svetlana Zhukov
Brunfelsia americana - 94853869 © Zeren
Brunfelsia pauciflora - 248345636 © Irina Opachevsk
Buddleja davidii - 78935605 © Caymi
Buddleja madagascariensis - 242064830 © Hguerri
Bulbine latifolia - 223984382 © Karin De Mamie
Butia capitata - 299985534 © Marinodenisenk
Calendula officinalis - 7948243 © Liane
Calliandra eriophylla - 243884394 © Ruan Whit
Calliandra tweediei - 137829204 © Emilia Salafranca Barrio
Calodendrum capense - 149266800 © Mariagrot
Camellia japonica - 27475148 © Odrachenk
Campsis grandiflora - 326986017 © Orest Lyzhechk
Campsis radicans flava - 75693686 © Macsstoc
Canarina canariensis - 304457305 © Robert Buche
Cantua buxifolia - 130366288 © Eddydegroo
Capparis spinosa - 249728371 © Joseph Khour
Caragana arborescens - 113720441 © Irina Borsuchenk
Carica papaya - 191546226 © Aiacob
Carissa macrocarpa - 164114366 © Maksims Grigorjev
Carnegiea gigantea - 4073675 © Joao Virissim
Carpenteria californica - 145969399 © Westhima
Carpobrotus edulis - 53123696 © Alvaro Trabazo Riva
Caryopteris clandonensis - 262321990 © Cristina Ionesc
Catananche caerulea - 151647630 © Tom Meake
Ceanothus impressus - 247758340 © Alain Wacquie

Ceiba speciosa - 68214532 © Emkapli
Cenchrus alopecuroides - 77955915 © Barmalin
Centaurea cineraria - 244484340 © Dizzizzme
Cerastium glomeratum - 137509961 © Apugach
Ceratostigma plumbaginoides - 202548791 © Anthony Bagget
Cercis siliquastrum - 91545871 © Eamesbo
Cestrum aurantiacum - 236418747 © Rob Lumen Captum
Cestrum parqui - 309140106 © Rob Lumen Captu
Chaenomeles speciosa - 58336538 © Stickas
Chamelaucium uncinatum - 151127016 © Karen Blac
Chasmanthe floribunda - 251601187 © Barmalin
Chilopsis linearis - 257000595 © Rob Lumen Captu
Choisya ternata - 254401354 © Unique9
Chorizema cordatum - 127923338 © Teddy OHear
Cistus aguilari - 119596743 © Dev
Cistus albidus - 255367448 © Unique9
Cleistocactus strausii - 237313573 © Karin De Mamie
Cleistocactus winteri - 151306078 © Lauraciesla
Clematis cirrhosa - 134155603 © Dav Hanso
Clematis montana var. grandiflora - 92446150 © Delstudi
Cleome spinosa - 27053265 © Reinout Van Wagtendon
Cleretum bellidiforme - 240386204 © RukiMedi
Clianthus puniceus - 240216623 © Hans Wismeije
Clivia miniata - 176524046 © Michal Paulu
Cobaea scandens - 158690249 © Renata Bobe
Colchicum autumnale - 88314090 © Office200
Colquhounia coccinea - 224627015 © Rattanakorn Songreno
Colutea arborescens - 255709548 © Rob Lumen Captu
Conicosia pugioniformis - 277371645 © Hannator9
Convolvulus cneorum - 238758258 © Rob Lumen Captu
Coprosma kirkii variegata - 194201538 © Simona Pava
Coprosma repens - 238681628 © Igor Abramovyc
Coprosma repens 'Marginata' - 285427013 © Nurchabib Jamaludi
Coreopsis lanceolata - 225879605 © Meunier
Coronilla valentina - 260657939 © Nahha
Cortaderia selloana - 85043928 © Lukeluke6
Corynabutilon vitifolium - 289034203 © Tom Meake
Cosmos bipinnatus - 37449418 © Shih Hao Lia
Cota tinctoria - 29387625 © Tosha1
Cotinus coggygria - 185323106 © Michal Paulu
Cotoneaster lacteus - 81219827 © Plazaccamerama
Crassula ovata - 91101816 © Tverkhovinet
Crocus chrysanthus - 282101690 © Wirestoc
Cupressus sempervirens - 262374412 © Wirestoc
Curio rowleyanus - 97854710 © Tkgraphicdesig
Cyathea dealbata - 80069897 © Rafael Ben Ar
Cyclamen hederifolium - 199369314 © Dpimboroug
Cydonia oblonga - 237499762 © Nataliia Melnychu
Cytisus praecox albus - 152264755 © Zanozar
Cytisus scoparius - 55645099 © Jose Goula
Dasylirion wheeleri - 283577979 © Eutoc
Datura innoxia - 136773194 © Apugach
Delairea odorata - 83772008 © Ricardo De Paula Ferreir
Delonix regia - 18944029 © Aleksey Solodo
Dendromecon rigida - 255168912 © Jared Quenti
Dianella tasmanica variegata - 310176321 © Aditya Riski Azi
Dianthus caryophyllus - 114700188 © Darya Fedorov
Dierama pulcherrimum - 192855706 © Suganya Sopa
Digitalis canariensis - 252726957 © Christopher Moswitze
Dimorphotheca sinuata - 317118775 © Ec
Dimorphotheca spectabilis - 68469241 © Alvaro Trabazo Riva
Dioon edule - 251233577 © Horst Liebe
Dodonaea viscosa purpurea - 223898865 © Karin De Mamie
Doronicum columnae - 151866233 © Shalom
Dracaena draco - 28116872 © Dekanarya
Dracaena marginata - 265255816 © arjuna anggar
Dracunculus vulgaris - 213427923 © Konstantin Basi
Drimia maritima - 246881086 © Iva Vagnerov
Drosanthemum floribundum - 251161800 © Yuri Arcur
Dyckia fosteriana - 58776902 © Pimonpim Tangoso
Eccremocarpus scaber - 267448725 © Tom Meake
Echeveria agavoides 'Red Tip' - 171002891 © Ericaimam
Echeveria 'Perle Von Nurnberg' - 138151388 © Fotoko
Echinacea purpurea - 311553131 © Stockavalepsa
Echinopsis oxygona - 325641224 © Jcasorey
Echium candicans - 215753910 © Guilherme Soare
Echium wildpretii - 246632389 © Yorozu Kitamur
Elaeagnus angustifolia - 184700930 © Mrehssan
Elaeagnus ebbingei - 195174688 © John Cale
Encephalartos altensteinii - 263843980 © Konstantin Shishki
Epacris longiflora - 51011855 © Caroline Marschne
Epilobium canum - 76797321 © Westhima
Eremurus isabellinus 'cleopatra' - 307613979 © Olga So
Erica arborea - 288485825 © Tom Meake
Erica australis - 245656929 © Jessicahyd
Eriobotrya japonica - 45176277 © Viovit
Eriocapitella hupehensis - 219090360 © Nikolai Kurzenk
Eriocephalus africanus - 173511393 © Josieelia
Eryngium amethystinum - 86217857 © Ciro Amedeo Orabon
Eryngium maritimum - 20248761 © Gl0ck3
Erythrina caffra - 246432044 © Rob Lumen Captu
Erythrostemon gilliesii - 251958042 © Unique9
Escallonia bifida - 121131315 © Nahha
Eschscholzia californica - 105152289 © Alonfrma
Eucalyptus polyanthemos - 125293237 © Gene Zhan
Euonymus fortunei 'Emerald n Gold' - 274066876 © Maryia Afanasyev
Euonymus japonicus 'ovatus aureus' - 248127199 © Svetlana Zhukov
Euphorbia characias 'wulfenii' - 217801946 © Dav Maddoc
Euphorbia pulcherrima - 187443020 © Matyas Reha
Evolvulus pilosus - 265640030 © Riosihombin
Fargesia murielae - 254835943 © Wirestoc
Felicia amelloides - 284749242 © Svetlana Zhukov
Ferocactus acanthodes - 318752160 © Oleg Kovtu
Ferocactus pilifer - 327467778 © Natalia Pavlov
Ferula communis - 309210768 © Hans Wismeije

Festuca glauca - 216515803 © Svetlana Zhukov
Ficus pumila - 31345148 © Scenery
Freesia corymbosa x hybrids - 215454437 © Joan Carles Juare
Fremontodendron californicum - 164742993 © Westhima
Fritilaria imperialis - 148457888 © Natali2220
Gaillardia grandiflora - 189587235 © Natalia Pavlov
Garrya elliptica - 233898236 © Tom Cardric
Gazania rigens - 150103095 © Clearvist
Gelsemium sempervirens - 68341889 © Bervol
Genista hispanica - 263796372 © Jon Benito Iz
Geranium maderense - 310795804 © Victoria Sharrat
Gerbera jamesonii - 40508318 © Westhima
Gladiolus grandiflorus - 183538500 © Khuruzer
Glandora diffusa - 238423605 © Rob Lumen Captu
Gleditsia triacanthos - 319725095 © Stockavalepsa
Gomphocarpus fruticosus - 86582988 © Woravit Vijitpany
Graptopetalum paraguayense - 147123828 © Simona Pava
Grevillea robusta - 91756530 © Foster Euban
Grevillea rosmarinifolia - 248247643 © Key123
Haemanthus coccineus - 235957179 © Barbarag5
Hakea laurina - 159912897 © Karin De Mamie
Hardenbergia violacea - 189618425 © Ken Griffith
Helianthemum nummularium - 253195525 © Rob Lumen Captu
Helichrysum italicum - 249248407 © Fedecandon
Helichrysum petiolare - 262522337 © Wirestoc
Hesperoyucca whipplei - 135817843 © Andreistanesc
Hibbertia scandens - 259619071 © Ken Griffith
Hibiscus syriacus - 147083168 © Gabriela Bertolin
Hippophae rhamnoides - 79560269 © Miroslav Hlavk
Hordeum jubatum - 43112132 © Pisotcki
Hyacinthus orientalis - 167273694 © Simona Pava
Hymenosporum flavum - 214974861 © Karin De Mamie
Hyophorbe lagenicaulis - 158332179 © Olesia Opymak
Iberis sempervirens - 211609881 © Iva Vagnerov
Ipheion uniflorum - 215546178 © Mario Krpa
Ipomoea purpurea - 228544995 © Nikolay Bodare
Iris pallida - 283113301 © Horst Liebe
Iris xiphium - 184795347 © Nikolai Kurzenk
Ismene deflexa - 126034125 © Nikolai Kurzenk
Isopogon anethifolius - 78200527 © Karen Blac
Isopogon formosus - 265271862 © InesPorad
Jacaranda mimosifolia - 238345484 © Marion Meye
Jacobaea maritima - 321724107 © Yorozu Kitamur
Jarava ichu - 291116448 © Tanjim Hasa
Jasminum mesnyi - 246096318 © Toshihisa Shimod
Jasminum officinale - 143442990 © Martin Lebe
Jubaea chilensis - 198239491 © Marinodenisenk
Kniphofia uvaria - 190362206 © Michelle K Woo
Koelreuteria paniculata seed pods - 124639925 © Tj87664829
Koelreuteria paniculata - 138963693 © Ivana Stevanosk
Kunzea ambigua - 201991490 © Karen Blac
Kunzea pulchella - 296878569 © Karen Blac
Lagerstroemia indica - 57761914 © Anan Punyo
Lagurus ovatus - 144668315 © Rontav12
Lampranthus glaucoides - 145331771 © Alexander Bernard
Lampranthus spectabilis - 241481936 © John Cale
Lantana camara - 74552730 © Phuon
Lantana montevidensis - 143382476 © Svetlana Bake
Laurus nobilis - 173781612 © Ehayd
Lavandula latifolia - 95075757 © Nancy Pauwel
Leonotis leonurus - 127765162 © Gene Zhan
Leschenaultia biloba - 204365904 © Dav Massi
Leucadendron argenteum - 232268632 © Craig Russel
Leucojum aestivum - 123182023 © Andreistanesc
Leucospermum cordifolium - 87693617 © Ninahass
Lilium candidum - 150569003 © Roadwind2
Lilium formosanum - 158021054 © Yorozu Kitamur
Limonium perezii - 146252806 © Westhima
Limonium sinuatum - 286179318 © Sheila Fitzgeral
Liquidambar formosana - 203658872 © Mikhail Gnatkovskiy
Lobularia maritima - 82880694 © Oleksandr Rad
Lomandra longifolia - 198514909 © Beautifulblosso
Lonicera etrusca - 226042828 © OLAYOL
Lonicera japonica - 176993242 © Mikhail Popo
Loropetalum chinense - 221397612 © Simona Pava
Lotus berthelotii - 143528999 © Severina7
Lupinus albifrons - 144334764 © Andreistanesc
Lupinus arboreus - 150944752 © Andreistanesc
Lycoris aurea - 45410643 © Moon123
Lycoris radiata - 244534106 © Jose Luis Lag
Macrozamia communis - 186479190 © Karin De Mamie
Malcolmia maritima - 244501425 © Anish P
Malva trimestris - 240308634 © Tom Meake
Matthiola incana - 180800443 © Yui Yuiz
Melaleuca nesophila - 123369484 © Andreistanesc
Melaleuca quadrifida - 216596530 © Jon Benito Iz
Melaleuca viminalis - 41968289 © Tomtsy
Melia azedarach - 231077185 © Max512
Melianthus major - 130835582 © Karin De Mamie
Mesembryanthemum cordifolium - 237577667 © Wirestoc
Metrosideros kermadecensis variegata - 190357391 © InesPorad
Mirabilis jalapa - 227759500 © Artist Kroly
Montanoa bipinnatifida - 245838602 © Rob Lumen Captu
Moraea setifolia - 266317313 © Ava Peatti
Moraea tricolor - 103070705 © Wiert
Muscari armeniacum - 114804478 © Paul Maguir
Muscari macrocarpum - 180854811 © Christian WeiÃ
Myoporum laetum - 135811020 © Andreistanesc
Myrtus communis - 73304851 © Ppy2010h
Nandina domestica - 111316557 © Simona Pava
Narcissus papyraceus - 236248517 © Kim Nelso
Nassella tenuissima - 259270474 © Unique9
Nemesia strumosa - 217879899 © Simona Pava
Nerium oleander - 125070475 © Moskw
Nicotiana glauca - 219787114 © Vladimir Bronniko
Nigella - 118977183 © Iva Vagnerov
Oenothera macrocarpa - 42069411 © Joe Ferre

Oenothera speciosa - 117409113 © Jacqueline F Coope
Olea europaea - 4088378 © Gian Marco Valent
Opuntia basilaris - 89612058 © Daniel Larso
Opuntia gosseliniana - 317996707 © Monica Lar
Ornithogalum arabicum - 121560996 © Simoncountry9
Ornithogalum dubium - 174897056 © N P
Orthrosanthus multiflorus - 193708250 © Chris De Blan
Osteospermum ecklonis - 101247923 © Westhima
Paeonia cambessedesii - 313551163 © Robert Buche
Pallenis maritima - 61058243 © Kewuw
Pancratium maritimum - 314215147 © Vicgin
Papaver atlanticum - 117026232 © Whiskybottl
Papaver commutatum - 252109626 © Golden Shar
Paraserianthes lophantha - 209156082 © Nemesio Jimenez Jimene
Pelargonium domesticum - 108937259 © Lubomir Jile
Pelargonium peltatum - 162861487 © Irina Borsuchenk
Penstemon barbatus - 241444411 © Inna Polietaiev
Penstemon heterophyllus - 120963038 © Anthony Bagget
Phlomis fruticosa - 317715509 © Yorozu Kitamur
Phoenix canariensis - 229032187 © Helga1
Photinia x fraseri - 255435670 © John Cale
Phygelius x rectus moonraker - 251857887 © Debu55
Physalis peruviana - 138012744 © Oleksandr Rad
Phytolacca dioica - 262220002 © Key123
Pistacia vera - 184845525 © Jessicahyd
Pittosporum tenuifolium variegatum - 318236752 © Unique9
Pittosporum tobira - 318273787 © Yorozu Kitamur
Plumbago auriculata - 33973 © Bob Denelze
Podranea ricasoliana - 236557434 © Irina Opachevsk
Polygala myrtifolia - 315584533 © Nataliav
Portulaca grandiflora - 28770868 © Graciela Ross
Protea cynaroides - 44615557 © Rafael Ben Ar
Protea eximia - 165051334 © Martine Banckaer
Prunus cerasifera pissardii - 141660959 © Apugach
Prunus lusitanica - 285842963 © Simona Pava
Pultenaea stipularis - 256247759 © Karen Blac
Punica granatum - 316359938 © Irina Opachevsk
Pyracantha coccinea - 63951664 © Arndal
Pyrostegia venusta - 240598789 © Mohan Kuma
Quercus coccifera - 64452247 © Whiskybottl
Retama monosperma - 138579354 © Tetyana Lyap
Retama sphaerocarpa - 214760797 © Alfredo Garcia Sa
Rhamnus alaternus - 111312840 © Marlene Vicent
Rhaphiolepis indica - 292611335 © Yanina Guimarayn
Rhodanthe chlorocephala ssp rosea - 228846165 © Rafael Ben Ar
Rhodomyrtus tomentosa - 30941185 © Happyboy200
Rhus typhina - 139804630 © Argenlan
Ricinus communis - 104044341 © Jeannemme
Robinia hispida - 316604150 © Hbcs008
Roldana petasitis - 310317225 © Antoniospapageorgiou198
Romneya coulteri - 303587930 © Anthony Bagget
Romulea bulbocodium - 312660400 © Robert Buche
Romulea monadelpha - 61042896 © Grobler Du Pree
Rosa banksiae - 143383673 © Svetlana Bake
Rosa laevigata - 180873909 © Yorozu Kitamur
Rosmarinus officinalis - 5200034 © Laurel Stewar
Ruscus aculeatus - 184870131 © Simona Pava
Ruta graveolens - 118257993 © Maren Winte
Salvia candidissima - 197453158 © Simona Pava
Salvia darcyi - 288210632 © Robert Buche
Salvia farinacea - 106994070 © Tristan Scholz
Salvia leucantha - 165043512 © Anubhab Ro
Salvia officinalis - 127384999 © Simona Pava
Salvia yangii - 175098860 © Agata Pietrza
Santolina chamaecyparissus - 121711815 © Jose Pedros
Scabiosa columbaria - 153605895 © Andreistanesc
Scadoxus multiflorus - 246980077 © Nh Mahfu
Scaevola aemula - 258494480 © Rob Lumen Captu
Schinus molle - 264752567 © Amovitani
Schotia brachypetala - 127767027 © Gene Zhan
Scilla peruviana - 216815493 © Yorozu Kitamur
Sedum acre - 120594380 © Belaruslad
Sedum morganianum - 264571016 © Rob Lumen Captu
Senecio macroglossus 'Variegatus' - Wouter Hagens | public domain
Senna alata - 193188341 © Sunasoa
Senna spectabilis - 134343480 © Tatiana Nazarov
Silene armeria - 129365191 © Sfagna
Solanum betaceum - 255106781 © Cecilia Di Di
Solanum laxum 'Album' - 210600070 © Estelle Bowde
Solanum wendlandii - 1155070 © Anke Van Wy
Sparaxis tricolor - 223984467 © Karin De Mamie
Spartium junceum - 56394727 © Saphire Ovadi
Sphaeralcea ambigua - 258732254 © Jared Quenti
Spirea cantoniensis - 183059260 © Supersomi
Stachys byzantina - 194303683 © James844
Strelitzia juncea - Andrew Massyn | public domain
Streptosolen jamesonii - 255888736 © Cindhy Hapsar
Styphnolobium japonicum - 277962707 © Jinfeng Zhan
Swainsona formosa - 150979053 © Rafael Ben Ar
Tamarix parviflora - 208104182 © Mikhail Gnatkovski
Tanacetum densum ssp amani - 219098069 © Nikolai Kurzenk
Tecoma stans - 128350639 © Khatawut Chaemchamra
Tecomaria capensis - 82299484 © Westhima
Telopea speciosissima - 34093888 © Anne Amphlet
Tetradenia riparia - 225026226 © Nancy Ayumi Kunihir
Teucrium fruticans - 219775052 © Yilmaz Savas Kanda
Thymus serpyllum - 318331629 © Gigell
Thymus x citriodorus - 42423207 © Marta Jonin
Tigridia pavonia - 102334365 © Sleepyhobbi
Tipuana tipu - 266085472 © Sanjiv Shukl
Tithonia rotundifolia - 258497173 © Rob Lumen Captu
Tradescantia sillamontana - 214977580 © Karin De Mamie
Tritonia crocata - 247265297 © Manfred Ruckszi
Tulbaghia violacea - 218258586 © Chih Chang Cho
Valeriana rubra - 248591043 © Anthony Bagget

Veltheimia bracteata - 247343210 © Karin De Mamie
Verbascum bombyciferum - 281762319 © Unique9
Verbena bonariensis - 258579981 © Rob Lumen Captu
Verticordia grandis - 241194120 © Karen Blac
Viburnum tinus - 215846192 © Rob Lumen Captu
Vinca major variegata - 250908128 © Ihor Hvozdetski
Viola odorata - 111336974 © Simona Pava
Vitex agnus-castus - 320619244 © Eutoc
Washingtonia filifera - 135812624 © Andreistanesc
Watsonia borbonica - 262376742 © Wirestoc
Wigandia urens - 315707714 © Callistemon
Xanthoceras sorbifolium - 85351428 © Rbiederman
Xanthorrhoea australis - 76835247 © Fritz Hiersch
Xeranthemum annuum - 190754829 © Iva Vagnerov
Xerochrysum bracteatum - 316194833 © Swee Ming Youn
Yucca aloifolia 'marginata' - 280495746 © Karin De Mamie
Yucca filamentosa - 179829121 © Anmbp
Yucca gigantea - 109645744 © Simona Pava
Zinnia elegans - 127125524 © Apugach

The following images are from Wikimedia Commons:
Amphilophium buccinatorium - © Mark Pilbeam, Shipston-on-Stour, UK
Corokia x virgata - © A. Barra
Daphne pontica - © Kurt Stüber
Daphne sericia - © Philippe Pechoux
Dicliptera squarrosa - © John Robert McPherson
Dudleya pulverulenta - © James M. Maley
Euryops pectinatus - © David J. Stang
Hedera canariensis 'Gloire de Marengo' - © David J. Stang
Hippeastrum aulicum - © Bullgirl
Hyphaene coriacea - © Krzysztof Ziarnek, Kenraiz
Lapageria rosea - © Ross Beever
Maurandella antirrhiniflora - © Katja Schulz, Washington D.C., USA
Pinus pinaster - © Miguel Angel Amsegosa Martinez
Prostanthera rotundifolia - © Kevin Sparrow
Reseda odorata - © Salicyna
Rhamnus alaternus 'Argenteovariegata' - © Myrabella
Zaluzianskya affinis - © SAplants
Zaluzianskya divaricata - © SAplants
Zaluzianskya violacea - © SAplants

All other photos are by the author, Graham Payne.

ENGLISH COMMON NAMES

Many people only know the common name of a plant. Below is the list of generally accepted English common names for the plants in this book, although there are many other names in use.

Abyssinian Fountain Grass – *Cenchrus longisetus*
Adam's Needle – *Yucca gloriosa*
Adam's Needle and Thread – *Yucca filamentosa*
African Blue Lily – Agapanthus
African Bush Daisy – *Euryops chrysanthemoides*
African Button-Flower – Dais
African Corn Flag – *Chasmanthe floribunda*
African Corn Lily – *Ixia maculata*
African Daisy – Gazania
African Daisy – Arctotis
African Daisy – *Dimorphotheca spectabilis*
African Daisy – Osteospermum
African Iris – *Dietes bicolor*
African Lily – *Agapanthus africanus*
African Walnut – *Schotia brachypetala*
African Wormwood – *Artemisia arborescens*
Airplane Plant – *Crassula perfoliata* var. *falcata*
Albanian Spurge – *Euphorbia characias* subsp. *wulfenii*
Aleppo Pine – *Pinus halepensis*
Algerian Ivy – *Hedera canariensis*
Alyssum – *Lobularia maritima*
Amarillo – Amaryllis
Amaryllis – Hippeastrum
Amethyst Eryngo – *Eryngium amethystinum*
Amethyst Sea Holly – *Eryngium amethystinum*
Angel's Fishing Rod – Dierama
Angels' Hair – *Artemisia schmidtiana*
Angels' Trumpet – *Datura innoxia*
Angels Trumpet – *Maurandya barclayana*
Annual Mallow – Malope
Annual Mallow – *Malva trimestris*
Apple Geranium – *Pelargonium odoratissimum*
Apricot mallow – *Sphaeralcea ambigua*
Argentine Senna – *Senna corymbosa*
Armenian Grape Hyacinth – *Muscari armeniacum*
Asiatic Poison Lily – Crinum
Asparagus Fern – *Asparagus densiflorus* 'Sprengeri'
Aspic Lavender – *Lavandula latifolia*
Atlas Poppy – *Papaver atlanticum*
Aurora Borealis Plant – *Kalanchoe fedtschenkoi* 'Marginata'
Australian Grasstree – *Xanthorrhoea australis*
Australian Brush Cherry – *Syzygium paniculatum*
Australian Clematis – *Clematis aristata*
Australian Frangipani – Hymenosporum

Australian Fuchsia – Correa
Australian Mock Orange – *Pittosporum undulatum*
Australian Willow Myrtle – *Agonis flexuosa*
Autumn Crocus – Colchicum
Autumn Daffodil – Sternbergia
Autumn Sage – *Salvia greggii*
Autumn Snowflake – *Acis autumnalis*
Aztec Lily – *Sprekelia formosissima*
Baboon Flowers – Babiana
Baja Fairy Duster – *Calliandra californica*
Balearic Islands Sage – *Phlomis italica*
Balearic Peony – *Paeonia cambessedesii*
Balga – *Xanthorrhoea preissii*
Balkan Anemone – *Anemonoides blanda*
Banksian Rose – *Rosa banksiae* 'Lutea'
Barberton Daisy – *Gerbera jamesonii*
Basket Evening Primrose – *Oenothera deltoides*
Basket Grass – *Lomandra longifolia*
Bat Faced Cuphea – *Cuphea llavea*
Bay Laurel – *Laurus nobilis*
Beach Wormwood – *Artemisia stelleriana*
Bearded Iris – *Iris* × *germanica*
Bear's Breeches – *Acanthus mollis*
Beavertail Prickly Pear – *Opuntia basilaris*
Belladonna Lily – Amaryllis
Bicol Wattle – *Paraserianthes lophantha*
Bidwill's Bottle Tree – *Brachychiton bidwillii*
Bigseed Tulp – *Moraea macrocarpa*
Bindweed – Convolvulus
Bindweeds – Evolvulus
Bird of Paradise – Strelitzia
Bird of Paradise Bush – *Erythrostemon gilliesii*
Birdcage Evening Primrose – *Oenothera deltoides*
Biting Stonecrop – *Sedum acre*
Bitter Aloe – *Aloe ferox*
Black Arum – *Dracunculus vulgaris*
Black Bamboo – *Phyllostachys nigra*
Black Calla – *Arum pictum*
Black Locust – *Robinia pseudoacacia*
Bladder Senna – Colutea
Bladderpod – Colutea
Blanket Flower – Gallardia
Blazing White Sage – *Salvia candidissima*
Blood Flower – *Asclepias curassavica*
Blood Flower – *Haemanthus coccineus*
Blood Lily – Haemanthus
Blood Lily – Scadoxus
Blood Red Trumpet Vine – *Amphilophium buccinatorium*
Bloodwoods – Corymbia
Blue Allium – *Allium caeruleum*
Blue Barrel Cactus – *Ferocactus glaucescens*
Blue Chalk Fingers – *Curio repens*
Blue Chalksticks – *Curio repens*
Blue Daisy – Felicia
Blue Fescue – *Festuca glauca*
Blue Flax Lily – *Dianella caerulea*
Blue Hesper Palm – *Brahea armata*
Blue Jacaranda – *Jacaranda mimosifolia*
Blue Leaf Wattle – *Acacia saligna*
Blue Leaved Cycad – *Encephalartos lehmannii*
Blue Leschenaultia – *Leschenaultia biloba*
Blue Marguerite – *Felicia amelloides*
Blue Mist – *Caryopteris* × *clandonensis*
Blue Potato Bush – *Lycianthes rantonnetii*
Blue Rock Bindweed – *Convolvulus sabatius*
Blue Spur Flower – *Plectranthus ecklonii*
Bluebeard – *Caryopteris* × *clandonensis*
Bluebell Creeper – *Billardiera heterophylla*
Blueblossom – *Ceanothus thyrsiflorus*
Bobtail Barley – *Hordeum jubatum*
Borage – *Borago officinalis*
Border or Garden Penstemon – Penstemon hybrids
Bottle Palm – Hyophorbe
Bottle Tree – Brachychiton
Bottlebrush – Melaleuca
Bowstring Hemp – *Dracaena trifasciata*
Branched Asphodel – *Asphodelus ramosus*
Bread Tree – *Encephalartos altensteinii*
Breckland thyme – *Thymus serpyllum*
Bridal Veil Broom – *Retama monosperma*
Bridal Wreath – *Spirea cantoniensis*
Broadleaved Lavender – *Lavandula latifolia*
Broad-Leaved Statice – *Limonium platyphyllum* (syn. *L. latifolium*)
Broom – Cytisus
Broom – Genista
Broom – Ruscus
Broussa Mullein – *Verbascum bombyciferum*
Brush Cherry – *Syzygium paniculatum*
Buckeye – Aesculus
Buckthorn – Rhamnus
Buddhist Bauhinia – *Bauhinia variegata*
Bull Bay – *Magnolia grandiflora*
Bull's-Eye – *Euryops chrysanthemoides*
Bunchleaf Penstemon – *Penstemon heterophyllus*
Burgundy Willow Myrtle – *Agonis flexuosa* 'Burgundy'
Burmese Plumbago – *Ceratostigma griffithii*
Bush Germander – *Teucrium fruticans*
Bush Poppy – *Dendromecon rigida*
Butcher's Broom – *Ruscus aculeatus*
Butterfly Bush – Buddleja
Butterfly Iris – Dietes
Byzantine Gladiolus – *Gladiolus communis* subsp. *byzantinus*
Cabbage Palm – Cordyline
Cabbage Tree – Cordyline
California Barrel Cactus – *Ferocactus acanthodes*
California Buckeye – *Aesculus californica*
California Fan Palm – *Washingtonia filifera*
California Flannelbush – *Fremontodendron californicum*
California Fuchsia – *Epilobium canum*
California Geranium – *Roldana petasitis*
California Lilac – Ceanothus
California Poppy – *Eschscholzia californica*
California Tree Poppy – *Romneya coulteri*
Canary Island Bird of Paradise – *Lotus berthelotii*
Canary Islands Bellflower – *Canarina canariensis*
Canary Islands Dragon Tree – *Dracaena draco*
Canary Islands Foxglove – *Digitalis canariensis*
Canary Islands Ivy – *Hedera canariensis*
Canary Islands Margeurite – *Argyranthemum foeniculaceum*
Canary Islands Palm – *Phoenix canariensis*
Canary Ivy – *Hedera canariensis*
Candelabra Euphorbia – *Euphorbia ingens*
Candelabra Plant – *Aloe arborescens*

Candelabra Tree – *Euphorbia ingens*
Candle Bush – *Senna alata*
Candytuft – Iberis
Cape Bugle Lily – *Watsonia borbonica*
Cape Chestnut – *Calodendrum capense*
Cape Figwort – Phygelius
Cape Fuchsia – Phygelius
Cape Gooseberry – *Physalis peruviana*
Cape Honeysuckle – *Tecomaria capensis*
Cape Ivy – *Senecio macroglossus*
Cape Jewels – *Nemesia strumosa*
Cape Leeuwin Wattle – *Paraserianthes lophantha*
Cape Mallow – Anisodontia
Cape Marguerite – *Dimorphotheca spectabilis*
Cape Plumbago – *Plumbago auriculata*
Cape Snow Bush – *Eriocephalus africanus*
Cape Strawflower – Phaenocoma
Cape Wattle – *Paraserianthes lophantha*
Caper Bush – *Capparis spinosa*
Caracus Wigandia – *Wigandia urens*
Caribbean Agave – *Agave angustifolia* 'Marginata'
Carolina Jasmine – *Gelsemium sempervirens*
Carrion Plant – *Duvalia corderoyi*
Cast-Iron Plant – *Aspidistra elatior*
Castor Oil Plant – *Ricinus communis*
Catmint – *Nepeta grandiflora*
Catnip – Nepeta
Caucasian Scarlet Poppy – *Papaver commutatum*
Century Plant – Agave
Chalk Dudleya – *Dudleya pulverulenta*
Chalk Lettuce – *Dudleya pulverulenta*
Chalk Liveforever – *Dudleya pulverulenta*
Chaste Tree – *Vitex agnus-castus*
Cheesewood – Pittosporum
Cherokee Rose – *Rosa laevigata*
Cherry Pie – *Heliotropium arborescens*
Chestnut Dioon – *Dioon edule*
Chile Cocopalm – *Jubaea chilensis*
Chilean Bellflower – Lapageria
Chilean Cestrum – *Cestrum parqui*
Chilean Glory Flower – *Eccremocarpus scaber*
Chilean Pitcher Sage – *Lepechinia salvia*
Chilean Potato Tree – *Solanum crispum*
Chilean Tree Mallow – *Corynabutilon vitifolium*
Chilean Wine Palm – *Jubaea chilensis*
Chinaberry – *Melia azedarach*
Chinese Flowering Chestnut – *Xanthoceras sorbifolium*
Chinese Flowering Quince – *Chaenomeles speciosa*
Chinese Fountain Grass – *Cenchrus alopecuroides*
Chinese Fringe Flower – Loropetalum
Chinese Jade Tree – *Crassula arborescens*
Chinese Juniper – *Juniperus chinensis*
Chinese Lanterns – Agapetes
Chinese Plumbago – *Ceratostigma willmottianum*
Chinese Scholar Tree – *Styphnolobium japonicum*
Chinese Trumpet Creeper – *Campsis grandiflora*
Chinese Witch Hazel – *Loropetalum chinense*
Christmas Berry – *Photinia × fraseri*
Christmas Candles – *Senna alata*
Christmas Kalanchoe – *Kalanchoe blossfeldiana*
Cigar Flower – *Cuphea ignea*
Cigar Plant – *Cuphea ignea*
Cigarette Flower – *Epacris longiflora*
Climbing Asparagus – *Asparagus setaceus*
Climbing Bell – *Gloriosa modesta*
Climbing Blueberry – *Billardiera heterophylla*
Climbing Guinea Flower – *Hibbertia scandens*
Climbing Lily – Gloriosa
Clove Pink – *Dianthus caryophyllus*
Coast Banksia – *Banksia integrifolia*
Coast Silk-Tassel – *Garrya elliptica*
Coastal Rosemary – *Westringia fruticosa*
Coastal Westringia – *Westringia fruticosa*
Cockscomb – *Erythrina crista-galli*
Cockspur Flower – *Plectranthus ecklonii*
Coleus – *Plectranthus glabratus*
Common Almond – *Prunus dulcis*
Common Asparagus Fern – *Asparagus setaceus*
Common Broom – *Cytisus scoparius*
Common Coral Tree – *Erythrina crista-galli*
Common Fennel – *Foeniculum vulgare*
Common Fig – *Ficus carica*
Common Geranium – *Pelargonium hortorum*
Common Hyacinth – *Hyacinthus orientalis*
Common Juniper – *Juniperus communis*
Common Mignonette – *Reseda odorata*
Common Morning-Glory – *Ipomoea purpurea*
Common Myrtle – *Myrtus communis*
Common Net Bush – *Melaleuca quadrifida*
Common Peony – *Paeonia officinalis*
Common Quince – *Cydonia oblonga*
Common Rock Rose – *Helianthemum nummularium*
Common Rosemary – *Rosmarinus officinalis*
Common Rue – *Ruta graveolens*
Common Sage – *Salvia officinalis*
Common White Jasmine – *Jasminum officinale*
Common Zinnia – *Zinnia elegans*
Compass Barrel Cactus – *Ferocactus acanthodes*
Cone Bush – Isopogon
Cone Bush – Leucadendron
Coneflowers – Echinacea
Coneflowers – Isopogon
Conesticks – Isopogon
Confederate Rose – *Hibiscus mutabilis*
Cootamundra – *Acacia baileyana*
Coppery Mesemb – *Malephora crocea*
Coral Gum – *Eucalyptus torquata*
Coral Pea – Hardenbergia
Coral Pea – Kennedia
Coral Plant – Russelia
Coral Tree – Erythrina
Coral Vine – Antigonon
Cork Oak – *Quercus suber*
Corn Flag – *Gladiolus communis* subsp. *byzantinus*
Cornflowers – Centaurea
Costa Rican Nightshade – *Solanum wendlandii*
Cotton Lavender – *Santolina chamaecyparissus*
Cow Itch Tree – *Lagunaria patersonia*
Cranesbill – Geranium
Crape Myrtle – *Lagerstroemia indica*
Creeping Juniper – *Juniperus horizontalis*
Creeping Rubber Plant – *Ficus pumilla*
Crested Wattle – *Paraserianthes lophantha*
Crimean Iris – *Iris lutescens*
Crimson Bottlebrush – *Melaleuca citrinus*

Crimson-Spot Rockrose – *Cistus ladanifer*
Crinum Lily – Crinum
Crown Imperial – *Fritillaria imperialis*
Crown of Thorns – *Euphorbia milii*
Crystalline Ice Plant – *Cleretum bellidiforme*
Cup and Saucer Plant – *Cobaea scandens*
Cupid's Dart – *Catananche caerulea*
Curry Plant – *Helichrysum italicum*
Curved-Leaved Spanish Dagger – *Yucca gloriosa* var. *tristis*
Curve-Leaf Yucca – *Yucca gloriosa* var. *tristis*
Cut Leaved Mallow – *Malva alcea*
Cypress – Cupressus
Daffodil – Narcissus
Daisy Bush – *Brachyglottis greyi*
Daisy Bush – Olearia
Daisy Tree – *Montanoa bipinnatifida*
Dalmatian Iris – *Iris pallida*
Darcy's Mexican Sage – *Salvia darcyi*
Darling Pea – *Swainsona galegifolia*
Desert Barrel Cactus – *Ferocactus acanthodes*
Desert Catalpas – Chilopis
Desert Hollyhock – *Sphaeralcea ambigua*
Desert Rose – Adenium
Desert Willows – Chilopis
Devil's Backbone – *Kalanchoe daigremontiana*
Dew Flower – *Drosanthemum floribundum*
Dew Plant – *Mesembryanthemum cordifolium*
Donkey Tail – *Sedum morganianum*
Doum Palm – *Hyphaene coriacea*
Downy Thorn-Apple – *Datura innoxia*
Drago – *Dracaena draco*
Dragon Arum – *Dracunculus vulgaris*
Dragon Lily – *Dracunculus vulgaris*
Drumstick Allium – *Allium sphaerocephalon*
Duck Egg Blue Ixia – *Ixia viridiflora*
Dusky Coral Pea – *Kennedia rubicunda*
Dusty Miller – *Artemisia stelleriana*
Dusty Miller – *Centaurea cineraria*
Dusty Miller – *Jacobaea maritima*
Dutch Hyacinth – *Hyacinthus orientalis*
Dutch Iris – *Iris xiphium*
Dwarf Blue Thunbergia – *Thunbergia natalensis*
Dwarf Morning Glories – Evolvulus
Dwarf Plumbago – *Ceratostigma plumbaginoides*
Early Virgin's Bower – *Clematis cirrhosa*
Easter Lily – Amaryllis
Easter Lily – *Lilium longiflorum*
Easter Lily Cactus – *Echinopsis oxygona*
Elephant's Foot – Beaucarnea
Eleven O'Clock – *Portulaca grandiflora*
Emperor's Candlesticks – *Senna alata*
Empress Candle Plant – *Senna alata*
Emu Bush – Eremophila
English Lavender – *Lavandula latifolia*
English Violet – *Viola odorata*
Etruscan Honeysuckle – *Lonicera etrusca*
Evening Primrose – Oenothera
Evening Trumpet Flower – *Gelsemium sempervirens*
Evergreen Candytuft – *Iberis sempervirens*
Evergreen Lupine – *Lupinus albifrons*
Evergreen Oak – *Quercus ilex*
Everlasting Daisy – *Rhodanthe chloro-cephala* ssp. *rosea*
Fairy Duster – Calliandra
Fairy Fan Flower – *Scaevola aemula*
Fairy Iris – Dietes
Fairybells – Dierama
False Acacia – *Robinia pseudoacacia*
False Heather – *Cuphea hyssopifolia*
False Mallows – Sphaeralcea
False Red Agave – *Beschorneria yuccoides*
Fan Aloe – *Kumara plicatilis*
Feather Grass – Stipa
Featherflowers – Verticordia
Feathertop – *Cenchrus longisetus*
Feathery Cassia – *Senna artemisioides*
Felt Plant – *Kalanchoe beharensis*
Fennel – Foeniculum
Fern-Leaf Yarrow – *Achillea filipendulina*
Ferocious Aloe – *Aloe ferox*
Ferocious Blue Cycad – *Encephalartos horridus*
Feverfew – *Tanacetum argenteum*
Fig – Ficus
Fire Lily – Gloriosa
Fire Lily – *Hippeastrum* hybrids
Firecracker Fern – *Russelia equisetiformis*
Firecracker Plant – *Cuphea ignea*
Firecracker Plant – *Dicliptera squarrosa*
Firecracker Plant – Russelia
Firecracker Vine – *Ipomoea lobata*
Firethorn – Pyracantha
Fishpole Bamboo – *Phyllostachys aurea*
Flamboyant Tree – Delonix
Flame Bush – *Calliandra californica*
Flame Lily – Gloriosa
Flame Tree – *Brachychiton acerifolius*
Flame Vine – *Pyrostegia venusta*
Flaming Katy – *Kalanchoe blossfeldiana*
Flannel Bush – Fremontodendron
Flax Lily – Dianella
Flax Lily – Phormium
Florist Kalanchoe – *Kalanchoe blossfeldiana*
Florist's Sea Lavender – *Limonium platyphyllum* (syn. *L. latifolium*)
Floss Silk Tree – *Ceiba speciosa*
Flowering Maple – *Corynabutilon vitifolium*
Flowering Quince – Chaenomeles
Flowering Senna – *Senna corymbosa*
Flowering Tobacco – *Nicotiana alata*
Flowering Yellowhorn – *Xanthoceras sorbifolium*
Foothill Beardtongue – *Penstemon heterophyllus*
Foothill Penstemon – *Penstemon heterophyllus*
Forest Gardenia – *Gardenia thunbergia*
Forest Lily – *Veltheimia bracteata*
Formosa Lily – *Lilium formosanum*
Formosa Sweet Gum – *Liquidambar formosana*
Fortnight Lily – *Dietes bicolor*
Fountain Bamboo – Fargesia
Fountain Bush – *Russelia equisetiformis*
Fountain Butterfly Bush – *Buddleja alternifolia*
Fountain Plant – *Russelia equisetiformis*
Four O'clock Plant – Mirabilis
Fox Tail Agave – *Agave attenuata*
Foxgloves – Digitalis
Foxtail Barley – *Hordeum jubatum*
Foxtail Fern – *Asparagus densiflorus*
Foxtail Lily – *Eremurus* × *isabellinus* 'Cleopatra'
Franchet's Cotoneaster – *Cotoneaster franchetii*
French Forget-Me-Not – *Malcolmia maritima*
French Lavender – *Lavandula dentata*
Fried Egg Plant – *Romneya coulteri*
Friendship Plant – *Billbergia nutans*
Fuchsia Heath – *Epacris longiflora*
Garden Candytuft – *Iberis umbellata*
Garden Grape Hyacinth – *Muscari armeniacum*

Garden Hyacinth – *Hyacinthus orientalis*
Garden Mignonette – *Reseda odorata*
Garden Star of Bethlehem – *Ornithogalum umbellatum*
Garden Thyme – *Thymus vulgaris*
Garden Verbena – *Verbena × hybrida*
George lily – *Cyrtanthus elatus*
Geraniums – Pelargonium
German Bearded Iris – *Iris × germanica*
German Ivy – *Delairea odorata*
Germander – Teucrium
Ghost Plant – *Graptopetalum paraguayense*
Giant Allium – *Allium giganteum*
Giant Crinum – *Crinum asiaticum*
Giant Feather Grass – *Stipa lagascae*
Giant Fennel – *Ferula communis*
Giant Herb-Robert – *Geranium maderense*
Giant Montbretia – *Crocosmia masoniorum*
Giant Potato Vine – *Solanum wendlandii*
Giant Protea – *Protea cynaroides*
Giant Reed – *Arundo donax*
Giant Silver Mullein – *Verbascum bombyciferum*
Giant Spurge – *Euphorbia ingens*
Giant Tuberose – *Solanum wendlandii*
Giant Viper's-Bugloss – *Echium pininana*
Gingerbread Palm – *Hyphaene thebaica*
Glaucous Barrel Cactus – *Ferocactus glaucescens*
Globe Candytuft – *Iberis umbellata*
Globe Mallows – Sphaeralcea
Globe Thistles – Echinops
Glory Lily – Gloriosa
Glossy Abelia – *Linnaea chinensis*
Goat's Beard – *Clematis aristata*
Gold Coin Daisy – *Pallenis maritima*
Golden Bamboo – *Phyllostachys aurea*
Golden Crocus – *Crocus chrysanthus*
Golden Easter Lily Cactus – *Echinopsis aurea*
Golden Everlasting – *Xerochrysum bracteatum*
Golden Garlic – *Allium moly*
Golden Ice Plant – *Lampranthus glaucoides*
Golden Marguerite – *Cota tinctoria* syn. *Anthemis tinctoria*
Golden Mimosa – *Acacia baileyana*
Golden Oats – *Stipa lagascae*
Golden Rain Tree – *Koelreuteria paniculata*
Golden Rat Tail – *Cleistocactus winteri*
Golden Shower – *Pyrostegia venusta*
Golden Spider Lily – *Lycoris aurea*
Golden Swan Tritonia – *Crocosmia masoniorum*
Golden Yarrow – *Achillea filipendulina*
Goldmoss Sedum – *Sedum acre*
Goldmoss Stonecrop – *Sedum acre*
Grandma's Freesias – *Freesia refracta*
Grape Hyacinth – Muscari
Grass Gum-Tree – *Xanthorrhoea preissii*
Grass Tree – Xanthorrhoea
Grass-Leaved Scabiosa – *Scabiosa graminifolia*
Greater Periwinkle – *Vinca major*
Grecian Windflower – *Anemonoides blanda*
Greek Acanthus – *Acanthus mollis*
Greek Mullein – *Verbascum olympicum*
Green Cestrum – *Cestrum parqui*
Grey Cotoneaster – *Cotoneaster franchetii*
Ground Cherry – Physalis
Ground Morning Glory – *Convolvulus sabatius*
Groundsel – Roldana
Guadeloupe Fan Palm – *Brahea edulis*
Guernsey Lily – *Nerine sarniensis*
Guinea Gold Flower – *Hibbertia scandens*
Gum – Liquidambar
Gum Cistus – *Cistus ladanifer*
Gum Tree – Eucalyptus
Hairbells – Dierama
Hairy Dewflower – *Drosanthemum hispidum*
Handsome Bush–Pea – *Pultenaea stipularis*
Hare's Tail Grass – *Lagurus ovatus*
Harlequin Flower – Sparaxis
Heart-leaf Flame Pea – *Chorizema cordatum*
Heather – Erica
Heavenly Bamboo – *Nandina domestica*
Hedge Wattle – *Acacia paradoxa*
Hedgehog Cacti – Echinopsis
Hesper Palm – Brahea
Highway Ice Plant – *Carpobrotus edulis*
Himalayan Lantern – *Agapetes serpens*
Himalayan Mint Shrub – *Colquhounia coccinea*
Holly Flame Pea – *Chorizema cordatum*
Holly Oak – *Quercus ilex*
Hollyhock Mallow – *Malva alcea*
Hollyhocks – Alcea
Holm Oak – *Quercus ilex*
Honey Bush – *Melianthus major*
Honey Flower – Melianthus
Honeypot – *Protea cynaroides*
Horse Chestnut – Aesculus
Hottentot Fig – *Carpobrotus edulis*
Ice Plant – Carpobrotus
Ice Plant – *Cleretum bellidiforme*
Ice Plant – *Drosanthemum floribundum*
Ice Plant – Lampranthus
Iceplant – *Hylotelephium spectabile*
Immortelle – *Helichrysum italicum*
Indian Apple – *Datura innoxia*
Indian Bead Tree – *Melia azedarach*
Indian Hawthorn – *Rhaphiolepis indica*
Indian Fig – *Opuntia ficus-indica*
Ironbark – Eucalyptus
Ismene Lily – *Ismene narcissiflora*
Italian Arum – *Arum italicum*
Italian Buckthorn – *Rhamnus alaternus*
Italian Cypress – *Cupressus sempervirens*
Italian Eryngo – *Eryngium amethystinum*
Italian Gladiolus – *Gladiolus italicus*
Italian Strawflower – *Helichrysum italicum*
Ivy – Hedera
Ivy Leaved Geranium – *Pelargonium peltatum*
Ivy Leaved Cyclamen – *Cyclamen hederifolium*
Jacaranda – *Jacaranda mimosifolia*
Jacobean Lily – *Sprekelia formosissima*
Jade Plant – *Crassula sarmentosa*
Jade Tree – *Crassula sarmentosa*
Japanese Anemone – *Eriocapitella hupehensis*
Japanese Camellia – *Camellia japonica*
Japanese Cheesewood – *Pittosporum tobira*
Japanese Honeysuckle – *Lonicera japonica*
Japanese Laurel – *Aucuba japonica*
Japanese Mock Orange – *Pittosporum tobira*
Japanese Pagoda Tree – *Styphnolobium japonicum*
Japanese Sago Palm – *Cycas revoluta*
Japanese Spindle – *Euonymus japonicus*
Japonica – Chaenomeles
Jasmine – *Jasminum azoricum*
Jasmine Daphne – *Daphne oleoides*
Jasmine Tobacco – *Nicotiana alata*
Jelly Palm – *Butia capitata*

Jelly Palms – Butia
Jersey Lily – Amaryllis
Jerusalem Sage – *Phlomis fruticosa*
Joseph's Coat – *Amaranthus tricolor*
Judas Tree – *Cercis siliquastrum*
Kaleidoscope Abelia – *Linnaea chinensis* 'Kaleidoscope'
Kangaroo Apple – *Solanum aviculare*
Kangaroo Paw – *Anigozanthos flavidus*
Kangaroo Tail – *Xanthorrhoea preissii*
Kangaroo Thorn – *Acacia paradoxa*
Kapokbossie – *Eriocephalus africanus*
Karo – *Pittosporum crassifolium*
Karoo Cycad – *Encephalartos lehmannii*
Kermes Oak – *Quercus coccifera*
King Protea – *Protea cynaroides*
King Sago Palm – *Cycas revoluta*
King Sugar Bush – *Protea cynaroides*
King's Spear – *Asphodeline lutea*
Klip Dagga – Leonotis
Knapweeds – Centaurea
Kohuhu – *Pittosporum tenuifolium*
Korokia–Tarango – *Corokia cotoneaster*
Korokio – *Corokia buddleioides*
Lace Fern – *Asparagus setaceus*
Laceleaf Tickseed – *Coreopsis lanceolata*
Lad's Love – *Artemisia abrotanum*
Lady of the Night – *Brunfelsia americana*
Lady Washington Geranium – *Pelargonium domesticum*
Ladybird Poppy – *Papaver commutatum*
Lambs' Ears – *Stachys byzantina*
Large Leaf Bush Pea – *Pultenaea daphnoides*
Laurel-Leaf Cistus – *Cistus laurifolius*
Laurestinus – *Viburnum tinus*
Leadwort – Plumbago
Leadworts – Ceratostigma
Lemon Bottlebrush – *Melaleuca citrinus*
Lemon Geranium – *Pelargonium graveolens*
Lemon Thyme – *Thymus* × *citriodorus*
Lemon Verbena – *Aloysia triphylla*
Lemon-Scented Gum – *Corymbia citriodora*
Lemon-Scented Jasmine – *Jasminum azoricum*
Lentisc – *Pistacia lentiscus*
Leopard's Bane – Doronicum
Lesser Periwinkle – *Vinca minor*
Lilac Vine – *Hardenbergia comptoniana*
Lily Leak – *Allium moly*
Lily of the Incas – Alstroemeria
Lily of the Nile – Agapanthus
Lily of the Orinoco – *Crinum moorei*
Lily of the Palace – *Hippeastrum aulicum*
Lilyturfs – Liriope
Lion's Ear – Leonotis
Lions Tail – *Leonotis leonurus*
Liquorice Plant – *Helichrysum petiolare*
Little Kurrajong – *Brachychiton bidwillii*
Live-For-Ever – Hylotelephium
Livingstone Daisy – *Cleretum bellidiforme*
Lobster Claw – *Clianthus puniceus*
Locusts – Robinia
Looking Glass Bush – *Coprosma repens*
Loquat – *Eriobotrya japonica*
Lord's Candlestick – *Yucca gloriosa*
Lords and Ladies – Arum
Love-in-a-Mist – *Nigella damascena*
Love-Lies-Bleeding – *Amaranthus caudatus*
Lucky Bean Tree – *Erythrina caffra*
Madagascan Butterfly Bush – *Buddleja madagascariensis*
Madagascar Dragon Tree – *Dracaena marginata*
Madagascar Periwinkle – Catharanthus
Madeira Stork's Bill – *Geranium maderense*
Madonna Lily – *Lilium candidum*
Madrones – Arbutus
Magic Tree – Cantua
Maguey – *Agave angustifolia* 'Marginata'
Majorcan Peony – *Paeonia cambessedesii*
Mallow – Malva
Mangles' Kangaroo Paw – *Anigozanthos manglesii*
Mangles' Everlasting – *Rhodanthe manglesii*
Marguerite – *Leucanthemum vulgare*
Marguerite Daisy – Argyranthemum
Marigolds – Calendula
Maritime Pine – *Pinus pinaster*
Marmalade Bush – *Streptosolen jamesonii*
Marvel of Peru – *Mirabilis jalapa*
Mastic Tree – *Pistacia lentiscus*
Mat Rushes – Lomandra
Maternity Plant – *Kalanchoe daigremontiana*
Matilija Poppy – Romneya
Mauritius Nightshade – *Solanum mauritianum*
Meadow Saffron – *Colchicum autumnale*
Mealy-Cup Sage – *Salvia farinacea*
Mediterranean Beach Daisy – *Pallenis maritima*
Mediterranean Cypress – *Cupressus sempervirens*
Mediterranean Fan Palm – *Chamaerops humilis*
Mediterranean Field Gladiolus – *Gladiolus italicus*
Mediterranean Meadow Saffron – *Colchicum cupanii*
Mediterranean Shrub Mallow – *Malva subovata*
Mediterranean Spurge – *Euphorbia characias* subsp. *wulfenii*
Mediterranean Sweet Scabious – *Scabiosa atropurpurea*
Mesembs – Malephora
Mexican Abelia – *Linnaea floribunda*
Mexican Blue Palm – *Brahea armata*
Mexican Cigar – *Cuphea ignea*
Mexican Creeper – *Antigonon leptopus*
Mexican Fan Palm – *Washingtonia robusta*
Mexican Feather Grass – *Nassella tenuissima*
Mexican Flame Bush – *Calliandra tweediei*
Mexican Hat Plant – *Kalanchoe daigremontiana*
Mexican Heather – *Cuphea hyssopifolia*
Mexican Honeysuckle – *Lonicera pilosa*
Mexican Lily – *Beschorneria yuccoides*
Mexican Lime Cactus – *Ferocactus pilifer*
Mexican Orange Blossom – *Choisya ternata*
Mexican Primrose – *Oenothera speciosa*
Mexican Rose – *Portulaca grandiflora*
Mexican Sage Bush – *Salvia leucantha*
Mexican Shell Flower – *Tigridia pavonia*
Mexican Sunflower – Tithonia
Mexican Viper – *Maurandya barclayana*
Mexican Zinnia – *Zinnia elegans*
Milk Bush – *Gomphocarpus fruticosus*
Milkweed – Euphorbia
Milkweed – *Gomphocarpus fruticosus*
Mimosa – Acacia
Mindiyet – *Melaleuca nesophila*
Miniature Date Palm – *Phoenix roebelenii*
Miniature Pig Face – *Drosanthemum hispidum*
Mint Bush – Prostanthera
Mirror Bush – *Coprosma repens*

Missouri Evening Primrose – *Oenothera macrocarpa*
Misty Plume Bush – *Tetradenia riparia*
Montbretia – Crocosmia
Moonflower – Datura
Moore's Crinum Lilly – *Crinum moorei*
Morning Glory – Ipomoea
Morning Iris – *Orthrosanthus multiflorus*
Moroccan Daisy – *Rhodanthemum atlanticum*
Moroccan Poppy – *Papaver atlanticum*
Moses-In-The-Cradle – *Tradescantia spathacea*
Moss Locust – *Robinia hispida*
Moss Rose – *Portulaca grandiflora*
Mossy Stonecrop – *Sedum acre*
Mother of Pearl Plant – *Graptopetalum paraguayense*
Mother-In-Law's Tongue – *Dracaena trifasciata*
Mount Etna Broom – *Genista aetnensis*
Mountain Cabbage Tree – *Cordyline indivisa*
Mousehole Tree – *Myoporum laetum*
Mullein – Verbascum
Myers Fern – *Asparagus densiflorus* 'Myersii'
Naked Ladies – Colchicum
Naked Lady – Amaryllis
Narbonne Star-of-Bethlehem – *Ornithogalum narbonense*
Narrow Leaved Peppermint – *Eucalyptus nicholii*
Narrow Leaved Drumsticks – *Isopogon anethifolius*
Narrow Leafed Ice Plants – Conicosia
Narrow Leaved Bird of Paradise – *Strelitzia juncea*
Narrow Leaved Century Plant – *Agave angustifolia* 'Marginata'
Narrow Leaved Iceplant – *Conicosia pugioniformis*
Natal Blue Thunbergia – *Thunbergia natalensis*
Natal Ivy – *Senecio macroglossus*
Natal Lilly – *Crinum moorei*
Natal Plum – *Carissa macrocarpa*
Necklacepod – Styphnolobium
Needle Grass – Stipa
Needle Grass – Achnatherum
New Zealand Christmas Tree – *Metrosideros excelsa*
Nodding Pincushion – *Leucospermum coros excelsa*
New Zealand Flax – *Phormium tenax difolium*
Norfolk Island Hibiscus – *Lagunaria patersonia*
Notch Leaf Marsh Rosemary – *Limonium sinuatum*
Nutmeg Bush – *Tetradenia riparia*
Oak – Quercus
Old Man's Beard – *Clematis aristata*
Oleander – *Nerium oleander*
Oleaster – Elaeagnus
Olive – Olea
Olympian Mullein – *Verbascum olympicum*
One–sided Bottlebrush – *Melaleuca quadrifida*
Onion – Allium
Orange Bulbine – *Bulbine frutescens*
Orange Cestrum – *Cestrum aurantiacum*
Orange Cotoneaster – *Cotoneaster franchetii*
Orange Jessamine – *Cestrum aurantiacum*
Orchid Rockrose – *Cistus × purpureus*
Ornamental Pincushion – *Leucospermum cordifolium*
Our Lord's Candle – *Hesperoyucca whipplei*
Ox-Eye Daisy – *Leucanthemum vulgare*
Oyster Plant – *Tradescantia spathacea*
Pagoda Tree – *Styphnolobium japonicum*
Paintbrush – *Haemanthus albiflos*
Paintbrush Lily – Scadoxus
Palmiste Gargoulette – *Hyophorbe lagenicaulis*
Palqui – *Cestrum parqui*
Pampas Grass – *Cortaderia selloana*
Panda Plant – *Kalanchoe tomentosa*
Panicgrass – Panicum
Pansy – Viola
Paper Daisies – *Xerochrysum bracteatum*
Paper Daisy – *Xeranthemum annuum*
Paper Flower – Bougainvillea
Paper White Narcissus – *Narcissus papyraceus*
Paperbark – Melaleuca
Paris Daisy – *Argyranthemum frutescens*
Parrot's Beak – *Clianthus puniceus*
Parrot's Beak – *Lotus berthelotii*
Pawpaw – *Carica papaya*
Pea Tree – Caragana
Peacock Flowers – Tigridia
Pendulous Yucca – *Yucca gloriosa* var. *tristis*
Peony – Paeonia
Pepper Tree – *Schinus molle*
Peppermint Tree – *Agonis flexuosa*
Periwinkle – Vinca
Persian Ivy – *Hedera colchica*
Persian Lilac – *Melia azedarach*
Peruvian Daffodil – *Ismene × deflexa*
Peruvian Feather Grass – *Jarava ichu*
Peruvian Lily – Alstroemeria
Peruvian Magic Tree – *Cantua buxifolia*
Peruvian Scilla – *Scilla peruviana*
Petticoat Palm – *Washingtonia filifera*
Phillip Island Hibiscus – *Hibiscus insularis*
Pigface – Carpobrotus
Pigroot – *Conicosia pugioniformis*
Pincushion Coneflower – *Isopogon dubius*
Pincushion Flower – Scabiosa
Pincushion Tree – *Hakea laurina*
Pindo Palms – Butia
Pine Echium – *Echium pininana*
Pineapple Flowers – Eucomis
Pineapple Guava – *Feijoa sellowiana*
Pineapple Lilies – Eucomis
Pink Evening Primrose – *Oenothera speciosa*
Pink Melaleuca – *Melaleuca nesophila*
Pink or Common Heath – *Epacris impressa*
Pink Sunray – *Rhodanthe manglesii*
Pink Trumpet Vine – *Podranea ricasoliana*
Pink Ladies – *Oenothera speciosa*
Pistachio – Pistacia
Pitcher Sages – Lepechinia
Plumbago – Ceratostigma
Plume Albizia – *Paraserianthes lophantha*
Poet's Jasmine – *Jasminum grandiflorum*
Pohutukawa – Metrosideros
Poinsettia – *Euphorbia pulcherrima*
Poison Bulb – Crinum
Poker Plant – *Kniphofia uvaria*
Pokeweed – Phytolacca
Pomegranate – *Punica granatum*
Pompon Tree – *Dais cotinifolia*
Ponga – *Cyathea dealbata*
Ponytail Palm – Beaucarnea
Popcorn Shrub – *Xanthoceras sorbifolium*
Popcorn-Bush – *Senna didymobotrya*
Poppy Anemone – *Anemone coronaria*

Pork and Beans – *Sedum rubrotinctum*
Portugal Laurel – *Prunus lusitanica*
Portuguese Broom – *Chamaecytisus elongatus*
Portuguese Heath – *Erica lusitanica*
Portuguese Lavender – *Lavandula latifolia*
Pot Marigold – *Calendula officinalis*
Potato Vine – *Solanum laxum*
Pouch Nemesia – *Nemesia strumosa*
Poverty Bush – *Kunzea ambigua*
Powder Puff Plant – Calliandra
Prickly Cycad – *Encephalartos altensteinii*
Prickly Juniper – *Juniperus oxycedrus*
Prickly Pear – Opuntia
Prickly Wattle – *Acacia paradoxa*
Pride of Bolivia – *Tipuana tipu*
Pride of India – *Koelreuteria paniculata*
Pride of Madeira – *Echium candicans*
Primrose Jasmine – *Jasminum mesnyi*
Primrose Tree – *Lagunaria patersonia*
Prince's Feather – *Amaranthus cruentus*
Propeller Plant – *Crassula perfoliata* var. *falcata*
Punga – *Cyathea dealbata*
Purple Coral Pea – *Hardenbergia violacea*
Purple Heart – *Tradescantia pallida* 'Purpurea'
Purple Morning Glory – *Ipomoea purpurea*
Purple Pinwheels – *Aeonium arboreum* 'Velour'
Purple Queen – *Tradescantia pallida* 'Purpurea'
Purple-Leaved Plum – *Prunus cerasifera* 'Pissardii'
Purslanes – Portulaca
Pussy Ears – *Kalanchoe tomentosa*
Pygmy Date Palm – *Phoenix roebelenii*
Pyramidal Star-of-Bethlehem – *Ornithogalum narbonense*
Queen Palm – *Syagrus romanzoffiana*
Queen Sago – *Cycas circinalis*
Queen's Tears – *Billbergia nutans*
Queen's Wreath Vine – Antigonon
Quince – Cydonia
Red Aloe – *Aloe cameronii*
Red Amaranth – *Amaranthus cruentus*
Red Buckeye – *Aesculus pavia*
Red Fairy Duster – *Calliandra californica*
Red Flowering Gum – *Corymbia ficifolia*
Red Hot Poker – Kniphofia
Red Ice Plant – *Malephora crocea*
Red Magic Lily – *Lycoris radiata*
Red Spider Lily – *Lycoris radiata*
Red Tip Photinia – *Photinia × fraseri*
Red Valerian – *Valeriana rubra*
Redbuds – Cercis
Redgum – Liquidambar
Reeve's Spiraea – *Spirea cantoniensis*
Regal Mallow – *Malva trimestris*
Regal Pelargonium – *Pelargonium domesticum*
Rigid Bottlebrush – *Melaleuca linearis* var. *linearis*
Rock Rose – Cistus
Rock Rose – Helianthemum
Rock Rose – *Portulaca grandiflora*
Rockspray Cotoneaster – *Cotoneaster franchetii*
Rockspray Cotoneaster – *Cotoneaster microphyllus*
Rose Acacia – *Robinia hispida*
Rose Coneflower – *Isopogon formosus*
Rose Mallow – *Malva trimestris*
Rose Moss – *Portulaca grandiflora*
Rose Myrtle – *Rhodomyrtus tomentosa*
Rose of Sharon – *Hibiscus syriacus*
Rosebay – *Nerium oleander*
Round Headed Allium – *Allium sphaerocephalon*
Round Headed Leek – *Allium sphaerocephalon*
Round Leaved Mint Bush – *Prostanthera rotundifolia*
Royal Mallow – *Malva trimestris*
Royal Poinciana – Bauhinia
Royal Poinciana – Delonix
Rue – Ruta
Russian Olive – *Elaeagnus angustifolia*
Russian Sage – *Salvia yangii*
Sacred Bamboo – *Nandina domestica*
Sacred Flower of the Andes – Cantua
Sacred Flower of the Inca – Cantua
Sage – Salvia
Sage-Leaf Rockrose – *Cistus salviifolius*
Sago Palm – Cycas
Saguaros – Carnegiea
Sallowthorn – Hippophae
Sandankwa Viburnum – *Viburnum suspensum*
Sandthorn – Hippophae
Santa Barbara Ceanothus – *Ceanothus impressus*
Satin-Walnut – Liquidambar
Savin Juniper – *Juniperus sabina*
Scarborough lily – *Cyrtanthus elatus*
Scarlet Beard–Tongue – *Penstemon barbatus*
Scarlet Bugler – *Penstemon centranthifolius*
Scarlet Feather Flower – *Verticordia grandis*
Scarlet Paintbrush – *Crassula perfoliata* var. *falcata*
Scarlet Flowered Colquhounia – *Colquhounia coccinea*
Scotch Broom – *Cytisus scoparius*
Sea Aster – *Pallenis maritima*
Sea Buckthorn – *Hippophae rhamnoides*
Sea Daffodil – *Pancratium maritimum*
Sea Eryngo – *Eryngium maritimum*
Sea Holly – *Eryngium maritimum*
Sea Lavender – Limonium
Sea Onion – *Drimia maritima*
Sea Pink – Armeria
Sea Pink – *Limonium sinuatum*
Sea Thrift – *Armeria maritima*
Seaberry – Hippophae
Seashore Lily – Crinum
Sedum – Hylotelephium
Shaggy Dwarf Morning-Glory – *Evolvulus pilosus*
Shasta Daisy – Leucanthemum
Shaving Brush Plant – *Haemanthus coccineus*
Shell Flowers – Tigridia
Shiny Leaf Yellowhorn – *Xanthoceras sorbifolium*
Showy Honey-Myrtle – *Melaleuca nesophila*
Siberian Pea Shrub – *Caragana arborescens*
Silk Tassel Bush – *Garrya elliptica*
Silkweed – Asclepias
Silky Eremophila – *Eremophila nivea*
Silver Dollar Gum – *Eucalyptus polyanthemos*
Silver Dust – *Centaurea cineraria*
Silver Fern – *Cyathea dealbata*
Silver Jade Plant – *Crassula arborescens*
Silver Lupine – *Lupinus albifrons*
Silver Mound – *Artemisia schmidtiana*
Silver Ragwort – *Centaurea cineraria*
Silver Torch – *Cleistocactus strausii*
Silver Tree – *Leucadendron argenteum*
Silver Tree-Fern – *Cyathea dealbata*
Silver Wattle – *Acacia dealbata*
Silver Waves Pig's Ear – *Cotyledon orbiculata* 'Silver Waves'

Silverberry – Elaeagnus
Silverbush – *Convolvulus cneorum*
Silvergrass – Miscanthus
Silverleaf Cotoneaster – *Cotoneaster franchetii*
Slender Vervain – *Verbena rigida*
Small Scabious – *Scabiosa columbaria*
Smallflower Tamarisk – *Tamarix parviflora*
Smoke Bush – Cotinus
Smoke Tree – Cotinus
Smokebush – *Buddleja madagascariensis*
Snake Vine – *Hibbertia scandens*
Snow on the Mountain – *Euphorbia marginata*
Snowflake – Leucojum
Snowflakes – Acis
Snow-In-Summer – *Cerastium tomentosum*
Society Garlic – *Tulbaghia violaceae*
Solar Fire – *Ursinia anthemoides*
South African Sage Wood – *Buddleja salviifolia*
South African Tree Daphne – *Dais cotinifolia*
Southern Globe Thistle – *Echinops ritro*
Southern Magnolia – *Magnolia grandiflora*
Southern Star-of-Bethlehem – *Ornithogalum narbonense*
Southernwood – *Artemisia abrotanum*
Sowbread – Cyclamen
Spanish Bayonet – *Yucca aloifolia*
Spanish Broom – *Genista hispanica*
Spanish Broom – *Retama monosperma*
Spanish Broom – *Spartium junceum*
Spanish Dagger – *Yucca gloriosa*
Spanish Flag Vine – *Ipomoea lobata*
Spanish Heath – *Erica australis*
Spanish Iris – Dietes
Spanish Iris – *Iris xiphium*
Spanish Jasmine – *Jasminum grandiflorum*
Spanish Lavender – *Lavandula stoechas*
Spanish Marigold – *Anemone coronaria*
Spanish Oats – *Stipa lagascae*
Spanish Poppy – *Papaver atlanticum*
Spider Flowers – Cleome
Spider Lily – Lycoris
Spiderworts – Tradescantia
Spike Lavender – *Lavandula latifolia*
Spiky-Headed Mat-Rush – *Lomandra longifolia*
Spindle Palm – *Hyophorbe verschaffeltii*
Spindle Tree – Euonymus
Spineless Yucca – *Yucca gigantea*
Spinning Gum – *Eucalyptus perriniana*
Spiny-Head Mat-Rush – *Lomandra longifolia*
Spotted Arum – *Arum dioscoridis*
Spotted Laurel – *Aucuba japonica*
Spring Star Flower – *Ipheion uniflorum*
Spurge – Euphorbia
Squills – *Drimia maritima*
Squirrel-tail Barley – *Hordeum jubatum*
St James Lily – *Sprekelia formosissima*
Stag's Horn Sumach – *Rhus typhina*
Star Gum – Liquidambar
Star of Bethlehem – Ornithogalum
Starfish Flower – *Duvalia corderoyi*
Statice – Limonium
Stiff Bottlebrush – *Melaleuca linearis* var. *linearis*
Stocks – Matthiola
Stonecrop – Hylotelephium
Stonecrop – Sedum
Stone Pine – *Pinus pinea*
Straw Flower – *Xerochrysum bracteatum*
Strawberry Tree – Arbutus
String of Beads – *Curio rowleyanus*
Sugarbushes – Protea
Sumach – Rhus
Summer Lilac – *Buddleja davidii*
Summer Snowflake – *Leucojum aestivum*
Sun Rose – Cistus
Sun Rose – Helianthemum
Sun Rose – *Portulaca grandiflora*
Sun Star – *Ornithogalum dubium*
Suncups – Oenothera
Sundrops – Oenothera
Sunrose – *Helianthemum nummularium*
Surprise Lilies – Lycoris
Swans Neck Agave – *Agave attenuata*
Sweet Bay – *Laurus nobilis*
Sweet Iris – *Iris pallida*
Sweet Pea Shrub – *Polygala myrtifolia*
Sweet Scented Geranium – *Pelargonium graveolens*
Sweet Tobacco – *Nicotiana alata*
Sweet Violet – *Viola odorata*
Sweet William Catchfly – *Silene armeria*
Sweetgum – Liquidambar
Swinebread – Cyclamen
Switchgrass – *Panicum virgatum*
Sydney Golden Wattle – *Acacia longifolia*
Taiwanese Lily – *Lilium formosanum*
Tall Morning-Glory – *Ipomoea purpurea*
Tamarillo – *Solanum betaceum*
Tasman Flax Lily – *Dianella tasmanica* Variegata
Taupata – *Coprosma repens*
Terebinth – *Pistacia terebinthus*
Thornapples – Datura
Three-Leaved Snowflake – *Acis longifolia*
Thrift – Armeria
Tick Bush – *Kunzea ambigua*
Tiger–Flowers – Tigridia
Tipu Tree – Tipuana
Tobacco Plant – Nicotiana
Torch Plant – *Aloe arborescens*
Torch-Lily – Kniphofia
Tower of Jewels – *Echium pininana*
Trailing African Daisy – *Osteospermum fruticosum*
Trailing Gazania – *Gazania rigens*
Trailing Ice Plant – *Lampranthus spectabilis*
Trailing Mauve Daisy – *Dimorphotheca jucunda*
Transvaal Daisy – *Gerbera jamesonii*
Treasure Flower – *Gazania* hybrids
Tree Aloe – *Aloe arborescens*
Tree Anemone – *Carpenteria californica*
Tree Daisies – Olearia
Tree Echium – *Echium pininana*
Tree Fuchsia – *Schotia brachypetala*
Tree Gardenia – *Gardenia thunbergia*
Tree Goldenhorn – *Xanthoceras sorbifolium*
Tree Heath – *Erica arborea*
Tree Lupin – *Lupinus arboreus*
Tree Mallow – *Malva arborea*
Tree Poke – *Phytolacca dioica*
Tree Poppy – Dendromecon
Tree Poppy – Romneya
Tree Tobacco – *Nicotiana glauca*
Tree Tobacco – *Solanum mauritianum*
Tree Tomato – *Solanum betaceum*
Tree Wisteria – *Bolusanthus speciosus*
Tree Wormwood – *Artemisia arborescens*
Tree Poppy – *Dendromecon rigida*
Tropical Milkweed – Asclepias
Trumpet Bush – *Tecoma stans*
Trumpet Creeper – Campsis
Trumpet Vine – Campsis
Trumpet Vine – *Eccremocarpus scaber*
Trumpetbush – Tecoma
Tuberous Vervain – *Verbena rigida*
Tunisian Carpet – *Pallenis maritima*

Turkish Mullein – *Verbascum bombyciferum*
Turk's Cap Cactus – Melocactus
Turpentine Tree – *Pistacia terebinthus*
Turquoise Ixia – *Ixia viridiflora*
Twin Flowered Agave – *Agave geminiflora*
Two Flowered Agave – *Agave geminiflora*
Umbra Tree – *Phytolacca dioica*
Umbrella Bamboo – Fargesia
Umbrella Pine – *Pinus pinea*
Umbrellaworts – Mirabilis
Valerian – Valeriana
Vampire Lily – *Dracunculus vulgaris*
Van Staden's River Daisy – *Dimorphotheca spectabilis*
Vanwykshout – *Bolusanthus speciosus*
Variegated Dianella – *Dianella tasmanica* Variegata
Variegated Flax Lily – *Dianella tasmanica* Variegata
Variegated Mauritius Hemp – *Furcraea foetida* 'Variegata'
Variegated Spider Plant – *Chlorophytum comosum*
Velvet Elephant Ear – *Kalanchoe beharensis*
Velvet Groundsel – *Roldana petasitis*
Velvet Rose – *Aeonium canariense*
Venetian Shumach – *Cotinus coggygria*
Vervain – Verbena
Victorian Box – *Pittosporum undulatum*
Vinca – *Catharanthus roseus*
Violet – Viola
Violet Climbing Snapdragon – *Maurandella antirrhiniflora*
Violet Pricklypear – *Opuntia gosseliniana*
Virginian Stock – *Malcolmia maritima*
Virgin's Palm – *Dioon edule*
Walking Iris – Trimezia
Wandering Jews – Tradescantia
Wandflower – *Sparaxis tricolor*
Wandflowers – Dierama
Waratah – Telopea
Warminster Broom – *Cytisus* × *praecox*
Wattle – Acacia
Wavyleaf Sea Lavender – *Limonium sinuatum*
Wavyleaf Silktassel – *Garrya elliptica*
Waxflowers – Chamelaucium
Weeping Bottlebrush – *Melaleuca viminalis*
Weeping Lantana – *Lantana montevidensis*
White Bird of Paradise – *Strelitzia nicolai*
White Correa – *Correa alba*
White Escallonia – *Escallonia bifida*
White Gardenia – *Gardenia thunbergia*
White Jasmine – *Jasminum polyanthum*
White Kunzea – *Kunzea ambigua*
White Leaved Rockrose – *Cistus albidus*
White Orchid Tree – *Bauhinia variegata*
White Rockrose – *Cistus aguilari*
White Spanish Broom – *Chamaecytisus elongatus*
White Virgin's Bower – *Clematis montana* var. *grandiflora*
White-Edged Swedish Ivy – *Plectranthus glabratus*
White-Flowered Asphodel – *Asphodelus albus*
White-Leaf Bush Lupine – *Lupinus albifrons*
Wild Carnation – *Dianthus caryophyllus*
Wild Clematis – *Clematis aristata*
Wild Cotton – *Gomphocarpus fruticosus*
Wild Gardenia – *Gardenia thunbergia*
Wild Iris – Dietes
Wild Peony – *Paeonia mascula*
Wild Rosemary – *Eriocephalus africanus*
Willow Leaf Cotoneaster – *Cotoneaster salicifolius*
Willow-Leaved Jessamine – *Cestrum parqui*
Windflower – Anemone
Winged Tobacco – *Nicotiana alata*
Wintercreeper – *Euonymus fortunei*
Wire Netting-Bush Korokio – *Corokia cotoneaster*
Wood Anemone – *Anemonoides nemorosa*
Woolly Torch – *Cleistocactus strausii*
Wormwood – *Artemisia schmidtiana*
Yarrow – Achillea
Yatay Palm – *Butia yatay*
Yellow Asphodel – *Asphodeline lutea*
Yellow Bells – *Tecoma stans*
Yellow Bush Lupine – *Lupinus arboreus*
Yellow Chamomile – *Cota tinctoria* syn. *Anthemis tinctoria*
Yellow Chincherinchee – *Ornithogalum dubium*
Yellow Elder – *Tecoma stans*
Yellow Flowered Garlic – *Allium flavum*
Yellow Grape Hyacinth – *Muscari macrocarpum*
Yellow Jessamine – *Gelsemium sempervirens*
Yellow Wild Iris – *Dietes bicolor*
Yesterday Today Tomorrow – *Brunfelsia pauciflora*
Zonal Geranium – *Pelargonium hortorum*

First published in 2025 by
The Crowood Press Ltd
Ramsbury, Marlborough
Wiltshire SN8 2HR

enquiries@crowood.com
www.crowood.com

British Library Cataloguing-in-Publication Data
A catalogue record for this book is available from the British Library.

For product safety-related questions, contact:
productsafety@crowood.com

ISBN 978 0 7198 4532 1

Typeset by Envisage IT

Cover design by Samantha Rolfe-Hoang

Printed and bound in India by Nutech Print Services

Dedication

A very special thanks must go to my husband and partner for 50 years, Dr David Sturge. Without his practical help in checking and editing the book, his unflagging encouragement and support, I may never have finished this book. Also, grateful thanks to all the people that kindly allowed me to photograph their plants or gardens.

I would also like to thank Dr Charles Clarke, Curator of Cairns Botanic Garden, for his helpful advice and encouragement.